AUTOCOURSE™

THE WORLD'S LEADING GRAND PRIX ANNUAL

CMG
PUBLISHING

CONTENTS

AUTOCOURSE 2006–2007

is published by
Crash Media Group Ltd
Number One
The Innovation Centre
Silverstone Circuit
Silverstone
Northants NN12 8GX
United Kingdom
Tel: +44 (0)870 3505044
Fax: +44 (0)870 3505088
Email: info@crash.net
Website: www.crashmediagroup.com

Printed in England by
Butler and Tanner Ltd,
Frome, Somerset

ISBN: 1-905334-15-X

DISTRIBUTORS

Gardners Books,
1 Whittle Drive, Eastbourne,
East Sussex, BN23 6QH
Tel: +44 (0)1323 521555
Email: sales@gardners.com

Menoshire Ltd
Unit 13
21 Wadsworth Road
Perivale
Middlesex UB6 7LQ
Tel: +44 (0)20 8566 7344
Fax: +44 (0)20 8991 2439

NORTH AMERICA
Motorbooks International
PO Box 1
729 Prospect Avenue
Osceola
Wisconsin 54020, USA
Tel: (1) 715 294 3345
Fax: (1) 715 294 4448

Dust jacket: Fernando Alonso,
double drivers' world champion
for Renault.

**Title page: Michael Schumacher
leads his championship rival
Fernando Alonso in the San
Marino Grand Prix at Imola.**
Photographs: James Moy/wwwcrashpa.net

editor
ALAN HENRY

publisher
BRYN WILLIAMS

text editor
SUZANNE ARNOLD

results and statistics
DAVID HAYHOE

advertising sales
DEBBIE THOMAS
SIMON MOORE

art editor
STEVE SMALL

design and production
ROSANNE DAVIS
MIKE WESTON

office manager
WENDY SALISBURY

chief photographer
JAMES MOY

chief contributing photographers
RUSSELL BATCHELOR

PAUL-HENRI CAHIER

LAURENT CHARNIAUX

JEAN-FRANÇOIS GALERON

LUKAS GORYS

PETER NYGAARD

JAD SHERIF

BRYN WILLIAMS

f1 illustrations
ADRIAN DEAN
f1artwork@blueyonder.co.uk

Editor's Acknowledgements

The Editor of AUTOCOURSE wishes to thank the following for their assistance in compiling the 2006–2007 edition.
France: ACO; Fédération Française du Sport Automobile; FIA (Max Mosley, Bernie Ecclestone, Alan Donnelly, Richard Woods, Christel Picot, Julia Brillard, Alexandra Scherin, Charlie Whiting, Herbie Blash and Pat Behar); Michelin (Nick Shorrock, Andy Pope and Severine Ray); Renault F1 (Flavio Briatore, Pat Symonds, Patrizia Spinelli and Bradley Lord); **Germany:** Formula 3 Vereinigung; Mercedes-Benz (Norbert Haug, Wolfgang Schattling, Frank Reichert and Tanya Severin); Sabine Kehm; **Great Britain:** Autocar; Martin Brundle; Mark Blundell; Bob Constanduros; Paul Edwards; Maurice Hamilton; Cosworth Engineering (Tim Routsis, Bernard Ferguson and Denise Proctor); Ford (Jost Capito); Red Bull Racing (Helmut Marko, Christian Horner, Adrian Newey, Tina Sponer, Britta Roeske and Katie Tweedle); McLaren (Ron Dennis, Martin Whitmarsh, Justine Bowen, Beverley Keynes, Ellen Kolby, Clare Robertson, Claire Bateman, Lyndy Redding, Simon Points, Neil Oatley, Steve Hallam and Peter Stayner); Midland F1/Spyker (Colin Kolles, Ian Phillips, Charlotte Anderson and Ron Fine); Nigel Roebuck; Eric Silbermann; Sir Jackie Stewart; Professor Sid Watkins; Jason Swales; Holly Samos; Fiona Winterburn; David Croft; WilliamsF1 (Sir Frank Williams, Patrick Head, Sam Michael, Chris Chapple, Frank Dernie, Jonathan Williams, Claire Williams, Jim Wright, Silvia Hoffer Frangipane, Katie Aspinall and Liam Clogger); **Italy:** Commisione Sportiva Automobilistica Italiana; Scuderia Ferrari (Jean Todt, Ross Brawn, Rory Byrne, Antonio Ghini, Luca Colajanni, Matteo Bonciani, Stefania Bocci and Regine Rettner); Scuderia Toro Rosso (Gerhard Berger, Franz Tost and Fabiana Valenti); 'George' Piola; **Japan:** Bridgestone (Hirohide Hamashima, Hiroshi Yasukawa, Hisao Suganuma, Adrian Atkinson and Rachel Ingham); Honda Racing (Nick Fry, Yasahiro Wada, Alastair Watkins, Tracy Novak, Nicola Armstrong, Jane Chapman, Jules Kulpinski, Robert Watherston and Charlie Reid); Toyota (Tsutomu Tomita, John Howett, Mike Gascoyne, Andrea Ficarelli, Fernanda Vilas, Marieluise Mammitsch and Alastair Moffat); **Switzerland:** BMW Sauber (Mario Theissen, Peter Sauber, Hanspeter Brack, Ann Bradshaw, Heike Bartsch and Jörg Kottmeier); **USA:** ChampCar; Daytona International Speedway; Indianapolis Motor Speedway; NASCAR; Roger Penske; SportsCar.

Photographs published in AUTOCOURSE 2006–2007 have been contributed by:
Chief photographer: James Moy of Crashpa.net; *Chief contributing photographers:* Bryn Williams and Mike Weston of Crashpa.net; A1 GP Media Service; ALMS Media; Russell Batchelor, Emily Davenport Marco Miltenberg and Breloer of XPB.cc; Brousseau Photo; Michael C. Brown; Paul-Henri Cahier; Laurent Charniaux, Jean-François Galeron and Jad Sherif of World Racing Images; David Cole/eKartingNews.com; Crashpa.net archive; Jakob Ebrey Motorsport Photography; Lukas Gorys; GP2 Media Services; LAT Photographic; (Phillip Abbott, Autostock, Richard Dole, Mike Levitt, Lesley-Ann Miller, Dan Streck, F.Pierce Williams, LAT South and PWS Consultancy/Autoracingone.com-US/LAT); Todd McCall; Peter Nygaard/GP Photo; Hiroyuki Orihara; Photo 4/XPB.cc; Chris Walker/www.kartpix.net.

www.autocourse.com

more THAN YOU *expect,* *no less* THAN YOU *deserve.*

ExecuJet - your partner for customised business aviation solutions

- Aircraft Sales
- Aircraft Management
- Business Jet Charter
- Aircraft Completion Management
- FBO Services

Contact ExecuJet:

Business Aviation Centre, P.O.Box 1, CH-8058, Zurich Airport
Telephone: +41 44 804 16 16   **Facsimile:** +41 44 804 16 17
Email: enquiries@execujet.ch   **Website:** www.execujet.ch

ExecuJet

Now you're flying.

Image provided courtesy of Bombardier Inc

FOREWORD by FERNANDO ALONSO

TWELVE months ago, I wrote that Renault and I had a mountain to climb to win the world championship again. And now, in late 2006, here we are – at the top of the mountain. This was an incredible season for Formula 1. At Renault, we had the best of times – such as at Barcelona and Monaco – and the worst of times, such as the weekends at Hockenheim and Monza. There were decisions that we did not understand. But all the way through, I had the conviction that time would put everybody in their right place. We deserved these championships, because they are the proof that the sport still comes first above everything else.

Our fight this year was different from the one in 2005. We were up against Ferrari and Michael Schumacher, legends in the sport. We had to be aggressive all year. We had to fight hard, to conquer our challenges and to win out on the track, where it mattered. Renault and Michelin taught me a lesson about sporting spirit that I will remember for the rest of my life.

It has been an honour to fight against Michael. His name will live forever in the history books, and to fight against him meant more stress, more attention and more pressure. To beat him, and to be the champion for the last two seasons of his career, also brings more prestige. It was a fantastic battle and I wish him the very best for his new life.

Finally, I must say thank you to all the fans who supported me, and especially my people in Spain. They are the best in the world. There were times this year when everybody thought the championship was lost but from them, I only had more support and more belief. These titles are theirs as well. They are all double world champions.

For me, it is now time for a new adventure, but I will never forget these years with Renault. They were my family in Formula 1. We grew up together and we have enjoyed amazing success. No matter what happens in the future, they will always be in my heart.

OPEN FOR BUSINESS

Besides the Gulf Air Bahrain Grand Prix, The Bahrain International Circuit hosts a wide variety of national and international races that offer exclusive hospitality for you and your guests. And for those interested in business, BIC offers excellent opportunities. With Corporate Driving Days, you and your business partners can come as a group and experience the adrenalin of on-track speed and the adventures of off-road action. With Track Hire you can hire one of our several world-class tracks to cater to any of your corporate needs. Driver Training offers you comprehensive driving skills, and with Facility Rental you can rent superb venues with state-of-the-art infrastructure. Simply put, we're open for business.

DOUBLE CHAMPION ALONSO ENDS THE SCHUMACHER ERA

Fernando Alonso's performances in 2006 proved him to be a worthy successor to the newly retired Michael Schumacher.
Photograph: Peter Nygaard/GP Photo

BY any standards it was a great F1 season, rich in both competition and controversy. Fernando Alonso drove with a consistent brilliance to notch up his second straight world championship title as Michael Schumacher called time on an epic grand prix career in a season that may have fallen short of delivering his eighth title crown but certainly consolidated his reputation as the defining star of his generation – even though I have positioned Alonso above him in my top ten drivers' rating, which reflects a tight focus on the single past season.

Alonso impressed overwhelmingly through his on-track consistency and the mental firepower he brought to bear on the task of retaining his championship. What made it doubly impressive was the fact that he did it knowing that he was leaving the Renault squad at the end of the year. Yet, in a sense, Schumacher faced a similar dilemma. His campaign

was shaded by the fact that, sooner or later, he would have to make a decision about his professional future. Should he quit driving at the end of the year? Or should he stay on and face the challenge of confronting Kimi Räikkönen – arguably the fastest driver in the F1 business – in equal cars and with equal treatment? He opted for the former and most insiders judged it a shrewd and timely call.

At the end of the season there was an upsurge of debate over whether Michael jumped ship or was in fact given a discreet push. Certainly it seemed a little difficult to believe that the future security of Felipe Massa's F1 career was a key factor that, he claimed, led him to reach his retirement conclusion as early as the US GP at Indianapolis.

Yet there were factions within the Maranello ranks that hinted that the Schumacher-Jean Todt axis had become too powerful even for president Luca di Montezemolo's comfort. This is all wild speculation, of course, but I offer it for the readers' consideration as an indication of how F1 insider gossip can become all-pervading. More likely, Michael simply judged that he might be able to keep the lid on Räikkönen for another season or two but it would still be best to check out while he could still lay claim to being the best of his generation. As Britain's first F1 world champion Mike Hawthorn observed on hanging up his helmet at the end of 1958, 'The question "Why did you retire?" is so much nicer than "Why *don't* you retire?"'

Yet right to the end of the very last lap of his career Schumacher kept people wondering just why he *was* retiring. He gave no quarter to his younger rivals and for that reason alone he will be missed hugely. It will take a couple of seasons fully to recalibrate F1's heroic perspective without him.

Of course, Renault and Ferrari totally dominated the 2006 scene, the first season of the new 2.4-litre F1 regulations. Only Jenson Button's welcome, but long overdue, triumph for Honda in Hungary gatecrashed a party that, in normal circumstances, one would have expected to be attended by Williams and McLaren-Mercedes. You can read within these pages how Britain's two blue-riband F1 teams disappointingly under-performed while, of the other potential big guns, Toyota had a simply terrible time, singularly failing to build on its 2005 promise and emphasising very publicly just what a difficult and demanding business F1 can be.

No F1 season would be complete, of course, without its helping of controversy and 2006 was certainly no exception in that respect. The superb on-track competition was played out against a backdrop of simmering strife and bad feeling as the governing body, the FIA, drove through its new philosophy for the long-term evolution of F1, the most contentious element of which was fixed-specification 'homologated' engines for a four-year period from the start of 2007.

This was very much perceived as FIA president Max Mosley's personal crusade, driven by deep concern that the spending levels presently existing within F1 are simply not sustainable in the longer term. Perhaps inevitably, the uncompromising zeal with which Mosley espoused his cause prompted accusations from some competing teams that he seemed hell-bent on 'dumbing down' F1 for no good reason and that the FIA was operating outside its remit. What on earth, they inquired, has the issue of how much private companies spend on their businesses got to do with the sport's regulator?

Mosley's nanny-knows-best *modus operandi* continues to drive many of the competing teams around the bend but, in this instance – although he never answered the question directly – it appears that the governing body has acted in the interests of the sport's long-term sustainability. Ironically, of course, you might conclude that FIA cost-cutting measures designed to aid the smaller, less-well-financed teams will in fact offer bigger benefits to the richer teams that have big-money sponsors in place for the longer term. Their profit margins – and therefore their ability to invest in sophisticated off-track simulation systems – will ensure that the gap between the haves and the have-nots in this business will

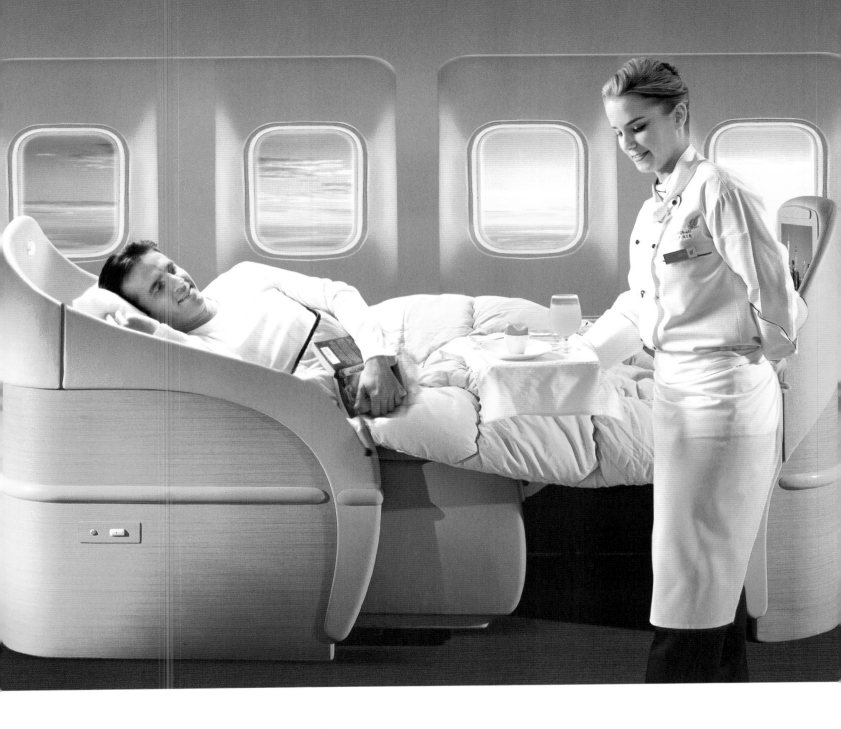

Sky Bed. Sky Chef.
First Class experience

With only eight seats in First Class you can settle into your own private space. Enjoy the supreme comfort of your fully flat Sky Bed and experience the award-winning meals prepared and served by your own personal Sky Chef. It is a unique First Class experience. For more information and reservations call your local travel agent or visit **www.gulfairco.com**

Join our award-winning Frequent flyer programme
Official airline and sponsor of the Gulf Air Bahrain Grand Prix 2007

Sky Beds are available on our A330 aircraft and selected A340's

GULF AIR

continue to expand rather than contract.

Beyond F1 there was a huge reservoir of bubbling new talent almost banging the door down in its enthusiasm to be admitted to the sport's senior category. For the second straight season the fledgling GP2 category offered closer and more spectacular racing than just about any other series in recent memory. McLaren protégé Lewis Hamilton emerged as the man of the moment, taking the title after a succession of brilliant drives that virtually guaranteed him a fast-track ride into F1 for next season.

Hamilton saw off Nelson Piquet Jr to take the GP2 crown but there were several other names – including Timo Glock, Alexandre Prémat and Ernesto Viso – who had moments of promise that suggested they have bright futures. Farther down the pecking order, Mike Conway marked himself out as a man to watch with victory in the British F3 championship, where he saw off a challenge from his Räikkönen Robertson team-mate Bruno Senna, nephew of the late triple world champion.

In the F3 Euro Series Paul di Resta just pipped Sebastian Vettel to the title crown, although the latter has already achieved a foothold in F1 as the third BMW Sauber driver and is forging himself quite a reputation as a capable operator.

The sports car racing scene continued to attract its loyal devotees on both sides of the Atlantic, with Audi dominating not only Le Mans, yet again, but also the increasingly prestigious American Le Mans Series. This year the German car maker pushed the technological boundaries of diesel engineering with its Shell-fuelled machine, which became the first car so powered to win a major international endurance event. Audi's love affair with Le Mans seems more enduring than ever and its success with its diesel-engined contender has sparked similar interest from at least two other manufacturers.

On the opposite side of the Atlantic, F1 happily survived the embarrassment of its 2005 fiasco at the US GP and this year's race duly took place against an optimistic backdrop of speculation that there might be other venues on the continent that are interested in applying for an F1 fixture. Yet F1 commercial rights holder Bernie Ecclestone's apparent enthusiasm for more calendar expansion in the Far East and Pacific Rim areas and the huge interest generated by the established US forms of racing make this seem unlikely.

NASCAR continues to thrive as motor sport's biggest attraction in North America and, with Toyota now committed long-term to the series, the two national single-seater categories seem destined to be consigned to an everlasting supporting role. Granted, the emergence of a third-generation Andretti and a second-generation Rahal may give the perception of single-seater racing something of a boost in the USA, but the real benefit would be derived from a rapprochement between the IRL and ChampCar. At one point in 2006 we were tempted to believe this might be on the cards, but it proved to be just one of many false dawns.

Ultimately, of course, the 2006 season proved that global motor sport in general, and F1 in particular, is in rude health. Doomsayers may have predicted that the departure of the tobacco companies from the F1 sponsorship scene would scupper the prospect of big-budget operations in the future, but the fact remains that all manner of high-profile and high-technology international companies have stepped forward to fill the void. This all suggests that F1 is doing something right, even though its critics may be sceptical about just what sort of a sport will be shaped by the FIA's latest raft of changes. Time alone will tell.

Alan Henry,
Tillingham, Essex
November 2006

Audi wins Le Mans 2006. This time without petrol.

For the sixth time, Audi has won the legendary Le Mans 24 Hour race. No surprise there. That we won the toughest race in the world in the diesel-powered R10 might surprise a few. **Vorsprung durch Technik**

continued
the winning streak

2006 – Yet another year in which our brakes and clutches excelled.

Since the current Formula 1 World Championship series began in 1950, AP Racing products have been at the front of almost every grid and, more often than not, first past the chequered flag.

A total of 597 Grand Prix victories, where we supplied the winner in each race with clutch, brakes – or both – is no mean feat. But it's one our designers, engineers and technicians plan to repeat in 2007.

Whatever formula you race in, you will not find a more comprehensive and integrated range of clutch, brake and associated products than that at AP Racing.

If your aim is to get off the line quicker and brake deeper, more reliably into every corner, speak to our Technical Sales Team. They've got the science covered.

If you would like more information on these or any other of our products, call our Technical Sales Team.

AP RACING

WHELER ROAD

COVENTRY

CV3 4LB

ENGLAND

TEL +44 (0)24 7663 9595

FAX +44 (0)24 7663 9559

EMAIL: sales@apracing.co.uk

the science of friction

www.apracing.com

AP-WS-3

FIA FORMULA 1
WORLD CHAMPIONSHIP 2006

TOP TEN DRIVERS

Chosen by the editor, taking into account their racing
performances and the equipment at their disposal

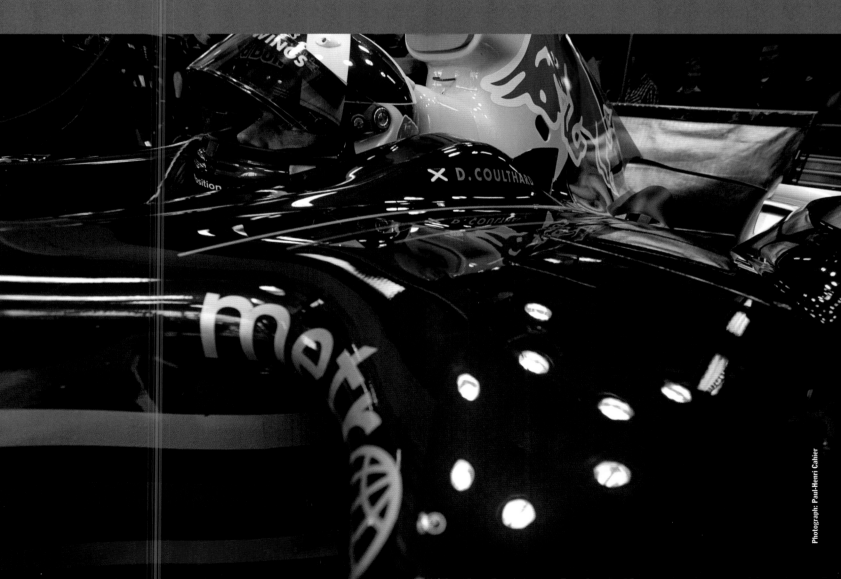

FERNANDO ALONSO

Born: 29 July 1981 • **Team: Mild Seven Renault F1 Team** • **2006** **Grand prix starts: 18** • **Championship placing: 1st** • **Wins: 7** • **Poles: 6** • **Points: 134**

FERNANDO Alonso's only significant mistake en route to his 2005 world championship crown was clipping the wall at Montreal, a slip that forced him to retire from the race with deranged suspension. Putting your finger on a corresponding mistake in 2006 was much more difficult. Despite the fact that he had committed himself to McLaren Mercedes long before he'd raced the new Renault R26 for the first time, Alonso and Renault impressively kept their focus and mutual commitment to brilliant effect.

That Pat Symonds, Renault's executive director of engineering, was able to make a joke out of the fact that the only mistake Fernando had made all year was to sign for McLaren underlined just how well the relationship between team and driver was sustained throughout what might otherwise have been a tense and difficult championship campaign. From the very outset Alonso had no doubts over how close the battle might be against Michael Schumacher and the Ferrari squad. In truth, Alonso's was almost a perfect canvas with only the very slightest of blemishes stemming from a distant, frustrated fifth in the German GP at Hockenheim, a race in which the team was struggling to regain its equilibrium in the face of a ban on its mass damper system, a revised suspension geometry and possibly the wrong tyre choice.

The reigning title holder opened the season with six wins out of the first nine races, building up what seemed to be an unassailable points lead by the time he'd finished the Canadian GP. Thereafter he was very much in damage limitation mode as the Ferrari-Bridgestone revival seemingly reversed the tide in Michael Schumacher's direction. The mathematics would not have been anywhere near so tight had not a problem with a rear wheel hub written him out of the Hungarian GP, where he looked a likely candidate for a magnificent victory despite a practice penalty that consigned him to 15th on the grid.

Overwhelmingly, Alonso is both composed and mature, his only sign of irritation generated by what he continues to feel was a totally unjust qualifying penalty at Monza for allegedly 'impeding' Felipe Massa. He can at least derive consolation from the fact that the majority of the F1 community agrees with his opinion.

1

MICHAEL SCHUMACHER

Born: 3 January 1969 • Team: Scuderia Ferrari Marlboro • 2006 Grand prix starts: 18 • Championship placing: 2nd • Wins: 7 • Poles: 4 • Points: 121

WHAT more is there to say about Michael Schumacher? At Interlagos he drove the 249th and last race of his F1 career with all the commitment and zest he'd applied to his first such outing, with the Jordan team at Spa-Francorchamps 15 years earlier. But for a rare Ferrari engine failure at Suzuka, Michael might well have signed off with a record eighth world championship crown and an unparalleled 92 GP wins, which would have equalled the combined career totals achieved by Ayrton Senna and Alain Prost. Even so, Schumacher leaves a legacy of statistical achievement that one cannot imagine ever being eclipsed.

Ferrari struggled with its Bridgestones in the early races and perhaps if Schumacher had not missed a crucial early-season tyre test at Jerez this slight performance shortcoming might have been earlier identified. He won for the first time of the year at Imola, where astute Ferrari tactics enabled him to out-fumble Alonso's Renault in what amounted to a reversal of the previous year's even tighter result. He then won again at the Nürburgring, settled for second in Spain, where a race-day change in track temperature just flipped the winning coin in the Alonso-Renault-Michelin direction.

Then came Monaco, where events were largely overshadowed by the amazing arrogance of Schumacher and the Ferrari team, who were found guilty of breaking the rules by the stewards after the seven-times world champion parked his car out on the circuit during qualifying in a deliberate attempt to prevent Alonso from taking pole position.

It triggered a row that brought back to the surface all the old Schumacher controversies, from the time he collided with Damon Hill's Williams at Adelaide 12 years ago through the moment he rammed Jacques Villeneuve's Williams at Jerez in 1997 and on to putting Fernando Alonso on the grass going down to Stowe at 190 mph on the opening lap of the 2004 British GP.

Despite what must be judged a brilliant final season, it was sad that Schumacher's last few races should take place in the long shadow of such questionable episodes. For all that, Michael was the defining driver of his era – a towering genius – and his departure removes a key reference point by which others can judge their efforts.

JENSON BUTTON

Born: 19 January 1980 • **Team: Lucky Strike Honda Racing F1 Team** • **2006 Grand prix starts: 18** • **Championship placing: 6th** • **Wins: 1** • **Poles: 1** • **Points: 56**

JENSON BUTTON rounded off seven years of F1 endeavour and a succession of thwarted efforts in 112 world championship outings by breaking his run of disappointment to win the 2006 Hungarian GP, finally putting his name into the motor racing record book as one of the élite who have claimed their place on the upper step of the winners' rostrum.

He brought his Honda home 30.8s ahead of Pedro de la Rosa's McLaren-Mercedes and the BMW-Sauber of Nick Heidfeld at the end of an afternoon that had been transformed into a wildly unpredictable lottery by heavy rain, which began falling just before the start of the 70-lap race. Yet there was much, much more significance attached to Jenson's success than the simple statistic that he'd at last won a grand prix. It altered his entire personality and perception.

From the moment Honda no. 12 swept past the chequered flag at the Hungaroring, Button changed. He'd always projected a pleasantly gregarious personality, but now he developed a relaxed assurance that hadn't quite been there before. Although he may have believed it to be present already, he also matured in an almost indefinable manner. Post-Hungary, if you watched him strolling through the paddock you saw a sleek gloss about him, a new-found sheen of confidence that had hitherto not been obvious. It was a fascinating transformation.

At a stroke, he could bury memories of the season's indifferent opening races. The pole position in Australia that ended with an ignominious, fiery engine failure. The embarrassing spin into retirement at Silverstone on his own oil. Now he sprinted to the end of the season with a fifth, three fourths and finally a stupendous third place at Interlagos, where he came storming though from 13th on the grid after being beset by traction control problems during qualifying.

Crucially, he also nailed the lie that Jenson Button can't overtake. All told, a season that had begun amid uncertainty and insecurity was transformed by that one victory into the possible foundation for future success. Who knows what Jenson might be able to deliver now?

KIMI RÄIKKÖNEN

Born: **17 October 1979** • Team: **Team McLaren Mercedes** • **2006** Grand prix starts: **18** • Championship placing: **5th** • Wins: **0** • Poles: **3** • Points: **65**

SEASONED McLaren insiders could judge it perfectly: once Kimi Räikkönen arrived in the team's garage on a Friday morning, within an hour they would know whether the race weekend would involve his pitching in as a top contender or if they could write off the grand prix as a waste of time. Kimi, they reckoned, was that easy to read.

To a very large degree, any assessment of Räikkönen's 2006 season must be seen in the context of the enduring uncertainty of his relationship with McLaren. Ostensibly the team was keen to re-sign him for 2007, to partner Fernando Alonso, but the McLaren top brass could never quite get an accurate picture from his management regarding his contractual status. Had he signed for Ferrari or not? Only when Maranello confirmed at Monza that Räikkönen would be on its driving strength in 2007 did it become clear that he'd signed the deal a year before.

For all that, Räikkönen continued to hone his reputation as an instinctive, seat-of-the-pants driver throughout the 2006 season, possible wins at Monaco and Hungary unfortunately slipping through his fingers. He was dynamically quick when the McLaren MP4-21 allowed him to be, which was certainly not all the time.

Behind the scenes, however, life seems to have become considerably more complex. Rumours of a personal rift between Räikkönen and the McLaren team had been circulating for more than a year since Ron Dennis, McLaren's chairman, wrote to his driver offering some unsolicited advice on how to conduct his personal lifestyle.

According to sources close to Ferrari, Räikkönen was so infuriated at this that it was only another couple of months before he signed a firm deal to join Ferrari in 2007. Yet Kimi was still champing at the bit for more victories and at Shanghai looked likely to break McLaren's 2006 duck – until throttle mechanism failure spelled the end of his efforts. He rounded off the year translating second on the grid at Interlagos into a less-than-inspired fifth at the chequered flag. Perhaps he had finally run out of energy.

FELIPE MASSA

Born: 25 April 1981 • Team: **Scuderia Ferrari Marlboro** • 2006 Grand prix starts: **18** • Championship placing: **3rd** • Wins: **2** • Poles: **3** • Points: **80**

There had always been something of a question mark over Felipe's ultimate capability, right since the very start of his F1 career with Sauber in 2002. He was undeniably quick but one always wondered whether his wild and unpredictable streak could be kept under control. Moreover, when the pleasant Brazilian was signed up to partner Michael Schumacher in the Ferrari squad there were more than a few raised eyebrows in the paddock. Felipe is managed by Nicolas Todt, the son of Ferrari MD Jean Todt. Not quite a conflict of interests, but pretty close in some people's opinions.

As it turned out, Ferrari's choice of Massa to succeed Rubens Barrichello was only one step removed from inspired. Granted, by the time he'd smashed up a couple of cars at Melbourne – one in qualifying, the other at the first corner of the race – you began to wonder whether he'd been over-promoted. But then Felipe settled into his stride and a whole succession of top-six placings came his way.

He scored his first podium with third at the Nürburgring, took second at Indianapolis and Hockenheim, then qualified on pole in Turkey and won the race pretty much unchallenged after he and Michael had to be queued in the pit lane during their first refuelling stop under the safety car, allowing Alonso to leapfrog Schumacher from second place. There was no legitimate opportunity for Ferrari to get Schumacher through into the lead, so it was all down to Felipe to hold the fort, a task he performed with faultless precision to score his maiden GP victory.

At Interlagos, fuel pressure problems for Schumacher left Maranello's team leader down in tenth place on the grid and Massa had a clear run to pole. The Bridgestone-shod Ferrari 248 was the class of the field come race day and Massa ran away to win in confident style, never putting a wheel wrong and having the great good humour to confess the race had been a piece of cake, possibly his easiest ever.

Most F1 insiders believe Räikkönen will have Massa for breakfast next year. Felipe's reaction to that is simple: 'Bring him on…'

GIANCARLO FISICHELLA

Born: 14 January 1973 • Team: Mild Seven Renault F1 Team • 2006 Grand prix starts: 18 • Championship placing: 4th • Wins: 1 • Poles: 1 • Points: 72

Just as he had done at Melbourne the previous year, Giancarlo delivered a copybook performance from pole position to deliver Renault a superb victory in the 2006 Malaysian Grand Prix, so in a sense he was the obvious candidate for sixth place in these rankings because nobody below him in the drivers' championship top ten managed to score a single race victory.

On the other hand, the sceptical might feel that there is little to choose between four of the last five in this AUTOCOURSE list, all 30-somethings possibly with their best days behind them and assailed on all sides by a bright crop of thrusting new talent. And yet Fisichella's reward for a middling 2006 season has been a contract to remain with Renault until the end of next year.

But, to be fair, Fisichella delivered some noteworthy performances during this season's championship campaign. Third in Spain, beaten only by Alonso and Schumacher; the upper hand over his team-mate and a strong third at Indianapolis; fourth in Italy; third in China and Japan; and finally a dogged run to sixth at Interlagos, where he strained every sinew to keep Schumacher's much quicker Ferrari behind him for as long as he possibly could.

You might argue that it was clear Fisichella would eventually make the crucial slip that would allow Schumacher to squeeze past. Yet many in the Renault squad praised him for withstanding the pressure for as long as he did, defusing the prospect of any pressure on Alonso, who was on course to secure the championship.

Ultimately Fisichella underlined his role as an effective and dependable team player, although not a driver of Alonso's calibre. The key test comes in 2007: can he assert his position as *de facto* team leader or will be quickly find himself eclipsed by new boy Heikki Kovalainen?

RUBENS BARRICHELLO

Born: 23 May 1972 • Team: Lucky Strike Honda Racing F1 Team • 2006 Grand prix starts: 18 • Championship placing: 7th • Wins: 0 • Poles: 0 • Points: 30

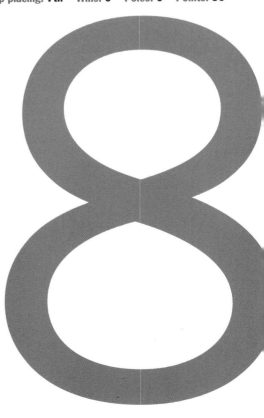

THERE was a wistful and downbeat edge to Rubens Barrichello's demeanour for a large part of the 2006 season, in which he was dramatically eclipsed by Jenson Button not only in the championship points table but more crucially in the private race to become the first contemporary Honda GP winner. In the end, it was not to be the popular Brazilian's tenth career victory, but Jenson's first.

He had not meant it to be like this. When Barrichello turned his back on Ferrari at the end of last season to join Honda it was with the optimistic intention of creating a springboard for his own world championship ambitions after six years in a dutiful supporting role to Michael Schumacher.

Barrichello's first year with Honda was more difficult than he imagined it would be, but the team was impressed with the balance and maturity he brought to the equation in terms of experience garnered in a front-line team. Both Jenson Button and Honda sporting director Gil de Ferran judged Barrichello's contribution to be well worth having, but he certainly experienced more than a few problems in the early races of the season coming to terms with the particular characteristics of the Honda's traction control system.

Not until the European GP, round five of the title chase, did Barrichello out-qualify Button for the first time, but he never quite managed to pull off a podium finish all season. He qualified third at the Hungaroring and the timing of his pit stops was such that he was almost in contention for victory at one point, but in the end he had to settle for fourth. Jenson, by contrast, came through from 14th on the grid to snatch that elusive win.

Barrichello is an energetic and popular member of the Honda F1 squad, but even allowing for the transitional nature of his first season in the team he may have to raise his game appreciably next year if he wants to be retained beyond the expiry of his current contract. It would be ironic if he had swapped the job as 'wing man' to Michael Schumacher for a similarly demanding team-mate against whom he struggled to get the upper hand.

JARNO TRULLI

Born: **13 July 1974** • Team: **Panasonic Toyota Racing** • **2006** Grand prix starts: **18** • Championship placing: **12th** • Wins: **0** • Poles: **0** • Points: **15**

JARNO TRULLI had a disappointing season, but the Toyota management retained sufficient confidence in the pleasant Italian driver to extend his contract to 2009, a welcome bonus for the man who delivered such a resounding 2004 Monaco GP victory for the Renault squad. On that day he looked absolutely unstoppable and in 2005 he showed repeated signs of that flair during his first season with Toyota.

Trulli freely admits to being slightly baffled by the way in which his experiences with the Japanese car maker have unfolded. In 2005 he expected a modest season but he over-delivered on results. In 2006 he anticipated a further step forward but his fortunes dwindled. Seldom did the Toyota look particularly convincing, although a strong run to fourth place at Indianapolis after starting from the pit lane served as a reminder of just how well Trulli could perform.

For all that, there are some who believe that a touch of emotional fragility remains Trulli's Achilles heel. Although not the most gregarious character in the pit lane, he has a sunny disposition and is very much his own man, not conforming to any F1 stereotypes. Jarno can also be a tough customer, as his team-mate Ralf Schumacher found to his cost in this year's Japanese GP. Battling with graining tyres after a refuelling stop, Trulli refused to let Schumacher past – he knew that it was the team policy to permit the two drivers to compete against each other. Trulli stuck to that principal and let Ralf make his own arrangements.

The closest he came to a podium finish was at Monaco, where he was holding third place in the closing stages only to succumb to hydraulic failure. Suggest to him that this might somehow have been his most satisfying race of the year and he shakes his head vigorously. It wasn't, he insists, because he failed to finish the job.

NICO ROSBERG

Born: 27 June 1985 • **Team: WilliamsF1 Team** • **2006** **Grand prix starts: 18** • **Championship placing: 17th** • **Wins: 0** • **Poles: 0** • **Points: 4**

NO matter who you are, no matter how well you have done in the junior formulae, there is just nothing easy about the F1 business. Competing in the sport's most senior category as a raw novice is unquestionably a bruising experience, as reigning GP2 champion Nico Rosberg discovered when he arrived in the Williams-Cosworth squad as Mark Webber's running mate.

The season started on a sunny note. In Bahrain he recovered superbly to finish seventh after losing his nose cone in a first-corner collision. In Malaysia he qualified third, but retired from the race. Thereafter his season nose-dived into a slough of despondency and despair as the Williams FW28 development programme seemed to come off the rails. Thankfully for Nico, the Williams squad was well aware of his talent, which had been emphasised throughout a busy season of test and development work in 2005. Frank Williams and director of engineering Patrick Head knew this was a mature and rounded young man with all the basic qualities needed to develop into a capable F1 driver. Consequently there was no hesitation when it came to extending Nico's contract for 2007.

Sure enough, Nico made a few mistakes, crashing in practice at Imola and flying off the road in the opening stages at Hockenheim. But that's where he was lucky in driving for Williams, where the management fully accepts that if you employ young drivers they are bound to damage a few cars as they go through the learning process.

Next year will be more difficult for Nico. The team is determined to fight back from its current poor position and the pressure will be on its driving line-up to aid that process by delivering both competitively and dependably. Only then will we truly see whether this second-generation Rosberg is a chip off the old block.

Photograph: Peter Nygaard/GP Photo

DAVID COULTHARD

Born: 27 March 1971 • Team: **Red Bull Racing** • 2006 Grand prix starts: **18** • Championship placing: **13th** • Wins: **0** • Poles: **0** • Points: **14**

IT was an acutely frustrating season for David Coulthard. After a promising start for the newly branded Red Bull team last year, life took something of a downward lurch once the team switched engine suppliers from Cosworth to Ferrari. The high spot of the season was Monaco – where a third-placed podium finish put a smile on the team's face – but there were too many occasions when the Red Bull RB2 bounced along outside the top ten and a final championship tally ten points shy of what Coulthard had achieved the previous year was hardly something to be proud of.

Yet Coulthard has certainly been a rock of stability for the Red Bull team, his huge experience playing a key role in calming frayed tempers and helping to signal the road ahead. At 35 he looked fitter, leaner and more motivated than ever throughout a season that was obviously frustrating and disheartening, not only for the Scot but for the entire team. But he has a passion for racing that remains undimmed despite all his years of endeavour.

There were many F1 insiders who voiced the opinion that Coulthard should have called it a day at the end of the 2004 season. He'd had a good run for his money, so why did he feel it was worth sinking into the mid-grid anonymity that seemed certain to go hand-in-hand with a switch to the fledgling Red Bull squad?

Coulthard feels that his critics have missed the point entirely. 'I love F1 – it's what I do,' he insists with just a tinge of exasperation at being required to justify his involvement in the sport. 'I love being part of a team, interacting with young and motivated people to improve performance and get a result.'

There is no doubt that DC firmly believes he has a few more good years remaining. And if circumstances can lead him into the cockpit of an Adrian Newey-designed Red Bull-Renault for 2007, there could well still be some sunny days on the rostrum to come.

champs 1992 • Estoril 1993 • Sao Paulo 1993 • Aida 1994 • Imola 1...

real 1994 • Magny Cours 1994 • Ungarnring 1994 • Jerez 1994 • S...

e Carlo 1995 • Magny Cours 1995 • Hockenheim 1995 • Spa-Fran...

...a 1995 • Suzuka 1995 • Barcelona 1996 • Spa-Francorchamps 199...

Montreal 1997 • Magny Cours 1997 • Spa-Francorchamps 1997 • ...

...ntreal 1998 • Magny Cours 1998 • Silverstone 1998 • Budapest 19...

...999 • Melbourne 2000 • Sao Paulo 2000 • Imola 2000 • Nürburgri...

...polis 2000 • Suzuka 2000 • Kuala Lumpur 2000 • Melbourne 2001 •

FAREWELL, SCHUMI;

Paulo 1995 •
champs 1995 •
• Monza 1996 •
zuka 1997 •
8 • Monza 1998 •
2000 • Montreal 2000 •
Kuala Lumpur 2001

Main: A special helmet for a special driver, Michael Schumacher. His staggering total of 91 grand prix victories is recorded for posterity.
Photograph: Paul-Henri Cahier

Below: The dominant force of his generation.
Photograph: Jad Sherif/WRI

IT'S BEEN GREAT

By MICHAEL SCHMIDT,
Formula 1 editor, *Auto Motor und Sport*

Below: Like father like son. A proud Rolf Schumacher was in Brazil to see Michael's final race.
Photograph: James Moy/www.crashpa.net

Bottom: A banner at Monza reflects the fans' deep-rooted appreciation of all that Michael has contributed to the Ferrari legend.
Photograph: Paul-Henri Cahier

THE moment when the most successful driver in F1 history announced his retirement was understandably expected to be something special. An unforgettable moment. An event of historic dimension. Yet, when it happened, Michael Schumacher's victory at Monza was the only thing that properly fitted in the picture.

Before he communicated to the world the most important decision of the 2006 F1 season, Schumacher had won another grand prix – his 90th. As soon as he sat down in front of the microphones, the show was over. His retirement left more question marks than answers. Typical Michael. He was never a man of great gestures, never showed any talent as an entertainer. He usually gave his answers with his right foot.

The manner of the announcement did not honour the man who dominated grand prix racing over the past 15 years. Ferrari handed out a piece of paper, which Niki Lauda described as 'an obituary'. The atmosphere during the announcement resembled a funeral. Michael repeated his explanation again and again, in English and in German, almost exactly identical to the official communiqué, as if it were coming from a tape. He declined to elaborate any further. You got the impression that he himself could not believe that he had decided to retire.

The reason he gave seemed cursory in the extreme: 'I doubt whether I will find in the future the determination and the motivation that are necessary to compete on the highest level over one season.' Anything less would not be enough. He loves racing, but only with one caveat: that he should win. Schumacher has never been a *competitor* such as Mario Andretti, who raced for the sake of it.

Michael Schumacher invested a lot of effort in his success. It was more than talent that made him so special. 'I would never say that I am the most talented driver,' he admitted. 'It is well possible that there are guys around who have more talent than me.' But most of them lacked the commitment of Schumacher. His put him ahead of the others. He never took anything for granted. For instance, at Benetton he had a speedometer on the dashboard to check his corner exit speeds for each line he tried.

Once, Eddie Irvine was faster than him in the last sector at Silverstone. Michael sat over the telemetry prints late into the night. 'I lost time entering the slow corners,' he said. 'Eddie had been always very strong on the brakes, so I tried to find out what made the difference.' That was what set the two men apart. 'For Eddie, it was acceptable that I took half a second from him in the first two corners,' said Michael. His colleagues might have been too proud to copy others. Not so Schumacher. 'One of my strong points always has been that I am flexible in the way I drive. If I see something in a competitor that could gain me time, I'll take it over.'

Now, he is 37, and his commitment has paid off yet again. After a disappointing 2005 season Schumacher intensified his preparation for what would be his last year in F1. Over the winter he spent more hours in the gym than ever before. He completed more than 17,000 test kilometres, a personal record. He even started testing before the start of the new year, something he had not done for seven seasons. All the time, he was asking himself whether he would be prepared to do it again.

Times have changed since Michael came into F1 like a shooting star in 1991. Today, a test day covers not 250 but 500 km, because modern racing cars do not fail. The technology is more complex. There are briefings for tyres, engines, electronics, aero set-up and strategy. His main rivals Fernando Alonso and Kimi Räikkönen are as fit as he is and they are capable of producing 20 qualifying laps if necessary. But they have the advantage of youth. Michael could not ignore the fact that they were ten and 12 years younger than him.

Racing was still in his blood but the price of enjoying it had got higher and higher. When Michael came to his decision around the time of the US Grand Prix, it was probably when he was aware, more than ever, of all these problems. It was an action-packed time, halfway through the season. Many people at Ferrari and Bridgestone still could not believe that Michael would leave. Those

who worked closely with him could see no sign of fatigue.

'At Monza, the way he was discussing tyre choice and insisting on running a risky race strategy with a low fuel level... that does not come from a man who wants to quit,' one engineer said. He added, 'It was a decision from his head, not his heart.' Another one expressed it differently: 'I got the feeling that he did not retire because he wanted it. No, he retired because he had to do it.'

There is some truth in that. Nobody *told* Michael Schumacher to retire – but the prevailing circumstances made it easier for him to reach that decision.

On top of the increased level of commitment, other considerations were pushing him towards the end of his career. Public appearances and the pressure from the media had increasingly become negative elements of F1. In the past two years, Schumacher had hidden as much as possible. No one did fewer sponsor days. No one gave fewer interviews. In the end, he communicated mainly through his loyal German TV channel, RTL. No controversial questions, no critical reflections, none of those painful interpretations when something went wrong.

Times at Ferrari had changed, as well. When team principal Jean Todt had asked him early in 2005 whether he could anticipate extending his contract beyond 2006, Michael had been unable to give a definitive answer. He accepted that Ferrari therefore had to enter the driver market. Alonso was

not in the equation due, in part, to lingering bad feeling over an earlier offer from Todt that had fallen through. So the only choice was Kimi Räikkönen. Everybody seemed to be targeting the McLaren driver, so Ferrari could not wait to sign a contract with him.

Michael had nothing against this, although most people in the paddock thought otherwise. But Michael had always been a team player. He knew what he owed to Ferrari. Mindful of the support the team had given him since 1996, he could not block its future. So for a while he prepared to face Räikkönen as the ultimate challenge of his career. Maybe Kimi would be superior in terms of pure speed, but Michael felt confident that he could match that with his work ethos, his experience, his understanding of the car and his special relationship with the key people at Maranello. On the other hand, it made it easier for him to quit because, with Kimi in his place, there would be no vacuum left behind him.

Michael also learned quite early that technical director Ross Brawn planned to take a sabbatical. The fact that he never tried to convince Brawn to stay shows that he was already thinking about his own retirement last winter. Ross is an important factor at Ferrari. He is a true leader, somebody who has authority within the whole team, who makes decisions and takes the responsibility if something goes wrong. A Ferrari insider sees replacing Ross as the biggest challenge facing Ferrari. Michael probably sees it the same

Above: Did he go, or did he receive a subtle push? It seems almost inconceivable, but some F1 insiders believe that Michael was encouraged to go.
Photograph: Paul-Henri Cahier

controversial behaviour. There was the crash with Damon Hill in 1994 at Adelaide, which secured Michael's first championship. The attempt to shove Jacques Villeneuve off the road in 1997 at Jerez. The moment when he pushed Heinz-Harald Frentzen into the gravel trap coming out of the pit lane at Montreal in 1998. His parking manoeuvre this year at Monte Carlo. Other times he shouldered the collective blame – for example, when Ferrari decided at the A1-Ring in 2002 that he should switch positions with Rubens Barrichello. Or in 1998 at Silverstone, when the team delayed Michael's stop-and-go penalty for overtaking under a yellow flag until the final lap and he crossed the 'finish line' in the pit lane before even entering his pit box, thus avoiding his punishment.

From so many victories, it is difficult to select the outstanding ones. There was the win in 1995 at Spa, starting from 16th. His first Ferrari win in 1996, at Barcelona, when it was pouring with rain and even Jacques Villeneuve admitted that 'Michael was driving on a different planet that day'. And Michael's battles with Mika Häkkinen at Imola and Suzuka in 2000 will never been forgotten. Or the race in Malaysia in 2001, where he lost 72 seconds in the pit lane waiting behind Rubens Barrichello. Still he won. Nor should we forget Imola 2003; his mother died the night before win number 65. A few races later, at the A1-Ring, he crossed the line first even though his Ferrari had caught fire during refuelling. At Barcelona in 2004 not even a broken exhaust could stop him.

Michael will be remembered for his record-breaking, but will he be remembered long-term as a personality? Niki Lauda thinks not: 'The only thing Michael has to offer is his success. Too rarely has he shown his emotions.' The racing world remembers Juan-Manuel Fangio as the gentleman, Jim Clark as the driving genius, James Hunt as the playboy, Niki Lauda as the one who flirted with death, Alain Prost as the professor and Ayrton Senna as the magician.

And Michael? To say he has no emotions is not quite fair. On the rostrum he could celebrate like a child. He enjoyed his 90th victory just as much as his first one, in 1992 at Spa. From time to time he even lost his temper, such as after colliding with David Coulthard during the horrendously wet 1998 Belgian GP. Remember when he won at Monza and cried in the media conference. And he gave a donation of $10 million to the victims of the 2004 tsunami in south-east Asia.

Michael Schumacher has no firm plans for the future. The first part of the off-season will pass as usual: playing with his kids at home in Switzerland, moving to Norway for the Christmas holiday. But then, with some distance after the last race, the fire will reignite and that is probably the moment Michael is fearing most. Around Christmas time, he always hankered to get back into a car. 'More than once he was calling Ferrari in early January asking, "Don't you have anything for me to test?"' his manager Willy Weber says. He thinks that within a few months Michael will miss F1.

That doesn't mean he'll return. All the reasons that made him retire will still be valid in a year's time. Probably even more so. He will be 38, Räikkönen will be accustomed to his new team, Alonso will be fully integrated at McLaren and young drivers such as Robert Kubica or Heikki Kovalainen may be challenging the leaders. The new generation of cars for 2008, without any driver aids, won't suit him – he has always been a supporter of the electronic toys of F1's modern era. A bit surprising, you might think, because the quality of a driver should shine even more if the cars are difficult to drive. But Schumacher says, 'I got faster lap times out of the electronic systems because I knew how to adapt them to my driving style. I loved to work with the engineers in this particular area.'

Willy Weber thinks Michael will take on a role within Ferrari. Not an office job; more like that of an ambassador. He will offer his input for new sports cars for the road as much as scouting for new racing talents for the Scuderia. And if the urge to drive a Formula 1 car becomes too great, he could still test at Fiorano and Mugello. And it would not be a surprise if Michael proved faster than the regular drivers.

way, although he would never say so. But it was just another factor that helped convince him that it was time to go.

What will F1 be like without Michael Schumacher? It will certainly survive, just as it did after Juan-Manuel Fangio, Jim Clark, Niki Lauda and Ayrton Senna left the stage. In Germany, the TV ratings will decrease by three to four million viewers, according to RTL's calculations. Ferrari will be a different team, 'but not necessarily a worse one,' says Brawn. The records Michael set will probably remain unbeaten for ever. The absolute numbers are very impressive, but so are the averages. Take the average of his grid positions and he never started lower than the second row. He collected 5.5 points per start. He won 87 percent of his qualifying battles against his various team-mates. He celebrated more than 150 times on the rostrum.

As for victories, pole positions, fastest race laps and kilometres in the lead, Michael collected more than the combined total of the other 21 men who participated in the 2006 Italian GP. 'I cannot imagine that there will ever be a driver who shows that commitment over such a long period and has the luck to be always in a top team,' says Alonso.

The fans and experts are divided. For many, Schumacher is the greatest ever. For others, he has been a reckless driver who wanted to win by any means and not all of his actions have been sporting ones. Despite all his titles, wins, pole positions and fastest laps, he also carries the burden of

181,000 litres
of Shell V-Power

8,330 litres
of Shell Helix

1066 points

72 wins

53 fastest laps

58 pole positions

5 world titles

one big thank you

A world-renowned fuel and motor oil, a car feared by every team in Formula One
and a driver that has swept past the chequered flag five times as a world champion with Ferrari.
Our partnership with Ferrari and Michael Schumacher has made history.
Congratulations Michael on an unforgettable career.
Working with you has helped us develop winning formulas for Shell V-Power and Shell Helix
that drivers around the world rely on every day. And thanks to you, and our continuing partnership
with Ferrari, we're confident that we will continue to make history.

Made to move

KEEPING IT SIMPLE
by NIGEL ROEBUCK – Grand Prix Editor, Autosport

TAKES no prisoners, Flavio Briatore. He was never your standard team principal, steeped in motor racing; never a mechanic who came up through the ranks, or whatever. Until he took over running the Benetton team, he knew nothing of Formula 1 and cared less. To this day he will tell you he understands little of the technology intrinsic to the sport and he couldn't care less about that, either. He is there to run the place and that's it. He is a manager. 'It's the people who make a company,' he is fond of saying. 'Not a company that makes the people.'

It is perhaps no surprise, then, that Briatore is a huge admirer of Carlos Ghosn, the Brazilian who not long ago became president of Renault. 'For me,' he says, 'it's a privilege to work with one of the best managers in the world. The way he takes decisions is very simple and very quick. And he's a brilliant strategist – he really thinks about the future. It's quite exciting to have direct contact with someone like Carlos.

'For me a good manager is a very simple person. Look at Formula 1: you see people who are very simple and people who are very complicated – and the complicated ones don't get the results. Carlos isn't like that – he's very clear and straightforward. It's a pleasure working with him and it's exciting to see the Renault Group more and more involved with F1. When Carlos became president, obviously he had different priorities, but now I think he realises that F1 is very, very important.'

If Briatore esteems Ghosn's management qualities, how does he define his own? 'I like to keep things as simple as possible. I like to be in control – to know what's going on, all the time. The important thing is to get the right people in senior positions in the company and then keep them, by making them feel they're trusted and supported. Some teams pay much more than Renault, but there are other things in life that make people happy, too. I think there is almost a family atmosphere about Renault and people like a good environment to work in. They're loyal to me and I am to them.'

London, one of which is in Harrods, and 15 more are in the pipeline. 'There are three in Japan, three in Russia and others in Dubai, Las Vegas, Beverly Hills…'

Not in New York, though, which is a surprise given Briatore's familiarity with the place. Compared with setting up the Benetton operation in Manhattan, Briatore suggests, running an F1 team is simplicity itself. It was after living there for several years, as Benetton's man in America, that he returned to Europe to run the company's F1 team, which years later was bought by Renault.

Flav was installed in the job simply because he was a proven manager and initially it caused considerable resentment in some quarters, for the existing management people – all greatly experienced in F1 – were swiftly removed.

This was 1993 and in '94 Benetton, with Michael Schumacher, won the world championship. Mention this and Briatore starts to laugh.

'People ask me what I think of F1 and I tell them it's wonderful, because if it wasn't the way it is, I would be nowhere in it – I'm serious! I arrived in the Benetton team with my T-shirts – and the year after, we won the world championship. Tell me: what other business in the world is there where you come into it and immediately be number one? I have to say thank you very much to everybody!

'Now I want it to stay like that. I've found a really good environment and I think I have a good background in F1 now. I have a good team, I buy teams, I sell teams, in 2007 I'll be managing 20 to 30 percent of the drivers in F1: [Fernando] Alonso, [Heikki] Kovalainen, [Mark] Webber and another on the way…

'So I think it's all great and I love it. Honestly!'

More laughter. 'I'm very happy to have all this confusion about the rules and God knows what – I'll just do my job. For a guy who came from the world of T-shirts, I haven't done so bad! But I tell you, if I've made a success in F1, it's not because I'm so good – it's because a lot of people aren't good at all.'

Left: Flavio Briatore runs the Renault F1 operation in his own uniquely individualistic style.
Photograph: James Moy/www.crash.pa.net

Left: Renault top man Carlos Ghosn has pledged that the company will have a long term F1 involvement, a stance which can be taken as a strong endorsement of Flavio's operational methods.
Photograph: XPB.cc

Aside from running the Renault F1 operation, Briatore has other interests, most of which he refers to as 'hobby businesses'. One that is not is Pierrel, a pharmaceutical company.

'I have a 50-percent shareholding in it,' says Flavio, 'and a friend of mine has the other 50 percent. We bought the company eight years ago – it was very small then and we built it up. Now it's a big company – we're number one in Europe in the manufacture of anaesthetic – and we launched it on the stock market in Italy last spring.'

The 'hobby businesses' are not exactly small-time, either. There are the Cipriani restaurants in London and Sardinia, and also in Sardinia is a club appropriately named Billionaire. 'Very big turnover – I would say it's the number-one club in Europe now,' says the unassuming owner, 'and there is also another big club, in Tuscany. It's called Twiga, which is Swahili for "giraffe". I called it that because I love Kenya.'

Then there is Billionaire Couture. There are two shops in

Then Flav becomes more serious. He approaches F1 just as he approached the clothing business: if you are trying to sell a product, make it as good as you can and folk will buy it. To Briatore F1 is just as much a product as a sweater is and, while he is gratified by the success his team has achieved, he has great misgivings about the product called Formula 1.

'We are in the entertainment business, aren't we? Sure, you need technology – but a lot of people forget that we're supposed to be *racing*. Everybody talks all the time about technology and a lot of them are people who never won a championship – never won a *race!* Okay, fine, if that's what they want to do, but I don't understand them – I just do my job, I go and win the championship…

'Formula 1 is a product and the product is very good – but we need to understand what the customer wants. It makes no sense to spend huge amounts of money on something the customer doesn't understand and doesn't want. The whole mass damper thing is a good example…'

Opposite page: The double world champion Fernando Alonso's career has been astutely handled by Briatore

Bottom: Max Mosley, the FIA president, has not always agreed with Briatore, but always feels his views on any particular subject are worth listening to.
Photographs: James Moy/www.crashpa.net

Simply put, mass damper systems, mounted in the nose, were conceived to help make the best use of the front tyres. They were judged acceptable by the FIA, which governs F1, and used throughout 2005 and most of '06, until suddenly it was decided they constituted 'a moveable aerodynamic device', which the rules do not permit. Several teams used the systems, Renault to particularly good effect. When they were banned, Briatore's team was hurt more than any other and for a time the overall competitiveness of the car was compromised.

Flav was not impressed. 'People don't care about mass damper systems – why should they? But I think what they do care about is that there is something wrong in the system of F1, simple as that. In Italy they knew there was something wrong in the football world. Same thing.

'I'll say it again, we have to consider what people – our customers – want. And what people don't understand is why we spend so much money to make sure the race is boring! I agree with them – I don't understand, either!

'Part of the problem with F1, I think, is that a lot of people at the top of teams started as engineers, rather than as businessmen. An engineer gets his satisfaction from technology – he doesn't care about making F1 a successful business. Of course technology is important but if it costs a lot of money and makes F1 less entertaining, something is wrong, I think.

'Another fundamental problem is this stupid thing about unanimous agreement being needed to change anything. Jesus, you don't manage a *house* with unanimous agreement! If you need the agreement of everyone – your kids, everybody – you're going nowhere.

'Also, very few people have a vision of the future of F1. Everyone thinks in terms of a little garden or a little garage – because this is their background.

'And every time somebody – Bernie [Ecclestone, F1's rights holder], Max [Mosley, FIA president] or whoever – proposes something "different", before people have even thought about it their instinctive response is "no". If I see something to make me change my mind about something, I do it – only the stupid never change their minds. And it seems to me that a lot of people in F1 never change their minds.

'Why do we need the FIA to impose all these rules about engine homologation? Why – if we're business people – don't we achieve an agreement on our own? Together, we spend $1.4 billion a year on engines – and we put on this lousy show!'

Briatore believes that many of his fellow team principals, out there in the real world, would not long survive. He despairs of the waste – of both time and money – in F1 and also of what he sees as blind complacency.

'We sit and look into our crystal balls – and all the time we're losing sponsors. And at the same time we beat up the price – crazy! Our job is racing – our job is entertaining people. And we look completely the opposite of that. If what you spend is proportional to the show, then I'm very happy – but the more we spend, the worse the show, because the more technology you put into the car, the less show you have.

'Why are the races interesting when it's raining? Simple – because there's no grip! Look at the race in Hungary: okay, for us, for Renault, it was no good, but for the people watching on TV it was spectacular. If people are watching a good show, they'll carry on watching it and they'll tell other people how good it is. I don't understand why some people can't see that. Ten people sit down and this one agrees, then he disagrees, then someone else agrees, then the next day doesn't agree...

'We're all in the right place at the right time, because Bernie has built up a fantastic business – but we're doing everything we can to destroy it! Everyone always talks all the time about technology – never about the show. Never about the *product.*'

It was Ecclestone and Briatore who brought GP2 into

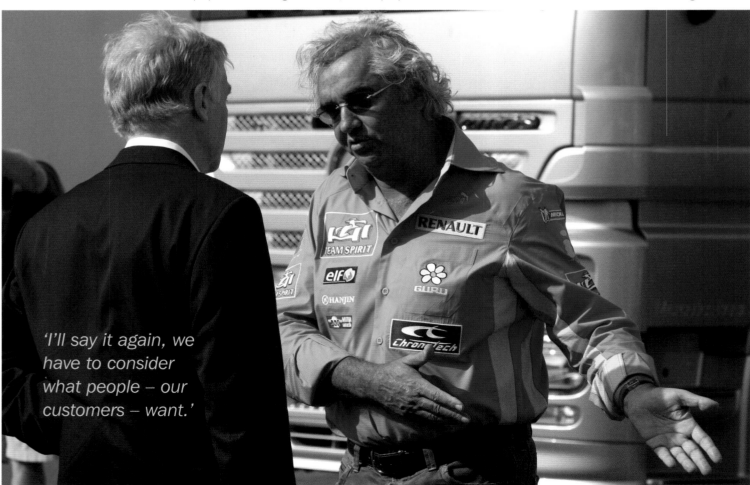

'I'll say it again, we have to consider what people – our customers – want.'

Top: GP2 cars at Monza. Nelson Piquet in a typically frentic piece of action.

Above: Flavio makes his point in characteristically emphatic style.

Inset right: Having the biggest motor home in the paddock is of no concern to Briatore.

Opposite page: Briatore has always been comfortable with the management style he deploys at Renault – and the strong results it has delivered.

Photographs: James Moy/www.crash.net

the world and by common consent it has been a tremendous success.

'Well, there are just two of us involved,' says Flavio. 'We sit and discuss whether we need to change this or that – and that's it. And it's working! No one was interested in F3000 [GP2's predecessor], so why is everyone watching GP2? Because the racing's fantastic – and that's because the product is right.'

Many have suggested that here could be a blueprint for the F1 of the future. GP1, if you like. Eight hundred horse-power, relatively simple aerodynamics, slicks, no 'driver aids'... With cars like that, driven by the likes of Alonso and Kimi Räikkönen, Briatore suggests, it could be a fantastic show.

'And it would cost you three million, instead of 300 million! As it is, we always educate our people to work for the maximum expenditure – an F1 guy, looking for a birthday present for somebody, goes straight to Bulgari or Cartier!

'He always thinks of the most expensive. If it doesn't cost a fantastic amount of money, it can't be good – that's the thinking in this bloody paddock. Everyone has to have the biggest factory, the biggest motorhome, and for what? Does a factory work better because it's bigger? No! Probably it's the opposite. Everyone has to make everything so much more complicated, so much more *difficult* than it needs to be.

'When we started GP2, which doesn't have too much technology, all the F1 team managers said, "You'll never succeed..." Now, though, everybody watches it – and why?

Because the race is good.

'I tell you, if I were not in F1 I wouldn't watch it. I don't want to waste two hours of my time watching a boring race. If two hours is too long, maybe we could have two races of 45 minutes each. And if qualifying is too boring, maybe we do it the same way as GP2 – put the quick drivers back in the pack.

'We – are – in – the – entertainment – business. And, as things are, the more we spend, the more boring we are. We spend top money – and put on the most boring top event in the world. It only gets interesting and exciting when it's raining – or when something unexpected happens in qualifying and gives us a strange grid, with the quick guys behind: look at Japan last year [Räikkönen won from the back of grid after rain in qualifying].

'The thing is, when we talk about "racing" in F1, these days we're really talking about "strategy". In football people don't want to see 0-0; they want to see 4-3. And in racing overtaking is like a goal. We don't need 350 overtaking moves in every race – it would mean nothing if it happened easily – but for sure you need five or six.

'We've created a big television sport in the world, a very solid foundation, a fantastic base – but we need to improve it because we've got much more competition these days than we used to have. Now we're going down and down and down – and why? Because our product isn't good enough. It's simple...'

So now you know.

'...so why is everyone watching GP2? Because the racing's fantastic – and that's because the product is right.'

'Everyone has to have the biggest factory, the biggest motorhome, and for what?'

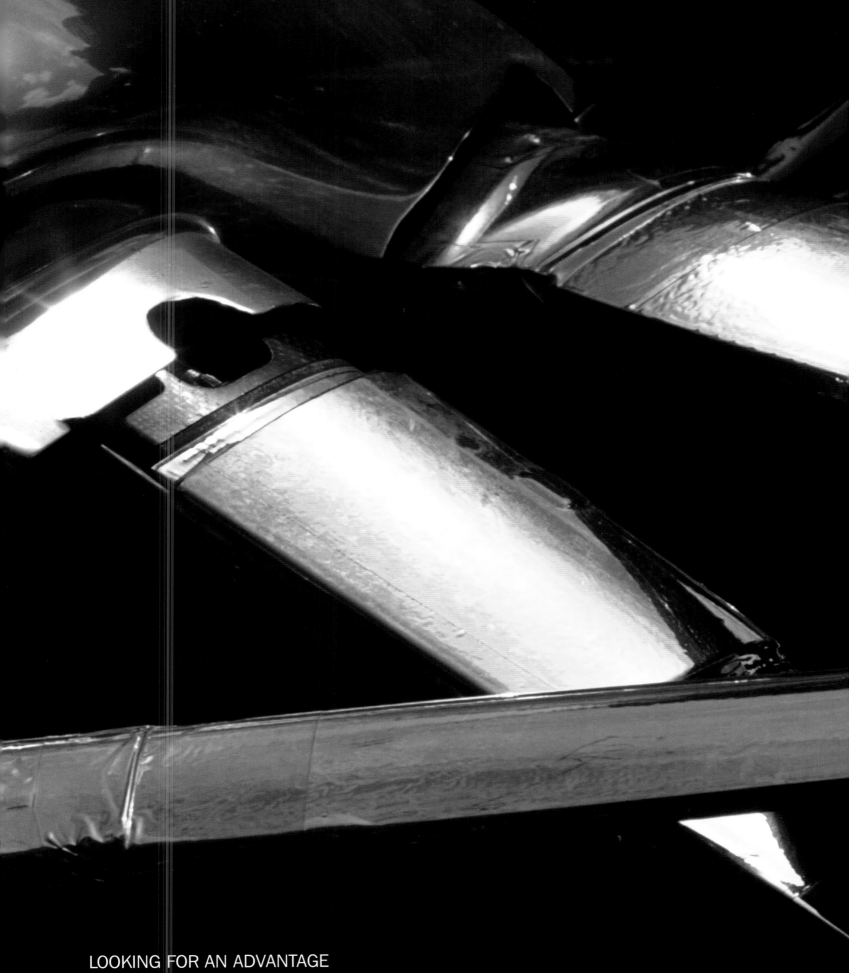

LOOKING FOR AN ADVANTAGE
PUSHING THE BOUNDARIES
by MARK HUGHES, F1 consultant editor, *Autosport*

FORMULA 1 has always served up controversy. Regardless of whether that's good or bad, it's part of the sport's DNA. Yet again this year the intense competitive drive of F1's participants went up against its unyielding rule book, perhaps the most infamous example being Michael Schumacher's 'parking incident' in the final seconds of Monaco qualifying, the seven-times world champion apparently losing control of his Ferrari at all of 14 mph at Rascasse corner, blocking the track and preventing anyone from beating his provisional pole position time.

It started early in the season, when Ferrari's rivals got themselves in a tizzy about the apparently flagrant way the 248's rear wing flexed, lowering at speed and thereby reducing its drag, yet passed the FIA's stationary deflection test.

Later in the year Fernando Alonso – stung into retribution, perhaps, for his qualifying time penalty in Hungary after a trifling incident with another driver – spotted a golden opportunity in a later practice session. With the red flags out, he saw arch-rival Schumacher behind him in the Renault's mirrors. Midway through the penultimate corner he slowed to a crawl and Schumacher unthinkingly passed him on his way to the pits, thereby incurring an Alonso-matching penalty.

There was also the issue of Renault's mass dampers: accepted by the FIA as perfectly legal when the team sought permission late in 2005, then deemed illegal halfway through 2006.

The sport has always been this way, as anyone who remembers the 'fan car' Brabham of 1978, the twin-chassis Lotus 88 of '81 or the hydraulic-ride Brabham BT49 of the

same year will attest. Or, a year later, the outrageously underweight Cosworth cars with the great water-tank scam.

An outside observer might get the impression that F1 competitors are a bunch of cheats. Gordon Murray – the man behind the fan car and the hydraulic-ride Brabham that got around the minimum ride height rule and who enthusiastically embraced the underweight cars with 'water-cooled brakes' – insists it's not so.

'No, it's not intentional cheating,' he says, trying to explain the mindset of an F1 warrior. 'I wouldn't even say that it's about looking for a loophole – though I accept that's how it will look from the outside. But a loophole implies you sit down and look through the rules thinking, "Right, how can we screw them?" and it doesn't work like that. You are attacking your task and assessing all the possibilities and limitations – and it's only towards the end of that process that you look at the regulations to see if there's a way you can do it.

'A classic example of this was the fan car. Once we'd understood the total energy Lotus was getting from its ground-effect venturis in the sidepods, and that we had a flat-12 engine making the concept a non-starter for us, I explored all the possibilities without even going near the regs. At first I was going to do a twin-chassis car: move the engine behind the driver, have the fuel tank behind the engine, with a propshaft running through the tank. That way the primary pipes and cylinder heads could be out of the way of the venturis. Then I did the weight calculation and found it added around 23 kg so that was a non-starter. So then I had another think about what I could do – and thought about sealing the

underside of the car and sucking all the air out. *Then* you go to the regs to see if you can do it and there was a bit of wording there that allowed us to do it – the primary function clause. You weren't allowed moveable aerodynamic devices but you could have something on the car that had an aerodynamic effect as long as that was not its primary purpose. So we said the primary purpose of the fan was for cooling. So the regulation bit came way down the line in the conception of that idea. It wasn't like we looked at the regs first.

'You have to consider the intensity of it all. I can liken it only to how I imagine it was in World War II when the enemy had come up with a new tank or some other new technology and you had to respond – with a virtually limitless engineering budget at your disposal. People used to ask how we could make 30 changes to the car in the six days that it was back at the factory between races. That's why – because you are alternately responding and trying to pull clear all the bloody time. The regs come a long way down the list.'

Imagine the shock in the F1 paddock when Brabham turned up to the '78 Swedish Grand Prix with a huge engine-driven fan mounted on the rear of the BT46B and sealing skirts around the underbody. In scrutineering an official asked

that the engine be revved while he observed the rear ride height so he could see if the fan created a suction. This was duly done and the scrutineer noted no change in the ride height. The engine was switched off and only then did one of the Brabham mechanics remove his foot from under the car's skirts, where it had prevented the skirt from sealing…

That Brabham mechanic was Herbie Blash, now part of the governing body's technical team. He assists FIA technical chief Charlie Whiting – another former Brabham mechanic – in applying a rule book vastly thicker than it was in the fan car's time.

Today, although that intense competitive striving is the same as it ever was, the way it all plays out is very different. You still could in theory simply show up with an innovation outside the spirit of the regulations – but you'd be running the risk of being thrown out for the 'crime' of not having sought permission first. When someone comes up with an idea that isn't adequately covered in the existing technical rules he has to explain the idea to Whiting, who will then rule on whether it is permissible. If he says yes the team simply turns up and begins racing with it and other teams do not get informed. If the answer is no, all the teams are informed about the query

Above centre: The Brabham BT46B 'fan car' won in Sweden – and was promptly banned.

Above: Gordon Murray, still a welcome grand prix visitor, retains his ever-enquiring F1 mind.

Left: Niki Lauda is as interested in Murray's creation as the photographers in the Anderstorp paddock back in 1978.
Photographs: www.crashpa.net

decided they want to control the teams and the sport, almost to the extent of manipulation. The mass damper was a case in point. If mass dampers are to be considered aerodynamic devices, then logically so are the tyres. They too are not part of the sprung mass, but they are moveable and have an effect on the aerodynamics. Therefore you should have steel tyres! Or the carbon wishbones that all the cars now have. They move all the time and are not attached to the sprung mass. Therefore you should have no suspension! It's not about the logic of the argument; it's about control.'

This is the tortured screaming of a free technical mind asked to contemplate rigid subservience to someone else's rules. It was the same for Lotus boss Colin Chapman when his twin chassis 88 was banned.

This was a conceptually brilliant way of getting around ground effect's major downside. With ground effect, a car would begin to 'porpoise', a violent bouncing as the airflow through the car's underbody alternately stalled and re-attached, the car sucked down on its springs then released. This would make the car virtually undriveable. To get around this, the 88 had a separate inner chassis for the driver, attached via soft springing to an outer chassis that was sprung stiffly enough to withstand the aero loads the underbody was capable of generating by maintaining a more consistent ride height.

The man behind the concept, Peter Wright, explains: 'There was nothing in the rule book that made that car illegal. But it was pretty obvious it was never going to be allowed to run. Colin got deeply trenchant about it because he was fighting for the right to innovate. When the affair was all over he told me he would keep going until the John Player sponsorship deal ran its course but after that he was going to leave F1. He died not long after saying that, but even had he lived I'm pretty sure he would have left.'

That was probably the earliest example of the governing body pushing through its interpretation of the intent of its regs regardless of their wording, the first time it almost explicitly said, 'I don't care what I said; I meant this.' Interestingly, and conforming to a pattern, Wright is now a retained FIA technical consultant.

But although getting past the technical regulations is a much more torturous process than in Murray's day, the driver is still faced with split-second decisions between the intent of the sporting regulations and any foul play that might be difficult to detect. This appears to

and the response. So the potential for finding any loophole is within much tighter constraints – and is entirely dependent upon the governing body's response.

The only way to pull a fast one now is to hoodwink Whiting about the true purpose of the development. Given that he used to be on the other side, that's no easy task. However, Whiting insists that his initial acceptance of Renault's mass dampers in 2005 was as a result of exactly this process. Partway through 2006 a rival team to Renault gave its interpretation of why mass dampers should be considered aerodynamic devices that were not part of the sprung mass of the car (and therefore moveable and illegal). Whiting agreed and duly changed his original ruling.

Renault continues to insist that the only benefit it sought from the devices was to equalise the contact patch loads on the tyres, to soften out the variations arising from the car's pitching and bouncing.

The FIA is at liberty to interpret the arguments any way it sees fit. Such a system will always be open to accusations of favouritism – and the FIA has been thus accused. But it uses this liberty ostensibly to ensure that no one gains an advantage from beating the intention of the regulations.

For Murray, this is where it all goes wrong. 'Using this system they have virtually killed any technical innovation,' he argues. 'With the major masses of the cars and the concept and dimensions of the engines pretty much predefined, it's now almost a one-make formula. It's no longer about the merit of the technical developments and how they relate to the rules; it's about control. They [F1's rule-makers] have

have been what Schumacher was banking on when he opted to 'lose control' at parking speeds during Monaco qualifying. The stewards were having none of it and were able to demand the telemetry traces from his car. After trawling through the data and comparing them with the in-car camera, they threw Schumacher to the back of the grid and issued the following statement: 'Having compared all the relevant data the stewards can find no justifiable reason for the driver to have braked with such undue, excessive and unusual pressure at this part of the circuit and are therefore left with no alternative but to conclude that the driver deliberately stopped his car on the circuit.'

When Murray was in charge of Bernie Ecclestone's Brabham team, his driver Carlos Reutemann would routinely cruise around the track slowly, balking his rival's quick laps after he'd set a good time. 'Absolutely,' says Murray. 'Under my specific instructions. It's called motor racing.'

There's the essence of a competitor's attitude to rules and regulations. At the core they are a distant secondary to competing. 'I don't believe the governing body should be there to control,' Murray says. 'It should be largely unheard and simply run the sport, not control it. Just as a government should be serving you, not controlling you.'

KEITH DUCKWORTH, who died in December 2005 just after the last edition of AUTOCOURSE was published, was widely acclaimed in F1 as possibly the most imaginative and resourceful engineer of the post-war era. His Cosworth DFV grand prix engine changed the sport's landscape for good after its introduction at the 1967 Dutch Grand Prix, where it powered Jim Clark's epochal Lotus 49 to a dominant début victory.

The availability of an off-the-shelf F1 engine that was rugged, dependable and easy to operate opened up to a whole raft of new independent teams the possibility of competing in the championship. Between Clark's win in Holland and Michele Alboreto's in the 1983 Detroit GP, the Cosworth DFV and its derivatives won no fewer than 155 world championship rounds.

A sometimes bluff and always direct Lancastrian, Duckworth's path to motor racing fame started when he left Lotus in 1958 to start his own race engine development company in partnership with Mike Costin, a fellow ex-Lotus engineer. The name Cosworth engineering sprang logically to mind and thus the seeds of what was to become a hugely successful enterprise were sown.

Duckworth was born in Blackburn in 1933. His father Frank owned a weaving business and sold cotton on the Manchester Cotton Exchange. The Duckworth family was comfortably off, but its relative affluence was the product of much hard work and application, qualities that Keith consistently demonstrated as he carved his own niche in his chosen business.

Educated at Giggleswick in Yorkshire, Duckworth later did national service with the RAF, although his aspirations to become a service pilot received a severe dent within hours of his being awarded his wings: Keith actually dozed off in the cockpit and was ejected from the course for 'dangerous and incompetent night flying'. Later in life he became an accomplished and meticulous helicopter pilot, relinquishing his licence only after a heart attack in 1973.

Cosworth's fortunes really took off at the start of the 1960s, when the company began building Ford Anglia-based engines for the new 1,100-cc Formula Junior, from which point the name Cosworth became increasingly synonymous with light, efficient and reliable racing engines. The company had started in distinctly down-at-heel premises in Frien Barnet before moving to Edmonton in 1961 and finally to what would become its spiritual home in St James Mill Road, Northampton, at the end of 1964.

Duckworth's big break as an engineer came in 1965 when Colin Chapman, the Lotus founder, persuaded Ford to finance the design and manufacture of a new engine for the new 3-litre F1 formula that was due to start in 1966. Thanks to the shrewd and perceptive influence of Walter Hayes, head of Ford's public affairs department, Lotus, Ford and Cosworth were all brought together. Hayes successfully sold the idea to Patrick Hennessey, the Ford of Britain chairman, and approval for the project duly followed from Ford's world headquarters in Detroit.

Cosworth was thus commissioned to design, develop and build the 3-litre V8 F1 engine, and the four-cylinder FVA F2 engine, for a fee of £100,000. Forty years later Ford veterans still describe it as 'the bargain of the age'. Duckworth set up his drawing board in the quiet of his home, away from the Cosworth factory, and settled down to his design work. The project took just under two years from his putting pen to paper to the first Cosworth DFV's being handed over to Team Lotus in April 1967. The designer frequently worked 16-hour days during the initial nine-month design period, during which he lost 40 pounds in weight. Although modestly self-effacing about the effort he expended, Duckworth was undeniably proud of the result.

Prompted by his heart attack and the possible death duty implications of his 85-percent stake in the company, Cosworth was sold in 1980 to United Engineering Industries, a Manchester-based engineering firm. Yet Duckworth continued to work as hard as ever, to the eventual further detriment of his health, and had to undergo open-heart surgery in 1987. Soon afterwards, he relinquished the role of company chairman to Mike Costin.

Left: Keith Duckworth, the creative genius behind the brilliantly successful Ford Cosworth-DFV engine.

Bottom left: The Lotus 49-Ford V8 on its début at Zandvoort in 1967. The BRM team has come down the pit lane to look-see at the new machine. Jackie Stewart and Chris Irwin are with Duckworth (far left), while Mike Spence and Tony Rudd are in discussion to the right.
Photographs: LAT Photographic

STALWART South African F1 privateer Doug Serrurier died this year at the age of 85, some 43 years after making his début in his country's home grand prix at East London. Serrurier, who came from Germiston in the Transvaal, drove an Alfa four-cylinder-engined LDS Special but retired 20 laps from the end of the race in which Graham Hill was crowned champion at the wheel of his BRM. He raced in only two other grands prix, both in South Africa.

By the mid '60s Serrurier had switched to sports car racing with a Lola T70 before trying his hand at rallying and powerboat racing. He then ran a highly regarded classic car restoration business near Johannesburg until he was in his mid 70s.

JOHNNY SERVOZ-GAVIN

Right: Johnny Servoz-Gavin's Matra MS10-Cosworth leads Derek Bell's Ferrari at Monza in 1968. Servoz-Gavin scored a career-best second place in the Ken Tyrrell-entered car.

Below right: The charismatic Frenchman in his prime.

Photographs: LAT Photographic

Above: Doug Serrurier in his self-built LDS-Alfa about to passed by Innes Ireland in the 1962 South African Grand Prix at East London. He retired the car with a leaking radiator.

Photograph: LAT Photographic

Photograph: crashpa archive

JOHNNY SERVOZ-GAVIN, who died at the age of 64 on 29 May, forged a reputation as one of France's most promising young F1 drivers even though he competed in only 12 world championship grands prix before abruptly deciding to retire after failing to qualify his Tyrrell team March 701 for the 1970 Monaco race.

The high spot of his career came in the 1968 Italian GP at Monza, where he was competing as Jackie Stewart's team-mate in Ken Tyrrell's Matra International squad.

After Stewart retired his Matra-Ford MS10 with engine failure, Servoz-Gavin kept the sister car in the thick of the high-speed battle all the way to the chequered flag and just pipped the Ferrari of Jacky Ickx for second place behind Denny Hulme's McLaren.

Georges-Francis Servoz-Gavin was born in Grenoble and became universally known as 'Johnny' from his days as a teenage ski instructor on the slopes above his home town. With his long blond hair and easy manner, the young Frenchman was hugely popular with the ladies and quickly developed something of a playboy image, which he never quite managed to shrug aside.

At the age of 21, Servoz-Gavin started competing in French national rally events, but after attending the racing drivers' school at the Magny-Cours circuit, near Nevers, he quickly decided that he wanted to race single seaters. He acquired a Brabham BT18 for 1965 and his promising performances attracted the attention of Jean-Luc Lagardère, the racing director of the Matra aerospace group that was establishing itself as an emergent motor racing force at that time.

Lagardère arranged for Servoz-Gavin to have a works F3 Matra drive in 1966 and the young driver rewarded his confidence by winning the French championship in decisive style. In 1967 he drove a Matra F2 car in the Monaco Grand Prix, but failed to finish. The following year he returned to the streets of the Principality, where he fumbled the biggest opportunity of his career.

Jackie Stewart had been forced to miss the race after a practice accident in a Matra at an F2 race at Jarama left him with a damaged wrist. Team owner Ken Tyrrell conferred with Elf, the French fuel company that was his major sponsor, and they agreed that Servoz-Gavin should act as Stewart's stand-in.

Driving his first grand prix at the wheel of a fully fledged Formula 1 car, Servoz-Gavin qualified on the front row of the grid and burst into an immediate lead at the start. For three glorious laps he dominated the race, then he made a slight slip coming through the very fast waterfront chicane and clipped the newly installed guard rail with his left-rear wheel.

The previous year a similar mistake had cost the life of the Ferrari driver Lorenzo Bandini, whose car had mounted the straw bales that had previously delineated the left-hand side of the circuit, flipped over and caught fire. Servoz-Gavin's only penalty was a broken driveshaft, damaged in the impact, which caused his retirement from the race.

In 1969 Servoz-Gavin won the prestigious European F2 championship for Matra and drove the experimental four-wheel-drive Matra MS84 in the Canadian, United States and Mexican GPs. For 1970 Tyrrell selected him to drive alongside Jackie Stewart on a regular basis, but the British team started the year using uncompetitive March 701 chassis because Tyrrell wanted to keep using Ford V8 engines and Matra would continue supplying its chassis only if Tyrrell switched to using Matra's own V12 engines, which Tyrrell resolutely refused to do.

Servoz-Gavin finished fifth in the Spanish Grand Prix, but was already worried about problems with his vision after suffering a slight eye injury when a tree branch struck him in the face while he was driving an off-road vehicle the previous winter. After again hitting the chicane at Monaco and failing to qualify for the grand prix, he told Ken Tyrrell he was retiring immediately.

Servoz-Gavin never raced again. He died from a pulmonary embolism after a period of ill-health and is survived by his second wife Annicke and his son from his first marriage.

B.R.M

V12-44-BN

BRM
BERNARD RICHARDS MANUFACTURE

www.brm-manufacture.com

For stockist enquiries please telephone +33 (0)1 61 02 00 25

réalisation Art - Channel 2006 Tél +33 (0)1 34 76 60 60 - photos Luc Virgeaux

Photograph: Paul-Henri Cahier

Contributors
BOB CONSTANDUROS
MAURICE HAMILTON
ALAN HENRY

F1 illustrations
ADRIAN DEAN

MILD SEVEN RENAULT F1 TEAM

FERNANDO ALONSO

GIANCARLO FISICHELLA

Photographs: James Moy/www.crashpa.net

WHEN you reach the season's halfway point having won seven of the nine races, the championship must surely be a formality. Renault did not see it that way. Some of its victories had not been as easy as Fernando Alonso had made them appear. In Spain, for instance, Alonso and Giancarlo Fisichella may have locked out the front row of the grid but the Renault team arrived at the circuit on race day uncertain of victory at Fernando's home track. Had it not been for a rise in temperature just as the race was starting, Michael Schumacher might have made it three wins in a row. As it was, the Ferrari driver outpaced Fisichella to take second. Alonso, meanwhile, did enough with three exquisite laps that left Schumacher breathless. The sixth round of the championship was as finely balanced as that and, in many ways, it summed up the first half of the season.

'Everything may have been perfect up to Canada [round 9],' said Pat Symonds, Renault's executive director of engineering, 'but we were under no illusions. We'd had plenty of alarm bells. Imola had been the reverse of the previous year: we had a quicker car and lost, whereas, in 2005, we'd had a slower car and won. At the Nürburgring [like Imola, won by Schumacher], we were not as quick as Ferrari. Barcelona had not looked particularly promising until our hopes went up with the temperature. So weren't sitting back thinking it was easy. But, equally, we didn't expect things to swing quite so dramatically after Canada.'

That said, trouble had been anticipated for the US Grand Prix a week later thanks to Michelin's taking an understandably conservative route following the embarrassing fiasco in 2005, when Michelin had withdrawn all its runners for safety reasons. Fisichella finished

© ADRIAN DEAN

RENAULT R26

SPONSORS	**Mild Seven • Renault • Elf • Michelin • Hanjin • i-mode • Telefonica • Mutua Madrilena • Chronotech • Guru • PVAXX**
ENGINE	Type: **Renault RS26** No. of cylinders (vee angle): **V8 (90°)** Sparking plugs: **Champion** Electronics: **Magneti Marelli Step 11** Fuel: **Elf** Oil: **Elf**
TRANSMISSION	Gearbox: **Renault F1 7-speed longitudinal** Semi-auto: **Electro-hydraulic actuation of gearchange, clutch and differential** Hand-operated: **Clutch and gearchange** Driveshafts: **Renault F1 integrated tri-lobe** Clutch: **AP Racing**
CHASSIS	Front and rear suspension: **Double wishbone/pushrod operating torsion bar** Dampers: **Penske** Wheel diameter: **330 mm front and rear** Wheels: **OZ** Tyres: **Michelin** Brake pads: **Hitco** Brake discs: **Hitco** Brake calipers: **AP Racing** Steering: **Renault F1 hydro-mechanical servo system (power-assisted)** Radiators: **Marston** Fuel tanks: **ATL** Instruments: **Renault F1 Team**
DIMENSIONS	Track, front: **1,450 mm** rear: **1,420 mm** Gearbox weight: **40 kg** Chassis weight (tub): **60 kg** Formula weight: **605 kg including driver**

Va Va Voom x F1=197

The new Clio Renaultsport 197. Like our F1 car, it has a rear diffuser that reduces rear-end lift. Because less lift equals more control. And now, when you're not glued to the road, you can be glued to your mobile. Text 'Game' to 85101 to download your free mobile driving game. For details, or to see more of the Renaultsport range, visit www.renaultsport.co.uk

Below: Flavio Briatore presided over another world championship success in his characteristically laid-back fashion.

Right: Fernando Alonso clinched his second title with a good run to second place behind Felipe Massa in the Brazilian GP.

Centre: Heikki Kovalainen, Renault's test driver, steps up to the plate next season in a bid to fill Alonso's shoes.

Far right: Pat Symonds continued to play a pivotal role in the Renault team's success.
Photographs: James Moy/www.crashpa.net

RENAULT F1 TEAM

President: Alain Dassas

Managing director: Flavio Briatore

**Deputy managing directors, France:
Rob White, André Lainé**

Technical director: Bob Bell

**Executive director of engineering:
Pat Symonds**

**Head of race engineering (engine):
Denis Chevrier**

Chief designer: Tim Densham

**Deputy chief designer:
Martin Tolliday**

**Engine project leader (RS26):
Léon Taillieu**

Head of aerodynamics: Dino Toso

Team manager: Steve Nielsen

Chief mechanic: Gavin Hudson

Engineering co-ordinator: Paul Seaby

**Race engineer, car no. 1,
Fernando Alonso: Rod Nelson**

**Race engineer, car no. 2, Giancarlo
Fisichella: Alan Permane**

third, two places ahead of Alonso, who confessed that Indy was his least favourite track of all those on the F1 calendar.

Alonso made it to the podium at the next race, in France, where finishing second to Schumacher was an indication of the struggle to keep the Ferrari in sight. If Renault thought that was bad, there was a rude shock (no pun intended) awaiting at Hockenheim.

It was there that the term 'mass damper' became the F1 buzz word of 2006 as Alonso and Fisichella struggled into fifth and sixth places after Renault felt it had no option but to remove the device from its cars. With a summer testing ban in place, the reigning champions had been clumsily shoved onto the back foot. Whether you considered this an unfortunate coincidence depended on whom you spoke to. Renault, for its part, was baffled because the mass damper had been a simple but integral part of the car since its inception.

The R26, the handiwork of a team led by Bob Bell and Tim Densham, was a logical development of the beautifully sculpted car that had brought the Anglo-French partnership the championship in 2005. Part of the front suspension included a tuned mass damper (TMD), which, as the name implies, works at one frequency. Renault tuned the front TMD to damp the pitch frequency; when a rear damper was added later, it damped the bounce frequency.

Having asked the FIA's opinion on the safety aspect of placing a TMD at the front of the car – and having let the officials see detailed drawings in the process – Renault, believing the device to be perfectly legal in the first place, assumed all was well when no objections were raised. The effect of the TMD was to improve both mechanical and aerodynamic grip by helping keep the tyres in more regular contact with the track while keeping the car's ride height more constant. Other teams had fitted TMDs but none seemed able to make them work as well as Renault, which, unlike the rest, had designed its car from scratch around the damper.

As the season wore on, concerns were raised about the aerodynamic influence of the TMD and the idea arose that this could be a moveable aerodynamic device – and therefore illegal. When the stewards at Hockenheim found no fault with the TMD, their decision was hastily questioned by the FIA and a

date set for an appeal. Renault was sure it would win but, in the meantime, raced without the damper at Hockenheim. The appalling performance – by Renault's standards – appeared to indicate the value of the mass damper.

'Hockenheim was a disaster,' said Symonds. 'We reckoned the mass damper was worth three-tenths of a second and it's bloody hard work getting that back. But this coincided with what was probably our worst tyre choice of the season and our worst balance on the car. We'd had a couple of days' testing at Jerez without the mass damper but we hadn't really optimised the car to run without it. The net result was a real struggle for us – particularly for Fernando, who used his tyres more than Fisi and suffered terrible blistering.

'We went off to Hungary still without the mass damper but having had a little more time to think and to do some theoretical optimisation. Fernando was stunningly quick and that wasn't just because the Michelin wet tyre was better than the Bridgestone wet; he was quicker than any Michelin car and very quick as it dried out. That was a race that he was going to win by miles.'

Leaving the pits after his final stop, Alonso got no farther than the second corner, where the right-rear wheel nut came off thanks to a problem with the locking pin. There was better fortune to be had in Turkey, where the appearance of the safety car played into Renault's hands and worked against Schumacher.

Then came Monza and another wild swing of the pendulum, starting with a puncture for Alonso during qualifying. Alonso drove a phenomenal lap to fifth on the grid with a damaged car and then suffered the penalty of losing his three fastest times after an absurd decision by the stewards that he had impeded the Ferrari of Felipe Massa. A computer simulation showed that, without the tyre damage, Alonso would have been on the front row but any speculation was made irrelevant by a rare failure of the Renault V8. This was a surprise because the V8, another excellent product from Rob White and his team at Viry-Châtillon, had been more or less trouble-free from its first pre-season test.

'We had an absolute stupidity in Bahrain,' recalled Symonds. 'We'd had a throttle problem on Fisi's car in practice and

The Mégane Renaultsport 225 Cup.
Feel it for yourself.

Lap up the F1 experience in the Mégane Renaultsport 225 Cup. With its 18" spoked alloys, sharper steering and racing car-inspired chassis as standard, it's more than just another road car. To get in a few practice laps, text 'GAME' to 85101 for your free Renaultsport phone game. Or visit www.renaultsport.co.uk for more details.

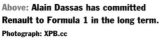

Above: Alain Dassas has committed Renault to Formula 1 in the long term.
Photograph: XPB.cc

Above right: Giancarlo Fisichella ahead of Fernando Alonso at Hockenheim; it was rare indeed for the Italian to get the upper hand.

Below: The entire team celebrates another world championship, with the Brazilian GP trophy taking centre stage.
Photographs: James Moy/www.crashpa.net

we fixed that without realising that an actuator seal had been damaged: the fluid drained away in the race. Other than that – and apart from blowing up one or two engines during testing, which is what tests are all about – we had been trouble free.

'We had a failure in the test at Monza and we went into the race aware that there was a potential problem. We did limit the performance of the engines for the Monza race by a reasonable amount – but unfortunately by not quite enough. Fernando's failed after he had worked his way into third. Fisi's engine was on its second race and, when we pulled it out after the race, we discovered it was within a couple of laps of doing the same.'

Fisichella led from pole in Malaysia and didn't put a foot wrong. It was one of the Italian's more impressive weekends in a season when he was more inconsistent than the team would have liked. It was almost as if Fisichella was psyched out by the undeniable speed of his team-mate.

Renault had begun the season knowing that Alonso would be leaving at the end of it. Symonds is quick to point out that his planned departure had no detrimental effect on what had always been an excellent working relationship.

'Apart from making a little joke with Fernando from time to time, I don't think anyone has given it a second thought,' said Symonds.

'We have been so focused on the job in hand. You have to live for today and just get on with it. If we had not been having such a good season, there might have been some little niggles creeping in – but that was simply not the case. Fernando has driven better than ever. He did not make a single mistake – except signing for McLaren, of course!'

Maurice Hamilton

Only a CHAMPION can be No.1 in Formula 1

RENAULT F1 Team *Supplier*

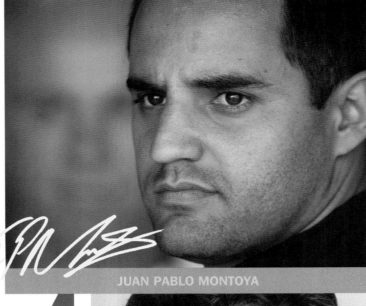

TEAM McLAREN MERCEDES

KIMI RAIKKÖNEN

JUAN PABLO MONTOYA

PEDRO DE LA ROSA

Photographs: James Moy/www.crashpa.net

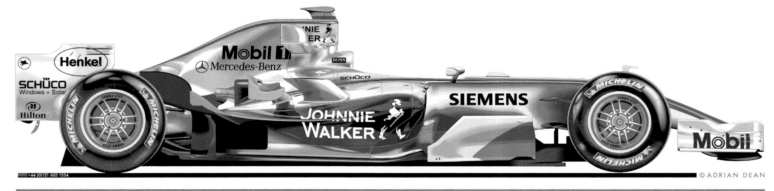

© ADRIAN DEAN

McLAREN MP4-21

SPONSORS	**Technology partners:** EXXONMobil • Siemens • Michelin • BAE Systems • Sun Microsystems, Inc
	Corporate partners: Johnnie Walker • SAP • Emirates • Hugo Boss • AT&T • Hilton International • Schüco • TAG Heuer
	Associate partners: Steinmetz Diamond Group
	Official suppliers: Henkel • Nescafé Xpress • Sonax • Advanced Composites Group • Charmilles • GS Yuasa • Yamazaki Mazak • Enkei • Sports Marketing Surveys • Kenwood • 3D Systems • Sparco • Silicon Graphics
ENGINE	**Type:** Mercedes FO 108S **No. of cylinders:** V8 **Electronics:** McLaren Electronics Systems **Fuel:** Mobil Unleaded **Lubricants:** Mobil 1 products
TRANSMISSION	**Gearbox:** 7 forward speeds and 1 reverse; semi-auto **Driveshafts:** McLaren **Clutch:** Hand-operated
CHASSIS	**Front and rear suspension:** Inboard torsion bar/damper system operated by pushrod and bell crank with a double wishbone arrangement **Suspension dampers:** McLaren **Wheels:** Enkei **Tyres:** Michelin **Steering:** McLaren power-assisted **Battery:** GS Yuasa **Instruments:** McLaren Electronic Systems
DIMENSIONS	**Formula weight:** 600 kg including driver

Above: Kimi Räikkönen took three pole positions in 2006, but was unable to translate any of them into race victories during his final season at McLaren.

Left to right: Norbert Haug, the Mercedes Motorsport vice president, continued to look after the interests of the 40-percent shareholder; Martin Whitmarsh, McLaren's F1 CEO, at least could identify some promising trends; but group chairman Ron Dennis found the year a painful experience.

Photographs: James Moy/www.crashpa.net

McLaren had an impressive 2005 campaign, winning ten of the season's 18 races, although neither the team nor its drivers managed to claim either world championship. So there was sufficient pre-season optimism to sustain the view that the new MP4-21 and its Mercedes 2.4-litre V8 would offer Kimi Räikkönen and Juan Pablo Montoya the chance to challenge regularly for race wins.

From the outset, Ron Dennis, the McLaren chairman, reiterated his belief that both drivers would attack the season with as much motivation as usual. But he made no apology for signing Fernando Alonso more than a year before the Spanish driver was scheduled to slip into the cockpit of a McLaren for the first time.

'I am very confident that our two current drivers would be ranked by anybody in the top five,' he said in Bahrain. 'Speculation in the media [about their motivation] is understandable, but irrelevant. We all have choices to make every day of our lives, and Kimi told us that he would like to try his car and have a few races before he makes a decision as to whether or not he leaves the team. We're happy to give him the time he needs.' It later became clear that Räikkönen had already signed a long-term contract to drive for Ferrari from the start of 2007, even before he drove the MP4-21 for the first time.

However Dennis made it clear that he regarded criticism over the manner in which he approached Alonso – voiced by F1 commercial rights holder Bernie Ecclestone and Renault team principal Flavio Briatore – as misplaced. 'The maximum integrity and fairness were used to bring this project to fruition,' he said.

In terms of their predicted track performance, Räikkönen and Montoya were pinning their hopes on the new Mercedes FO 108S V8 engines, which had proved fast but fragile during winter testing.

'Over 28 test days, Kimi, Juan Pablo and Pedro de la Rosa covered a total of 8,692 km, which is on average one grand prix distance per day and therefore equates to a total of 28 grand prix distances in preparation for the first races,' said Norbert Haug, Mercedes Motorsport vice president.

'The lap times improved continuously throughout the tests and the long runs were okay compared with the fastest. Several times, our new V8 engine stood the strain of two race weekends and up to 50 percent more, on the circuits at Barcelona and Valencia as well as on the dynamometers.'

Team hopes were raised in Bahrain when Räikkönen proved right on the pace from the outset, recovering from a rear suspension breakage in qualifying to move from 22nd on the grid to third at the chequered flag. Kimi followed that up with a distant second to Alonso at Melbourne, although he was matching the Renault pace in the closing stages, after which the MP4-21 package drifted away from the front-running pace, with the notable exception of Monaco – where the car was a potential winner, shadowing Alonso until a smouldering heat shield in the engine bay caught fire and put him out of the race.

'I think when we analyse the comparative paces of the top three Michelin and top three Bridgestone runners, Bridgestone clearly made a significant leap forward at Indianapolis,' said

TEAM McLAREN MERCEDES

Team principal: **Ron Dennis**

CEO, Formula 1: **Martin Whitmarsh**

Vice president, Mercedes-Benz Motorsport: **Norbert Haug**

Managing director, McLaren: **Jonathan Neale**

Managing director, Mercedes High Performance Engines: **Ola Kaellenius**

Design and development director: **Neil Oatley**

Chief designer: **Mike Coughlan**

Chief engineer, (MP4-21): **Tim Goss**

Chief engineer, vehicle dynamics: **Mark Williams**

Team manager: **Dave Ryan**

Chief mechanic: **Peter Vale**

Race engineer, car no. 3, Kimi Räikkönen: **Mark Slade**

Race engineer, car no. 4, Pedro de la Rosa/Juan Pablo Montoya: **Phil Prew**

McLaren CEO Martin Whitmarsh. 'But at the time I think we at McLaren perhaps thought the Bridgestone [upsurge] at that point was possibly a characteristic of the circuit, or the fact that perhaps we'd [Michelin] been a bit too conservative and we didn't quite recognise the full implication of Bridgestone's step forward at that point. Since then it's been something of a fightback.

'As far as the car was concerned, we frankly threw away the opportunity to win in Monaco, where we undeniably had the best package. I think we started the season second to Renault in terms of competitiveness, but then Ferrari improved, did an extremely good job. The reality is that every element of our package needs to be better, so we're working hard to improve that situation next year.'

One of the MP4-21's problems was that it had inherited its predecessor's quality of being very easy on its rear tyres. That was certainly a bonus when one set of tyres had to last a race distance, but with tyre changes reintroduced for 2006 suddenly the difficulty was getting enough heat into the rear Michelins for qualifying runs.

The fact that he was already committed to Ferrari in no way shaded Räikkönen's determination behind the wheel and only a slight lapse of concentration at Budapest – when he was listening to a radio message from the pit wall telling him to let his fuel-light team-mate Pedro de la Rosa overtake – lost him another possible win. He looked up and, before he could respond, slammed straight into the back of Vitantonio Liuzzi. McLaren made much of the fact that Liuzzi came and apologised for backing off on the racing line but Kimi later confessed to the Italian that it had been his own fault.

McLaren's self-confidence in managing drivers also took something of a knock during the season. Despite the management's inclination – at least in public – to look on the bright side when it came to the issue of whether Räikkönen might stay with the team, either they were in denial or they simply did not believe what the Finn's management team was telling them. Why else would they have signed Alonso so early?

You could at least forgive Räikkönen because he was so naturally and dramatically quick.

By contrast, Juan Pablo Montoya never recovered from a combination of being frozen out by Ron Dennis over his 'tennis accident' last year – which caused him to miss two races – and overwhelmed by Räikkönen's speed.

Team insiders suggest that Montoya's decline hit rock bottom when he screwed up in Australia, spinning three times, shouting at the pit crew when he had to queue behind Kimi in the pit lane and then punching a hole through the bottom of the chassis over a kerb, which triggered the default mechanism and switched off the engine.

The final disappointments for Montoya came in the two North American races. He clipped a wall and broke his car's suspension at Montreal and ran into the back of Räikkönen in the multi-car first-corner pile-up at Indianapolis. By then the Colombian was fed-up and felt marginalised within the team. So he decided to jump – before he was firmly pushed – and signed a deal to join the Ganassi NASCAR team for 2007, a move that guaranteed the feisty Colombian a racing future in the USA, where he had always felt so relaxed and at home. It certainly wasn't how Montoya or McLaren had anticipated events unfolding when Juan Pablo joined the team at the start of 2005.

Alan Henry

Above: Gary Paffett continued to fulfil a crucial role on the test team throughout the year.

Left: The McLaren steering wheel is literally a work of technological art.

Below: Pedro de la Rosa drove gamely to stand in for the departed Juan Pablo Montoya and took a strong second place in the Hungarian GP.
Photographs: James Moy/www.crashpa.net

SCUDERIA FERRARI MARLBORO

5

6

MICHAEL SCHUMACHER

Photograph: XPB.cc

FELIPE MASSA

Photograph: James Moy/www.crashpa.net

© ADRIAN DEAN

FERRARI 248 F1

SPONSORS	Title sponsor: **Philip Morris** Major sponsors: **Fiat • Vodafone • Shell • Bridgestone • Martini • Acer • AMD**
ENGINE	Type: **Ferrari 056** No. of cylinders (vee angle): **V8 (90°)** Sparking plugs: **NGK** Electronics: **Magneti Marelli** Fuel: **Shell V-power** Oil: **Shell SL-0932**
TRANSMISSION	Gearbox: **Ferrari longitudinal gearbox, limited-slip differential; semi-automatic sequential electronically controlled gearbox**
	Number of gears: **7 plus reverse** Clutch: **AP Racing**
CHASSIS	Front and rear suspension: **Independent suspension, pushrod-activated torsion springs** Dampers: **Sachs**
	Wheel diameter: **330 mm front and rear** Wheels: **BBS** Tyres: **Bridgestone** Brake discs: **Brembo ventilated carbon-fibre disc brakes**
	Brake pads: **Brembo/Carbon Industrie** Brake callipers: **Brembo**
DIMENSIONS	Wheelbase: **3,050 mm** Length: **4,545 mm** Width: **1,796 mm** Height: **959 mm**
	Formula weight: **605 kg including driver**

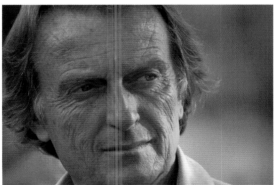

Above: **Michael Schumacher and Felipe Massa developed into a formidable partnership as the season unfolded.**

Far left: **Luca di Montezemolo was in charge at Ferrari when Michael Schumacher arrived in 1996 and was still in the driving seat when Michael quit at the end of this season.**

Left: **Jean Todt was appointed CEO of Ferrari as a whole only days after the season-ending Brazilian GP. He will also remain head of the Gestione Sportiva.**
Photographs: James Moy/www.crashpa.net

EQUAL on wins in the drivers' championship, one more win than its closest rival in the constructors' series – you might have thought that Ferrari had done all it needed to do to win both championships and yet it came away with two seconds and a third. It may have been a whole lot better than 2005 but it was still a disappointment.

After round nine, Canada, both team and drivers had slipped steadily. Renault led the constructors by 34 points; Fernando Alonso led Michael Schumacher by 25. Then began the fantastic fightback. Steadily, both margins decreased. After round 15, Italy, Ferrari led Renault by three points; Michael was two points behind Alonso. A race later, Michael was equal on points with Alonso but Renault was back in the lead by a point. But then it drifted away in the final two races. Ferrari lost the constructors' title by five points; Michael lost the drivers' by 13 points.

It was the end of an era. Michael had already decided to quit Formula 1; Kimi Räikkönen will replace him. Jean Todt was made CEO; Ross Brawn's retirement for at least a year was confirmed – Mario Almondo will replace him. Paolo Martinelli is off to Fiat; Stefano Domenicali will become sporting director. Team Schumacher – whether you like the expression or not – is breaking up.

There had been a shake-up at the end of the 2004 season. Aerodynamicists Nikolas Tombazis and James Allison left; John Iley arrived. John had to establish himself and get the group working with the vision he had and 2005 was tough in that respect, explained technical director Ross Brawn.

The year had been tough in other ways, too, yet had its benefits. 'The big change for us from 2004 to 2005 was on the tyre front: our car had been designed around virtual sprint racing; the tyres had been designed around sprint racing and suddenly we had to face up to the fact that tyres had to last the whole race,' said Ross.

'And then of course, we reached a stage in the season when it wasn't worth wasting resources on 2005; we had to really commit to 2006. In 2006 we were going back to multi-tyre races but, interestingly, in trying to make the tyres last a whole race we found quite a lot of performance in the construction of the tyre in the latter part of 2005 and over the winter of 2005–06, so a lot of the things that we started to work on with Bridgestone really started to come together in the winter.'

The change of regulations allowing tyre changes during the race also played into Ferrari's hands. 'It made a big difference for us. You could argue that it played to our strengths, because I think we have a team of people who are very creative in that area: [chief race engineer] Luca Baldisserri, the drivers, the race engineers, the team. They're not afraid to attack when it comes to strategy. This year was exciting, the multi-tyre races opened up the strategy field again and for me it was far more enjoyable.

SCUDERIA FERRARI MARLBORO

President: **Luca di Montezemolo**

Managing director and team principal: **Jean Todt**

Technical director: **Ross Brawn**

Engine director: **Paolo Martinelli**

Team manager: **Stefano Domenicali**

Head of car design: **Aldo Costa**

Chief designer (2007): **Nikolas Tombazis**

Chief aerodynamicist: **John Iley**

Electronics: **Roberto Dalla**

Chief race engineer: **Luca Baldisserri**

Race and test technical manager: **Nigel Stepney**

Race engineer, car no. 5, Michael Schumacher: **Christopher Dyer**

Race engineer, car no. 6, Felipe Massa: **Rob Smedley**

'I think the 2006 car was really the first car that [designer] Aldo Costa had to take full responsibility for. Luckily we managed to retain Rory Byrne on the team but Rory was handing over the baton to Aldo and 2005 was a bit of a transitional year. But Aldo did a great job; 2006 was reconfirming his role within the team. Nikolas came back – the prodigal son came back – so he was obviously an asset to us.

'We didn't do anything specific on the car; we just said this [2005] car is not fast enough and we all know what makes the performance of the car. It's the suspension geometry; it's the weight distribution; it's the centre of gravity; and primarily it's the aerodynamics. We just went through the whole organisation and said we've got to make a step up; what do we need to do to make a step forward? And we probably did more work on suspension than we've ever done since I've been at Ferrari, and I must say a lot of it was very productive.'

Another area was the diffuser and rear wing. 'That was a much-needed package,' says Brawn. 'Because the regulations didn't change much from 2005 to 2006, we took a fresh look at those regulations and I think the team did a great job on the transmission, the rear crash structure, the rear wing. We went to the centrally mounted rear wing, which gave us a lot more flexibility to change the diffuser and to change the lower wing, and so that became something that could be developed consistently during the year. It's structural but it's not a critical structure, as it was before, so there's a lot more potential there.'

Pre-season testing revealed a number of problems. 'We did get a lot of the groundwork done testing in Bahrain, which proved to be a very consistent track to test on,' says Brawn. 'But we started to have the beginnings of a clutch control problem that really hurt us at the beginning of the season. If I look at the year overall, we made too slow a start to the season and because we had problems with the car in January and February we didn't get the team as well polished as we would have liked, so when we got to those first few races, things were not as smooth as we knew they could be.

'In Bahrain, we had a little bit of a tardy pit stop, we didn't pick the right tyres in Australia, in Malaysia we had the engine problems… so we really made a poor start to the season and that related a lot to the reliability issues we had at the end of testing and the beginning of the season.'

Cracked pistons caused problems in the first two races but Ferrari was quick to correct the problem. 'We had to stabilise that situation because, with two-race engines, if you start having problems, particularly prior to a race and even during a race, you pay for it over quite a long period. I think the development during the year was pretty normal. We weren't desperately looking for engine developments that might cause risk in the overall picture.'

Even so, there was a reasonable amount of development given the fact that it was a new formula. 'Everything,' says Brawn. 'Top end, bottom end, friction, everything, so the engine made a reasonable step during the year, and of course on driveability and all the other aspects.'

Brawn feels that it was sad and unjust that engine reliability issues should return in the last few races to thwart the team's championship chances after that fightback. Felipe Massa had a valve failure that the team had had problems with before and Schumacher suffered similarly in Japan, but this time with the top stem of the valve, which proved crucial to his title hopes.

Schumacher had said at the beginning of the season that the key would be development. Brawn agrees, explaining, 'I think the rate of progress with this car is the strongest I've ever seen at Ferrari. There were aerodynamic improvements at almost every race and there were suspension developments every few races, and new tyres every few races, so it was a great effort by everyone. Why it was different this year, I don't know. The 2005 season was a wake-up call – it wasn't good enough and I think everyone then was determined to show what they could do.'

Massa matured significantly during the year to become a two-times winner and a fine support for Schumacher, outqualifying him on several occasions. He teamed up with test team engineer Rob Smedley, who came in to replace his race engineer Gabriele Delli Colli at the European Grand Prix.

Ferrari's head count has stayed pretty stable for four or five years. There are a few areas where changes are made, but the team has had to react to regulations such as the limitation of track testing by moving resources to simulation at the factory.

In his last season, however, Brawn's principal satisfaction was in the performance of the car, even if it didn't win titles. 'There were a couple of races where we didn't pick the right tyres or we didn't have the right tyres for the conditions, such as in Hungary and Australia. But overall, Bridgestone did a fantastic job and we had a very, very good car. When we put the two together we had races such as Hockenheim, Magny-Cours and the last race, in Brazil. The performance was just incredible. Put all those things together, hit the sweet spot and we had a margin over the others that truly surprised me.'

Bob Constanduros

Above: Ross Brawn decided he would take his cue from Schumacher and leave Maranello at the end of the season. But he could be back at some point in the future.
Photograph: Paul-Henri Cahier

Top left: Luca Badoer has been Ferrari's longest-serving F1 test driver of all.

Top right: Marc Gené continued in his behind-the-scenes role as a key member of the test team.

Left: Paolo Martinelli will be relinquishing control of the F1 engine programme to Gilles Simon from 2007 as career promotion takes him to a senior role in the Fiat group.

Opposite page: Felipe Massa grew in stature throughout the season, distinguishing himself with two masterly grand prix victories.
Photographs: James Moy/www.crashpa.net

RALF SCHUMACHER

Photograph: James Moy, www.crashpa.net

JARNO TRULLI

Photograph: Lukas Gorys

TOYOTA'S six-year $1 billion investment in F1 was supposed to pay off in 2006, with the team's senior management predicting that the team was heading for its first GP victory and would beat Ferrari over the course of the world championship campaign.

That was the bullish message at the formal unveiling of the new Toyota TF106 challenger at the Japanese car maker's manufacturing facility at Valenciennes in northern France. Ralf Schumacher and Jarno Trulli smiled for the world's media, their confidence apparently well buttressed by the fact that their new car had been track testing since late November and was the very first of the new-generation 2.4-litre V8-engined machines to be ready for action.

'We feel that we have to stand up to Ferrari and take them on and beat them,' said John Howett, the Toyota motorsport president, whose team employs around 1,000 personnel on the Formula 1 programme at its base in Cologne.

'The first ambition is that we really would like to be the quickest Bridgestone team and we definitely want to challenge to have our first victory in this year.

'We realise that we have still got to work very hard and push in every area but we have a growing confidence that we can do that.'

Mike Gascoyne, the team's British technical director who previously headed the Renault F1 design team, was also confident that the early testing début of the TF106 had given Toyota a crucial head start over its rivals in terms of progressing its development programme once the season got under way.

But it just didn't happen. Drivers Jarno Trulli and Ralf Schumacher struggled for much of the year, battling for balance and grip in many of the races and seldom looking anything more than bit-part members of the supporting cast.

Moreover, only three days after Ralf delivered the best result of the year – a run to third place in the Australian GP at Melbourne – Gascoyne was dismissed following an acrimonious disagreement over development strategy with the Cologne-based team's senior management.

'Due to a fundamental difference of opinion with regard to the technical operations of its Formula 1 team, Toyota Motorsport has suspended its technical director, Mike Gascoyne, until further notice,' said a spokesman. 'Toyota Motorsport will not make any additional comments on this matter at this time.'

Gascoyne slipped away quietly for a period of 'gardening leave' before joining the newly rebranded Spyker – formerly Midland – squad at the end of the year. Neither party wished

© ADRIAN DEAN

TOYOTA TF106B

SPONSORS	Panasonic • Denso • BMC Software • Bridgestone • Dassault Systemes • Ebbon-Dacs • EMC 2• Denso • Esso • Intel • KDDI Magneti Marelli • Time Inc
ENGINE	Type: **Toyota RVX-06** No. of cylinders: **V8** Sparking plugs: **Denso** Electronics: **Magneti Marelli** Fuel: **Esso** Oil: **Esso**
TRANSMISSION	Gearbox: **7-speed sequential, electro-hydraulic, Toyota-designed maincase with Toyota/Xtrac internals** Clutch: **Hand-operated**
CHASSIS	Front suspension: **Carbon-fibre double wishbone arrangement, with carbon-fibre trackrod and pushrod. Pushrod activates rocker, torsion bar, damper and anti-roll bar** Rear suspension: **Carbon-fibre double wishbone arrangement, with carbon-fibre toelink and pushrod. Pushrod activates rocker, torsion bar, damper and anti-roll bar** Dampers: **Penske** Wheel diameter: **330 mm front and rear** Wheels: **BBS** Tyres: **Bridgestone** Brake discs: **Hitco** Brake pads: **Hitco** Brake callipers: **Brembo** Steering: **Toyota power-assisted** Radiators: **Denso** Fuel tank: **ATL** Instruments: **Toyota/Marelli**
DIMENSIONS	Wheelbase: **3,090 mm** Length **4,530 mm** Width: **1,800 mm** Height **950 mm** Formula weight: **600 kg including driver and camera**

PANASONIC TOYOTA RACING

Team principal: Tsutomu Tomita

Team president: John Howett

Executive vice president:
Yoshiaki Kinoshita

Senior general manager (engine):
Luca Marmorini

Senior general manager (chassis):
Pascal Vasselon

Director, technical co-ordination:
Noritoshi Arai

Team manager: **Richard Cregan**

Chief race and test engineer:
Dieter Gass

to elaborate on the reasons for the split, leaving the rest of the paddock to speculate that the British engineer's chippy and to-the-point *modus operandi* sat uneasily with the structured Japanese formality within the senior management echelons of the cash-rich car maker known as 'the Bank of Japan'.

The roots of Toyota's problem stemmed from not having built a completely new car from the outset – and the cause of that in turn went back to Tokyo's imposition of a switch from Michelin to Bridgestone. In reality, the TF106 was little more than last year's car with a V8 engine. The TF106B, introduced at Monaco, was what should have been up and running during winter testing.

The first car still had the keel from the TF105/105B even though it now had 'zero keel' type front suspension. So Toyota had the worst of both worlds –the smaller range of suspension set-up that a zero-keel type suspension limits you to (because the top and lower wishbones have to be closer together) and the aerodynamic limitation of the keel.

This first problem was exacerbated by the switch from Michelin to Bridgestone. The latter required more camber on the suspension to work properly – the very factor that the keel-less suspension limited. The whole zero-keel layout had been developed by Gascoyne in 2005.

Another problem with the initial TF106 was that the engine, despite being significantly shorter than the V10, was still in the same place as the V10. It hadn't been brought forward like everyone else's, to offer scope for better airflow around the back, particularly around the lower body (the 'coke bottle') section.

This was because Toyota – for whatever reason – could not develop a new gearbox in time. The TF106B had the new, longer gearbox and the engine moved into the proper place.

The general consensus was that the Toyota V8 was not good enough, either. When Williams ran back-to-back tests with the Cosworth, it found the Toyota to be 25 bhp down – and that was quite late in the season, after plenty of development on the Toyota and not much on the Cossie. A realistic estimate is that by the end of the season the Toyota was 40 bhp down on the Ferrari – that's 0.4s a lap.

'To be honest, when I joined Toyota I expected worse results than we actually had in 2005,' said Trulli reflectively. 'I expected a difficult season, but apart from a period in the middle of the year when we had a run of bad luck that cost us some podium finishes, it was a really good first season with the team. By contrast, the 2006 season has been disappointing.

'In reality, things have been the other way around from what I'd originally expected. I thought we would struggle in 2005 and then get things much more together in 2006. But as Ferrari has proved with its return to competitiveness this season, F1 is always a question of keeping pushing, improving from both good and bad experiences.'

Ralf Schumacher added, 'This year we started very poorly, worse than expected, but fought our way through it. In the second half of the season we began to see the trend we wanted to see, but we never quite managed to translate that into hard results.

'In a sense there was nowhere to hide after the season we'd had in 2005, no choice but to be optimistic and predict we would be challenging for victories. We played the game and

certainly the development did not go as well with the new car as we expected; a couple of [other] teams came out with better packages to start with. Then it took a while to get on top of the performance of the new [Bridgestone] tyre, but no regrets for this year because the team has shown how stable it can be in very hard and difficult times.'

Both men gave the impression that they were trying to be polite. All in all, it had been a disastrous year with the far-removed senior management in Tokyo imposing a fundamental technical decision on its racing team for what seemed little more than commercial reasons. Throw in a messy divorce with the team's technical director and one is really bound to wonder why they should have expected any better.

Alan Henry

Above: Jarno Trulli had the stronger season overall even though his team-mate Ralf Schumacher claimed Toyota's only podium finish of 2006.

Top left: Ralf Schumacher flew the flag for Toyota by qualifying third in Japan.

Top right: Toyota motorsport president John Howett had little to smile about when it came to surveying the 2006 season.

Centre: Seasoned test driver Ricardo Zonta will be making the switch to Renault in 2007.

Photographs: James Moy/www.crashpa.net

WILLIAMSF1 TEAM

9

10

MARK WEBBER

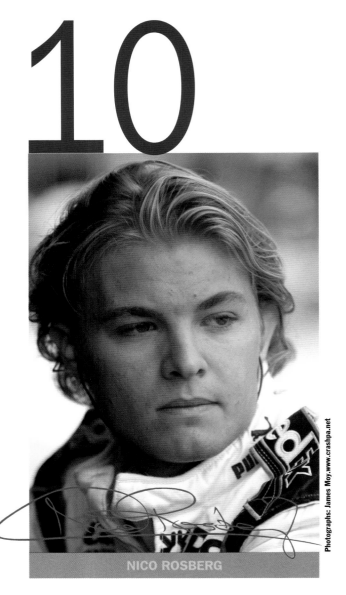

NICO ROSBERG

Photographs: James Moy, www.crashpa.net

© ADRIAN DEAN

WILLIAMS FW28

SPONSORS	RBS • Allianz • Bridgestone • FedEx • Mobilecast • Petrobras • Qinetiq • TATA • Accenture • Battery • Budweiser • Hamleys • Oris • Phillips • Reuters
ENGINE	Type: **Cosworth CA2006** No. of cylinders: **V8** Sparking plugs: **Champion** Electronics: **Pi/Cosworth** Fuel: **Esso** Oil: **Castrol**
TRANSMISSION	Gearbox: **WilliamsF1 7-speed seamless sequential semi-automatic shift plus reverse gear in an aluminium maincase with Xtrac internals, gear selection electro-hydraulically actuated** Clutch: **Hand-operated**
CHASSIS	Front suspension: **Carbon-fibre double wishbone arrangement, with composite toelink and pushrod-activated torsion springs** Rear suspension: **Wishbone and pushrod-activated torsion springs and rockers** Dampers: **WilliamsF1** Wheels: **OZ Racing** Tyres: **Bridgestone** Brake discs: **Carbone Industrie** Brake pads: **Carbone Industrie** Callipers: **AP Racing** Steering: **WilliamsF1 power-assisted** Radiators: **Marston** Fuel tank: **ATL**
DIMENSIONS	Wheelbase: **3,100 mm** Length: **4,500 mm** Width: **1,800 mm** Height: **950 mm** Formula weight: **605 kg with driver, camera and ballast**

NOT for the first time in recent years, Williams entered the new season genuinely hoping it would be better than the last. Not only was 2006 even worse than before – it was one of the most disappointing in this team's distinguished history. Finishing eighth in the constructors' championship holds about as much interest for Sir Frank Williams and Patrick Head as learning that their drivers had crashed into each other on the opening lap of the final race. That incident just about summed up the season for WilliamsF1.

It was a sad way to end the team's two-year relationship with Mark Webber and a single season with Cosworth. But, more than that, it removed the final opportunity to salvage something worthwhile from a year in which two sixth places had been the unremarkable highlights.

There had been flashes of potential but, when a podium at Monaco beckoned, Webber was let down by a mechanical failure that was not the first in a catalogue of disappointment previously unheard of within a team that has won nine constructors' championships. The FW28 was rarely on the pace and that had little to do with the switch to Cosworth, although the move from Michelin to Bridgestone did present a few difficulties at the start.

'The Bridgestone tyres have been excellent,' said Head. 'But we gave ourselves an added difficulty initially because we were not familiar with the range of compounds thanks to having no carry-over experience from the previous year. When we were testing over the winter, we were extremely slow – well off the pace. Our long runs didn't look too bad but our single laps and first laps were very poor and generally the winter running on cold tracks did not teach us very much. That improved when we got to hotter climates but you could see quite clearly from Michael Schumacher's performance that the tyres have been excellent and fully capable of winning a championship.'

Similarly, despite an engine failure in Malaysia and the need to reduce performance as a precaution during the next few races, Head has no complaints about the Cosworth CA2006 V8 that replaced the BMW V10.

Above: **Nico Rosberg in action at Silverstone, where he could manage only ninth place in the British GP.**
Photograph: Bryn Williams/www.crashpa.net

Left: **Sir Frank Williams is looking for better times ahead when his team switches to Toyota engines for the 2007 season.**

Below left: **Director of engineering Patrick Head was acutely embarrassed and unhappy about the team's failure to perform with the FW28.**
Photographs: James Moy/www.crashpa.net

WILLIAMSF1 TEAM

Managing director and team principal: **Sir Frank Williams**

Director of engineering: **Patrick Head**

Chief executive officer: **Chris Chapple**

Technical director: **Sam Michael**

Chief operating officer: **Alex Burns**

Chief aerodynamicist: **Loïc Bigois**

Race-team manager: **Tim Newton**

Race engineer: car, no 9, Mark Webber: **Xevi Pujolar**

Race engineer: car, no 10, Nico Rosberg: **Tony Ross**

Right: Narain Karthikeyan contributed to the test programme.

Far right: Alex Wurz offered hope to all test drivers by gaining promotion to a Williams race seat for 2007.
Photographs: James Moy/www.crashpa.net

Above: Mark Webber delivered a strong showing at Monaco – he was heading for a podium but he retired from third place.
Photograph: James Moy/www.crashpa.net

'Once Cosworth got on top of the early problem, the V8 returned to being an extremely good, fully competitive engine,' said Head. 'I have no doubt that it would have been capable had our car been a match. The FW28 had a poor handling characteristic at the rear, particularly entering corners. It's about the worst characteristic you can have because there are all sorts of follow-on problems. For example, it causes you to put on more wing and, of course, that makes you slow on the straights.'

The performance shortfall was one thing but the spate of unreliability was quite another for a team that prides itself on attention to such significant detail. Webber was heading for third in Monaco when an exhaust collector cracked and leaked hot gas onto a wiring loom.

'That was a particularly low point,' said Head. 'Mark was in very good shape. He could see that [Fernando] Alonso in front was in trouble with his rear tyres, whereas our Bridgestones were just getting stronger and stronger. Monaco is a bit of a special case in terms of the engine cycle and traction control, which give the exhaust a bit of a hard time. But this type of unreliability went on all year. Some of those problems came from design, some from quality control and some from maybe trying too hard and taking risks that didn't pay off.

'It has caused us to take a very good look at ourselves. We have identified areas of weakness and reorganised ourselves internally. We have restructured the design office under heads of departments who have to deliver to the chief designer. We have promoted internally and we have taken one or two people from other teams because we needed a bit of fresh blood.'

Speaking of fresh blood, Williams took a gamble by signing Nico Rosberg. The 2005 GP2 champion scored two points in his first race but, for the rest of the season, Rosberg showed

just how difficult it is to step up to Formula 1, particularly with the limitation on Friday running – a time when the novice should have been learning the tracks, many of which were new to him.

'The Bahrain result had the effect of making the rest of Nico's season look disappointing,' said Head. 'But if you look closely you will see that, surprisingly, he was better than Mark on his first visit to Suzuka, which is not an easy track. Equally, he had one or two races – Hockenheim, for example – where he didn't cover himself with glory. But we had an option on him for 2007 and we had no hesitation in taking it up.

'It's been a very disappointing year for both drivers. They have done a perfectly good job and, if we had given them better and more reliable equipment, they could have had some good places. There have been a number of races where we could have picked up points. It wouldn't have been respectable but it would have been very easy, had we had reliability, to finish fifth or sixth in the championship.

'I don't believe in luck but there were a few times when things could have gone better for us – Turkey, for example, where we were fourth and sixth with a lot of fuel on board and the bloody safety car came out and completely screwed us.

'But the simple fact is that we can't run an independent company on the basis of finishing eighth. As you know, Frank is a very competitive person and I hope I'm still the same. The only problem is, we have been coming out with the same story for too long: "You watch us next year; it will be better!" So I'm not making any predictions. But you can take it as read that we're not happy. Not happy at all.'

Maurice Hamilton

New talent.

New power.

New dawn.

Make it happen.

As the 2006 season ends there's only one way to look.
Forwards. For the WilliamsF1 Team that means looking forward
to working with a new engine partner and a new driver.
In the new season, the entire team will be totally focused
and determined to make it happen.

rbs.com

Make it happen

The Royal Bank of Scotland Group

11

RUBENS BARRICHELLO

12

JENSON BUTTON

Photographs: James Moy/www.crashpa.net

© ADRIAN DEAN

© ADRIAN DEAN

HONDA RA106

PARTNERS	**BAT • Michelin • Eneos • Intercond • NTN • Celerant • Ray Ban • Seiko • Asahi Soft Drinks**
ENGINE	Type: **Honda RA806E** No. of cylinders (vee angle): **V8 (90°)** Fuel: **Elf** Oil: **Eneos**
TRANSMISSION	Gearbox: **Honda maincase and internals; 7-speed unit** Clutch: **Carbon plate**
CHASSIS	Front and rear suspension: **Wishbone and pushrod-activated torsion springs and rockers; mechanical anti-roll bar** Dampers: **Showa**
	Wheel diameter, front: **312 mm** rear: **340 mm** Wheels: **BBS forged magnesium** Tyres: **Michelin** Brake discs: **Carbon** Brake pads: **Carbon**
	Steering: **Honda power-assisted rack and pinion** Fuel tank: **ATL** Instruments: **Honda steering-wheel dash display**
DIMENSIONS	Wheelbase: **3,140 mm** Track, front: **1,460 mm** rear: **1,420 mm** Length: **4,675 mm** Width: **1,800 mm** Height: **950 mm**
	Formula weight: **600 kg including driver**

A shaky start, but one that gave way to a happy ending. Half a dozen races into the season there were cynical voices questioning what on earth Honda had been thinking about, purchasing the 55-percent balance of the shareholding in British American Racing. The deal, flagged up at a reputedly modest $30 million was inked just before the 2005 Japanese GP, supposedly clearing the decks for a serious tilt at the world championship in 2006.

It was understandable that the uncomfortable statistical reality behind Jenson Button's paucity of F1 achievement continued to cast a long shadow over the launch of the all-new Honda RA106 challenger at Barcelona early in the year. The initial testing promise displayed by the new car was certainly positive, but by the time the team prepared to fly off to the Canadian GP – round nine of the 18-race series – the whole programme had come so badly unravelled that technical director Geoff Willis found himself consigned to the subs' bench.

After a succession of disappointing results, culminating in a fiery oil leak that caused Button to spin into retirement from his home race at Silverstone, Honda's senior management appointed Shuhei Nakamoto to the position of senior technical director to shake up the Brackley-based organisation.

This placed the 49-year-old engineer above Willis in the team's hierachy and placed a question mark over his future with the organisation. 'Discussions are currently taking place [with Willis] regarding his future role with the team,' said an official communiqué.

This news came less than a fortnight after it was announced that Willis would be attending fewer races over the balance of the season in order to concentrate on developing the new full-scale wind tunnel that recently came on-stream at the team's headquarters. Geoff left the team mid-season by mutual agreement.

'Honda has set itself some very tough targets for its F1 team and made a considerable investment in order to achieve them, so we have to ensure that we do everything necessary to pursue those objectives,' said Nick Fry, the team's chief executive officer.

'Before the season, in winter testing, the car seemed to be quite fast, close to the pace of the Renault and Ferrari, but only on the first few laps,' said engineering director Jacky Eeckelaert. 'On longer runs we lacked some pace. You could see it in the first races, where we qualified much better than we raced.

'Jenson qualified on pole in Australia but the race pace was not there and it got worse as the season went on, when our qualifying pace also started to desert us.

'We were a little behind in different areas of development. One of the reasons was that the new wind tunnel was in its final stages as the season started and a lot of effort went into setting it up and so the development on the aerodynamic side was lagging. The aero department was growing, we were hiring new people and that all eats up time, so the development was not quite following the path foreseen.'

Rubens Barrichello also struggled to adjust to the traction control system on the RA106 and took some time getting it working to his liking.

'Rubens had a few problems at the start of the year and I can understand that because, for the past six years at Sauber, I was used to the Ferrari engine and software, and I knew exactly where he was coming from,' said Eeckelaert.

'You could set up the Ferrari traction control so that coming out of low-speed corners you could floor the throttle and it would catch the car when it went into oversteer. That was not the case at Honda. It was optimised more for traction in a straight line but in the corners it was not as far developed.

Above: Rubens Barrichello leads team-mate Jenson Button in the first race of the year, in Bahrain. The Brazilian did not retain his edge for long.
Photograph: James Moy/www.crashpa.net

HONDA RACING F1 TEAM

Chief executive officer: **Nick Fry**

President, HRD: **Yasuhiro Wada**

Senior technical director, Honda Racing F1: **Shuhei Nakamoto**

Sporting director: **Gil de Ferran**

Engineering director: **Jacky Eeckelaert**

Deputy technical director: **Gary Savage**

Chief designer: **Kevin Taylor**

Chief race engineer: **Craig Wilson**

Race engineer, car no. 11, Rubens Barrichello: **Jock Clear**

Race engineer, car no. 12, Jenson Button: **Andrew Shovlin**

Race-team manager: **Ron Meadows**

Chief mechanic: **Alastair Gibson**

Right: **Sporting director Gil de Ferran.**

Centre: **Team principal Nick Fry did not always find much to smile about.**

Far right: **Test driver Anthony Davidson did a good job as usual and will be racing for Super Aguri in 2007.**

Photographs: James Moy/www.crashpa.net

Above: **That glorious moment. Jenson Button and the team celebrating that long-overdue win in Hungary.**

Far right: **Jenson wore a specially liveried helmet for his home GP at Silverstone, but it brought him no good fortune – he spun off when oil leaked over his rear tyres.**

Photographs: James Moy/www.crashpa.net

Jenson had no problems with that because he is very smooth on the throttle. Rubens, meanwhile: as soon as the nose was pointing in the right direction he was used to just flooring the throttle and letting the TC do the rest with him just controlling the car's attitude a little.' Honda responded and developed new software, which did the trick.

Honda ownership gave the team initial renewed impetus, which translated into some encouraging pre-season test outings that the RA106 carried into the first few races.

'We didn't adequately sustain that development and paid the price around the middle of the season. However, we responded by ramping up our development programme and this stood us in good stead from Hockenheim,' Fry reflected.

'We scored points in every race since, with Jenson securing seven consecutive points finishes. From the unforgettable day that we won our first race, in Hungary, Jenson achieved more points than any other driver, and Rubens scored points in ten out of 18 opportunities in his first year with our team.'

Fry acknowledges that Jenson's win was the icing on the cake for Honda. On that day, he feels, both team and Jenson were simply the best, and winning has made a difference to the way they subsequently operated.

'With regard to the engine, after a slightly shaky start to the season we embarked on a relentless development programme to end the year with the early introduction of next year's engine, a significant step forward in performance, meeting the homologation requirements for 2007,' said Fry.

'In 2006 we also made the investment required for us to compete on a level playing field with the other top teams. A magnificent effort from all concerned led to our new full-scale wind tunnel being completed three months ahead of schedule and this certainly benefited us in the second half of the season.

'We now have a fantastic springboard for 2007 and we know we are on the right trajectory. There is a great deal of opportunity for improvement and we will be working at 150 percent over the winter to ensure that we are bona fide championship contenders next season.' Don't bet against it.

Alan Henry

RED BULL RACING

DAVID COULTHARD

14

15

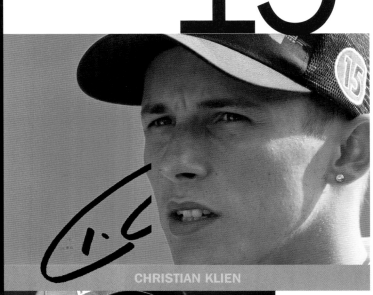

CHRISTIAN KLIEN

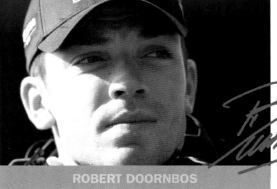

ROBERT DOORNBOS

Photographs: James Moy, www.crashpa.net

© ADRIAN DEAN

RED BULL RB2

PARTNERS	Rauch • Alpinestars • Quehenberger • Michelin
ENGINE	Type: **Ferrari 056** No. of cylinders (vee angle): **V8 (90°)** Sparking plugs: **NGK** Electronics: **Magneti Marelli** Fuel: **Shell** Oil: **Shell**
TRANSMISSION	Gearbox: **7-speed gearbox, longitudinally mounted with hydraulic shift and clutch operation** Clutch: **AP Racing pull-type clutch**
CHASSIS	Front and rear suspension: **Aluminium uprights, upper and lower carbon wishbones and pushrods, torsion bar springs and anti-roll bars** Dampers: **Multimatic** Wheels: **Avus Racing** Wheel diameter, front: **320 mm** rear: **340 mm** Tyres: **Michelin** Brake discs: **Hitco** Brake pads: **Hitco** Brake callipers: **Brembo** Steering: **Red Bull Racing** Radiators: **Marston/Red Bull Racing** Fuel tank: **ATL/Red Bull Racing** Instruments: **Magneti Marelli/Red Bull Racing**
DIMENSIONS	Formula weight: **600 kg including driver**

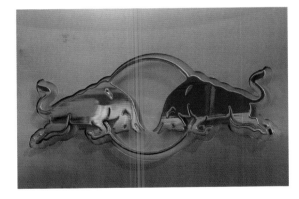

THE second season of Red Bull's ownership of the former Jaguar team delivered less than had been expected. Granted, David Coulthard seized the team's first podium finish after a suitably bullish drive to third place through the streets of Monaco, but the sense of anticipation engendered by the switch from Cosworth to Ferrari engines was certainly not matched by the subsequent track performance, in which Red Bull seldom broke free of the mid-field ruck.

In a sense, Red Bull was on a hiding to nothing. Its first season, in 2005, had been distinctly promising, but it had unquestionably built on the momentum generated by inheriting Jaguar's hardware. This year things would be very different as Red Bull simultaneously attempted to get the best out of its new RB2 and concentrated on the long-term development of the 2007 RB3 under the guidance of newly recruited chief technical officer Adrian Newey, who came on board at the start of the year.

Earlier, a *volte-face* prior to a crucial F1 Commission meeting

led Red Bull to vote in favour of reintroducing in-race tyre changes for 2006 – for a Michelin runner this was the F1 equivalent of turkeys voting for an early Christmas – which infuriated many of the team's rivals, who'd originally been convinced that RBR would vote against such a proposition.

The switch from Cosworth to Ferrari power was intended to offer a boost to the team's performance and credibility. It improved neither. The track record for teams using Ferrari customer engines has historically been average and Red Bull was no exception. Maranello looks on these arrangements as purely commercial alliances designed to enhance the Ferrari company's financial bottom line. Progressing the deal into a meaningful technical collaboration didn't really appear to be on the Prancing Horse's agenda.

The Red Bull deal with Ferrari was for two years, but by the end of 2006 the new team had put Ferrari's back up by indicating that it wanted to switch its contract to Scuderia Toro Rosso, clearing the way for Red Bull to use Renault engines in

Above: Christian Klien's tenure with the team came to an abrupt end after a patchy season.

Top: David Coulthard leads temporary team-mate Robert Doornbos at Suzuka.

Above centre left: Sporting director Christian Horner displayed an upbeat temperament, always trying to look on the bright side.

Centre left: Red Bull sustains a vibrant presence in the paddock.
Photographs: James Moy/www.crashpa.net

Above: GP2 exponent Michael Ammermüller took over the third drive when Doornbos received his late-season promotion.

Top: Red Bull founder Dietrich Mateschitz seems happy to continue investing in F1, aiming for long-term success.

Above right: Just a part of the huge Red Bull team posing for an end of season photo in Brazil.
Photographs: James Moy/www.crashpa.net

Right: Helmut Marko continued his role in developing driver talent.
Photograph: Peter Nygaard/GP Photo

Far right: Adrian Newey's intensive personnel recruitment campaign throughout 2006 should pay off for Red Bull next season.
Photograph: James Moy/www.crashpa.net

RED BULL RACING

Team principal: Christian Horner

**Chief technical officer:
Adrian Newey**

Chief designer: Rob Marshall

Team manager: Jonathan Wheatley

**Head of aerodynamics:
Ben Agathangelou**

**Chief aerodynamicist:
Peter Prodromou**

Technical director: Mark Smith

**Head of R&D controls and
development: Anton Stipinovich**

**Head of R&D, testing and
vehicle dynamics: Andrew Green**

2007. At the end of October this change of engine supply arrangements was finally confirmed.

'I think that this year has really been about consolidation,' explained sporting director Christian Horner. 'We have changed the technical group and a lot of factors within the company during the past 12 months and really this year has been a settling-down period with that group coming together and it's obvious that it has been a slightly frustrating year on circuit.

'We've had issues that we took a little bit of time to get on top of and, some time ago, we made the decision to really focus our attentions on Adrian and what will be his first Red Bull car, for next year.

'There are a lot of good things in the pipeline and I think this year we really consolidated where we are and that group is now working together as a cohesive unit and I think we should start to see the results of that in Adrian's first car for us next year.'

When Newey arrived, his priority was the RB3 programme, so he wasn't directly involved in all the pre-season strife with the overheating problems on the Ferrari-engined car, a combination of assumptions made on the basis of the relationship with Cosworth and the basic fact that the new generation of V8s has more cooling demands than the recent V10s had.

The team lost about 50 percent of its hoped-for pre-season testing time due to this problem, which, embarrassingly, left Red Bull initially testing the RB2 with hacked-about bodywork as engineers struggled to get the problem under control. Once the car settled into its racing programme its strongest card turned out to be its performance on lower-speed circuits; Horner acknowledged that it lost out on the higher-speed tracks. 'Happily, high-speed-circuit performance has traditionally been the forte of Adrian's designs,' he said, 'which I hope bodes

well for the future.'

For Coulthard, third place at Monaco was a satisfying achievement, but there were too few other upbeat days to brighten his season. Only three times in the 18 races did he manage to qualify in the top ten and by the end of the year at Suzuka he looked glum and steely-eyed when he told ITV, 'We're slower than [we were with] last year's car. The year started badly and we never made it up. This team needs to look at its personnel. We have a new car next year and I'm nervous.'

In fairness to DC, he usually took a positive and upbeat attitude towards the team's potential. 'Now we're in a building process,' he explained. 'We want to make ourselves into the best team in the business but that won't happen overnight. But in the meantime, we can make an effort to have the slickest pit stops, the cleanest garage and so on, while working towards that aim.'

In the number-two seat Christian Klien made a good start to the season, but his performance was eventually deemed too patchy for a driver in his third year in F1. He was eventually stood down in favour of third driver Robert Doornbos, who performed respectably in China, Japan and Brazil.

Mark Webber moves across from Williams to join DC in the Red Bull squad next year. If they end up using Renault engines and if Newey performs another display of his aerodynamic wizardry, this pair of 30-somethings may well find themselves in among the best seats in the house. If that happens, it will be fascinating to see which of them winds up getting the upper hand.

Alan Henry

NICK HEIDFELD

Photograph: James Moy/www.crashpa.net

JACQUES VILLENEUVE

ROBERT KUBICA

Photographs: James Moy/www.crashpa.net

IT was on 22 June, 2005 that BMW announced that it would be taking over Sauber on 1 January, 2006. It would safeguard the team built up by Peter Sauber and turn it into another wholly owned manufacturer team, combining BMW's mechanical base in Munich and Sauber's operations base at Hinwil in Switzerland.

Of course, this would take time. There were major expansion plans, integration was important and a whole new structure had to be implemented. It was a two-year project to get the team to a fully competitive stage, said team principal Mario Theissen. 'We started in 2006 but we are in a two-year transition phase. We will have all the people on board by the end of 2007. The factory expansion will also be ready by the end of next year, so we should have everything in place to be competitive and challenge the top teams in 2008. Right from the start, we said it would be a two-year project.'

So 2006 was a transitional year but already the signs were good, as Theissen explained. 'For our first year on the grid, we set ourselves the goal of halving the 1.5s per lap deficit to the leading cars that the Saubers were running at in 2005 and improving on eighth place in the constructors' championship.

'But the most positive thing for me is that since the existence of the original Sauber team, 2006 was the first season in which competitiveness increased over the season, instead of decreased. That shows best that the effort made behind the scenes is bearing fruit. Obviously it is very positive as well to have podium finishes in the first ramp-up season, which we didn't expect.'

Truth be told, the project is lasting more than two years, because BMW Sauber's plans for the future began virtually the day that the takeover was announced, even if control didn't actually pass into BMW's hands until the start of 2006. What was important was to have a package that was ready to be as competitive as possible right from the start of the 2006 season, and build from there. Indeed, BMW invested in the 2006 car even before it had taken over the team.

At the same time, it sought to lay off some of the additional costs, with some success, Theissen explained. 'After having put the first bits and pieces in place on the technical side last year, over the winter we focused on finding partners and we have

+44 (0)121 603 1554   © ADRIAN DEAN

BMW SAUBER F1.06

SPONSORS	**Petronas • Intel • Credit Suisse • O²**
PARTNERS	**Certina • Dalco • Fluent • Man • NGK • Puma • Walter Meier • Gore-Tex • Wurth**
ENGINE	Type: **BMW P86** No. of cylinders: **V8** Sparking plugs: **NGK** Electronics: **BMW** Fuel: **Petronas** Oil: **Petronas**
TRANSMISSION	Gearbox: **Longitudinally mounted 7-speed transmission** Clutch: **AP Racing hand-operated carbon clutch**
CHASSIS	Suspension: **Upper and lower wishbones (front and rear), inboard springs and dampers, actuated by pushrods (Sachs Race Engineering)**
	Chassis electronics: **Magneti Marelli** Wheel diameter: **330 mm front and rear** Wheels: **OZ** Tyres: **Michelin** Brake pads and discs: **Brembo/Carbon Industrie**
	Brake callipers: **6-piston, Brembo** Steering: **Power-assisted BMW Sauber F1 Team** Radiators: **Calsonic, Modine**
DIMENSIONS	Wheelbase: **3,110 mm** Track, front: **1,470 mm** rear: **1,410 mm** Length: **4,610 mm** Width: **1,800 mm** Height: **1,000 mm**
	Formula weight: **600 kg (including driver, ready to drive; tank empty)**

found very strong partners in terms of know-how contribution and financial contribution,' he said. 'So I can say that for BMW the entire operation is not more expensive than its role as an engine supplier used to be over the years before, so the company doesn't spend more money.'

But that doesn't necessarily take into account the increase in personnel or facilities. 'We have decided on a personnel expansion of some 150 staff, plus the factory expansion, so that's certainly extra capital expenditure,' continued the BMW motor sport chief.

Over in Munich, where BMW's Formula 1 force is stable at 250 people, work had started on the new BMW P86 V8 in November 2004. The first specification completed its brake tests in May 2005 and another spec was tested in a Williams in July 2005. The first V8-powered Sauber ran in winter testing in late November 2005.

The chassis, meanwhile, had been developed at Hinwil, once again under the technical directorship of Willy Rampf. During the year he would see his team strengthened by many appointments. Willem Toet took over the aerodynamics and Sauber's top-level wind tunnel from Seamus Mullarkey. Jörg Zander joined from Williams as chief designer in April. Former head of F1 engine development at Mercedes Markus Duesmann is due to take over as head of powertrain from Heinz Paschen on 1 January, 2007.

Like every other team, Sauber had to cope with the reduction of engine size and horsepower and, therefore, speed. 'We had to estimate what would be the new top speed and end up with a figure to reduce the drag by,' said Rampf. 'When you give this figure to the aerodynamicists they almost had to start with a new car. Reducing drag meant taking off a lot of the components because the cross section is the same and the tyre size, which normally dictates most of the drag, was also the same, so we had to shrink the bodywork wherever possible.

'We started with a baseline car for the rollout and decided, in December, to introduce the next evolution mid-February. So, pre-season, we froze the design and told the aero guys to keep developing.'

Like many of its competitors, Sauber found two problems.

First, the V8 had a different vibration pattern from the V10. 'The vibrations are ranged in the area above 16,000 rpm,' said Theissen, 'which means the area where the engine spends the most time. These challenges came under control but we had to cope with a general shortage of R&D time for the new V8. It would normally take us 18 months to develop an entirely new engine concept but we've had less time than that. Usually we would do what we did in April in January, so we were developing the engine into the season.'

That shortcoming resulted in engine failures in Bahrain, Australia and Spain for Jacques Villeneuve, and Malaysia for Nick Heidfeld.

The other problem concerned tyres, which the teams were now able to change during races. 'I think most people found that they couldn't go as soft with the tyres as they expected,' explained Rampf. 'In reality, with less torque on the wheels there is more capacity for lateral force and the cornering speeds

Top: Heidfeld was a consistent performer scoring points for the team in ten of the eighteen races.
Photograph: James Moy/www.crash.net

Above: Jacques Villeneuve looks pensive below his image on the side of the BMW Sauber transporter. Neither he, nor his image, would last out the season.
Photograph: Jad Sherif/WRI

Right: BMW Motorsport chief Mario Theissen was well satisfied with the steady progress made by the team throughout the year.
Photograph: James Moy/www.crashpa.net

Centre right: Willy Rampf steadily consolidated an expanding and promising technical department under the new BMW regime.

Far right: 19-year old Sebastian Vettel became the youngest-ever participant in a GP weekend.
Photographs: XPB.cc

Above: Robert Kubica's strong run to third place in the Italian GP was one of the outstanding drives of the season.
Photograph: James Moy/www.crashpa.net

BMW SAUBER F1 TEAM

BMW Motorsport director:
Mario Theissen

Former team owner, advisor:
Peter Sauber

Technical director, chassis:
Willy Rampf

Technical director, powertrain:
Heinz Paschen

Head of aerodynamics: Willem Toet

Head of track engineering:
Mike Krack

Team manager: Beat Zehnder

Chief mechanic: Urs Kuratle

Race engineer, car no. 16,
Nick Heidfeld: Andy Borme

Race engineer, car no. 17, R. Kubica/
J. Villeneuve: Giampaolo Dall'ara

increased quite a lot, and everybody was surprised about this. More lateral load on the tyres meant that you could even end up with a harder tyre in some cases.'

Sauber also took a leaf out of Renault's book by working hard on its race starts. By the later stages of the season, the drivers were regularly gaining places. 'You can improve the starts by changing weight distribution,' says Rampf, 'but that causes problems elsewhere. We looked at what we could do to use the tyres to the maximum and we were happy to see the performance we had without compromising the car itself.'

Development really began for the San Marino Grand Prix and thereafter they concentrated on improvements for every race. Such was their aerodynamicists' appetite for invention that they fell foul of the FIA for the rear flex-wing introduced in Canada and the so-called twin towers in France. Both were initially approved and subsequently banned. The wind tunnel was being used more and more: a second shift per day was added in January, with a third being used on occasions by the end of October, earlier than planned.

By mid-season, the drivers were regularly scoring points, particularly Nick Heidfeld. The team had secured his services a season early after signing him for 2007–08; Williams let him go early. Jacques Villeneuve had had a contract with Sauber for 2006 before BMW bought the team but at mid-season Theissen commented that, 'He's highly motivated and right back on top form, which puts a smile on my face.'

However, waiting in the wings was the team's very promising third driver, Robert Kubica, and when Villeneuve crashed heavily

at Hockenheim and subsequently complained of headaches the Pole was an instant replacement for the next weekend's race in Hungary. 'We wanted to evaluate the options for next year,' said Theissen, 'and that impacted on Jacques' position for the rest of the season.'

Even though Jacques had outqualified his team-mate seven–five at that stage of the season, on the slippery Hungary surface Heidfeld upped his game and finished third, BMW's first podium, and Kubica came home in seventh only to be disqualified.

A final highlight was Monza. 'As in Canada, we considered all the bodywork and whether it still made sense and was efficient enough,' said Rampf of the team's low-downforce set-up. 'I think we proved there that it was the right direction to go, to start from scratch for a low-downforce car and then concentrate just on the drag target to make it efficient.'

Efficient it was; Kubica finished on the podium in only his third race. In the meantime, his 19-year-old replacement Sebastian Vettel had also proved immensely promising, setting the fastest time in his first day of Friday testing, just like his predecessor.

BMW Sauber, then, finished the season on a high, battling with Toyota over fifth in the championship and coming out on top. Now the team would have to improve again in its second transitional year, to be ready to fight for victories in 2008.

Bob Constanduros

Some think
heat, rubber,
and asphalt.

**We think the
right solution.**

Investment Banking • Private Banking • Asset Management

In Formula One it's often the equipment that decides the race. The BMW Sauber F1 Team makes their tire choice based on their race strategy, the circuit, and the prevailing weather conditions. That's why know-how and precision determine success. These are the qualities that we share with the racing team, and that inspire us to find the best solution for you. www.credit-suisse.com/f1

Thinking New Perspectives.

SPYKER MF1 TEAM

TIAGO MONTEIRO

CHRISTIJAN ALBERS

JORDAN finally disappeared, the once-familiar yellow making way for Midland's mix of grey, black and bright red. The transformation was supposed to mark the way forward for the Silverstone-based team after a holding year following the hurried buy-out of Jordan at the beginning of 2005. By the end of 2006, however, the team had changed hands once more and, in between, this tightly knit outfit had somehow survived with a meagre budget that some leading teams would consider derisory.

Alex Shnaider made only a handful of appearances, the Midland Group chairman leaving Colin Kolles to run the team. Having suffered a difficult F1 baptism in 2005, the Romania-born Kolles used his knowledge to run a tight ship with help from the experienced Ian Phillips (officially the manager of business affairs but, equally, the vital link between the team and those controlling F1's politics) and Andy Stevenson, team manager and long-time Jordan man. Johnny Herbert once again played out an important role as advisor to the team and front man with the media.

There was, in truth, not a great deal for Herbert to talk about in 2006. The main aim was to move from the back row of the grid (an easy enough task given the arrival of Super Aguri) and take the fight to Torro Rosso. Tiago Monteiro, who remained on board for his second year in F1, was joined by Christijan Albers, the Dutchman moving from Minardi to replace Narain Karthikeyan.

A motley collection of Friday test drivers summed up Midland's situation: financial interests simply had to take priority over the preferred option of consistent feedback from a single experienced driver. And yet progress was made, the M16 undergoing gradual development that occasionally allowed at least one car to make it into the second phase of qualifying,

Photograph: Russell Batchelor/XPB.cc

SPYKER M16

© ADRIAN DEAN

© ADRIAN DEAN

MIDLAND M16

PARTNERS	Bridgestone • Rhino's Energy • Mingya.cn • JVC • Lbi Midland Group plc, • Portugal • MAN Trucks • Garcia • Dremel • Lost Boys • LeasePlan RotoZip • Trust • Philoderm • EuroPoker.com • Zim Intergrated Shipping Services Ltd • Superfund • F1Racing.net • Trekstor • Futurecom.
ENGINE	Type: **Toyota RVX-06** No. of cylinders: **V8** Sparking plugs: **Denso**
TRANSMISSION	Gearbox: **In-house Midland MF1 Racing design. 7-speed + reverse longitudinal gearbox with electro-hydraulic sequential gear change** Clutch: **AP hand operated**
CHASSIS	Front and rear suspension: **Composite pushrods activating chassis mounted in-line dampers and torsion bars, unequal length composite aerodynamic wishbones, front anti-roll bar and cast uprights** Dampers: **Penske** Wheels: **BBS** Tyres: **Bridgestone** Brake discs: **Hitco** Brake pads: **Hitco** Brake calipers: **AP** Steering: **Midland power assisted** Radiators: **Marston** Fuel tank: **ATL** Fuel-tank capacity: **more than 90 kg** Instruments: **Toyota/Magneti-Marelli**
DIMENSIONS	Formula weight: **601 kg including driver and camera**

Left: Christijan Albers will be remaining with what is now regarded as his national team for 2007.

Below left: Occupants of the third car during the year included (from left to right), Giorgio Mondini, Markus Winkelhock, Adrian Sutil, Alexandre Prémat and Ernesto Viso.

Below: (Clockwise from top left) Dr Colin Kolles, Victor P. Muller, James Key and Mike Gascoyne.

Bottom left: Spyker's director of racing Michiel Mol and the re-liveried car for the balance of the season under Spyker.

Photographs: James Moy/www.crashpa.net

14th on the grid (Albers at Indianapolis) being as good as it got. From mediocre starting positions, point scoring would never be more than a slim hope.

'It was never going to be easy,' said Herbert. 'But, saying that, we achieved a lot more than we thought we would. Basically, we were starting afresh, running as Midland. We had a very difficult start to the year because we had not been able to do much testing. Changing the name and image of the team is a major job and we were always playing catch-up. We had no chance of getting through to the second round of qualifying – no chance at all.

'But, to give the technical guys [led by James Key] credit, we improved as the season went on. We got very, very close to second qualifying a couple of times. Finally, we got one car [Monteiro's] through, at Silverstone, and came very close with the other. That was a very respectable achievement because it had been through a lot of hard work on very limited resources. I really don't think a lot of people understand how limited it had been and what a damn good job the boys had actually done.'

Midland experienced the perennial F1 problem once the season got going: nothing stands still. Improve your car and the opposition will have done like-wise. It was a credit to Midland, therefore, that moving into the second qualifying session became a valid expectation rather than a pipe dream. Unfortunately for the team – and Albers in particular – much of the promise was nullified by a spate of engine problems and the subsequent ten-place penalties on the grid. It was unfortunate timing that these failures should occur just as Toyota announced a switch of supply from Midland to Williams for 2007.

'Bad timing – but no more than that,' said Herbert. 'The relationship with Toyota has been excellent. We built a really good rapport. There has been no sense of, "Well, we are Toyota, this is the package: just get on with it!" They have been very helpful and very flexible at the same time. That is a boon when you are struggling under constrained circumstances.'

The team, however, was not helped by having its drivers collide on two occasions. Having started 16th at Monaco, Albers eased Monteiro into the wall as he tried to come alongside at the start, earning a drive-through penalty. Two races later, the roles were reversed when Monteiro locked up and accidentally collided with Albers. Generally, however, the drivers worked hard with frequently difficult cars, their efforts matching those of the team. Although Herbert would not quote a figure, reliable sources say Midland got by on $50 million.

'When you take into account the flyaway races and the cost of just getting the cars out, there is very little left to run

the wind tunnel with all the man-hours that requires,' said Herbert. 'I was quoted in an article that we were getting by on £1.95 and the guys stuck that on the wall of the design office! It was a joke, of course. But the meaning was understood.'

For 2007 things look much brighter. The Dutch high-performance car maker Spyker completed its purchase of the team at the Italian Grand Prix and the new consortium's seriousness of purpose was confirmed when it announced that the team would be using customer Ferrari V8 engines in 2007.

Disappointingly, they also dispensed with the cheery Johnny Herbert's services, but there seemed little doubt that the new investors could see great commercial potential in being involved in the F1 business.

They insisted that they were in for the long haul.

Maurice Hamilton

Photographs: James Moy/www.crashpa.net

SPYKER MF1 TEAM

CEO, Spyker Cars: Victor P. Muller

Director of Formula 1 racing: Michiel Mol

Team principal and MD: Colin Kolles

Director of business affairs: Ian Phillips

Chief technical officer: Mike Gascoyne

Chief race and test engineer: Dominic Harlow

Chief designer: John McQuilliam

Head of aerodynamics: Simon Phillips

Head of electronics: Mike Wroe

Production manager: Simon Shinkins

Technical director: James Key

Team manager: Andy Stevenson

Chief mechanic: Andy Deeming

Race engineer, car no. 18, Tiago Monteiro: Brad Joyce

Race engineer, car no. 19, Christijan Albers: Jody Eggington

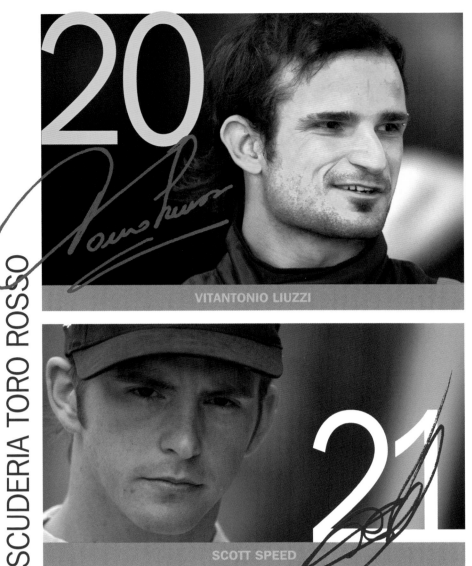

20

VITANTONIO LIUZZI

21

SCOTT SPEED

SCUDERIA TORO ROSSO

YOU hear the term 'transitional year' used many times in team reviews, but it probably could not have applied to any team in 2006 more than Scuderia Toro Rosso. Just about everything either had already changed since 2005 or would change during the year, apart from the former Minardi team's base in Faenza.

Gone was former head Paul Stoddart, who announced the new owner, Red Bull, at Spa in 2005. He had negotiated the continued use of Cosworth's V10 engine to guarantee his team's future, but this became a millstone rather than salvation.

Taking charge on a day-to-day basis was Franz Tost, reporting to new team principal Gerhard Berger, who announced his part-ownership of Toro Rosso with Red Bull in mid-February. Gone too was the previous technical department headed by Gabriele Tredozi, who cut a sorry figure when he turned up at Monza, seeing out his contract.

During the year the team grew from 108 employees to 125, with another 12 being sought for work in quality control and fabrication. There were eight engineers initially, but that had grown to 12, with a couple more being sought.

Perhaps the most comprehensive change was the team's ethos. 'The goal for Red Bull was, of course, from the outset, to renew the position and to try and make a competitive team out of it,' explained Berger. 'It was also to change Minardi into Toro Rosso – not with the Minardi culture, but to build up a Toro Rosso culture, which is very close to a Red Bull culture.

'We know how difficult it is to move forward from last place on the grid to a better position, to build up a team, how much time it takes to build up a culture in a team. It's not something you do in two months; it's a process of three, five, ten years. As long as you are aware of the complexity of the whole thing and you respect it, then I don't think you're going to have a bad surprise.

'The first step to get off the back of the grid is difficult, but it's reachable in a shorter term and we did it,' he continued. 'Today, at the end of the season, we are already respected in the paddock as a team having continuously good preparation and being competitive, even if it's more towards the back of the field.

'But at the same time, I think we've been able to be better than Suzuki [Super Aguri] and Midland [Spyker]. That was the first goal but the next step, when you look forward, is already to challenge Red Bull, Williams, sometimes BMW, sometimes Toyota. For us to be better than Williams would take time and it's not going to happen overnight.'

© ADRIAN DEAN

TORO ROSSO STR01

SPONSOR	**Red Bull**
OFFICIAL SUPPLIERS	**UGS • MSC Software • Sabelt • Avus • Michelin • Cosworth • Liquid Cosworth • Alpinestars**
ENGINE	Type: **Cosworth TJ2005-2** No. of cylinders (vee angle): **V10 (90°)** Sparking plugs: **Champion** Electronics: **Pi VCS System** Fuel: **Shell**
TRANSMISSION	Gearbox: **7-speed gearbox, longitudinally mounted with hydraulic shift and clutch operation** Clutch: **AP Racing pull-type clutch**
CHASSIS	Front and rear suspension: **Cast titanium uprights, pushrods, carbon-fibre upper and lower wishbones** Dampers: **Koni** Wheels: **Avus Racing** Tyres: **Michelin** Brake discs: **Hitco** Brake pads: **Hitco** Brake callipers: **AP** Steering: **Power-assisted** Radiators: **Marston/Red Bull Racing** Fuel tank: **Castrol Racing Fuel** Instruments: **Pi**
DIMENSIONS	Formula weight: **600 kg including driver**

Left: Scott Speed is quite aptly named and is the first American in F1 since Michael Andretti.

Below: Third driver Neel Jani was kept busy with his Friday driving duties.
Photographs: James Moy/www.crashpa.net

The team had four main obstacles in 2006. Some were perceived, others real. First was that V10 engine. In order for it to run without being more competitive than the V8s, the FIA limited its revs to 16,700 with a 77-mm restrictor and no development was allowed. Immediate rivals came up with scare stories – that its torque would be a massive advantage around tight circuits such as Monaco and the Hungaroring – that turned out to be rubbish, even though the team was allowed another 300 rpm for qualifying as continued development had allowed V8 manufacturers to raise their revs to 20,000.

But, on top of that, the aerodynamics had to be compromised due to the greater size of the V10. And however much torque the V10 may have produced, most of its advantage was cancelled out by traction control. Sure, the team tried to limit that disadvantage as much as possible via the software but it couldn't change anything in the engine itself. 'We didn't do well in Monaco or at Budapest,' said Tost. 'I think they were our worst races.'

Second, the team had two novice drivers – Vitantonio Liuzzi and Scott Speed – who had very little Formula 1 experience. Tost praised their development but also appreciated that the restructuring within the team didn't give them the best environment. Of course, having different equipment from the rest of the field's meant it was also harder to evaluate them.

Third, the team was often the centre of controversy for running what was sometimes perceived as a copy car. With the loss of Tredozi and his team, Toro Rosso didn't seem to have its own design team and it relied on Red Bull Racing in Milton Keynes for the hardware. Critics said that this was against the rules.

Tost, however, would admit that 'this year's car is a development of the RB1, last year's Red Bull car. It was changed a little bit on the aerodynamic side and on the mechanical side, but many components were carried over from

the RB1. Next year's car will be a completely new construction.' Ex-Cosworth engineer Alex Hitzinger has been appointed as technical director.

Fourth, the team wasn't able to undertake any tyre testing. This was because Toro Rosso switched from Bridgestones to Michelins after the 2005 season and, because of a lack of capacity, Michelin decided that only Red Bull Racing could test tyres, and not Toro Rosso. In what was known as the Tree House, a structure built above their race trucks, race engineers from both teams worked closely at races to find the correct tyres. However, Toro Rosso benefited from a test team, a luxury not always afforded to its previous incarnation.

During the year, the team developed the car in spite of spending very limited time in a full-scale wind tunnel in Stuttgart. 'We were there for a couple of days,' said Tost, 'but we were very well prepared and I think we tested around 120 parts. It was a very good test. It led to some key steps on the aerodynamic side: front end plates, then side pods, the side pod cooling intakes and some small mechanical parts. The brake system was also changed, starting with discs during the winter tests, then callipers around Monaco time and master cylinders at the Nürburgring. Some drivers feel better with Heatco equipment, some with Brembo material. We basically changed from AP to Heatco and Brembo; we mixed it up.'

Tost would admit that 'there were a couple of highs. First the really good race from Scott in Australia and then the first point for Tonio at Indy. Disappointing were Budapest and Shanghai. The rest of the season was average, it was okay.

'The philosophy of Red Bull and Toro Rosso is that sooner or later the team will be a front runner. Look at the rear wing on our cars: *Red Bull Gives You Wings*. I hope that we will have these wings and therefore we are pushing very hard.'

Bob Constanduros

Above: Team celebrations after Tonio Liuzzi scores its first point at Indianapolis.

Far left: Gerhard Berger has a 50-per cent stake in the STR operation.

Centre left: The highly regarded Franz Tost was recruited as team principal.
Photographs: James Moy/www.crashpa.net

SCUDERIA TORO ROSSO

Team principal: **Franz Tost**

Team co-owner: **Gerhard Berger**

Technical director: **Gabriele Tredozi**

General manager:
Gianfranco Fantuzzi

Chief engineer: **Laurent Mekies**

Team manager: **Massimo Rivola**

Race engineer, car no. 20,
Tonio Liuzzi: **Brunetto Calderoni**

Race engineer, car no. 21,
Scott Speed: **Stefano Pieranoni**

YUJI IDE

SAKON YAMAMOTO

TAKUMA SATO

FRANCK MONTAGNY

22

23

MANY people would suggest that it's almost impossible to start an F1 team from scratch these days – unless you are a major manufacturer such as Toyota, for instance. To start one up in a matter of months is impossible. Aguri Suzuki would admit that that is true, even though he did just that to establish Formula 1's newest team.

Aguri already had Formula Nippon, GT and IndyCar teams – all with Honda – as well as a go-kart team and series. 'Early last year [2005], in February or March, I started this project as an idea,' explained former grand prix driver Aguri. 'I discussed it with my business partner [one of three] and he said, "I want to get into Formula 1."'

Their first thoughts were to invest in BAR, because owner BAT was pulling out in the wake of tobacco bans in Europe, but, after initially approving their idea, Honda decided that it wanted to take over BAR 100 percent. Jordan had already been bought by Midland so then Aguri considered Minardi, but Red Bull was moving in on that.

'So, okay, I try to make a new team,' said Aguri. 'At the beginning of August I discussed it more deeply with Honda and they agreed to supply me with engines. Then I called Daniel [Audetto] because I knew he was working at Menard Engineering in the old Arrows factory and he said the factory was empty.'

Aguri visited it in September 2005. 'There was nothing in the factory – it was like a garage; nothing. And so after that I started this project, this crazy impossible project. At the beginning of October, we had five people: me, Daniel, Kevin Lee [chief operations officer], Mick Ainsley-Cowlishaw [team manager] and Wayne Humphreys [chief financial officer].'

After that, things moved fast – they had to. Yasuhiro Wada, president of Honda Racing Development, announced at the 2005 Brazilian Grand Prix that Honda would be supporting a new team, but rather left the announcement hanging by being unable to say who was involved. The level of support from Honda was also in doubt. At one time BAR's winter test chassis was offered, but Honda put a block on that.

Steadily, however, information emerged. Humphreys negotiated the acquisition of the 2002 Sergio Rinland-designed Arrows chassis from Paul Stoddart and Mark Preston was recruited as chief technical officer. 'We had four monocoques,' he said, 'one doing the crash test, two that were destined to be race cars and one that was initially a systems car because Honda was supplying all the electronics and codes to help us integrate that with the old Arrows chassis and gearbox. Every day there was a problem; every day a solution.'

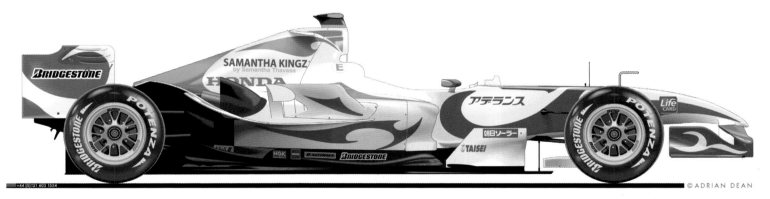

SAMANTHA KINGZ
by Samantha Thavasa

HONDA

© ADRIAN DEAN

SUPER AGURI SA06

SPONSORS	**Honda • Bridgestone • Samantha Kingz • Life Card • ANA • NGK**
ENGINE	Type: **Honda RA806-E** No. of cylinders (vee angle): **V8 (90°)** Sparking plugs: **Champion** Electronics: **Pi VCS System** Fuel: **Elf** Oil: **Elf**
TRANSMISSION	Gearbox: **7-speed, longitudinally mounted with hydraulic system for power shift and clutch operation** Clutch: **Sachs**
CHASSIS	Front and rear suspension: **Wishbones, pushrod-operated torsion bars and dampers. Mechanical anti-roll bar** Dampers: **Ohlins** Wheels: **BBS**
	Tyres: **Bridgestone** Brake discs: **Hitco** Brake pads: **Hitco** Brake callipers: **AP** Steering: **Super Aguri power-assisted** Fuel tank: **ATL**
	Instruments: **Super Aguri**
DIMENSIONS	Wheelbase: **3,090 mm** Length: **4,666 mm** Width: **1,800 mm** Height: **950 mm**
	Formula weight: **600 kg including driver**

Left: **Takuma Sato in characteristically exuberant action.**

Below, clockwise from top left:
Team founder Aguri Suzuki; managing director Daniel Audetto; chief technical officer Mark Preston; team manager Mick Ainsley-Cowlishaw.
Photographs: James Moy/www.crashpa.net

Prior to the start of the season, the team initiated a five-week programme in the 50-percent British Maritime Technology wind tunnel at Teddington, formerly used by McLaren. 'Obviously the old Arrows – now known as the SA05 – had run to less stringent aero regulations,' explained Preston. 'When we drew an aero graph it was just phenomenal. It started at a fairly high aero level and immediately dropped more than 20 percent when it was adapted to the current rules. It didn't take long to get back up there.

'We focused on the body during the first week in the wind tunnel. The second week was top bodies, then wings and nose box. We first did three not-so-reliable days of testing at Barcelona at the end of February. That car was the old Arrows with the same old aero package and, in parallel, we had one car being modified to the 2006 rules and crash tested.

'The gearbox was probably the most difficult technical challenge. We were going to introduce the new one earlier but we had some timing issues and so used the old gearbox to start with.'

Initially, there were also problems with the entry. It was confirmed only on 26 January, after Aguri had lodged his $48-million bond. 'My most important job is to get that back,' he said.

When the team flew out to Bahrain, it was just under 80 strong. By the end of the season, it had virtually doubled. Leading the driving team was Takuma Sato, with newcomer Yuji Ide. Amazingly, after three races, Sato had completed more racing kilometres than any other driver!

But as far as Suzuki was concerned, the season was just one big winter test. Sadly, Ide did not come up to scratch and lost his Superlicence after five races. 'He was a good talent but he had no experience in Formula 1, how to use Formula 1 tyres,' said Suzuki. 'He didn't know the circuits and we hadn't had any tests before the grands prix. And his English wasn't good enough – I had to translate everything for the engineers.' He was replaced by Franck Montagny, who did a more-than-adequate job.

The big focal point for the team was the development and then introduction of the SA06. Initially the team had been disappointed with the level of support from Honda, but the arrival of Shuhei Nakamoto as the senior technical director of Honda's F1 team freed up the supply channels, even if there were only two engine specifications during the year. The new quick-shift gearbox was primary among the SA06's features and Bridgestone had worked hard to help develop new suspension. However, a five-day breakdown at the wind tunnel eventually delayed its introduction until the German Grand Prix, coinciding with the race début of Sakon Yamamoto.

'This development really has focused on the rear end of the car and the new gearbox,' said Preston at the time. 'With the new gearbox comes a lot of integration. The rear end is now a lot neater; the gearbox is obviously made for the engine, to

fit the hydraulics. Added to that, the SA05 had suspension from 2002 and tyres have moved on a long way since then, so the rear suspension needed a lot of attention.

'Integrating the gearbox and the engine in a more efficient way, we've saved a lot of weight, so we now have a reasonable amount of ballast [20 kg] on the car and a reduced centre of gravity. We have done a lot more work on aerodynamics and the SA06 has new sidepods and new-style radiator inlet ducts; we've got a new top body; and the heat shielding across the gearbox now integrates properly with the engine. Under-body and over-body flow is a lot better because of changes to the rear end – a twin pylon arrangement that has allowed the lower main plane to become much more aerodynamic.'

Downforce gain was estimated at 10 percent, thanks to nearly ten weeks in the wind tunnel, and new front suspension arrived for the Turkish Grand Prix, as did a third SA06.

Before Monza, Super Aguri had formed its own test team and, as the season ended, chief designer Peter McCool had a staff of just under 20 that had come up with an update package for the final three races. Super Aguri had worked miracles to get to Bahrain and had completed the season with honour – winter test or not.

Bob Constanduros

SUPER AGURI F1 TEAM

Team principal: **Aguri Suzuki**

Managing director: **Daniel Audetto**

Chief operations officer: **Kevin Lee**

Chief technical engineer:
Mark Preston

Chief designer: **Peter McCool**

Team manager:
Mick Ainsley-Cowlishaw

Chief mechanic: **Phill Spencer**

Race engineer, car no. 22,
Takuma Sato: **Gerry Hughes**

Race engineer, car no. 23,
Sakon Yamamoto/Franck Montagny/
Yuji Ide: **Antonio Cuquerella**

Whittlebury Park

The Ideal Base for a Day at Silverstone

Become a Corporate Member of Whittlebury Park and you and your guests can meet and play golf in superb surroundings; dine in style in the magnificent Atrium Clubhouse, Pavilion or Orangery and stroll into Silverstone Circuit for any of the major race meetings, including the British Grand Prix.

Private Boardroom and Dining facilities from 20 to 250 guests.

FAST TRACK ACCESS INTO THE CIRCUIT plus use of Whittlebury Park's extensive facilities including the largest campsite.

Whittlebury Park
Towcester
Northamptonshire
NN12 8WP

Tel: 01327 850 000
Fax: 01327 850 001

Email: Enquiries@whittlebury.com
www.whittlebury.com

SHOOTING & ARCHERY

PILOT BUGGIES

2.5 MILE 4x4 COURSE

36 HOLES OF CHAMPIONSHIP GOLF

QUAD BIKE TREKS

GRASS CARTS

GRANDS PRIX 2006 by ALAN HENRY & DAVID TREMAYNE

Photograph: James Moy/www.crashpa.net

Fernando Alonso acknowledges his first victory
of the 2006 F1 season, the new Renault R26 with
its 2.4-litre V8 ensuring him a seamless transition
from his title-winning efforts of the previous season.
Photograph: Bryn Williams/www.crashpa.net

BAHRAIN GP

SAKHIR

Top inset: Rubens Barrichello and Nick Fry listen attentively to Honda's Yasuhiro Wada at the start of what would be a roller-coaster season for the Britain-based team.
Photograph: Bryn Williams/www.crashpa.net

Centre inset: Takuma Sato gives the Arrows-based Super Aguri its race debut after a heroic effort on the part of the Leafield-based team.
Photograph: James Moy/www.crashpa.net

Main photograph: Ferrari new boy Felipe Massa did an excellent job in qualifying, his time bettered only by his team leader Michael Schumacher.
Photograph: Russell Batchelor/XPB.cc

Bottom inset: Like mother, like son. Sina Rosberg gives a poster of new Williams driver Nico an admiring appraisal.
Photograph: Jean-François Galeron/WRI

SAKHIR QUALIFYING

FRIDAY'S free practice sessions offered what many in the paddock thought was a preview of the future if in fact the sport gravitates to two-day grands prix with Friday set aside for open testing. BMW Sauber's Polish test driver Robert Kubica wrote his own slice of motorsport history by setting the fastest time in the first hour-long practice session, but generally this was a day when the superstars spent most of the time kicking their heels in the pits while their test drivers – or compliant number-twos – did the hard work checking out tyre compounds for the following day.

On the face of it new knock-out qualifying format looked straightforward to implement and explain. But the more you looked at the intricacies of the rules, the more complicated it all became. The first two 15-minute sessions looked simple enough, but the final 20-minute shoot-out for the top ten positions was complicated by the fact that at the end of the session the teams would have to top up their tanks for the race to the level at which they started the session based on a 'fuel credit' rate prescribed for each circuit on the calendar; in Bahrain's case it was 2.75 kg per lap.

Also, given that all the top contenders for pole would be wanting to run on fresh tyres and the lightest possible fuel load right at the end of the session, you faced the prospect of them all cruising around slowly on worn rubber for the first part of the session in order to burn off their fuel load before going for their ultimate lap time.

Finally, if their slowest lap at any time was more than 110 percent of their best time, they would receive no fuel credit for that lap. So, as Renault tech chief Pat Symonds pointed out, you could be on pole by half a second – but with only enough fuel in your car for an eight-lap opening stint. In the event, it didn't happen, but it could have done.

In gusty and unpredictable conditions, even by Sakhir's standards, Ferrari's decision to carry out extended pre-season tests at the Bahrain track seemed to have paid off handsomely. Admittedly carrying slightly less fuel than his key Michelin-shod rivals, Schumacher equalled the late Ayrton Senna's record of 65 pole positions by lapping just 0.047s faster than his impressive new team-mate Felipe Massa.

'All winter we knew that we seemed to have a good package but then you have to wait for the final confirmation of all the hard work,' said Michael. 'We have had some struggles over the winter and we couldn't always [complete] the whole [testing programmes] we wanted to, but nevertheless we came here very focused, very concentrated and very organised.'

Behind Massa, Jenson Button was the fastest Michelin runner in the Honda RA106, just edging out Fernando Alonso's Renault R26 for a place on the inside of row two. Sharing the third row were Juan Pablo Montoya's McLaren MP4-21 and Rubens Barrichello in the other Honda, the Brazilian grappling with a slight handling imbalance that slowed his efforts.

Kimi Räikkönen's hopes took a spectacular dive at the start of the session when his McLaren suffered a right-rear suspension failure. The wayward rear wheel then flicked up, removing the rear wing and sending him spinning down the track and consigning him to 22nd and last place on the starting grid. Could Kimi's race chances be salvaged by McLaren's well-tried back-of-the-grid ploy of fuelling up to the brim and running a very long opening stint? It was a conundrum that preoccupied the team engineers through to race morning as they factored in the high levels of tyre contamination generated by the sand on the circuit and wondered whether the risk might be too high if the Finn got stuck behind other fuel-heavy competitors in the opening stages. In the end, McLaren opted for a one-stop strategy, figuring that Kimi would deliver the value-added quotient to their finely balanced equation. He did.

Meanwhile, farther back, the decision to allow the Scuderia Toro Rosso to use rev-limited 3-litre Cosworth V10 engines for 2006, rather than obliging it to switch to more costly 2.4-litre V8s, continued to be a serious bone of contention. After the former Minardi team's drivers Vitantonio Liuzzi and Scott Speed lapped much faster than expected during the Friday free practice session, rival Midland team chief Colin Kolles again expressed his annoyance with the so-called equivalency formula. The new rules were supposed to ensure the V10s would have no competitive advantage, but several teams believed that the FIA, the governing body, had got its calculations incorrect.

'The equivalency is wrong and this is what we have said all along,' said Kolles. 'Everybody has to think about this. People are investing lots of development money into V8 engines and then you simply come with an old car and a restricted V10 and you are competitive.'

However, Toro Rosso co-owner Gerhard Berger defended his team's use of the old engines. 'We took over the team from Minardi and that came with a contract to use the engine. Should we be penalised for using it or should the FIA try to put it into perspective by limiting its performance?'

Looking at the team's grid positions in Bahrain, it seemed unlikely that the Toro Rosso cars would prove much of a threat. Not yet, at least.

Left: Kimi Räikkönen's season gets off to a lurid start when a rear suspension breakage negates any prospect of a proper qualifying effort and consigns him to the back of the grid.

Photograph: Emily Davenport/XPB.cc

Left: Even before his victorious start to the 2006 season, Fernando Alonso had dropped the bombshell that he would be moving to McLaren for 2007.
Photograph: James Moy/www.crashpa.net

Below: Hold on tight! A close moment as Alonso anchors up hard to avoid the pirouetting Felipe Massa's Ferrari.
Photograph: Peter Nygaard/GP Photo

McLAREN MOOD UNCERTAIN AFTER ALONSO SIGNING

AMOOD of tantalising uncertainty suffused the McLaren Mercedes team as it put the finishing touches to its preparations for the opening round of the world championship at the sun-baked Sakhir circuit, knowing before the first car turned a wheel in the first free practice session that at least one of its star drivers would be packing his trap and moving on at the end of the season.

Yet if either Kimi Räikkönen or Juan Pablo Montoya was unsettled by the McLaren management's decision to sign Fernando Alonso for 2007, he was doing a good job of concealing it.

In any case, Räikkönen remained at the centre of speculation that he would join Ferrari in 2007 and, even though Kimi continued to shrug off rumours that he had already decided to make the move, Ferrari's managing director Jean Todt offered an unqualified endorsement of the Finn's ability, claiming he was ideally qualified to be a future member of the Italian team.

'If Ferrari needed him and found him available, the answer would be yes,' Todt told the *Gazzetta dello Sport*. 'He's very strong, he never complains, he doesn't blame others if he loses.'

As for Montoya, he cheerfully concealed any depth of feeling on the matter beneath a veneer of free-wheeling charm that bordered on the mischievous. In his mind at least there seemed little doubt that Räikkönen would end up driving for Ferrari in 2007, but he was open minded as to whether that would guarantee his own presence at McLaren as Alonso's running mate.

'I just need to get myself into a position where I can secure my best option for the future,' said Montoya, who was starting his second season with McLaren. 'I have to look around and see what offers the best prospect, whether or not that is staying with McLaren. When I finally see the option I am happy with, I will take it.'

Ron Dennis, the McLaren chairman, meanwhile reiterated his belief that both his current drivers would attack the season with as much motivation as usual. But he made no apology for signing Alonso more than a year before the Spanish driver was scheduled to slip into the cockpit of a McLaren for the first time.

'I am very confident that our two current drivers would be ranked by anybody in the top five,' he said. 'Speculation in the media [about their motivation] is understandable, but irrelevant. We all have choices to make every day of our lives, and Kimi told us that he would like to try his car and have a few races before he makes a decision as to what he wants to do and whether or not he leaves the team. We're happy to give him the time that he needs.'

However Dennis made it clear that he regarded criticism over the manner in which he approached Alonso, voiced by Bernie Ecclestone and the Renault team principal Flavio Briatore, as misplaced. 'Let's get real,' he said. 'If a girl likes the look of you and asks you to dance, you don't say, "Let me think about it and I'll get back to you." In a situation like this, you're not going to phone up [Briatore] and present him with an opportunity to convince him [Alonso] not to do it!

'All I will say is that the maximum integrity and fairness were used to bring this project to fruition.'

IT was as if there had been no off-season, such was the seamless perfection of the almost imperceptible transition. As if to issue a timely reminder to Michael Schumacher that he was bidding for the crown as the most convincing contemporary F1 performer, Fernando Alonso opened 2006 as he'd closed 2005: by winning a grand prix at the wheel of a very impressive Renault.

Much had happened since the young Spaniard took the chequered flag in Shanghai the previous October. Most notably, he'd controversially thrown in his lot with McLaren for 2007, a sensational switch that had been one of the very best-kept secrets of the F1 business during the off-season. But if McLaren thought it might have a chance of destabilising the Renault squad by pulling off such a coup, the first signs betrayed no evidence of creaking tensions within the French F1 team.

Alonso's focus allied to Renault's well-honed professionalism seemed set brilliantly to keep the show on the road. The only different element in the equation was the backdrop. Since 1996 the season had kicked off at Melbourne's uniquely hospitable Albert Park circuit, but the staging of this year's Commonwealth Games in the Australian city meant that the F1 fixture had to be juggled back to third place in the schedule. Now the season would get under way at the Sakhir desert circuit in Bahrain, followed a week later by the Malaysian GP at Sepang: two punishingly hot races in quick succession calculated to stretch every one of the new 2.4-litre V8 technical packages on the starting grid.

Shadowing Schumacher's Ferrari 248 from the start, Alonso squeezed his Renault R26 ahead of the seven-times champion at the second round of refuelling stops and thereafter kept his cool to take the chequered flag just over a second ahead.

The reigning world champion had started from fourth place on the grid with a slightly heavier fuel load than his immediate rival's, which gave him a marginal strategic advantage from the outset because he was able to run a few laps farther than Schumacher on his two stints before refuelling.

Schumacher eased into the lead on the sprint to the first corner while his new team-mate Felipe Massa, who'd qualified admirably in second place, did his level best to keep ahead of Alonso in order to give Michael a strategic cushion for the first few laps. But it didn't work. Alonso was through into second place by the time they reached Turn Four, completing the opening lap 1.4s behind the Ferrari. Then came Massa, Juan Pablo Montoya's McLaren MP4-21, the Hondas of Rubens Barrichello and Jenson Button, Giancarlo Fisichella in the other Renault R26 and Mark Webber's Williams FW28.

Kimi Räikkönen was already up to 13th after starting at the back due to his qualifying woes, while new boy Nico Rosberg came straight into the pits at the end of the opening lap for a new nose section to be fitted to his Williams after pitching Nick Heidfeld into a spin at the first corner.

Button, meanwhile, was rueing his poor start – due to a clutch problem – and was embroiled in a very precise and disciplined wheel-to-wheel tussle with Barrichello. But his opening phase behind Montoya's McLaren lost him crucial track time. 'Had I not had such a bad start, this could have been a great race for us,' he later reflected after finishing an obviously disappointed fourth. 'The pace of the car was absolutely there but the strategy didn't pan out because we were not where we needed to be when it came to the pit stop.'

Alonso came within a few inches of disaster going into lap eight in second place when Massa spun across his Renault's bows during a bungled overtaking manoeuvre. The Brazilian's Ferrari pirouetted wildly in a spectacular cloud of tyre smoke.

Massa pitted immediately for fresh rubber only to be badly delayed by a problem changing the right-rear tyre, with the result that he dropped well down the field. 'When he came in for the pit stop we had a problem with the right-rear gun,' explained an exasperated Ross Brawn, Ferrari's technical director, after the race. 'The back-up system didn't work, either, so we're going to have a careful look and see what caused this error.'

Schumacher made his first 8.2s stop from the lead at the end of lap 15 and Button made an 8.5s stop from what was fleetingly second place at the end of lap 18. Meanwhile Alonso had been piling on the pressure at the head of the field and darted in to make his first scheduled stop (8.0s) at the end of lap 19. It wasn't enough for him to snatch the advantage and he resumed third behind Michael, the pair of them moving back into first and second places when Montoya pitted from the lead for an 8.8s stop at the end of lap 23.

If things were going well for Alonso, his Renault team-mate Giancarlo Fisichella was having yet another dollop of what looked like becoming his customary bad luck. Fisichella had been frustrated by a sudden loss of power and had been unable to qualify better than ninth. That loss of power returned during the race, he slowed suddenly and finally retired with a hydraulic leak. Small wonder he let rip with some fruity expletives for which he later politely apologised to his team, who felt awful about the failures anyway.

The defining moment came on lap 36 of the 57-lap race, when Schumacher ducked into the pits for his second refuelling stop. The Ferrari was stationary for just 8.8s and resumed in third place behind Alonso and Jenson Button's Honda. For the next three laps Alonso stretched himself again before coming in for his own second stop of 7.7s. Button briefly went through into the lead before making his second stop at the end of lap 39.

But as Alonso accelerated back down the pit lane Schumacher's Ferrari was slamming across the start-finish line.

As Michael entered the braking area for the tight right-hander beyond the pits, so Alonso's blue Renault popped out from behind the barrier and began to converge on him as they both hit their brake pedals. For a few fleeting seconds the cars were absolutely abreast but, with Schumacher on the wide outside line, all Alonso had to do was stick to his position. For a moment it seemed as though Schumacher might force the issue on the outside, but Alonso didn't yield a spare centimetre.

Fernando was through and away, resuming the lead when Button made his scheduled stop next time around.

Alonso was understandably elated, emphasising that he'd always felt his Renault had a slight edge over its immediate rivals. 'This was a good fighting win and I want to dedicate it to the team, the mechanics and the right strategy,' he said.

Yet it might so easily have been a different outcome because Schumacher was marginally disadvantaged by losing one lap's top-up 'fuel credit' in qualifying after one of his laps was outside 110 percent of his pole-winning time, reducing by one the number of laps he could run up to his first refuelling stop. This new rule might just have been enough to cost him victory.

'All in all this is an excellent result and I'm certainly not complaining about finishing second,' said Schumacher. 'If someone had told us over the winter months that this was the way we would finish the first race of the season, I would not have believed them. This year the fight for the championship will be very close. There are several good teams capable of battling for the title and it's great to be in one of them.'

By any standards this was a superbly close-fought race with wheel-to-wheel battles raging right down the field. Third place fell to Räikkönen's McLaren-Mercedes MP4-21 after a quite remarkable climb through the field from 22nd, running on a one-stop strategy after suffering a spectacular crash in qualifying when his car's rear suspension broke and a wayward rear wheel ripped off the rear wing.

'This is a great result after the disappointment of yesterday,' said Räikkönen. 'The first few laps were crucial to this result and luckily I managed to pass a lot of cars on the run to the first corner. I was up to 13th by lap two even though the cars in front were lighter than mine.' For Button, fourth was less by far than he had been hoping for, but it was still a respectable performance to split the two McLarens of Räikkönen and Montoya.

Fuelling the sport's nostalgia quotient was the superb maiden drive by Rosberg in the Williams-Cosworth FW28. After his spin on the first corner, the 20-year-old son of the 1982 world champion Keke stormed back to an eventual seventh place behind his team-mate Mark Webber. 'Nico made a mistake at Turn One that cost him 45s on his in-lap and pit stop,' said Sam Michael, the Williams technical director. 'Without this he would have been on the podium and he did record the fastest lap. For his first race it's a fantastic result.'

Christian Klien did well to take eighth place and the final championship point on offer, but his team-mate David Coulthard had a frustrating weekend in the other Ferrari-engined Red Bull RB2. At one stage it looked as though he was on course for a finish in the points, but after flat-spotting a tyre when he locked a wheel under braking during a battle with Nick Heidfeld's BMW-Sauber, he was troubled by serious vibration through to the end of the race and dropped to tenth.

'There's so much vibration when that occurs, you lose visibility, your eyes are shaking in your head and it feels like you're sitting on top of a spin drier,' said Coulthard. 'You can't read the pit board or the displays in the car. The team wanted me to do an oil transfer, but I had to ask them what colour the button was that I needed to press, because you can't read anything when it's like that. It's horrible and rounds off a pretty disappointing weekend.'

2006 TEAM LINE-UPS

MILD SEVEN RENAULT F1 TEAM
Poised for a seamless transition into 2006 as reigning world champion with the new R26 powered by a 2.4-litre V8 engine showing good winter testing form in the hands of Fernando Alonso and Giancarlo Fisichella. Test driver Heikki Kovalainen was being groomed in the wings for future stardom.

TEAM McLAREN MERCEDES
In upbeat mood after landing a nifty double blow on its rivals by bagging Fernando Alonso and Ferrari sponsor Vodafone for 2007. Meanwhile Kimi Räikkönen and Juan Pablo Montoya faced the new season in the new McLaren MP4-21, which proved quick in testing despite reliability problems with its new Mercedes FO 108S V8 power unit.

SCUDERIA FERRARI MARLBORO
Urgently chasing a return to competitive form with new type 248 F1 car powered by Ferrari 056 V8 engine. Michael Schumacher still led the team for the 11th straight season, with Felipe Massa moving in to fill the number-two seat vacated by the Honda-bound Rubens Barrichello.

PANASONIC TOYOTA RACING
Ready to test well before Christmas with the new TF106 challenger, which displayed considerable consistency and mechanical reliability during the pre-season shakedowns. Ralf Schumacher and Jarno Trulli continued as the team's driver line-up, but now running on Bridgestone tyres after a switch from Michelin.

WILLIAMSF1 TEAM
Frank's squad underwent a major makeover during the winter. Out went the partnership with BMW; in came a new engine supply deal with Cosworth to use the British company's new V8. Out went Michelin; in came Bridgestone – and out went Nick Heidfeld and in came 20-year-old novice Nico Rosberg as Mark Webber's team-mate.

LUCKY STRIKE HONDA RACING F1 TEAM
Now owned totally by Honda, the former BAR squad covered thousands of reliable testing miles with its new RA806E V8 engine. Driver line-up had Jenson Button partnered with Ferrari refugee Rubens Barrichello, who the team felt confident would make a worthwhile contribution to its operational strength in depth.

RED BULL RACING
Heralded in the new F1 regulations by switching from Cosworth V10s to Ferrari V8s and earning a feather in its cap by recruiting Adrian Newey from McLaren as technical director. Driver line-up of David Coulthard and Christian Klien remained unchanged.

BMW SAUBER F1 TEAM
Having purchased the Sauber squad as a springboard for its F1 ambitions, BMW was expecting very much a low-key transitional season with Nick Heidfeld and Jacques Villeneuve doing their best behind the wheel.

MF1 RACING
Now totally rebranded under Alex Shnaider's Midland banner, the former Jordan squad continued to use customer Toyota engines but with Christijan Albers joining Tiago Monteiro in the driver line-up.

SCUDERIA TORO ROSSO
Red Bull's second division team not only took advantage of an FIA provision permitting the use of detuned V10s – Cosworth in this case – but also surprised its rivals by using last year's Red Bull RB1 chassis badged as the STR01. Vitantonio Liuzzi and young American Scott Speed were entrusted with driving duties.

SUPER AGURI F1 TEAM
A late 11th entry for the championship, Super Aguri's presence on the grid was sanctioned only by unanimous agreement of the other ten F1 entrants. The team had special dispensation to use uprated Arrows A23 chassis acquired from Paul Stoddart (known as the SA05), but powered by Honda V8 engines for an all-Japanese line-up of Takuma Sato and new boy Yuji Ide.

Coulthard's frustration was compounded when his car suffered an engine failure on the slowing-down lap. This meant he would have to take an engine change penalty prior to the second race of the season the following Sunday in Malaysia, because engines were supposed to last for two grand prix weekends. 'If they'd told me quickly enough that there was a problem, I could have pulled up on the last lap and not been forced to take the penalty,' he shrugged.

Scuderia Toro Rosso's Vitantonio Liuzzi and Scott Speed – the US's first F1 driver since Michael Andretti – finished 11th and 13th, sandwiching Nick Heidfeld's BMW-Sauber, the *équipe*'s sole survivor after Jacques Villeneuve dropped out with a fiery engine failure.

At least the Red Bull guys could console themselves that they'd done a better job than the big-budget Toyota squad, for whom Ralf Schumacher and Jarno Trulli finished an appalling 14th and 16th respectively after the latest TF106 challenger proved reluctant to generate decent tyre temperatures all weekend. 'The first grand prix weekend of 2006 has been a shocking way to start the year,' said team principal Tsutomo Tomita. At least you couldn't accuse him of mincing his words.

Alan Henry

Left: The newly rebranded Midland team's livery looked astonishingly similar to the latest McLaren paint job. Here Tiago Monteiro lines up on the grid ready to kick off the new season.
Photograph: James Moy/www.crashpa.net

NEW RULES FOR A NEW YEAR

TYRES

Instead of having to make one set of tyres last through qualifying and the race, it was now possible to change tyres again, subject to a maximum of seven sets per car over the course of the GP weekend. Race strategy seemed likely once again to become a complex balancing act between fuel loads and tyre performance.

The idea behind this move was to improve the spectacle by eliminating the sight of competitive cars slowing dramatically in the closing stages of the race in order to conserve their fast-diminishing reserves of grip. The downside was that serious contenders would probably opt not to run in Friday's free practice in order to conserve precious sets of tyres.

On the face of it this rule change looked likely to help the leading Bridgestone teams – Ferrari, Williams and Toyota – because the Japanese tyres have historically had the most trouble lasting a race distance without being replaced. Michelin, however, started the season confident that it could be every bit as competitive as Bridgestone under the new rules.

ENGINES

The old breed of 3-litre V10 engines was replaced by a new generation of 2.4-litre V8s, a costly decision for which the teams blamed the FIA and the governing body blamed the teams. Only Scuderia Toro Rosso continued to use V10s, rev-limited under a special dispensation for cash-strapped teams.

In terms of entertainment, this change seemed unlikely to make any difference at all as far as the fans in the grandstand were concerned. The cars would hardly be more than a couple of seconds slower than they were last year, although cornering speeds were slightly reduced, which helps with safety.

QUALIFYING FORMAT

There was a new knock-out format for determining the grid order, with qualifying now split into three blocks of 15 minutes, 15 minutes and 20 minutes. After the first session the slowest six cars dropped out; after the second session the next six slowest dropped out – thereby determining the grid order from 11th to 22nd – leaving the final ten to battle for the top ten places.

Those who didn't make the top ten could add as much fuel to their cars as they liked for Sunday's race. But the top ten runners now had to start the final session with their race fuel loads and, after the session was over, be topped up again under FIA supervision so that they would start the race with the same weight as they had on board at the start of the final 20 minutes of qualifying.

On the face of it, this looked like a terrific bonus for the spectator, with the attraction of seeing all 22 cars crowding the circuit for the first 15 minutes of qualifying. It eliminated the monotony of single-car qualifying which, although conceived with the best of intentions, had proved a tedious failure in entertainment terms over the previous few years.

FIA F1 WORLD CHAMPIONSHIP • ROUND 1

GULF AIR
BAHRAIN GRAND PRIX

SAKHIR 10–12 MARCH 2006

BAHRAIN INTERNATIONAL CIRCUIT, SAKHIR

Turn 13 200/124
Turn 4 150/93
Turn 6 118/74
Turn 12 245/152
Turn 9 173/277
Turn 8 55/88
Turn 11 175/109
Turn 14 125/78
Turn 10 52/83
Turn 2 120/75
317/198
Turn 1 105/93

116/187 **mph/kmh**

Photograph: James Moy/www.crashpa.net

Circuit: 3.363 miles / 5.412 Km   Gear

RACE RESULTS

Pos.	Driver	Nat.	No.	Entrant	Car/Engine	Tyres	Laps	Time/Retirement	Speed (mph/km/h)	Gap to leader	Fastest race lap	
1	Fernando Alonso	E	1	Mild Seven Renault F1 Team	Renault R26-RS26 V8	M	57	1h 29m 46.205s	128.014/206.018		1m 32.534s	21
2	Michael Schumacher	D	5	Scuderia Ferrari Marlboro	Ferrari 248 F1-056 V8	B	57	1h 29m 47.451s	127.984/205.970	+1.246s	1m 32.523s	38
3	Kimi Räikkönen	FIN	3	Team McLaren Mercedes	McLaren MP4-21-Mercedes FO 108S V8	M	57	1h 30m 05.565s	127.555/205.280	+19.360s	1m 32.864s	29
4	Jenson Button	GB	12	Lucky Strike Honda Racing F1 Team	Honda RA106-RA806E V8	M	57	1h 30m 06.197s	127.540/205.256	+19.992s	1m 32.729s	39
5	Juan Pablo Montoya	COL	4	Team McLaren Mercedes	McLaren MP4-21-Mercedes FO 108S V8	M	57	1h 30m 23.253s	127.139/204.610	+37.048s	1m 32.771s	21
6	Mark Webber	AUS	9	WilliamsF1 Team	Williams FW28-Cosworth CA2006 V8	B	57	1h 30m 28.137s	127.024/204.426	+41.932s	1m 32.660s	25
7	Nico Rosberg	D	10	WilliamsF1 Team	Williams FW28-Cosworth CA2006 V8	B	57	1h 30m 49.248s	126.532/203.634	+1m 03.043s	1m 32.408s	42
8	Christian Klien	A	15	Red Bull Racing	Red Bull RB2-Ferrari 056 V8	M	57	1h 30m 52.976s	126.446/203.495	+1m 06.771s	1m 33.212s	40
9	Felipe Massa	BR	6	Scuderia Ferrari Marlboro	Ferrari 248 F1-056 V8	B	57	1h 30m 56.112s	126.373/203.378	+1m 09.907s	1m 32.739s	28
10	David Coulthard	GB	14	Red Bull Racing	Red Bull RB2-Ferrari 056 V8	M	57	1h 31m 01.746s	126.243/203.168	+1m 15.541s	1m 33.376s	26
11	Vitantonio Liuzzi	I	20	Scuderia Toro Rosso	Toro Rosso STR01-Cosworth TJ2005-2 V10	M	57	1h 31m 12.202s	126.002/202.780	+1m 25.997s	1m 33.480s	26
12	Nick Heidfeld	D	16	BMW Sauber F1 Team	BMW Sauber F1.06-BMW P86 V8	M	56			+1 lap	1m 33.772s	26
13	Scott Speed	USA	21	Scuderia Toro Rosso	Toro Rosso STR01-Cosworth TJ2005-2 V10	M	56			+1 lap	1m 33.108s	45
14	Ralf Schumacher	D	7	Panasonic Toyota Racing	Toyota TF106-RVX-06 V8	B	56			+1 lap	1m 34.112s	25
15	Rubens Barrichello	BR	11	Lucky Strike Honda Racing F1 Team	Honda RA106-RA806E V8	M	56			+1 lap	1m 33.840s	14
16	Jarno Trulli	I	8	Panasonic Toyota Racing	Toyota TF106-RVX-06 V8	B	56			+1 lap	1m 34.852s	24
17	Tiago Monteiro	P	18	MF1 Racing	Midland M16-Toyota RVX-06 V8	B	55			+2 laps	1m 35.940s	41
18	Takuma Sato	J	22	Super Aguri F1 Team	Super Aguri SA05-Honda RA806E V8	B	53			+4 laps	1m 37.104s	17
	Yuji Ide	J	23	Super Aguri F1 Team	Super Aguri SA05-Honda RA806E V8	B	35	Engine			1m 38.302s	11
	Jacques Villeneuve	CDN	17	BMW Sauber F1 Team	BMW Sauber F1.06-BMW P86 V8	M	29	Engine			1m 33.694s	20
	Giancarlo Fisichella	I	2	Mild Seven Renault F1 Team	Renault R26-RS26 V8	M	21	Hydraulics			1m 34.320s	15
	Christijan Albers	NL	19	MF1 Racing	Midland M16-Toyota RVX-06 V8	B	0	Driveshaft			No time	-

Fastest lap: Nico Rosberg on lap 42, 1m 32.408s, 131.009 mph/210.838 km/h.

Lap record: Michael Schumacher (Ferrari F2004 V10), 1m 30.252s, 134.263 mph/216.074 km/h (2004) (3.366-mile/5.417-km circuit).

All results and data © FOM 2006

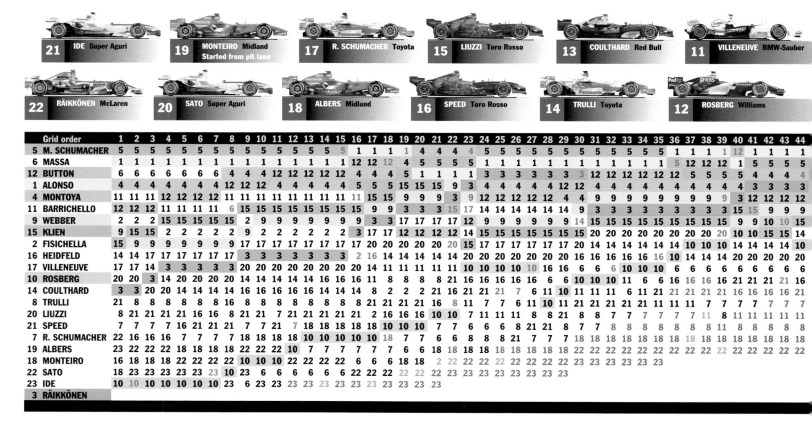

21 IDE Super Aguri | 19 MONTEIRO Midland Started from pit lane | 17 R. SCHUMACHER Toyota | 15 LIUZZI Toro Rosso | 13 COULTHARD Red Bull | 11 VILLENEUVE BMW-Sauber

22 RÄIKKÖNEN McLaren | 20 SATO Super Aguri | 18 ALBERS Midland | 16 SPEED Toro Rosso | 14 TRULLI Toyota | 12 ROSBERG Williams

Grid order	1	2	3	4	5	6	7	8	9	10	11	12	13	14	15	16	17	18	19	20	21	22	23	24	25	26	27	28	29	30	31	32	33	34	35	36	37	38	39	40	41	42	43	44
5 M. SCHUMACHER	5	5	5	5	5	5	5	5	5	5	5	5	5	5	1	1	1	1	4	4	4	4	5	5	5	5	5	5	5	5	5	5	5	1	1	1	1	12	1	1	1	1		
6 MASSA	1	1	1	1	1	1	1	1	1	1	1	1	1	1	12	12	12	4	5	5	5	5	1	1	1	1	1	1	1	1	1	1	1	5	12	12	12	1	5	5	5	5		
12 BUTTON	6	6	6	6	6	4	4	4	12	12	12	12	12	4	4	4	5	1	1	1	3	3	3	3	3	3	12	12	12	12	12	12	5	5	5	5	4	4	4	4	4	4		
1 ALONSO	4	4	4	4	4	4	12	12	12	4	4	4	4	4	5	15	15	9	9	12	12	12	12	4	4	4	4	4	4	4	3	3	3											
4 MONTOYA	11	11	11	12	12	12	12	11	11	11	11	11	11	11	11	11	11	15	15	9	9	9	3	9	12	12	12	12	4	9	9	9	9	9	9	9	3	12	12	12				
11 BARRICHELLO	12	12	12	11	11	11	11	6	15	15	15	15	15	15	15	9	9	3	3	3	15	17	14	14	14	14	14	9	3	3	3	3	3	3	3	3	15	15	9	9	9			
9 WEBBER	2	2	2	15	15	15	15	15	2	9	9	9	9	9	9	9	3	3	17	17	17	17	12	9	9	9	9	9	14	15	15	15	15	15	15	15	9	9	10	10	15			
15 KLIEN	9	15	15	2	2	2	2	9	2	2	2	2	2	2	3	17	17	12	12	12	12	14	15	15	15	15	15	15	20	20	20	20	20	20	20	10	10	15	15	14				
2 FISICHELLA	15	9	9	9	9	9	17	17	17	17	17	17	17	17	20	20	20	20	15	17	17	17	17	20	14	14	14	14	14	14	10	10	14	14	14	14	10							
16 HEIDFELD	14	14	14	17	17	17	17	17	3	3	3	3	3	3	2	16	14	14	14	14	11	11	16	16	16	16	16	16	16	14	14	20	20	20	20	20								
17 VILLENEUVE	17	17	14	3	3	3	3	20	20	20	20	20	20	20	14	11	11	11	11	11	10	10	10	10	10	16	16	6	6	10	10	10	6	6	6	6	6	6	6					
10 ROSBERG	20	20	3	14	20	20	20	14	14	14	14	14	16	16	16	11	8	8	8	21	16	16	16	6	6	10	10	10	11	6	8	16	16	16	16	21	21	21	21	16				
14 COULTHARD	3	3	20	20	14	14	14	14	16	16	16	16	14	14	14	2	2	21	16	21	21	7	6	11	10	11	10	11	6	11	11	21	21	21	16	16	16	21						
8 TRULLI	21	8	8	8	8	8	8	16	8	8	8	8	8	8	8	21	21	16	2	16	14	14	11	7	7	6	11	7	7	7	7	7	7	7										
20 LIUZZI	8	21	21	21	21	16	16	16	8	21	21	21	21	21	21	16	10	10	7	7	6	6	8	8	7	7	8	8	11	11	11	11	11	11										
21 SPEED	7	7	7	7	16	21	21	21	7	7	21	7	18	18	18	18	10	10	10	7	6	6	21	21	8	8	8	8	8	8	8	11	8	8										
7 R. SCHUMACHER	22	16	16	16	7	7	7	18	18	18	18	18	10	10	10	10	10	18	7	7	6	8	21	7	7	18	18	18	18	18	18	18	18	18	18									
19 ALBERS	23	22	22	22	18	18	18	22	22	22	10	7	7	7	7	7	6	6	18	18	18	18	18	22	22	22	22	22	22	22	22	22	22	22	22									
18 MONTEIRO	16	18	18	22	22	22	10	10	10	22	22	22	6	6	18	18	2	22	22	22	22	22	23	23	23	23	23	23	23															
22 SATO	18	23	23	23	23	23	23	10	23	6	6	6	6	6	22	22	22	22	23	23	23	23	23																					
23 IDE	10	10	10	10	10	10	10	23	6	23	23	23	23	23	23	23	23	23	23	23	23	23																						
3 RÄIKKÖNEN																																												

PRACTICE 1 (FRIDAY)
Sunny/light wind (track 36–38ºC, air 29–30ºC)

Pos.	Driver	Laps	Time
1	Robert Kubica	20	1m 32.170s
2	Alexander Wurz	18	1m 32.184s
3	Kimi Räikkönen	6	1m 33.388s
4	Michael Schumacher	5	1m 33.469s
5	Christian Klien	6	1m 34.800s
6	Neel Jani	15	1m 34.831s
7	Juan Pablo Montoya	6	1m 34.887s
8	Felipe Massa	6	1m 34.925s
9	David Coulthard	4	1m 35.017s
10	Vitantonio Liuzzi	8	1m 35.083s
11	Robert Doornbos	15	1m 35.203s
12	Scott Speed	7	1m 35.371s
13	Tiago Monteiro	9	1m 36.542s
14	Christijan Albers	9	1m 36.930s
15	Markus Winkelhock	16	1m 37.918s
16	Takuma Sato	15	1m 38.190s
17	Yuji Ide	15	1m 40.782s
18	Anthony Davidson	2	No time
19	Fernando Alonso	2	No time
20	Giancarlo Fisichella	2	No time
21	Jarno Trulli	2	No time
22	Ralf Schumacher	1	No time
23	Nick Heidfeld	1	No time
24	Jacques Villeneuve	1	No time

PRACTICE 2 (FRIDAY)
Sunny/overcast (track 36–38ºC, air 30–31ºC)

Pos.	Driver	Laps	Time
1	Anthony Davidson	28	1m 31.353s
2	Michael Schumacher	15	1m 31.751s
3	Alexander Wurz	27	1m 31.764s
4	Felipe Massa	13	1m 32.175s
5	Fernando Alonso	13	1m 32.538s
6	Vitantonio Liuzzi	24	1m 32.703s
7	Robert Doornbos	24	1m 32.926s
8	Giancarlo Fisichella	14	1m 33.215s
9	Jenson Button	12	1m 33.226s
10	Robert Kubica	26	1m 33.244s
11	Christian Klien	8	1m 33.557s
12	Kimi Räikkönen	11	1m 33.577s
13	Juan Pablo Montoya	15	1m 33.726s
14	Nick Heidfeld	9	1m 33.848s
15	Neel Jani	24	1m 33.900s
16	Scott Speed	22	1m 34.284s
17	Mark Webber	5	1m 34.333s
18	Rubens Barrichello	9	1m 34.384s
19	David Coulthard	7	1m 34.432s
20	Tiago Monteiro	14	1m 34.459s
21	Nico Rosberg	5	1m 34.953s
22	Ralf Schumacher	18	1m 35.170s
23	Markus Winkelhock	24	1m 35.686s
24	Jarno Trulli	11	1m 35.898s
25	Jacques Villeneuve	8	1m 36.264s
26	Christijan Albers	16	1m 36.314s
27	Takuma Sato	19	1m 37.588s
28	Yuji Ide	21	1m 39.021s

QUALIFYING (SATURDAY)
Sunny/dry (track 30ºC, air 22ºC)

Pos.	Driver	First	Second	Third
1	Michael Schumacher	1m 33.310s	1m 32.025s	1m 31.431s
2	Felipe Massa	1m 33.579s	1m 32.014s	1m 31.478s
3	Jenson Button	1m 32.603s	1m 32.025s	1m 31.549s
4	Fernando Alonso	1m 32.433s	1m 31.215s	1m 31.702s
5	Juan Pablo Montoya	1m 33.233s	1m 31.487s	1m 32.164s
6	Rubens Barrichello	1m 33.922s	1m 32.322s	1m 32.579s
7	Mark Webber	1m 33.454s	1m 32.309s	1m 33.006s
8	Christian Klien	1m 34.308s	1m 32.106s	1m 33.112s
9	Giancarlo Fisichella	1m 32.934s	1m 31.831s	1m 33.496s
10	Nick Heidfeld	1m 33.374s	1m 31.958s	1m 33.926s
11	Jacques Villeneuve	1m 33.882s	1m 32.456s	
12	Nico Rosberg	1m 32.945s	1m 32.620s	
13	David Coulthard	1m 33.678s	1m 32.850s	
14	Jarno Trulli	1m 33.987s	1m 33.066s	
15	Vitantonio Liuzzi	1m 34.439s	1m 33.416s	
16	Scott Speed	1m 33.995s	1m 34.606s	
17	Ralf Schumacher	1m 34.702s		
18	Christijan Albers	1m 35.724s		
19	Tiago Monteiro	1m 35.900s		
20	Takuma Sato	1m 37.411s		
21	Yuji Ide	1m 40.270s		
22	Kimi Räikkönen	No time		

PRACTICE 3 (SATURDAY)
Cloudy/rainy (track 15–16ºC, air 13–14ºC)

Pos.	Driver	Laps	Time
1	Jenson Button	16	1m 31.857s
2	Michael Schumacher	8	1m 31.868s
3	Fernando Alonso	11	1m 31.975s
4	Giancarlo Fisichella	12	1m 32.050s
5	Felipe Massa	6	1m 32.826s
6	Jacques Villeneuve	14	1m 32.913s
7	Jarno Trulli	16	1m 33.038s
8	Kimi Räikkönen	12	1m 33.262s
9	Ralf Schumacher	14	1m 33.523s
10	Mark Webber	11	1m 33.876s
11	Christian Klien	14	1m 33.944s
12	Rubens Barrichello	15	1m 34.009s
13	Nick Heidfeld	11	1m 34.094s
14	David Coulthard	16	1m 34.142s
15	Juan Pablo Montoya	11	1m 34.406s
16	Nico Rosberg	11	1m 34.434s
17	Christijan Albers	14	1m 34.541s
18	Tiago Monteiro	14	1m 35.026s
19	Vitantonio Liuzzi	13	1m 35.351s
20	Scott Speed	13	1m 35.532s
21	Takuma Sato	15	1m 36.994s
22	Yuji Ide	10	1m 41.889s

CHASSIS LOG BOOK

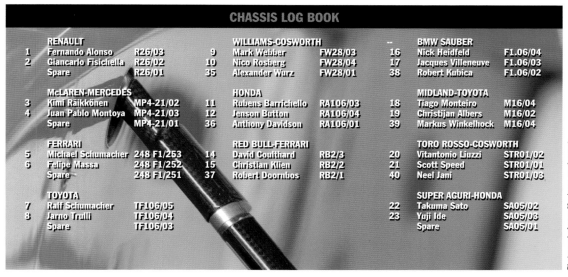

	RENAULT			WILLIAMS-COSWORTH			BMW SAUBER	
1	Fernando Alonso	R26/03	9	Mark Webber	FW28/03	16	Nick Heidfeld	F1.06/04
2	Giancarlo Fisichella	R26/02	10	Nico Rosberg	FW28/04	17	Jacques Villeneuve	F1.06/03
	Spare	R26/01	35	Alexander Wurz	FW28/01	38	Robert Kubica	F1.06/02

	McLAREN-MERCEDES			HONDA			MIDLAND-TOYOTA	
3	Kimi Räikkönen	MP4-21/02	11	Rubens Barrichello	RA106/03	18	Tiago Monteiro	M16/04
4	Juan Pablo Montoya	MP4-21/03	12	Jenson Button	RA106/04	19	Christijan Albers	M16/02
	Spare	MP4-21/01	36	Anthony Davidson	RA106/01	39	Markus Winkelhock	M16/04

	FERRARI			RED BULL-FERRARI			TORO ROSSO-COSWORTH	
5	Michael Schumacher	248 F1/253	14	David Coulthard	RB2/3	20	Vitantonio Liuzzi	STR01/02
6	Felipe Massa	248 F1/252	15	Christian Klien	RB2/2	21	Scott Speed	STR01/01
	Spare	248 F1/251	37	Robert Doornbos	RB2/1	40	Neel Jani	STR01/03

	TOYOTA						SUPER AGURI-HONDA	
7	Ralf Schumacher	TF106/05				22	Takuma Sato	SA05/02
8	Jarno Trulli	TF106/04				23	Yuji Ide	SA05/03
	Spare	TF106/03					Spare	SA05/01

Photograph: James Moy/www.crashpa.net

| 9 FISICHELLA Renault | 7 WEBBER Williams | 5 MONTOYA McLaren | 3 BUTTON Honda | 1 M. SCHUMACHER Ferrari |

| 10 HEIDFELD BMW-Sauber | 8 KLIEN Red Bull | 6 BARRICHELLO Honda | 4 ALONSO Renault | 2 MASSA Ferrari |

RACE DISTANCE:
57 laps
191.530 miles/308.238 km

RACE WEATHER:
Sunny/breezy
track 29–34ºC, air 20–23ºC

	47	48	49	50	51	52	53	54	55	56	57	•
	1	1	1	1	1	1	1	1	1	1	1	1
5	5	5	5	5	5	5	5	5	5	5	5	2
3	3	3	3	3	3	3	3	3	3	3	3	3
2	12	12	12	12	12	12	12	12	12	12	12	4
4	4	4	4	4	4	4	4	4	4	4	4	5
9	9	9	9	9	9	9	9	9	9	9	9	6
5	15	15	15	15	15	15	15	15	10	10		7
4	14	14	10	10	10	10	10	10	15	15		8
0	10	10	14	14	14	14	14	6	6	6	6	
4	20	6	6	6	6	6	14	14	14	14		
6	6	20	20	20	20	20	20	20	20	20	20	
6	16	16	16	16	16	16	16	16	16	16		
21	21	21	21	21	21	21	21	21	21	21		
7	7	7	7	7	7	7	7	7	7	7		
1	11	11	11	11	11	11	11	11	11	11		
8	8	8	8	8	8	8	8	8	8	8		
8	18	18	18	18	18	18	18	18	18			
2	22	22	22	22	22	22	22					

t stop
rive-through penalty
ne lap or more behind leader

FOR THE RECORD

FIRST GRAND PRIX START: Yuji Ide, Nico Rosberg, Scott Speed (above), BMW Sauber, Midland, Super Aguri, Toro Rosso
FIRST GRAND PRIX POINTS: Nico Rosberg
FASTEST LAP ON DEBUT: Nico Rosberg
200TH GRAND PRIX START: BMW engine
250th POINT: Fernando Alonso

POINTS

DRIVERS

1	Fernando Alonso	10
2	Michael Schumacher	8
3	Kimi Räikkönen	6
4	Jenson Button	5
5	Juan Pablo Montoya	4
6	Mark Webber	3
7	Nico Rosberg	2
8	Christian Klien	1

CONSTRUCTORS

1	Renault	10
2	McLaren	10
3	Ferrari	8
4	Honda	5
5	Williams	5
6	Red Bull	1

Photographs: James Moy/www.crashpa.net

Cheered to the echo, Giancarlo Fisichella's Renault R26 sprints for the chequered flag after a dominant performance by the Italian at Sepang.
Photograph: Lukas Gorys

FIA F1 WORLD CHAMPIONSHIP/ROUND 2

MALAYSIAN GP

IT had looked as though Jenson Button might be on pole position at this circuit where he scored his first F1 podium two years ago with third place, but in the final moments he was edged out by the impressive Giancarlo Fisichella.

It was certainly an emotional moment for Giancarlo. 'I want to dedicate my pole position to Pietro, a childhood friend who died last Sunday,' he said. 'This is the best pole position I have had so far.'

Unfortunately, due to a problem with his refuelling rig, Fernando Alonso found himself carrying more fuel than he'd intended during the crucial top ten shoot-out, with the result that he had to be satisfied with seventh place in the final starting order.

For his part, Button was delighted with the performance of his Honda RA106 after a slightly disappointing Friday free practice. 'We had some balance problems in the first two sessions,' said Jenson, 'but the team did a brilliant job improving the set-up overnight and the car really came alive in the first qualifying session. We made a few adjustments to the differential and the traction control and the car felt really good.'

Yet for the second time in a week it was 20-year-old rookie Nico Rosberg who monopolised everybody's attention. Six days after finishing seventh on his GP début in Bahrain, the new Williams driver qualified his Cosworth-powered FW28 third fastest ahead of Michael Schumacher's Ferrari and a philosophical Mark Webber.

At least Nico had the good manners to come to the press conference perspiring profusely. It would have been too much for the other guys up there if he'd turned up looking as cool as a cucumber.

'I'm really pleased to be starting from the second row of the grid because it is important for me to make a good first impression,' said Nico. 'Getting here has not been easy at all, but I have been working really well with my engineers and the team generally. It may be tough in the heat for some drivers, but I didn't find the conditions in Bahrain a problem at all.'

For Michael Schumacher and the Maranello squad, life was more complicated. Ferrari man Felipe Massa and the

Ferrari-propelled David Coulthard had incurred ten-place qualifying penalties after their cars both needed new engines prior to the start of Friday free practice and it was soon Michael's turn to hit trouble: an acoustic analysis of his car's exhaust note alerted rival teams to a possible problem with the V8 that had powered him to second place in Bahrain.

Massa did not contest qualifying, but Michael, DC, Ralf Schumacher (Toyota) and Rubens Barrichello (Honda) all took engine-change penalties from their original qualifying positions. All were ten-place penalties but Ralf was demoted to the back of the grid because his occurred in qualifying.

'I'll be starting from the seventh row, which isn't too bad considering the penalty inflicted for the engine change,' said the Ferrari team leader. 'It'll certainly be interesting to see whether overtaking will be possible and how much fuel the others have on board. During unofficial practice we've seen our race pace was fine.'

Ferrari was also the focal point of critical attention from its rivals on race morning, with threats of a protest based on the alleged flexibility of its front and rear wings, the interaction of which they believed gave the Italian team an illegal advantage. Ferrari tech chief Ross Brawn received a deputation from McLaren's Martin Whitmarsh, Pat Symonds from Renault and Honda's Geoff Willis. They secured Brawn's assurance that the matter would be resolved by the FIA before the Australian GP on 2 April, so the trio agreed to put any objections on hold.

Farther down the grid there were no real surprises over who was consigned to the back in the first qualifying stint, but Rubens Barrichello was clearly extremely disappointed at not having made the cut into the contest for the first ten slots. He'd been uncomfortable with the set-up of his RA106 all weekend and then suffered an engine problem during the Saturday morning free practice, so the team – with nothing now to lose – switched him to the T-car fitted with a fresh engine. He duly lined up at the back of the grid.

'We decided that the chassis change might give us a better chance for the race,' he admitted. 'It's sure to be tough, but I'll give it my best shot.'

The Toyota-owned Fuji circuit is confirmed as the venue for the Japanese GP from 2007. It replaces Suzuka, which has held the race for 20 years.

Paul Stoddart, the former owner of the Minardi F1 team, closes down his new Australian charter airline Ozjet due to lack of business.

IRL founder Tony George and Champcar boss Kevin Kalkhoven admit that merger talks between the two US single-seater series have now been scheduled.

Jörg Zander, the Williams F1 team's chief designer, who joined from BAR in September 2005, leaves the Grove-based team with immediate effect for personal reasons.

Left: Vitantonio Liuzzi survived a first-lap tangle in his Toro Rosso but had to pit to replace a damaged nose. He wound up a distant 11th, hampered for much of the race by locking brakes.

Photograph: Jean-François Galeron/WRI

Below: Nico Rosberg performed superbly in qualifying to bag third place on the grid, although things went badly wrong for him in the race.

Photograph: Brousseau Photo

Above: **Giancarlo Fisichella neatly gets the jump on Jenson Button's Honda and the two warring Williams as they accelerate away from the starting grid.**
Photograph: James Moy/www.crashpa.net

Bottom right: **No love lost here. Michael Schumacher elbows his Ferrari inside Jacques Villeneuve's BMW-Sauber with no room to spare.**
Photograph: Peter Nygaard/GP Photo

GIANCARLO Fisichella took a giant stride towards reviving his reputation as a front-line F1 performer by posting a dominant victory in the punishing humidity of Malaysia ahead of his team-mate Fernando Alonso, taking advantage of a refuelling glitch prior to the final qualifying session that left the world champion's Renault R26 burdened with a heavier-than-planned fuel load in the opening stages of the 56-lap second round of the championship battle.

This was only the second Renault one-two success in F1 history, duplicating the result of the 1982 French GP at Paul Ricard in which René Arnoux ignored team orders to trounce colleague Alain Prost in a straight fight. Although at Sepang there were no such instructions, the French team delivered a similarly dominant performance with the perceived number-two having his moment in the sun.

By any standards, this was certainly a copybook performance for the 33-year-old from Rome and was arguably the most impressive of his three GP victories to date. Running a two-stop strategy and refuelling on laps 17 (11.1s) and 38 (6.9s), he was never headed all the way to the chequered flag.

Yet as Giancarlo made a perfect getaway from the front row of the grid, Alonso was already making up for his qualifying problems with a stunning start from seventh. First he dodged to the right, but with Nico Rosberg – who'd bagged a magnificent third on the grid in only his second GP – moving the same way in a bid to squeeze out his Williams team-mate Mark Webber, suddenly Fernando saw a huge gap opening to the left of him.

The world champion dodged back across to the left and ran right around the outside of both Frank's boys to complete the opening lap third behind Fisichella and Jenson Button's Honda RA106. 'I knew Webber was lighter than me and [I] would have let him go if he had tried to pass,' said Alonso. 'But I had the speed in spite of the heavy fuel load. After that it was just a question of pushing and letting the strategy work itself out.'

Fernando duly conserved his tyres throughout his long opening stint, moving up into second place behind Button

'Having said that, I was held up by traffic a few times – not least by Scott Speed, before the second pit stop. Had that not happened, maybe I could have come out of the pits ahead of Alonso. Regardless of that, though, we have two weeks [before the Australian GP] and a test in Vallelunga to work through our issues and hopefully we can look forward to better things in Melbourne in two weeks' time.'

It was a disappointing day for Williams, too. Webber and Rosberg ran impressively fourth and seventh in the opening stages, but Nico was out with a spectacular engine failure on lap seven and Webber lasted only another nine laps before being sidelined by a hydraulic failure.

Rubens Barrichello wound up tenth after taking a drive-through penalty for speeding in the pit lane, his second disappointment in seven days, although his fastest race lap was 0.6s slower than team-mate Button's.

Below left: Fans of both kinds were welcome in the heat!
Photograph: James Moy/www.crashpa.net

Below centre left: Jarno Trulli had another frustrating race. Hit from behind in the first corner, the Toyota driver battled with a broken diffuser and struggled home ninth, out of the points.
Photograph: Jean-François Galeron/WRI

Below: Fernando Alonso works out without his Renault R26.
Photograph: Laurent Charniaux/WRI

after Fisichella made his first pit stop. Button made his first stop on lap 19 (7.9s) and resumed in fourth place behind Juan Pablo Montoya's McLaren MP4-21. Alonso now led by 5.4s from Fisichella with only 10.4s covering the top four. Spots of rain began falling at around the 20-lap mark but nothing serious developed and Alonso duly made his first stop on lap 26 (7.3s), resuming in third behind Button and then leapfrogging ahead of the British driver to round off the Renault grand slam.

For Button, however, the second race in seven days ended in disappointment. He'd been fourth in Bahrain, but after qualifying second to Fisi this time he really thought that his maiden GP victory was beckoning. But it just didn't happen.

'I'm obviously pleased to be back on the podium,' shrugged Jenson, 'but it was the top step that we [the team and I] had in mind, so we are a little disappointed. We want to be winning races and today showed that we are in the fight, but there is still a lot of work to be done before we can achieve that target.

RENAULT SUPPORTS FIA COST-CUTTING

FLAVIO Briatore, the Renault F1 team principal, wrote to the FIA president Max Mosley more than a year ago urging support for the cost-cutting regulations that the governing body was poised to force through for the 2008 season, it emerged during the week following the Malaysian GP.

The FIA's new rules would require the engine suppliers to freeze the specifications of their power units for three seasons, together with major restrictions on aerodynamic development. Mosley intended to put further pressure on the Grand Prix Manufacturers' Association, which was threatening a breakaway championship for 2008, by opening the entry for the 2008 world championship on the Friday following Sepang. It would close on 31 March. Only teams that had entered by that date were to be allowed a voice in the discussion process that would result in the new technical regulations being finalised by the end of June.

It had also emerged that the GPMA wrote to Mosley two days after the Malaysian Grand Prix outlining some aspects of the regulations that the manufacturers were unhappy about, including plans to freeze engine development programmes.

Mosley duly responded to the GPMA in a letter in which he criticised the car manufacturers for not having shown interest in the regulations before. 'The World Motor Sport Council took account of the contents of your letter, but noted that it contained no proposals that could be substituted for any of those in front of the Council, sent to you on 1 March and then again, with minor modifications, on 15 March,' wrote Mosley.

'The World Motor Sport Council has also noticed that none of you attended the meetings that were held in 2005 to discuss the 2008 regulations, despite repeated invitations to do so, and that the proposals that you promised to deliver to us in June 2005 are still not at hand.'

It was clear that Briatore's thinking, which could almost certainly help the Renault management to maintain its commitment to F1 in the longer term, broadly coincided with the governing body's plans to slash costs and restrict technology. Briatore asked that 'the technical and sporting regulations should be frozen for a minimum of three years. Only in extreme cases should changes be introduced, for safety reasons, during this period.' He also called for restrictions on testing and suggested that the format of GP weekends should be reduced to two days, leaving Fridays for testing and promotional events, a move that some believed could lead to an increase from 18 to 20 races in the near future.

Over at McLaren, Kimi Räikkönen's race ended on the opening lap when he spun off after a nudge from Christian Klien's Red Bull broke the MP4-21's suspension. Juan Pablo Montoya took fourth behind Button, grappling with understeer in the opening stages and then cutting his revs to conserve the engine in the closing stages when it became clear he was not going to catch the Honda.

McLaren was also suffused by renewed speculation over Kimi Räikkönen's long-term plans. The Finn's unruffled confidence was underpinned not only by his obvious role as a potential 2006 world championship contender but also by the knowledge that his choice of team for next season would play a pivotal role in shaping an F1 landscape that would look very different if Michael Schumacher finally called time on his racing career at the end of the current season.

The less Räikkönen said – and that's not much at the best of times – the more he fuelled speculation about whether or not his personal horizons extended beyond the McLaren team after the expiry of his current contract following the 16 races remaining on this year's schedule.

'Kimi is under no pressure,' said his manager Steve Robertson. 'There are several top teams out there who would like to secure his services for next season but he doesn't need to be hurried into any decision. We will evaluate all his options very carefully and ultimately he will make the decision. But it certainly won't be a decision solely driven by money.'

In reality there were only three teams – McLaren, Ferrari and Renault – in with a sporting chance of signing Räikkönen, teams whose offers he would seriously consider at around the $20 million a year mark. Obviously staying with McLaren was one option, but persuading him to renew his contract depended on his being convinced that the current MP4-21 was capable of being developed into a serious world championship contender.

Nevertheless, with Räikkönen out of the equation on the opening lap, Button convincingly saw off Montoya's McLaren, which must have been faintly worrying for the Woking brigade.

'The car was good today and I think we had a solid race,' said the Colombian. 'We lost a lot of time in the first stint because my front tyres were graining, but as soon as we changed the tyres the car came back to life and if you look at my pace against Button's later on, it was pretty much the same. With the hot temperatures here we did have to look after the engine, which means we had to sacrifice downforce, so finishing fourth is encouraging. The team has scored more points and I think we look strong going into the next race.'

Ironically, the McLaren team's biggest plus-point over the first two races had been the reliability of its Mercedes V8s. A month before the start of the season, if you'd bet the McLaren top brass that they'd get through the hottest two races on the calendar without a single engine failure, they would probably have bitten your hand off in the rush to take your money. As it was, the Mercs steamed through Bahrain and Malaysia without missing a beat. Impressive stuff.

After a promising performance from Michael Schumacher in Bahrain, the Ferrari 248 struggled in both qualifying and the race at Sepang, the lead driver in particular mindful of the Bridgestone wear problems that the team battled against in last year's race. Schumi ran a two-stop strategy from 14th place on the grid, Felipe Massa a one-stopper from 21st. In the end Massa just pipped Schumacher for fifth place, but although many commentators seemed eager to read into this some

suggestion of a dwindling lack of motivation on the part of the seven-times champion, he was plagued by a mysterious lack of grip on his second set of tyres and finished the afternoon in a sanguine frame of mind about the result.

'We [the team and I] can accept this result, considering everything that has happened over the weekend,' he said. 'I don't think we could have expected much more. On my second stint I wasn't as quick as I was on my first and third ones, so now we really need to understand the reasons why.

'All things said and done, the race went basically as I had expected, even though one always hopes for something more. During my first pit stop I had to wait for a fraction of a second before going out because another car was coming down the pit lane. This was a wise decision from a safety point of view. In the closing stages I was unable to get past Felipe because I just wasn't fast enough and he didn't make any mistakes.'

Behind the Ferraris, Jacques Villeneuve was the sole surviving BMW Sauber runner in seventh place, just squeezing home 0.827s ahead of Ralf Schumacher's energetically driven Toyota TF106. The Canadian driver had been held up behind Jarno Trulli's Toyota in the opening stages and, after getting past the Italian, admitted that it was just a question of running through to the finish. 'Physically it was an easier race than I had expected and I knew I should be in good shape mechanically because it was the first race for my engine,' said Villeneuve.

His team-mate Nick Heidfeld had a painfully disappointing afternoon. Following a great start he was running ahead of Massa's Ferrari after his second refuelling stop and was holding a strong fifth when a sudden engine failure sidelined him without warning on lap 49.

Ralf's performance in the Toyota was certainly pretty heartening after he was forced to start from the back of the grid. The decision was taken to put him on a three-stop strategy, which worked well to yield the Japanese constructor its first championship point of the year.

Trulli, hobbled from the start after he was hit from behind and sustained a broken diffuser, struggled to finish ninth. 'After I was hit I was suffering a mixture of understeer and oversteer and it was a big struggle, so I just concentrated on driving as quickly as possible,' he said. 'We tried to adjust the car at the pit stops, but obviously with the diffuser broken we could do very little.'

In the Red Bull camps there was but one survivor at the chequered flag, Vitantonio Liuzzi bringing his Toro Rosso home 11th. His team-mate Scott Speed succumbed to a problem with the clutch mechanism on his machine.

After Christian Klien ran into the back of Räikkönen, he had limped into the pits with broken front suspension, which was duly repaired. He was sent out again but eventually retired due to a hydraulics failure similar to that which sidelined David Coulthard's RB2 after only ten laps.

The Malaysian GP ended with much guarded optimism on the part of several potentially front-running teams, but the hard facts of the matter were that Renault had looked pretty well bullet-proof in the opening two races of the season and the firm message was that Honda and McLaren Mercedes were already being left trailing in terms of their world championship ambitions.

The big mystery, of course, was just where Ferrari stood in the overall pecking order, but the F1 community would have to wait another five weeks until Imola before getting the first firm signal from Maranello.

Alan Henry

PETRONAS
MALAYSIAN GRAND PRIX

KUALA LUMPUR 17–19 MARCH 2006

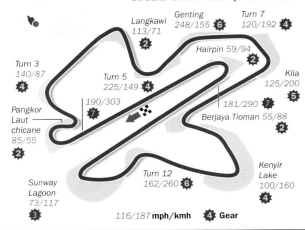

SEPANG INTERNATIONAL CIRCUIT, KUALA LUMPUR

Circuit: 3.444 miles / 5.543 km

Langkawi 113/71 • Genting 248/155 • Turn 7 120/192
Turn 3 140/87 • Turn 5 225/149 • Hairpin 59/94 • Klia 125/200
190/303 • 181/290 • Berjaya Tioman 55/88
Pangkor Laut chicane 85/55 • Turn 12 162/260 • Kenyir Lake 100/160
Sunway Lagoon 73/117

116/187 mph/kmh • Gear

Photograph: James Moy/www.crashpa.net

RACE RESULTS

Pos.	Driver	Nat.	No.	Entrant	Car/Engine	Tyres	Laps	Time/Retirement	Speed (mph/km/h)	Gap to leader	Fastest race lap	
1	Giancarlo Fisichella	I	2	Mild Seven Renault F1 Team	Renault R26-RS26 V8	M	56	1h 30m 40.529s	127.628/205.397		1m 35.294s	16
2	Fernando Alonso	E	1	Mild Seven Renault F1 Team	Renault R26-RS26 V8	M	56	1h 30m 45.114s	127.520/205.224	+4.585s	1m 34.803s	45
3	Jenson Button	GB	12	Lucky Strike Honda Racing F1 Team	Honda RA106-RA806E V8	M	56	1h 30m 50.160s	127.402/205.034	+9.631s	1m 35.604s	35
4	Juan Pablo Montoya	COL	4	Team McLaren Mercedes	McLaren MP4-21-Mercedes FO 108S V8	M	56	1h 31m 19.880s	126.711/203.922	+39.351s	1m 35.566s	39
5	Felipe Massa	BR	6	Scuderia Ferrari Marlboro	Ferrari 248 F1-056 V8	B	56	1h 31m 23.783s	126.621/203.776	+43.254s	1m 35.954s	51
6	Michael Schumacher	D	5	Scuderia Ferrari Marlboro	Ferrari 248 F1-056 V8	B	56	1h 31m 24.383s	126.607/203.754	+43.854s	1m 35.647s	44
7	Jacques Villeneuve	CDN	17	BMW Sauber F1 Team	BMW Sauber F1.06-BMW P86 V8	M	56	1h 32m 00.990s	125.767/202.403	+1m 20.461s	1m 36.002s	43
8	Ralf Schumacher	D	7	Panasonic Toyota Racing	Toyota TF106-RVX-06 V8	B	56	1h 32m 01.817s	125.749/202.373	+1m 21.288s	1m 35.686s	34
9	Jarno Trulli	I	8	Panasonic Toyota Racing	Toyota TF106-RVX-06 V8	B	55			+1 lap	1m 36.380s	52
10	Rubens Barrichello	BR	11	Lucky Strike Honda Racing F1 Team	Honda RA106-RA806E V8	M	55			+1 lap	1m 36.188s	54
11	Vitantonio Liuzzi	I	20	Scuderia Toro Rosso	Toro Rosso STR01-Cosworth TJ2005-2 V10	M	54			+2 laps	1m 37.387s	40
12	Christijan Albers	NL	19	MF1 Racing	Midland M16-Toyota RVX-06 V8	B	54			+2 laps	1m 38.198s	34
13	Tiago Monteiro	P	18	MF1 Racing	Midland M16-Toyota RVX-06 V8	B	54			+2 laps	1m 39.510s	39
14	Takuma Sato	J	22	Super Aguri F1 Team	Super Aguri SA05-Honda RA806E V8	B	53			+3 laps	1m 40.199s	14
	Nick Heidfeld	D	16	BMW Sauber F1 Team	BMW Sauber F1.06-BMW P86 V8	M	48	Engine			1m 35.751s	41
	Scott Speed	USA	21	Scuderia Toro Rosso	Toro Rosso STR01-Cosworth TJ2005-2 V10	M	41	Clutch			1m 37.313s	25
	Yuji Ide	J	23	Super Aguri F1 Team	Super Aguri SA05-Honda RA806E V8	B	33	Engine			1m 42.833s	18
	Christian Klien	A	15	Red Bull Racing	Red Bull RB2-Ferrari 056 V8	M	26	Hydraulics			1m 36.867s	14
	Mark Webber	AUS	9	WilliamsF1 Team	Williams FW28-Cosworth CA2006 V8	B	15	Hydraulics			1m 36.771s	12
	David Coulthard	GB	14	Red Bull Racing	Red Bull RB2-Ferrari 056 V8	M	10	Hydraulics			1m 38.078s	4
	Nico Rosberg	D	10	WilliamsF1 Team	Williams FW28-Cosworth CA2006 V8	B	6	Engine/fire			1m 37.366s	6
	Kimi Räikkönen	FIN	3	Team McLaren Mercedes	McLaren MP4-21-Mercedes FO 108S V8	M	0	Accident			No time	

Fastest lap: Fernando Alonso on lap 45, 1m 34.803s, 130.791 mph/210.487 km/h.

Lap record: Juan Pablo Montoya (Williams FW26-BMW V10), 1m 34.223s, 131.596 mph/211.782 km/h (2004).

All results and data © FOM 2006

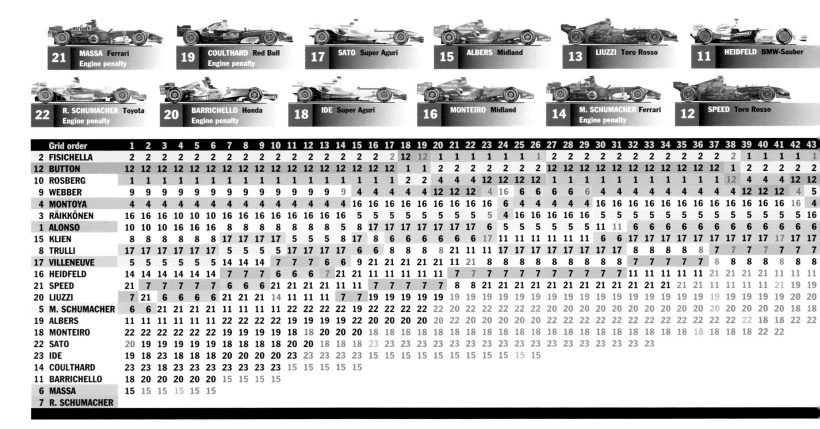

21	MASSA Ferrari Engine penalty	19	COULTHARD Red Bull Engine penalty	17	SATO Super Aguri	15	ALBERS Midland	13	LIUZZI Toro Rosso	11	HEIDFELD BMW-Sauber
22	R. SCHUMACHER Toyota Engine penalty	20	BARRICHELLO Honda Engine penalty	18	IDE Super Aguri	16	MONTEIRO Midland	14	M. SCHUMACHER Ferrari Engine penalty	12	SPEED Toro Rosso

Grid order	1	2	3	4	5	6	7	8	9	10	11	12	13	14	15	16	17	18	19	20	21	22	23	24	25	26	27	28	29	30	31	32	33	34	35	36	37	38	39	40	41	42	43
2 FISICHELLA	2	2	2	2	2	2	2	2	2	2	2	2	2	2	2	2	2	12	12	1	1	1	1	1	1	2	2	2	2	2	2	2	2	2	2	2	2	2	1	1	1	1	1
12 BUTTON	12	12	12	12	12	12	12	12	12	12	12	12	12	12	12	12	12	1	2	2	2	2	2	2	2	12	12	12	12	12	12	12	12	12	12	12	1	2	2	2	2	2	2
10 ROSBERG	1	1	1	1	1	1	1	1	1	1	1	1	1	1	1	1	1	2	2	4	4	12	12	12	12	1	1	1	1	1	1	1	1	1	1	12	4	4	4	12	12		
9 WEBBER	9	9	9	9	9	9	9	9	9	9	9	9	9	9	9	4	4	4	4	12	12	12	4	16	6	6	6	6	6	6	4	4	4	4	4	4	4	12	12	12	4	5	
4 MONTOYA	4	4	4	4	4	4	4	4	4	4	4	4	4	4	4	16	16	16	16	16	16	16	6	4	4	16	16	16	16	16	16	16	16	16	16	16	16	16	16	16	16	4	
3 RÄIKKÖNEN	16	16	16	10	10	10	16	16	16	16	16	16	16	16	16	5	5	5	5	5	5	5	5	4	16	5	5	5	5	5	5	5	5	5	5	5	5	5	5	5	5	6	
1 ALONSO	10	10	10	16	16	16	8	8	8	8	8	8	8	8	5	8	17	17	17	17	17	17	6	5	5	5	5	5	11	6	6	6	6	6	6	6	6	6	6	6	6	6	
15 KLIEN	8	8	8	8	8	8	17	17	17	5	5	5	8	17	8	6	6	6	6	6	17	11	11	11	11	11	6	17	17	17	17	17	17	17	17	17	17	17					
8 TRULLI	17	17	17	17	17	17	5	5	5	17	17	17	17	6	6	8	8	8	21	11	11	17	17	17	17	17	17	8	8	8	8	8	7	7	7	7	7	7					
17 VILLENEUVE	5	5	5	5	5	5	14	14	14	7	7	7	6	9	21	21	21	21	11	21	11	8	8	8	8	8	8	7	7	7	7	8	8	8	8	8	8	8					
16 HEIDFELD	14	14	14	14	14	14	7	7	7	6	6	6	7	21	11	11	11	11	11	7	7	7	7	7	7	7	7	11	11	11	11	11	11	21	21	21	11	11					
21 SPEED	21	7	7	7	7	6	6	6	21	21	21	21	11	11	7	7	7	7	8	8	21	21	21	21	21	21	21	21	21	21	21	11	11	11	11	11	21	19	19				
20 LIUZZI	7	21	6	6	6	21	21	21	14	11	11	11	7	7	19	19	19	19	19	19	19	19	19	19	19	19	19	19	19	19	19	19	19	19	19	19	19	20					
5 M. SCHUMACHER	6	6	21	21	21	21	11	11	22	22	22	22	22	22	22	20	22	20	20	20	22	22	20	20	20	20	20	20	20	20	20	20	20	20	20	18	18						
19 ALBERS	11	11	11	11	11	11	22	22	22	19	19	19	19	20	20	20	20	22	22	22	20	20	22	22	22	22	22	22	22	18	18	18	18	18	18	22	22						
18 MONTEIRO	22	22	22	22	22	19	18	19	19	18	18	20	20	18	20	22	22	18	18	18	18	18	18	18	18	18	18	18	18	18	18	18	18	22	22								
22 SATO	20	19	19	19	19	18	19	18	18	20	20	18	18	23	18	23	18	23	23	23	23	23	23	23	23																		
23 IDE	19	18	23	18	18	18	20	20	20	23	23	23	23	15	15	15	15	15	15	23																							
14 COULTHARD	23	23	18	23	23	23	23	23	23	15	15	15	15	15																													
11 BARRICHELLO	18	20	20	20	20	20	15	15	15	15																																	
6 MASSA	15	15	15	15	15	15																																					
7 R. SCHUMACHER																																											

PRACTICE 1 (FRIDAY)

Sunny/cloudy (track 36°C, air 33°C)

Pos.	Driver	Laps	Time
1	Alexander Wurz	19	1m 34.946s
2	Robert Kubica	22	1m 35.733s
3	Anthony Davidson	25	1m 35.997s
4	Juan Pablo Montoya	4	1m 36.709s
5	David Coulthard	7	1m 37.042s
6	Michael Schumacher	4	1m 37.043s
7	Felipe Massa	18	1m 37.557s
8	Robert Doornbos	18	1m 37.604s
9	Ralf Schumacher	9	1m 37.826s
10	Christian Klien	5	1m 38.448s
11	Neel Jani	21	1m 38.668s
12	Jarno Trulli	8	1m 38.837s
13	Scott Speed	14	1m 39.599s
14	Tiago Monteiro	8	1m 39.899s
15	Giorgio Mondini	22	1m 40.092s
16	Vitantonio Liuzzi	8	1m 40.123s
17	Christijan Albers	12	1m 40.608s
18	Takuma Sato	18	1m 41.072s
19	Yuji Ide	19	1m 43.449s
20	Kimi Räikkönen	1	No time
21	Fernando Alonso	2	No time
22	Giancarlo Fisichella	2	No time
23	Jacques Villeneuve	1	No time
24	Nick Heidfeld	1	No time

PRACTICE 2 (FRIDAY)

Sunny/cloudy (track 43°C, air 37°C)

Pos.	Driver	Laps	Time
1	Anthony Davidson	14	1m 35.041s
2	Alexander Wurz	30	1m 35.388s
3	Fernando Alonso	14	1m 35.806s
4	Felipe Massa	22	1m 35.924s
5	Kimi Räikkönen	15	1m 36.132s
6	Giancarlo Fisichella	14	1m 36.182s
7	Michael Schumacher	17	1m 36.617s
8	Jenson Button	12	1m 36.661s
9	Jacques Villeneuve	9	1m 37.045s
10	Rubens Barrichello	13	1m 37.270s
11	Jarno Trulli	23	1m 37.317s
12	Nick Heidfeld	7	1m 37.418s
13	Robert Kubica	28	1m 37.457s
14	Juan Pablo Montoya	12	1m 37.463s
15	Vitantonio Liuzzi	22	1m 37.590s
16	David Coulthard	8	1m 37.603s
17	Ralf Schumacher	20	1m 37.695s
18	Neel Jani	23	1m 37.831s
19	Scott Speed	21	1m 37.926s
20	Mark Webber	5	1m 38.081s
21	Nico Rosberg	6	1m 38.205s
22	Giorgio Mondini	20	1m 38.256s
23	Christian Klien	10	1m 38.644s
24	Christijan Albers	20	1m 38.918s
25	Robert Doornbos	28	1m 39.105s
26	Tiago Monteiro	20	1m 39.416s
27	Takuma Sato	22	1m 41.549s
28	Yuji Ide	16	1m 43.164s

QUALIFYING (SATURDAY)

Scattered clouds (track 46–50°C, air 34–36°C)

Pos.	Driver	First	Second	Third
1	Giancarlo Fisichella	1m 35.488s	1m 33.623s	1m 33.840s
2	Jenson Button	1m 35.023s	1m 33.527s	1m 33.986s
3	Nico Rosberg	1m 35.105s	1m 34.563s	1m 34.626s
4	Michael Schumacher	1m 35.810s	1m 34.574s	1m 34.668s
5	Mark Webber	1m 35.252s	1m 34.279s	1m 34.672s
6	Juan Pablo Montoya	1m 34.536s	1m 34.568s	1m 34.916s
7	Kimi Räikkönen	1m 34.667s	1m 34.351s	1m 34.983s
8	Fernando Alonso	1m 35.514s	1m 33.997s	1m 35.747s
9	Christian Klien	1m 35.171s	1m 34.537s	1m 38.715s
10	Ralf Schumacher	1m 35.214s	1m 34.586s	No time
11	David Coulthard	1m 34.839s	1m 34.614s	
12	Rubens Barrichello	1m 35.526s	1m 34.683s	
13	Jarno Trulli	1m 35.517s	1m 34.702s	
14	Jacques Villeneuve	1m 35.391s	1m 34.752s	
15	Nick Heidfeld	1m 35.588s	1m 34.783s	
16	Felipe Massa	1m 35.091s	No time	
17	Scott Speed	1m 36.297s		
18	Vitantonio Liuzzi	1m 36.581s		
19	Christijan Albers	1m 37.426s		
20	Tiago Monteiro	1m 37.819s		
21	Takuma Sato	1m 39.011s		
22	Yuji Ide	1m 40.720s		

PRACTICE 3 (SATURDAY)

Sun/scattered cloud (track 42–44°C, air 32–33°C)

Pos.	Driver	Laps	Time
1	Michael Schumacher	16	1m 34.126s
2	Fernando Alonso	13	1m 34.180s
3	Giancarlo Fisichella	13	1m 34.585s
4	Jenson Button	20	1m 34.616s
5	Christian Klien	12	1m 34.815s
6	Kimi Räikkönen	10	1m 34.854s
7	Ralf Schumacher	7	1m 35.040s
8	Nico Rosberg	14	1m 35.242s
9	David Coulthard	14	1m 35.639s
10	Jarno Trulli	19	1m 35.690s
11	Mark Webber	11	1m 35.700s
12	Jacques Villeneuve	9	1m 36.144s
13	Nick Heidfeld	13	1m 36.505s
14	Vitantonio Liuzzi	15	1m 36.549s
15	Rubens Barrichello	13	1m 36.655s
16	Juan Pablo Montoya	8	1m 37.053s
17	Felipe Massa	21	1m 37.148s
18	Christijan Albers	18	1m 37.232s
19	Scott Speed	19	1m 37.437s
20	Tiago Monteiro	17	1m 37.900s
21	Takuma Sato	15	1m 38.821s
22	Yuji Ide	18	1m 40.542s

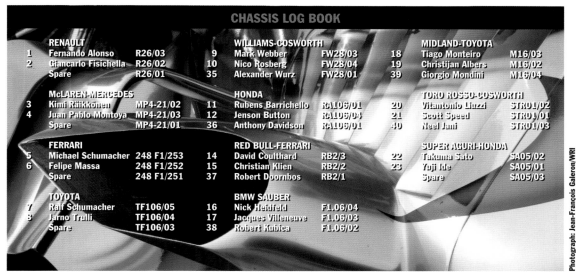

CHASSIS LOG BOOK

RENAULT
1	Fernando Alonso	R26/03
2	Giancarlo Fisichella	R26/02
	Spare	R26/01

McLAREN-MERCEDES
3	Kimi Räikkönen	MP4-21/02
4	Juan Pablo Montoya	MP4-21/03
	Spare	MP4-21/01

FERRARI
5	Michael Schumacher	248 F1/253
6	Felipe Massa	248 F1/252
	Spare	248 F1/251

TOYOTA
7	Ralf Schumacher	TF106/05
8	Jarno Trulli	TF106/04
	Spare	TF106/03

WILLIAMS-COSWORTH
9	Mark Webber	FW28/03
10	Nico Rosberg	FW28/04
19	Alexander Wurz	FW28/01

HONDA
11	Rubens Barrichello	RA106/01
12	Jenson Button	RA106/04
	Anthony Davidson	RA106/01

RED BULL-FERRARI
14	David Coulthard	RB2/3
15	Christian Klien	RB2/2
	Robert Doornbos	RB2/1

BMW SAUBER
16	Nick Heidfeld	F1.06/04
17	Jacques Villeneuve	F1.06/03
38	Robert Kubica	F1.06/02

MIDLAND-TOYOTA
18	Tiago Monteiro	M16/03
19	Christijan Albers	M16/02
	Giorgio Mondini	M16/04

TORO ROSSO-COSWORTH
20	Vitantonio Liuzzi	STR01/02
21	Scott Speed	STR01/01
	Neel Jani	STR01/03

SUPER AGURI-HONDA
22	Takuma Sato	SA05/02
23	Yuji Ide	SA05/01
	Spare	SA05/03

Photograph: Jean-François Galeron/WRI

 9 TRULLI Toyota

 7 ALONSO Renault

 5 MONTOYA McLaren

 3 ROSBERG Williams

 1 FISICHELLA Renault

 10 VILLENEUVE BMW-Sauber

 8 KLIEN Red Bull

 6 RÄIKKÖNEN McLaren

 4 WEBBER Williams

 2 BUTTON Honda

RACE DISTANCE:
56 laps
192.879 miles/310.408 km

RACE WEATHER:
Overcast
track 37–40°C, air 32–33°C

4	45	46	47	48	49	50	51	52	53	54	55	56	•
2	2	2	2	2	2	2	2	2	2	2	2	2	1
1	1	1	1	1	1	1	1	1	1	1	1	1	2
2	12	12	12	12	12	12	12	12	12	12	12	12	3
5	5	4	4	4	4	4	4	4	4	4	4	4	4
4	4	16	16	16	6	6	6	6	6	6	6	6	5
6	16	6	6	6	5	5	5	5	5	5	5	5	6
6	6	5	5	5	17	17	17	17	17	17	17	17	7
7	17	17	17	17	7	7	7	7	7	7	7	7	8
7	7	7	7	7	8	8	8	8	8	8	8		
8	8	8	8	8	11	11	11	11	11	11	11		
1	11	11	11	11	20	20	20	20	20	20			
9	19	19	19	20	19	19	19	19	19				
0	20	20	20	19	18	18	18	18	18				
8	18	18	18	18	22	22	22	22					
2	22	22	22	22									

Pit stop
One lap or more behind leader

FOR THE RECORD

Photograph: James Moy/www.crashpa.net

100th GRAND PRIX START: Nick Heidfeld
FIRST POINTS: BMW Sauber

POINTS

DRIVERS
1	Fernando Alonso	18
2	Michael Schumacher	11
3	Jenson Button	11
4	Giancarlo Fisichella	10
5	Juan Pablo Montoya	9
6	Kimi Räikkönen	6
7	Felipe Massa	4
8	Mark Webber	3
9	Nico Rosberg	2
10	Jacques Villeneuve	2
11	Ralf Schumacher	1
12	Christian Klien	1

CONSTRUCTORS
1	Renault	28
2	Ferrari	15
3	McLaren	15
4	Honda	11
5	Williams	5
6	BMW Sauber	2
7	Toyota	1
8	Red Bull	1

Photograph: Jean-François Galeron/WRI

AUSTRALIAN GP
MELBOURNE

Fernando Alonso leads the McLarens of Kimi
Räikkönen and Juan Pablo Montoya. The
Finn had a strong run to second behind
the world champion's Renault but JPM had
a dire afternoon and failed to finish.
Photograph: Laurent Charniaux/WRI

Above: Rubens Barrichello heads Honda team-mate Jenson Button in damp free practice. It was a bad race day for both men, despite Button's starting from an impressive pole position.

Photograph: Paul-Henri Cahier

Left: Barrichello looked pensive after struggling home ninth, grappling with brake problems in a car that did not yet suit his driving style.

Photograph: Emily Davenport/XPB.cc

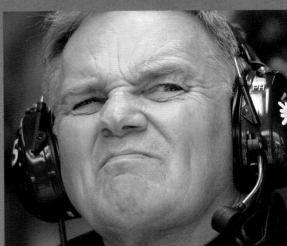

Right: Toro Rosso boss Gerhard Berger looks glum after a stressful weekend for Scott Speed and Vitantonio Liuzzi.

Photograph: James Moy/www.crashpa.net

Centre right: Patrick Head looks even less amused after both his Williams FW28s fail to make it to the finish.

Photograph: Paul-Henri Cahier

HONDA CRISIS OVER RUBENS?

THE Honda F1 team was left pondering a potential major crisis after Rubens Barrichello, the former Ferrari driver, was again totally outclassed by Jenson Button in the Australian GP. Barrichello's morale hit rock bottom in qualifying when he could manage only a distant 17th on a day when Button stormed to a superb pole position in an identical car. In the race, Barrichello finished a disappointing seventh.

'I need to get to the bottom of my problems before I say that I'm happy or not,' said Rubens, who was being paid $10 million a year on a firm three-year contract. 'Right now I'm just disappointed, because something has happened in these two hot races, where the grip is lower than in the test. I'm struggling on brakes and traction quite a lot. Jenson is just used to the car and he's doing a superb job. I'm not too concerned about my pace to him; I'm concerned that I'm below my own expectations on the driving. It's not a mind game now; I'm just relearning something on the car.'

The 33-year-old Brazilian veteran of 218 races, with nine GP victories to his credit, confessed to feeling overshadowed by the highly motivated Button, who had already shaped the team around himself just as Michael Schumacher had done at Ferrari.

'It was disappointing in the way that I really felt on top of my problems,' said Barrichello as he reflected on his battle to get the best out of the new Honda RA106 during pre-season testing. 'I like the car set up a bit differently, so every Friday [free practice session] seems to be a small struggle before I actually get on top of it.'

Team insiders suggested that the Honda's fundamental handling characteristics did not suit Barrichello's taste and that Button's more precise and economical driving style, especially as regards steering and braking, had enabled him to keep the upper hand.

DIARY

Damon Hill is nominated to succeed Sir Jackie Stewart as president of the British Racing Drivers' Club.

Toyota signals that it may reconsider its long-term F1 involvement unless the FIA offers an unambiguous reassurance that the car companies are welcome in the world championship.

Bruno Senna, Ayrton's nephew, wins three out of the four F3 supporting races at Melbourne.

Adrian Sutil wins the opening round of the All-Japan F3 series in his TOM'S Dallara-Toyota.

Vitantonio Liuzzi, currently racing in Red Bull's junior team, is invited to test the Red Bull-Ferrari RB2.

MELBOURNE QUALIFYING

MELBOURNE was still fizzing with enthusiasm over the successful Commonwealth Games, which had dominated the headlines throughout the previous fortnight, but as the F1 circus rolled into town the most pressing priority for the competitors was to find a way of erecting a road block to slow the Renault bandwagon that powered reigning world champion Fernando Alonso and Giancarlo Fisichella to victories in the first two races of the season.

Yet although both of the Renault R26s featured in the thick of the pole position battle in an action-packed qualifying session, Fisichella (1m 25.635s) and Alonso (1m 25.778s) were eventually elbowed back into second and third places as Jenson Button (pictured below) stormed to the third pole position of his career in the Honda RA106 with a 1m 25.229s best.

'We were really struggling for grip early on,' said Button at the end of a gusty session punctuated by a fleeting rain shower on this challenging track where competitors spend more than 70 percent of the lap running under full throttle. 'But it's fantastic to take pole position after all that. We juggled with the differential and traction control settings, plus the tyre pressures and the front wing adjustments, and then the car was good – *very* good – on new tyres right at the end.'

He added, 'Conditions were very windy, with very low grip, and the track is bumpy so it would have been easy to make a mistake. It was really tough to get [sufficient] heat into the tyres, but we're in the best position we possibly could be.'

The Renault twins nevertheless remained fairly confident for their race prospects. 'At the end the car balance was quite good,' said Fisichella. 'On my second lap we were quicker but I made a couple of mistakes in the first part of the lap, but we have a great pace for the race. The target is to be first into the first corner.'

By contrast, Alonso seemed a little deflated after having had his best run ruined when he came up behind Nick Heidfeld. 'I caught him and lost half a second in the last sector,' he explained. 'But the car performed very well. We will be extremely competitive in the race.'

The two McLaren-Mercedes were next up, Kimi Räikkönen (1m 25.822s) ahead of Juan Pablo Montoya (1m 25.976s), and the signs tended to suggest that they would be quick in the race. It was more difficult to judge the race speed of Ralf Schumacher (1m 26.612s) and Mark Webber (1m 26.937s), who qualified sixth and seventh. The BMWs were next, a better result than might have been expected. Jarno Trulli was the last man in the top ten but did not participate in the run-off because of a gearbox problem.

With Jacques Villeneuve dropping away because of a ten-place penalty on the grid, Michael Schumacher (1m 26.718s), who missed the cut in the second qualifying session because of the sudden rain flurry, would start tenth ahead of David Coulthard (1m 27.023s) in the fastest of the Red Bull-owned quartet – although not by much. Tonio Liuzzi was only 0.2s farther back, a very good effort with the Toro Rosso on 1m 27.219s.

It was a bad day for Ferrari. Felipe Massa went off and hit the wall in a bizarre incident that looked like a rear suspension failure, but according to the team he lost control when he ran over a kerb. He ended up 15th on 1m 28.868s behind Christian Klien (1m 27.757s) and Nico Rosberg (1m 28.351s), who struggled to get temperature into his tyres and missed out in the second qualifying session.

Photograph: Russell Batchelor/XPB.cc

FERNANDO Alonso delivered yet another consummate performance in his Renault R26 to dominate the Australian GP at Melbourne's Albert Park circuit and extend his world championship points lead, defeating the McLaren-Mercedes challenge before easing off in the closing stages to take a close win by just 1.8s from a hard-charging Kimi Räikkönen. The Finn had flat-spotted a front tyre as he muscled his way ahead of Jenson Button's Honda in the opening stages, thereafter losing pace as he grappled with a serious vibration problem that prevented him from keeping up with the leading Renault.

'This was a very different race from the other two so far this season,' said an effusive Alonso as he stepped down from the podium. 'In Bahrain I was fighting with Michael [Schumacher] all the way; in Malaysia it was Jenson I was battling for second place. But today it was quite comfortable. There were no fights and I was very relaxed for a lot of the race.'

Thwarted by understeer after the vibration threw off a front wing strake, Kimi changed the MP4-21's nose section at his second refuelling stop but, from a spectacular race punctuated by spins, accidents and no fewer than four periods with the field running behind the safety car, he was moderately satisfied with the outcome.

Meanwhile Jenson Button and the Honda team were left wondering precisely what they had to do to achieve a decent result after a simply dismal event in which the British driver slipped from a brilliant pole position to an ignominious retirement with a massive, fiery engine failure within sight of the chequered flag. It dropped him from fifth to tenth in literally the last few yards of the race.

The third round of the world championship was a wild and woolly affair with most competitors battling for tyre grip on a dusty track surface in conditions that were dramatically cool after the earlier sweltering heat. The Honda squad unfortunately opted to use the softer tyre choice – against Michelin's advice – with the result that Button grappled with graining rubber and struggled to generate sufficient temperature.

'The tyres weren't too bad when they built up some temperature,' said Button, 'but in the long periods running slowly behind the safety car they just lost all grip. Coming through the right-hander onto the pit straight it was as if we'd got no wings on the car. It was understeer, oversteer… there was just nothing I could do about it.'

The Honda management may have patted itself on the back, claiming that, with great strategic judgement, Button's engineers told him to stop his crippled car just before the timing line so that he would not be classified as a race finisher, thereby avoiding the need to take an engine change penalty in qualifying for the San Marino GP at Imola on 23 April. But in fact the V8's stopping point was preordained after such a massive mechanical failure and Jenson had little choice in the matter.

Alonso, who almost hit pole sitter Button on the run down to the first corner, found himself having to tuck in behind the Honda as the first safety car period was triggered just seconds into the race when Felipe Massa crashed spectacularly in his Ferrari, taking out novice Nico Rosberg's Williams in the process.

Massa was slightly sheepish, if not exactly apologetic, after this unfortunate incident, claiming that he'd received a helping hand from another competitor. 'Not much to say,' shrugged the

Brazilian. 'At the first turn I had [Christian] Klien on my left and [Scott] Speed on my right. Christian touched me, which spun me round and to the right, then I hit Rosberg and ended up in the barrier.'

He added, 'There was nothing I could do; I was basically a passenger in my car. I am very unhappy because I am sure I could have had a good race. It's been a weekend to forget.'

The first lap also claimed Jarno Trulli's Toyota after an inexplicable incident with David Coulthard's Red Bull. 'This was a disastrous weekend for me and it was a shame to be punted out of the race so early,' said the Italian. 'A couple of corners in I was following Coulthard, who was going very slowly and zigzagging on the straight. I went to the inside to overtake him and I was ahead at the corner, but he just closed the door on me, hitting me in the back. I was just being careful and overtaking a slower car so I don't understand how it happened and I was surprised by what he did.' To cap it all, a painful ear infection delayed Trulli's return to Europe by 24 hours.

At the restart Fernando neatly got the jump on Button to take the lead into the first corner but the pack had hardly got into its stride before the safety car was deployed a second time, from laps seven to nine, while debris from Christian Klien's crashed Red Bull was swept up from the circuit.

At the next restart Räikkönen jumped Button for second going into the first corner and Juan Pablo Montoya – who'd embarrassingly spun on the pre-race formation lap – was now up to fourth place and pressing Button hard. After the leading bunch made its first round of refuelling stops, the Australian crowd was delighted as Mark Webber surged through into the lead in the Williams-Cosworth FW28,

but it proved a short-lived moment of joy for the locals: his gearbox failed after only two laps at the head of the field.

During the week prior to the race the F1 fraternity had become consumed in an arcane debate over the legality of the so-called flexible front wings on the Ferrari 248, which may or may not have conferred an aerodynamic advantage on the Italian car. Thankfully, before things had a chance to get ugly and protests started flying about the paddock, Ferrari changed the suspect components, although it insisted it had taken this step in the pursuit of performance rather than because of any formal ruling from the governing body, the FIA.

Not that the question of wings figured prominently in Ferrari's race weekend. After Massa checked out at the first corner, Michael was hunting down Button for fifth place when, coming up to complete his 33rd lap, he ran wide coming out of the last right-hander and slammed into the wall. The wrecked Ferrari bounced back across the track to stop almost in front of its own pit – though Michael amused everybody by escaping from the pit lane through the Toyota garage.

'I was pushing to the maximum to try and close on Jenson and pass him,' said Schumi. 'Probably he had some problems because he was not very quick. I tucked in behind him and unexpectedly I got some heavy understeer and finished on the grass.' Had not a rain shower prevented Michael from trying a softer Bridgestone tyre during Saturday morning's free practice session the result might well have been very different; his brother Ralf successfully used that choice of rubber to climb through to third place in the Toyota TF106.

'Our main problem was keeping the tyres up to temperature,' Michael said, 'especially in the first part of the race and also

Above: Giancarlo Fisichella drove a terrific race to fifth, without telemetry during the opening stint, after a problem with the anti-stall mechanism stopped his engine on the grid and forced him to take the restart from the pit lane.

Centre left: Michael Schumacher climbs to safety after crashing his Ferrari coming onto the start-line straight.
Photographs: XPB.cc

Top left: Felipe Massa also ended his day with a pile-up, this one at the first corner of the race.
Photograph: Jean François Galeron/WRI

Left: Jarno Trulli was unfortunate to be eliminated in this first-lap skirmish with David Coulthard's Red Bull, but the Scot went on to take eighth place after a post-race stewards' meeting.
Photograph: Paul-Henri Cahier

because there were a few safety car periods. We had chosen this compound specifically for the race and once they reached the right operating temperature they were going well, as was obvious after the pit stop. At first, though, it was difficult to drive because after locking the wheels a few times the tyres were completely finished. It's clear we have a lot of work to do.'

Meanwhile Ralf had raced strongly near the front of the pack from the outset, only to lose crucial time due to a drive-through penalty. Thereafter he made the best use of the safety car periods to pull through the pack.

'The penalty was my fault because I accidentally hit the [speed limiter on-off] button twice,' he confessed. 'But I was lucky and due to the safety car periods I achieved a lot more than we [the team and I] ever thought before the weekend.

'At the start we were sliding around and locking up wheels, but while we've had some problems warming our tyres in earlier races others seemed to struggle with that today. We are still some way from the top teams, so we have to work, but I have no doubt that our crew is able to do that. We're strong people

and pushing hard, so I'm looking forward to the next few races.'

Over in the BMW Sauber squad there was a similar level of elation for, although the team missed out on a podium finish, both its F1.06s stormed home in the championship points: Nick Heidfeld was fourth and Jacques Villeneuve sixth.

'I am really happy about this result,' enthused Heidfeld. 'We were already competitive in practice, but we were even stronger in the race. My only problem was that I could not get any heat into the tyres immediately after each safety car period. It was particularly bad after the last one, when Kimi was all over me and we touched lightly in Turn Four. Then I braked too late for Turn Six because the front tyres were not up to temperature and as I ran wide he was able to pass me. So was Ralf, within metres of the yellow flags.'

Villeneuve was similarly satisfied with his run through from the back of the grid on a full fuel load.

There had, meanwhile, been tension in the McLaren camp. Juan Pablo Montoya had a spin during the first period behind the safety car that dropped him back behind Ralf Schumacher's

Toyota and Mark Webber's Williams. Another safety car period on lap 34 triggered the second round of refuelling stops, with Kimi coming in for a 16.7s stop during which a new nose section was fitted to cure his car's understeer. Montoya followed him in for his second stop and they resumed with Kimi third and Juan Pablo sixth. At the end of lap 46 Juan Pablo ran wide onto the kerb at the last corner and the impact forced him to retire.

Montoya explained, 'I think I could have finished on the podium, but as I was pushing to get past Ralf I hit the kerb at the start of the straight and went into a bit of a wobble, but managed to save it. Unfortunately the impact triggered a default system, which switched off the engine.' The Colombian would later voice some criticism of the team for forcing him to queue behind Räikkönen for his second stint, which prompted the McLaren management to observe crisply that it was pretty disappointed with its badly damaged MP4-21 chassis.

Young Scott Speed finished eighth in his Toro Rosso after a great dice with Red Bull's David Coulthard to become the first American driver since Michael Andretti in 1993 to score a championship point. Except that he didn't. He had a 25s time penalty added to his race time, which dropped him to ninth behind Coulthard, and also collected a $5,000 fine for using abusive language in the stewards' meeting.

Yet the star of the race was unquestionably Renault's hapless Giancarlo Fisichella. His car's anti-stall mechanism failed on the starting grid, cutting the engine and forcing him to relinquish his place on the outside of the front row and to start from the pit lane. Then his telemetry packed up, forcing him to monitor his fuel load and keep his engineers appraised of it over the radio. That was followed by understeer and clutch failure, but he kept thrashing along hard to take a fine fifth as Button ground to a halt within sight of the chequered flag. It was an epic performance.

Alan Henry

FIA F1 WORLD CHAMPIONSHIP • ROUND 3

FOSTER'S AUSTRALIAN GRAND PRIX

MELBOURNE 31 MARCH–2 APRIL 2006

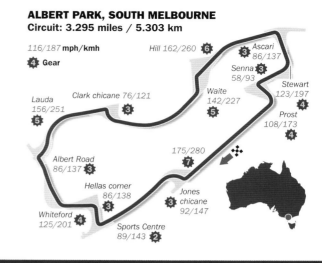

ALBERT PARK, SOUTH MELBOURNE
Circuit: 3.295 miles / 5.303 km

116/187 mph/kmh

Gear

Hill 162/260

Ascari 86/137

Senna 58/93

Stewart 123/197

Waite 142/227

Clark chicane 76/121

Prost 108/173

Lauda 156/251

175/280

Albert Road 86/137

Hellas corner 86/138

Jones chicane 92/147

Whiteford 125/201

Sports Centre 89/143

Photograph: James Moy/www.crashpa.net

RACE RESULTS

Pos.	Driver	Nat.	No.	Entrant	Car/Engine	Tyres	Laps	Time/Retirement	Speed (mph/km/h)	Gap to leader	Fastest race lap	
1	Fernando Alonso	E	1	Mild Seven Renault F1 Team	Renault R26-RS26 V8	M	57	1h 34m 27.870s	119.297/191.990		1m 26.189s	49
2	Kimi Räikkönen	FIN	3	Team McLaren Mercedes	McLaren MP4-21-Mercedes FO 108S V8	M	57	1h 34m 29.699s	119.259/191.928	+1.829s	1m 26.045s	57
3	Ralf Schumacher	D	7	Panasonic Toyota Racing	Toyota TF106-RVX-06 V8	B	57	1h 34m 52.694s	118.777/191.153	+24.824s	1m 27.810s	45
4	Nick Heidfeld	D	16	BMW Sauber F1 Team	BMW Sauber F1.06-BMW P86 V8	M	57	1h 34m 58.902s	118.647/190.944	+31.032s	1m 27.700s	49
5	Giancarlo Fisichella	I	2	Mild Seven Renault F1 Team	Renault R26-RS26 V8	M	57	1h 35m 06.291s	118.494/190.697	+38.421s	1m 27.561s	53
6	Jacques Villeneuve	CDN	17	BMW Sauber F1 Team	BMW Sauber F1.06-BMW P86 V8	M	57	1h 35m 17.424s	118.263/190.326	+49.554s	1m 28.321s	56
7	Rubens Barrichello	BR	11	Lucky Strike Honda Racing F1 Team	Honda RA106-RA806E V8	M	57	1h 35m 19.774s	118.214/190.247	+51.904s	1m 27.690s	32
8	David Coulthard	GB	14	Red Bull Racing	Red Bull RB2-Ferrari 056 V8	M	57	1h 35m 21.853s	118.171/190.178	+53.983s	1m 28.250s	32
9	Scott Speed*	USA	21	Scuderia Toro Rosso	Toro Rosso STR01-Cosworth TJ2005-2 V10	M	57	1h 35m 46.687s	117.661/189.357	+1m 18.817s	1m 28.367s	26
10	Jenson Button	GB	12	Lucky Strike Honda Racing F1 Team	Honda RA106-RA806E V8	M	56	Engine		+1 lap	1m 27.799s	17
11	Christijan Albers	NL	19	MF1 Racing	Midland M16-Toyota RVX-06 V8	B	56			+1 lap	1m 29.238s	53
12	Takuma Sato	J	22	Super Aguri F1 Team	Super Aguri SA05-Honda RA806E V8	B	55			+2 laps	1m 30.574s	54
13	Yuji Ide	J	23	Super Aguri F1 Team	Super Aguri SA05-Honda RA806E V8	B	54			+3 laps	1m 33.737s	49
	Juan Pablo Montoya	COL	4	Team McLaren Mercedes	McLaren MP4-21-Mercedes FO 108S V8	M	45†	Spin/electrics			1m 27.464s	45
	Tiago Monteiro	P	18	MF1 Racing	Midland M16-Toyota RVX-06 V8	B	39	Hydraulics			1m 29.687s	31
	Vitantonio Liuzzi	I	20	Scuderia Toro Rosso	Toro Rosso STR01-Cosworth TJ2005-2 V10	M	37	Accident			1m 27.988s	25
	Michael Schumacher	D	5	Scuderia Ferrari Marlboro	Ferrari 248 F1-056 V8	B	32	Accident			1m 27.180s	27
	Mark Webber	AUS	9	WilliamsF1 Team	Williams FW28-Cosworth CA2006 V8	B	22	Gearbox			1m 27.800s	19
	Christian Klien	A	15	Red Bull Racing	Red Bull RB2-Ferrari 056 V8	M	4	Brakes/accident			1m 41.351s	4
	Jarno Trulli	I	8	Panasonic Toyota Racing	Toyota TF106-RVX-06 V8	B	0	Accident			No time	
	Nico Rosberg	D	10	WilliamsF1 Team	Williams FW28-Cosworth CA2006 V8	B	0	Accident			No time	
	Felipe Massa	BR	6	Scuderia Ferrari Marlboro	Ferrari 248 F1-056 V8	B	0	Accident			No time	

†Although officially classified with 46 laps, Montoya abandoned the car just before terminating lap 46. A couple of minutes later the car was pushed into the pitlane by the track stewards and in the process crossed the finish line, completing lap 46.

Race scheduled for 58 laps but reduced due to aborted start when Montoya's car blocked the grid. *Scott Speed's time includes a 25s penalty for overtaking David Coulthard under yellow flags.

Fastest lap: Kimi Räikkönen on lap 57, 1m 26.045s, 137.864 mph/221.869 km/h.

Lap record: Michael Schumacher (Ferrari F2004 V10), 1m 24.125s, 141.010 mph/226.933 km/h (2004).

All results and data © FOM 2006

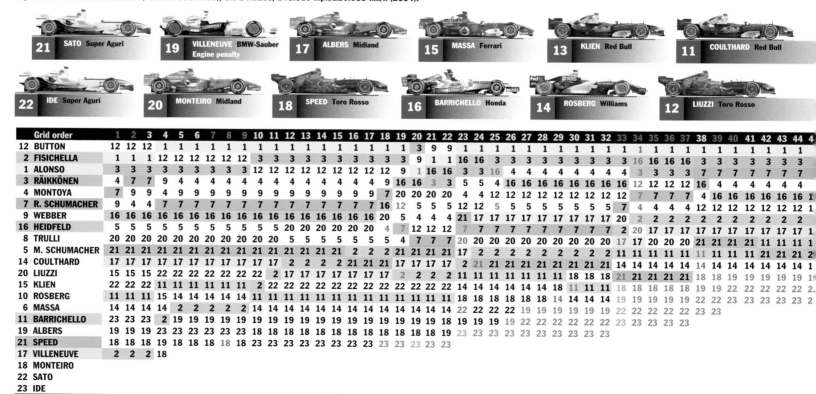

Grid order	1	2	3	4	5	6	7	8	9	10	11	12	13	14	15	16	17	18	19	20	21	22	23	24	25	26	27	28	29	30	31	32	33	34	35	36	37	38	39	40	41	42	43	44	44
12 BUTTON	12	12	12	1	1	1	1	1	1	1	1	1	1	1	1	1	1	1	1	3	9	9	1	1	1	1	1	1	1	1	1	1	1	1	1	1	1	1	1	1	1	1	1	1	1
2 FISICHELLA	1	1	1	12	12	12	12	12	12	3	3	3	3	3	3	3	3	3	3	9	1	1	16	16	3	3	3	3	3	3	3	3	16	16	16	16	3	3	3	3	3	3	3	3	3
1 ALONSO	3	3	3	3	3	3	3	3	12	12	12	12	12	12	12	12	9	1	16	16	3	3	16	4	4	4	4	4	4	4	4	3	3	3	7	7	7	7	7	7	7	7	7		
3 RÄIKKÖNEN	4	7	7	9	4	4	4	4	4	4	4	4	4	4	4	9	16	16	3	3	5	5	4	16	16	16	16	16	16	16	12	12	12	12	16	4	4	4	4	4	4			
4 MONTOYA	7	9	4	4	9	9	9	9	9	9	9	9	9	9	9	7	20	20	20	20	4	4	12	12	12	12	12	12	12	12	7	7	7	4	4										
7 R. SCHUMACHER	9	4	4	7	7	7	7	7	7	7	7	7	7	7	7	12	12	5	5	12	12	5	5	7	4	4	4	4	16	16	16	16	16	16	1										
9 WEBBER	16	16	16	16	16	16	16	16	16	16	16	16	16	16	16	20	5	4	4	21	17	17	17	17	17	17	17	17	20	2	2	2	2	2	2	2	2	2							
16 HEIDFELD	5	5	5	5	5	5	5	5	5	20	20	20	20	20	4	7	12	12	12	7	7	7	7	7	7	7	7	2	20	17	17	17	17	17	17	17	17	1							
8 TRULLI	20	20	20	20	20	20	20	20	20	5	5	5	5	5	5	4	7	7	7	20	20	20	20	20	20	20	20	17	17	20	20	20	21	21	21	21	11	11	1						
5 M. SCHUMACHER	21	21	21	21	21	21	21	21	21	21	21	21	21	21	2	2	21	21	21	17	2	2	2	2	2	2	2	11	11	11	11	11	11	11	11	11	21	21	2						
14 COULTHARD	17	17	17	17	17	17	17	17	17	2	2	2	21	21	21	2	21	21	21	21	21	11	11	14	14	14	14	14	14	14	14	14	14	14	14	14									
20 LIUZZI	15	15	15	22	22	22	22	22	22	2	17	17	17	17	17	2	2	2	21	21	11	11	11	11	18	18	18	21	21	21	21	18	18	19	19	19	19	19							
15 KLIEN	22	22	22	11	11	11	11	11	11	11	11	2	2	2	14	14	14	14	18	11	11	11	18	18	18	18	18	18	18	18	19	19	22	19	22	22	22								
10 ROSBERG	11	11	11	15	14	14	14	14	14	14	14	14	14	14	11	11	11	11	18	18	18	18	14	14	14	19	19	19	19	19	19	22	23	23	23	23	2								
6 MASSA	14	14	14	14	2	2	2	2	14	14	14	14	14	14	14	14	22	22	22	19	19	19	19	19	22	22	23	23	23																
11 BARRICHELLO	23	23	23	2	19	19	19	19	19	19	19	19	19	18	18	18	19	19	19	22	22	22	22	23	23	23	23																		
19 ALBERS	19	19	19	23	23	23	23	23	23	18	18	18	18	19	19	19	18	18	18	23	23	23	23																						
21 SPEED	18	18	18	19	18	18	18	18	18	23	23	23	23	23	23	23	23	23	23																									
17 VILLENEUVE	2	2	2	18																																								
18 MONTEIRO																																													
22 SATO																																													
23 IDE																																													

PRACTICE 1 (FRIDAY)

Cloudy (track 23ºC, air 21ºC)

Pos.	Driver	Laps	Time
1	Anthony Davidson	26	1m 28.259s
2	Robert Doornbos	19	1m 28.559s
3	Jacques Villeneuve	16	1m 28.595s
4	Kimi Räikkönen	5	1m 28.713s
5	Felipe Massa	7	1m 29.025s
6	Michael Schumacher	5	1m 29.041s
7	Ralf Schumacher	5	1m 29.411s
8	Alexander Wurz	19	1m 29.461s
9	Robert Kubica	13	1m 29.576s
10	Christian Klien	7	1m 29.601s
11	David Coulthard	9	1m 29.676s
12	Scott Speed	8	1m 31.017s
13	Christijan Albers	9	1m 31.039s
14	Tiago Monteiro	10	1m 31.812s
15	Takuma Sato	9	1m 34.036s
16	Yuji Ide	19	1m 36.684s
17	Markus Winkelhock	17	1m 36.859s
18	Neel Jani	4	1m 40.818s
19	Fernando Alonso	2	No time
20	Giancarlo Fisichella	2	No time
21	Jarno Trulli	2	No time
22	Juan Pablo Montoya	1	No time
23	Nick Heidfeld	1	No time
24	Rubens Barrichello	1	No time
25	Vitantonio Liuzzi	2	No time

PRACTICE 2 (FRIDAY)

Cloudy (track 26ºC, air 23ºC)

Pos.	Driver	Laps	Time
1	Anthony Davidson	28	1m 26.822s
2	Alexander Wurz	27	1m 26.832s
3	Robert Kubica	25	1m 27.200s
4	Jenson Button	12	1m 27.213s
5	Fernando Alonso	14	1m 27.443s
6	Michael Schumacher	16	1m 27.658s
7	Kimi Räikkönen	16	1m 27.773s
8	Rubens Barrichello	20	1m 28.075s
9	Juan Pablo Montoya	15	1m 28.200s
10	Felipe Massa	17	1m 28.227s
11	Giancarlo Fisichella	11	1m 28.280s
12	Jacques Villeneuve	22	1m 28.440s
13	David Coulthard	18	1m 28.531s
14	Mark Webber	10	1m 28.860s
15	Nick Heidfeld	5	1m 29.053s
16	Jarno Trulli	20	1m 29.138s
17	Scott Speed	18	1m 29.196s
18	Ralf Schumacher	16	1m 29.379s
19	Tiago Monteiro	21	1m 29.713s
20	Robert Doornbos	32	1m 29.876s
21	Christian Klien	9	1m 29.879s
22	Nico Rosberg	11	1m 29.933s
23	Neel Jani	26	1m 30.686s
24	Vitantonio Liuzzi	14	1m 30.734s
25	Christijan Albers	18	1m 30.830s
26	Markus Winkelhock	25	1m 31.260s
27	Takuma Sato	27	1m 32.556s
28	Yuji Ide	22	1m 34.224s

QUALIFYING (SATURDAY)

Intermittent sun/rain showers (track 25–26ºC, air 16–17ºC)

Pos.	Driver	First	Second	Third
1	Jenson Button	1m 28.081s	1m 26.337s	1m 25.229s
2	Giancarlo Fisichella	1m 27.765s	1m 26.196s	1m 25.635s
3	Fernando Alonso	1m 28.569s	1m 25.729s	1m 25.778s
4	Kimi Räikkönen	1m 27.193s	1m 26.161s	1m 25.822s
5	Juan Pablo Montoya	1m 27.079s	1m 25.902s	1m 25.976s
6	Ralf Schumacher	1m 28.007s	1m 26.596s	1m 26.612s
7	Mark Webber	1m 27.669s	1m 26.075s	1m 26.937s
8	Nick Heidfeld	1m 27.796s	1m 26.014s	1m 27.579s
9	Jacques Villeneuve	1m 28.460s	1m 26.714s	1m 29.239s
10	Jarno Trulli	1m 27.748s	1m 26.327s	No time
11	Michael Schumacher	1m 28.228s	1m 26.718s	
12	David Coulthard	1m 28.408s	1m 27.023s	
13	Vitantonio Liuzzi	1m 28.999s	1m 27.219s	
14	Christian Klien	1m 28.757s	1m 27.591s	
15	Nico Rosberg	1m 28.351s	1m 29.422s	
16	Felipe Massa	1m 28.868s	No time	
17	Rubens Barrichello	1m 29.943s		
18	Christijan Albers	1m 30.226s		
19	Scott Speed	1m 30.426s		
20	Tiago Monteiro	1m 30.709s		
21	Takuma Sato	1m 32.279s		
22	Yuji Ide	1m 36.164s		

PRACTICE 3 (SATURDAY)

Rain/cloud/wind (track 14–15ºC, air 14ºC)

Pos.	Driver	Laps	Time
1	Nick Heidfeld	10	1m 35.335s
2	Jacques Villeneuve	16	1m 36.281s
3	Vitantonio Liuzzi	10	1m 36.373s
4	Giancarlo Fisichella	13	1m 36.414s
5	Ralf Schumacher	10	1m 36.445s
6	Felipe Massa	11	1m 36.506s
7	Michael Schumacher	10	1m 37.332s
8	Rubens Barrichello	15	1m 37.481s
9	Jarno Trulli	10	1m 37.492s
10	Scott Speed	11	1m 37.852s
11	Christian Klien	12	1m 37.947s
12	Mark Webber	7	1m 38.036s
13	Jenson Button	11	1m 38.505s
14	David Coulthard	15	1m 38.683s
15	Nico Rosberg	11	1m 39.401s
16	Tiago Monteiro	7	1m 39.515s
17	Fernando Alonso	11	1m 39.654s
18	Yuji Ide	18	1m 40.261s
19	Takuma Sato	5	1m 41.448s
20	Juan Pablo Montoya	3	1m 44.350s
21	Kimi Räikkönen	3	1m 48.284s
22	Christijan Albers	3	No time

CHASSIS LOG BOOK

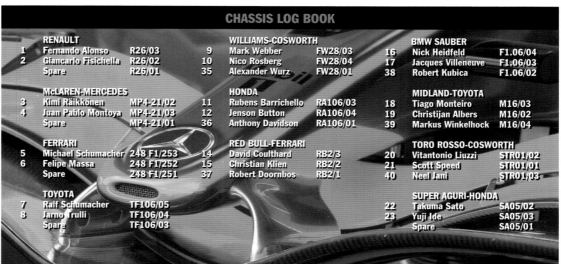

RENAULT		
1	Fernando Alonso	R26/03
2	Giancarlo Fisichella	R26/02
	Spare	R26/01

McLAREN-MERCEDES		
3	Kimi Räikkönen	MP4-21/02
4	Juan Pablo Montoya	MP4-21/03
	Spare	MP4-21/01

FERRARI		
5	Michael Schumacher	248 F1/253
6	Felipe Massa	248 F1/252
	Spare	248 F1/251

TOYOTA		
7	Ralf Schumacher	TF106/05
8	Jarno Trulli	TF106/04
	Spare	TF106/03

WILLIAMS-COSWORTH		
9	Mark Webber	FW28/03
10	Nico Rosberg	FW28/04
35	Alexander Wurz	FW28/01

HONDA		
11	Rubens Barrichello	RA106/03
12	Jenson Button	RA106/04
36	Anthony Davidson	RA106/01

RED BULL-FERRARI		
14	David Coulthard	RB2/3
15	Christian Klien	RB2/2
37	Robert Doornbos	RB2/1

BMW SAUBER		
16	Nick Heidfeld	F1.06/04
17	Jacques Villeneuve	F1.06/03
38	Robert Kubica	F1.06/02

MIDLAND-TOYOTA		
18	Tiago Monteiro	M16/03
19	Christijan Albers	M16/02
39	Markus Winkelhock	M16/04

TORO ROSSO-COSWORTH		
20	Vitantonio Liuzzi	STR01/02
21	Scott Speed	STR01/01
40	Neel Jani	STR01/03

SUPER AGURI-HONDA		
22	Takuma Sato	SA05/02
23	Yuji Ide	SA05/03
	Spare	SA05/01

9 TRULLI Toyota

7 WEBBER Williams

5 MONTOYA McLaren

3 ALONSO Renault

1 BUTTON Honda

10 M. SCHUMACHER Ferrari

8 HEIDFELD BMW-Sauber

6 R. SCHUMACHER Toyota

4 RÄIKKÖNEN McLaren

2 FISICHELLA Renault

RACE DISTANCE:
57 laps
187.822 miles/302.271 km

RACE WEATHER:
Sunny/cloudy
(track 22–27ºC, air 16–19ºC)

46	47	48	49	50	51	52	53	54	55	56	57	•
1	1	1	1	1	1	1	1	1	1	1	1	1
3	3	3	3	3	3	3	3	3	3	3	3	2
7	7	7	7	7	7	7	7	7	7	7	7	3
16	16	16	16	16	16	16	16	16	16	16	16	4
12	12	12	12	12	12	12	12	12	12	12	2	5
2	2	2	2	2	2	2	2	2	2	2	17	6
17	17	17	17	17	17	17	17	17	17	17	11	7
11	11	11	11	11	11	11	11	11	11	11	21	8
21	21	21	21	21	21	21	21	21	21	21	14	9
14	14	14	14	14	14	14	14	14	14	14		
19	19	19	19	19	19	19	19	19	19	19		
22	22	22	22	22	22	22	22	22	22			
4	23	23	23	23	23	23	23	23	23			
23												

Pit stop
One lap or more behind leader
Safety car deployed on laps shown

FOR THE RECORD

500th POINT: David Coulthard (above)
TENTH GRAND PRIX WIN:
Fernando Alonso

POINTS

DRIVERS

1	Fernando Alonso	28
2	Giancarlo Fisichella	14
3	Kimi Räikkönen	14
4	Michael Schumacher	11
5	Jenson Button	11
6	Juan Pablo Montoya	9
7	Ralf Schumacher	7
8	Nick Heidfeld	5
9	Jacques Villeneuve	5
10	Felipe Massa	4
11	Mark Webber	3
12	Rubens Barrichello	2
13	Nico Rosberg	2
14	David Coulthard	1
15	Christian Klien	1

CONSTRUCTORS

1	Renault	42
2	McLaren	23
3	Ferrari	15
4	Honda	13
5	BMW Sauber	10
6	Toyota	7
7	Williams	5
8	Red Bull	2

SAN MARINO GP

IMOLA

Michael Schumacher hangs on ahead
of Fernando Alonso on his way to a great
tactical victory at Imola, neatly reversing
the outcome of his battle with the Renault
driver 12 months earlier.
Photograph: Laurent Charniaux/WRI

Above: Christian Klien makes heavy
weather of his weekend as he bounces his
Red Bull-Ferrari over one of the kerbs.

Above right: Ferrari sponsor Martini turned
the clock back 30 years by presenting
ex-Brabham men Gordon Murray, Bernie
Ecclestone and Herbie Blash with classic
Martini Brabham jackets to celebrate
its fresh involvement in F1.

Photographs: Peter Nygaard/GP Photo

Centre right: Jacques Villeneuve joins
his mother Joanne at a function to
name a street in Imola after his father,
the legendary Gilles.

Photograph: Lukas Gorys

Top right: The powers behind Ferrari,
Luca di Montezemolo and Jean Todt.

Photograph: Brousseau Photo

Bottom right: Juan Pablo Montoya
had a good run to third place in the
McLaren-Mercedes MP4-21.

Photograph: Jean-François Galeron/WRI

IMOLA QUALIFYING

MICHAEL Schumacher (1m 22.795s) and his team-mate Felipe Massa (1m 23.702s) were separated in the final grid order by Honda twins Jenson Button (1m 22.988s) and the revitalised Rubens Barrichello (1m 23.242s), both of whom admitted they were pleasantly surprised with their qualifying performances after battling for grip in Friday and Saturday free practice. They'd more realistically expected to be on the third or fourth rows of the grid.

'The car was a lot better in qualifying than it was this morning and in the first half of the weekend generally, especially in terms of grip and with the handling over the kerbs,' said Button afterwards. 'We did a lot of work overnight and through this morning and I'm much happier for the race. We'll have to see how things pan out, though, because we won't know until later what everyone has been doing through free practice, but I think we should feel quite confident.'

Renault also found itself slightly wrong-footed by Honda, Fernando Alonso having to be content with fifth place in his R26 on 1m 23.709s, although it was clear that he could probably run farther on his opening race stint than his closest rivals could. 'There was a lot of traffic during the third part of qualifying,' said the world champion, 'but when it came to doing my really quick laps at the end of the session the car felt good and the track was clear.'

Then came Ralf Schumacher's Toyota (1m 23.772s) followed by the two McLarens, with Juan Pablo Montoya (1m 24.021s) ahead of Kimi Räikkönen (1m 24.158s). It was a particularly disappointing performance for the Finn, who lost crucial fractions on the final sector of his qualifying lap and paid a high price as a result.

Next in line were Jarno Trulli's Toyota (1m 24.172s) and the Williams of Mark Webber (1m 24.795s).

The obvious name missing from the top ten was that of Giancarlo Fisichella, the second Renault driver, who had failed to make the cut at the end of the second qualifying quarter-hour.

'What can I say?' shrugged Fisichella. 'The balance of the car felt much better than it did yesterday, so we should have been in the top ten for sure. I think we may have made a mistake about the way we managed the second session, because I think we could have run again at the end, but this is something we will learn for the future.'

Also out after the second session were Jacques Villeneuve's BMW, Nico Rosberg's Williams, David Coulthard's Red Bull, Nick Heidfeld's BMW (which the German spun at the end of the mini-session) and Tonio Liuzzi's Toro Rosso – though Liuzzi had done well to get through the first qualifying quarter-hour.

Rosberg, in particular, had a bruising time after crashing his race car in free practice, which meant that his engine had to be switched into the spare FW28 chassis for his qualifying round. 'I must say thanks to the mechanics who managed to get the T-car ready for me in time for qualifying,' he said. 'But when we got into the second qualifying session it was difficult because the balance of the car had become a bit worse and I made two mistakes going wide, which wasted valuable tenths.' It was all part of the learning process for an F1 novice.

MICHAEL Schumacher put the Ferrari team right back in the F1 headlines on Maranello's home turf with a brilliantly judged tactical victory in the San Marino Grand Prix ahead of the world champion Fernando Alonso, whose Renault was just 2s behind at the chequered flag after a race-long battle that raised memories of the previous year's contest, from which the Spaniard had emerged victorious after a similarly close confrontation.

Yet as Schumacher celebrated his first victory of 2006, a success that seemed likely to accelerate his decision to continue driving into next season, he seemed both delighted and highly relieved that the flickering early promise displayed by the Ferrari 248 in the first few races of the season had now been firmly translated into a much more tangible performance bedrock.

'The result shows that work pays off and that the effort put in by everybody has delivered its reward,' he said. 'The key moment was staying ahead after the second round of pit stops. As we saw last year, overtaking at this track is almost impossible unless the guy in front makes a mistake.

'With all my years of experience, I knew that what I wanted to do was to keep Alonso behind me – but at my pace, not pushing flat out, and that's what I did.'

Nevertheless, although it seemed from the start that Schumacher's 85th career victory might be well within his grasp, he clearly was not going to have an easy ride. From second place on the front row of the grid, Jenson Button's Honda led the pursuit and dropped only 3.7s on the leading Ferrari 248 by the time Button came in for his first refuelling stop on lap 15. This left Felipe Massa's Ferrari running second but, when he stopped on lap 19, Alonso was up to second behind Schumacher and the Renault surged into the lead when the top Ferrari refuelled for the first time on lap 20.

Alonso pitted on lap 25 and, while he dropped back behind Schumacher, the fact that he had run an opening stint ten laps longer than Button's meant that he easily retained second place when he rejoined the fray 11.2s behind the Ferrari.

Alonso's prospects of victory now depended on some clever strategy from the Renault boffins on the pit wall. But as they crunched their way through complex computer calculations, they suddenly realised that their man was slashing great chunks out of Schumacher's advantage as the Ferrari driver apparently grappled with deteriorating grip on his second set of Bridgestones. In fact, Michael was running as gently as he dared, a strategy that had two effects. First, it kept his tyres

**Below: Christijan Albers was launched
into this spectacular roll by Yuji Ide on
the opening lap of the race. The Dutchman
was lucky to be unhurt.**

Photographs: Laurent Charniaux/WRI

in the best possible condition for his crucial in-lap prior to his final stop. Second, it may have sent out a slightly misleading signal to Renault that the red car looked slightly more tactically vulnerable than in fact it was.

From 11.2s on lap 26 Alonso trimmed Schumacher's lead to 0.4s on lap 34. The Renault team judged that the only real chance of passing the Ferrari would be if they could out-fox their rivals in the pits at their last stop.

Alonso came in on lap 41, Schumacher on the following lap. But it just wasn't enough for Alonso to leapfrog ahead. For the rest of the race he was left to hound the Ferrari but, when Alonso made a mistake and ran wide over a kerb with three laps to go, the German driver knew he was home and dry.

'It was great,' said Schumacher. 'What else can you say? Ferrari had an amazing weekend. We did a lot of work over the weekend. There was a big push from everybody and it paid off.'

Alonso finished the day in a sanguine frame of mind. 'Second place and eight points is the perfect result for me this afternoon,' said the world champion, a tad unconvincingly for a man more used to racking up the race wins.

'We suspected that we had qualified with more fuel than the others had and the race showed that we were right to pick that strategy. At a normal circuit, we could have won, but this is Imola, where overtaking is almost impossible. I could see that I was faster than Michael in the second stint and I was just trying to put pressure on him in the hope that he would make a mistake.'

He added, 'We did not plan to make our second stop when we did. We pitted early to try and overtake him but it didn't quite work. So I stayed in his slipstream and in the last five laps piled on all the revs the engine had and tried to overtake. But the Ferrari was a lot quicker in the end and it just didn't happen.'

Meanwhile Jenson Button was left rueing yet another lost opportunity as his prospects of a strong result from second on the grid evaporated in a bizarre episode at his second refuelling stop. This was the circuit where he'd started from pole in 2004 and led the opening phase of the race, so the Englishman started his weekend with high hopes of a strong result.

Button ran confidently in second place from the start, dropping only 3.7s to Schumacher's Ferrari 248 by the time he brought the Honda RA106 in for an early first stop at the end of lap 15, which unfortunately dropped him back to seventh. He was back to third place behind Schumacher and Alonso by the time he steered his Honda RA106 into the pit lane to fill up at the end of lap 30. It seemed as though the

**Above: Scott Speed delights over
his lampooning in the *Red Bulletin*,
F1's irreverent 'school magazine'.**

Photograph: XPB.cc

Happy or what? Spontaneous delight is written all over Michael Schumacher's face as he holds the winner's trophy aloft for all the crowd to see.

Photograph: James Moy/www.crashpa.net

Left: One of the Honda tyre men awaits
the split-second arrival of his charge.
Photograph: James Moy/www.crashpa.net

Below: The stylish new F1 logo for a whole
new range of quality merchandise.
Photograph: Jean-François Galeron/WRI

Below centre: Fernando Alonso, who finished second,
is obscured by the 'lollipop' during a Renault pit stop.
Photograph: Paul-Henri Cahier

Above: Ross Brawn and Michael Schumacher carry
the elated Felipe Massa towards the podium for the
first visit of his career.
Photograph: Peter Nygaard/GP Photo

Left: Michael Schumacher and Felipe Massa run in
team formation against the towering backdrop of
the huge Mercedes grandstand dominating the first
turn at the Nürburgring.
Photograph: James Moy/www.crashpa.net

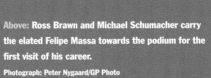

Above: Rubens Barrichello confers with his hugely experienced Honda engineer Jock Clear.
Photograph: Paul-Henri Cahier

Right: Franck Montagny joins the Super Aguri race team as Yuji Ide's replacement.
Photograph: Jean-François Galeron/WRI

Below: Christijan Albers prepares for a quick getaway.
Photograph: James Moy/www.crashpa.net

FERNANDO Alonso underscored his star quality in qualifying. Just as it seemed Michael Schumacher was allowing himself a flicker of a self-satisfied grin at having buttoned up a Ferrari/Bridgestone pole position in his personal backyard, the world champion came from nowhere to trump him by 0.2s.

Michael tried to conceal his disappointment but his fixed expression said it all. 'I am happy to be on the front row,' he said coolly. 'I have been strong all weekend so I can be optimistic about tomorrow's race. The fact that the Renault is on pole does not surprise me but I think I have a great chance of fighting for the win.'

For his part Alonso was guardedly confident, running a fuel load similar to his closest rivals' for the Renault's qualifying sprint. 'At previous races we have had problems with traffic or the fuel load, but today everything went smoothly and that made things much easier for me.'

Easy was certainly not how Giancarlo Fisichella found his qualifying session. He felt he had been badly balked by Jacques Villeneuve's BMW-Sauber and, despite the Canadian's protestations that he had not intended to get in Fisichella's way, the stewards disallowed Jacques's fastest time, which moved him down to tenth on the grid – though he then went up to ninth because Mark Webber ahead of him had an engine change penalty. That was still two ahead of Fisichella's eventual starting place and the Italian was scarcely mollified by the penalty.

'All I can say is that I am really angry, as people probably saw from the TV this afternoon,' he fumed. 'For me, Villeneuve's behaviour was unacceptable. As drivers, we know that if you are on the out-lap, you give way to the guys going past on their quick laps. But Villeneuve did not move over; he held me up all the way through the final sector and lost me a lot of time.'

Jacques, for his part, looked almost contrite. 'I am not exactly sure what happened,' he said. 'I thought I was ahead of him and I was trying to get out of his way; maybe I slowed him down a little bit, but I never thought he was that close to me. I will go and talk to him because it was not done on purpose.'

For the first time this year Rubens Barrichello seemed to have got on top of the handling of the Honda RA106 to take fourth place on the starting grid, two places ahead of the team's regular pace-setter Jenson Button, who confessed that the Nürburgring was a circuit on which he had always struggled.

'I couldn't get a good balance, which is pretty normal for me around here,' said Button. 'The car didn't feel good, so I wasn't feeling comfortable. I locked up into Turn One, which didn't help my last lap time but it didn't cost much – it probably wouldn't even have cost me a [grid] place.'

McLaren's Kimi Räikkönen lined up an eventual fifth, three places ahead of team-mate Juan Pablo Montoya. 'I am happy with the result today,' said the Finn, 'because we were not entirely comfortable with the car in the Friday sessions. Today was much better and I was able to push and get the best out of the car. Everyone has worked very hard and the balance of the car has really improved.'

By contrast, Montoya admitted that he was struggling slightly with the car's set-up and he didn't have a great qualifying lap as a result. Juan Pablo eventually took eighth on the grid behind Jarno Trulli's Toyota after Villeneuve took his one-place grid penalty.

With the Williams twosome taking their engine change penalties, Ralf Schumacher, Fisichella, David Coulthard's Red Bull and Nick Heidfeld's BMW-Sauber moved up to take positions ten to 12. For his part, Heidfeld – who'd been on pole here in 2005 with the Williams-BMW – was extremely disappointed to be outpaced by his team-mate.

'Of course I'm unhappy with my lap time and position,' he simmered. 'The car was not bad, although in the second half of the lap I had some understeer and the overall grip was not ideal. I don't know why I didn't manage to record a better time; we definitely didn't have the difficulties today we had here on Friday or at Imola.'

The remainder of the grid was made up by the usual suspects, with Vitantonio Liuzzi's Toro Rosso and Christian Klien's Red Bull lining up close behind Heidfeld, and Christijan Albers' Minardi just edging Scott Speed's Toro Rosso for 16th.

MONTAGNY REPLACES IDE AT SUPER AGURI

SUPER AGURI F1 confirmed that Frenchman Franck Montagny would replace Yuji Ide in the race team starting at the European Grand Prix only a fortnight after the inexperienced Japanese novice pitched Christijan Albers into a spectacular roll on the opening lap at Imola.

After Ide struggled to get on pace with his Japanese team-mate Takuma Sato in the first four races, the team demoted him to a testing role, acting on the advice of the governing body the FIA. Montagny therefore made his first Formula 1 start at the Nürburgring – the first French driver on the GP scene since Olivier Panis retired in 2004.

Team principal Aguri Suzuki said, 'We accept the advice offered by the FIA to allow Yuji to accrue the mileage he requires to improve in F1 during our testing days only. The team has made every effort to ensure that Yuji settled into his new F1 surroundings and I think that he has coped incredibly well under the circumstances.

'I wish that I could have given Yuji more time in the car before the start of the season, but with the team's being put together so rapidly we were unable to allow him the proper testing that he should have experienced. I will continue to look after Yuji's interests and support his continuing efforts within the team, including his path back to an F1 race seat. As a result, Franck Montagny will drive for us in the second race seat in the European Grand Prix.'

DIARY

Lewis Hamilton scores two dominant GP2 victories on the European GP supporting programme.

Former Jaguar F1 chief Tony Purnell is awarded £75,000 in damages and £132,000 in costs against _Business F1_ magazine after a UK High Court libel action.

Ray Bellm, the former BRDC chairman who resigned after a confrontation with then-president Sir Jackie Stewart, is voted back onto the board of the company that owns Silverstone.

Indy 500 veteran Al Unser Jr is confirmed as an entrant for the 2006 Memorial Day classic driving a Dallara-Honda under the A1 Team USA banner.

MICHAEL Schumacher sent another strong message to his rivals not to count on his imminent retirement from F1 by delivering a classic winning performance in the European Grand Prix, brilliantly turning the tables on reigning world champion Fernando Alonso at the last round of refuelling stops to post the 86th race victory of his career.

Alonso had qualified superbly on pole position for the first time this year and accelerated his Renault R26 cleanly into the lead at the start with the Ferrari 248s of Schumacher and Felipe Massa slotting into line astern formation in his wake and Jenson Button's Honda RA106 leading the pursuit from fourth place.

For the first 15 laps barely a second separated the two leaders, with Alonso demonstrating great composure under relentless pressure from the man he deposed as title holder at the end of last season. Neither man so much as put a wheel out of place and both drove with such disciplined precision that it quickly became clear that the race's outcome would almost certainly be decided by the unpredictable vagaries of their respective pit stop strategies.

On this occasion there seemed little to choose between Bridgestone and Michelin, although the former seemed to have a slight edge on single-lap pace from new. In fact, there was mounting evidence through free practice in the run-up to qualifying that Bridgestone might have the upper hand when it came to the race, possibly due to the fact that Michelin had offered too many compounds for its contracted teams to assess in the run-up to the Nürburgring event.

Newcomer Franck Montagny's Super Aguri, David Coulthard's Red Bull RB2 and Vitantonio Liuzzi's Toro Rosso tangled at the first corner, Liuzzi hobbling only midway around the opening lap in an attempt to return to the pits before a deflated right-rear tyre finally came off its rim and spun him out of the race.

'At the first corner Ralf [Schumacher] moved across and touched Tonio, who got knocked into the air and onto me,' explained Coulthard. 'It was just one of those racing incidents.' Coulthard pitted for a new nose cone, but there was further damage that the team was unable to repair and he stopped for good at the end of the second lap.

The safety car had been deployed so that the debris on the circuit could be cleared up and when it was withdrawn at the end of lap three Alonso and Schumacher settled into a fast rhythm, pulling steadily away from the rest of the pack. Massa held third from Button, Kimi Räikkönen, Jarno Trulli's Toyota and Rubens Barrichello in the other Honda. The third retirement of the day came on lap 13, when Mark Webber's Williams FW28 rolled to a standstill, an acutely disappointing end to a weekend in which the Australian had started from a distant 19th on the grid after both he and team-mate Nico Rosberg incurred penalties following engine changes at the end of Saturday morning practice.

'It was going fantastically well until what we think was a hydraulics problem meant that I lost all the controls,' said Webber. 'I'd made up seven places and I was still carrying a lot of fuel – enough to get me a long way into the race – so I'm sure it would have been easy to score some points today. From here, if we fix the hydraulic problem, I am sure we will run near the front.' In fact, team insiders suggested that he would not have refuelled until lap 34 and they reckoned that he might have been fifth by the end of the race, which would have been a good result from such a lowly starting position.

Alonso made his first scheduled refuelling stop at the end of lap 17 (7.5s), which allowed Michael ahead fleetingly until he brought the Ferrari in for its first stop next time around (7.9s). Schumi duly resumed in fourth, a few lengths behind Alonso, while Kimi Räikkönen's McLaren stormed across the line now leading the race by 9.1s from Button's Honda. Kimi remained out in the lead until bringing his MP4-21 in to refuel in 7.8s at the end of lap 23. That allowed Alonso back into the lead 2.1s ahead of Schumacher, with Massa still third and the Finn popping back into the queue in fourth.

Button's race finished on lap 29 with an engine failure just as Christian Klien's Red Bull rolled to a halt with transmission problems. 'It was a disappointing end to a fairly tough weekend, really,' said Jenson.

'I got a strong start and had a good tussle with Räikkönen through Turns One, Two and Three before I got ahead of him to take fourth place. But the car was inconsistent throughout the race. Some of it was down to the wind – it was quite gusty out there today – but the balance wasn't there and it was changing from corner to corner.

'In my second stint it was starting to come good as the fuel load came down and I would have been happy to finish fifth in a car I wasn't happy with and get four points. Instead, I had a big loss of power, the engine tightened and I lost drive so I had to pull over. Let's hope for better things in Spain.'

In the end it was Barrichello who picked up fifth at the chequered flag, but the Brazilian was only slightly less underwhelmed than his team-mate. 'Fifth is not what the team was hoping for, but at the end of the day we just didn't have the pace,' he admitted. 'I was struggling with the balance of the car

and it was just a case of surviving and doing the best I could.'

Alonso duly led into the second round of stops, coming in for a second time at the end of lap 38 for 8.8s. Michael immediately slammed in three very quick laps before coming in at the end of lap 41 when, aided in by an in-lap almost three seconds faster than Fernando's, he converted a 1.2s deficit into a 7.7s lead. Schumacher then cruised home to victory backed up admirably by his team-mate Felipe Massa, who took a strong third ahead of Kimi Räikkönen's McLaren-Mercedes MP4-21.

'On the car side, the engine side, the tyre side it was perfect,' said Schumacher. 'I thought we might have taken the lead at the first round of stops but I made a slight mistake at Turn Six [on my in-lap], but we knew from the start that we had the race pace.' Typically, the German driver was easy on his tyres and conserved just enough grip to pile on the pressure as soon as it was strategically necessary.

'It was an interesting race for me this afternoon,' said Alonso, with masterly understatement. 'I had a good start from pole position and controlled the race in the opening stint. The first stop went okay but I came in a couple of laps earlier than the Ferraris for the second stop and they had the speed to move ahead.'

Michelin would later hint that its prime runners Renault and McLaren had opted for a tyre choice that was too cool for the conditions on the Sunday, although the track temperature was almost exactly the same on race day as it had been during Saturday qualifying.

'I agree that we went too hard in our choice of tyre,' said Martin Whitmarsh, the McLaren chief executive, after Räikkönen came home a close fourth, having posted the second-fastest

Point of impact at the first corner as Vitantonio Liuzzi's Toro Rosso brushes David Coulthard's Red Bull, which then tags the sister car of Christian Klien.

Photographs: Breloer/XPB.cc

135

Above: **Felipe Massa, seen here running ahead of Rubens Barrichello, was delighted with his fine third for Ferrari.**

Top right: **Michael Schumacher gives Massa a champagne shampoo.**
Photographs: James Moy/www.crashpa.net

Centre: **Kimi Räikkönen looks glum after settling for fourth behind Massa.**
Photograph: Brousseau Photo

Centre right: **Job done, Michael Schumacher and his manager Willi Weber head for the door.**
Photograph: Peter Nygaard/GP Photo

Bottom right: **Jacques Villeneuve took the final point for BMW Sauber.**
Photograph: XPB.cc

lap of the race. 'If we'd selected the right tyre from Michelin's portfolio, we [Kimi] could have beaten the Ferraris.'

Unfortunately there was only one McLaren still running at the finish. Juan Pablo Montoya, mired in traffic for much of the distance after losing out badly at the first corner, suffered an engine failure six laps from the end while holding eighth place.

For his part, Massa was understandably delighted to have seen off Räikkönen's McLaren on his way to the first podium finish of his F1 career. 'The whole car was quite strong,' reported the elated Brazilian, 'especially at the beginning when I and Michael were pushing Fernando, and then suddenly they [Renault] got the pace.

'My car was quite consistent all race and the tyres were working well. Only in the last stint, when I had scrubbed tyres, were they not working so well. I had a great start and the strategy was perfect, too.'

Rounding off the points scorers were Giancarlo Fisichella's Renault in sixth ahead of the excellent Nico Rosberg's one-stopping Williams and Jacques Villeneuve's BMW-Sauber. Rosberg's was an outstanding performance from the back of the grid on a heavy fuel load, which went largely overlooked on a day when most attention was focused on the front of the field.

Fisichella was only 1.53s behind Barrichello as they crossed the line, the Italian having experienced an eventful race to climb back through the pack from 11th on the grid, a worthwhile reward for a mix of aggressive driving, good pit strategy and a couple of timely retirements.

'I had only one or two clear laps in the entire race,' said Fisi. 'It was hard to show my real pace, but I had a good strategy and was able to gain positions. The second pit stop [on lap 40] was a very nice point. I was very aggressive on the pit entry because I knew that this was the one real opportunity to pass Villeneuve, then the team did a fantastic job and got me out very quickly. I had a nice fight with Montoya going into Turn One, as well; it was not easy, but I managed to hold my position.'

Toyota had a disappointing time in its role as an 'adopted' German home team. Ralf Schumacher was delayed by the first-corner fracas, then used a long first stint to excellent effect to vault through to sixth by the time he made his first refuelling stop. He was well on course for a helping of points when his engine failed with eight laps to go.

'The car felt strong and we were doing competitive times,' he explained, 'but I was unlucky not to make it past Barrichello at the second stop. Of course we [at Toyota] are disappointed, because we were stronger in the race than expected.'

It was therefore left to Jarno Trulli to make it to the end alone, the Italian struggling for handling balance for much of the way to finish a lapped ninth between the BMW-Saubers of Villeneuve and Nick Heidfeld.

It had been a copybook performance from Michael in his own backyard. Now we had to wait and see what Fernando could deliver on *his* patch at Barcelona the following weekend.

Alan Henry

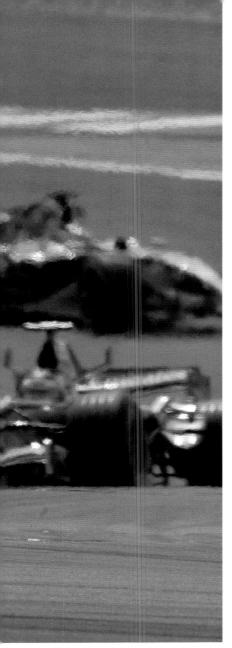

GRAND PRIX OF EUROPE

NÜRBURGRING 5–7 MAY 2006

NÜRBURGRING, NÜRBURG/EIFEL
Circuit: 3.199 miles / 5.148 km

Photograph: James Moy/www.crashpa.net

Dunlop-Kurve 60/96 **2**
Ford-Kurve 64/104 **2**
Audi-S 166/266 **5**
116/187 **mph/kmh** **4** Gear
Castrol-S 58/93 **1**
Michelin 84/136 **3**
Coca-Cola Kurve 80/128 **3**
Mercedes-Arena 113/182 **3**
Bit-Kurve 110/177 **4**
NGK-Schikane 170/273 **6**
Rheinland-Pfalz-Bogen 170/273 **6**

RACE RESULTS

Pos.	Driver	Nat.	No.	Entrant	Car/Engine	Tyres	Laps	Time/Retirement	Speed (mph/km/h)	Gap to leader	Fastest race lap	
1	Michael Schumacher	D	5	Scuderia Ferrari Marlboro	Ferrari 248 F1-056 V8	B	60	1h 35m 58.765s	119.974/193.080		1m 32.099s	39
2	Fernando Alonso	E	1	Mild Seven Renault F1 Team	Renault R26-RS26 V8	M	60	1h 36m 02.516s	119.897/192.955	+3.751s	1m 32.532s	37
3	Felipe Massa	BR	6	Scuderia Ferrari Marlboro	Ferrari 248 F1-056 V8	B	60	1h 36m 03.212s	119.882/192.931	+4.447s	1m 33.099s	19
4	Kimi Räikkönen	FIN	3	Team McLaren Mercedes	McLaren MP4-21-Mercedes FO 108S V8	M	60	1h 36m 03.644s	119.873/192.917	+4.879s	1m 32.472s	43
5	Rubens Barrichello	BR	11	Lucky Strike Honda Racing F1 Team	Honda RA106-RA806E V8	M	60	1h 37m 11.351s	118.481/190.677	+1m 12.586s	1m 33.952s	59
6	Giancarlo Fisichella	I	2	Mild Seven Renault F1 Team	Renault R26-RS26 V8	M	60	1h 37m 12.881s	118.450/190.627	+1m 14.116s	1m 32.964s	46
7	Nico Rosberg	D	10	WilliamsF1 Team	Williams FW28-Cosworth CA2006 V8	B	60	1h 37m 13.330s	118.441/190.612	+1m 14.565s	1m 33.579s	48
8	Jacques Villeneuve	CDN	17	BMW Sauber F1 Team	BMW Sauber F1.06-BMW P86 V8	M	60	1h 37m 28.129s	118.141/190.130	+1m 29.364s	1m 34.037s	38
9	Jarno Trulli	I	8	Panasonic Toyota Racing	Toyota TF106-RVX-06 V8	B	59			+1 lap	1m 33.953s	58
10	Nick Heidfeld	D	16	BMW Sauber F1 Team	BMW Sauber F1.06-BMW P86 V8	M	59			+1 lap	1m 34.035s	47
11	Scott Speed	USA	21	Scuderia Toro Rosso	Toro Rosso STR01-Cosworth TJ2005-2 V10	M	59			+1 lap	1m 34.091s	57
12	Tiago Monteiro	P	18	MF1 Racing	Midland M16-Toyota RVX-06 V8	B	59			+1 lap	1m 35.504s	41
13	Christijan Albers	NL	19	MF1 Racing	Midland M16-Toyota RVX-06 V8	B	59			+1 lap	1m 35.428s	35
	Ralf Schumacher	D	7	Panasonic Toyota Racing	Toyota TF106-RVX-06 V8	B	52	Engine			1m 33.607s	27
	Juan Pablo Montoya	COL	4	Team McLaren Mercedes	McLaren MP4-21-Mercedes FO 108S V8	M	52	Engine			1m 33.571s	47
	Takuma Sato	J	22	Super Aguri F1 Team	Super Aguri SA05-Honda RA806E V8	B	45	Hydraulics			1m 36.706s	26
	Franck Montagny	F	23	Super Aguri F1 Team	Super Aguri SA05-Honda RA806E V8	B	29	Hydraulics			1m 37.214s	21
	Jenson Button	GB	12	Lucky Strike Honda Racing F1 Team	Honda RA106-RA806E V8	M	28	Engine			1m 34.042s	9
	Christian Klien	A	15	Red Bull Racing	Red Bull RB2-Ferrari 056 V8	M	28	Transmission			1m 34.553s	16
	Mark Webber	AUS	9	WilliamsF1 Team	Williams FW28-Cosworth CA2006 V8	B	12	Hydraulics			1m 35.415s	11
	David Coulthard	GB	14	Red Bull Racing	Red Bull RB2-Ferrari 056 V8	M	2	Accident damage			2m 24.500s	2
	Vitantonio Liuzzi	I	20	Scuderia Toro Rosso	Toro Rosso STR01-Cosworth TJ2005-2 V10	M	0	Accident			No time	

All results and data © FOM 2006

Fastest lap: Michael Schumacher on lap 39, 1m 32.099s, 125.037 mph/201.226 km/h.

Lap record: Michael Schumacher (Ferrari F2004 V10), 1m 29.468s, 128.714 mph/207.144 km/h (2004).

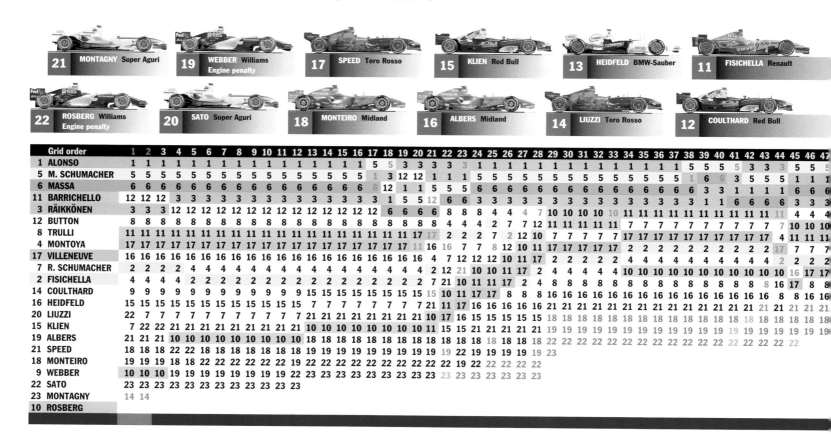

21 MONTAGNY Super Aguri
19 WEBBER Williams Engine penalty
17 SPEED Toro Rosso
15 KLIEN Red Bull
13 HEIDFELD BMW-Sauber
11 FISICHELLA Renault
22 ROSBERG Williams Engine penalty
20 SATO Super Aguri
18 MONTEIRO Midland
16 ALBERS Midland
14 LIUZZI Toro Rosso
12 COULTHARD Red Bull

Grid order	1	2	3	4	5	6	7	8	9	10	11	12	13	14	15	16	17	18	19	20	21	22	23	24	25	26	27	28	29	30	31	32	33	34	35	36	37	38	39	40	41	42	43	44	45	46	47
1 ALONSO	1	1	1	1	1	1	1	1	1	1	1	1	1	1	1	1	1	5	5	3	3	3	3	1	1	1	1	1	1	1	1	1	1	1	1	1	1	5	5	5	3	3	3	5	5	5	
5 M. SCHUMACHER	5	5	5	5	5	5	5	5	5	5	5	5	5	5	5	5	1	3	12	12	1	1	1	5	5	5	5	5	5	5	5	5	5	5	5	5	5	1	6	6	3	5	5	1	1	1	
6 MASSA	6	6	6	6	6	6	6	6	6	6	6	6	6	6	12	1	1	5	5	6	6	6	6	6	6	6	6	6	6	6	6	6	3	3	1	1	1	1	6	6	6						
11 BARRICHELLO	12	12	12	3	3	3	3	3	3	3	3	3	3	3	3	3	5	12	6	3	3	3	3	3	3	3	3	3	3	3	1	6	6	6	3	3	3										
3 RÄIKKÖNEN	3	3	3	12	12	12	12	12	12	12	12	12	12	12	12	6	6	6	8	8	4	4	7	10	10	10	10	11	11	11	11	11	11	11	6	6	6	3	3	3							
12 BUTTON	8	8	8	8	8	8	8	8	8	8	8	8	8	8	8	8	8	4	4	2	7	12	11	11	11	11	7	7	7	7	7	7	7	10	10												
8 TRULLI	11	11	11	11	11	11	11	11	11	11	11	11	11	11	11	11	17	2	2	7	2	12	10	7	7	7	7	17	17	17	17	17	17	17	4	11	11	11									
4 MONTOYA	17	17	17	17	17	17	17	17	17	17	17	17	17	17	17	11	16	7	7	8	12	10	11	17	17	17	2	2	2	2	2	2	17	7	7	7											
17 VILLENEUVE	16	16	16	16	16	16	16	16	16	16	16	16	16	16	4	7	12	12	10	11	17	17	17	2	2	2	4	4	4	4	4	2	2	2													
7 R. SCHUMACHER	2	2	2	4	4	4	4	4	4	4	4	4	4	4	2	12	11	10	11	17	2	4	10	10	10	10	10	10	10	10	8	8	8	8													
2 FISICHELLA	4	4	4	2	2	2	2	2	2	2	2	2	2	2	7	21	10	11	11	17	2	4	8	8	8	8	8	8	8	8	8	16	17	17													
14 COULTHARD	9	9	9	9	9	9	9	9	15	15	15	15	15	15	15	10	11	17	17	16	16	16	16	16	16	16	16	16	16	16	16	8	16	8	16												
16 HEIDFELD	15	15	15	15	15	15	15	7	7	7	7	7	7	7	21	16	16	16	16	21	21	21	21	21	21	21	21	21	21	21	21	21	21	21													
20 LIUZZI	22	21	21	21	21	21	21	21	21	21	21	21	21	21	16	15	15	15	15	18	18	18	18	18	18	18	18	18	18	18	18	18	18	18													
15 KLIEN	7	22	22	21	21	21	21	21	21	21	21	21	21	15	15	15	15	18	18	19	19	19	19	19	19	19	19	19	19	19	19	19															
19 ALBERS	21	21	21	10	10	10	10	10	10	10	10	10	18	18	18	18	18	22	22	22	22	22	22	22	22	22	22	22	22	22	22																
21 SPEED	18	18	18	22	22	18	18	18	18	18	18	18	19	19	19	19	19	19	23																											
18 MONTEIRO	19	19	19	18	18	22	22	22	22	22	22	22	22	22	19	22	22	22																												
9 WEBBER	10	10	10	19	19	19	19	19	19	19	19	23	23	23	23	23	23	23	23	23	23	23	23																							
22 SATO	23	23	23	23	23	23	23	23	23	23																																					
23 MONTAGNY	14	14																																													
10 ROSBERG																																															

PRACTICE 1 (FRIDAY)

Sunny (track 23–26ºC, air 17–18ºC)

Pos.	Driver	Laps	Time
1	Alexander Wurz	20	1m 32.079s
2	Anthony Davidson	29	1m 32.399s
3	Robert Kubica	22	1m 32.852s
4	Michael Schumacher	4	1m 32.858s
5	Robert Doornbos	19	1m 32.944s
6	Jenson Button	7	1m 33.635s
7	Rubens Barrichello	6	1m 34.213s
8	Kimi Räikkönen	5	1m 34.402s
9	Ralf Schumacher	6	1m 34.995s
10	Adrian Sutil	21	1m 35.332s
11	Neel Jani	19	1m 35.365s
12	Scott Speed	8	1m 35.612s
13	Christijan Albers	8	1m 35.985s
14	Tiago Monteiro	10	1m 36.062s
15	Takuma Sato	20	1m 37.817s
16	Franck Montagny	16	1m 37.933s
17	Fernando Alonso	2	No time
18	Giancarlo Fisichella	2	No time
19	Jarno Trulli	1	No time
20	Juan Pablo Montoya	1	No time
21	Christian Klien	1	No time
22	David Coulthard	1	No time
23	Vitantonio Liuzzi	2	No time

PRACTICE 2 (FRIDAY)

Sunny (track 30–32ºC, air 19–20ºC)

Pos.	Driver	Laps	Time
1	Alexander Wurz	27	1m 32.675s
2	Fernando Alonso	14	1m 33.579s
3	Michael Schumacher	14	1m 33.619s
4	Robert Doornbos	25	1m 33.799s
5	Anthony Davidson	29	1m 33.870s
6	Ralf Schumacher	19	1m 33.883s
7	Jenson Button	12	1m 33.920s
8	Robert Kubica	30	1m 33.991s
9	Giancarlo Fisichella	19	1m 34.030s
10	Adrian Sutil	23	1m 34.179s
11	Nico Rosberg	19	1m 34.215s
12	Christijan Albers	23	1m 34.472s
13	Kimi Räikkönen	13	1m 34.536s
14	Felipe Massa	18	1m 34.546s
15	Rubens Barrichello	11	1m 34.631s
16	Mark Webber	14	1m 34.825s
17	Juan Pablo Montoya	14	1m 34.968s
18	Christian Klien	19	1m 35.066s
19	David Coulthard	14	1m 35.241s
20	Nick Heidfeld	12	1m 35.308s
21	Vitantonio Liuzzi	19	1m 35.406s
22	Neel Jani	26	1m 35.479s
23	Scott Speed	21	1m 35.669s
24	Jacques Villeneuve	12	1m 35.688s
25	Tiago Monteiro	18	1m 35.902s
26	Takuma Sato	25	1m 36.255s
27	Franck Montagny	16	1m 36.665s
28	Jarno Trulli	5	No time

QUALIFYING (SATURDAY)

Sunny/breezy (track 30–32ºC, air 20ºC)

Pos.	Driver	First	Second	Third
1	Fernando Alonso	1m 31.138s	1m 30.336s	1m 29.819s
2	Michael Schumacher	1m 31.235s	1m 30.013s	1m 30.028s
3	Felipe Massa	1m 31.921s	1m 30.732s	1m 30.407s
4	Rubens Barrichello	1m 31.671s	1m 30.469s	1m 30.754s
5	Kimi Räikkönen	1m 31.263s	1m 30.203s	1m 30.933s
6	Jenson Button	1m 31.420s	1m 30.755s	1m 30.940s
7	Jarno Trulli	1m 31.809s	1m 30.733s	1m 31.419s
8	Jacques Villeneuve	1m 31.545s	1m 30.865s	1m 31.542s*
9	Juan Pablo Montoya	1m 31.774s	1m 30.671s	1m 31.880s
10	Mark Webber	1m 31.712s	1m 30.892s	1m 33.405s
11	Ralf Schumacher	1m 31.470s	1m 30.944s	
12	Nico Rosberg	1m 32.053s	1m 31.194s	
13	Giancarlo Fisichella	1m 31.574s	1m 31.197s	
14	David Coulthard	1m 31.742s	1m 31.227s	
15	Nick Heidfeld	1m 31.457s	1m 31.422s	
16	Vitantonio Liuzzi	1m 32.621s	1m 31.728s	
17	Christian Klien	1m 32.901s		
18	Christijan Albers	1m 32.936s		
19	Scott Speed	1m 32.992s		
20	Tiago Monteiro	1m 33.658s		
21	Takuma Sato	1m 35.239s		
22	Franck Montagny	1m 46.505s		

*Fastest time disallowed for blocking; Villeneuve dropped two grid slots

PRACTICE 3 (SATURDAY)

Sunny/breezy (track 23–28ºC, air 16–17ºC)

Pos.	Driver	Laps	Time
1	Michael Schumacher	12	1m 30.788s
2	Felipe Massa	10	1m 31.093s
3	Ralf Schumacher	21	1m 31.395s
4	Jacques Villeneuve	13	1m 31.531s
5	Giancarlo Fisichella	12	1m 31.584s
6	Fernando Alonso	14	1m 31.807s
7	Jenson Button	16	1m 32.104s
8	Christian Klien	13	1m 32.197s
9	Vitantonio Liuzzi	17	1m 32.290s
10	Kimi Räikkönen	11	1m 32.320s
11	Nico Rosberg	15	1m 32.459s
12	Scott Speed	18	1m 32.505s
13	Rubens Barrichello	18	1m 32.534s
14	Mark Webber	16	1m 32.711s
15	Nick Heidfeld	16	1m 32.773s
16	David Coulthard	15	1m 32.779s
17	Juan Pablo Montoya	12	1m 32.989s
18	Jarno Trulli	24	1m 33.120s
19	Tiago Monteiro	19	1m 33.744s
20	Christijan Albers	21	1m 34.469s
21	Franck Montagny	20	1m 35.706s
22	Takuma Sato	15	1m 36.082s

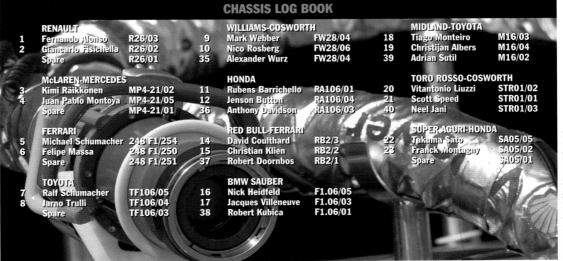

CHASSIS LOG BOOK

	RENAULT		
1	Fernando Alonso	R26/03	
2	Giancarlo Fisichella	R26/02	
	Spare	R26/01	35

	McLAREN-MERCEDES		
3	Kimi Räikkönen	MP4-21/02	
4	Juan Pablo Montoya	MP4-21/05	
	Spare	MP4-21/01	36

	FERRARI		
5	Michael Schumacher	248 F1/254	
6	Felipe Massa	248 F1/250	
	Spare	248 F1/251	37

	TOYOTA		
7	Ralf Schumacher	TF106/05	
8	Jarno Trulli	TF106/04	
	Spare	TF106/03	38

	WILLIAMS-COSWORTH		
9	Mark Webber	FW28/04	
10	Nico Rosberg	FW28/06	
	Alexander Wurz	FW28/04	39

	HONDA		
11	Rubens Barrichello	RA106/01	
12	Jenson Button	RA106/04	
	Anthony Davidson	RA106/03	40

	RED BULL-FERRARI		
14	David Coulthard	RB2/3	
15	Christian Klien	RB2/2	
	Robert Doornbos	RB2/1	

	BMW SAUBER		
16	Nick Heidfeld	F1.06/05	
17	Jacques Villeneuve	F1.06/03	
	Robert Kubica	F1.06/01	

	MIDLAND-TOYOTA		
18	Tiago Monteiro	M16/03	
19	Christijan Albers	M16/04	
	Adrian Sutil	M16/02	

	TORO ROSSO-COSWORTH		
20	Vitantonio Liuzzi	STR01/02	
21	Scott Speed	STR01/01	
	Neel Jani	STR01/03	

	SUPER AGURI-HONDA		
22	Takuma Sato	SA05/05	
23	Franck Montagny	SA05/02	
	Spare	SA05/01	

Photograph: James Moy/www.crashpa.net

Grid

9 VILLENEUVE BMW-Sauber — Misdemeanour penalty

7 TRULLI Toyota

5 RÄIKKÖNEN McLaren

3 MASSA Ferrari

1 ALONSO Renault

10 R. SCHUMACHER Toyota

8 MONTOYA McLaren

6 BUTTON Honda

4 BARRICHELLO Honda

2 M. SCHUMACHER Ferrari

RACE DISTANCE:
60 laps
191.919 miles/308.863 km

RACE WEATHER:
Sunny/breezy
track 29–30ºC, air 19–20ºC

Lap chart

48	49	50	51	52	53	54	55	56	57	58	59	60	
5	5	5	5	5	5	5	5	5	5	5	5	5	1
1	1	1	1	1	1	1	1	1	1	1	1	1	2
6	6	6	6	6	6	6	6	6	6	6	6	6	3
3	3	3	3	3	3	3	3	3	3	3	3	3	4
10	10	11	11	11	11	11	11	11	11	11	11	11	5
4	11	7	7	7	2	2	2	2	2	2	2	2	6
11	7	2	2	2	10	10	10	10	10	10	10	10	7
7	2	10	10	10	17	17	17	17	17	17	17	17	8
2	4	4	4	4		8	8	8	8	8	8	8	
17	17	17	17	17		16	16	16	16	16	16	16	
8	8	8	8	21	21	21	21	21	21	21			
16	16	16	16	16	18	18	18	18	18	18	18		
21	21	21	21	21	19	19	19	19	19	19	19		
18	18	18	18	18									
19	19	19	19	19									

Pit stop
One lap or more behind leader
Safety car deployed on laps shown

FOR THE RECORD

600th GRAND PRIX START: McLaren
150th GRAND PRIX START: Ralf Schumacher
FIRST GRAND PRIX START:
Franck Montagny
TENTH POLE POSITION: Fernando Alonso
FIRST PODIUM: Felipe Massa (above)
70th FASTEST LAP: Michael Schumacher
300th POINT: Kimi Räikkönen

POINTS

	DRIVERS				CONSTRUCTORS	
1	Fernando Alonso	44		1	Renault	62
2	Michael Schumacher	31		2	Ferrari	46
3	Kimi Räikkönen	23		3	McLaren	38
4	Giancarlo Fisichella	18		4	Honda	19
5	Felipe Massa	15		5	BMW Sauber	11
6	Juan Pablo Montoya	15		6	Williams	10
7	Jenson Button	13		7	Toyota	7
8	Ralf Schumacher	7		8	Red Bull	2
9	Rubens Barrichello	6				
10	Mark Webber	6				
11	Jacques Villeneuve	6				
12	Nick Heidfeld	5				
13	Nico Rosberg	4				
14	David Coulthard	1				
15	Christian Klien	1				

Photographs: James Moy/www.crashpa.net

Out on his own to the delight of his countrymen, Fernando Alonso in the Renault R26 interrupted a run of two straight Ferrari victories. The reigning world champion won dominantly from the front.
Photograph: Brousseau Photo

FIA F1 WORLD CHAMPIONSHIP/ROUND 6

SPANISH GP

CATALUNYA

CATALUNYA QUALIFYING

MICHAEL Schumacher's best grid time was a 1m 14.970s, 0.3s away from Fernando Alonso's pole winner. But before taking on his race fuel at the start of the third qualifying segment he'd posted an absolute fastest overall lap of 1m 14.637s, during the second qualifying stint. The message was clear: Michael was running slightly more fuel than the Renaults in the final shoot-out. But it didn't help.

'I don't think even 66 laps tomorrow will be enough for me to enjoy this race,' said Alonso after trumping the opposition. 'It's fantastic to be on pole because the times have been very close all the way through practice, probably because we test a lot at this circuit, and we expected the qualifying session to be tough. In fact, we [everyone in the Renault team] were more nervous about the second than the third session before qualifying started. Like at the Nürburgring, we were not so happy in the second part, but we managed to find something extra in the third session, so I am really happy to take my second consecutive pole.'

Fisichella was delighted to join the world champion on the front row of the grid, but never remotely underestimated the challenge posed by the two Ferraris lined up side by side on the second row.

On the next row, Rubens Barrichello took fifth with 1m 15.885s, ahead of the Toyota TF106s of Ralf Schumacher (1m 15.885s) – equalling the Honda to three decimal points – and Jarno Trulli (1m 15.976s). Both the Toyota boys were pretty satisfied, although Trulli had a touch too much understeer for his liking. Looking on the bright side, though, Jarno reckoned the team had worked hard to eliminate problems with tyre graining, which opened the prospect of a reasonably promising race.

Jenson Button, Kimi Räikkönen and Nick Heidfeld were the other runners who'd made it through to the top ten shoot-out, but both Williams drivers, Juan Pablo Montoya and the other BMW-Sauber of Jacques Villeneuve had to be content with placings outside the top ten. In fact, it got far worse for Jacques when he had to take a ten-place penalty for an engine change, which dropped him right to the back of the grid. The V8 had been dropped in transit to Barcelona and could not be used.

'We got a bit of an idea in testing that maybe it was going to be a little bit difficult for us here,' said Mark Webber, who had to be content with an 11th-fastest 1m 15.502s – although if he'd got through into third qualifying and turned that time it would have been good enough for fifth overall on the grid. 'But you only really confirm this on the day and we found out that we were just a sniff away from making it into the top ten. This was the first time this year that I didn't make it.'

Nico Rosberg wound up 13th on 1m 15.804s, the Williams duo sandwiching Montoya, who could post only a 1m 15.801s at the wrong moment. 'I'm really disappointed,' shrugged Juan Pablo. 'There was a problem when I came in to get my car refuelled; my tyres lost a lot of heat and we should have changed to a new set. These things happen, I'm afraid, but they are very frustrating.'

Completing the second-session runners were Christian Klien's Red Bull and Vitantonio Liuzzi's Toro Rosso, while the Italian's team-mate Scott Speed was just outside the next cut-off point in 17th. Those bumped from the contest in the first session included the usual suspects, with the honourable exception of David Coulthard, whose efforts were thwarted after he spun early on due to a technical problem.

F1 COMMERCIAL DEAL AGREED AT LAST

ON the morning of the Spanish GP it seemed as though Christmas had come early for the 11 currently competing F1 teams, with the resolution of a battle for more cash that has raged for more than three years between the competitors and Bernie Ecclestone, the sport's commercial rights holder, who last year sold his holding company SLEC to the investment company CVC Capital Partners.

The finishing touches to the new contract were finalised behind the smoked-glass windows of Ecclestone's $2-million motor home, which dominated the entrance to the paddock at the Circuit de Catalunya throughout the weekend, as it does at most grands prix.

Under the complex new deal, the precise details of which were being kept secret by the parties involved, the teams stood to double their income from the sport's commercial rights pot. It was anticipated that the top ten teams would now share 50 percent of the sport's total $700-million income rather than 47 percent of the $450m generated solely from television coverage and race promotion fees.

The teams had originally demanded 60 percent from the start of 2008 but Ecclestone stuck firm with an offer of 50 percent, leaving the negotiations apparently deadlocked ten days earlier, immediately prior to the San Marino Grand Prix. Finally the deadlock seemed to have been broken with Ecclestone and CVC sticking on 50 percent but agreeing to backdate the rise to come into force immediately, rather than from the start of 2008 when the current Concorde Agreement covering all the commercial and reglementary aspects of the sport expires.

The deal brought the five teams grouped loosely under the Grand Prix Manufacturers' Association alliance – Toyota, Renault, BMW Sauber, McLaren Mercedes and Honda – into line with those other teams which had already signed a commercial deal with Ecclestone. Those already committed included Ferrari, Williams, Midland, Red Bull, Toro Rosso and Super Aguri.

The Renault F1 squad was quick to confirm that it had reinforced its commitment to the sport after agreeing to sign a deal with Bernie Ecclestone's F1 administration empire to guarantee the French car maker's participation in the world championship beyond 2008.

'The agreement the team has reached today with the FOA expresses [Renault's] commitment to F1,' said the new Renault F1 president, Alain Dassas. 'Having entered the 2008 world championship last month, this is the next, logical step to guarantee the financial stability and competitiveness of the team.' Dassas, interestingly, did not rule out rebranding the Renault team under the title of its Nissan or Infiniti associated companies at some point in the future.

Norbert Haug, the Mercedes Motorsport vice president, added that he was now upbeat and optimistic about the sport's future. 'I think the prospects for F1 are better than ever,' he said. 'I think there is a positive and fruitful process in place. The manufacturers and their teams are in this for the long term, I'm quite sure. I'm certainly much more optimistic than I was three or five years ago.'

WAS it a decisive shift in the balance of F1 power? Or was it simply a Rafael Nadal-style backhander across the net designed to unsettle Michael Schumacher and remind the seven-times world champion that Fernando Alonso's second crown was a more likely outcome from the 2006 season than the Ferrari driver's eighth? It was obviously difficult to judge the significance of the moment before the Spaniard's home race had slipped into the context of the season. But, for now, all that mattered was that Fernando had brilliantly turned the tables on his most formidable rival to score a memorable home victory in front of a 130,000-strong crowd of his most passionate supporters.

'Fantastic,' said a delighted Alonso as he stepped down from the podium after receiving his trophy from King Juan Carlos. 'During the last five or six laps I saw that Michael was slowing down as well and not pushing anymore, so there were four or five laps when I was cruising to the end.

'Winning in front of everyone – my people, my supporters – it was the best feeling in an F1 car; it was equal to Brazil [last year], winning my championship, but there I finished third after a lot of problems and I didn't enjoy that race as much as today's.'

Going into the weekend, most F1 insiders believed that the potential performance differential between the Michelin-shod Renault and the Bridgestone-equipped Ferrari would be very close, but while Michael Schumacher performed with all the single-mindedness he could muster, there was no way he could find that extra pace that would have allowed him to compete with Alonso at the front of the pack.

Alonso burst into the lead from the start, completing the first of the afternoon's 66 gruelling laps already 1.4s ahead of his Renault team-mate Giancarlo Fisichella. Schumacher ran third ahead of his Ferrari colleague Felipe Massa, but confessed that he never quite had the speed to get on terms with Fisichella, let alone Alonso, in the opening phase of what promised to be yet another strategic contest.

With only four laps completed, Alonso was already 3.8s ahead of Fisichella and 5.7s covered the leading threesome. Massa was dropping away slightly in fourth ahead of Kimi Räikkönen's McLaren MP4-21 and the Honda RA106s of Rubens Barrichello and Jenson Button.

When Alonso came in for his first refuelling stop after only 17 laps, Fisichella briefly inherited the lead, but he made his first stop next time around, allowing Schumacher to surge confidently to the head of the field, where he stayed until he too dodged in for fuel, at the end of lap 23.

Michael proved quick enough to vault ahead of Fisichella for second place through this first round of stops, then settled down for a lonely run. Alonso made his second stop on lap 40, allowing the Ferrari back ahead again, but he regained the lead when Schumacher stopped on lap 46, after which the Spanish hero had it all his own way.

'We were expecting a very close race and that's what we got,' said Ferrari chief Jean Todt, 'although obviously we were hoping that it would work out in our favour. We had opted for a strategy that meant carrying a bit more fuel at the start than those ahead of us on the grid, but it did not work out for us and our rivals were stronger.'

After dominating at Imola and the Nürburgring, Schumacher seemed relaxed about being pushed back to the inside of the second row behind Renault twins Alonso and Fisichella in Saturday's qualifying session. In a bid to avoid tyre graining on a track surface washed clean by overnight rain on Thursday

Above: Juan Pablo Montoya abandons his McLaren MP4-21 after spinning off over a kerb.

Left: How many? Felipe Massa ponders Fernando Alonso's winning advantage.
Photographs: Jad Sherif/WRI

Centre left: Christijan Albers finds it all a bit depressing and decides that he's heard enough for now.
Photograph: James Moy/www.crashpa.net

Far left: Tiago Monteiro and Franck Montagny continue the car bashing between Midland and Super Aguri Racing.
Photograph: Lukas Gorys

and Friday, the two Ferrari drivers opted for the harder of the two Bridgestone compounds and the seven-times champion was well satisfied with the result.

Fisichella, who always relishes the challenge thrown up by the Circuit de Catalunya, could hardly have been more satisfied with his eventual third place in such exalted company. 'I got a fantastic start and things were close with Fernando into the first corner, but he had the advantage so I let him go,' said the Italian.

'After that the balance of the car was not perfect and so even though I was pulling away from Michael in the [opening] stint, it was not enough to stay ahead of him at the stops. We made some changes to give less oversteer and so when I came out behind him I was pushing hard. But then I made a small mistake that put me in the gravel at Turn Three. But I didn't lose a position and I just kept pushing hard to keep

Massa behind me in the second stops. I kept third quite easily, then after that I just looked after everything to the finish.'

Farther back, McLaren had a disappointing race, with Kimi Räikkönen battling lack of rear-end grip on the high-speed corners to bring his Mercedes-engined challenger home fifth on a day when team-mate Juan Pablo Montoya blotted his copybook by spinning off. 'McLaren was the second-fastest Michelin team,' said McLaren's Martin Whitmarsh. You could see his point, even though it offered little by way of consolation. For his part, Räikkönen just described it as 'a rather uneventful race for me.'

Montoya's post-race comments suggested a touch of bewilderment on the part of the Colombian driver. 'I made a dreadful start off the line and lost three or four places but managed to gain ground again in the first corner to end up 11th,' he explained. 'Then I don't know quite what happened, but

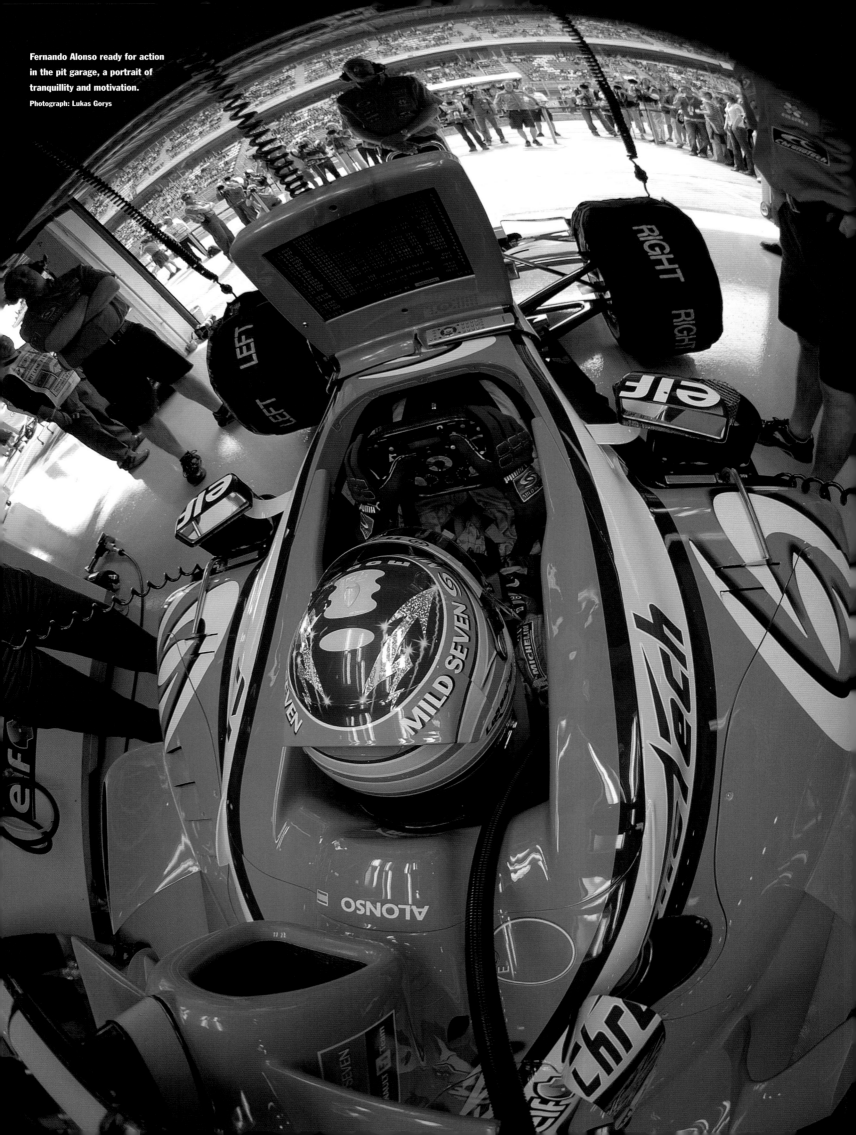

Fernando Alonso ready for action in the pit garage, a portrait of tranquillity and motivation.
Photograph: Lukas Gorys

Below: Jenson Button had to settle for fifth, his Honda still not quite quick enough to run in the leading bunch.
Photograph: Laurent Charniaux/WRI

I lost the car and got stuck on the kerb and that was it. The strategy I was running meant that I carried a lot of fuel and I think with the way things were I could have scored some points today. Overall it was a difficult weekend for us [the team].'

Jenson Button yet again played no more than a supporting role for Honda, qualifying eighth after grappling with too much understeer, then coming home sixth ahead of his team-mate Rubens Barrichello, who was lapped by Alonso's Renault.

In qualifying, Button had been shaded by Barrichello, having made a front-wing adjustment that left him with a serious handling imbalance. 'I'm extremely disappointed to qualify in eighth position,' he said. 'The car balance was fine until I asked for a little more front wing. Normally you would expect to get a better front end on the car but I had massive understeer – far more than we would have expected.'

Come the race, things were, thankfully, slightly better. 'The car worked well and it was pretty much a faultless race, although I was behind Rubens in the first stint and Räikkönen was able to pull away,' said Jenson. 'As soon as I had clear air the car worked very well and the balance was good – probably the best it has been since Malaysia. I was quite happy, reeling in Räikkönen every lap by a tenth or two, but it would have been a closer fight had I not been hampered by problems that stemmed from yesterday's qualifying.'

Button's fans, many of whom were poised to make the trip to Monaco to cheer on their hero a fortnight later, were left hoping that the high-downforce environment through the streets of Monte Carlo might help Button deliver the best result of his season so far. Jenson started the year hoping against hope for a win but, coming out of another disappointment at Barcelona, a repeat of his 2004 second place to Jarno Trulli's Renault would do nicely.

Still, for a sliver of consolation the Honda squad could at least be satisfied that it had a better day in Spain than close rival Toyota, whose Ralf Schumacher drove into the back of his team-mate Jarno Trulli. Both men shrugged it off as a racing accident but in reality it was a notably absurd incident between a couple of highly paid, supremely experienced F1 competitors who should have known better.

'Early on when Ralf and I were racing we were on similar strategies,' explained Trulli. 'But I was on old tyres and suffering from graining and he was quicker. When he made the move on me, I just took my usual driving line. I didn't deliberately close the door and I didn't do anything unusual. No one was to blame; it just goes down as a racing incident.'

For his part, Ralf was correspondingly conciliatory. 'At Toyota we go to the grid as racing drivers and in a race we are allowed to overtake each other,' he agreed. 'So that means sometimes things like this can happen.' Trulli went on to finish tenth but his team-mate eventually retired with an electronics problem.

Behind Barrichello, the remaining point for eighth place went to Nick Heidfeld, who at least ended the day a whole lot happier than BMW Sauber team-mate Jacques Villeneuve, who could manage no better than 12th, separated from his German colleague by Mark Webber's Williams, Trulli's Toyota and Nico Rosberg's Williams.

'I had a good start,' said Villeneuve, 'but the two Super Aguris had amazing starts and then there were cars in front and there was nowhere to go. It was a question of braking late. I was next to David Coulthard, but then he pushed me wide a little bit, which was fair. I lost six seconds in the first two or three laps and that was it.'

Neither Williams driver was at all satisfied about coming away from the grand prix without any championship points and the race gave Rosberg his first experience of being lapped at the wheel of an F1 car. It amused him no more than it did the rest of the team personnel.

There wasn't much to shout about in the Red Bull camp, either. Coulthard trailed home 14th behind team-mate Christian Klien after what he described as 'a bit of a long, lonely race'. He added, 'I had a problem with the brakes while driving to the grid and locked up about three or four times, and I wasn't able to attack the corners for the entire race.'

From that standpoint it was clear that Alonso and Schumacher were inhabiting pretty much a different planet. For now and for the foreseeable future.

Alan Henry

DIARY

Nelson Piquet Jr emerges from the weekend still just leading the GP2 championship after taking fourth and second in the two races.

Fernando Alonso hits out at criticism from Bernie Ecclestone, who says that the world champion does not do enough to promote F1.

Plans for a possible second Spanish F1 race – at Valencia, perhaps titled the Mediterranean GP – continue to be the focus of much speculation.

GRAN PREMIO TELEFÓNICA DE ESPAÑA
CATALUNYA 12–14 MAY 2006

CIRCUIT DE CATALUNYA, MONTMELO, BARCELONA

Renault 142/228 **4**
Repsol 84/135 **3**
Seat 55/88 **2**
Campsa 124/200 **3**
Europcar 80/128 **2**
Banc Sabadell 80/128 **2**
Würth 85/136 **2**
Elf 87/139 **2**
La Caixa 50/80 **2**
190/305 **7**
New Holland 140/225 **4**

Circuit:
2.875 miles/ 4.627 km
116/187 mph/kmh
4 Gear

Photograph: Russell Batchelor/XPB.cc

RACE RESULTS

Pos.	Driver	Nat.	No.	Entrant	Car/Engine	Tyres	Laps	Time/Retirement	Speed (mph/km/h)	Gap to leader	Fastest race lap	
1	Fernando Alonso	E	1	Mild Seven Renault F1 Team	Renault R26-RS26 V8	M	66	1h 26m 21.759s	131.777/212.074		1m 16.723s	39
2	Michael Schumacher	D	5	Scuderia Ferrari Marlboro	Ferrari 248 F1-056 V8	B	66	1h 26m 40.261s	131.308/211.320	+18.502s	1m 16.922s	43
3	Giancarlo Fisichella	I	2	Mild Seven Renault F1 Team	Renault R26-RS26 V8	M	66	1h 26m 45.710s	131.171/211.099	+23.951s	1m 17.083s	38
4	Felipe Massa	BR	6	Scuderia Ferrari Marlboro	Ferrari 248 F1-056 V8	B	66	1h 26m 51.618s	131.022/210.859	+29.859s	1m 16.648s	42
5	Kimi Räikkönen	FIN	3	Team McLaren Mercedes	McLaren MP4-21-Mercedes FO 108S V8	M	66	1h 27m 18.634s	130.346/209.772	+56.875s	1m 17.357s	40
6	Jenson Button	GB	12	Lucky Strike Honda Racing F1 Team	Honda RA106-RA806E V8	M	66	1h 27m 20.106s	130.309/209.713	+58.347s	1m 17.367s	40
7	Rubens Barrichello	BR	11	Lucky Strike Honda Racing F1 Team	Honda RA106-RA806E V8	M	65			+1 lap	1m 17.399s	40
8	Nick Heidfeld	D	16	BMW Sauber F1 Team	BMW Sauber F1.06-BMW P86 V8	M	65			+1 lap	1m 17.869s	49
9	Mark Webber	AUS	9	WilliamsF1 Team	Williams FW28-Cosworth CA2006 V8	B	65			+1 lap	1m 17.900s	61
10	Jarno Trulli	I	8	Panasonic Toyota Racing	Toyota TF106-RVX-06 V8	B	65			+1 lap	1m 18.465s	42
11	Nico Rosberg	D	10	WilliamsF1 Team	Williams FW28-Cosworth CA2006 V8	B	65			+1 lap	1m 17.861s	51
12	Jacques Villeneuve	CDN	17	BMW Sauber F1 Team	BMW Sauber F1.06-BMW P86 V8	M	65			+1 lap	1m 18.050s	62
13	Christian Klien	A	15	Red Bull Racing	Red Bull RB2-Ferrari 056 V8	M	65			+1 lap	1m 18.516s	59
14	David Coulthard	GB	14	Red Bull Racing	Red Bull RB2-Ferrari 056 V8	M	65			+1 lap	1m 17.862s	55
15	Vitantonio Liuzzi	I	20	Scuderia Toro Rosso	Toro Rosso STR01-Cosworth TJ2005-2 V10	M	63	Hydraulics		+3 laps	1m 18.488s	52
16	Tiago Monteiro	P	18	MF1 Racing	Midland M16-Toyota RVX-06 V8	B	63			+3 laps	1m 19.265s	38
17	Takuma Sato	J	22	Super Aguri F1 Team	Super Aguri SA05-Honda RA806E V8	B	62			+4 laps	1m 20.411s	42
	Christijan Albers	NL	19	MF1 Racing	Midland M16-Toyota RVX-06 V8	B	48	Front wing/spin			1m 19.532s	28
	Scott Speed	USA	21	Scuderia Toro Rosso	Toro Rosso STR01-Cosworth TJ2005-2 V10	M	47	Engine			1m 18.541s	41
	Ralf Schumacher	D	7	Panasonic Toyota Racing	Toyota TF106-RVX-06 V8	B	31	Electronics			1m 18.621s	24
	Juan Pablo Montoya	COL	4	Team McLaren Mercedes	McLaren MP4-21-Mercedes FO 108S V8	M	17	Spin			1m 19.482s	17
	Franck Montagny	F	23	Super Aguri F1 Team	Super Aguri SA05-Honda RA806E V8	B	10	Driveshaft			1m 22.389s	9

Fastest lap: Felipe Massa on lap 42, 1m 16.648s, 135.037 mph/217.320 km/h.

Lap record: Giancarlo Fisichella (Renault R25 V10), 1m 15.641s, 136.835 mph/220.213 km/h (2005).

All results and data © FOM 2006

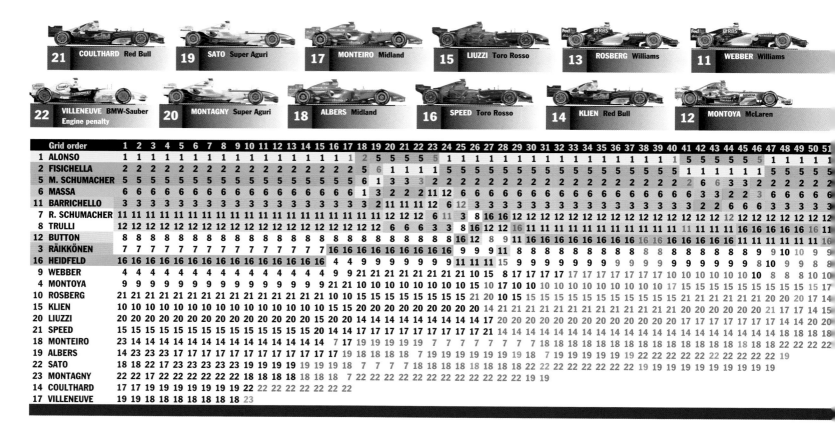

Grid order	1	2	3	4	5	6	7	8	9	10	11	12	13	14	15	16	17	18	19	20	21	22	23	24	25	26	27	28	29	30	31	32	33	34	35	36	37	38	39	40	41	42	43	44	45	46	47	48	49	50	51
1 ALONSO	1	1	1	1	1	1	1	1	1	1	1	1	1	1	1	1	1	2	5	5	5	5	5	1	1	1	1	1	1	1	1	1	1	1	1	1	1	1	1	1	5	5	5	5	5	5	1	1	1	1	1
2 FISICHELLA	2	2	2	2	2	2	2	2	2	2	2	2	2	2	2	2	5	6	1	1	1	1	5	5	5	5	5	5	5	5	5	5	5	5	5	5	5	5	1	1	1	1	1	5	5	5	5
5 M. SCHUMACHER	5	5	5	5	5	5	5	5	5	5	5	5	5	5	5	5	6	1	3	3	3	2	2	2	2	2	2	2	2	2	2	2	2	2	2	2	2	2	6	3	3	2	2	2	2	2
6 MASSA	6	6	6	6	6	6	6	6	6	6	6	6	6	6	6	6	1	3	2	2	11	12	6	6	6	6	6	6	6	6	6	6	6	6	6	6	6	6	3	6	6	6	6	6
11 BARRICHELLO	3	3	3	3	3	3	3	3	3	3	3	3	3	3	3	3	3	2	11	11	12	6	12	3	3	3	3	3	3	3	3	3	3	3	3	3	3	2	2	6	6	3	3	3
7 R. SCHUMACHER	11	11	11	11	11	11	11	11	11	11	11	11	11	11	11	11	11	12	12	12	6	11	3	8	16	16	12	12	12	12	12	12	12	12	12	12	12	12	12	12	12	12	12	12
8 TRULLI	12	12	12	12	12	12	12	12	12	12	12	12	12	12	12	12	6	6	6	3	3	8	16	12	12	16	11	11	11	11	11	11	11	11	11	11	11	11	16	16	16	16	16	11
12 BUTTON	8	8	8	8	8	8	8	8	8	8	8	8	8	8	8	8	8	8	16	12	8	9	11	16	16	16	16	16	16	16	16	16	16	16	16	16	16	11	11	11	11	11	11	16
3 RÄIKKÖNEN	7	7	7	7	7	7	7	7	7	7	7	7	7	7	7	16	16	16	16	16	16	16	9	9	9	11	8	8	8	8	8	8	8	8	8	8	8	8	8	9	10	10	9	9
16 HEIDFELD	16	16	16	16	16	16	16	16	16	16	16	16	16	16	4	4	9	9	9	9	9	9	11	11	11	15	9	9	9	9	9	9	9	9	9	9	9	9	9	8	10	9	8	8
9 WEBBER	4	4	4	4	4	4	4	4	4	4	9	21	21	21	21	21	21	21	15	8	17	17	17	17	17	17	17	17	17	10	10	10	10	10	10	8	10	8	8	10	10
4 MONTOYA	9	9	9	9	9	9	9	9	9	9	21	10	10	10	10	10	10	10	10	15	10	17	10	10	10	10	10	10	10	17	15	15	15	15	15	15	15	17
10 ROSBERG	21	21	21	21	21	21	21	21	21	21	10	15	15	15	15	15	20	20	20	10	15	10	15	15	15	15	15	15	15	15	20	20	20	20	20	20	20	20	20	17	14
15 KLIEN	10	10	10	10	10	10	10	10	10	10	15	20	20	20	20	20	14	21	21	21	21	21	21	21	21	21	21	21	21	21	21	17	17	14	15
20 LIUZZI	20	20	20	20	20	20	20	20	20	20	20	14	14	14	14	14	17	14	14	14	14	14	14	14	14	14	14	14	14	14	14	21	17	17	14	14
21 SPEED	15	15	15	15	15	15	15	15	15	15	14	14	17	17	17	17	14	17	17	17	17	17	14	14	14	14	14	14	14	7	7	7	18	18	18	18
18 MONTEIRO	23	14	14	14	14	14	14	14	14	14	14	14	14	14	7	17	19	19	19	7	7	7	7	18	18	18	18	18	18	18	18	18	18	18	22	22
19 ALBERS	14	23	23	23	17	17	17	17	17	17	17	17	17	17	19	18	18	18	18	18	18	18	7	19	19	19	19	19	19	19	19	22	22	22	22	19
22 SATO	18	18	22	17	23	23	23	23	23	23	19	19	19	19	19	7	7	7	7	18	18	18	18	22	22	22	22	22	22	19	19	19	19	19	19
23 MONTAGNY	22	22	17	22	22	22	22	22	18	18	18	18	18	18	7	2	2	2	18	22	22	22	22	22	22	22	22	19	19	19	19	19	19
14 COULTHARD	17	17	19	19	19	19	19	19	22	19	22	22	22	22	18	22	22	22	22	22
17 VILLENEUVE	19	19	18	18	18	18	18	18	18	18	23

148

PRACTICE 1 (FRIDAY)
Overcast then sunny (track 22–28°C, air 18–20°C)

Pos.	Driver	Laps	Time
1	Felipe Massa	4	1m 15.796s
2	Michael Schumacher	4	1m 16.099s
3	Alexander Wurz	21	1m 16.125s
4	Robert Kubica	21	1m 16.628s
5	Anthony Davidson	24	1m 16.961s
6	Robert Doornbos	20	1m 17.424s
7	Neel Jani	20	1m 19.720s
8	Giorgio Mondini	21	1m 20.708s
9	Takuma Sato	9	1m 20.744s
10	Franck Montagny	3	No time
11	Scott Speed	3	No time
12	Mark Webber	1	No time
13	Jarno Trulli	1	No time
14	Christijan Albers	1	No time
15	Nico Rosberg	1	No time
16	Tiago Monteiro	1	No time
17	Ralf Schumacher	1	No time
18	Jenson Button	1	No time
19	Vitantonio Liuzzi	1	No time
20	Nick Heidfeld	1	No time
21	Juan Pablo Montoya	1	No time
22	Jacques Villeneuve	2	No time
23	David Coulthard	1	No time
24	Christian Klien	1	No time
25	Rubens Barrichello	1	No time
26	Fernando Alonso	2	No time
27	Giancarlo Fisichella	2	No time

PRACTICE 2 (FRIDAY)
Sunny (track 33–36°C, air 23–25°C)

Pos.	Driver	Laps	Time
1	Anthony Davidson	38	1m 16.533s
2	Robert Doornbos	29	1m 16.824s
3	Fernando Alonso	16	1m 16.860s
4	Alexander Wurz	30	1m 17.075s
5	Christian Klien	10	1m 17.086s
6	Michael Schumacher	21	1m 17.100s
7	Giancarlo Fisichella	17	1m 17.291s
8	Jenson Button	12	1m 17.414s
9	Rubens Barrichello	16	1m 17.417s
10	Ralf Schumacher	25	1m 17.506s
11	Jarno Trulli	30	1m 17.610s
12	Nick Heidfeld	18	1m 17.622s
13	Robert Kubica	34	1m 17.844s
14	Mark Webber	14	1m 17.908s
15	Kimi Räikkönen	4	1m 17.933s
16	Jacques Villeneuve	13	1m 18.007s
17	Felipe Massa	19	1m 18.223s
18	Juan Pablo Montoya	5	1m 18.261s
19	Nico Rosberg	18	1m 18.283s
20	David Coulthard	6	1m 18.410s
21	Neel Jani	32	1m 18.774s
22	Giorgio Mondini	22	1m 18.910s
23	Scott Speed	22	1m 19.257s
24	Vitantonio Liuzzi	18	1m 19.334s
25	Christijan Albers	15	1m 19.358s
26	Takuma Sato	30	1m 19.616s
27	Tiago Monteiro	19	1m 20.311s
28	Franck Montagny	21	1m 22.222s

QUALIFYING (SATURDAY)
Sunny (track 34–37°C, air 24–26°C)

Pos.	Driver	First	Second	Third
1	Fernando Alonso	1m 15.816s	1m 15.124s	1m 14.648s
2	Giancarlo Fisichella	1m 16.046s	1m 14.766s	1m 14.709s
3	Michael Schumacher	1m 16.049s	1m 14.637s	1m 14.970s
4	Felipe Massa	1m 16.359s	1m 15.245s	1m 15.442s
5	Rubens Barrichello	1m 16.266s	1m 15.258s	1m 15.885s
6	Ralf Schumacher	1m 16.234s	1m 15.164s	1m 15.885s
7	Jarno Trulli	1m 16.174s	1m 15.068s	1m 15.976s
8	Jenson Button	1m 16.054s	1m 15.150s	1m 16.008s
9	Kimi Räikkönen	1m 16.613s	1m 15.422s	1m 16.015s
10	Nick Heidfeld	1m 16.322s	1m 15.468s	1m 17.144s
11	Mark Webber	1m 16.685s	1m 15.502s	
12	Juan Pablo Montoya	1m 16.195s	1m 15.801s	
13	Nico Rosberg	1m 17.213s	1m 15.804s	
14	Jacques Villeneuve	1m 16.066s	1m 15.847s	
15	Christian Klien	1m 16.627s	1m 15.928s	
16	Vitantonio Liuzzi	1m 17.105s	1m 16.661s	
17	Scott Speed	1m 17.361s		
18	Tiago Monteiro	1m 17.702s		
19	Christijan Albers	1m 18.024s		
20	Takuma Sato	1m 18.920s		
21	Franck Montagny	1m 20.763s		
22	David Coulthard	No time		

PRACTICE 3 (SATURDAY)
Cloudy (track 22–29°C, air 20–23°C)

Pos.	Driver	Laps	Time
1	Michael Schumacher	14	1m 15.658s
2	Giancarlo Fisichella	14	1m 15.707s
3	Nick Heidfeld	13	1m 16.057s
4	Christian Klien	12	1m 16.277s
5	David Coulthard	16	1m 16.352s
6	Rubens Barrichello	16	1m 16.399s
7	Felipe Massa	15	1m 16.410s
8	Fernando Alonso	10	1m 16.595s
9	Juan Pablo Montoya	9	1m 16.660s
10	Kimi Räikkönen	9	1m 16.705s
11	Jenson Button	18	1m 16.999s
12	Scott Speed	13	1m 17.004s
13	Ralf Schumacher	19	1m 17.199s
14	Vitantonio Liuzzi	19	1m 17.240s
15	Nico Rosberg	14	1m 17.645s
16	Mark Webber	14	1m 17.743s
17	Jacques Villeneuve	16	1m 17.924s
18	Jarno Trulli	18	1m 18.411s
19	Tiago Monteiro	22	1m 18.747s
20	Takuma Sato	20	1m 18.857s
21	Christijan Albers	19	1m 19.587s
22	Franck Montagny	24	1m 20.031s

CHASSIS LOG BOOK

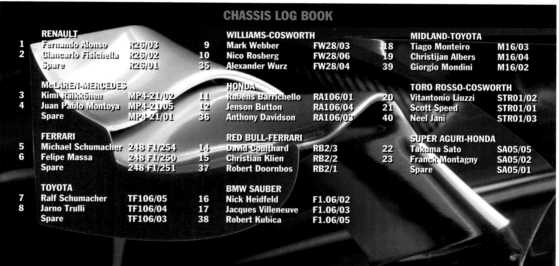

RENAULT
1	Fernando Alonso	R26/03
2	Giancarlo Fisichella	R26/02
	Spare	R26/01

McLAREN-MERCEDES
3	Kimi Räikkönen	MP4-21/02
4	Juan Pablo Montoya	MP4-21/05
	Spare	MP4-21/01

FERRARI
5	Michael Schumacher	248 F1/254
6	Felipe Massa	248 F1/250
	Spare	248 F1/251

TOYOTA
7	Ralf Schumacher	TF106/05
8	Jarno Trulli	TF106/04
	Spare	TF106/03

WILLIAMS-COSWORTH
9	Mark Webber	FW28/03
10	Nico Rosberg	FW28/06
35	Alexander Wurz	FW28/04

HONDA
11	Rubens Barrichello	RA106/01
12	Jenson Button	RA106/04
36	Anthony Davidson	RA106/03

RED BULL-FERRARI
14	David Coulthard	RB2/3
15	Christian Klien	RB2/2
37	Robert Doornbos	RB2/1

BMW SAUBER
16	Nick Heidfeld	F1.06/02
17	Jacques Villeneuve	F1.06/03
38	Robert Kubica	F1.06/05

MIDLAND-TOYOTA
18	Tiago Monteiro	M16/03
19	Christijan Albers	M16/04
39	Giorgio Mondini	M16/02

TORO ROSSO-COSWORTH
20	Vitantonio Liuzzi	STR01/02
21	Scott Speed	STR01/01
40	Neel Jani	STR01/03

SUPER AGURI-HONDA
22	Takuma Sato	SA05/05
23	Franck Montagny	SA05/02
	Spare	SA05/01

 9 RÄIKKÖNEN McLaren
 7 TRULLI Toyota
 5 BARRICHELLO Honda
 3 M. SCHUMACHER Ferrari
 1 ALONSO Renault
 10 HEIDFELD BMW-Sauber
 8 BUTTON Honda
 6 R. SCHUMACHER Toyota
 4 MASSA Ferrari
 2 FISICHELLA Renault

RACE DISTANCE: 66 laps
189.677 miles/305.256 km
RACE WEATHER: Sunny
track 36–38°C, air 25–26°C

Lap chart

52	54	55	56	57	58	59	60	61	62	63	64	65	66	
1	1	1	1	1	1	1	1	1	1	1	1	1	1	1
5	5	5	5	5	5	5	5	5	5	5	5	5	5	2
2	2	2	2	2	2	2	2	2	2	2	2	2	2	3
6	6	6	6	6	6	6	6	6	6	6	6	6	6	4
3	3	3	3	3	3	3	3	3	3	3	3	3	3	5
12	12	12	12	12	12	12	12	12	12	12	12	12		6
11	11	11	11	11	11	11	11	11	11	11	11	11		7
16	16	16	16	16	16	16	16	16	16	16	16	16		8
9	9	9	9	9	9	9	9	9	9	9	9	9		
8	8	8	8	8	8	8	8	8	8	8	8			
10	10	10	10	10	10	10	10	10	10	10	10			
17	17	17	17	17	17	17	17	17	17	17	17			
15	15	15	15	15	15	15	15	15	15	15	15			
15	20	20	20	20	20	20	20	20	20	20	14	14		
20	14	14	14	14	14	14	14	14	14	14				
18	18	18	18	18	18	18	18	18	18					
22	22	22	22	22	22	22	22	22	22					

Pit stop
One lap or more behind leader

FOR THE RECORD

150th POLE POSITION: Renault engine
FIRST FASTEST LAP: Felipe Massa

POINTS

	DRIVERS			CONSTRUCTORS	
1	Fernando Alonso	54	1	Renault	78
2	Michael Schumacher	39	2	Ferrari	59
3	Kimi Räikkönen	27	3	McLaren	42
4	Giancarlo Fisichella	24	4	Honda	24
5	Felipe Massa	20	5	BMW Sauber	12
6	Jenson Button	16	6	Williams	10
7	Juan Pablo Montoya	15	7	Toyota	7
8	Rubens Barrichello	8	8	Red Bull	2
9	Ralf Schumacher	7			
10	Nick Heidfeld	6			
11	Mark Webber	6			
12	Jacques Villeneuve	6			
13	Nico Rosberg	4			
14	David Coulthard	1			
15	Christian Klien	1			

Photograph: James Moy/www.crashpa.net
Photograph: Russell Batchelor/XPB.cc

Fernando Alonso's Renault R26 sprints towards Ste Devote en route to another powerful and decisive race victory.

Photograph: Michael C. Brown

MONACO GP

MONTE CARLO

Right: Michael Schumacher's Ferrari is pushed into the pit lane after skidding to a halt at Rascasse on his final qualifying run.
Photograph: XPB.cc

Above: Michael looks bewildered by the whole business.
Photograph: Jean-François Galeron/WRI

MONTE CARLO QUALIFYING

FERNANDO Alonso's fourth win of the year was largely overshadowed by the controversial performance of Michael Schumacher and the Ferrari team, who were found guilty of breaking the rules after the seven-times world champion parked his car out on the circuit during qualifying in a deliberate attempt to prevent the Renault team leader from taking pole position.

The Monaco stewards reviewed the available evidence for several hours before announcing that they found Schumacher guilty and were sending him to the back of the grid for Sunday's race. The stewards decreed that they were 'left with no alternative but to conclude that the driver deliberately stopped his car on the circuit in the last few minutes of qualifying at a time at which he had thus set the fastest lap time'.

They added that they had examined all the relevant data supplied by the team and found that 'having set a fast time in sector one the driver lost time in sector two, arrived at Turn 18 [Rascasse] at a speed little if any different from his previous fastest lap and braked with such force that his front wheels locked up, requiring the driver to regain control of the car. The driver ultimately did so without hitting the barrier on the outside of Turn 18. The engine of the car subsequently stalled with the result that the car partially blocked the track.'

Rather than accept the stewards' ruling with a modicum of dignity and good grace, Ferrari boss Jean Todt let rip with an indignant critique of the decision, which reawakened memories of his self-absorbed defence of the team's decision to oblige Rubens Barrichello to relinquish victory in the 2002 Austrian GP.

'Ferrari notes with great displeasure the decision of the race stewards,' he fumed, 'which is to delete the times set by Michael Schumacher in qualifying for the Monaco Grand Prix.

'We totally disagree with it. Such a decision creates a very serious precedent, ruling out the possibility of driver error. Michael was on his final timed lap and he was trying to put his first place beyond doubt, as could be seen from the fact that his first split time was the best and could have seen him do another very good lap. With no real evidence, the stewards have assumed he is guilty.'

Any other team principal committing such an act of defiance against the governing body's officials might well have found himself summoned before the FIA World Motor Sport Council for bringing the sport into disrepute, so many onlookers felt that Todt could have counted himself lucky to get away without further penalty. For his part, FIA president Max Mosley said that it would be unfair to brand Schumacher a cheat, but some people expressed the view that the stewards had imposed the minimum penalty possible and that Schumacher was fortunate not to have been excluded from the meeting.

Schumacher had 'clinched' his apparent pole position in circumstances that were as controversial as they were improbable in the extreme. With Alonso already 0.3s faster at the second timing split and on course to knock the Ferrari team leader off pole position, Schumi made an amateurish hash of Rascasse, locked up and skidded to a convenient halt on the racing line, thereby thwarting Fernando's sprint for fastest time.

It was quite clear from Alonso's body language that he reckoned he'd been deliberately slowed by his Ferrari rival. Down in the pits Renault boss Flavio Briatore was fit to be tied. 'It was disgusting,' he said. 'This is the way Ferrari manages.'

Others also failed to pull their punches. 'It was the cheapest, dirtiest thing I've ever seen in F1,' said 1982 world champion Keke Rosberg. 'He should leave F1 and go home. I think he's underestimated our intelligence by trying to claim it was a driving mistake. I mean, give me a break.'

Alonso was duly promoted to pole position (1m 13.962s), although he referred to the Schumacher incident discreetly in passing. 'I would have been on pole for sure today without the problem on the final lap,' he noted before Schumacher's demotion was announced. Renault had its own problems when Giancarlo Fisichella had his fastest three qualifying times disallowed for holding up David Coulthard's Red Bull, dropping him to ninth on the grid.

Mark Webber did a superb job to place his Williams FW28 alongside Alonso on the front row in 1m 14.082s ahead of the all-McLaren second row, Kimi Räikkönen (1m 14.140s) ahead of Juan Pablo Montoya (1m 14.664s), the Colombian hampered only by picking up a touch too much understeer on new tyres. Rubens Barrichello – seventh-quickest on 1m 15.804s, but fifth in the final starting order just ahead of Jarno Trulli's debutant Toyota TF106B (1m 15.857s) – did a fine job on a relatively heavy fuel load, but Jenson Button failed to make the top ten run-off and languished down in 14th on 1m 14.982s.

'I'd love to win at Monaco, but that's not really on the cards,' said Jenson. 'We're not going to be as quick as the Renaults or the Ferraris; no way. They beat us by a minute at Barcelona – almost a second a lap.'

It was a particularly disappointing outcome after a promising test the previous week at the Vallelunga circuit near Rome, where an artificial chicane was installed to duplicate the need for low-speed traction and crisp engine response, which are key requirements through the tortuous streets of the Mediterranean principality.

Button's efforts were not helped when his colleague Anthony Davidson, the Honda test driver, crashed heavily at the Ste Devote right-hander, badly damaging his car and losing valuable tyre testing mileage on Friday.

David Coulthard (1m 16.426s) and Nico Rosberg (1m 16.636s) were promoted to seventh and eighth on the grid ahead of the demoted, frustrated Fisichella, who was ninth ahead of Ralf Schumacher (1m 14.398s) in the other Toyota.

Christian Klien (1m 14.747s) did a good job to line up his Red Bull RB2 ahead of Vitantonio Liuzzi's Toro Rosso (1m 14.969s), while behind Button were the two BMW-Saubers, with Jacques Villeneuve (1m 15.052s) just edging out Nick Heidfeld (1m 15.137s).

Right at the back of the grid was Felipe Massa, who'd crashed his Ferrari at Casino Square in the opening moments of the first qualifying stint, writing himself out of the equation as a result.

McLAREN'S MONACO RECORD

POSSIBLY the most quietly significant moment of the Monaco GP came when the television cameras swung upward to frame a hotel balcony, fixing on the face of Lewis Hamilton, Britain's brightest rising star, watching the race with Lisa Dennis, the wife of the McLaren chairman.

It was just 24 hours since Hamilton had dominated the Monaco GP2 race from start to finish, laying down a marker for the future at this circuit where McLaren has won an all-time record 13 victories since making its F1 début here some 40 years ago. Many insiders were already tipping the 21-year-old to be back in the streets of the Principality in 2007 at the wheel of an F1 McLaren alongside Fernando Alonso.

When Bruce McLaren made his team's F1 début in the Ford V8-propelled M2B it was painted in a distinctive white livery with a central green stripe designed to double for a car from the fictional Yamura team featuring in the late John Frankenheimer's film *Grand Prix*, which was filmed throughout the 1966 season prior to its launch the following year.

The few thousand dollars paid to McLaren for obligingly respraying his car to fill the role of Hollywood extra generated a welcome boost to his slim finances on a weekend when just four employees assisted him in preparing the car.

How things change. For the 2006 race the team took no fewer than 137 personnel to Monaco, including drivers, engineers, mechanics, support crew and marketing and hospitality personnel. It was an operation on a scale that McLaren, who was killed testing one of his own Can-Am sports cars at Goodwood in 1970, could never have envisaged in his most optimistic dreams.

Ironically, although McLaren would field generations of competitive F1 cars, which carried Emerson Fittipaldi and James Hunt to the world championship in 1974 and 1976 respectively, it was not until 1984 that a car bearing the New Zealander's name finally raced to victory through the streets of Monte Carlo.

On that occasion, Alain Prost's TAG-engined MP4-2B just scraped home to a rain-soaked half-points victory ahead of a Toleman-Hart driven by one Ayrton Senna, a man who would win five of his record six Monaco wins driving for McLaren. Prost won again in 1985 and completed a hat trick of victories in 1986, heading a one-two success for the team in front of his team-mate Keke Rosberg.

In 1988 Senna joined Prost at McLaren, triggering a personal rivalry that crackled like high-tension static right through to the French driver's retirement at the end of 1993. They spent only two seasons together at McLaren, with Prost winning at Monaco in 1988 after Senna, nursing a half-minute lead, slid into the wall at the Portier right-hander leading onto the waterfront.

Nevertheless Senna, who had scored his first Monaco victory in 1987 at the wheel of a Lotus-Honda, made amends by posting an uninterrupted run of five victories from 1989 to 1993, topping Graham Hill's record of five wins in this historic event.

'I think my father would have approved of his record finally being beaten by a driver of Ayrton's calibre,' said Damon Hill after finishing second in his Williams-Renault behind Senna's McLaren in the 1993 race.

McLaren would have to wait until Mika Häkkinen's success in 1998 before winning again, followed by David Coulthard's two victories in 2000 and 2002, a third having slipped from the Scot's grasp in 2001 when he qualified on pole position only for his car to stall on the starting grid prior to the formation lap. Kimi Räikkönen added a 13th win last year.

This time Coulthard's third place ensured that there were McLaren drivers past, present and future – Fernando Alonso joins McLaren for 2007 – sharing the Monaco F1 podium. Nobody would bet against Hamilton's joining that élite group in the not-too-distant future.

FERNANDO Alonso yet again showcased his imperturbable confidence and matchless precision with a flawless victory, this time in the most demanding race on the Formula 1 calendar, completing 78 gruelling laps around the unforgiving streets of Monte Carlo without a single slip. It was a triumph that served further to extend his lead in the world championship points table while at the same time enhancing his image as possibly the most complete performer in the business.

Alonso may have paradoxically have been aided in his quest for pole position by Michael Schumacher's unsporting behaviour in Saturday's qualifying session, a slip by the Ferrari team leader that guaranteed the reigning world champion his position at the very front of the grid.

At the start, Alonso accelerated his Renault R26 cleanly into the lead as the pack aimed for that narrowing ribbon of asphalt that is the slightly off-camber, uphill right-hander at Ste Devote. Alonso confidently swung into the corner ahead of Mark Webber's Williams FW28 knowing that the man he really had to worry about, Kimi Räikkönen in the McLaren-Mercedes MP4-21, was right behind the Australian driver in third place as they scrambled up the hill to Casino Square for the first time.

At the end of the opening lap Alonso led Webber by 0.5s but, as they rounded Ste Devote for the second time, Räikkönen dodged out from behind the Williams and squeezed audaciously past, his right-hand wheels almost shaving the unyielding guard rail as he did so. By the end of lap three Räikkönen had trimmed Alonso's advantage to 0.4s and his McLaren's nose cone was almost touching the rear end of the Renault as they braked for the two tight hairpins at the opposite end of the circuit.

With six laps completed Alonso was still hanging on ahead, looking as though he was right on the limit of adhesion, but in reality the Spaniard was pacing himself in as disciplined a fashion as he could, secure in the knowledge that, so long as he did not make a mistake, Räikkönen would have little choice but to follow in his wheel tracks.

Alonso admitted that he was driving quite conservatively, mindful of the need to watch his rear-tyre wear, so it was little surprise when Webber began to close in from third place after a dozen or so laps, while at the same time Juan Pablo Montoya was moving in to make it a foursome at the front.

Räikkönen came in from second place to make his first refuelling stop (10.2s) at the end of lap 22, followed two laps later by Alonso (7.9s), who just managed to squeeze back into the fray ahead of the Finn's McLaren. Webber led before making his own first stop (7.8s) at the end of lap 25, after which they all resumed their original positions in the high-speed procession.

By lap 33 the leaders were well into lapping some of the slower cars and Alonso got a breather as he nipped ahead of his team-mate Giancarlo Fisichella, who had started from ninth on the grid following his post-qualifying penalty. 'With the strategy we had it was impossible to do anything from so far back,' shrugged the Italian, 'so I just had to go out there and push to the maximum. That was all I could do.'

On lap 47 Webber's great run came to a premature finish with an engine-bay fire caused by an exhaust failure that allowed hot gas to burn through the wiring loom. He parked his steaming car on the hill after Ste Devote, striding purposefully away in a fury without a backward glance.

'I am very disappointed, of course,' said Webber with characteristic composure. 'It felt like we deserved something

Right: Rubens Barrichello swapped his helmet colours for the race with his IRL compatriot Tony Kanaan, who was competing in the Indy 500 that weekend.

Below: Juan Pablo Montoya drove smoothly to inherit second place after his McLaren team-mate Kimi Räikkönen retired.

Photographs: James Moy/www.crashpa.net

Bottom: Mark Webber's Williams FW28 ran with the leaders until another technical failure sidelined the Australian.

Photograph: XPB.cc

today, but reliability has let us down. There is no rewind button and all the hard work we did over the past few days is invisible now. [But] we were quick here, I was going a lot longer than Juan Pablo in the second stint and he wasn't really a threat, so the podium was there.'

The safety car was immediately deployed to slow the pack while the Williams was retrieved, but the cooling on Räikkönen's McLaren was overtaxed by running slowly in such hot conditions immediately following a routine refuelling stop and a heat shield in the engine bay caught fire – also damaging his wiring loom – two laps after Webber pulled up. Soon after, Nico Rosberg suffered an identical failure to Webber's, which contributed to the throttle's sticking open, pitching him into the barrier coming onto the start-line straight while running sixth close behind Rubens Barrichello's Honda.

There were 25 laps of this unforgiving race still to run but, with the second-placed Montoya now held up amid a huge gaggle of slower cars that he was in the process of lapping, all Alonso had to do was cut his engine revs, conserve his brakes and tyres and reel off the laps to the chequered flag.

'To be honest, I was quite surprised by Räikkönen's speed,' said Fernando, 'but I knew I had to control the pace as well to look after the tyres. We seemed to have more problems

with the rear wear than our competitors, but I managed the situation to keep the tyres fresh for the end of the stints and to build a gap when I needed it.'

Montoya was satisfied with his second place, although he admitted that heavy traffic in the closing stages prevented him from launching an attack on Alonso, and David Coulthard gave the Red Bull squad a welcome boost going into the British Grand Prix with third ahead of Rubens Barrichello's Honda – Rubens had survived a drive-through penalty for speeding in the pit lane – and Michael Schumacher's Ferrari.

It was a lively and action-packed race for DC and the Red Bull squad, who switched from a two- to a one-stop refuelling strategy. 'It's been a couple of years since I've been on the podium,' said Coulthard, 'so it's especially great to finish on it here at Monaco. This is always a hard and physical race that takes a lot out of you. Once you get into it, you think you've done about 50 laps, but then you see that you've only done about 12.'

Schumacher started from the pit lane on a two-stop strategy, but the team switched him to a one-stop halfway through, which worked brilliantly to leapfrog him through the field, and he crossed the finishing line only a couple of lengths behind his erstwhile team-mate.

'I think we were very unlucky with the safety car coming out at just the wrong time,' said Ferrari's Ross Brawn, 'but the car was very good in the race, with good balance and performance. Obviously it's frustrating not to have had the results we could have had with the car this weekend, but it will make us even more determined for the rest of the season.'

Nick Heidfeld finished a contented seventh after a good run with the BMW-Sauber, making up for Jacques Villeneuve's drive-through penalty, which contributed to his distant 14th place. Ralf Schumacher's Toyota was eighth, but only after team-mate Jarno Trulli lost a superb third in the closing stages when hydraulic failure intervened. Felipe Massa's Ferrari was next, ahead of Vitantonio Liuzzi's Toro Rosso and the hapless Jenson Button's Honda.

For Button there was to be no dream result in this glamorous setting. Beset by acute oversteer in qualifying, he could line up only 13th on the grid and he trailed home 11th, grappling with the same handling problems, which lost him seconds to his rivals through the two tight hairpins. At his one stop the team reduced front downforce and fitted a set of scrubbed rear tyres. It was better, but not what he was hoping for. Jenson had meant it to be so very different.

Alan Henry

Above: Red Bull's very own Superman David Coulthard scored the team's first ever podium finish.
Photograph: Paul-Henri Cahier

Top left: David Coulthard and girlfriend Karen Minier, happy together.

Top centre: A furious Kimi Räikkönen heads for the seclusion of a yacht after another bruising retirement.

Centre: Ralf Schumacher with his wife Cora.
Photographs: XPB.cc

Right: Red Bull sporting director Christian Horner keeps his promise to jump into the swimming pool to celebrate the team's first podium finish – wearing only a Superman cape.
Photograph: James Moy/crashpa.net

Main photo: Räikkönen chases race leader Fernando Alonso towards Casino Square.
Photograph: Paul-Henri Cahier

Above: A Marlboro grid girl adds to the glamour.

Photograph: James Moy/crashpa.net

Left: Michael Schumacher's Ferrari slices through the backmarkers on the opening lap.

Photograph: Jean-François Galeron/WRI

GRAND PRIX DE
MONACO
MONTE-CARLO 25–28 MAY 2006

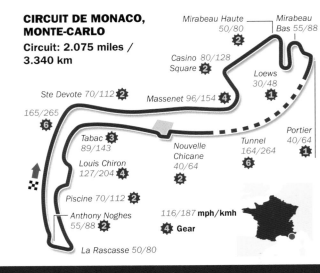

CIRCUIT DE MONACO, MONTE-CARLO

Circuit: 2.075 miles / 3.340 km

Mirabeau Haute 50/80 — Mirabeau Bas 55/88
Casino 80/128 Square
Loews 30/48
Ste Devote 70/112
Massenet 96/154
165/265
Tabac 89/143
Nouvelle Chicane 40/64
Tunnel 164/264
Portier 40/64
Louis Chiron 127/204
Piscine 70/112
Anthony Noghes 55/88
116/187 mph/kmh
Gear
La Rascasse 50/80

Photograph: Breloer/XPB.cc

RACE RESULTS

Pos.	Driver	Nat.	No.	Entrant	Car/Engine	Tyres	Laps	Time/Retirement	Speed (mph/km/h)	Gap to leader	Fastest race lap	
1	Fernando Alonso	E	1	Mild Seven Renault F1 Team	Renault R26-RS26 V8	M	78	1h 43m 43.116s	93.645/150.707		1m 15.671s	11
2	Juan Pablo Montoya	COL	4	Team McLaren Mercedes	McLaren MP4-21-Mercedes FO 108S V8	M	78	1h 43m 57.683s	93.426/150.355	+14.567s	1m 16.008s	20
3	David Coulthard	GB	14	Red Bull Racing	Red Bull RB2-Ferrari 056 V8	M	78	1h 44m 35.414s	92.865/149.451	+52.298s	1m 17.849s	45
4	Rubens Barrichello	BR	11	Lucky Strike Honda Racing F1 Team	Honda RA106-RA806E V8	M	78	1h 44m 36.453s	92.850/149.427	+53.337s	1m 17.320s	67
5	Michael Schumacher	D	5	Scuderia Ferrari Marlboro	Ferrari 248 F1-056 V8	B	78	1h 44m 36.946s	92.842/149.415	+53.830s	1m 15.143s	74
6	Giancarlo Fisichella	I	2	Mild Seven Renault F1 Team	Renault R26-RS26 V8	M	78	1h 44m 45.188s	92.720/149.219	+1m 02.072s	1m 15.919s	58
7	Nick Heidfeld	D	16	BMW Sauber F1 Team	BMW Sauber F1.06-BMW P86 V8	M	77			+1 lap	1m 17.319s	72
8	Ralf Schumacher	D	7	Panasonic Toyota Racing	Toyota TF106B-RVX-06 V8	B	77			+1 lap	1m 17.540s	72
9	Felipe Massa	BR	6	Scuderia Ferrari Marlboro	Ferrari 248 F1-056 V8	B	77			+1 lap	1m 16.612s	40
10	Vitantonio Liuzzi	I	20	Scuderia Toro Rosso	Toro Rosso STR01-Cosworth TJ2005-2 V10	M	77			+1 lap	1m 17.660s	75
11	Jenson Button	GB	12	Lucky Strike Honda Racing F1 Team	Honda RA106-RA806E V8	M	77			+1 lap	1m 17.300s	59
12	Christijan Albers	NL	19	MF1 Racing	Midland M16-Toyota RVX-06 V8	B	77			+1 lap	1m 17.603s	77
13	Scott Speed	USA	21	Scuderia Toro Rosso	Toro Rosso STR01-Cosworth TJ2005-2 V10	M	77			+1 lap	1m 17.481s	77
14	Jacques Villeneuve	CDN	17	BMW Sauber F1 Team	BMW Sauber F1.06-BMW P86 V8	M	77			+1 lap	1m 17.767s	74
15	Tiago Monteiro	P	18	MF1 Racing	Midland M16-Toyota RVX-06 V8	B	76			+2 laps	1m 17.329s	71
16	Franck Montagny	F	23	Super Aguri F1 Team	Super Aguri SA05-Honda RA806E V8	B	75			+3 laps	1m 19.104s	72
17	Jarno Trulli	I	8	Panasonic Toyota Racing	Toyota TF106B-RVX-06 V8	B	72	Hydraulics		+6 laps	1m 17.180s	30
	Christian Klien	A	15	Red Bull Racing	Red Bull RB2-Ferrari 056 V8	M	56	Transmission			1m 17.930s	19
	Nico Rosberg	D	10	WilliamsF1 Team	Williams FW28-Cosworth CA2006 V8	B	51	Exhaust			1m 17.227s	43
	Kimi Räikkönen	FIN	3	Team McLaren Mercedes	McLaren MP4-21-Mercedes FO 108S V8	M	50	Engine overheating/fire			1m 15.325s	19
	Mark Webber	AUS	9	WilliamsF1 Team	Williams FW28-Cosworth CA2006 V8	B	48	Exhaust/fire			1m 15.680s	23
	Takuma Sato	J	22	Super Aguri F1 Team	Super Aguri SA05-Honda RA806E V8	B	46	Electrics			1m 18.793s	39

Fastest lap: Michael Schumacher on lap 74, 1m 15.143s, 99.429 mph/160.014 km/h.

Lap record: Michael Schumacher (Ferrari F2004 V10), 1m 14.439s, 100.369 mph/161.528 km/h (2004).

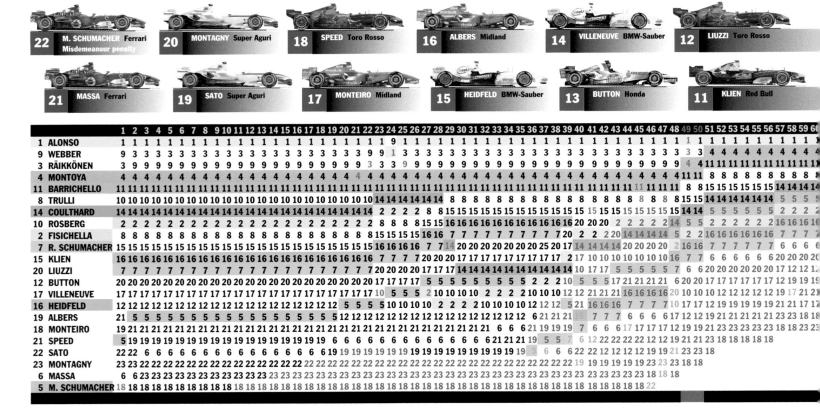

All results and data © FOM 2006

PRACTICE 1 (THURSDAY)

Sunny/light breeze (track 33–35°C, air 22–24°C)

Pos.	Driver	Laps	Time
1	Fernando Alonso	13	1m 16.712s
2	Anthony Davidson	31	1m 16.872s
3	Giancarlo Fisichella	12	1m 16.888s
4	Michael Schumacher	8	1m 16.973s
5	Juan Pablo Montoya	7	1m 17.458s
6	Robert Kubica	19	1m 17.869s
7	Alexander Wurz	28	1m 17.949s
8	Jenson Button	12	1m 18.329s
9	Robert Doornbos	23	1m 18.394s
10	Rubens Barrichello	12	1m 18.406s
11	David Coulthard	10	1m 18.447s
12	Nico Rosberg	15	1m 18.480s
13	Mark Webber	17	1m 18.571s
14	Felipe Massa	15	1m 18.695s
15	Jarno Trulli	11	1m 18.703s
16	Ralf Schumacher	14	1m 19.021s
17	Jacques Villeneuve	16	1m 19.246s
18	Christian Klien	10	1m 19.543s
19	Neel Jani	25	1m 19.651s
20	Giorgio Mondini	29	1m 19.669s
21	Tiago Monteiro	17	1m 19.730s
22	Vitantonio Liuzzi	16	1m 19.857s
23	Scott Speed	13	1m 20.137s
24	Christijan Albers	17	1m 20.552s
25	Takuma Sato	23	1m 21.144s
26	Franck Montagny	21	1m 21.594s
27	Kimi Räikkönen	3	2m 06.592s
28	Nick Heidfeld	1	No time

PRACTICE 2 (THURSDAY)

Sunny (track 37–39°C, air 24°C)

Pos.	Driver	Laps	Time
1	Alexander Wurz	27	1m 15.907s
2	Anthony Davidson	15	1m 16.075s
3	Juan Pablo Montoya	24	1m 16.138s
4	Fernando Alonso	18	1m 16.221s
5	Robert Doornbos	36	1m 16.292s
6	Kimi Räikkönen	18	1m 16.707s
7	Giancarlo Fisichella	23	1m 16.721s
8	David Coulthard	19	1m 16.870s
9	Jenson Button	20	1m 16.903s
10	Felipe Massa	25	1m 17.251s
11	Jarno Trulli	25	1m 17.325s
12	Tiago Monteiro	30	1m 17.439s
13	Rubens Barrichello	24	1m 17.456s
14	Giorgio Mondini	30	1m 17.497s
15	Michael Schumacher	25	1m 17.603s
16	Vitantonio Liuzzi	31	1m 17.638s
17	Mark Webber	19	1m 17.744s
18	Ralf Schumacher	26	1m 17.793s
19	Nico Rosberg	15	1m 17.845s
20	Jacques Villeneuve	13	1m 17.874s
21	Christian Klien	22	1m 18.123s
22	Nick Heidfeld	10	1m 18.257s
23	Scott Speed	29	1m 18.420s
24	Christijan Albers	24	1m 18.430s
25	Franck Montagny	19	1m 18.731s
26	Robert Kubica	22	1m 19.273s
27	Neel Jani	27	1m 19.445s
28	Takuma Sato	31	1m 19.803s

QUALIFYING (SATURDAY)

Sunny (track 40–42°C, air 25–26°C)

Pos.	Driver	First	Second	Third
1	Michael Schumacher	1m 15.118s	1m 13.709s	1m 13.898s*
2	Fernando Alonso	1m 14.232s	1m 13.622s	1m 13.962s
3	Mark Webber	1m 14.305s	1m 13.728s	1m 14.082s
4	Kimi Räikkönen	1m 13.887s	1m 13.532s	1m 14.140s
5	Giancarlo Fisichella	1m 14.614s	1m 13.647s	1m 14.396s†
6	Juan Pablo Montoya	1m 14.483s	1m 14.295s	1m 14.664s
7	Rubens Barrichello	1m 14.766s	1m 14.312s	1m 15.804s
8	Jarno Trulli	1m 14.883s	1m 14.211s	1m 15.857s
9	David Coulthard	1m 15.090s	1m 13.687s	1m 16.426s
10	Nico Rosberg	1m 14.888s	1m 13.909s	1m 16.636s
11	Ralf Schumacher	1m 14.412s	1m 14.398s	
12	Christian Klien	1m 14.489s	1m 14.747s	
13	Vitantonio Liuzzi	1m 15.314s	1m 14.969s	
14	Jenson Button	1m 15.085s	1m 14.982s	
15	Jacques Villeneuve	1m 15.316s	1m 15.052s	
16	Nick Heidfeld	1m 15.324s	1m 15.137s	
17	Christijan Albers	1m 15.598s		
18	Tiago Monteiro	1m 15.993s		
19	Scott Speed	1m 16.236s		
20	Takuma Sato	1m 17.276s		
21	Franck Montagny	1m 17.502s		
22	Felipe Massa	No time		

*Times disallowed for blocking track during qualifying; M. Schumacher sent to back of grid
†Fastest time disallowed for blocking; Fisichella dropped four grid slots

PRACTICE 3 (SATURDAY)

Sunny (track 34–36°C, air 22–23°C)

Pos.	Driver	Laps	Time
1	Fernando Alonso	19	1m 13.823s
2	Michael Schumacher	20	1m 14.031s
3	Giancarlo Fisichella	20	1m 14.056s
4	David Coulthard	19	1m 14.550s
5	Nico Rosberg	17	1m 14.623s
6	Juan Pablo Montoya	21	1m 14.785s
7	Mark Webber	16	1m 14.804s
8	Felipe Massa	24	1m 14.842s
9	Jenson Button	21	1m 15.020s
10	Kimi Räikkönen	17	1m 15.124s
11	Rubens Barrichello	19	1m 15.283s
12	Christian Klien	19	1m 15.476s
13	Nick Heidfeld	20	1m 15.591s
14	Tiago Monteiro	26	1m 15.809s
15	Christijan Albers	26	1m 16.066s
16	Vitantonio Liuzzi	27	1m 16.147s
17	Scott Speed	21	1m 16.201s
18	Jacques Villeneuve	27	1m 16.285s
19	Jarno Trulli	24	1m 16.456s
20	Takuma Sato	24	1m 17.148s
21	Ralf Schumacher	21	1m 17.860s
22	Franck Montagny	21	1m 17.934s

CHASSIS LOG BOOK

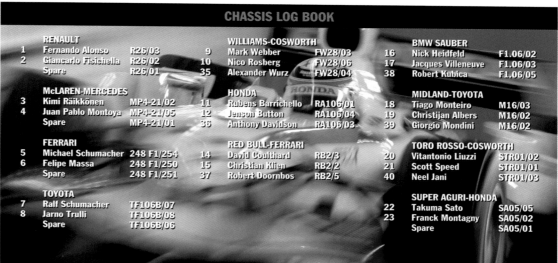

	RENAULT				WILLIAMS-COSWORTH				BMW SAUBER	
1	Fernando Alonso	R26/03	9		Mark Webber	FW28/03	16		Nick Heidfeld	F1.06/02
2	Giancarlo Fisichella	R26/02	10		Nico Rosberg	FW28/06	17		Jacques Villeneuve	F1.06/03
	Spare	R26/01	35		Alexander Wurz	FW28/04	38		Robert Kubica	F1.06/05

	McLAREN-MERCEDES				HONDA				MIDLAND-TOYOTA	
3	Kimi Räikkönen	MP4-21/02	11		Rubens Barrichello	RA106/01	18		Tiago Monteiro	M16/03
4	Juan Pablo Montoya	MP4-21/05	12		Jenson Button	RA106/04	19		Christijan Albers	M16/02
	Spare	MP4-21/01	36		Anthony Davidson	RA106/03	39		Giorgio Mondini	M16/02

	FERRARI				RED BULL-FERRARI				TORO ROSSO-COSWORTH	
5	Michael Schumacher	248 F1/254	14		David Coulthard	RB2/3	20		Vitantonio Liuzzi	STR01/02
6	Felipe Massa	248 F1/250	15		Christian Klien	RB2/2	21		Scott Speed	STR01/01
	Spare	248 F1/251	37		Robert Doornbos	RB2/5	40		Neel Jani	STR01/03

	TOYOTA								SUPER AGURI-HONDA	
7	Ralf Schumacher	TF106B/07						22		Takuma Sato	SA05/05
8	Jarno Trulli	TF106B/08						23		Franck Montagny	SA05/02
	Spare	TF106B/06								Spare	SA05/01

Photograph: James Moy/www.crashpa.net

RACE DISTANCE:
78 laps
161.880 miles/260.520 km

RACE WEATHER:
Sunny/scattered cloud
track 39–40°C, air 23°C

10 R. SCHUMACHER Toyota

8 ROSBERG Williams

6 TRULLI Toyota

4 MONTOYA McLaren

2 WEBBER Williams

9 FISICHELLA Renault
Misdemeanour penalty

7 COULTHARD Red Bull

5 BARRICHELLO Honda

3 RÄIKKÖNEN McLaren

1 ALONSO Renault

62	63	64	65	66	67	68	69	70	71	72	73	74	75	76	77	78	•	
1	1	1	1	1	1	1	1	1	1	1	1	1	1	1	1	1		1
4	4	4	4	4	4	4	4	4	4	4	4	4	4	4	4	4		2
8	8	8	8	8	8	8	8	14	14	14	14	14	14					3
14	14	14	14	14	14	14	14	11	11	11	11	11	11					4
11	11	11	11	11	11	11	11	5	5	5	5	5	5					5
5	5	5	5	5	5	5	5	2	2	2	2	2	2					6
2	2	2	2	2	2	2	2	16	16	16	16	16	16					7
16	16	16	16	16	16	16	16	7	7	7	7							8
7	7	7	7	7	7	7	7	6	6	6								
6	6	6	6	6	6	6	6	20	20	20	20							
20	20	20	20	20	20	20	20	12	12	12	12							
12	12	12	12	12	12	12	12	19	19	19	19							
19	19	19	19	19	19	19	19	21	21	21								
21	21	21	21	21	21	21	21	17	17	17								
17	17	17	17	17	17	17	17	18	18									
18	18	18	18	18	18	18	18	23	23									
23	23	23	23	23	23	23	23											

49

Pit stop
One lap or more behind leader
Drive-through penalty
Safety car deployed on laps shown

FOR THE RECORD

200th GRAND PRIX START: David Coulthard
40th ANNIVERSARY: McLaren
30th WIN: Renault
FIRST PODIUM: Red Bull (above)
500th POINT: Rubens Barrichello
300th POINT: Juan Pablo Montoya
200th POINT: Giancarlo Fisichella

POINTS

DRIVERS

1	Fernando Alonso	64
2	Michael Schumacher	43
3	Giancarlo Fisichella	27
4	Kimi Räikkönen	27
5	Juan Pablo Montoya	23
6	Felipe Massa	20
7	Jenson Button	16
8	Rubens Barrichello	13
9	Ralf Schumacher	8
10	Nick Heidfeld	8
11	David Coulthard	7
12	Mark Webber	6
13	Jacques Villeneuve	6
14	Nico Rosberg	4
15	Christian Klien	1

CONSTRUCTORS

1	Renault	91
2	Ferrari	63
3	McLaren	50
4	Honda	29
5	BMW Sauber	14
6	Williams	10
7	Toyota	8
8	Red Bull	8

Photographs: Russell Batchelor/XPB.cc

FIA F1 WORLD CHAMPIONSHIP/ROUND 8

BRITISH GP

SILVERSTONE

Main: Fernando Alonso's finger points to another dominant performance from the reigning world champion, this time after a display of precision driving on the fast open swerves at Silverstone.
Photograph: Jad Sherif/WRI

Insets: The jubilant Fernando celebrates with his trophy as the delighted fans show their appreciation of his singular talent.
Photographs: Paul-Henri Cahier

SILVERSTONE QUALIFYING

Above: Rubens Barrichello doesn't want to hear any over-optimistic predictions as to the Honda team's possible Silverstone form.

Top right: A spontaneous grin from David Coulthard as he gets himself togged up for the afternoon's proceedings.

Photographs: Paul-Henri Cahier

Bottom right: Michael Schumacher battles for control during an unexpectedly grassy moment at the wheel of his Ferrari.

Photograph: Laurent Charniaux/WRI

FERRARI came to Silverstone believing that its cars might – just might – be able to go head-to-head with Fernando Alonso's Renault R26 on the fast open swerves of the Northamptonshire circuit. But the world champion did the job superbly, buttoning up pole position with a 1m 20.253s best, which was enough to ease out Kimi Räikkönen's McLaren by just over a tenth of a second.

'On my first lap I had a little mistake in the last sector,' said Fernando, 'and they [the team] told me on the radio that we were second just behind Michael [Schumacher]. So I thought, well, maybe I've lost the pole with this mistake, but we had a second chance with the second set of tyres and I did a normal lap with no mistakes.'

It was Alonso's fourth consecutive pole, which obviously gave him huge satisfaction, although Räikkönen reckoned there was no way in which he could have challenged the Renault in such circumstances despite the fact that his efforts had ensured that it was an all-Michelin front row.

Schumacher (1m 20.574s) was clearly disappointed. 'We [Ferrari] haven't been here testing [this year] so we don't know what it was like then, but according to the lap times they [the other Bridgestone runners] were doing, something is different here. It's significantly slower.'

He added, 'But it's the same conditions for everybody. It was tricky yesterday [Friday] to adapt the car to the conditions, but we managed reasonably today for our qualifying runs.'

Felipe Massa's Ferrari (1m 20.764s) lined up on the outside of the second row while Giancarlo Fisichella's Renault (1m 20.919s) and Rubens Barrichello's Honda (1m 20.943s) shared row three to complete the top six. It was a respectable enough performance for Rubens, in dire contrast to that of Jenson Button (1m 23.247s), who failed to get beyond the first session cut-off point and wound up languishing in a distant 19th place for his home race.

'I'm obviously massively disappointed for myself, the team and all the fans,' shrugged Jenson. 'My first run wasn't quick enough because we had quite low grip. If the car isn't working well on the first run, you don't want to push it to the limit because the penalty for going off the track and not completing the lap is so high.

'The circuit was improving massively all the time and we thought we would get a second chance to do a run, but then I got called onto the weighbridge and that effectively finished my session.' By any standards, this was a crushing disappointment.

In the second McLaren, Juan Pablo Montoya could not get close to his team-mate and had to be content with a 1m 21.107s, fractionally behind Ralf Schumacher's Toyota (1m 21.073s) but just ahead of the two BMW-Saubers of Nick Heidfeld (1m 21.329s) and Jacques Villeneuve (1m 21.599s).

'I am happy,' enthused Heidfeld. 'It's really good we have got both cars in the top ten, especially when you consider who is behind us. This confirms for me the impression I had from the test at Barcelona that the latest changes to the car have meant a step forward for the team.'

David Coulthard (1m 21.442s) was the best of those who failed to make it into the top ten. He managed to get himself embroiled in a controversy with Montoya, whom he believed had held him up on one of his quick laps. DC made some unflattering remarks about the Colombian driver, although Juan Pablo was absolved of any blame by a stewards' inquiry and Coulthard later apologised.

Nico Rosberg had the fastest Williams FW28, on 1m 21.567s, five places ahead of team-mate Mark Webber (1m 23.129s). 'I am relatively disappointed considering where we were at Monaco,' said Nico. 'My lap time today wasn't enough for me to make it into the top ten but I think we're still a bit behind on circuits like this where aerodynamics are really important.'

Webber complained about lack of rear-end grip and made it clear that the car was simply not quick enough. 'I think it's going to be a very long race tomorrow,' he predicted. There was no way he could have guessed how wide of the mark that statement was.

Splitting the Williams twosome was a trio of Red Bull-backed contenders in the shape of Vitantonio Liuzzi's Toro Rosso (1m 21.699s), Christian Klien's Red Bull RB2 (1m 21.990s) and Scott Speed's Toro Rosso (1m 22.076s).

Rounding off the grid were the two Super Aguris of Takuma Sato (1m 26.158s) and Franck Montagny (1m 26.316s), and right at the back was Jarno Trulli's Toyota after its engine change.

HAD he so chosen, Fernando Alonso could have been back in his Oxford apartment for a late Sunday lunch after a brisk 90-minutes work-out winning the British Grand Prix at Silverstone in that familiar dominant fashion that seemed increasingly likely to ensure that he retain his world championship crown at the end of the season.

Alonso qualified superbly on pole position and, despite pre-race speculation that McLaren's Kimi Räikkönen and Ferrari team leader Michael Schumacher might turn the tables on him during the 60-lap race, he brilliantly handled the torrid conditions, in which track temperatures touched the 45-degree mark, to win in convincing and commanding fashion.

Alonso broke his opposition with a blinding pace in the opening phase of the race, such that he effectively had victory in the bag by the time he came in for his first refuelling stop at the end of lap 22. Schumacher, who many insiders believed was running a heavier fuel load and could therefore run a longer opening stint, in fact came in to make his own first stop on lap 18, closing off any realistic chance of challenging for victory.

On the first lap the American novice Scott Speed triggered a multiple accident going through the fast Becketts ess-bend when he tapped the back of Ralf Schumacher's Toyota. The Toyota snapped sideways and lurched back to the right, side-swiping Mark Webber's passing Williams. Both Schumacher and Webber were out of the race on the spot but, with debris all over the circuit, the safety car had to be deployed for a couple of laps while the mess was cleared up by the marshals.

Webber was understandably exasperated because this was another major setback for him in a season that had delivered precious little in terms of hard results so far.

'I had a pretty good start and made up a few places off the line,' he shrugged. 'It looked like Scott Speed tapped Ralf on the right rear going into Becketts, causing the Toyota to spin and end up right in my path. Ralf was obviously trying to save his car, which is fair enough, but he came directly back across the track when I was on the outside trying to get a clean run out, so I had nowhere to go. We [the team and I] have had a tough weekend, so it's a shame we couldn't get something out of it.'

The safety car was withdrawn and the pack unleashed again at the end of lap three. Alonso came through Woodcote to lead lap four already 0.5s ahead of Räikkönen's McLaren with Michael Schumacher right on its tail, then Felipe Massa's Ferrari, Giancarlo Fisichella's Renault and Nick Heidfeld's BMW-Sauber. Kimi hung on to the leading Renault gamely, but by lap nine Fernando was 1.4s ahead of the McLaren and clearly asserting the upper hand.

'We had set up the Renault to be handling at its best towards the end of each stint,' said Alonso. 'For the first two laps after the safety car was withdrawn, Kimi was very quick behind me, but lap by lap my car's initial understeer went away and I could start edging away.

'To be honest, to win in Spain, then in Monaco and now at Silverstone – just 20 minutes away from my home in Oxford – is a really great feeling.'

Schumacher provided some of the closest wheel-to-wheel jousting of the afternoon as he jostled to get past Räikkönen's McLaren in the opening stages, boldly trying the outside line

into the tight left-hand Abbey chicane only to be squeezed by the Finn to the point where 'there was only the thickness of a piece of paper between our side pods.' Michael was forced to decide that discretion was the better part of valour on that occasion and he eventually leapfrogged ahead of his rival to take second place at the second round of refuelling stops.

Yet both Schumacher and Räikkönen admitted that neither of their cars was quick enough to get on terms with Alonso's Renault. 'It is all a bit difficult to analyse, but at the end of the day we just didn't have the speed,' said the seven-times world champion.

Räikkönen put his own dilemma more succinctly. 'The car was a bit too slow on the straight to challenge anyone,' he shrugged. 'There wasn't much for us [the team], but I did the best I could. We lost a lot of rear-end grip and I had to work hard to keep Fisichella behind me because his Renault was very quick through the first sector of the lap.'

Just scoring a modest tally of world championship points would have been enough for Jenson Button on his home circuit but his pre-race predictions of a modest result turned into a painfully self-fulfilling prophecy. After managing only a dismal 19th place on the 22-car starting grid in a qualifying session fraught with problems, the Briton was up to 12th by lap nine when his Honda erupted in flames: its engine had dumped all its oil over the rear tyres, spinning him unceremoniously into a gravel trap and out of the race.

All that was left for Button was to walk back to the pits, trying to keep his mind off the fact that Alonso, the man who

Above: **Jenson Button's home grand prix comes to a spectacular and premature end in a cloud of smoke after an oil leak onto the rear tyres sends his Honda RA106 pirouetting into the gravel trap.**

Centre: **Nick Fry looks pensive and absorbed as he reflects on the vagaries of Honda's fortunes.**

Photographs: **James Moy/www.crashpa.net**

Top left: **Jacques Villeneuve prepares for action.**

Photograph: **Paul-Henri Cahier**

Bottom left: **Kimi Räikkönen's McLaren strives to gain an early advantage over Michael Schumacher's Ferrari. The Finn eventually lost out in the battle for second place behind Fernando Alonso.**

Photograph: **Lukas Gorys**

DIARY

Former Williams driver Riccardo Patrese says he believes it is unacceptable that Michael Schumacher should be subjected to a witch hunt after his qualifying 'error' at Monaco.

Jacques Villeneuve resigns from the Grand Prix Drivers' Association immediately after a meeting convened to consider Michael Schumacher's behaviour at Monaco. 'Personally I'm not happy that someone can run the GPDA and act like that,' says the Canadian.

Commenting on cost reductions planned for 2008, FIA president Max Mosley warns, 'We must save the teams from themselves, which means restricting scope for development.'

replaced him in the Renault squad three years ago, was heading for his fifth win out of the eight races so far this season – and the 13th of his career.

'The race was going pretty well for me and the car felt pretty good,' said Button. 'I wasn't as quick as the leaders, but the car was working well and had a good balance. I was absolutely loving it out there, working my way through the field, and, given the fuel load, I was doing pretty well. When I walked back in it was quite emotional because there were lots of cheers and flags being waved. The fans' support this weekend has been fantastic.'

By lap 15 Alonso had eked out a 3.2s lead over Räikkönen as the leading group approached the first pit stop window. Schumacher dodged in from third at the end of lap 18, followed by Räikkönen and Massa next time around, but Alonso stayed out until lap 22, a lap after team-mate Fisichella. That put Alonso back in the lead 5.5s ahead of Nick Heidfeld's BMW-Sauber, which was running a long opening stint and did not come in to refuel until the end of lap 25.

BERNIE SAYS F1 IS DAMAGED BY DISPUTE

ONLY weeks after all the teams signed up to race in the championship beyond the expiry at the end of 2007 of the current Concorde Agreement governing the sport, Bernie Ecclestone admitted that the protracted dispute over the way F1 is administered had done 'a lot of damage to F1'.

'I think we are all losers,' said Ecclestone, the F1 commercial rights holder, in the run-up to the British GP. 'The FIA [the governing body] is a loser, because it was forced to adopt a position. We [the FOM, his Formula One Management group] are losers because we were forced to defend our position. The manufacturers and the teams have suffered more than anybody because the sponsors started putting a question-mark against F1 where there had never been a question mark before.'

Ecclestone also defended reducing the final offer to the competing teams from 60 to 50 percent of the sport's estimated $800 million annual income stream from television, race promoters' fees, trackside advertising and corporate hospitality. Ecclestone had controlled these rights exclusively through the FOM until he sold a controlling interest last year to CVC Capital Partners, which also owns the AA.

'The offer of 60 percent had been made on the assumption that the manufacturers would sign as manufacturers,' he said. 'But they didn't want to do that and they sent their relevant teams. The new owners are business people who have to value the risks. For them a signature from BMW is worth more than the one from BMW Sauber. They could have had 60 percent at any time, had they signed in their own names. But they didn't; they said that they couldn't make the commitment.'

When Heidfeld finally made his stop – which was frustrated by a problem engaging first gear as he went to rejoin the race – so Räikkönen went back into second place some 12.6s behind the leading Renault. Within another ten laps Schumacher was seriously hunting down the second-placed McLaren, to the point where only a second separated the two cars by the end of lap 35.

On lap 41 Michael came in for his second stop, a lap before Kimi's, and, thanks to really brisk in- and out-laps, he just managed to vault ahead of the McLaren.

'Second place was the best I could manage today,' said Schumacher after taking the chequered flag. 'Although there were no real problems with the car this weekend, we [the team] were simply not quick enough to win. Even though I am now 23 points behind Alonso I don't think the fight for the championship is over.'

Behind Räikkönen, Fisichella did a good job to storm home fourth ahead of Massa. 'It was a good race for me,' enthused Giancarlo. 'I had a competitive and consistent pace and was

much quicker than the cars around me. I suffered tyre graining during the second stint, just like Fernando, but it cleared up on the final set of tyres and I was really able to push.

'In the final laps I was much quicker than Räikkönen in the first sector, but he was a little bit quicker in the second and third sectors because he was running a bit more downforce than me. As I got near him I lost grip due to the turbulence and I couldn't get close enough to overtake.'

Behind Fisichella, Felipe Massa brought the other Ferrari home fifth ahead of Juan Pablo Montoya's McLaren, and the BMW-Saubers of Nick Heidfeld and Jacques Villeneuve completed the points-scoring positions in seventh and eighth. Despite his gearchange problem at the first pit stop, Heidfeld still managed to keep ahead of his team-mate, who had had a brush with Juan Pablo Montoya's McLaren on the first corner.

'I was on the inside and he was following another car on the outside,' said Villeneuve. 'He came across the track, took his line and didn't see I was there. I locked my wheels and ran into him but there was luckily no damage.'

Nico Rosberg was a frustrated ninth and Rubens Barrichello could do no better than tenth, wrestling his ill-handling Honda for much of the distance. The Brazilian finished ahead of Jarno Trulli's Toyota, which started the race from the back of the grid following a Saturday engine failure.

'It was always going to be a hard day's work out there from the back of the grid,' said the Italian. 'Silverstone is never the easiest place to overtake, but I still made it past a lot of people at the start and over the first three or four laps. The car was well balanced and I was fighting really hard throughout.'

Twice-British-GP-winner David Coulthard had a disappointing time in the Red Bull-Ferrari, ending the race a lapped 12th. 'The car had a lot of understeer during the race,' he said. 'I thought I might have done some damage to its underside when I was pushed wide over the kerb at the exit of Stowe on lap one during a battle with Jacques Villeneuve.'

For Button, however, just to finish the race would have seemed like a dream.

Alan Henry

Above: Fernando Alonso leads Kimi Räikkönen, Michael Schumacher, Felipe Massa and Giancarlo Fisichella around in front of the packed BRDC clubhouse.
Photograph: James Moy/crashpa.net

Left: Bernie Ecclestone – still forthright in his negotiating stance over the division of the sport's finances.
Photograph: Jean-François Galeron/WRI

SILVERSTONE GRAND PRIX CIRCUIT

116/187 mph/kmh

⚙ 4 Gear

Club 2 125/200 ⚙4
Club 1 50/80 ⚙2
Luffield 62/100 ⚙3
Bridge 6 181/290
Stowe 112/180 ⚙4
Abbey 2 75/120
Priory 96/155 ⚙
Woodcote 162/260 ⚙5
Brooklands 56/90 ⚙2
Hangar straight 190/305 ⚙6
Maggotts 155/250 ⚙5
Chapel 146/235 ⚙5
Becketts 131/210 ⚙4
Copse 165/265 ⚙5

Photograph: James Moy/www.crashpa.net

Circuit: 3.194 miles/5.141 km

FIA F1 WORLD CHAMPIONSHIP • ROUND 8

FOSTER'S
BRITISH GRAND PRIX
SILVERSTONE 9–11 JUNE 2006

RACE RESULTS

Pos.	Driver	Nat.	No.	Entrant	Car/Engine	Tyres	Laps	Time/Retirement	Speed (mph/km/h)	Gap to leader	Fastest race lap	
1	Fernando Alonso	E	1	Mild Seven Renault F1 Team	Renault R26-RS26 V8	M	60	1h 25m 51.927s	133.886/215.468		1m 21.599s	21
2	Michael Schumacher	D	5	Scuderia Ferrari Marlboro	Ferrari 248 F1-056 V8	B	60	1h 26m 05.878s	133.524/214.886	+13.951s	1m 21.934s	53
3	Kimi Räikkönen	FIN	3	Team McLaren Mercedes	McLaren MP4-21-Mercedes FO 108S V8	M	60	1h 26m 10.599s	133.402/214.690	+18.672s	1m 22.461s	15
4	Giancarlo Fisichella	I	2	Mild Seven Renault F1 Team	Renault R26-RS26 V8	M	60	1h 26m 11.903s	133.369/214.636	+19.976s	1m 22.238s	42
5	Felipe Massa	BR	6	Scuderia Ferrari Marlboro	Ferrari 248 F1-056 V8	B	60	1h 26m 23.486s	133.070/214.156	+31.559s	1m 22.371s	43
6	Juan Pablo Montoya	COL	4	Team McLaren Mercedes	McLaren MP4-21-Mercedes FO 108S V8	M	60	1h 26m 56.696s	132.223/212.793	+1m 04.769s	1m 22.780s	38
7	Nick Heidfeld	D	16	BMW Sauber F1 Team	BMW Sauber F1.06-BMW P86 V8	M	60	1h 27m 03.521s	132.051/212.515	+1m 11.594s	1m 22.706s	43
8	Jacques Villeneuve	CDN	17	BMW Sauber F1 Team	BMW Sauber F1.06-BMW P86 V8	M	60	1h 27m 10.226s	131.881/212.242	+1m 18.299s	1m 22.921s	46
9	Nico Rosberg	D	10	WilliamsF1 Team	Williams FW28-Cosworth CA2006 V8	B	60	1h 27m 10.935s	131.864/212.214	+1m 19.008s	1m 22.916s	47
10	Rubens Barrichello	BR	11	Lucky Strike Honda Racing F1 Team	Honda RA106-RA806E V8	M	59			+1 lap	1m 23.224s	38
11	Jarno Trulli	I	8	Panasonic Toyota Racing	Toyota TF106B-RVX-06 V8	B	59			+1 lap	1m 22.744s	19
12	David Coulthard	GB	14	Red Bull Racing	Red Bull RB2-Ferrari 056 V8	M	59			+1 lap	1m 23.995s	42
13	Vitantonio Liuzzi	I	20	Scuderia Toro Rosso	Toro Rosso STR01-Cosworth TJ2005-2 V10	M	59			+1 lap	1m 24.221s	25
14	Christian Klien	A	15	Red Bull Racing	Red Bull RB2-Ferrari 056 V8	M	59			+1 lap	1m 23.712s	30
15	Christijan Albers	NL	19	MF1 Racing	Midland M16-Toyota RVX-06 V8	B	59			+1 lap	1m 23.977s	27
16	Tiago Monteiro	P	18	MF1 Racing	Midland M16-Toyota RVX-06 V8	B	58			+2 laps	1m 24.636s	25
17	Takuma Sato	J	22	Super Aguri F1 Team	Super Aguri SA05-Honda RA806E V8	B	57			+3 laps	1m 26.520s	23
18	Franck Montagny	F	23	Super Aguri F1 Team	Super Aguri SA05-Honda RA806E V8	B	57			+3 laps	1m 27.167s	26
	Jenson Button	GB	12	Lucky Strike Honda Racing F1 Team	Honda RA106-RA806E V8	M	8	Oil leak/spin			1m 25.207s	8
	Scott Speed	USA	21	Scuderia Toro Rosso	Toro Rosso STR01-Cosworth TJ2005-2 V10	M	1	Accident			No time	
	Ralf Schumacher	D	7	Panasonic Toyota Racing	Toyota TF106B-RVX-06 V8	B	0	Accident			No time	
	Mark Webber	AUS	9	WilliamsF1 Team	Williams FW28-Cosworth CA2006 V8	B	0	Accident			No time	

Fastest lap: Fernando Alonso on lap 21, 1m 21.599s, 140.934 mph/226.811 km/h.

Lap record: Michael Schumacher (Ferrari F2004 V10), 1m 18.739s, 146.053 mph/235.049 km/h (2004).

All results and data © FOM 2006

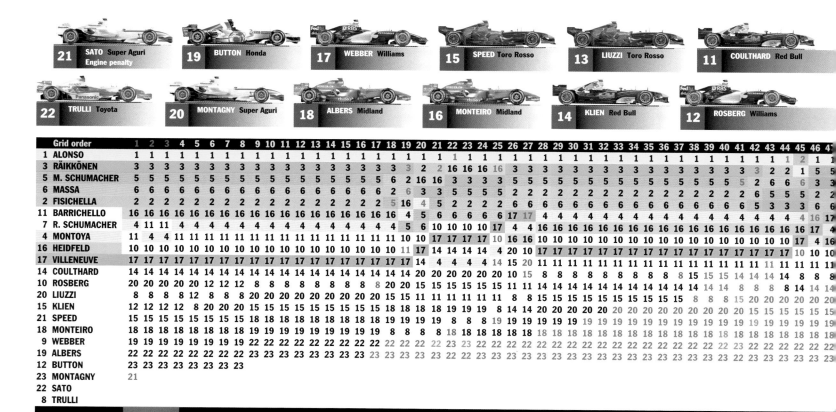

21	SATO	Super Aguri Engine penalty
19	BUTTON	Honda
17	WEBBER	Williams
15	SPEED	Toro Rosso
13	LIUZZI	Toro Rosso
11	COULTHARD	Red Bull
22	TRULLI	Toyota
20	MONTAGNY	Super Aguri
18	ALBERS	Midland
16	MONTEIRO	Midland
14	KLIEN	Red Bull
12	ROSBERG	Williams

Grid order		
1	ALONSO	
3	RÄIKKÖNEN	
5	M. SCHUMACHER	
6	MASSA	
2	FISICHELLA	
11	BARRICHELLO	
7	R. SCHUMACHER	
4	MONTOYA	
16	HEIDFELD	
17	VILLENEUVE	
14	COULTHARD	
10	ROSBERG	
20	LIUZZI	
15	KLIEN	
21	SPEED	
18	MONTEIRO	
9	WEBBER	
19	ALBERS	
12	BUTTON	
23	MONTAGNY	
22	SATO	
8	TRULLI	

TIME SHEETS

PRACTICE 1 (FRIDAY)

Sunny (track 29–32°C, air 23–24°C)

Pos.	Driver	Laps	Time
1	Alexander Wurz	26	1m 21.946s
2	Anthony Davidson	31	1m 22.003s
3	Robert Kubica	30	1m 22.365s
4	Jarno Trulli	7	1m 22.877s
5	Michael Schumacher	3	1m 22.925s
6	Rubens Barrichello	5	1m 23.128s
7	Jenson Button	6	1m 23.415s
8	Felipe Massa	4	1m 23.816s
9	Christijan Albers	6	1m 24.019s
10	Tiago Monteiro	6	1m 24.070s
11	Giorgio Mondini	19	1m 24.087s
12	Neel Jani	22	1m 24.145s
13	Takuma Sato	10	1m 27.724s
14	Sakon Yamamoto	22	1m 29.678s
15	Robert Doornbos	9	No time
16	Franck Montagny	3	No time
17	Ralf Schumacher	2	No time
18	Fernando Alonso	1	No time
19	Giancarlo Fisichella	1	No time
20	Christian Klien	1	No time
21	David Coulthard	1	No time
22	Kimi Räikkönen	1	No time
23	Juan Pablo Montoya	1	No time
24	Scott Speed	1	No time
25	Jacques Villeneuve	1	No time
26	Nick Heidfeld	1	No time
27	Vitantonio Liuzzi	1	No time

PRACTICE 2 (FRIDAY)

Sunny (track 37°C, air 26–27°C)

Pos.	Driver	Laps	Time
1	Robert Kubica	29	1m 21.082s
2	Giancarlo Fisichella	3	1m 22.294s
3	Alexander Wurz	30	1m 22.300s
4	Anthony Davidson	34	1m 22.310s
5	Jarno Trulli	17	1m 22.437s
6	Felipe Massa	19	1m 22.476s
7	Fernando Alonso	13	1m 22.603s
8	Michael Schumacher	14	1m 22.825s
9	Mark Webber	15	1m 23.099s
10	Rubens Barrichello	17	1m 23.104s
11	Ralf Schumacher	22	1m 23.114s
12	Robert Doornbos	25	1m 23.140s
13	Tiago Monteiro	23	1m 23.194s
14	Juan Pablo Montoya	10	1m 23.199s
15	Christijan Albers	14	1m 23.499s
16	Giorgio Mondini	25	1m 23.529s
17	Jenson Button	18	1m 23.707s
18	Jacques Villeneuve	13	1m 23.750s
19	Nico Rosberg	16	1m 23.816s
20	Nick Heidfeld	14	1m 23.895s
21	Kimi Räikkönen	4	1m 23.915s
22	Vitantonio Liuzzi	19	1m 24.012s
23	Christian Klien	12	1m 24.158s
24	Scott Speed	19	1m 24.167s
25	David Coulthard	13	1m 24.392s
26	Neel Jani	22	1m 24.666s
27	Takuma Sato	26	1m 25.870s
28	Franck Montagny	22	1m 26.248s
29	Sakon Yamamoto	27	1m 27.908s

QUALIFYING (SATURDAY)

Sunny (track 44–45°C, air 29°C)

Pos.	Driver	First	Second	Third
1	Fernando Alonso	1m 21.018s	1m 20.271s	1m 20.253s
2	Kimi Räikkönen	1m 21.648s	1m 20.497s	1m 20.397s
3	Michael Schumacher	1m 22.096s	1m 20.659s	1m 20.574s
4	Felipe Massa	1m 21.647s	1m 20.846s	1m 20.764s
5	Giancarlo Fisichella	1m 22.411s	1m 20.594s	1m 20.919s
6	Rubens Barrichello	1m 22.965s	1m 20.929s	1m 20.943s
7	Ralf Schumacher	1m 22.886s	1m 21.043s	1m 21.073s
8	Juan Pablo Montoya	1m 22.169s	1m 20.816s	1m 21.107s
9	Nick Heidfeld	1m 21.670s	1m 20.629s	1m 21.329s
10	Jacques Villeneuve	1m 21.637s	1m 20.672s	1m 21.599s
11	David Coulthard	1m 22.424s	1m 21.442s	
12	Nico Rosberg	1m 23.083s	1m 21.567s	
13	Vitantonio Liuzzi	1m 22.685s	1m 21.699s	
14	Christian Klien	1m 22.773s	1m 21.990s	
15	Scott Speed	1m 22.541s	1m 22.076s	
16	Tiago Monteiro	1m 22.860s	1m 22.207s	
17	Mark Webber	1m 23.129s		
18	Christijan Albers	1m 23.210s		
19	Jenson Button	1m 23.247s		
20	Takuma Sato	1m 26.158s		
21	Franck Montagny	1m 26.316s		
22	Jarno Trulli	No time		

PRACTICE 3 (SATURDAY)

Sunny (track 41–42°C, air 27°C)

Pos.	Driver	Laps	Time
1	Michael Schumacher	13	1m 20.919s
2	Nick Heidfeld	13	1m 21.361s
3	Felipe Massa	15	1m 21.633s
4	Kimi Räikkönen	12	1m 21.771s
5	Giancarlo Fisichella	12	1m 21.859s
6	Fernando Alonso	13	1m 21.870s
7	Rubens Barrichello	12	1m 22.023s
8	Jacques Villeneuve	14	1m 22.229s
9	Vitantonio Liuzzi	18	1m 22.456s
10	Scott Speed	14	1m 22.532s
11	Jenson Button	15	1m 22.596s
12	David Coulthard	15	1m 22.681s
13	Tiago Monteiro	19	1m 22.812s
14	Christian Klien	14	1m 22.921s
15	Juan Pablo Montoya	7	1m 23.412s
16	Jarno Trulli	13	1m 23.459s
17	Mark Webber	12	1m 23.964s
18	Nico Rosberg	11	1m 24.010s
19	Ralf Schumacher	12	1m 24.386s
20	Franck Montagny	10	1m 27.229s
21	Takuma Sato	12	1m 27.525s
22	Christijan Albers	3	No time

CHASSIS LOG BOOK

RENAULT
1	Fernando Alonso	R26/03	9
2	Giancarlo Fisichella	R26/04	10
	Spare	R26/01	35

McLAREN-MERCEDES
3	Kimi Räikkönen	MP4-21/06	11
4	Juan Pablo Montoya	MP4-21/05	12
	Spare	MP4-21/04	36

FERRARI
5	Michael Schumacher	248 F1/254	14
6	Felipe Massa	248 F1/250	37
	Spare	248 F1/251	

TOYOTA
7	Ralf Schumacher	TF106B/07	16
8	Jarno Trulli	TF106B/08	17
	Spare	TF106B/06	38

WILLIAMS-COSWORTH
	Mark Webber	FW28/03	18
	Nico Rosberg	FW28/06	19
	Alexander Wurz	FW28/04	39

HONDA
	Rubens Barrichello	RA106/01	20
	Jenson Button	RA106/04	21
	Anthony Davidson	RA106/03	40

RED BULL-FERRARI
	David Coulthard	RB2/3	22
	Christian Klien	RB2/2	23
	Robert Doornbos	RB2/5	41

BMW SAUBER
16	Nick Heidfeld	F1.06/04	
17	Jacques Villeneuve	F1.06/08	
38	Robert Kubica	F1.06/03	

MIDLAND-TOYOTA
	Tiago Monteiro	M16/03	
	Christijan Albers	M16/02	
	Giorgio Mondini	M16/02	

TORO ROSSO-COSWORTH
	Vitantonio Liuzzi	STR01/02	
	Scott Speed	STR01/01	
	Neel Jani	STR01/03	

SUPER AGURI-HONDA
	Takuma Sato	SA05/01	
	Franck Montagny	SA05/02	
	Sakon Yamamoto	SA05/01	

Starting grid

9 HEIDFELD BMW-Sauber

7 R. SCHUMACHER Toyota

5 FISICHELLA Renault

3 M. SCHUMACHER Ferrari

1 ALONSO Renault

10 VILLENEUVE BMW-Sauber

8 MONTOYA McLaren

6 BARRICHELLO Honda

4 MASSA Ferrari

2 RÄIKKÖNEN McLaren

RACE DISTANCE:
60 laps
191.603 miles/308.355 km

RACE WEATHER:
Sunny
track 36–39°C, air 26–27°C

Lap chart

8	49	50	51	52	53	54	55	56	57	58	59	60	•
1	1	1	1	1	1	1	1	1	1	1	1	1	1
5	5	5	5	5	5	5	5	5	5	5	5	5	2
3	3	3	3	3	3	3	3	3	3	3	3	3	3
2	2	2	2	2	2	2	2	2	2	2	2	2	4
6	6	6	6	6	6	6	6	6	6	6	6	6	5
4	4	4	4	4	4	4	4	4	4	4	4	4	6
7	16	16	16	16	16	16	16	16	16	16	16	16	7
6	17	17	17	17	17	17	17	17	17	17	17	17	8
0	10	10	10	10	10	10	10	10	10	10	10	10	9
1	11	11	11	11	11	11	11	11	11	11	11		10
8	8	8	8	8	8	8	8	8	8	8	8	8	11
4	14	14	14	14	14	14	14	14	14	14	14	14	12
0	15	15	20	20	20	20	20	20	20	20	20	20	13
5	15	15	15	15	15	15	15	15	15	15	15	15	14
9	19	19	19	19	19	19	19	19	19	19	19	19	15
8	18	18	18	18	18	18	18	18	18	18	18		16
2	22	22	22	22	22	22	22	22	22				17
3	23	23	23	23	23	23	23	23					18

Pit stop
One lap or more behind leader
Safety car deployed on laps shown

FOR THE RECORD

200th GRAND PRIX START: Renault

50th POINT: Felipe Massa

POINTS

DRIVERS
1	Fernando Alonso	74
2	Michael Schumacher	51
3	Kimi Räikkönen	33
4	Giancarlo Fisichella	32
5	Juan Pablo Montoya	26
6	Felipe Massa	24
7	Jenson Button	16
8	Rubens Barrichello	13
9	Nick Heidfeld	10
10	Ralf Schumacher	8
11	David Coulthard	7
12	Jacques Villeneuve	7
13	Mark Webber	6
14	Nico Rosberg	4
15	Christian Klien	1

CONSTRUCTORS
1	Renault	106
2	Ferrari	75
3	McLaren	59
4	Honda	29
5	BMW Sauber	17
6	Williams	10
7	Toyota	8
8	Red Bull	8

Photograph: James Moy/www.crashpa.net

Photographs: James Moy/www.crashpa.net

Main: The sound of thunder at the start of the Canadian Grand Prix, with the whole pack successfully negotiating the first corner of the Circuit Gilles Villeneuve.

Photograph: Jean-François Galeron

Inset: Winner Fernando Alonso goes through his very special celebratory routine.

Photograph: Paul-Henri Cahier

FIA F1 WORLD CHAMPIONSHIP/ROUND 9

CANADIAN GP

MONTREAL

DID SCHUMACHER HOLD THE KEY TO RÄIKKÖNEN SWITCH?

FERRARI may have paid Kimi Räikkönen a one-off $3-million fee not to sign for any other team prior to 31 May this year in a bid to keep open its rights to his services for 2007 should Michael Schumacher decide to retire, it emerged from well-placed sources in the paddock at Montreal.

If true, this latest wild twist to the who-drives-what saga for next season seemed to leave the Ferrari team leader holding all the negotiating cards because he had made it clear that he would not be making public his final decision over whether to continue racing until the Italian GP in September.

Räikkönen also continued to be linked to a possible transfer to Renault, which was believed to be an initiative driven by Bernie Ecclestone, the F1 commercial rights holder, who wanted to have all three top teams featuring a star driver in 2007.

However, despite assertions from Renault's senior management two months earlier that the French car maker would pay whatever was necessary to secure one of the top three drivers – Fernando Alonso, Schumacher or Räikkönen – there remained considerable doubt over whether they would actually pay the $20 million required to sign the Finn.

Most people believed that Räikkönen was firmly committed to Ferrari, whatever Schumacher eventually decided to do.

Meanwhile McLaren had 'a cupboard-full of good drivers' available, according to a team source. Should it opt to keep GP2 star Lewis Hamilton on an F1 testing contract in 2007, it could supposedly choose from Juan Pablo Montoya, Pedro de la Rosa or Gary Paffett to keep the seat warm alongside Alonso while Hamilton amassed more experience and testing miles. Montoya would soon drop from that equation, of course.

MONTREAL QUALIFYING

DURING pre-race testing in Europe, Ferrari, Toyota and Williams had all concluded that their latest Bridgestone tyres would offer them the real prospect of challenging Fernando Alonso's Renault and the other Michelin runners in a no-holds-barred confrontation. Yet when it came to the battle for pole position Alonso and his team-mate Giancarlo Fisichella commandingly locked out the front row of the starting grid.

'Five pole positions in a row is something I have never experienced and it is a fantastic feeling,' said the world champion, who posted a 1m 14.942s to ease out his team-mate by just 0.24s. 'The competition between myself, Fisico and [Kimi] Räikkönen has been very close all weekend and that is how it turned out in qualifying this afternoon.'

With Räikkönen's McLaren (1m 15.386s) on the inside of the second row alongside Jarno Trulli's Toyota TF106B (1m 15.968s), Michael Schumacher found his Ferrari struggling for grip and he could do no better than fifth fastest to line up on the inside of row three on a 1m 15.986s. Nursing a 23-point deficit to Alonso, he clearly felt his championship chances were slipping away.

'Obviously we [the team and I] can't be happy with this result, especially in the light of the championship situation,' said Schumacher. 'We have made some progress compared with yesterday, but we are still suffering from a lack of grip. This could be down to the cars, the tyres or the set-up. At the moment we cannot be sure which. What is sure is that, starting from fifth on the grid, we can expect a very tough race.'

Nico Rosberg did an excellent job to qualify his Williams FW28 sixth (1m 16.012s) despite glancing one of the trackside walls and attracting criticism from both his team-mate Mark Webber and Honda's Rubens Barrichello for what they regarded as balking them unacceptably during this crucial session.

Barrichello just squeezed into ninth on 1m 16.912s, 0.3s slower than team-mate Jenson Button, who was immediately ahead of him on the grid. 'We were on the borderline for the first qualifying session and I nearly got put out of it by Rosberg holding me up,' said the Brazilian.

'Apart from that our qualifying hour ran smoothly enough. In the last sector of my final lap I went a little wide onto the marbles, which cost a little time, so I'm happy with my position.'

Felipe Massa completed the top ten on 1m 17.209s, just easing out Jacques Villeneuve's BMW-Sauber (1m 15.832s), which failed to make the top ten cut on the Canadian's home turf. 'The track heated up, we lost the balance of the car and couldn't get it to work anymore,' said Jacques. 'It is very disappointing because I'm now in the middle of the pack for the first corner. I should be all right once the race gets going, but I just need to keep my nose clean at the first corner.'

Christian Klien did a steady job to qualify his Red Bull on 1m 15.833s ahead of Nick Heidfeld's BMW-Sauber, Ralf Schumacher's Toyota and Vitantonio Liuzzi's Toro Rosso, leaving David Coulthard to pip Mark Webber as the last runner to make it through into the second spell of qualifying.

'I had a lot of oversteer during qualifying, which I've had all weekend, and it basically means I can't carry speed into the corners,' said DC. 'That's where you lose time here, so it doesn't surprise me we're at the back end of the second qualifying group. We can't really change anything on the car before the race, apart from front wing adjustments and, because I think we've got bigger issues than that, we're just going to have to do the best we can.'

Immediately behind Webber came Scott Speed in his Toro Rosso, a fraction ahead of the two Midlands and the Super Aguri duo. 'For some reason we picked up a lot more oversteer in this session than in the others,' said Speed, slightly perplexed. 'The car felt completely different and was sliding a lot. The track temperature was a lot higher, so we adjusted tyre pressures accordingly and maybe that's where we didn't get it quite right.'

Left: Kimi Räikkönen was not happy at having to settle for third place in Montreal.
Photograph: James Moy/www.crashpa.net

Above: Tiago Monteiro collided with team-mate Christijan Albers on the opening lap of the race.
Photograph: James Moy/www.crashpa.net

Left: Mark Webber, having failed to beat the cut in qualifying for the second time in a row, struggled throughout the race with lack of grip caused by tyre graining and trailed home out of the points.
Photograph: Paul-Henri Cahier

Above: Jarno Trulli had a heartening run to score his first points of the season for the Toyota squad.

Photographs: James Moy/www.crashpa.net

Centre right: Nick Heidfeld managed seventh place for BMW Sauber, adding another two points to his personal tally.

Bottom right: Jean Todt oversees the final preparations to Michael Schumacher's Ferrari on the starting grid.

Photographs: Paul-Henri Cahier

FERNANDO Alonso yet again underlined his metronomic consistency under intense pressure as he fended off a strong initial challenge from Kimi Räikkönen's McLaren-Mercedes to win for Renault at the evocatively titled Circuit Gilles Villeneuve. To compound Räikkönen's acute disappointment, Michael Schumacher forced his Ferrari past the McLaren on the penultimate lap to take runner-up spot.

This was Alonso's 14th career victory – and his sixth this season, which further confirmed his relentless progress towards his second world championship crown as well as celebrating the centenary of the French car maker's victory in the first ever GP at Le Mans on 26 June 1906.

'It was perfect all weekend,' said Alonso, who had never finished on the podium at the Montreal circuit before. 'Obviously without the safety car the gap would have been much bigger and the race easier, but the safety car sometimes helps you and sometimes not. But the important thing is to win again.

'The race was quite difficult because off the line there was a lot of dirt and a lot of dust coming from the tyres and you cannot do many mistakes. You go a little bit off line and you lose one or two seconds and we saw a lot of this type of incident in the race.'

In front of a capacity crowd of more than 100,000 spectators, Alonso eased smoothly into the lead of the 70-lap race on the sprint from the grid to the first tight left-hander. Giancarlo Fisichella slightly jumped the start and fell back to third as Kimi Räikkönen came storming through to second in his McLaren.

Midway around the second lap Juan Pablo Montoya, running sixth in his McLaren, lunged inside Nico Rosberg's fifth-placed Williams going into one of the fast ess-bends on the back of the circuit. The two cars made smart contact but while Montoya got away with only a bent left-front wheel Rosberg was pitched unceremoniously into the wall and out of the race.

Just before their coming together, JPM had pulled level with the Williams under braking for the ess-bend before the pits. Montoya had the inside line, but Nico tried to sit it out with him and straight-lined the chicane, emerging still ahead of the McLaren. Racing etiquette suggested that Nico would have been better advised to concede the position – and save himself much grief half a lap later.

'I claimed one place off the start and I thought the car felt really good and we could possibly be in with a chance of some points today,' said Rosberg ruefully. 'I was aware that Montoya was close behind me, but I knew I could defend my position because the car was really good on the brakes. I chose an outside line and left enough room for him to come inside me into the chicane, because I knew that if he did pass me I would

174

get ahead again coming out of the corner. However, he came in really tight and we were never going to make it around the corner together. I felt him hit me from the rear once, then again and that was it: my race was over.'

Moments after the Rosberg episode it was announced that the stewards had decided to impose a drive-through penalty on Fisichella. He came in to take his punishment at the end of lap seven, dropping from third to fifth as he did so, behind Jarno Trulli's Toyota and Michael Schumacher's Ferrari.

Meanwhile there was, understandably, a rather edgy atmosphere in the Midland team garage after Tiago Monteiro spun out his team-mate Christijan Albers on the opening lap of the race. Tiago continued to finish 17th, but the Dutchman

was out on the spot. 'I think it's quite clear what happened,' he said crisply. 'So let's leave it at that and move on.'

Räikkönen now began to show his real mettle, harrying Alonso relentlessly and on one occasion actually pulling level with the Spaniard on the 195-mph straight before the pits. Yet Alonso refused to be intimidated and, yard by yard, gradually edged away until he was 1.1s ahead with 20 laps completed.

Alonso made his first scheduled refuelling stop at the end of lap 23, leaving Räikkönen to stay out in the lead for another two laps before coming in for his stop, a strategy that McLaren hoped would vault him into the lead. Unfortunately a sticking right-rear wheel-securing nut delayed him and he went back into the fray still holding second place.

DIARY

Toyota confirms that it regards winning Le Mans as unfinished business. The Japanese marque's F1 boss John Howett says, 'Le Mans is something we would consider again. If we did, there's no way we would do it in addition to F1. It would have to be one or the other.'

AJ Almendinger wins the Cleveland Champcar race after series leader Sébastien Bourdais is pushed off in a first-lap shunt.

Durban is confirmed as the venue for this year's South African round of the Grand Prix Masters series, replacing Kyalami.

Indy boss Tony George denies stories that a rapprochement between Champcar and the IRL is close to being finalised.

Right: Michael Schumacher, Fernando Alonso and Kimi Räikkönen, alone with their thoughts on the podium.

Photograph: Paul-Henri Cahier

Below: Michelin celebrates its well-deserved 100th grand prix victory.

Photograph: Jean-François Galeron

Schumacher had a lucky escape when his Ferrari's right-front wheel grazed the wall on the fast left-hander before the start line – he got away with it and was up to third by the time of the first round of refuelling stops. Montoya was less lucky, hitting the wall rather harder before pulling his McLaren to a halt at the trackside with broken suspension at the end of lap 13.

'That was a bit of a mess,' said Montoya with masterly understatement as he reviewed the debris of his race. 'I was battling with Nico Rosberg in the opening laps but then we touched. I thought I had damaged the nose and as the safety car came out I went into the pits. The team did a precautionary tyre change and I changed my strategy to give me a good chance of a strong finishing position.

'I had a good battle with DC [David Coulthard], then with Ralf [Schumacher] and was making progress. The car was great, but I was sliding about quite a bit because I had lost a deflector and consequently was a bit light on downforce. I was trying to make up positions, but then I touched the wall and damaged the rear, so that was the end of the race for me.'

McLaren's fortunes took another dive on lap 53 when Räikkönen came in for his second refuelling stop, losing more time when he stalled the engine. He just scrambled back out onto the track ahead of the third-placed Michael Schumacher, but any chance of catching the impeccable Alonso was now gone for good.

The safety car came out again on lap 60, because Jacques Villeneuve crashed, and was withdrawn with seven laps to go, allowing Alonso to sprint home the winner ahead of Räikkönen, Schumacher and an understandably dejected Fisichella. Running on a one-stop refuelling strategy, Felipe Massa was quite satisfied with his eventual fifth place as the last of the unlapped runners. 'Even with a heavy fuel load the car and tyres performed well and I was able to run at a competitive pace,' he said. 'Only after the safety car did I feel a slight lack of grip, but in this particular situation we were in much better shape than yesterday.'

Sixth place fell to Jarno Trulli's Toyota TF106B, this – amazingly – being the first time in 2006 that the Italian driver had managed to score world championship points. Even so, Jarno found himself grappling with a misfire so bad that he was having to run the engine in 'recover mode' to conserve it for the second part of the race.

Track conditions were undeniably appalling in the closing stages, with treacherous build-ups of rubber debris from the tyres waiting for anybody who dared stray off the racing line. The most spectacular departure from the race was that of local hero Villeneuve, who momentarily got out of the groove while lapping Ralf Schumacher's limping Toyota. It was as if he had hit a patch of black ice and he was in the wall almost before his hands had time to apply any corrective lock.

'Ralf was running slowly for quite a few laps and I think he was having trouble with his car,' explained Jacques, who had seemed on course for an eighth-place finish behind his BMW Sauber team-mate Nick Heidfeld. 'When he decided to let me through it was on a corner. He lifted off and just to avoid him I had to go wide where there was old rubber from the tyres – it was like being on an ice rink. This is always a tough race and sometimes it doesn't work out.'

At the final restart, Coulthard's Red Bull was running behind Jenson Button's Honda, but keen radio listeners heard DC's engineer Mark Hutcheson shouting over the radio link for his man to make a huge effort 'because Jenson is always slow off the mark when it comes to the restarts'. In fact, Button ran wide onto the marbles and handed David the place.

'It's been a very frustrating day for me,' reflected Button. 'I had no grip with either the front or rear tyres, as well as understeer and a lack of traction. The difficulty with this circuit is that there is just so much rubber going down, which leaves marbles on every corner.

'If you make a slight mistake or lock up, you go off-line and then you lose a few seconds trying to get the tyres back up to temperature. The car was difficult to drive all day and it's very disappointing indeed to have finished outside the points.'

Scott Speed's Toro Rosso was just 0.4s farther back in tenth place, followed home by Christian Klien's Red Bull and Mark Webber, who had a simply dismal time battling with tyre graining for much of the distance.

'For this event we picked the wrong tyres,' said Webber, 'and we didn't have any grip at all due to the high levels of degradation that those tyres suffered. I got a little bit of grip back towards the end of the stints, but when all four tyres were completely grained, it was unfortunately impossible to drive the car. We were just too far off the pace today.'

At just after 9pm, the first of 69 huge articulated transporters rumbled onto the freeway outside Montreal at the start of a 22-hour non-stop journey carrying the F1 cars, spares and supplies towards the American border and on down to Indianapolis, for what the racing community feared might possibly be the last US GP the following weekend.

Last year's fiasco of a race, in which Michael Schumacher's Ferrari scored an inconsequential victory at the head of a six-car field after all the Michelin teams withdrew following a spate of tyre failures, was one of the sport's lowest moments and left the European racing community facing the exacting task of mending fences with the US race fans. Now that rebuilding task would be put to the test as a matter of urgency.

Alan Henry

FIA F1 WORLD CHAMPIONSHIP • ROUND 9

GRAND PRIX DU CANADA
MONTRÉAL 23–25 JUNE 2006

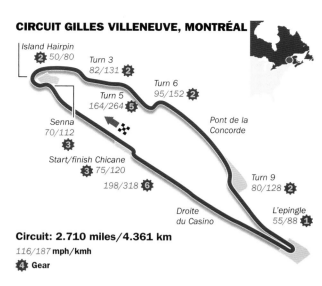

CIRCUIT GILLES VILLENEUVE, MONTRÉAL

Island Hairpin
2 50/80

Turn 3
82/131 **2**

Turn 6
95/152 **2**

Turn 5
164/264 **5**

Senna
70/112 **3**

Pont de la Concorde

Start/finish Chicane
3 75/120

198/318 **6**

Turn 9
80/128 **2**

Droite du Casino

L'epingle
55/88 **1**

Photograph: James Moy/www.crashpa.net

Circuit: 2.710 miles/4.361 km
116/187 **mph/kmh**
4 Gear

RACE RESULTS

Pos.	Driver	Nat.	No.	Entrant	Car/Engine	Tyres	Laps	Time/Retirement	Speed (mph/km/h)	Gap to leader	Fastest race lap	
1	Fernando Alonso	E	1	Mild Seven Renault F1 Team	Renault R26-RS26 V8	M	70	1h 34m 37.308s	120.281/193.572		1m 15.911s	22
2	Michael Schumacher	D	5	Scuderia Ferrari Marlboro	Ferrari 248 F1-056 V8	B	70	1h 34m 39.419s	120.235/193.500	+2.111s	1m 15.993s	68
3	Kimi Räikkönen	FIN	3	Team McLaren Mercedes	McLaren MP4-21-Mercedes FO 108S V8	M	70	1h 34m 46.121s	120.094/193.272	+8.813s	1m 15.841s	22
4	Giancarlo Fisichella	I	2	Mild Seven Renault F1 Team	Renault R26-RS26 V8	M	70	1h 34m 52.987s	119.949/193.039	+15.679s	1m 16.669s	49
5	Felipe Massa	BR	6	Scuderia Ferrari Marlboro	Ferrari 248 F1-056 V8	B	70	1h 35m 02.480s	119.749/192.718	+25.172s	1m 17.308s	31
6	Jarno Trulli	I	8	Panasonic Toyota Racing	Toyota TF106B-RVX-06 V8	B	69			+1 lap	1m 17.503s	15
7	Nick Heidfeld	D	16	BMW Sauber F1 Team	BMW Sauber F1.06-BMW P86 V8	M	69			+1 lap	1m 17.454s	52
8	David Coulthard	GB	14	Red Bull Racing	Red Bull RB2-Ferrari 056 V8	M	69			+1 lap	1m 17.619s	39
9	Jenson Button	GB	12	Lucky Strike Honda Racing F1 Team	Honda RA106-RA806E V8	M	69			+1 lap	1m 18.001s	21
10	Scott Speed	USA	21	Scuderia Toro Rosso	Toro Rosso STR01-Cosworth TJ2005-2 V10	M	69			+1 lap	1m 17.720s	52
11	Christian Klien	A	15	Red Bull Racing	Red Bull RB2-Ferrari 056 V8	M	69			+1 lap	1m 17.576s	55
12	Mark Webber	AUS	9	WilliamsF1 Team	Williams FW28-Cosworth CA2006 V8	B	69			+1 lap	1m 17.705s	17
13	Vitantonio Liuzzi	I	20	Scuderia Toro Rosso	Toro Rosso STR01-Cosworth TJ2005-2 V10	M	68			+2 laps	1m 18.078s	50
14	Tiago Monteiro	P	18	MF1 Racing	Midland M16-Toyota RVX-06 V8	B	66			+4 laps	1m 19.291s	5
15	Takuma Sato	J	22	Super Aguri F1 Team	Super Aguri SA05-Honda RA806E V8	B	64	Accident		+6 laps	1m 20.490s	40
	Jacques Villeneuve	CDN	17	BMW Sauber F1 Team	BMW Sauber F1.06-BMW P86 V8	M	58	Accident			1m 17.394s	29
	Ralf Schumacher	D	7	Panasonic Toyota Racing	Toyota TF106B-RVX-06 V8	B	58	Handling			1m 18.793s	19
	Juan Pablo Montoya	COL	4	Team McLaren Mercedes	McLaren MP4-21-Mercedes FO 108S V8	M	13	Accident			1m 18.493s	5
	Rubens Barrichello	BR	11	Lucky Strike Honda Racing F1 Team	Honda RA106-RA806E V8	M	11	Engine			1m 19.286s	10
	Franck Montagny	F	23	Super Aguri F1 Team	Super Aguri SA05-Honda RA806E V8	B	2	Engine			2m 07.709s	2
	Nico Rosberg	D	10	WilliamsF1 Team	Williams FW28-Cosworth CA2006 V8	B	1	Accident			No time	–
	Christijan Albers	NL	19	MF1 Racing	Midland M16-Toyota RVX-06 V8	B	0	Accident			No time	–

All results and data © FOM 2006

Fastest lap: Kimi Räikkönen on lap 22, 1m 15.841s, 128.628 mph/207.006 km/h.

Lap record: Rubens Barrichello (Ferrari F2004 V10), 1m 13.622s, 132.505 mph/213.246 km/h (2004).

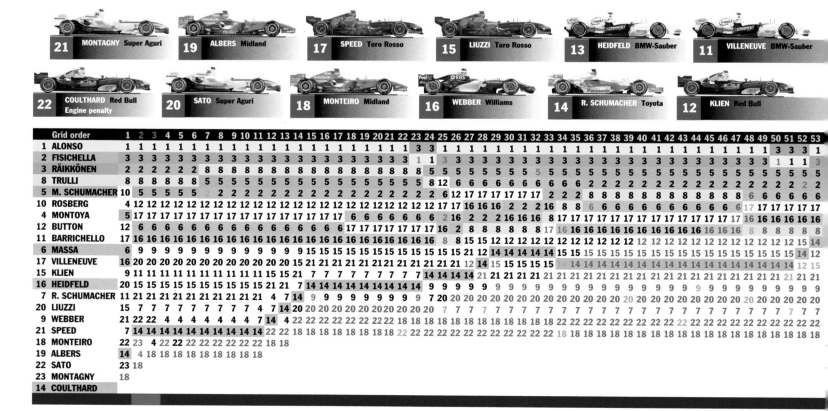

Grid order	1	2	3	4	5	6	7	8	9	10	11	12	13	14	15	16	17	18	19	20	21	22	23	24	25	26	27	28	29	30	31	32	33	34	35	36	37	38	39	40	41	42	43	44	45	46	47	48	49	50	51	52	53
1 ALONSO	1	1	1	1	1	1	1	1	1	1	1	1	1	1	1	1	1	1	1	1	1	1	3	3	1	1	1	1	1	1	1	1	1	1	1	1	1	1	1	1	1	1	1	1	1	1	1	1	1	3	3	3	1
2 FISICHELLA	3	3	3	3	3	3	3	3	3	3	3	3	3	3	3	3	3	3	3	3	3	3	1	1	3	3	3	3	3	3	3	3	3	3	3	3	3	3	3	3	3	3	3	3	3	3	3	3	3	1	1	1	3
3 RÄIKKÖNEN	2	2	2	2	2	2	8	8	8	8	8	8	8	8	8	8	8	8	8	8	8	8	5	5	5	5	5	5	5	5	5	5	5	5	5	5	5	5	5	5	5	5	5	5	5	5	5	5	5	5	5	5	3
8 TRULLI	8	8	8	8	8	5	5	5	5	5	5	5	5	5	5	5	5	5	5	5	5	5	8	12	6	6	6	6	6	6	6	6	2	2	2	2	2	2	2	2	2	2	2	2	2	2	2	2	2	2	2	2	2
5 M. SCHUMACHER	10	5	5	5	5	5	2	2	2	2	2	2	2	2	2	2	2	2	2	2	2	2	6	12	17	17	17	17	17	2	2	2	8	8	8	8	8	8	8	8	8	6	6	6	6	6	6	6	6	6	6	6	6
10 ROSBERG	4	12	12	12	12	12	12	12	12	12	12	12	12	12	12	12	12	12	17	16	16	16	2	16	2	2	2	16	8	6	6	6	6	6	6	6	6	6	6	6	6	17	17	17	17	17	17	17	17				
4 MONTOYA	5	17	17	17	17	17	17	17	17	17	17	17	17	17	17	6	6	6	6	6	6	6	16	2	2	16	16	8	17	17	17	17	17	17	17	17	17	17	17	17	16	16	16	16	16	16	16						
12 BUTTON	12	6	6	6	6	6	6	6	6	6	6	6	6	6	6	17	17	17	17	17	17	16	2	8	8	8	8	17	16	16	16	16	16	16	16	16	16	16	16	8	8	8	8	8	8								
11 BARRICHELLO	17	16	16	16	16	16	16	16	16	16	16	16	16	16	16	16	16	16	16	16	16	8	8	15	12	12	12	12	12	12	12	12	12	12	12	12	12	12	12	12	12	12	12	12	15	14							
6 MASSA	6	9	9	9	9	9	9	9	9	9	9	9	9	9	9	9	9	9	15	15	15	15	14	14	15	15	15	15	15	15	15	15	15	15	15	15	15	15	15	15	15	15	15	15	14	12							
17 VILLENEUVE	16	20	20	20	20	20	20	20	20	20	20	20	20	15	21	21	21	21	21	21	21	14	15	15	15	15	14	14	14	14	14	14	14	14	14	14	14	14	14	14	14	14	14	14	12	15							
15 KLIEN	9	11	11	11	11	11	11	11	11	15	15	15	21	7	7	7	7	7	7	7	7	21	21	21	21	21	21	21	21	21	21	21	21	21	21	21	21	21	21	21	21	21	9										
16 HEIDFELD	20	15	15	15	15	15	15	15	15	21	7	14	14	14	14	14	14	14	14	14	9	9	9	9	9	9	9	9	9	9	9	9	9	9	9	9	9	9	9	9	9	9											
7 R. SCHUMACHER	11	21	21	21	21	21	21	21	4	7	14	9	9	9	9	9	9	9	9	9	7	20	20	20	20	20	20	20	20	20	20	20	20	20	20	20	20	20	20	20	20	20											
20 LIUZZI	15	7	7	7	7	7	7	4	7	14	20	20	20	20	20	20	20	20	20	20	7	7	7	7	7	7	7	7	7	7	7	7	7	7	7	7	7	7	7	7	7	7											
9 WEBBER	21	22	22	4	4	4	4	4	14	4	22	22	22	22	18	18	18	18	18	18	18	18	22	22	22	22	22	22	22	22	22	22	22	22	22	22	22	22	22	22	22	22											
21 SPEED	7	14	14	14	14	14	14	14	14	14	18	18	18	18	22	22	22	22	18	18	22	22	18	18	18	18	18	18	18	18	18	18	18	18	18	18	18	18	18	18	18	18											
18 MONTEIRO	22	23	4	22	22	22	22	22	22	18	18																																										
19 ALBERS	14	4	18	18	18	18	18	18	18	18																																											
22 SATO	23	18																																																			
23 MONTAGNY	18																																																				
14 COULTHARD																																																					

PRACTICE 1 (FRIDAY)
Cloudy (track 26ºC, air 20ºC)

Pos.	Driver	Laps	Time
1	Robert Kubica	30	1m 16.390s
2	Anthony Davidson	26	1m 18.306s
3	Alexander Wurz	23	1m 18.941s
4	Michael Schumacher	5	1m 18.994s
5	Rubens Barrichello	6	1m 19.070s
6	Jenson Button	6	1m 19.165s
7	Neel Jani	24	1m 19.258s
8	Robert Doornbos	20	1m 19.681s
9	Vitantonio Liuzzi	7	1m 20.154s
10	Christijan Albers	9	1m 20.646s
11	Tiago Monteiro	8	1m 20.799s
12	Ralf Schumacher	6	1m 20.861s
13	Franck Montagny	17	1m 21.783s
14	Takuma Sato	20	1m 21.891s
15	Sakon Yamamoto	29	1m 23.159s
16	Felipe Massa	5	1m 23.179s
17	Jarno Trulli	7	1m 24.029s
18	Giorgio Mondini	2	No time
19	Fernando Alonso	2	No time
20	Giancarlo Fisichella	1	No time
21	Christian Klien	1	No time
22	Scott Speed	1	No time
23	Jacques Villeneuve	1	No time
24	David Coulthard	1	No time
25	Nick Heidfeld	1	No time

PRACTICE 2 (FRIDAY)
Broken cloud (track 33–41ºC, air 24ºC)

Pos.	Driver	Laps	Time
1	Robert Kubica	33	1m 16.965s
2	Fernando Alonso	15	1m 17.095s
3	Alexander Wurz	21	1m 17.337s
4	Kimi Räikkönen	10	1m 17.490s
5	Anthony Davidson	32	1m 17.627s
6	Giancarlo Fisichella	21	1m 17.805s
7	Mark Webber	13	1m 17.848s
8	Vitantonio Liuzzi	18	1m 18.009s
9	Nick Heidfeld	13	1m 18.015s
10	Jacques Villeneuve	14	1m 18.035s
11	Robert Doornbos	32	1m 18.201s
12	Rubens Barrichello	16	1m 18.279s
13	Jenson Button	18	1m 18.429s
14	Christian Klien	20	1m 18.503s
15	Michael Schumacher	17	1m 18.549s
16	Ralf Schumacher	23	1m 18.614s
17	Juan Pablo Montoya	14	1m 18.761s
18	Christian Klien	15	1m 18.865s
19	Jarno Trulli	17	1m 18.868s
20	Scott Speed	21	1m 18.907s
21	Nico Rosberg	10	1m 19.048s
22	Felipe Massa	15	1m 19.099s
23	Giorgio Mondini	24	1m 19.138s
24	David Coulthard	15	1m 19.313s
25	Neel Jani	28	1m 19.541s
26	Takuma Sato	22	1m 19.624s
27	Sakon Yamamoto	26	1m 20.197s
28	Tiago Monteiro	18	1m 20.262s
29	Franck Montagny	22	1m 21.434s

QUALIFYING (SATURDAY)
Scattered cloud/sunny (track 38–42ºC, air 24–26ºC)

Pos.	Driver	First	Second	Third
1	Fernando Alonso	1m 15.350s	1m 14.726s	1m 14.942s
2	Giancarlo Fisichella	1m 15.917s	1m 15.295s	1m 15.178s
3	Kimi Räikkönen	1m 15.376s	1m 15.273s	1m 15.386s
4	Jarno Trulli	1m 16.455s	1m 15.506s	1m 15.968s
5	Michael Schumacher	1m 15.716s	1m 15.139s	1m 15.986s
6	Nico Rosberg	1m 16.404s	1m 15.269s	1m 16.012s
7	Juan Pablo Montoya	1m 16.251s	1m 15.253s	1m 16.228s
8	Jenson Button	1m 16.594s	1m 15.814s	1m 16.608s
9	Rubens Barrichello	1m 16.735s	1m 15.601s	1m 16.912s
10	Felipe Massa	1m 16.259s	1m 15.555s	1m 17.209s
11	Jacques Villeneuve	1m 16.493s	1m 15.832s	
12	Christian Klien	1m 16.585s	1m 15.833s	
13	Nick Heidfeld	1m 15.906s	1m 15.885s	
14	Ralf Schumacher	1m 16.702s	1m 15.888s	
15	Vitantonio Liuzzi	1m 16.581s	1m 16.116s	
16	David Coulthard	1m 16.514s	1m 16.301s	
17	Mark Webber	1m 16.985s		
18	Scott Speed	1m 17.016s		
19	Tiago Monteiro	1m 17.121s		
20	Christijan Albers	1m 17.140s		
21	Takuma Sato	1m 19.088s		
22	Franck Montagny	1m 19.152s		

PRACTICE 3 (SATURDAY)
Sunny (track 30–34ºC, air 21–23ºC)

Pos.	Driver	Laps	Time
1	Fernando Alonso	20	1m 15.455s
2	Giancarlo Fisichella	19	1m 15.521s
3	Jacques Villeneuve	13	1m 15.554s
4	Nick Heidfeld	12	1m 15.616s
5	Kimi Räikkönen	12	1m 15.902s
6	Michael Schumacher	13	1m 15.959s
7	Juan Pablo Montoya	12	1m 15.975s
8	Rubens Barrichello	17	1m 16.334s
9	Felipe Massa	18	1m 16.348s
10	Scott Speed	18	1m 16.493s
11	Christian Klien	17	1m 16.660s
12	Jenson Button	15	1m 16.673s
13	Mark Webber	13	1m 16.710s
14	David Coulthard	11	1m 16.765s
15	Nico Rosberg	19	1m 16.829s
16	Vitantonio Liuzzi	19	1m 16.928s
17	Jarno Trulli	24	1m 17.503s
18	Tiago Monteiro	18	1m 17.747s
19	Ralf Schumacher	18	1m 18.212s
20	Takuma Sato	18	1m 18.926s
21	Franck Montagny	19	1m 19.160s
22	Christijan Albers	16	1m 19.531s

CHASSIS LOG BOOK

RENAULT
1	Fernando Alonso	R26/03
2	Giancarlo Fisichella	R26/04
	Spare	R26/01

McLAREN-MERCEDES
3	Kimi Räikkönen	MP4-21/03
4	Juan Pablo Montoya	MP4-21/05
	Spare	MP4-21/04

FERRARI
5	Michael Schumacher	248 F1/254
6	Felipe Massa	248 F1/250
	Spare	248 F1/251

TOYOTA
7	Ralf Schumacher	TF106B/07
8	Jarno Trulli	TF106B/08
	Spare	TF106B/09

WILLIAMS-COSWORTH
9	Mark Webber	FW28/03
10	Nico Rosberg	FW28/06
35	Alexander Wurz	FW28/04

HONDA
11	Rubens Barrichello	RA106/01
12	Jenson Button	RA106/05
36	Anthony Davidson	RA106/03

RED BULL-FERRARI
14	David Coulthard	RB2/3
15	Christian Klien	RB2/2
37	Robert Doornbos	RB2/5

BMW SAUBER
16	Nick Heidfeld	F1.06/04
17	Jacques Villeneuve	F1.06/08
38	Robert Kubica	F1.06/03

MIDLAND-TOYOTA
18	Tiago Monteiro	M16/04
19	Christijan Albers	M16/02
39	Giorgio Mondini	M16/01

TORO ROSSO-COSWORTH
20	Vitantonio Liuzzi	STR01/02
21	Scott Speed	STR01/01
40	Neel Jani	STR01/03

SUPER AGURI-HONDA
22	Takuma Sato	SA05/05
23	Franck Montagny	SA05/02
41	Sakon Yamamoto	SA05/01

Photograph: James Moy/www.crashpa.net

9 BARRICHELLO Honda

7 MONTOYA McLaren

5 M. SCHUMACHER Ferrari

3 RÄIKKÖNEN McLaren

1 ALONSO Renault

10 MASSA Ferrari

8 BUTTON Honda

6 ROSBERG Williams

4 TRULLI Toyota

2 FISICHELLA Renault

RACE DISTANCE:
70 laps
189.686 miles/305.270 km

RACE WEATHER:
Scattered cloud, sunny
track 38–42ºC, air 24–26ºC

56	57	58	59	60	61	62	63	64	65	66	67	68	69	70	•
1	1	1	1	1	1	1	1	1	1	1	1	1	1	1	1
3	3	3	3	3	3	3	3	3	3	3	3	3	5	5	2
5	5	5	5	5	5	5	5	5	5	5	5	5	3	3	3
2	2	2	2	2	2	2	2	2	2	2	2	2	2	2	4
6	6	6	6	6	6	6	6	6	6	6	6	6	6	5	5
8	8	8	8	8	8	8	8	8	8	8	8	8	8	8	6
16	16	16	16	16	16	16	16	16	16	16	16	16	16	16	7
17	17	17	12	12	12	12	12	12	12	12	12	14	14	14	8
12	12	12	15	15	15	15	15	15	14	14	12	12	12		
	15	15	14	14	14	14	14	21	21	21	21				
15	14	14	21	21	21	21	15	15	15	15	15				
21	21	21	9	9	9	9	9	9	9	9	9				
20	20	20	22	22	22	22	22	20	20	20					
7	22	22	18	18	18	18	18	18							
22	18	18													
18	7	7													

Pit stop
One lap or more behind leader
Drive-through penalty
Safety car deployed on laps shown

FOR THE RECORD

Photograph: James Moy/www.crashpa.net

100th WIN: Michelin

100th ANNIVERSARY:
FIRST GRAND PRIX, 26 June 1906

POINTS

CONSTRUCTORS
1	Renault	121
2	Ferrari	87
3	McLaren	65
4	Honda	29
5	BMW Sauber	19
6	Toyota	11
7	Williams	10
8	Red Bull	9

DRIVERS
1	Fernando Alonso	84
2	Michael Schumacher	59
3	Kimi Räikkönen	39
4	Giancarlo Fisichella	37
5	Felipe Massa	28
6	Juan Pablo Montoya	26
7	Jenson Button	16
8	Rubens Barrichello	13
9	Nick Heidfeld	12
10	Ralf Schumacher	8
11	David Coulthard	8
12	Jacques Villeneuve	7
13	Mark Webber	6
14	Nico Rosberg	4
15	Jarno Trulli	3
16	Christian Klien	1

Photograph: XPB.cc

Mayhem at the first corner as Jacques Villeneuve and Kimi Räikkönen – in the foreground – try to avoid the chaos unfolding in their rear-view mirrors.

Photograph: Laurent Charniaux/WRI

INDIANAPOLIS QUALIFYING

ALL through the weekend there was a frisson about Ferrari. Yes, Michael Schumacher spun his Ferrari 248 rather clumsily in Turn Four and ended up stranded in the gravel on Friday morning – he put the left wheel on the grass and then, as one team insider put it, 'found that it braked less well on the green stuff than on the grey' – but the red cars always looked clean and quick, whereas the Renaults appeared to be floundering a little.

Perhaps, the feeling went, *les bleus* were just not yet showing their hand. Friday is largely a waste of time when it comes to trying to predict true form, such are the disparities in set-up configuration; but Saturday morning revealed the R26s still to be a long way off. Schumacher was fastest then with 1m 10.760s from Felipe Massa on 1m 11.039s; the next-best runner was Giancarlo Fisichella with 1m 11.940s. Alonso was only sixth on 1m 12.202s.

The Spaniard struggled to get his car balanced all through practice and was further hampered by having to run an older engine while Fisi, due for a fresh one, enjoyed the improved performance of the latest-specification V8 from Viry Châtillon. That was worth a couple of tenths, but it still didn't fully explain the champion's problem.

Qualifying, then, went Ferrari's way with insouciant ease. Schumi took pole, his 67th, with 1m 10.832s and Felipe Massa backed him perfectly with 1m 11.435s on slightly more fuel (one lap more, to be precise). Schumacher praised the consistency of his car and said he was very surprised how much of an advantage the red cars had.

Fisichella came next on 1m 11.920s and Alonso was fifth this time on 1m 12.449s, separated from his team-mate by Rubens Barrichello, who pushed his Honda to 1m 12.109s. It was Alonso's worst qualifying position of the year to date. Renault was confident that Honda would be stopping early (which proved correct), but that didn't help the mood.

Team personnel admitted privately that they were stunned by Ferrari's speed. But Michelin had clearly been conservative on its tyre choice – that was inevitable given the events of 2005 – and at this stage Renault's lack of grip was simply put down to that. After all, hadn't the R26 been in a class of its own at Montreal the previous weekend? The biggest

relief in the Michelin camp was that there had been absolutely no sign of any structural problems in the tyres.

Sixth place went to Jacques Villeneuve courtesy of a lap of 1m 12.479s, giving BMW Sauber its best grid place thus far in the season. Nick Heidfeld had been on a faster lap early in the session when his F1.06 rolled to a halt in Turn 12 with a recurrence of an obscure electronic problem that had arisen a couple of times previously, which left him tenth on the grid with 1m 15.280s. Jenson Button was seventh with 1m 12.523s, Honda claiming later that he was fuelled for a long opening stint, then came Ralf Schumacher on 1m 12.795s. Ralf was relieved to get through an Indy weekend without a major shunt, after his less fortunate experiences there in 2004 and 2005.

Kimi Räikkönen made it through to the final session, but team-mate Juan Pablo Montoya did not. The Finn was disappointed with his 1m 13.174s lap, which left him only ninth, but the secret there was that the team was gambling on a one-stop strategy because tyre wear is negligible at Indy. He thus ran with a lot of fuel. Montoya wound up 11th with 1m 12.150s, ahead of Mark Webber (1m 12.292s), local hero Scott Speed (1m 12.792s), Christijan Albers (1m 12.854s), Tiago Monteiro (1m 12.864s) and Christian Klien (1m 12.925s), who had all made it through to the second session prior to being eliminated from the top ten shoot out. Speed was the first American to start his home GP since Eddie Cheever in 1989, while Webber in particular did a good job given the fact that Williams wasn't getting anything like the performance out of Bridgestone's latest tyre that Ferrari and Toyota were.

David Coulthard (1m 13.180s), Takuma Sato (1m 13.496s), Nico Rosberg (1m 13.506s), Jarno Trulli (1m 13.787s), Tonio Liuzzi (1m 14.041s) and Franck Montagny (1m 16.036s) were the contenders eliminated after the first qualifying session. Both Coulthard and Liuzzi had serious understeer problems; Liuzzi's put him over a kerb in Turn Eight, after which his Toro Rosso lost all semblance of decent handling. Sato's was a fine performance – he outqualified Rosberg's Williams. The young German complained of vague handling that sapped his confidence. Trulli, meanwhile, having suffered sensor problems in practice, now had a rear suspension problem, which held him back. He would start from the pit lane, fuelled to the brim.

Top: A local Red Bull Racing fan looks the part.

Above: Champcar top man Sébastien Bourdais makes a visit to keep an eye on F1 possibilities for the future.

Right: Photographers become bricklayers for a brief moment.
Photographs: James Moy/www.crashpa.net

Centre: F1 launches a charm offensive at Indy to make up for the 2005 fiasco.
Photograph: Jean-François Galeron

**Left: Fans crossing 16th street
on their way into the speedway.**

**Bottom left: The Fisichella family is
momentarily wrong-footed by the swipe-card
machine at the entrance to the paddock.**
Photographs: Jean-François Galeron/WRI

**Centre left: Why so gloomy, boys? ITV's
Martin Brundle and Mark Blundell take
a serious view of things.**
Photograph: James Moy/www.crashpa.net

**Below: Yes, they had, this year.
And they worked!**
Photograph: Lukas Gorys

BERNIE STICKS HIS OAR IN

SOME pointed and critical remarks from Bernie Ecclestone prior to the US GP inevitably focused attention on whether the contract with the Indianapolis Motor Speedway (IMS) would be renewed for 2007 and beyond. In the paddock, however, these were interpreted as preliminary positioning remarks for the forthcoming negotiations and few thought that taking the GP to Indy was anything but an inspired move that placed F1 right at the heart of US motor sport after fruitless years spent in wildernesses such as Detroit, Dallas, Phoenix or a car park in Las Vegas. Most people felt that the race belonged at the IMS, which makes a huge promotional effort each year.

IMS owner Tony George, perhaps perturbed that recent quotes he had given concerning a possible merger of the warring open-wheel factions of his breakaway Indy Racing League and the long-established Champcar series had not been interpreted quite the way he'd intended, relied on a written statement when faced with the much-asked question whether he would keep the grand prix.

'We appreciate the interest and support from everyone who has inquired about the future of this event,' his statement said. 'Many months ago, Bernie and I agreed to wait until the conclusion of the 2006 event to evaluate our future together. We expect to do that in the coming weeks. The good news is that we enjoy the partnership that has been forged and are committed to working towards continuing to build on the foundation that has been laid over the past seven years.'

Ecclestone, with whom George had talks earlier on the Friday of race weekend, appeared to have mellowed and gave a television interviewer what he wanted to hear in his practised style. 'Ask Tony George,' he said cheerfully. 'We are happy here and I hope we can build it up. Let's see. We are not anti, but it needs to be commercially viable for both of us. Everybody is being very positive and that's good. I'm happy. If we can make it happen, we will.'

Days after the US GP, Juan Pablo Montoya springs a huge surprise on the F1 fraternity by agreeing terms to join former Champcar entrant Chip Ganassi's NASCAR Nextel Cup team for 2007.

Immediately after the US GP, BMW sets about modifying its rear wing, having been told by the FIA stewards that it was outside the spirit of the regulations.

The argument over engine rules rumbles on in America, with a so-called 'Indianapolis Agreement' freezing development from 2007 to 2010 inclusive.

The FIA confirms soon after the US GP that Bridgestone has been appointed the sole tyre supplier for F1 from 2008 onwards, following the governing body's competitive tender offer.

Mario Andretti declares that his grandson Marco, 19, who drives for his son Michael in the IRL, will be ready to race in F1 within two years.

MICHAEL Schumacher has a habit of making Hoosiers see red. He did it for the fifth time at Indianapolis, doing much to lay the ghost of the previous year's six-race farce that had masqueraded as a grand prix. Where he was lucky then, for the 87th win of his career, was in so dominating that the only man who could keep him honest was his team-mate Felipe Massa.

The triumph enabled the German to claw back six valuable points on Fernando Alonso as Renault had, by its lofty standards, an appalling weekend, with its drivers struggling for grip. Giancarlo Fisichella brought his R26 home a damage-limiting third after a good drive, but the world champion struggled to only fifth place and was beaten home by Jarno Trulli's Toyota, which had started from the pit lane.

That was an indication of how conservatively Michelin played its cards on this weekend, desperate to avoid the expensive embarrassment that had played such a key role in the 2005 fiasco. But, and it was easy to miss the point in the slightly misleading circumstances, it was also a warning of the significant progress Bridgestone had made with its latest tyres.

The easy triumph made Schumacher Indianapolis's first five-times winner. Legends such as AJ Foyt, Al Unser Sr and Rick Mears had been quadruple winners of the famed 500-mile

race, and Jeff Gordon has won four Brickyard 400 NASCAR races. But Schumacher won the inaugural GP at Indianapolis in 2000, gifted the race to Ferrari team-mate Rubens Barrichello in a remarkable kerfuffle on the finish line in 2002 and took the 2003, 2004 and 2005 races, too.

'I'm not much on the history stuff, as you know,' he admitted, 'but this was an important victory for us [the team and I] that confirms that we are still very much in the hunt for the title.'

There was palpable relief among the spectators when all cars (except Trulli's Toyota, waiting at the end of the pit lane) came out onto the grid, as the spectre of the 14 Michelin runners pitting after the grid formation lap last year still haunted the place, but by the end of the first lap the field had been decimated once again.

Massa, on new tyres, made a great start to lead Schumacher but farther back, as the midfield raced four or even five abreast into the first corner, something had to give. In two separate incidents the McLaren drivers, Nick Heidfeld, Christian Klien, Scott Speed, Mark Webber and Franck Montagny were eliminated.

There was the inevitable funnelling and bottling effect, as Kimi Räikkönen, Jenson Button, Heidfeld, Juan Pablo Montoya and Speed all got caught up behind a group comprising Rubens Barrichello, Schumacher Jr and Jacques Villeneuve. On the inside for Turn Two, the left-hander, Räikkönen inevitably had

to brake. At the same time, Button was looking for a way around him in the middle of the track, with Heidfeld on the outside of him. As Räikkönen braked, Montoya ran straight into the back of his car.

Both McLarens sustained damage and spun. Montoya's car also caught Button's and the twitch that the Honda gave was enough to lead to contact with Heidfeld, who in turn flipped into an alarming barrel-roll that ended in the Turn Two gravel bed. The German was unharmed. Speed couldn't avoid either Button or Räikkönen and collided with them.

Farther back, Klien overcooked it under braking, spun and took out Webber before brushing Albers, and an innocent Montagny couldn't avoid hitting Klien's wrecked Red Bull. David Coulthard and Vitantonio Liuzzi gratefully avoided the mêlée, as did Trulli. Just as Massa was wondering whether he should concede the lead to his team leader, out came the safety car while the mess was cleared up.

The result of all this was immediate retirement for seven drivers – and Button retired after three stops to investigate the damage sustained. A radiator was leaking badly.

In 2005 six cars had come around at the end of the opening lap. This time there were 14 left and Button's Honda was doomed. Soon afterwards, another rash passing move from Takuma Sato took out himself and, indirectly,

Above: Nick Heidfeld's BMW-Sauber proves the most spectacular victim of the first-corner pile-up.
Photograph: Jean-François Galeron

Centre: Scott Speed abandons his wrecked Toro Rosso.
Photograph: Paul-Henri Cahier

Left: Pass the bin liner. Both McLarens were badly rumpled in what proved to be Juan Pablo Montoya's last outing for the team.
Photograph: Laurent Charniaux/WRI

an innocent Tiago Monteiro, whose Midland had sustained what would soon become terminal damage.

Alonso had very nearly squeaked his Renault ahead of Schumacher at the start and they went through the first two corners side by side before Michael was able to settle the issue with his superior grip. But when the safety car went back to the pits on lap six and the racing started again, Alonso could do nothing about the Ferraris. Massa held the lead easily until his pit stop on lap 30.

Schumacher had stopped on the previous lap and he made the first corner just before Massa did after rejoining. No surprise there. They settled down to a straightforward run to the flag. On this day Bridgestone had a small but crucial advantage.

Giancarlo Fisichella was clearly quicker than Alonso and breezed past him into Turn One on lap 15. He soon pulled away but though Alonso's Michelin-shod Renault wasn't that much slower on lap time, he fell steadily back. Before long the unthinkable happened and Alonso found Rubens Barrichello, Ralf Schumacher and Jacques Villeneuve (admittedly in cars running with lighter fuel loads) bottled up in his rear-view mirrors. He got some respite when Villeneuve's BMW blew its engine on lap 24 and Barrichello stopped for fuel, but Ralf pushed Alonso for another six laps before pitting on lap 30.

The Spaniard was clearly struggling and could not match Fisichella's times. He did, however, maintain his record of leading every 2006 race up to that point by taking the lead on lap 31 after Massa stopped, until he too pitted at the end of that lap. Worse still for him, however, it soon became clear that he could not keep ahead of Trulli's Toyota.

The Italian overtook him while Alonso was in the pits, lost the place with his own stop, then went ahead again as Alonso refuelled for the second time on lap 53. After that the Italian pulled away to take an excellent fourth place. Alonso could do nothing about that and trailed home a dejected fifth.

Barrichello boosted the battered Honda's spirits with sixth, while seventh was the subject of great dispute between Tonio Liuzzi and David Coulthard. The Italian monstered the Scot's

faster but heavier car all the way through to his own fuel stop on the 39th lap, but DC went even longer, not stopping until the 47th. That lengthy stint proved crucial and, as a result, Coulthard was well clear for seventh by the flag. Liuzzi fought strongly to catch and pass Nico Rosberg's Williams going into Turn One on the 47th lap and Schumacher Jr's retirement with a wheel bearing failure 11 laps from the flag rewarded Liuzzi with his first point of the season and Toro Rosso's first ever after a feisty performance. Rosberg, in ninth, was the final finisher. The German's car was no better in the race than it had been in qualifying. Christijan Albers' Midland broke its transmission after 37 laps.

The victory was a huge fillip for Ferrari. 'We performed extremely well all weekend,' Schumacher said. 'We prepared ourselves very hard for the two overseas races and knew we had a good car. Canada didn't work out but here it was spot-on. Having Felipe here alongside me is a dream result. Another step towards the championship, and a perfect weekend. Germany getting through to the semi-finals of the World Cup and my winning the race – you couldn't have a better result, really!'

The mood had really lifted in the Italian camp. There had been a feeling of despair after qualifying in Canada, which became delight when circumstance had helped Schumacher to second place behind Alonso. The demonstration run at the Brickyard was just like old times and the only thing wider than the margin of victory over Renault was Schumacher's grin, which was set to the maximum wattage.

'We can only hope to keep some of the edge we had this weekend and transform it into the European season,' he said as he looked ahead. 'There are eight races [left], so there are 80 points to come, so being 19 points behind is not a lot; it is not impossible at all. I think we can do it.'

There was resignation at Renault after what seemed like a body blow. 'Third was the best I could have done today,' Fisichella said glumly. 'To be on the podium at such a hard track for us is a strong result and I think things will get back to normal again at Magny-Cours.'

Alonso was similarly philosophical. What else could he be? 'Fifth was the maximum I could do today,' the champion said. 'I was not competitive all weekend and the car was lacking grip all the way through the race, as well as completing race two of a very hard cycle for the engine. So I did the maximum possible and made sure I scored points for the championship. Looking back to last year, I scored zero points in North America; this year, I have scored 14 and my championship position is still very strong. That's a big reason to stay positive. Ferrari and Bridgestone were quicker than us today, but in ten races we have had the better tyres for nine of them, so I am not worried for the next grands prix.

'We must carry on doing our job and know that sometimes we can win, sometimes not. I am already looking forward to the next race, where I think we will see a more usual balance of competitiveness between Renault and Ferrari.'

This was always going to be a tough weekend for Michelin. 'The tyres we brought this weekend were designed to give us a combination of durability and performance,' its F1 director Nick Shorrock said. 'We succeeded handsomely in the first part of our quest – witness David Coulthard's 47-lap stint – but, for once, we fell short in the second.'

Even the normally ebullient Flavio Briatore was subdued.

'Today was not our day,' he conceded. 'The competition was too strong for us and the maximum we could have got from the race was 11 points. In the end, we scored 10, so we limited the damage as much as possible.

'Giancarlo did a fantastic job to finish third; it was everything we could ask of him today. Fernando never got the car to his liking all weekend but still scored valuable points. The team has done a great job during two difficult races in North America and we all go to France determined to win again at our home race – and extend our advantage in the championship.'

As the teams headed back to Europe in differing frames of mind, most of the spectators went home happy. Those directly affected by the 2005 race will not forget it but Michelin paid for 20,000 free tickets for the aggrieved parties and did what it could to make amends.

The race attracted as many fans this year as last, with unofficial figures claiming 10,000 spectators on Thursday, 20,000 on Friday, 50,000 on Saturday and 130,000 on race day. So it seemed that America had forgiven F1 for its bloody suicide attempt. And the sudden surge in Ferrari's performance could barely have generated a better result to maintain interest in the title fight as the championship moved back to Europe.

David Tremayne

Above: Ross Brawn is force-fed his share of the bubbly by winner Michael Schumacher.
Photograph: Photo 4/XPB.cc

Left: Vitantonio Liuzzi made up for his team-mate's disappointment by scoring Toro Rosso's first championship point.
Photograph: Paul-Henri Cahier

187

FIA F1 WORLD CHAMPIONSHIP • ROUND 10

UNITED STATES GRAND PRIX

INDIANAPOLIS 30 JUNE–2 JULY 2006

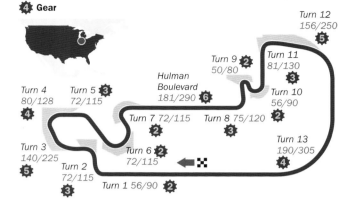

INDIANAPOLIS MOTOR SPEEDWAY, INDIANAPOLIS

Circuit: 2.605 miles/4.192 km

116/187 mph/kmh

4 Gear

Turn 12 156/250 **5**
Turn 9 50/80 **2**
Turn 11 81/130 **3**
Turn 4 80/128 **4**
Turn 5 72/115 **3**
Hulman Boulevard 181/290 **6**
Turn 10 56/90 **2**
Turn 7 72/115 **2**
Turn 8 75/120 **3**
Turn 3 140/225 **4**
Turn 6 72/115 **2**
Turn 13 190/305 **4**
Turn 2 72/115 **5**
Turn 1 56/90 **2**
3

Photograph: Photo4/XPB.cc

RACE RESULTS

Pos.	Driver	Nat.	No.	Entrant	Car/Engine	Tyres	Laps	Time/Retirement	Speed (mph/km/h)	Gap to leader	Fastest race lap	
1	Michael Schumacher	D	5	Scuderia Ferrari Marlboro	Ferrari 248 F1-056 V8	B	73	1h 34m 35.199s	120.619/194.117		1m 12.719s	56
2	Felipe Massa	BR	6	Scuderia Ferrari Marlboro	Ferrari 248 F1-056 V8	B	73	1h 34m 43.183s	120.450/193.845	+7.984s	1m 12.954s	29
3	Giancarlo Fisichella	I	2	Mild Seven Renault F1 Team	Renault R26-RS26 V8	M	73	1h 34m 51.794s	120.267/193.551	+16.595s	1m 13.131s	28
4	Jarno Trulli	I	8	Panasonic Toyota Racing	Toyota TF106B-RVX-06 V8	B	73	1h 34m 58.803s	120.119/193.313	+23.604s	1m 13.269s	37
5	Fernando Alonso	E	1	Mild Seven Renault F1 Team	Renault R26-RS26 V8	M	73	1h 35m 03.609s	120.018/193.150	+28.410s	1m 13.316s	72
6	Rubens Barrichello	BR	11	Lucky Strike Honda Racing F1 Team	Honda RA106-RA806E V8	M	73	1h 35m 11.715s	119.848/192.876	+36.516s	1m 13.611s	47
7	David Coulthard	GB	14	Red Bull Racing	Red Bull RB2-Ferrari 056 V8	M	72			+1 lap	1m 14.730s	33
8	Vitantonio Liuzzi	I	20	Scuderia Toro Rosso	Toro Rosso STR01-Cosworth TJ2005-2 V10	M	72			+1 lap	1m 14.286s	41
9	Nico Rosberg	D	10	WilliamsF1 Team	Williams FW28-Cosworth CA2006 V8	B	72			+1 lap	1m 14.707s	42
	Ralf Schumacher	D	7	Panasonic Toyota Racing	Toyota TF106B-RVX-06 V8	B	62	Wheel bearing			1m 13.225s	29
	Christijan Albers	NL	19	MF1 Racing	Midland M16-Toyota RVX-06 V8	B	37	Transmission			1m 14.731s	34
	Jacques Villeneuve	CDN	17	BMW Sauber F1 Team	BMW Sauber F1.06-BMW P86 V8	M	23	Engine			1m 13.934s	19
	Tiago Monteiro	P	18	MF1 Racing	Midland M16-Toyota RVX-06 V8	B	9	Accident			1m 22.036s	9
	Takuma Sato	J	22	Super Aguri F1 Team	Super Aguri SA05-Honda RA806E V8	B	6	Accident			1m 43.802s	6
	Jenson Button	GB	12	Lucky Strike Honda Racing F1 Team	Honda RA106-RA806E V8	M	3	Accident damage			2m 04.692s	2
	Kimi Räikkönen	FIN	3	Team McLaren Mercedes	McLaren MP4-21-Mercedes FO 108S V8	M	0	Accident			No time	
	Nick Heidfeld	D	16	BMW Sauber F1 Team	BMW Sauber F1.06-BMW P86 V8	M	0	Accident			No time	
	Juan Pablo Montoya	COL	4	Team McLaren Mercedes	McLaren MP4-21-Mercedes FO 108S V8	M	0	Accident			No time	
	Mark Webber	AUS	9	WilliamsF1 Team	Williams FW28-Cosworth CA2006 V8	M	0	Accident			No time	
	Scott Speed	USA	21	Scuderia Toro Rosso	Toro Rosso STR01-Cosworth TJ2005-2 V10	M	0	Accident			No time	
	Christian Klien	A	15	Red Bull Racing	Red Bull RB2-Ferrari 056 V8	M	0	Accident			No time	
	Franck Montagny	F	23	Super Aguri F1 Team	Super Aguri SA05-Honda RA806E V8	B	0	Accident			No time	

Fastest lap: Michael Schumacher on lap 56, 1m 12.719s, 128.951mph/207.527 km/h.

Lap record: Rubens Barrichello (Ferrari F2004 V10), 1m 10.399s, 133.201 mph/214.366 km/h (2004).

All results and data © FOM 2006

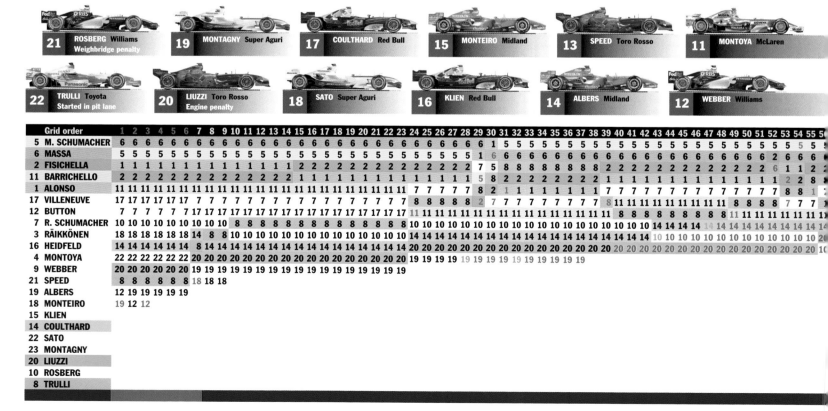

21	ROSBERG Williams Weighbridge penalty
19	MONTAGNY Super Aguri
17	COULTHARD Red Bull
15	MONTEIRO Midland
13	SPEED Toro Rosso
11	MONTOYA McLaren
22	TRULLI Toyota Started in pit lane
20	LIUZZI Toro Rosso Engine penalty
18	SATO Super Aguri
16	KLIEN Red Bull
14	ALBERS Midland
12	WEBBER Williams

Grid order	1	2	3	4	5	6	7	8	9	10	11	12	13	14	15	16	17	18	19	20	21	22	23	24	25	26	27	28	29	30	31	32	33	34	35	36	37	38	39	40	41	42	43	44	45	46	47	48	49	50	51	52	53	54	55
5 M. SCHUMACHER	6	6	6	6	6	6	6	6	6	6	6	6	6	6	6	6	6	6	6	6	6	6	6	6	6	6	6	6	6	1	5	5	5	5	5	5	5	5	5	5	5	5	5	5	5	5	5	5	5	5	5	5	5	5	5
6 MASSA	5	5	5	5	5	5	5	5	5	5	5	5	5	5	5	5	5	5	5	5	5	5	5	5	5	5	5	5	5	6	6	6	6	6	6	6	6	6	6	6	6	6	6	6	6	6	6	6	6	6	6	6	2	6	6
2 FISICHELLA	1	1	1	1	1	1	1	1	1	1	1	1	1	1	2	2	2	2	2	2	2	2	2	2	2	2	2	2	7	5	8	8	8	8	8	8	8	2	2	2	2	2	2	2	2	2	2	2	2	2	6	1	2		
11 BARRICHELLO	2	2	2	2	2	2	2	2	2	2	2	2	2	2	1	1	1	1	1	1	1	1	1	1	1	1	1	1	5	8	2	2	2	2	2	2	2	1	1	1	1	1	1	1	1	1	1	1	1	1	1	2	2	8	
1 ALONSO	11	11	11	11	11	11	11	11	11	11	11	11	11	11	11	11	11	11	11	11	11	11	11	7	7	7	7	7	8	2	1	1	1	1	1	1	1	7	7	7	7	7	7	7	7	7	7	7	7	7	8	8	1		
17 VILLENEUVE	17	17	17	17	17	17	7	7	7	7	7	7	7	7	7	7	7	7	7	7	7	7	7	8	8	8	8	2	7	7	7	7	7	7	7	7	7	8	11	11	11	11	11	11	11	11	8	8	8	8	7	7	7		
12 BUTTON	7	7	7	7	7	7	17	17	17	17	17	17	17	17	17	17	17	17	17	17	17	17	17	11	11	11	11	11	11	11	11	11	11	11	11	11	11	8	8	8	8	8	8	8	8	8	11	11	11	11	11	11	11		
7 R. SCHUMACHER	10	10	10	10	10	10	10	10	10	8	8	8	8	8	8	8	8	8	8	8	8	8	8	10	10	10	10	10	10	10	10	10	10	10	10	10	10	14	14	14	14	14	14	14	14	14	14	14	14	14	14	14	14		
3 RÄIKKÖNEN	18	18	18	18	18	18	14	8	8	10	10	10	10	10	10	10	10	10	10	10	10	10	10	14	14	14	14	14	14	14	14	14	14	14	14	14	14	10	10	10	10	10	10	10	10	10	10	10	10	10	10	10	20		
16 HEIDFELD	14	14	14	14	14	14	8	14	14	14	14	14	14	14	14	14	14	14	14	20	20	20	20	20	20	20	20	20	20	20	20	20	20	20	20	20	20	20	20	20	20	20	20	20	20	20	20	20	20	20	20	20	10		
4 MONTOYA	22	22	22	22	22	22	20	20	20	20	20	20	20	20	20	20	20	20	20	19	19	19	19	19	19	19	19	19	19	19	19	19																							
9 WEBBER	20	20	20	20	20	20	19	19	19	19	19	19	19	19	19	19	19	19	19																																				
21 SPEED	8	8	8	8	8	8	18	18	18																																														
19 ALBERS	12	19	19	19	19	19																																																	
18 MONTEIRO	19	12	12																																																				
15 KLIEN																																																							
14 COULTHARD																																																							
22 SATO																																																							
23 MONTAGNY																																																							
20 LIUZZI																																																							
10 ROSBERG																																																							
8 TRULLI																																																							

PRACTICE 1 (FRIDAY)

Cloudy (track 35–39°C, air 25–27°C)

Pos.	Driver	Laps	Time
1	Anthony Davidson	27	1m 12.083s
2	Michael Schumacher	3	1m 12.458s
3	Robert Kubica	31	1m 13.008s
4	Rubens Barrichello	5	1m 13.090s
5	Jenson Button	6	1m 13.189s
6	Neel Jani	24	1m 13.710s
7	Giorgio Mondini	33	1m 14.654s
8	Alexander Wurz	38	1m 14.745s
9	Scott Speed	8	1m 14.791s
10	Robert Doornbos	22	1m 15.018s
11	Tiago Monteiro	8	1m 15.091s
12	Vitantonio Liuzzi	8	1m 15.532s
13	Christijan Albers	10	1m 15.647s
14	Takuma Sato	17	1m 15.971s
15	Sakon Yamamoto	31	1m 16.116s
16	Franck Montagny	17	1m 16.489s
17	Jarno Trulli	2	No time
18	Ralf Schumacher	2	No time
19	Giancarlo Fisichella	3	No time
20	Fernando Alonso	1	No time
21	Christian Klien	1	No time
22	Kimi Räikkönen	1	No time
23	David Coulthard	1	No time
24	Juan Pablo Montoya	1	No time
25	Nick Heidfeld	1	No time
26	Jacques Villeneuve	2	No time

PRACTICE 2 (FRIDAY)

Heavy cloud (track 37–39°C, air 27–28°C)

Pos.	Driver	Laps	Time
1	Anthony Davidson	38	1m 12.013s
2	Robert Kubica	39	1m 12.809s
3	Giancarlo Fisichella	14	1m 12.933s
4	Felipe Massa	26	1m 13.264s
5	Giorgio Mondini	33	1m 13.327s
6	Michael Schumacher	18	1m 13.346s
7	Tiago Monteiro	21	1m 13.387s
8	Jenson Button	16	1m 13.397s
9	Fernando Alonso	14	1m 13.474s
10	Kimi Räikkönen	9	1m 13.554s
11	Scott Speed	26	1m 13.688s
12	Mark Webber	15	1m 13.691s
13	Nick Heidfeld	14	1m 13.725s
14	Vitantonio Liuzzi	24	1m 13.735s
15	Juan Pablo Montoya	10	1m 13.825s
16	Jacques Villeneuve	17	1m 13.857s
17	Neel Jani	31	1m 13.946s
18	Rubens Barrichello	20	1m 14.011s
19	Alexander Wurz	39	1m 14.050s
20	Christian Klien	15	1m 14.084s
21	Christijan Albers	19	1m 14.169s
22	Takuma Sato	24	1m 14.391s
23	Jarno Trulli	16	1m 14.449s
24	Nico Rosberg	17	1m 14.562s
25	David Coulthard	18	1m 14.676s
26	Robert Doornbos	13	1m 14.839s
27	Ralf Schumacher	10	1m 15.063s
28	Sakon Yamamoto	33	1m 15.120s
29	Franck Montagny	2	No time

QUALIFYING (SATURDAY)

Sunny (track 44–46°C, air 31–32°C)

Pos.	Driver	First	Second	Third
1	Michael Schumacher	1m 11.588s	1m 10.636s	1m 10.832s
2	Felipe Massa	1m 11.088s	1m 11.146s	1m 11.435s
3	Giancarlo Fisichella	1m 12.287s	1m 11.200s	1m 11.920s
4	Rubens Barrichello	1m 12.156s	1m 11.263s	1m 12.109s
5	Fernando Alonso	1m 12.416s	1m 11.877s	1m 12.449s
6	Jacques Villeneuve	1m 12.114s	1m 11.724s	1m 12.479s
7	Jenson Button	1m 12.238s	1m 11.865s	1m 12.523s
8	Ralf Schumacher	1m 11.879s	1m 11.673s	1m 12.795s
9	Kimi Räikkönen	1m 12.777s	1m 12.135s	1m 13.174s
10	Nick Heidfeld	1m 11.891s	1m 11.718s	1m 15.280s
11	Juan Pablo Montoya	1m 12.477s	1m 12.150s	
12	Mark Webber	1m 12.935s	1m 12.292s	
13	Scott Speed	1m 13.167s	1m 12.792s	
14	Christijan Albers	1m 12.711s	1m 12.854s	
15	Tiago Monteiro	1m 12.627s	1m 12.864s	
16	Christian Klien	1m 12.773s	1m 12.925s	
17	David Coulthard	1m 13.180s		
18	Takuma Sato	1m 13.496s		
19	Nico Rosberg	1m 13.506s*		
20	Jarno Trulli	1m 13.787s		
21	Vitantonio Liuzzi	1m 14.041s		
22	Franck Montagny	1m 16.036s		

*Times disallowed for missing a call to the weighbridge; Rosberg sent to back of grid

PRACTICE 3 (SATURDAY)

Sunny (track 33–39°C, air 20–26°C)

Pos.	Driver	Laps	Time
1	Michael Schumacher	15	1m 10.760s
2	Felipe Massa	8	1m 11.039s
3	Giancarlo Fisichella	15	1m 11.940s
4	Nick Heidfeld	18	1m 12.049s
5	Rubens Barrichello	13	1m 12.149s
6	Fernando Alonso	15	1m 12.202s
7	Jenson Button	18	1m 12.269s
8	Jacques Villeneuve	13	1m 12.327s
9	Kimi Räikkönen	13	1m 12.569s
10	Juan Pablo Montoya	10	1m 12.592s
11	Vitantonio Liuzzi	18	1m 12.675s
12	Mark Webber	15	1m 12.904s
13	Tiago Monteiro	18	1m 12.913s
14	Jarno Trulli	21	1m 13.091s
15	Ralf Schumacher	19	1m 13.101s
16	Scott Speed	17	1m 13.103s
17	Christian Klien	15	1m 13.113s
18	Christijan Albers	19	1m 13.172s
19	Nico Rosberg	12	1m 13.230s
20	David Coulthard	17	1m 13.364s
21	Takuma Sato	16	1m 13.806s
22	Franck Montagny	10	1m 14.454s

CHASSIS LOG BOOK

RENAULT
1	Fernando Alonso	R26/03
2	Giancarlo Fisichella	R26/04
	Spare	R26/01

McLAREN-MERCEDES
3	Kimi Räikkönen	MP4-21/03
4	Juan Pablo Montoya	MP4-21/05
	Spare	MP4-21/04

FERRARI
5	Michael Schumacher	248 F1/254
6	Felipe Massa	248 F1/252
	Spare	248 F1/251

TOYOTA
7	Ralf Schumacher	TF106B/07
8	Jarno Trulli	TF106B/08
	Spare	TF106B/09

WILLIAMS-COSWORTH
9	Mark Webber	FW28/03
10	Nico Rosberg	FW28/04
35	Alexander Wurz	FW28/06

HONDA
11	Rubens Barrichello	RA106/01
12	Jenson Button	RA106/05
36	Anthony Davidson	RA106/03

RED BULL-FERRARI
14	David Coulthard	RB2/3
15	Christian Klien	RB2/2
37	Robert Doornbos	RB2/5

BMW SAUBER
16	Nick Heidfeld	F1.06/04
17	Jacques Villeneuve	F1.06/02
38	Robert Kubica	F1.06/03

MIDLAND-TOYOTA
18	Tiago Monteiro	M16/04
19	Christijan Albers	M16/02
39	Giorgio Mondini	M16/01

TORO ROSSO-COSWORTH
20	Vitantonio Liuzzi	STR01/02
21	Scott Speed	STR01/01
40	Neel Jani	STR01/03

SUPER AGURI-HONDA
22	Takuma Sato	SA05/05
23	Franck Montagny	SA05/02
41	Sakon Yamamoto	SA05/01

 9 RÄIKKÖNEN McLaren
 7 BUTTON Honda
 5 ALONSO Renault
 3 FISICHELLA Renault
 1 M. SCHUMACHER Ferrari
 10 HEIDFELD BMW-Sauber
 8 R. SCHUMACHER Toyota
 6 VILLENEUVE BMW-Sauber
 4 BARRICHELLO Honda
 2 MASSA Ferrari

RACE DISTANCE:
73 laps
190.150 miles/306.016 km

RACE WEATHER:
Sunny
track 46–49°C, air 35–37°C

	57	58	59	60	61	62	63	64	65	66	67	68	69	70	71	72	73	●	
	5	5	5	5	5	5	5	5	5	5	5	5	5	5	5	5	5	1	
	6	6	6	6	6	6	6	6	6	6	6	6	6	6	6	6	6	2	
	2	2	2	2	2	2	2	2	2	2	2	2	2	2	2	2	2	3	
	8	8	8	8	8	8	8	8	8	8	8	8	8	8	8	8	4	4	
	7	7	7	7	7	7	1	1	1	1	1	1	1	1	1	1	1	5	
	1	1	1	1	1	1	11	11	11	11	11	11	11	11	11	11	11	6	
	11	11	11	11	11	11							14	14	14	14	14	7	
	14	14	14	14	14	14	20	20	20	20	20	20	20	20	20			8	
20	20	20	20	20	20	10	10	10	10	10	10	10	10						
10	10	10	10	10	10														

Pit stop
One lap or more behind leader
1 **Safety car deployed on laps shown**

FOR THE RECORD

FIRST POINT: Toro Rosso

POINTS

DRIVERS
1	Fernando Alonso	88
2	Michael Schumacher	69
3	Giancarlo Fisichella	43
4	Kimi Räikkönen	39
5	Felipe Massa	36
6	Juan Pablo Montoya	26
7	Jenson Button	16
8	Rubens Barrichello	16
9	Nick Heidfeld	12
10	David Coulthard	10
11	Ralf Schumacher	8
12	Jarno Trulli	8
13	Jacques Villeneuve	7
14	Mark Webber	6
15	Nico Rosberg	4
16	Christian Klien	1
17	Vitantonio Liuzzi	1

CONSTRUCTORS
1	Renault	131
2	Ferrari	105
3	McLaren	65
4	Honda	32
5	BMW Sauber	19
6	Toyota	16
7	Red Bull	11
8	Williams	10
9	Toro Rosso	1

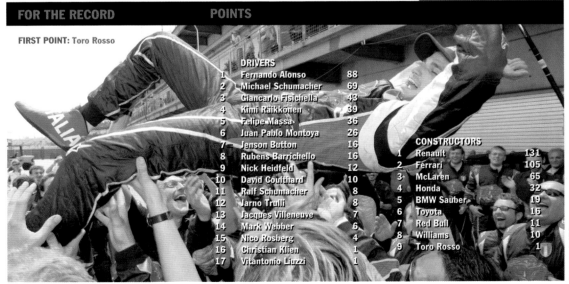

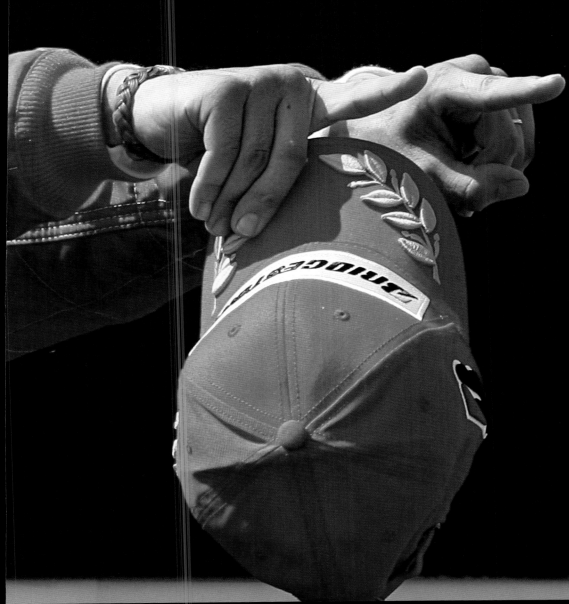

**Main: Maintaining the momentum.
Michael Schumacher signals his
congratulations to the Ferrari team
after another magnificent victory.**
Photograph: Paul-Henri Cahier

**Top left: One hundred years of grand prix
racing were celebrated at Magny-Cours.**
Photograph: Lukas Gorys

**Top right: Among the festivities,
Roger Waters, formerly of Pink Floyd,
performed *Dark Side of the Moon*.**
Photograph: Jad Sherif/WRI

MAGNY-COURS QUALIFYING

MICHAEL Schumacher took his 68th pole position at Magny-Cours, but at one stage there was a chance that the German's car wouldn't even be ready for the first qualifying session after a faulty heat shield caused his Ferrari 248 to catch fire in Saturday morning's practice session. Felipe Massa was also in trouble, with a clutch problem. For Ferrari, then, its second front-row start in succession was a tribute to the mechanics who got both drivers out in time. It was also a surprise because the problems had prevented assessment of further set-up options that morning.

The team was so confident in its choice of Bridgestone's softer compound offering that neither Schumacher nor Massa even tried the harder option, despite the smooth Magny-Cours track surface's reputation of being very hard on tyres. That enabled both drivers to generate sufficient heat straight away when it mattered, so it was no surprise to see Schumacher annex the pole after all, with 1m 15.493s, and Massa back him all the way with 1m 15.510s, a particularly strong performance from the charismatic little Brazilian.

Schumacher said cheerfully, 'I'm very happy with pole and that Felipe is so close to me in second place.' Massa was equally happy.

Renault had been second until the closing moment of a session now shortened by five minutes to improve the show, when Massa's time beat Alonso's 1m 15.785s.

Alonso and Schumacher staged a little bit of theatre as they scrapped for premier track position on leaving the pits at the start of the final session, but in the end *les bleus* did not quite have the answer to the reds, for the second race in succession. Alonso freely acknowledged later that third place was the best he could have hoped for as a track temperature rise gave the Bridgestones a slight edge over his Michelins.

It came as a shock to Renault to be toppled from its dominant perch, though team members did all they could to hide their concern. It wasn't as if the R26 was far off the pace but it was beginning to dawn on the team just what Ferrari's American success really meant.

'The important thing is to be back in the top three,' Alonso said. 'Indy was a bad weekend and it's good to come back here happier and more confident. The grip and balance were okay, so we didn't change the set-up too much. We were not quick enough over one lap so that was no surprise. My chance will come tomorrow.'

Alonso's view on tyres was borne out by the presence of the Toyotas of Jarno Trulli and Ralf Schumacher in fourth and fifth places, their best for a long time. The Italian lapped his TF106B in 1m 16.036s, the German 1m 16.091s.

That left the two McLarens slightly behind, with Kimi Räikkönen battling to sixth on 1m 16.281s and new boy Pedro de la Rosa on 1m 16.632s, which left the Spaniard eighth behind Giancarlo Fisichella, who recorded 1m 16.345s in his Renault.

Nico Rosberg and David Coulthard completed the top ten, the German taking his Williams to 1m 18.272s, the Scot his Red Bull to 1m 18.663s. Coulthard, however, started ninth because Rosberg needed an engine change on his FW28 and thus dropped to 19th.

Rosberg's team-mate Mark Webber made the top ten through his team-mate's misfortune, having been bumped from the knock-out session at the last moment by Coulthard. The Australian's best lap was 1m 16.129s, which left him ahead of Nick Heidfeld (1m 16.294s) and Christian Klien (1m 16.433s). Like Webber, Scott Speed found himself pushed down a place right at the end by Rubens Barrichello, who bettered the American's 1m 17.063s with 1m 17.027s. Christijan Albers had been the final man through from the first session thanks to a 1m 17.105s lap in his Midland.

Those knocked out in the first session were Tonio Liuzzi, who lapped his Toro Rosso in 1m 17.164s compared to Speed's best in that session of 1m 17.117s; Jacques Villeneuve, whose BMW was still in the pits when the session ended; Jenson Button, who for the second time in four races lost out, after a lap of 1m 17.495s in his Honda proved insufficient; Tiago Monteiro, who went autocrossing in his Midland before recording 1m 17.589s; and the Super Aguris of Franck Montagny (1m 18.637s) and Takuma Sato (1m 18.845s).

Above: Pedro de la Rosa takes Juan Pablo Montoya's seat in the McLaren line-up.

Below: Immediately after the French Grand Prix Takuma Sato poses with the Super Aguri SA06 at its first test at Silverstone.
Photographs: James Moy/www.crashpa.net

Above right: Tonio Liuzzi sports some suitably appropriate World Cup footwear.
Photograph: Laurent Charniaux/WRI

Right: BMW Sauber's vertical aero strakes were outlawed after this single race outing.
Photograph: Lukas Gorys

FIA DEMANDS GPMA BOW THE KNEE ON ENGINE RULES

THE French Grand Prix may have been a dull affair, but the argument over engine rules that went on behind the scenes – even, incredibly, during the race itself – would have made a political correspondent salivate.

It rumbled on all weekend and on Sunday morning the Grand Prix Manufacturers' Association (GPMA) finally issued a statement, hours before a notional 4pm deadline expired – which had previously been agreed by all parties and by which time it had to make counter-proposals to FIA president Max Mosley's intended development freeze that would limit engines for 2008 to the specifications appertaining on 1 June 2006.

Under the so-called Indianapolis Proposal, which allowed for a limited amount of development beginning in 2007 rather than a complete freeze in 2008 (when the new Concorde Agreement governing F1 comes into force), the GPMA offered to create a £7.5-million fund with which to support engine supply for independent teams. The FIA's reaction was published literally as the cars began their grid formation lap and by subsequent letter to the FIA the GPMA increased its offer to £10 million, which was the sum previously suggested by the governing body.

However, the latter insisted that the Indianapolis Proposal must be agreed unanimously by all the teams under the rules of the existing Concorde Agreement, which would not expire until the end of 2007. MF1 Racing and the Prodrive team, which was not due to join the circus until 2008, had not yet signed up to the GPMA's counter-proposal. During the race Renault took the extraordinary step of issuing a statement of its own which said, 'Renault and the Renault F1 Team wish to clarify that this statement [the GPMA's] was released without their agreement and that neither the manufacturer nor the team consider themselves to be party to it.'

Seeking to create an engine development fund for the benefit of the so-called independents might have been venturing into commercial areas into which a regulatory body ought not to step, but Mosley was determined that his 'full freeze' would come into effect unless viable counter-proposals were forthcoming – and quickly. As one FIA insider said ominously on the Sunday evening at Magny-Cours, 'If that doesn't happen, Jack Frost will be on his way.'

It remained to be seen whether the disgruntled engine manufacturers would then feel inclined to seek legal redress on the grounds of unfair restriction of competition. The FIA was adamant that unless unanimous agreement was forthcoming, it would simply impose the freeze and let manufacturers spend as much as they wanted to on engine development in 2007 knowing that they would be obliged to revert to mid-2006 specification engines a year later.

FIRST there was the football World Cup. Then the French Grand Prix. Both times the Italians emerged victorious, leaving the French to lick their wounds.

Michael Schumacher's victory at Indianapolis had been put down mainly to Michelin's understandable conservatism in the wake of the 2005 fiasco. Renault and Michelin expected to resume normal business on their home ground at Magny-Cours, but it did not take long for Ferrari and Bridgestone to show that they had indeed made significant progress in America and that F1's status quo had changed again. Now the pendulum had clearly swung back in Ferrari's favour.

Schumacher took his scarlet racer took off into the lead, but a super start from Fernando Alonso almost won his Renault second place. Having started from the second front-row slot, however, Felipe Massa just managed to squeeze ahead in the start of the long right-hander leading down to the Adelaide hairpin and the Spaniard wisely did not push the issue too far. It was close.

From the moment he took the initiative, Schumacher never looked back and he won the 70-lap event virtually as he pleased. Massa, however, failed to make it a Ferrari one-two after some cunning strategising by Renault.

Flavio Briatore's men had gone into the race clinging to the hope that Ferrari's soft Bridgestones would never go the distance, but very soon it became clear that that hope was forlorn. And with Massa grabbing second back so early on, it was clear their game plan needed revision. They took the decision just before Alonso's first pit stop on lap 17 to switch from a three-stop refuelling strategy similar to Ferrari's to only two stops. It enabled the champion to leapfrog past the second Ferrari driver.

'It was very close with Massa at the start,' Alonso confirmed. 'I was nearly on the grass and had to back off, but Felipe was correct. None of us wants to give away his place. After that I tried to overtake but we had to wait for the pit stops.'

Massa chuckled. 'I was a little in front of him and knew that he had more to lose than I did... But it was fair.' Indeed it was.

'We expected to have better consistency from our tyres and everything worked as planned,' Alonso continued. 'I think we lost maybe four or five seconds in the first stint, nothing more. It wasn't crucial to whether we could have won the race. Obviously after the stops I had a lot of fuel in the car and at the end of each stint the tyres were not in perfect condition because I had to push hard at the beginning of each one with a heavy car, but still it worked really nicely. We were two or three tenths of a second down on Michael all through, but to be second on a difficult weekend for us was really a perfect result.'

This had the tone of whistling to keep spirits up, but thus far it had been a season in which fortunes had ebbed and flowed between Renault and Ferrari, Michelin and Bridgestone, and in those races that the top contenders could not win they had to be sure of scoring as many points as they could.

Schumacher had no problem winning on this occasion and was in a class of his own as he became the first man ever

Below: The Toro Rosso brigade celebrates Italy's World Cup success.
Photograph: Jean-François Galeron/WRI

Bottom: The BMW Sauber lads put the finishing touches to Nick Heidfeld's car on the grid.

Left: Lost Boys' Michiel Mol with Midland's Colin Kolles.

Photographs: James Moy/www.crashpa.net

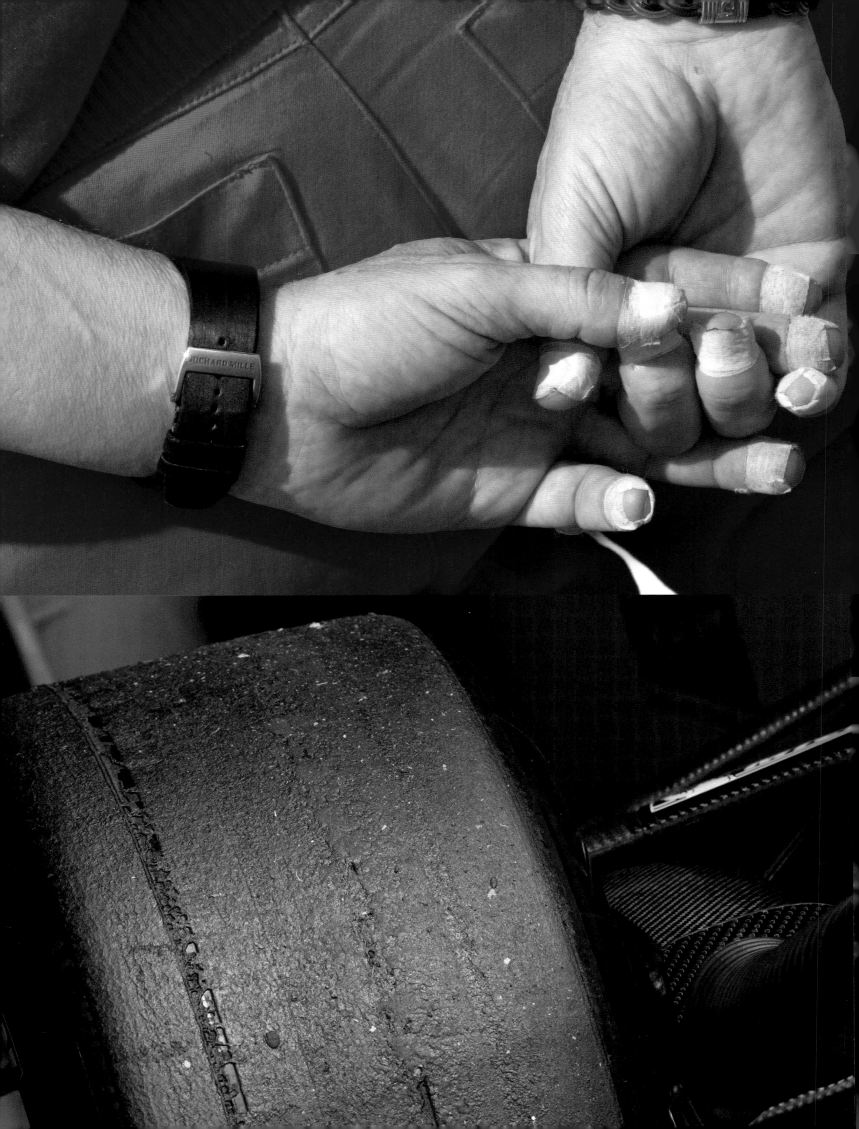

to win eight times in one particular race. The Spaniard finished 10s behind, but in reality the gap was nearer thirty seconds and Alonso got so close only because Schumacher backed off in the final laps.

The 88th victory of Schumacher's career was arguably one of the dullest, at least outwardly, but appearances were deceptive. The decision to use Bridgestone's softer tyre could have left Ferrari wallowing around avoiding graining or suffering from it in the early laps, but the German drove with all of his brilliance to keep his tyres healthy. It was a masterful performance.

The victory also yielded Schumacher's 150th podium finish and he was rightly a very happy man as he waved an Italian flag and embraced Ferrari sporting director Jean Todt. They had taken a huge gamble and it had rewarded them handsomely.

'We had a good start and drove our race from there,' he said. 'We were not sure how the race would go because our problems on Saturday prevented us from doing any long runs. But I have to say the car, the tyres, the whole package worked superbly. I'm sorry that Felipe couldn't keep his second place, but nevertheless third place means more points. It's a great result if we see how difficult this weekend has been at certain moments and how we didn't know at one stage whether we could go out to qualify. The mechanics are really special guys and as they repaired the cars we guessed the set-up, so the engineers worked very well together, too. Well done to the whole team.

'We have clearly made up ground and everybody here is giving everything for the last seven races. The championship is far from being over. What matters is how the car and the package match a circuit and we are confident ours will be a good match at Hockenheim [in Germany two weeks later]. We have to hope for the coming races that we can keep the momentum going. It's going to be a battle in the development of the car.'

Alonso remained philosophical. 'I'm not surprised at all by Ferrari's resurgence. Indy was a strange race and maybe that was us [Michelin] being too conservative. Here we were close but not quick enough, the same as we had been at the Nürburgring and Imola. After those races everybody thought Ferrari would win all the races, but then we [Renault and I] won four consecutively so hopefully that's going to happen again.'

This was not a great race and, as usual at Magny-Cours, there was barely any overtaking. Behind Massa, a two-stop strategy helped Ralf Schumacher to a good fourth place for Toyota ahead of three-stopping Kimi Räikkönen, two-stopping Giancarlo Fisichella and three-stopping Pedro de la Rosa, who scored two more points on his return for McLaren but came to a smoky halt on the slowing-down lap. Toyota thus kept up its recent momentum with five more points, overtaking BMW for fifth place overall and creeping ever closer to arch-rival Honda.

The departure of Juan Pablo Montoya, which was announced with immediate effect after he signed to race in America's NASCAR for 2007, did not outwardly appear too disruptive for McLaren as Pedro de la Rosa got back into the swing of racing. Team-mate Kimi Räikkönen said he was really happy with the handling of his MP4-21 on his way to fifth place, as was the Spaniard after claiming his two points. Each of them suffered in traffic, which blunted their challenge, but the Silver Arrows were certainly quick and took over from Renault the mantle of Michelin's fastest runner. Schumacher set the fastest lap in 1m 17.111s, with Massa close behind on 1m 17.141s, but the McLarens were next with 1m 17.625s for Räikkönen and 1m 17.717s for De la Rosa. That put both of them ahead of Alonso, whose best was only 1m 17.770s.

The final point went to two-stopping Nick Heidfeld and BMW ahead of David Coulthard and Scott Speed. They were all a lap down and Heidfeld's passing move on Coulthard at Adelaide on the opening lap proved decisive in their battle: Coulthard was right behind him to the flag. Heidfeld was far from pleased, however, about having moved over to let De la Rosa through when he was unfairly and incorrectly shown the blue flag. Jacques Villeneuve, Christian Klien and Tonio Liuzzi followed them home.

Villeneuve believed his BMW-Sauber F1.06 was very good, but could never fight his way out of the midfield traffic, while Klien's Red Bull lost revs with overheating and Liuzzi dropped from 17th on the grid to last because his tired Cosworth V10 needed changing. Nico Rosberg was 14th, two laps adrift, ahead of Christijan Albers and Franck Montagny. Albers had problems with his gearbox that included loss of first and subsequent selection difficulties, while the Frenchman was having his last scheduled race for Super Aguri: Sakon Yamamoto was due to replace him from Hockenheim onwards.

Super Aguri lost Takuma Sato early. The Japanese racer had trouble leaving the grid for the formation lap in his SA05, which was having its last outing, and made it only to Turn Six on the first lap before the car rolled to a halt with a clutch problem. Tiago Monteiro retired on the 12th lap after spinning behind Montagny in the final chicane and then damaging his Midland's hydraulics as it took off after hitting the kerb.

Jarno Trulli's chances of fourth place evaporated with a brake problem after 39 laps – the pedal movement just got longer and longer until the Italian deemed the situation dangerous. Similarly, Mark Webber's hopes of a much-needed point for Williams were dashed by overheating of the inside shoulder of a rear Bridgestone, which caused the tyre to throw a tread. The resultant spin damaged a wheel rim and caused other damage that led to the Australian's retirement after 53 laps. He had run as high as eighth. Team-mate Rosberg also lost time after being called in for a precautionary check.

The team with the greatest problem, however, was Honda, whose despair deepened as neither Rubens Barrichello nor Jenson Button finished, having been able to stage only weak performances. Both men tried to put an optimistic spin on a terrible race but the facts were all too apparent. Barrichello never ran higher than 12th before succumbing to an engine-related problem after 18 laps and Button lasted until lap 62, albeit without rising above 11th position.

Then his engine appeared to suffer a similar fate. Metaphorically holding his head in his hands as his much-vaunted team's pathetic form continued, the Briton commented, 'I felt a loss of power as I came on to the back straight as I was changing up through the gears on lap 61.'

When the dust had settled, the gap between Alonso and Schumacher was still 17 points after Renault's clever bit of damage limitation, but the writing was on the wall: Renault and Michelin had an awful lot to do before Hockenheim.

Schumacher, Ferrari and Bridgestone had turned the tables in remarkable style at Magny-Cours, proving that Indianapolis owed a lot more than was at the time thought to the stunning progress that the Japanese tyre manufacturer had suddenly made. With seven races left to run, however, Alonso was still in the relatively luxurious position of being able to finish second even if Schumacher were to win all of them. But that situation was also soon to change.

David Tremayne

DIARY

Ferrari and Red Bull are locked in conflict over engine supply for 2007, the second year of their contract. Red Bull wants to pass the supply down to its sister team Toro Rosso, and use Renault V8s itself, but Ferrari insists that the contract is with Red Bull Racing itself, not the parent company, and that RBR must stick with its engines.

The French Grand Prix marks Franck Montagny's last F1 race outing. Super Aguri plans Sakon Yamamoto's début for Germany, together with its new SA06 chassis.

Pedro de la Rosa is confirmed as having at least three races as Juan Pablo Montoya's McLaren successor.

Bernie Ecclestone praises efforts by the Wallonia local government to have the Belgian Grand Prix reinstated in 2007.

Top left: Stickered fingers? Jean Todt's taped-up fingers – his bid to protect himself from nervous chewing trackside.
Photograph: Laurent Charniaux/WRI

Bottom left: A slick testimony to the intensity of the F1 tyre war.
Photograph: James Moy/www.crashpa.net

FIA F1 WORLD CHAMPIONSHIP • ROUND 11
GRAND PRIX DE FRANCE
MAGNY-COURS 14–16 JULY 2006

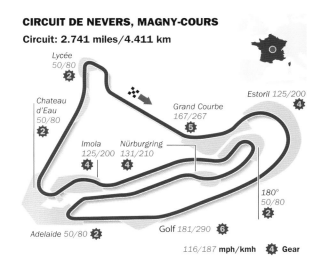

CIRCUIT DE NEVERS, MAGNY-COURS

Circuit: 2.741 miles/4.411 km

Lycée 50/80 **2**

Chateau d'Eau 50/80 **2**

Grand Courbe 167/267 **5**

Estoril 125/200 **4**

Imola 125/200 **4**   Nürburgring 131/210 **4**

180° 50/80 **2**

Adelaide 50/80 **2**   Golf 181/290 **6**

116/187 mph/kmh   **4** Gear

Photograph: James Moy/www.crashpa.net

RACE RESULTS

All results and data © FOM 2006

Pos.	Driver	Nat.	No.	Entrant	Car/Engine	Tyres	Laps	Time/Retirement	Speed (mph/km/h)	Gap to leader	Fastest race lap	
1	Michael Schumacher	D	5	Scuderia Ferrari Marlboro	Ferrari 248 F1-056 V8	B	70	1h 32m 07.803s	124.875/200.967		1m 17.111s	46
2	Fernando Alonso	E	1	Mild Seven Renault F1 Team	Renault R26-RS26 V8	M	70	1h 32m 17.934s	124.646/200.599	+10.131s	1m 17.770s	23
3	Felipe Massa	BR	6	Scuderia Ferrari Marlboro	Ferrari 248 F1-056 V8	B	70	1h 32m 30.349s	124.368/200.151	+22.546s	1m 17.141s	18
4	Ralf Schumacher	D	7	Panasonic Toyota Racing	Toyota TF106B-RVX-06 V8	B	70	1h 32m 35.015s	124.264/199.983	+27.212s	1m 17.809s	19
5	Kimi Räikkönen	FIN	3	Team McLaren Mercedes	McLaren MP4-21-Mercedes FO 108S V8	M	70	1h 32m 40.809s	124.134/199.774	+33.006s	1m 17.717s	30
6	Giancarlo Fisichella	I	2	Mild Seven Renault F1 Team	Renault R26-RS26 V8	M	70	1h 32m 53.068s	123.861/199.335	+45.265s	1m 18.057s	20
7	Pedro de la Rosa	E	4	Team McLaren Mercedes	McLaren MP4-21-Mercedes FO 108S V8	M	70	1h 32m 57.210s	123.769/199.187	+49.407s	1m 17.625s	34
8	Nick Heidfeld	D	16	BMW Sauber F1 Team	BMW Sauber F1.06-BMW P86 V8	M	69			+1 lap	1m 18.809s	48
9	David Coulthard	GB	14	Red Bull Racing	Red Bull RB2-Ferrari 056 V8	M	69			+1 lap	1m 18.978s	56
10	Scott Speed	USA	21	Scuderia Toro Rosso	Toro Rosso STR01-Cosworth TJ2005-2 V10	M	69			+1 lap	1m 18.674s	66
11	Jacques Villeneuve	CDN	17	BMW Sauber F1 Team	BMW Sauber F1.06-BMW P86 V8	M	69			+1 lap	1m 17.906s	56
12	Christian Klien	A	15	Red Bull Racing	Red Bull RB2-Ferrari 056 V8	M	69			+1 lap	1m 18.968s	56
13	Vitantonio Liuzzi	I	20	Scuderia Toro Rosso	Toro Rosso STR01-Cosworth TJ2005-2 V10	M	69			+1 lap	1m 18.241s	54
14	Nico Rosberg	D	10	WilliamsF1 Team	Williams FW28-Cosworth CA2006 V8	B	68			+2 laps	1m 18.796s	62
15	Christijan Albers	NL	19	MF1 Racing	Midland M16-Toyota RVX-06 V8	B	68			+2 laps	1m 19.356s	67
16	Franck Montagny	F	23	Super Aguri F1 Team	Super Aguri SA05-Honda RA806E V8	B	67			+3 laps	1m 20.113s	53
	Jenson Button	GB	12	Lucky Strike Honda Racing F1 Team	Honda RA106-RA806E V8	M	61	Engine			1m 18.510s	47
	Mark Webber	AUS	9	WilliamsF1 Team	Williams FW28-Cosworth CA2006 V8	B	53	Tyre/spin/wheel rim			1m 18.859s	34
	Jarno Trulli	I	8	Panasonic Toyota Racing	Toyota TF106B-RVX-06 V8	B	39	Brakes			1m 18.036s	16
	Rubens Barrichello	BR	11	Lucky Strike Honda Racing F1 Team	Honda RA106-RA806E V8	M	18	Engine			1m 20.094s	16
	Tiago Monteiro	P	18	MF1 Racing	Midland M16-Toyota RVX-06 V8	B	11	Differential/spin			1m 21.663s	8
	Takuma Sato	J	22	Super Aguri F1 Team	Super Aguri SA05-Honda RA806E V8	B	0	Clutch			No time	—

Fastest lap: Michael Schumacher, 1m 17.111s on lap 46, 127.960 mph/ 205.931 km/h.

Lap record: Michael Schumacher (Ferrari F2004 V10), 1m 15.377s, 130.904 mph/210.669 km/h (2004).

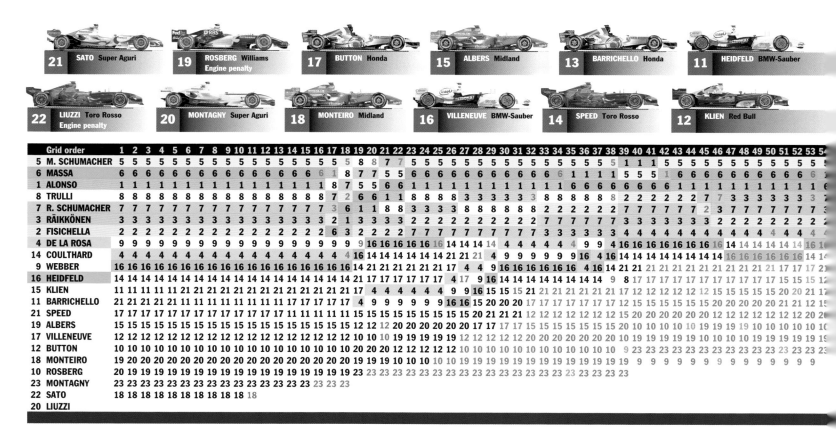

198

PRACTICE 1 (FRIDAY)

Sunny (track 38–43ºC, air 26–29ºC)

Pos.	Driver	Laps	Time
1	Robert Kubica	31	1m 16.794s
2	Anthony Davidson	29	1m 17.133s
3	Jenson Button	4	1m 18.160s
4	Ralf Schumacher	6	1m 18.752s
5	Adrian Sutil	32	1m 18.777s
6	Neel Jani	21	1m 18.962s
7	Alexander Wurz	17	1m 19.055s
8	Jacques Villeneuve	6	1m 19.063s
9	Robert Doornbos	20	1m 19.311s
10	Nico Rosberg	6	1m 19.401s
11	Christijan Albers	7	1m 19.465s
12	Jarno Trulli	7	1m 19.806s
13	Tiago Monteiro	7	1m 20.335s
14	Franck Montagny	11	1m 20.790s
15	Takuma Sato	10	1m 21.160s
16	Sakon Yamamoto	11	1m 23.891s
17	Giancarlo Fisichella	1	No time
18	Fernando Alonso	1	No time
19	Pedro de la Rosa	1	No time
20	Scott Speed	1	No time
21	Vitantonio Liuzzi	2	No time
22	David Coulthard	1	No time
23	Christian Klien	1	No time
24	Kimi Räikkönen	1	No time

PRACTICE 2 (FRIDAY)

Sunny/cloudy (track 46–50ºC, air 34–35ºC)

Pos.	Driver	Laps	Time
1	Robert Kubica	33	1m 16.902s
2	Fernando Alonso	14	1m 17.498s
3	Anthony Davidson	37	1m 17.750s
4	Alexander Wurz	29	1m 17.859s
5	Giancarlo Fisichella	13	1m 17.916s
6	Michael Schumacher	16	1m 17.938s
7	Adrian Sutil	31	1m 18.049s
8	Robert Doornbos	28	1m 18.175s
9	Ralf Schumacher	21	1m 18.274s
10	Neel Jani	32	1m 18.639s
11	Jarno Trulli	23	1m 18.721s
12	Jenson Button	18	1m 19.005s
13	Felipe Massa	20	1m 19.013s
14	Nick Heidfeld	15	1m 19.108s
15	Kimi Räikkönen	9	1m 19.140s
16	Christijan Albers	21	1m 19.183s
17	Rubens Barrichello	5	1m 19.259s
18	Mark Webber	10	1m 19.413s
19	Vitantonio Liuzzi	14	1m 19.589s
20	Nico Rosberg	19	1m 19.692s
21	Tiago Monteiro	19	1m 19.701s
22	Pedro de la Rosa	14	1m 19.809s
23	Takuma Sato	22	1m 19.996s
24	Scott Speed	12	1m 20.003s
25	David Coulthard	12	1m 20.135s
26	Jacques Villeneuve	11	1m 20.154s
27	Christian Klien	14	1m 20.409s
28	Franck Montagny	14	1m 21.132s
29	Sakon Yamamoto	32	1m 21.969s

QUALIFYING (SATURDAY)

Sunny (track 49–51ºC, air 33–34ºC)

Pos.	Driver	First	Second	Third
1	Michael Schumacher	1m 15.865s	1m 15.111s	1m 15.493s
2	Felipe Massa	1m 16.277s	1m 15.679s	1m 15.510s
3	Fernando Alonso	1m 16.328s	1m 15.706s	1m 15.785s
4	Jarno Trulli	1m 15.550s	1m 15.776s	1m 16.036s
5	Ralf Schumacher	1m 15.949s	1m 15.625s	1m 16.091s
6	Kimi Räikkönen	1m 16.154s	1m 15.742s	1m 16.281s
7	Giancarlo Fisichella	1m 16.825s	1m 15.901s	1m 16.345s
8	Pedro de la Rosa	1m 16.679s	1m 15.902s	1m 16.632s
9	Nico Rosberg	1m 16.534s	1m 15.926s	1m 18.272s
10	David Coulthard	1m 16.350s	1m 15.974s	1m 18.663s
11	Mark Webber	1m 16.531s	1m 16.129s	
12	Nick Heidfeld	1m 16.686s	1m 16.294s	
13	Christian Klien	1m 16.921s	1m 16.433s	
14	Rubens Barrichello	1m 17.022s	1m 17.027s	
15	Scott Speed	1m 17.117s	1m 17.063s	
16	Christijan Albers	1m 16.962s	1m 17.105s	
17	Vitantonio Liuzzi	1m 17.164s		
18	Jacques Villeneuve	1m 17.304s		
19	Jenson Button	1m 17.495s		
20	Tiago Monteiro	1m 17.589s		
21	Franck Montagny	1m 18.637s		
22	Takuma Sato	1m 18.845s		

PRACTICE 3 (SATURDAY)

Sunny (track 38–43ºC, air 29–30ºC)

Pos.	Driver	Laps	Time
1	Jacques Villeneuve	13	1m 17.005s
2	Nick Heidfeld	16	1m 17.049s
3	Jarno Trulli	18	1m 17.056s
4	Nico Rosberg	16	1m 17.188s
5	Mark Webber	12	1m 17.358s
6	Jenson Button	19	1m 17.476s
7	Kimi Räikkönen	12	1m 17.556s
8	Pedro de la Rosa	16	1m 17.653s
9	Ralf Schumacher	18	1m 17.666s
10	David Coulthard	19	1m 17.859s
11	Giancarlo Fisichella	17	1m 17.995s
12	Christijan Albers	24	1m 18.059s
13	Vitantonio Liuzzi	20	1m 18.199s
14	Michael Schumacher	5	1m 18.214s
15	Felipe Massa	8	1m 18.396s
16	Fernando Alonso	16	1m 18.447s
17	Tiago Monteiro	23	1m 18.487s
18	Scott Speed	20	1m 18.545s
19	Christian Klien	17	1m 18.631s
20	Rubens Barrichello	20	1m 18.961s
21	Franck Montagny	18	1m 19.497s
22	Takuma Sato	10	1m 21.497s

CHASSIS LOG BOOK

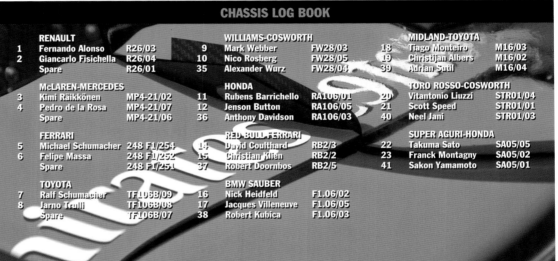

RENAULT
1	Fernando Alonso	R26/03
2	Giancarlo Fisichella	R26/04
Spare		R26/01

McLAREN-MERCEDES
3	Kimi Räikkönen	MP4-21/02
4	Pedro de la Rosa	MP4-21/07
Spare		MP4-21/06

FERRARI
5	Michael Schumacher	248 F1/254
6	Felipe Massa	248 F1/252
Spare		248 F1/251

TOYOTA
7	Ralf Schumacher	TF106B/09
8	Jarno Trulli	TF106B/08
Spare		TF106B/07

WILLIAMS-COSWORTH
9	Mark Webber	FW28/03
10	Nico Rosberg	FW28/05
35	Alexander Wurz	FW28/04

HONDA
11	Rubens Barrichello	RA106/01
12	Jenson Button	RA106/05
36	Anthony Davidson	RA106/03

RED BULL-FERRARI
14	David Coulthard	RB2/3
15	Christian Klien	RB2/2
37	Robert Doornbos	RB2/5

BMW SAUBER
16	Nick Heidfeld	F1.06/02
17	Jacques Villeneuve	F1.06/05
38	Robert Kubica	F1.06/03

MIDLAND-TOYOTA
18	Tiago Monteiro	M16/03
19	Christijan Albers	M16/02
39	Adrian Sutil	M16/04

TORO ROSSO-COSWORTH
20	Vitantonio Liuzzi	STR01/04
21	Scott Speed	STR01/01
40	Neel Jani	STR01/03

SUPER AGURI-HONDA
22	Takuma Sato	SA05/05
23	Franck Montagny	SA05/02
41	Sakon Yamamoto	SA05/01

 **9 COULTHARD** Red Bull
 **7 FISICHELLA** Renault
 **5 R. SCHUMACHER** Toyota
 **3 ALONSO** Renault
 **1 M. SCHUMACHER** Ferrari
 **10 WEBBER** Williams
 **8 DE LA ROSA** McLaren
 **6 RÄIKKÖNEN** McLaren
 **4 TRULLI** Toyota
 **2 MASSA** Ferrari

RACE DISTANCE:
70 laps
191.746 miles/308.586 km

RACE WEATHER:
Sunny
track 48–57ºC, air 34–36ºC

55	56	57	58	59	60	61	62	63	64	65	66	67	68	69	70	*	
5	5	5	5	5	5	5	5	5	5	5	5	5	5	5	5		1
1	1	1	1	1	1	1	1	1	1	1	1	1	1	1	1		2
6	6	6	6	6	6	6	6	6	6	6	6	6	6	6	3		3
7	7	7	7	7	7	7	7	7	7	7	7	7	7	7	7		4
3	3	3	3	3	3	3	3	3	3	3	3	3	3	3	5		5
2	2	2	2	2	2	2	2	2	2	2	2	2	2	2	6		6
4	4	4	4	4	4	4	4	4	4	4	4	4	4	4	7		7
16	16	16	16	16	16	16	16	16	16	16	16	16	16				8
14	14	14	14	14	14	14	14	14	14	14	14	14	14				
21	21	21	21	21	21	21	21	21	21	21	21	21	21				
12	12	12	12	12	12	12	17	17	17	17	17	17	17				
17	17	17	17	17	17	15	15	15	15	15	15	15	15				
15	15	15	15	15	20	20	20	20	20	20	20	20	20				
20	20	20	20	20	20	12	10	10	10	10	10	10	10				
10	10	10	10	10	10	10	19	19	19	19	19	19	19				
19	19	19	19	19	19	23	23	23	23	23	23	23					
23	23	23	23	23	23	23											

Pit stop
One lap or more behind leader

FOR THE RECORD

150th PODIUM: Michael Schumacher

POINTS

	DRIVERS				CONSTRUCTORS	
1	Fernando Alonso	96		1	Renault	142
2	Michael Schumacher	79		2	Ferrari	121
3	Giancarlo Fisichella	46		3	McLaren	71
4	Kimi Räikkönen	43		4	Honda	32
5	Felipe Massa	42		5	Toyota	21
6	Juan Pablo Montoya	26		6	BMW Sauber	20
7	Jenson Button	16		7	Red Bull	11
8	Rubens Barrichello	16		8	Williams	10
9	Ralf Schumacher	13		9	Toro Rosso	1
10	Nick Heidfeld	13				
11	David Coulthard	10				
12	Jarno Trulli	8				
13	Jacques Villeneuve	7				
14	Mark Webber	6				
15	Nico Rosberg	4				
16	Pedro de la Rosa	2				
17	Christian Klien	1				
18	Vitantonio Liuzzi	1				

GERMAN GP
HOCKENHEIM

HOCKENHEIM QUALIFYING

UNDERLINING McLaren's growing competitiveness, Kimi Räikkönen repeated his 2005 qualifying position on Saturday afternoon, pushing his MP4-21 around in 1m 14.070s when it mattered to beat Michael Schumacher, who recorded 1m 14.205s. But with Felipe Massa third, with a lap in 1m 14.569s, Ferrari continued to look very threatening. Both its drivers had complained of too much oversteer in the final session and everything would of course depend on respective fuel loads on Sunday, but the red cars seemed to be in great shape and events would endorse that view.

In the paddock on Saturday evening the feeling was that the Renaults had better be running a lot of fuel, otherwise they were in clear trouble. Giancarlo Fisichella could manage only fifth place with 1m 14.894s, while world champion Fernando Alonso seemed to be lost down in seventh with 1m 15.282s. The strain of the championship chase also seemed to be getting to him. At one point Schumacher cut across him as they left the pits, leaving the Spaniard screaming down his pit radio, 'Did you see what he just did? Did you see that?' It was another indication, as their battle grew more intense, that there is no love lost between the two contenders.

The other big surprise was the performance of Honda. Steady development programmes in a number of areas – principally engine, aerodynamics and suspension – had been put in train by Geoffrey Willis prior to his departure and taken up by former Sauber engineer Jacky Eeckelaert. Now, at last, they were beginning to bear fruit. Jenson Button set the fourth-fastest lap of qualifying in 1m 14.862s to give the team a major fillip, though the Englishman was concerned not to get too excited. 'We always seem to go well here,' he said, 'so let's reserve judgement and see what happens in the race.'

Rubens Barrichello placed the sister car sixth on the grid with 1m 14.943s, so there was an air of cautious optimism in the Brackley camp.

Ralf Schumacher had an adventurous session: he survived driving into Pedro de la Rosa's McLaren and puncturing the Spaniard's right-rear tyre and then nearly drove out of the Toyota pit into the side of Button, who had to take avoiding action. He was subsequently fined for his actions, but took eighth place with 1m 15.923s ahead of De la Rosa, who lapped his MP4-21 in 1m 15.936s. David Coulthard completed the top ten for Red Bull on 1m 16.326s.

The second session had had Michael Schumacher fastest on 1m 13.778s from Massa (1m 14.094s) and Button (1m 14.378s, which, when he recorded it, was the fastest time thus far over the weekend), and weeded out Williams's Mark Webber, who just missed getting through with 1m 15.094s, Christian Klien with 1m 15.141s for Red Bull, Toyota's Jarno Trulli with 1m 15.150s, Jacques Villeneuve with 1m 15.329s for BMW Sauber, Williams' Nico Rosberg with 1m 15.380s and Nick Heidfeld in the second F1.06 with 1m 15.397s. Unfortunately for Trulli, he had blown an engine that morning and been obliged to switch to the spare TF106B, which he didn't like. His resultant ten-place penalty dropped him to 20th on the grid, so it was small wonder he described this as one of his worst-ever weekends.

The first qualifying session was disastrous for Toro Rosso. Scott Speed had an accident in Turn One that really began in the last corner: his STR01 bounced down the grass opposite the pits before spinning and clobbering the inside wall in the first corner. Then Tonio Liuzzi was unable to squeeze any more out of his car and had to settle for 17th-fastest time, 1m 16.399s, the first man not to get through.

Neither Christijan Albers nor Tiago Monteiro made it for Midland, either, with 1m 17.093s and 1m 17.836s respectively. Albers, like Trulli, lost ten grid places because of an engine change and started 21st.

Super Aguri went to Germany with high hopes of getting through the first session for the first time, thanks to its new SA06. Takuma Sato did a fine job to post 1m 17.185s, but it wasn't enough. Rookie Sakon Yamamoto, replacing Franck Montagny, crashed his SA06 on Saturday morning and managed 1m 20.444s after being forced into the old SA05 spare chassis. He reverted to his repaired SA06 for the race, electing to start from the pit lane rather than 22nd on the grid.

On paper Ferrari looked set for a strong run in the race and to make a dent in Alonso's and Renault's championship leads. The race would prove that, on this occasion, qualifying appearances were not deceptive.

Top: Flavio Briatore helps Fernando Alonso to celebrate: the youngest world champion has reached the ripe old age of 25!
Photograph: Lukas Gorys

Above: Jacques Villeneuve confers with BMW Sauber technical director Willy Rampf. The calm before the storm, perhaps.

Right: Kimi Räikkönen put a smile on the faces of the Mercedes top brass after planting his McLaren MP4-21 firmly on pole position.

Below: Christian Klien, Tonio Liuzzi and Robert Doornbos share a quiet moment in the comfortable surroundings of the Red Bull Energy Station.
Photographs: Jean-François Galeron/WRI

MASS DAMPER FIASCO HITS RENAULT HARD

RENAULT'S championship campaign in Germany started to come off the rails early in the week, when F1's governing body, the FIA, decreed that the mass damper that the team used to control the R26 over bumps was illegal and sought to have it banned.

The dampers had been on the two cars all season, mounted within the nose cone, having been introduced on the R25s the previous year in Brazil. In 2005 they were cleared verbally by the FIA's safety delegate Charlie Whiting but not, apparently, in writing. Now – as he did over Michelin tyre-wear parameters prior to the race at Monza back in 2003 – Whiting had a change of heart and 'reinterpreted' his own interpretation. What had been deemed legal was now deemed not to be. At a stroke.

It was common knowledge that Ferrari, McLaren and Red Bull had also experimented with mass dampers, with varying levels of success. Their purpose was to help the engineers optimise the tyre contact patches by neutralising the car's vertical movement in reaction to bumps. The finger was pointed at McLaren as the culprit who drew the FIA's attention to the devices on the Renaults.

The FIA contended that, under article 3.15 of its technical regulations, mass dampers constituted a movable means of controlling the aerodynamics and were therefore illegal. Renault disagreed and the matter was investigated at Hockenheim by the FIA's own stewards, Tony Scott Andrews, Rafael Sierra and Waltraud Wuensch.

They concluded that mass dampers have less influence on the aerodynamics than would changes to the conventional dampers (by comparison with making the suspension settings stiffer, for example), and that because conventional dampers are not considered to be movable aerodynamic components neither should mass dampers be. The stewards suggested that, in comparison to conventional dampers', the effect of mass dampers on aerodynamic performance was 'negligible'.

The FIA was known to want mass dampers outlawed for 2007 and immediately confirmed to all of the teams its intention to appeal the decision of its own stewards. That meant, in theory at least, that if Renault were to run with mass dampers in Germany, the subsequent result could later be threatened if the FIA's appeal were upheld. That put *les bleus* into something of a quandary, but eventually the team bit the bullet and decided that running without them was the only sensible course of action.

Cynics who recalled the effect of Whiting's 'reinterpretation' of Michelin's wear parameters on McLaren's and Williams's championship campaigns in 2003 pointed out how convenient the timing again was: the summer testing ban had come into force, so Renault had no chance to re-optimise the R26 without the dampers in the week between Hockenheim and Hungary. It was thus hamstrung for two critical races.

Opening spread: Hockenheim traditionally attracts a huge crowd – and so does the packed starting grid on this occasion.

Left: The Renaults struggled for grip for much of the weekend. Here Giancarlo Fisichella has a slight edge over the pursuing Fernando Alonso.

Photographs: James Moy/www.crashpa.net

MICHAEL Schumacher's third victory in succession will be remembered as much for the controversy that surrounded another FIA 'reinterpretation' of its own rules as it will for the fact that Schumacher cut another six points from Fernando Alonso's championship lead. Because the FIA decreed that his Renault's mass damper was illegal, the Spaniard struggled home in only fifth place ahead of team-mate Giancarlo Fisichella, his once-dominant team looking confused and beaten.

Making things even worse for Renault – and so much better for Ferrari – Felipe Massa kept his team leader honest all the way through and finished second, the gap between them rarely more than a few seconds. After Schumacher eased off at the end they crossed the line only 0.7s apart.

A bold run from polesitter Kimi Räikkönen gave McLaren Mercedes the final podium position after the Finn had muscled past Jenson Button's revitalised Honda on the 58th lap.

Schumacher's triumph was his 70th for Ferrari, his fourth in his home grand prix and Bridgestone's 100th. But, as usual, the German was unimpressed by the pure statistics. All except one, that is. 'Numbers are never very important – but if you want one that is [important] right now,' he beamed, 'it's 11, the number of points left in Alonso's championship lead. To be

honest I was a bit surprised to be that much in front of him today, but I'll take it, really I'll take it. It is the right moment in time for such a performance to close the gap and keep the pressure on. It was a perfect weekend.'

As soon as early leader Räikkönen pitted for fuel on the tenth lap, the red cars ran away and hid. McLaren had not intended to run Räikkönen quite so light; this was not the sort of grandstanding other teams might indulge in, even if it was Mercedes-Benz's home ground. There was a sensor *snafu* in the camp prior to the final qualifying stint, as a result of which too little fuel was put into the tank.

'We had some problems with that yesterday,' Räikkönen admitted, deadpan. 'We got the pole but not with as much fuel as we had planned. But that actually worked out quite well because my tyres were on the limit by the time I stopped for fresh ones.'

With Räikkönen out of the way, further delayed in his stop by a sticking wheel nut, Ferrari ruled. Massa kept the pressure on Schumacher and very nearly grabbed the lead when the German had a poor-ish lap in traffic prior to his first refuelling stop on lap 20. They were side by side at one stage as he rejoined, but Massa is no fool. Ferrari needed this result desperately and he wasn't about to jeopardise it.

Below: David Coulthard's Red Bull is pitched into the air after tangling with Ralf Schumacher's Toyota. DC recovered to finish a lowly 11th.
Photograph: Lukas Gorys

Bottom: After finishing third, Kimi Räikkönen had to resort to picking up a fire extinguisher when his McLaren began to smoulder in *parc fermé*.

Left: Ferrari and Felipe Massa enjoy plenty of support.
Photographs: James Moy/www.crashpa.net

'This was our target today, especially after we showed such strong pace yesterday morning,' Massa said. 'It was a great job from the team and everybody. I'm getting used a little bit to the podium, but not yet to the first place!'

'With such a margin we could really drive safely,' Schumacher admitted. 'We were on pretty soft compounds here, so there was a lot of rubber off-line. Driving on the limit was probably very difficult, but we didn't really have to do that. The feeling in the team is superb and we just need to keep up that spirit and motivation.'

Button's strong performance in a revitalised Honda nearly yielded him the final podium place but, despite an electronic problem that at one stage robbed him of power and sent his gearshift awry, Räikkönen overtook him for the place as they exited the hairpin. Part of McLaren's upturn was down to a new front wing first tried at Jerez the previous week.

'Without the electronics problem I think we could have been a lot closer to the Ferraris,' said Räikkönen, who was the only front runner to make three refuelling stops. Team-mate Pedro de la Rosa should also have been a strong points contender, but he retired early with fuel pump failure.

As he eyed the Ferrari drivers alongside him on the podium, the Finn may silently have been celebrating his choices. The

Above: Jacques Villeneuve in the
BMW-Sauber shortly before he
crashed out of the race – and
the team – in unexpected fashion.
Photograph: Peter Nygaard/GP Photo

Opposite: Happy or what? Even by his
own standards, Michael seems unusually
ecstatic as he celebrates on the podium.
Photograph: James Moy/www.crashpa.net

F1 world was awash with a new wave of rumours that he would, after all, be taking Alonso's place at Renault for 2007, whereas he knew that his Ferrari contract was firm. It was simply a matter of which of the men who stood with him, Schumacher or Massa, would be his partner. And Schumacher's current form strongly suggested that he could win his eighth world title and retire gracefully at the end of the season.

Ferrari president Jean Todt gave the clearest indication of Ferrari's thinking when he said afterwards, 'The moment that I will keep in my mind from this day is the podium ceremony, which featured my three favourite drivers.'

Button's satisfaction was more evident. 'To get past both Renaults at the start and then past Kimi during the race felt very good and I had a lot of fun out there,' he grinned. 'But the last stint was really tough because I had massive amounts of tyre graining on the front left and a lot of rear locking, so I just couldn't fight off Räikkönen.'

The result was a huge boost for Honda, especially after Rubens Barrichello's RA106 had succumbed to engine failure after only 18 laps. 'I just have to hope that we can carry this progress through to Hungary [a week later] because everyone has been working so hard to make this step forward,' Barrichello said. Little did anyone know…

As Ferrari swept on majestically, the wheels on Renault's world championship campaign came well and truly loose. Both Alonso and Fisichella complained of blistering Michelin tyres, but nobody was prepared to try and estimate how much that might have been down to the decision not to run with the mass dampers. Alonso said his first set of tyres was poor, his second good and his third poor again. He blamed a big slide that put him onto the grass on the 61st lap on a combination of the blistering and the need to push hard after Button.

Had it not been for Fisichella's presence, the Spaniard would probably have lost fifth place to Jarno Trulli. Fisi reported that his first set of tyres was good, the second bad and the third good. Renault's strategy this weekend called for all of its race sets to be scrubbed, to try to avoid the graining to which new tyres are prey, but it didn't pay off.

Schumacher and Massa set the fastest race laps – 1m 16.357s and 1m 16.392s respectively; Alonso languished in ninth place (one behind Fisichella) on 1m 17.256s. Worse still, for Renault, those times were bettered by Räikkönen (1m 16.475s), Ralf Schumacher (1m 16.763s), Trulli (1m 16.807s), Mark Webber (1m 16.812s) and Button (1m 16.818s). Some of that was explainable because of the Bridgestones, but for Renault to have fallen behind fellow Michelin runners McLaren and Honda indicated the depth of its distress at Hockenheim.

What made things worse still was that the R26s had what the team described as their 'most significant' aerodynamic update of the season, yet they had fallen farther behind their opposition. Post-race head-scratching in the camp suggested that the combination of a revised rear suspension and the fact that Renault was the only team to go for a new-construction Michelin rear tyre had been its undoing.

'We were not competitive this weekend, but I did the maximum I could and so did the team,' Alonso said as a glum postscript. 'Without the blistering we experienced, the podium was a possibility. But the tyres then blistered. We did not have enough to fight Ferrari here.'

The ever-unlucky Mark Webber also made a solid contribution to Alonso's fifth place. The Australian should have left Germany with four valuable – read 'desperately needed' – points, having driven his heart out in the FW28. There had already been the disappointment of team-mate Nico Rosberg's second shunt of the weekend on the opening lap; then, with nine laps to go, Webber's Cosworth succumbed to, of all things, a water leak as he was in the running for fourth or fifth place. It was a bitter blow, especially because the points would have moved the team ahead of Red Bull Racing in the championship.

Toyota continued to hold on to the fifth place that it had taken from BMW at Magny-Cours, courtesy of Trulli's strong run to seventh place. Team-mate Ralf Schumacher had another torrid day, building on his adventures in qualifying. He collided with David Coulthard on the first lap, had a pit lane speeding penalty, then a driving lesson from Tonio Liuzzi, but his fourth-fastest lap showed that the TF106B was a contender for points now that its Bridgestone tyres were working well.

Christian Klien took the final point for Red Bull after a measured drive, while team-mate Coulthard was left disgruntled about the assault by Ralf and then being overtaken later on by Liuzzi's year-old Toro Rosso. The Scot refused to make any meaningful comment afterwards. The STR01s were quite competitive, Liuzzi and team-mate Scott Speed setting the tenth- and 11th-best lap times ahead of the two Red Bulls, but the Italian reported that this time he did not have the grunt to keep ahead of the two Toyotas.

Midland started two cars and finished both. Christijan Albers had a solid dice with Speed and was ahead when his Toyota engine began to lose power in the closing stages, costing him a place. Tiago Monteiro chose softer Bridgestones that were less durable and suffered accordingly, and his race was further compromised by a drive-through penalty for ignoring blue flags. He also had a spell chasing Takuma Sato's new Super Aguri

SA06, until the latter lost so much oil that its engine cried enough. Sato's team-mate Sakon Yamamoto made his F1 début from the pit lane on the race's second lap, but suffered an immediate retirement with a driveshaft failure. There was a final sting in the tail for Midland, however: both M16s were disqualified afterwards for having flexible rear wings.

The race was a disaster for BMW on its home ground. It had the worst possible opening lap as Jacques Villeneuve ran into the back of team-mate Nick Heidfeld in Turn Six. Both made pit stops at the end of the lap and the resultant damage to Heidfeld's brakes eventually prompted his retirement. Villeneuve got going again with a new nose, but serious oversteer caught him out in Turn 17 on lap 31 and he got off-line onto the marbles and crashed heavily. As with Juan Pablo Montoya at Indianapolis, nobody could know at the time that they had just witnessed the 1997 champion's last GP outing.

So now the championship had reached its two-thirds distance and Ferrari was on the warpath. It had once seemed unthinkable that anyone could catch Fernando Alonso and Renault, but suddenly that seemed likely after the progress made by Ferrari and Bridgestone.

Only ten points now separated Renault and Ferrari in the constructors' championship: 149 to 139. Renault would not have the same type of Michelins at the Hungaroring the following weekend and therein lay its hope of retrieving the ground lost so spectacularly. But Schumacher, Ferrari and Bridgestone exuded confidence. While church bells rang in Maranello in celebration of victory, at Renault's bases in Enstone and Viry-Châtillon the only bells sounding were alarms.

David Tremayne

DIARY

Ross Brawn gets himself into hot water at Hockenheim when he indicates that he will be taking a sabbatical in 2007 from his role as technical director at Ferrari because his contract will expire at the end of 2006 regardless of whether Michael Schumacher continues with the Scuderia. Ferrari hotly denies that Brawn will step down.

Ferrari president Jean Todt gives a strong indication of Ferrari's driver line-up for 2007 when he declares that the podium at Hockenheim contains his three favourite drivers.

Michael Schumacher's fourth victory at Hockenheim seems timely because Bernie Ecclestone announces that there will be only one F1 race in Germany next year and that it will be held at the Nürburgring.

Jarno Trulli's unhappy practice and qualifying sessions are offset by the revelation that he has signed a new three-year extension with Toyota.

Mark Webber makes it clear after the race that he will not be continuing with Williams in 2007. The team is unable to pay him the $5.5 million specified in an ongoing contract. Webber signs for Red Bull alongside David Coulthard.

Two days after the German GP, Williams confirms that Friday test driver Alexander Wurz will be stepping into Webber's vacated seat.

GRÖSSER MOBIL 1 PREIS VON DEUTSCHLAND

HOCKENHEIM 28–30 JULY 2006

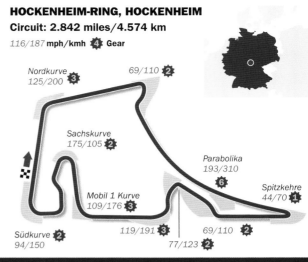

HOCKENHEIM-RING, HOCKENHEIM

Circuit: 2.842 miles/4.574 km

116/187 mph/kmh **4** Gear

Photograph: James Moy/www.crashpa.net

Nordkurve *125/200* **3**

69/110 **2**

Sachskurve *175/105* **2**

Parabolika *193/310* **6**

Mobil 1 Kurve *109/176* **3**

Spitzkehre *44/70* **1**

119/191 **3**

69/110 **2**

Südkurve *94/150* **2**

77/123 **2**

RACE RESULTS

Pos.	Driver	Nat.	No.	Entrant	Car/Engine	Tyres	Laps	Time/Retirement	Speed (mph/km/h)	Gap to leader	Fastest race lap	
1	Michael Schumacher	D	5	Scuderia Ferrari Marlboro	Ferrari 248 F1-056 V8	B	67	1h 27m 51.693s	130.039/209.277		1m 16.357s	17
2	Felipe Massa	BR	6	Scuderia Ferrari Marlboro	Ferrari 248 F1-056 V8	B	67	1h 27m 52.413s	130.021/209.249	+0.720s	1m 16.392s	18
3	Kimi Räikkönen	FIN	3	Team McLaren Mercedes	McLaren MP4-21-Mercedes FO 108S V8	M	67	1h 28m 04.899s	129.714/208.754	+13.206s	1m 16.475s	4
4	Jenson Button	GB	12	Lucky Strike Honda Racing F1 Team	Honda RA106-RA806E V8	M	67	1h 28m 10.591s	129.575/208.530	+18.898s	1m 16.818s	14
5	Fernando Alonso	E	1	Mild Seven Renault F1 Team	Renault R26-RS26 V8	M	67	1h 28m 15.400s	129.456/208.340	+23.707s	1m 17.256s	66
6	Giancarlo Fisichella	I	2	Mild Seven Renault F1 Team	Renault R26-RS26 V8	M	67	1h 28m 16.507s	129.430/208.297	+24.814s	1m 16.981s	18
7	Jarno Trulli	I	8	Panasonic Toyota Racing	Toyota TF106B-RVX-06 V8	B	67	1h 28m 18.237s	129.388/208.229	+26.544s	1m 16.807s	48
8	Christian Klien	A	15	Red Bull Racing	Red Bull RB2-Ferrari 056 V8	M	67	1h 28m 39.824s	128.862/207.384	+48.131s	1m 17.719s	49
9	Ralf Schumacher	D	7	Panasonic Toyota Racing	Toyota TF106B-RVX-06 V8	B	67	1h 28m 52.044s	128.567/206.909	+1m 0.351s	1m 16.763s	64
10	Vitantonio Liuzzi	I	20	Scuderia Toro Rosso	Toro Rosso STR01-Cosworth TJ2005-2 V10	M	66			+1 lap	1m 17.407s	51
11	David Coulthard	GB	14	Red Bull Racing	Red Bull RB2-Ferrari 056 V8	M	66			+1 lap	1m 17.811s	24
12	Scott Speed	USA	21	Scuderia Toro Rosso	Toro Rosso STR01-Cosworth TJ2005-2 V10	M	66			+1 lap	1m 17.450s	50
	Mark Webber	AUS	9	WilliamsF1 Team	Williams FW28-Cosworth CA2006 V8	B	59	Engine			1m 16.812s	43
	Takuma Sato	J	22	Super Aguri F1 Team	Super Aguri SA06-Honda RA806E V8	B	38	Gearbox oil leak			1m 19.413s	26
	Jacques Villeneuve	CDN	17	BMW Sauber F1 Team	BMW Sauber F1.06-BMW P86 V8	M	30	Accident			1m 18.904s	29
	Rubens Barrichello	BR	11	Lucky Strike Honda Racing F1 Team	Honda RA106-RA806E V8	M	18	Engine			1m 18.029s	16
	Nick Heidfeld	D	16	BMW Sauber F1 Team	BMW Sauber F1.06-BMW P86 V8	M	9	Accident/rear suspension			1m 19.264s	3
	Pedro de la Rosa	E	4	Team McLaren Mercedes	McLaren MP4-21-Mercedes FO 108S V8	M	2	Fuel pump			1m 19.649s	2
	Sakon Yamamoto	J	23	Super Aguri F1 Team	Super Aguri SA06-Honda RA806E V8	B	1	Driveshaft			No time	–
	Nico Rosberg	D	10	WilliamsF1 Team	Williams FW28-Cosworth CA2006 V8	B	0	Accident			No time	–
	Christijan Albers	NL	19	MF1 Racing	Midland M16-Toyota RVX-06 V8	B	66	Disqualified for illegal rear wing			1m 18.247s	35
	Tiago Monteiro	P	18	MF1 Racing	Midland M16-Toyota RVX-06 V8	B	65	Disqualified for illegal rear wing			1m 18.718s	46

Fastest lap: Michael Schumacher on lap 17, 1m 16.357s, 133.999 mph/215.650 km/h.

Lap record: Kimi Räikkönen (McLaren MP4-19B-Mercedes Benz V10), 1m 13.780s, 138.679 mph/223.182 km/h (2004).

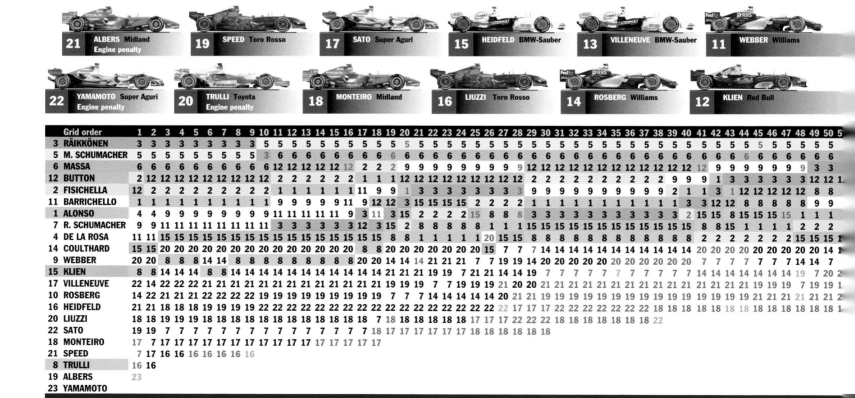

	Grid order	1	2	3	4	5	6	7	8	9	10	11	12	13	14	15	16	17	18	19	20	21	22	23	24	25	26	27	28	29	30	31	32	33	34	35	36	37	38	39	40	41	42	43	44	45	46	47	48	49	50
3	RÄIKKÖNEN	3	3	3	3	3	3	3	3	5	5	5	5	5	5	5	5	5	5	5	5	5	5	5	5	5	5	5	5	5	5	5	5	5	5	5	5	5	5	5	5	5	5	5	5	5	5	5	5	5	5
5	M. SCHUMACHER	5	5	5	5	5	5	5	5	3	6	6	6	6	6	6	6	6	6	6	6	6	6	6	6	6	6	6	6	6	6	6	6	6	6	6	6	6	6	6	6	6	6	6	6	6	6	6	6	6	6
6	MASSA	6	6	6	6	6	6	6	12	12	12	12	12	12	12	2	2	2	9	9	9	9	9	9	9	9	12	12	12	12	12	12	12	12	12	12	12	12	9	9	9	9	9	9	9	3	3				
12	BUTTON	2	12	12	12	12	12	12	6	6	2	2	2	2	2	1	1	1	12	12	12	12	12	12	12	12	2	2	2	2	2	2	2	2	9	9	9	1	3	3	3	3	3	3	3	12	12	1			
2	FISICHELLA	12	2	2	2	2	2	2	2	1	1	1	1	1	1	11	9	9	1	3	3	3	3	3	3	3	9	9	9	9	9	9	9	9	2	1	1	3	1	12	12	12	12	12	8	8					
11	BARRICHELLO	1	1	1	1	1	1	1	9	9	9	9	9	9	11	9	12	12	3	15	15	15	15	2	2	2	1	1	1	1	1	1	1	1	3	12	12	8	8	8	8	8	9	9							
1	ALONSO	4	4	9	9	9	9	9	11	11	11	11	11	11	9	3	11	3	15	2	2	2	2	15	8	8	3	3	3	3	3	3	3	3	15	15	8	15	15	15	15	15	1	1	1						
7	R. SCHUMACHER	9	9	11	11	11	11	11	11	11	3	3	3	3	3	12	3	15	2	8	8	8	8	1	1	1	15	15	15	15	15	15	15	15	8	15	1	1	1												
4	DE LA ROSA	11	11	15	15	15	15	15	15	15	15	15	15	15	15	15	8	1	1	1	1	1	20	15	15	8	8	8	8	8	8	8	8	8	8	2	2	2	2	2	2	15	15	15							
14	COULTHARD	15	15	20	20	20	20	20	20	20	20	20	20	20	8	20	20	20	20	20	20	15	7	7	7	14	14	14	14	14	14	14	14	20	20	20	20	20	20	20	20	14	1								
9	WEBBER	20	20	8	8	8	14	14	8	8	8	8	8	8	20	20	14	14	14	21	21	7	7	19	19	14	20	20	20	20	20	20	20	7	7	7	7	7	7	7	14	7									
15	KLIEN	8	8	14	14	14	8	8	14	14	14	14	14	14	14	14	21	21	21	19	7	21	14	14	19	7	7	7	7	7	7	7	7	14	14	14	14	14	19	7	20	2									
17	VILLENEUVE	22	14	22	22	22	21	21	21	21	21	21	21	21	21	21	14	21	21	21	14	21	21	21	21	21	21	21	21	21	21	21	21	21																	
10	ROSBERG	14	22	21	21	21	19	19	19	19	19	19	19	19	19	7	7	14	19	14	20	21	21	21	21	19	19	19	19	19	21	21	21	21	21	21	21	21	21	21	21	21									
16	HEIDFELD	21	21	18	18	18	18	19	19	19	18	18	18	18	18	22	18	22	22	22	22	22	22	17	17	17	18	18	18	18	18	18	18	18	18	18	18	18	18	18	18	18	1								
20	LIUZZI	18	18	19	19	19	19	18	18	18	16	16	16	16	18	18	18	18	17	17	17	17	22	22	22	18	18	18	18	18	18	22																			
22	SATO	19	19	7	7	7	7	7	7	7	7	7	7	7	7	18	17	17	17	17	17	18	18	18	18	18																									
18	MONTEIRO	17	17	17	17	17	17	17	17	17	17	17	17	17	17	17	17																																		
21	SPEED	7	17	16	16	16	16	16	16	16																																									
8	TRULLI	16	16																																																
19	ALBERS	23																																																	
23	YAMAMOTO																																																		

21 ALBERS Midland — Engine penalty
19 SPEED Toro Rosso
17 SATO Super Aguri
15 HEIDFELD BMW-Sauber
13 VILLENEUVE BMW-Sauber
11 WEBBER Williams
22 YAMAMOTO Super Aguri — Engine penalty
20 TRULLI Toyota — Engine penalty
18 MONTEIRO Midland
16 LIUZZI Toro Rosso
14 ROSBERG Williams
12 KLIEN Red Bull

PRACTICE 1 (FRIDAY)

Overcast (track 32–33ºC, air 26–27ºC)

Pos.	Driver	Laps	Time
1	Alexander Wurz	26	1m 16.349s
2	Anthony Davidson	29	1m 16.523s
3	Robert Kubica	29	1m 17.343s
4	Jenson Button	5	1m 17.439s
5	Robert Doornbos	25	1m 17.835s
6	Rubens Barrichello	6	1m 18.085s
7	Fernando Alonso	5	1m 18.328s
8	Neel Jani	24	1m 18.539s
9	Giancarlo Fisichella	6	1m 18.664s
10	David Coulthard	5	1m 18.795s
11	Markus Winkelhock	27	1m 18.964s
12	Jacques Villeneuve	6	1m 18.972s
13	Vitantonio Liuzzi	5	1m 19.214s
14	Nick Heidfeld	7	1m 19.507s
15	Takuma Sato	14	1m 20.102s
16	Christijan Albers	5	1m 20.132s
17	Tiago Monteiro	7	1m 20.575s
18	Scott Speed	7	1m 20.950s
19	Sakon Yamamoto	21	1m 21.218s
20	Nico Rosberg	3	1m 34.942s
21	Jarno Trulli	4	No time
22	Ralf Schumacher	4	No time
23	Christian Klien	1	No time
24	Pedro de la Rosa	1	No time
25	Kimi Räikkönen	1	No time

PRACTICE 2 (FRIDAY)

Overcast (track 30–38ºC, air 24–27ºC)

Pos.	Driver	Laps	Time
1	Robert Kubica	18	1m 16.225s
2	Michael Schumacher	14	1m 16.502s
3	Robert Doornbos	18	1m 16.549s
4	Kimi Räikkönen	9	1m 17.040s
5	Felipe Massa	11	1m 17.205s
6	Anthony Davidson	26	1m 17.294s
7	Mark Webber	6	1m 17.344s
8	Pedro de la Rosa	10	1m 17.516s
9	Rubens Barrichello	13	1m 17.519s
10	Jenson Button	13	1m 17.542s
11	Giancarlo Fisichella	10	1m 17.672s
12	Jarno Trulli	13	1m 17.844s
13	Ralf Schumacher	14	1m 17.895s
14	Markus Winkelhock	20	1m 17.962s
15	Fernando Alonso	8	1m 18.082s
16	Alexander Wurz	36	1m 18.164s
17	Christian Klien	13	1m 18.223s
18	Vitantonio Liuzzi	13	1m 18.366s
19	Neel Jani	19	1m 18.460s
20	David Coulthard	10	1m 18.616s
21	Nick Heidfeld	10	1m 18.636s
22	Christijan Albers	11	1m 18.643s
23	Tiago Monteiro	11	1m 18.991s
24	Jacques Villeneuve	9	1m 19.113s
25	Scott Speed	12	1m 19.232s
26	Takuma Sato	8	1m 19.365s
27	Sakon Yamamoto	2	No time

QUALIFYING (SATURDAY)

Sunny (track 41–44ºC, air 29–30ºC)

Pos.	Driver	First	Second	Third
1	Kimi Räikkönen	1m 15.214s	1m 14.410s	1m 14.070s
2	Michael Schumacher	1m 14.904s	1m 13.778s	1m 14.205s
3	Felipe Massa	1m 14.412s	1m 14.094s	1m 14.569s
4	Jenson Button	1m 15.869s	1m 14.378s	1m 14.862s
5	Giancarlo Fisichella	1m 15.916s	1m 14.540s	1m 14.894s
6	Rubens Barrichello	1m 15.757s	1m 14.652s	1m 14.934s
7	Fernando Alonso	1m 15.518s	1m 14.746s	1m 15.282s
8	Ralf Schumacher	1m 15.789s	1m 14.743s	1m 15.923s
9	Pedro de la Rosa	1m 15.655s	1m 15.021s	1m 15.936s
10	David Coulthard	1m 15.836s	1m 14.826s	1m 16.326s
11	Mark Webber	1m 15.719s	1m 15.094s	
12	Christian Klien	1m 15.816s	1m 15.141s	
13	Jarno Trulli	1m 15.430s	1m 15.150s	
14	Jacques Villeneuve	1m 16.281s	1m 15.329s	
15	Nico Rosberg	1m 16.183s	1m 15.380s	
16	Nick Heidfeld	1m 16.234s	1m 15.397s	
17	Vitantonio Liuzzi	1m 16.399s		
18	Christijan Albers	1m 17.093s		
19	Takuma Sato	1m 17.185s		
20	Tiago Monteiro	1m 17.836s		
21	Sakon Yamamoto	1m 20.444s		
22	Scott Speed	No time		

PRACTICE 3 (SATURDAY)

Scattered cloud/sun (track 33–37ºC, air 25–26ºC)

Pos.	Driver	Laps	Time
1	Christian Klien	14	1m 15.628s
2	Jenson Button	15	1m 15.651s
3	Rubens Barrichello	19	1m 15.963s
4	Felipe Massa	13	1m 15.977s
5	David Coulthard	14	1m 16.080s
6	Giancarlo Fisichella	16	1m 16.130s
7	Nick Heidfeld	14	1m 16.167s
8	Kimi Räikkönen	12	1m 16.218s
9	Michael Schumacher	11	1m 16.307s
10	Pedro de la Rosa	12	1m 16.322s
11	Fernando Alonso	15	1m 16.427s
12	Vitantonio Liuzzi	18	1m 16.532s
13	Scott Speed	17	1m 16.600s
14	Nico Rosberg	20	1m 16.690s
15	Mark Webber	16	1m 16.834s
16	Ralf Schumacher	17	1m 17.419s
17	Jacques Villeneuve	16	1m 17.740s
18	Tiago Monteiro	23	1m 17.793s
19	Sakon Yamamoto	19	1m 18.643s
20	Takuma Sato	21	1m 18.668s
21	Christijan Albers	15	1m 19.254s
22	Jarno Trulli	2	No time

CHASSIS LOG BOOK

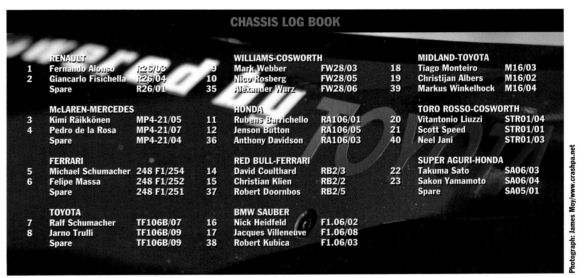

RENAULT
1	Fernando Alonso	R26/03	9
2	Giancarlo Fisichella	R26/04	10
	Spare	R26/01	35

McLAREN-MERCEDES
3	Kimi Räikkönen	MP4-21/05	11
4	Pedro de la Rosa	MP4-21/07	12
	Spare	MP4-21/04	36

FERRARI
5	Michael Schumacher	248 F1/254	14
6	Felipe Massa	248 F1/252	15
	Spare	248 F1/251	37

TOYOTA
7	Ralf Schumacher	TF106B/07	16
8	Jarno Trulli	TF106B/09	17
	Spare	TF106B/09	38

WILLIAMS-COSWORTH
Mark Webber	FW28/03	18
Nico Rosberg	FW28/05	19
Alexander Wurz	FW28/06	39

HONDA
Rubens Barrichello	RA106/01	20
Jenson Button	RA106/05	21
Anthony Davidson	RA106/03	40

RED BULL-FERRARI
David Coulthard	RB2/3	22
Christian Klien	RB2/2	23
Robert Doornbos	RB2/5	37

BMW SAUBER
Nick Heidfeld	F1.06/02	16
Jacques Villeneuve	F1.06/08	17
Robert Kubica	F1.06/03	38

MIDLAND-TOYOTA
Tiago Monteiro	M16/03	18
Christijan Albers	M16/02	19
Markus Winkelhock	M16/04	39

TORO ROSSO-COSWORTH
Vitantonio Liuzzi	STR01/04	20
Scott Speed	STR01/01	21
Neel Jani	STR01/03	40

SUPER AGURI-HONDA
Takuma Sato	SA06/03	22
Sakon Yamamoto	SA06/04	23
Spare	SA05/01	

9 DE LA ROSA McLaren

7 ALONSO Renault

5 FISICHELLA Renault

3 MASSA Ferrari

1 RÄIKKÖNEN McLaren

10 COULTHARD Red Bull

8 R. SCHUMACHER Toyota

6 BARRICHELLO Honda

4 BUTTON Honda

2 M. SCHUMACHER Ferrari

RACE DISTANCE:
67 laps
190.424 miles/306.458 km

RACE WEATHER:
Scattered cloud, sunny
track 45–46ºC, air 32ºC

	53	54	55	56	57	58	59	60	61	62	63	64	65	66	67	
5	5	5	5	5	5	5	5	5	5	5	5	5	5	5	5	1
6	6	6	6	6	6	6	6	6	6	6	6	6	6	6	2	2
3	3	3	3	12	12	3	3	3	3	3	3	3	3	3	3	3
2	12	12	12		3	12	12	12	12	12	12	12	12	12	12	4
9	9	9	9	9	9	1	1	1	1	1	1	1	1	1	5	5
1	1	1	1	1	2	2	2	2	2	2	2	2	2	2	6	
2	2	2	2	2	8	8	8	8	8	8	8	8	7	7	
8	8	8	8	8	9	15	15	15	15	15	15	15	15	8	
5	15	15	15	15	15	15	7	7	7	7	7	7	7	7	
7	7	7	7	7	7	7	20	20	20	20	20	20	20	20	
4	14	20	20	20	20	20	14	14	14	14	14	14	14	14	
20	20	14	14	14	14	14	21	21	21	21	21	21	21	21	
19	19	19	19	19	19	19	19	19	19	19	19	19	19	19	
21	21	21	21	21	21	9	18	18	18	18	18	18			
18	18	18	18	18	18	18	18								

Pit stop
One lap or more behind leader
Drive-through penalty

FOR THE RECORD

FIRST GRAND PRIX START:
Sakon Yamamoto (above)

100th WIN: Bridgestone

POINTS

DRIVERS
1	Fernando Alonso	100
2	Michael Schumacher	89
3	Felipe Massa	50
4	Giancarlo Fisichella	49
5	Kimi Räikkönen	49
6	Juan Pablo Montoya	26
7	Jenson Button	21
8	Rubens Barrichello	16
9	Ralf Schumacher	13
10	Nick Heidfeld	13
11	David Coulthard	10
12	Jarno Trulli	10
13	Jacques Villeneuve	7
14	Mark Webber	6
15	Nico Rosberg	4
16	Pedro de la Rosa	2
17	Christian Klien	2
18	Vitantonio Liuzzi	1

CONSTRUCTORS
1	Renault	149
2	Ferrari	139
3	McLaren	77
4	Honda	37
5	Toyota	23
6	BMW Sauber	20
7	Red Bull	12
8	Williams	10
9	Toro Rosso	1

HUNGARIAN GP

HUNGARORING

FERNANDO LOSES HIS COOL

RENAULT'S director of engineering, Pat Symonds, was at pains to stress that Fernando Alonso was being as calm as ever, but the evidence suggested that the pressure of the title battle was beginning to get to the Spaniard. There were stories of strong arguments within the team. Then when Michael Schumacher cut him up in the Hockenheim pit lane there had been an angry response over the radio. But what happened on Friday afternoon in Hungary was uncharacteristic of the normally placid champion.

Believing that Robert Doornbos had spoiled a lap, Alonso pulled alongside him going past the pits, gesticulated at the Dutchman and then weaved gently in his direction before moving back on-line. Then he brake-tested him in the first corner.

The stewards, led by permanent appointee Tony Scott Andrews, who had wielded the cane against Schumacher for stopping on-track during qualifying in Monaco, deemed such conduct 'unnecessary, unacceptable and dangerous' and levied a penalty of 1s on Alonso's fastest lap time in each qualifying session. In addition there was a 1s penalty for overtaking under waved yellow flags. Exit one world champion, bottom stinging.

Things thus looked very bleak for Renault – especially because the team had left its highly successful and, since Germany, controversial mass dampers in the garage rather than risk doing well with them and then having the FIA win its appeal against its own stewards on the matter in the court of appeal hearing in Paris that was scheduled for 22 August. It was as if Schumacher (who was in any case expected to dominate in Hungary) had been handed a bye for the weekend.

Then Jenson Button's engine blew up on Saturday morning. The session was red-flagged, but Alonso and Robert Kubica reported that Schumacher had passed them after the flag came out. There was a suspicion that the wily Alonso might have backed off prematurely to sucker his hated rival, but in any case the stewards decided that the German had committed the ultimate crime and handed him a 2s per lap per session penalty too. You couldn't make it up.

'With Michael penalised as well we have not lost so much,' a relieved Alonso said. Schumacher, meanwhile, gritted his teeth. 'I prefer not to go into a long explanation, but I'm really angry,' he said.

Just to compound the controversies, Renault chief Flavio Briatore went into overdrive, accusing the FIA of race-fixing after the sudden ban on mass dampers the previous week. It was one of those weekends.

HUNGARORING QUALIFYING

FERNANDO Alonso and Michael Schumacher do not like each other. In the F1 paddock that is less of a secret than it is elsewhere, but after practice and qualifying in Hungary nobody could have been in any doubt about it, nor that the strain of their world championship fight was getting to each of them (see separate story above).

The honours for pole position thus fell right at the very end of qualifying to McLaren's Kimi Räikkönen, whose lap of 1m 19.599s cost Felipe Massa the first pole of his career. The Ferrari driver had upheld team honours with 1m 19.886s, but his lap got a little wild at times after he'd had to slow down for Ralf Schumacher, who pulled out in front of him the pit lane, and thus lost some of the heat in his tyres letting the German get clear.

Even without the extra excitement of the penalties, this was always going to be an interesting session because the tyre manufacturers had come to Hungary expecting ambient temperatures around 43°C and instead encountered only slightly more than half that. The tyre situation was thus something of a lottery all through practice and qualifying. Both manufacturers encountered horrible graining on long runs with their softer compounds, obliging Ferrari to go for the harder Bridgestone and all of the Michelin runners except Honda to follow suit. Neither Rubens Barrichello nor Jenson Button could get his RA106 to generate sufficient temperature with the harder Michelin.

'The car has been very good all weekend and this pole is much better than last week's because there is no fuelling problem,' said Räikkönen, after setting the tenth pole of his career and his second in succession in 2006 in a McLaren that seemed to be the best car on the French tyres. 'We have set good lap times so I'm really looking forward to the race. It's up to the teams to choose the right tyres for the circuit, so it's not really Michelin's fault [Renault's recent problems]. It looks like this is a good tyre for us. I think we have an excellent chance to win the race.'

He conceded that it would have been more difficult with Schumacher and Alonso in contention, but added somewhat trenchantly, 'But it doesn't make any difference; there are rules and if you don't respect them, you get a penalty.'

Continuing their upturn in fortune since Hockenheim, the Hondas of Rubens Barrichello and Jenson Button were next up, with 1m 20.085s and 1m 20.092s respectively, the Brazilian opting for Michelin's softer compound. Unfortunately for Button, however, a morning engine failure had saddled him with a ten-grid-place penalty, so he started 14th. It did not seem a promising augury.

Pedro de la Rosa was fifth fastest with 1m 20.117s in the second McLaren, followed by Mark Webber, who did a good job for Williams with 1m 20.266s but was on a very low fuel load, Ralf Schumacher (1m 20.759s), Giancarlo Fisichella (1m 20.924s), Jarno Trulli (1m 21.132s) and the hugely impressive Robert Kubica, who would start his first grand prix from a corrected ninth place after lapping his BMW-Sauber in 1m 22.049s and consistently out-performing team-mate Nick Heidfeld.

Both Schumacher Jr and Kubica were a trifle fortunate, making it through from the second qualifying knock-out after Schumacher and Alonso had their penalties applied. Michael had been fastest in that session with 1m 18.875s, which thus became 1m 20.875; Fernando was second with 1m 19.364s, which became 1m 21.364s. Their penalties left them 11th and 15th respectively in the final line-up.

Nick Heidfeld, David Coulthard, Christian Klien and Tiago Monteiro all made it through to second qualifying but not into the top ten, lapping in 1m 20.623s, 1m 20.890s, 1m 21.207 and 1m 23.767s respectively.

The first session weeded out the Toro Rossos despite an extra 300 rpm allowed for the weekend from their restricted Cosworth V10s (Tonio Liuzzi with 1m 22.068s and Scott Speed with 1m 23.005s); Nico Rosberg (1m 22.084s); Takuma Sato (1m 22.967s); Christijan Albers (1m 23.146s); and Sakon Yamamoto (1m 24.016s).

THERE was a time, in 2004, when each successive race generated expectation of Jenson Button's breakthrough victory, but somehow it never came. Then 2005 disappointed and, after a poor start to 2006, Honda began to sink. So, when the great moment did finally arrive, in the uncharacteristically overcast conditions of the 2006 Hungarian Grand Prix, it took everyone by surprise. Not the least Button and his once beleaguered team.

And what a race! It was reminiscent of some of the Austrian GPs of yesteryear, in which the conditions allowed men such as Vittorio Brambilla and, at that time unfancied, Alan Jones to win their first races.

To use an apposite cliché, it was a goulash of a race. Fernando Alonso *should* have won it and Pedro de la Rosa *might* have but, for once, the cards finally fell Button's way and he richly deserved it. Honda's sudden turnaround in fortune was a match for Jordan's in 1998 and McLaren's in 2004.

The weather forecast had mostly been accurate during the unusually dull weekend, but rain on race morning was not supposed to be part of the script, which had called for cloud but a dry road. Instead, the field went to the line with no worries about which side of the grid offered better traction: neither did. But it was only damp, with a few serious wet patches farther around the lap. Most of the Michelin runners plumped for intermediate tyres, the exception being Rubens Barrichello, third on the grid. Down at Ferrari, Michael Schumacher and Felipe Massa went for Bridgestone's intermediate; so did Toyota's guys.

At the start of the first wet race since Spa 2005, Kimi Räikkönen pushed his McLaren into the lead from pole, with De la Rosa jumping up to second but quickly being supplanted by Barrichello. Farther back, from the 11th and 15th places to which they had been dropped by their practice penalties (for ignoring a red flag, and for brake-testing Robert Doornbos and overtaking under a yellow flag respectively), Schumacher and Fernando Alonso were already driving like men possessed, their class clearly showcased.

At the end of the lap Schumacher was an incredible fourth, ahead of Giancarlo Fisichella, who was already being hustled by Alonso. Felipe Massa had gone backwards, from second to seventh, and was chased by Robert Kubica, David Coulthard, Nick Heidfeld, Button (who started 14th instead of fourth thanks to a Saturday-morning engine failure and who later admitted that he had made 'a terrible start'), Ralf Schumacher, Tonio Liuzzi, Jarno Trulli *et al.* Sakon Yamamoto never made it past the first corner, his Super Aguri's engine stalling.

It was soon clear that Michelin's intermediates were the answer in the conditions, and that Bridgestone's weren't. By the fifth lap Barrichello was into the pits for intermediates, his original choice of tyre losing him his chance of victory. Mark Webber, who had dropped his Williams and damaged its front wing, was already out of the race; he was soon followed by Christian Klien, who put his Red Bull into the wall after making a mistake.

That was easy in the conditions, which was what made the performances of Schumacher, Alonso and a recovering Button so special. There is, of course, absolutely no love lost between Alonso and Schumacher and they went at it with a vengeance once the Spaniard passed the tardy Fisichella on the second lap. Alonso had already brushed wheels with Massa coming through to snatch sixth place in the last corner of the opening lap. Now he found another Ferrari being obstructive. Michael used all his wiles to block Fernando for two laps but the

inevitable happened on lap four as the champion exploited his superior grip and went around the outside of the German in Turn Seven. Great stuff!

He immediately set off after De la Rosa, who was hounding the soon-to-stop Barrichello, while farther back rookie Kubica blotted his copybook with a spin that dropped him from eighth to 16th behind Scott Speed's Toro Rosso.

Now the focus was on whether Fisichella could pass Schumacher, but the Italian is no Alonso and it took him until lap 17 to find the answer, by which time Button had passed him on lap six and Schumacher on seven. When Fisi's move finally came in Turn One, Schumacher resisted too much and suddenly found his front wing smashed, so he pitted early for a replacement and some fuel, retaining the same tyres.

Up front, De la Rosa had pitted on lap 16, and Räikkönen and Button on 17, so Alonso had the lead against all pre-race expectations and by lap 20 he was looking very comfortable. Räikkönen and De la Rosa had opened up such an advantage early on that they were still second and third respectively, while Button was fourth from Coulthard (who had yet to stop), Barrichello and Nick Heidfeld. Schumacher was down in eighth being chased by his brother. So where was Fisi? In the wall in Turn Eight, having spun his Renault backwards. He wouldn't be remembering this race with any fondness.

Kubica was also in trouble, again, breaking his BMW-Sauber's front wing in an incident in Turn Five and having to stop for a replacement.

By lap 25 Alonso had opened up a 39.1s gap over the McLarens, De la Rosa was clearly faster than Räikkönen, and Button was chasing them hard. Barrichello had overtaken Coulthard on lap 22 for fifth, and Heidfeld was still chasing down the Scot. Michael was barely keeping ahead of Ralf.

Things changed dramatically on the 26th lap, when the first real seeds of Button's triumph bore fruit. In a spiteful bit of spin doctoring, McLaren put these words into Räikkönen's mouth after he crashed into and over Tonio Liuzzi's Toro Rosso while

lapping it: 'I could do nothing to avoid the collision with Liuzzi. He really slowed down on the racing line and there was just nowhere to go.'

This turned out not to be the case. Räikkönen and Liuzzi are very close friends and the Finn later admitted to the Italian, who had been doing his best to keep out of the way, that he was actually looking in his mirrors, considering letting the faster De la Rosa through, at the time. When he looked back ahead he was unable to avoid colliding with Liuzzi's machine.

'Actually,' a McLaren insider confessed, 'it was worse than that. We were actually talking to Kimi over the radio, which also distracted him.'

Räikkönen (who had been on a two-stop strategy, in contrast to De la Rosa's three, hence the Spaniard's greater speed) was out on the spot, his McLaren badly damaged. Liuzzi crept around to the pits to retire, minus his rear wing.

The incident brought out the safety car and that was when things first began to go wrong for Alonso, who had actually lapped Schumacher on lap 23 but now at a stroke lost his big lead. Barrichello, Coulthard and Heidfeld all pitted on lap 26, Alonso on 27. The Spaniard was far enough ahead of Button, who had made capital out of De la Rosa's near miss in his team-mate's accident, to jump ahead into second place on lap 27, but Alonso cleared the pits without trouble and was still 6.5s ahead.

Button, however, had the bit between his teeth and brought the gap down to less than half a second by lap 45. True, he was running with what transpired to be a five-laps-lighter fuel load, but his performance at that stage of the race gave the lie to those who suggest he isn't quite at the top level as he and Alonso traded fastest laps. He refuelled on lap 46, rejoining still in second place, and began chasing Alonso all over again.

Behind them, lots was happening. De la Rosa was still third, Barrichello fourth. But as conditions improved and his tyres wore even more, Schumacher had been flying and was challenging Barrichello after a remarkable drive. Heidfeld was sixth, having passed Coulthard during their pit stops. A lap down, Kubica was the meat in a Ralf Schumacher-Jarno Trulli Toyota sandwich, with Massa gamely holding on behind them in one of his least convincing drives for a long time.

Alonso went five laps farther than Button before pitting and seemed to have the race in the bag despite a hiccough on the 34th lap when he accidentally hit neutral and momentarily slowed. But his refuelling stop on lap 51 was the prelude to disaster. As he rejoined he nearly went off in Turn One. Then the TV footage captured the moment when his right-rear wheel nut flew off, pitching him into a spin into the Turn Two barriers and out of the race. Initially it was thought to have been a driveshaft problem, but investigation subsequently revealed that the safety mechanism holding the wheel nut on did not

Below: Fernando Alonso, who looked on course for a decisive victory before his Renault retired, congratulates his compatriot Pedro de la Rosa on his best ever F1 result.

Photograph: Lukas Gorys

disengage in the stop; that in turn damaged the nut, which did not then reattach properly. Ten crucial points thus disappeared.

'These things happen,' Alonso said philosophically, 'but what an incredible race. The first part was fantastic and the car felt really good in the wet, even with a much bigger fuel load than our rivals'. I think it would have been a comfortable win today.'

As Button inherited the lead, Alonso's worst nightmare started to unfold. Schumacher had been flying on a drying track, retaining the same tyres in his pit stops and momentarily exploiting their increasing wear rate as if he were running on the

old type of slick tyre. But by lap 60 he was having to defend second place behind Button from De la Rosa and Heidfeld and his Bridgestones were finished. Instead of electing to settle for fourth place and five critical points, he forced the issue with both and had collisions with each.

He and De la Rosa ran side by side past the pits for four laps before De la Rosa finally squeezed through, but Schumacher brushed the Spaniard after refusing to give back to him the position Schumacher should have surrendered for overshooting the first chicane as De la Rosa overtook him. Heidfeld followed suit a lap later and again there was trouble as Schumacher ran into the back of the BMW. That damaged the Ferrari's steering and suddenly Alonso got his second big break of the weekend: Schumacher was forced to retire.

'He was defending his position a bit too much for his pace, already doing miracles to stay on the track, but I didn't expect him to battle that hard,' De la Rosa said, celebrating the first podium of his revived career. 'I just waited and waited and knew that I had to be patient. The second time around I made it, but he nearly caused me to crash because he jumped over the chicane, backed off and then when I went into Turn Eight on the inside, thinking he was letting me go past, he suddenly accelerated and we clashed wheels. I didn't understand.'

According to Heidfeld, 'Michael drove into the back of my car. His suspension was damaged and my steering wasn't straight any more, so I took it easy for the last few laps.'

Schumacher simply said, 'Of course I'm disappointed. We had a great opportunity but we did not take it. The track rod broke as Heidfeld went past. We touched, partly because the track was still a bit slippery. These things happen.'

Button reeled off the remaining laps and came home to a rousing reception, a winner at last after 113 races (or 114 if you count the 2005 US GP). De la Rosa and Heidfeld completed the podium, BMW's first, with Barrichello fourth to make Honda's day, Coulthard fifth, Ralf Schumacher sixth, Kubica a great seventh on his début and Massa eighth.

Schumacher was classified ninth ahead of the Midlands of Tiago Monteiro and Christijan Albers, and Scott Speed's Toro Rosso (the first car to try running dries, just before conditions would tolerate them, necessitating further delays switching back to intermediates). Jarno Trulli's prospects of points evaporated late in the race with engine failure, while Takuma Sato's Super Aguri was 13th, five laps down. Nico Rosberg had made an inelegant exit after 19 laps when an electrical problem cut his engine and sent him off-course.

There was a final sting in the tail for BMW: poor Kubica was thrown out because his car was 2kg underweight after the team got caught out by unexpectedly high tyre wear and therefore weight loss. That promoted Massa to seventh and Schumacher to eighth, trebling Ferrari's score. As Michael closed to within an even ten points of Alonso, the Scuderia was now only seven points adrift of the *Régie*.

None of that bothered Button or Honda on the Englishman's day of days.

'If my voice sounds funny it's because I've been screaming so much,' a jubilant Button said. 'It was fun closing down Alonso. We made a great choice of tyres and also our last stop was great. We were a real thinking team today. We thought hard about our strategy and we won not just because we had speed but also because we had the strategy. The last lap felt amazing.

In fact, over the last ten I didn't want the race to end. Normally when you are in the lead – I suppose – it seems to go on forever but I was loving it, I didn't want it to end, knowing I was on my way home to winning my first grand prix.

'This evening I'll run through it again. I've read a lot of stories about all the races I've done without winning, but they're not going to happen again. That's a big weight off my shoulders.'

He had finally made it and he did so in style. It was the most popular triumph of the season.

David Tremayne

Above: It doesn't get any better than this. Jenson Button celebrates with his father John.
Photograph: XPB.cc

Main: Button's Honda laps former Renault team-mate Giancarlo Fisichella at the height of the downpour.
Photograph: James Moy/www.crashpa.net

Fernando
ESP 🇪🇸 1

FIA F1 WORLD CHAMPIONSHIP • ROUND 13

MAGYAR NAGYDÍJ
BUDAPEST 4–6 AUGUST 2006

HUNGARORING, MOGYORÓD, BUDAPEST
Circuit: 2.722 miles/ 4.381 km
116/187 mph/kmh
Gear

Turn 1 75/120
Turn 2 50/80
Turn 3 137/220
Turn 4 125/200
Turn 5 135/2
Turn 6 56/90
Turn 7 61/98
Turn 8 75/120
Turn 9 80/128
Turn 10 140/225
Turn 11 115/185
Turn 12 66/106
Turn 13 55/88
Turn 14 85/136

Photograph: James Moy/www.crashpa.net

RACE RESULTS

Pos.	Driver	Nat.	No.	Entrant	Car/Engine	Tyres	Laps	Time/Retirement	Speed (mph/km/h)	Gap to leader	Fastest race lap	
1	Jenson Button	GB	12	Lucky Strike Honda Racing F1 Team	Honda RA106-RA806E V8	M	70	1h 52m 20.941s	101.764/163.773		1m 25.143s	57
2	Pedro de la Rosa	E	4	Team McLaren Mercedes	McLaren MP4-21-Mercedes FO 108S V8	M	70	1h 52m 51.778s	101.300/163.027	+30.837s	1m 24.315s	67
3	Nick Heidfeld	D	16	BMW Sauber F1 Team	BMW Sauber F1.06-BMW P86 V8	M	70	1h 53m 04.763s	101.106/162.715	+43.822s	1m 25.801s	65
4	Rubens Barrichello	BR	11	Lucky Strike Honda Racing F1 Team	Honda RA106-RA806E V8	M	70	1h 53m 06.146s	101.086/162.682	+45.205s	1m 24.678s	69
5	David Coulthard	GB	14	Red Bull Racing	Red Bull RB2-Ferrari 056 V8	M	69			+1 lap	1m 27.572s	65
6	Ralf Schumacher	D	7	Panasonic Toyota Racing	Toyota TF106B-RVX-06 V8	B	69			+1 lap	1m 25.247s	65
7	Felipe Massa	BR	6	Scuderia Ferrari Marlboro	Ferrari 248 F1-056 V8	B	69			+1 lap	1m 23.516s	65
8	Michael Schumacher	D	5	Scuderia Ferrari Marlboro	Ferrari 248 F1-056 V8	B	67	Track rod		+3 laps	1m 27.834s	57
9	Tiago Monteiro	P	18	MF1 Racing	Midland M16-Toyota RVX-06 V8	B	67			+3 laps	1m 28.178s	66
10	Christijan Albers	NL	19	MF1 Racing	Midland M16-Toyota RVX-06 V8	B	67			+3 laps	1m 26.117s	67
11	Scott Speed	USA	21	Scuderia Toro Rosso	Toro Rosso STR01-Cosworth TJ2005-2 V10	M	66			+4 laps	1m 26.249s	66
12	Jarno Trulli	I	8	Panasonic Toyota Racing	Toyota TF106B-RVX-06 V8	B	65	Engine		+5 laps	1m 25.779s	58
13	Takuma Sato	J	22	Super Aguri F1 Team	Super Aguri SA06-Honda RA806E V8	M	65			+5 laps	1m 30.957s	53
	Fernando Alonso	E	1	Mild Seven Renault F1 Team	Renault R26-RS26 V8	M	51	Wheel nut/spin			1m 29.408s	50
	Kimi Räikkönen	FIN	3	Team McLaren Mercedes	McLaren MP4-21-Mercedes FO 108S V8	M	25	Accident			1m 33.690s	7
	Vitantonio Liuzzi	I	20	Scuderia Toro Rosso	Toro Rosso STR01-Cosworth TJ2005-2 V10	M	25	Accident			1m 38.858s	8
	Nico Rosberg	D	10	WilliamsF1 Team	Williams FW28-Cosworth CA2006 V8	B	19	Electrics			1m 38.964s	9
	Giancarlo Fisichella	I	2	Mild Seven Renault F1 Team	Renault R26-RS26 V8	M	18	Accident			1m 35.550s	9
	Christian Klien	A	15	Red Bull Racing	Red Bull RB2-Ferrari 056 V8	M	6	Accident			1m 38.702s	6
	Mark Webber	AUS	9	WilliamsF1 Team	Williams FW28-Cosworth CA2006 V8	B	1	Accident			No time	–
	Sakon Yamamoto	J	23	Super Aguri F1 Team	Super Aguri SA06-Honda RA806E V8	B	0	Engine			No time	–
	Robert Kubica	POL	17	BMW Sauber F1 Team	BMW Sauber F1.06-BMW P86 V8	M	69	Disqualified for underweight car			1m 28.154s	55

Fastest lap: Felipe Massa on lap 65, 1m 23.516s, 117.343 mph/ 188.845 km/h.

Lap record: Michael Schumacher (Ferrari F2004 V10), 1m 19.071s, 123.939 mph/199.461 km/h (2004).

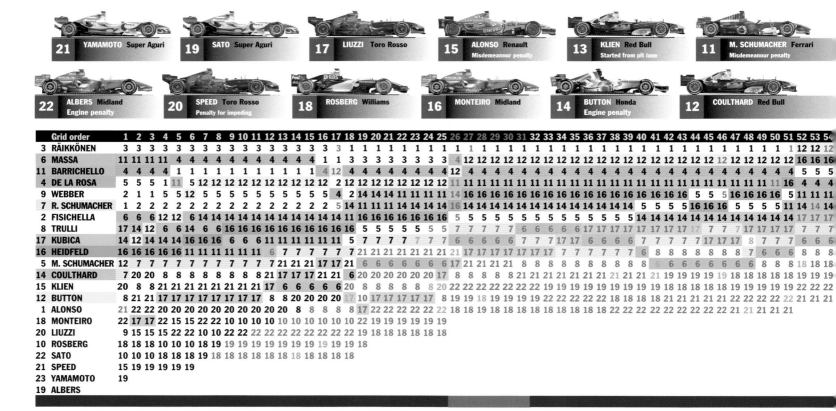

21 YAMAMOTO Super Aguri
19 SATO Super Aguri
17 LIUZZI Toro Rosso
15 ALONSO Renault — Misdemeanour penalty
13 KLIEN Red Bull — Started from pit lane
11 M. SCHUMACHER Ferrari — Misdemeanour penalty
22 ALBERS Midland — Engine penalty
20 SPEED Toro Rosso — Penalty for impeding
18 ROSBERG Williams
16 MONTEIRO Midland
14 BUTTON Honda — Engine penalty
12 COULTHARD Red Bull

Grid order	1	2	3	4	5	6	7	8	9	10	11	12	13	14	15	16	17	18	19	20	21	22	23	24	25	26	27	28	29	30	31	32	33	34	35	36	37	38	39	40	41	42	43	44	45	46	47	48	49	50	51	52	53	54
3 RÄIKKÖNEN	3	3	3	3	3	3	3	3	3	3	3	3	3	3	3	3	1	1	1	1	1	1	1	1	1	1	1	1	1	1	1	1	1	1	1	1	1	1	1	1	1	1	1	1	1	1	1	1	1	1	1	12	12	12
6 MASSA	11	11	11	11	4	4	4	4	4	4	4	4	4	4	4	1	3	3	3	3	3	3	3	4	12	12	12	12	12	12	12	12	12	12	12	12	12	12	12	12	12	12	12	12	12	12	12	12	12	12	12	16	16	16
11 BARRICHELLO	4	4	4	4	1	1	1	1	1	1	1	1	1	1	1	4	12	4	4	4	4	4	12	4	4	4	4	4	4	4	4	4	4	4	4	4	4	4	4	4	4	4	4	4	4	4	4	4	4	4	4	5	5	5
4 DE LA ROSA	5	5	5	1	11																																																		
9 WEBBER	2	1	1	5	12	5	5	5	5	5	5	5	5	5	5		4	2	14	14	14	14	14	11	11	11	11	11	11	11	11	16	16	16	16	16	16	16	16	16	16	16	16	5	5	16	16	16	16	16	5	11	11	11
7 R. SCHUMACHER	1	2	2	2	2	2	2	2	2	2	2	2	2	2	2	14	11	11	11	14	14	14	16	14	14	14	14	14	14	14	14	14	14	14	14	14	5	5	5	16	16	16	5	16	16	5	5	11	14	14
2 FISICHELLA	6	6	6	12	12	6	14	14	14	14	14	14	14	14	14	11	16	16	16	16	16	16	5	5	5	5	5	5	5	5	14	14	14	14	14	14	14	14	14	17	17	17
8 TRULLI	17	14	12	6	6	14	6	16	16	16	16	16	16	16	16	5	5	5	5	5	5	7	7	7	6	6	6	6	17	17	17	17	17	7	7	17	17	17	17	7	7	7
17 KUBICA	14	12	14	14	14	11	16	11	11	11	11	11	11	5	7	7	7	7	7	6	6	6	6	17	17	17	7	7	7	17	17	17	8	7	7	6	6	6
16 HEIDFELD	16	16	16	16	16	11	11	11	11	11	11	6	7	7	7	7	7	21	21	21	21	21	21	17	17	17	17	17	17	7	7	7	7	6	8	8	8	8	8	8	8
5 M. SCHUMACHER	12	7	7	7	7	7	7	7	7	7	7	21	21	21	17	17	21	6	6	6	6	6	6	17	21	21	21	8	8	8	8	8	8	8	8	6	6	6	6	6	6	8	8	8	18	18	18
14 COULTHARD	7	20	20	8	8	8	8	8	8	21	17	17	17	21	21	6	20	20	20	20	20	17	8	8	8	8	21	21	21	21	21	19	19	19	19	19	19	19	19	19	19
15 KLIEN	20	8	8	21	21	21	21	17	21	6	6	6	6	20	8	8	8	8	20	8	20	22	22	19	19	19	19	19	19	19	19	22	22	22	22	22
12 BUTTON	8	21	21	17	17	17	17	21	17	8	20	20	20	8	20	20	17	10	17	17	17	17	8	19	19	19	22	22	22	22	22	21	21	21	21	21
1 ALONSO	21	22	22	20	20	20	20	20	20	20	8	8	8	17	22	19	19	19	19	19	21	21	21	21	21
18 MONTEIRO	22	17	17	22	15	15	22	10	10	10	10	10	10	10	10	10	22	19	19	19	19	19
20 LIUZZI	9	15	15	15	22	22	10	10	22	22	22	22	22	22	22	22	19	18	18	18	18	18
10 ROSBERG	18	18	18	10	10	10	18	19	19	19	19	19	19	19	19	19	18
22 SATO	10	10	10	18	18	18	19	18	18	18	18	18	18	18	18	18
21 SPEED	15	19	19	19	19	19
23 YAMAMOTO	19
19 ALBERS	

218

TIME SHEETS

PRACTICE 1 (FRIDAY)

Overcast (track 20–24°C, air 17–19°C)

Pos.	Driver	Laps	Time
1	Kimi Räikkönen	5	1m 21.624s
2	Anthony Davidson	28	1m 22.396s
3	Michael Schumacher	5	1m 22.499s
4	Pedro de la Rosa	6	1m 22.730s
5	Alexander Wurz	25	1m 22.941s
6	Rubens Barrichello	6	1m 23.553s
7	Jenson Button	5	1m 23.659s
8	Robert Doornbos	27	1m 23.999s
9	Jarno Trulli	9	1m 24.620s
10	Markus Winkelhock	26	1m 25.194s
11	Neel Jani	17	1m 25.424s
12	Vitantonio Liuzzi	6	1m 25.477s
13	Scott Speed	7	1m 26.678s
14	Christian Albers	5	1m 26.680s
15	Tiago Monteiro	8	1m 27.321s
16	Takuma Sato	4	1m 29.765s
17	Ralf Schumacher	5	1m 30.110s
18	Sakon Yamamoto	12	1m 30.353s
19	Fernando Alonso	1	No time
20	Christian Klien	1	No time
21	David Coulthard	1	No time
22	Giancarlo Fisichella	1	No time

PRACTICE 2 (FRIDAY)

Overcast (track 24–25°C, air 19°C)

Pos.	Driver	Laps	Time
1	Felipe Massa	12	1m 21.778s
2	Fernando Alonso	15	1m 23.097s
3	Giancarlo Fisichella	14	1m 23.189s
4	Robert Doornbos	30	1m 23.195s
5	Anthony Davidson	31	1m 23.498s
6	Ralf Schumacher	19	1m 23.747s
7	Jarno Trulli	18	1m 23.771s
8	Michael Schumacher	19	1m 23.931s
9	Nick Heidfeld	11	1m 23.934s
10	Robert Kubica	11	1m 24.106s
11	Pedro de la Rosa	11	1m 24.252s
12	Markus Winkelhock	28	1m 24.381s
13	Rubens Barrichello	17	1m 24.445s
14	Jenson Button	15	1m 24.465s
15	Tiago Monteiro	8	1m 24.508s
16	Alexander Wurz	31	1m 24.609s
17	Takuma Sato	23	1m 24.623s
18	Nico Rosberg	12	1m 24.793s
19	Neel Jani	33	1m 24.854s
20	Christijan Albers	7	1m 25.038s
21	Scott Speed	16	1m 25.152s
22	Mark Webber	8	1m 25.393s
23	Christian Klien	14	1m 25.647s
24	David Coulthard	12	1m 25.843s
25	Kimi Räikkönen	11	1m 25.968s
26	Vitantonio Liuzzi	16	1m 26.198s
27	Sakon Yamamoto	20	1m 26.877s

QUALIFYING (SATURDAY)

Heavy cloud (track 27–29°C, air 21–22°C)

Pos.	Driver	First	Second	Third
1	Kimi Räikkönen	1m 20.080s	1m 19.704s	1m 19.599s
2	Felipe Massa	1m 19.742s	1m 19.504s	1m 19.886s
3	Rubens Barrichello	1m 21.141s	1m 19.783s	1m 20.085s
4	Jenson Button	1m 20.820s	1m 19.943s	1m 20.092s
5	Pedro de la Rosa	1m 21.288s	1m 19.991s	1m 20.117s
6	Mark Webber	1m 21.335s	1m 20.047s	1m 20.266s
7	Ralf Schumacher	1m 21.112s	1m 20.243s	1m 20.759s
8	Giancarlo Fisichella	1m 21.370s	1m 20.154s	1m 20.924s
9	Jarno Trulli	1m 21.434s	1m 20.231s	1m 21.132s
10	Robert Kubica	1m 20.891s	1m 20.256s	1m 22.049s
11	Nick Heidfeld	1m 21.437s	1m 20.623s	
12	Michael Schumacher	1m 21.440s	1m 20.875s	
13	David Coulthard	1m 21.163s	1m 20.890s	
14	Christian Klien	1m 22.027s	1m 21.207s	
15	Fernando Alonso	1m 21.792s	1m 21.364s	
16	Tiago Monteiro	1m 22.009s	1m 23.767s	
17	Vitantonio Liuzzi	1m 22.068s		
18	Nico Rosberg	1m 22.084s		
19	Takuma Sato	1m 22.967s		
20	Scott Speed	1m 23.005s*		
21	Christijan Albers	1m 23.146s		
22	Sakon Yamamoto	1m 24.016s		

* Set a time of 1m 22.317s but his three fastest times were disallowed for impeding a rival

PRACTICE 3 (SATURDAY)

Heavy cloud (track 25–27°C, air 20–21°C)

Pos.	Driver	Laps	Time
1	Michael Schumacher	11	1m 20.795s
2	Felipe Massa	11	1m 21.472s
3	Robert Kubica	18	1m 21.806s
4	Rubens Barrichello	18	1m 21.833s
5	Fernando Alonso	25	1m 22.119s
6	Giancarlo Fisichella	13	1m 22.340s
7	Christian Klien	15	1m 22.362s
8	Pedro de la Rosa	14	1m 22.424s
9	Vitantonio Liuzzi	13	1m 22.560s
10	Kimi Räikkönen	8	1m 22.599s
11	David Coulthard	14	1m 22.643s
12	Mark Webber	17	1m 22.839s
13	Tiago Monteiro	12	1m 23.819s
14	Scott Speed	16	1m 23.858s
15	Ralf Schumacher	13	1m 23.963s
16	Nico Rosberg	15	1m 24.381s
17	Jenson Button	4	1m 24.731s
18	Takuma Sato	15	1m 24.847s
19	Jarno Trulli	16	1m 25.373s
20	Nick Heidfeld	14	1m 25.597s
21	Christijan Albers	12	1m 26.047s
22	Sakon Yamamoto	19	1m 26.260s

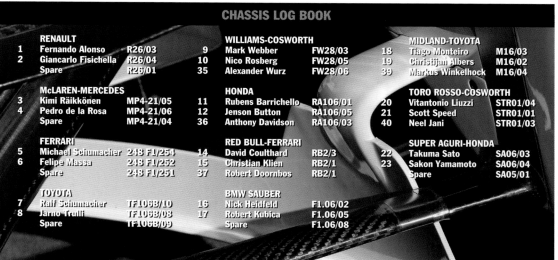

CHASSIS LOG BOOK

RENAULT
1	Fernando Alonso	R26/03	9
2	Giancarlo Fisichella	R26/04	10
	Spare	R26/01	35

McLAREN-MERCEDES
3	Kimi Räikkönen	MP4-21/05	11
4	Pedro de la Rosa	MP4-21/06	12
	Spare	MP4-21/04	36

FERRARI
5	Michael Schumacher	248 F1/254	14
6	Felipe Massa	248 F1/252	15
	Spare	248 F1/251	37

TOYOTA
7	Ralf Schumacher	TF106B/10	16
8	Jarno Trulli	TF106B/08	17
	Spare	TF106B/09	

WILLIAMS-COSWORTH
9	Mark Webber	FW28/03	18
10	Nico Rosberg	FW28/05	19
	Alexander Wurz	FW28/06	39

HONDA
11	Rubens Barrichello	RA106/01	20
12	Jenson Button	RA106/05	21
	Anthony Davidson	RA106/03	40

RED BULL-FERRARI
14	David Coulthard	RB2/3	22
15	Christian Klien	RB2/1	23
	Robert Doornbos	RB2/1	

BMW SAUBER
16	Nick Heidfeld	F1.06/02	
17	Robert Kubica	F1.06/05	
	Spare	F1.06/08	

MIDLAND-TOYOTA
18	Tiago Monteiro	M16/03	
19	Christijan Albers	M16/02	
	Markus Winkelhock	M16/04	

TORO ROSSO-COSWORTH
20	Vitantonio Liuzzi	STR01/04	
21	Scott Speed	STR01/01	
	Neel Jani	STR01/03	

SUPER AGURI-HONDA
22	Takuma Sato	SA06/03	
23	Sakon Yamamoto	SA06/04	
	Spare	SA05/01	

9 KUBICA BMW-Sauber

7 FISICHELLA Renault

5 WEBBER Williams

3 BARRICHELLO Honda

1 RÄIKKÖNEN McLaren

10 HEIDFELD BMW-Sauber

8 TRULLI Toyota

6 R. SCHUMACHER Toyota

4 DE LA ROSA McLaren

2 MASSA Ferrari

RACE DISTANCE:
70 laps
190.552 miles/306.663 km

RACE WEATHER:
Intermittent heavy rain
track 21–24°C, air 18–19°C

5	56	57	58	59	60	61	62	63	64	65	66	67	68	69	70	•	
2	12	12	12	12	12	12	12	12	12	12	12	12	12	12	12	1
6	5	5	5	5	5	5	5	5	5	4	4	4	4	4	2
4	4	4	4	4	4	4	4	4	16	16	16	16	3
5	16	16	16	16	16	16	16	16	16	11	11	11	11	11	4
1	11	11	11	11	11	11	11	11	11	11	5	14	14	5
4	14	14	14	14	14	14	14	14	14	14	7	7	6
7	17	17	17	17	17	17	17	17	7	7	7	17	17	7
7	7	7	7	7	7	7	17	17	17	6	6	8
6	6	6	6	8	8	8	8	6	6
8	8	8	8	6	6	6	6	6	18	18
8	18	18	18	18	18	18	18	18	18	19	19
9	19	19	19	19	19	19	19	19	19	21
2	22	22	22	22	22	22	21	21	21
1	21	21	21	21	21	21	22	22	22

26

Pit stop
One lap or more behind leader
Safety car deployed on laps shown

FOR THE RECORD

FIRST GRAND PRIX WIN: Jenson Button
FIRST GRAND PRIX PODIUM:
Pedro de la Rosa (above)
FIRST GRAND PRIX START:
Robert Kubica
TENTH POLE POSITION: Kimi Räikkönen
600th GRAND PRIX START:
Cosworth engine
300th GRAND PRIX START: Honda engine
100th POINT: Honda
50th POINT: Red Bull

POINTS

DRIVERS
1	Fernando Alonso	100
2	Michael Schumacher	90
3	Felipe Massa	52
4	Giancarlo Fisichella	49
5	Kimi Räikkönen	49
6	Jenson Button	31
7	Juan Pablo Montoya	26
8	Rubens Barrichello	21
9	Nick Heidfeld	19
10	Ralf Schumacher	16
11	David Coulthard	14
12	Pedro de la Rosa	10
13	Jarno Trulli	10
14	Jacques Villeneuve	7
15	Mark Webber	6
16	Nico Rosberg	4
17	Christian Klien	2
18	Vitantonio Liuzzi	1

CONSTRUCTORS
1	Renault	149
2	Ferrari	142
3	McLaren	85
4	Honda	52
5	Toyota	26
6	BMW Sauber	26
7	Red Bull	16
8	Williams	10
9	Toro Rosso	1

TURKISH GP

ISTANBUL

Main: A very tight moment going into the first corner as pole man Felipe Massa just squeezes in ahead of a wheel-locking Michael Schumacher's sister Ferrari, the Maranello duo successfully squeezing out Fernando Alonso's Renault on the outside line.

Inset: A jubilant Massa celebrates his first GP success.

Photographs: Breloer/XPB.cc

ISTANBUL QUALIFYING

Felipe Massa came of age in Turkey as he took the first pole position of his career with a performance that overshadowed vaunted team-mate Michael Schumacher. Bridgestone's tyre worked a lot better here than it did last year and the red cars were in the hunt all through Friday practice even though BMW's latest rookie – Sebastian Vettel – grabbed the headlines in the afternoon by setting the fastest time of the day in 1m 28.091s.

This might have been a case of 'boardroom lap times' but he acquitted himself well as he became, at 19 years and 53 days, the youngest driver ever officially to take part in a GP meeting. He also got done for pit lane speeding the first time he ventured onto the track...

Schumacher was a comfortable seven-tenths ahead of Fernando Alonso on Saturday morning so it was no surprise when Ferrari wrapped up the front row of the grid.

Giancarlo Fisichella and Fernando Alonso set the initial pace, with 1m 27.878s and 1m 28.071s respectively, but soon the Ferraris were on the warpath. Massa's 1m 27.307s made him fastest, until Schumacher recorded 1m 27.284s. There was a flurry of excitement as Jenson Button set the fastest sector-one time and appeared to be on a quick lap, but his effort fizzled into a 1m 27.790s, which left him only seventh.

Massa then improved to 1m 26.907s to leap ahead of his team-mate, who spoiled two runs with minor errors. The fact that Massa avoided them underlined the quality of his performance.

'This is a fantastic moment for me,' the little Brazilian beamed. 'Your first pole position is always much more important than the others. I'm really, really happy; this is a great moment for me.' Even Michael was impressed, musing, 'Felipe must have done a very good lap...'

The seven-times champion added, 'I ran wide in Turn One and didn't have an optimum lap. The tyres are basically good for one lap, take a certain dive and then stay there. I'm happy for Felipe, taking his first pole, and we are on the first row, which is what matters.'

Chez Renault, the continuing speed of Ferrari and Bridgestone did not lighten the mood. Alonso leapfrogged Fisichella to take third place on 1m 27.321s even though the Italian lowered his own to 1m 27.564s to take fourth. The Spaniard was resigned to the fact that his Michelin tyres lacked the one-lap performance to match the Bridgestones, having been obliged to switch from the softer compound to the harder for Saturday after graining problems on the first day of practice.

How much the upheld ban on the controversial mass dampers contributed to all that was anybody's guess, but he was still cautiously optimistic. 'I'm very happy, to be honest,' Alonso reported. 'We knew for one timed lap performance that Ferrari was too strong, but I believe more in our pace in the race. To be close behind the Ferraris, with Giancarlo close behind me, is the best the team could expect to do. I am very optimistic for tomorrow.'

Ralf Schumacher did a good job to take fifth with 1m 27.569s, exploiting Toyota's latest aero package, but that was negated because he would lose ten grid places after his TF106B required an engine change on Friday. Nick Heidfeld was BMW Sauber's lead runner with 1m 27.785s on Michelin's harder tyre, just ahead of Jenson Button. 'I was obviously hoping for something more from qualifying today,' Button admitted, 'although we have been struggling a little bit in the last sector here – on the long straight and the three very slow corners. That's where we have been losing out to Alonso.'

Kimi Räikkönen, who had been fastest on Friday morning, qualified eighth in 1m 27.866s, running his McLaren with a decent fuel load. The top ten was completed by Robert Kubica, who recorded 1m 28.167s in his BMW-Sauber on the softer Michelin, and Mark Webber, who lapped his Williams in 1m 29.436s.

Christian Klien got into the top ten on the grid thanks to Schumacher Jr's penalty, having lapped his Red Bull in 1m 27.852s, then came Pedro de la Rosa (1m 27.897s), Jarno Trulli (1m 27.973s), a glum Rubens Barrichello, who did not like his Honda's balance (1m 28.257s), Nico Rosberg (1m 28.386s) and Christijan Albers (1m 28.639s). Like Schumacher Jr, however, Albers got an engine change penalty, dropping to last place on the grid.

David Coulthard was the fastest of those to fall at the end of first qualifying, after lapping his Red Bull in 1m 29.136s to head the Toro Rossos of Scott Speed and Tonio Liuzzi (1m 29.158s and 1m 29.250s), Tiago Monteiro's Midland (1m 29.901s) and the Super Aguris of Sakon Yamamoto and Takuma Sato (1m 30.607s and 1m 30.850s).

'AN UNACCEPTABLE AND PROVOCATIVE PIECE OF THEATRE'

The Istanbul Park circuit is universally adored by the drivers, but the pleasure of seeing someone score his first F1 victory was soured the day after the race when a row blew up over the prize-giving ceremony on the podium.

The FIA, F1's governing body, launched a full investigation into the circumstances in which Mehmet Ali Talat was invited to present the victorious Felipe Massa with his trophy. Talat styles himself as the president of the northern Turkish republic of Cyprus but the Cypriot government, which does not recognise Talat, was quick to denounce the display as 'an unacceptable and provocative piece of theatre'.

This was a clear case of political exploitation. Cyprus became independent in 1960 but tensions remained between the Greek-Cypriot majority and the Turkish-Cypriot minority and resulted in frequent outbreaks of violence. In 1974 a Greek-sponsored attempt to seize control of the island resulted in Turkish troops invading the north. In 1983 Rauf Denktash annexed the northern part of Cyprus and declared it to be the independent Turkish Republic of Northern Cyprus, which is recognised only by Turkey.

The only internationally recognised government is that of the Greek Cypriots and, though Cyprus joined the European Union in May 2004, all EU obligations and rights apply only to the area under the control of the government and are suspended in the Turkish-controlled zone.

Bernie Ecclestone did not seem too perturbed – his Formula One Management company regards the track as one of the best facilities in the business and has no intention of dropping it. However, FIA president Max Mosley was apoplectic and the possibility arose that the Turks might lose their race. An FIA spokesman said, 'Political neutrality is fundamental to the FIA's role as the governing body of international motor sport. No compromise or violation of this neutrality is acceptable.'

Above: BMW Sauber's new test driver Sebastian Vettel is not only much younger than Nick Heidfeld and Robert Kubica, but also very much smaller.

Centre left: Bridgestone's was the tyre to beat at Istanbul, but the aerodynamic wheel discs on the Ferrari caused some controversy.

Photographs: James Moy/www.crashpa.net

223

THE 27th day of August, 2006, will go down in history not just as the day when Felipe Massa became the 87th man to win a grand prix but also as the day when circumstances outside Ferrari's control rewrote a script that had clearly called for his team-mate to be the victor. The man who made the difference was Tonio Liuzzi, for it was the demise of his uncompetitive Toro Rosso in Turn One on the 13th lap, with a seized differential, that prompted deployment of the safety car that disrupted the Scuderia's plans.

Massa had taken pole position with a fine performance and immediately jumped into the lead at the start of the race. Fernando Alonso, from third on the grid, got slightly ahead of Michael Schumacher but then had to back off as the two Ferraris pincered him in the run down to Turn One. As Alonso did this, his Renault team-mate Giancarlo Fisichella found himself short-braked and suddenly all hell broke loose.

In order to avoid running into his team-mate, Fisichella was forced to spin and was hit hard by Nick Heidfeld's pursuing BMW-Sauber. Behind them there was carnage as Kimi Räikkönen was hit from behind by Ralf Schumacher and Scott Speed, and a sideways Takuma Sato was hit by Tiago Monteiro, who retired on the spot. While that was happening, Schumacher Jr swept wildly across the track and collided lightly with team-mate Jarno Trulli. Ralf, Fisichella, Heidfeld, Speed, Räikkönen and Sato all pitted at the end of the lap before resuming, Sato many laps later.

Heidfeld's BMW had lost its front wing and resultant damage ruined his afternoon once he had pitted for a replacement. Schumacher Jr also needed a new nose and Speed needed repairs after hitting Räikkönen for the second time this year. The American recovered but, having pitted for a replacement rear tyre, Räikkönen crashed out after a lap when a detached floor cost him the downforce he needed at a critical moment in Turn Four.

There were several phenomenal avoidances, with the result that at the end of that first lap Massa led Schumacher,

Alonso, Mark Webber (a great start), Jenson Button, Nico Rosberg, Liuzzi (up from 18th) and Robert Kubica.

Massa and Schumacher quickly pulled away and few doubted that the latter would take the lead during the first pit stops. But Fate intervened. Liuzzi was struggling with his uncompetitive car and steadily dropped back down the order as his Toro Rosso could not sustain its position. Then its differential packed up suddenly, leaving him beached in a vulnerable position.

No safety car had been deployed after the initial carnage, despite the presence of sharp pieces of carbon-fibre all over the track, but now it came out and that changed the entire complexion of the race. On lap 14 there was a mass stampede to the pits. There was no way Ferrari could risk running Schumacher another lap – it had to exploit whatever was left of the 7.7s he had opened out over Alonso by lap 12 – so Michael had to wait in the queue as Massa's car was serviced first. With amazing efficiency Ferrari got the German back into the race with the loss of only one place but, crucially, that was to Alonso.

The order remained Massa, Alonso, Schumacher, Button until the next round of stops, which came on the 39th lap. By that stage the Brazilian was nine seconds ahead of the Spaniard. Alonso in turn was seven ahead of Schumacher, who had lost almost four seconds when he slid off the road in Turn Eight on the 28th lap while pushing hard to make up ground. Massa and Alonso dived into the pits, together with Button – who was no threat to any of them but was equally unchallenged in his Honda after deposing Webber on the second lap. That left Schumacher to take the lead and run four further laps.

Although Alonso's lap times were competitive with Massa's, it was clear that the Renault had no answer to the Brazilian's lead and soon it became a question of whether the champion could hold on to second place once Schumacher refuelled. When Michael finally pitted on the 43rd lap Massa resumed the lead and Alonso just squeaked by the other Ferrari into second place.

But all of his previous advantage over Schumacher had been eaten away. There was no love lost between these two and now it was going to be an all-out war for the remainder of a nail-biting contest.

Schumacher came within inches of snatching second place on the 50th lap but Alonso kept his nerve intact and the door closed and was able to exploit the Renault's superior performance through Turn Eight to eke out a breather four laps later as Schumacher made another small error. By the finish, however, the official timing could not split them as Alonso just got the verdict, having deliberately been slow into the final corner to frustrate any last-chance attack from Schumacher.

'I was lucky with the safety car; I overtook Michael there and managed to pull away,' Alonso said, 'but I was light on fuel in the second stint and Michael went wide in Turn Eight and probably that was the key to maintaining second place after the second stop. I was confident I could hold him behind and was playing with the revs a little bit, going down and up depending on the gap. In the last corner I just closed the door in case he tried a racing manoeuvre.'

Schumacher explained his busy afternoon thus: 'On my second set of tyres I didn't manage the speed I was supposed to go. There were some blisters on the rears because I had a pretty heavy fuel load. I lost significant time and had to make it up and probably overdrove the tyres a bit but there was nothing else I could do. It was a nice fight towards the end, but overall congratulations to Felipe. He did a superb job.'

Below left: Bernie Ecclestone confers with his right-hand-man Pasquale Lattuneddu.

Below: Michael Schumacher is not best pleased that team-mate Felipe Massa has grabbed pole position.
Photographs: James Moy/www.crash.net

Bottom: Fernando Alonso punches the air with delight as he holds off Michael Schumacher's Ferrari in a split-second sprint to the finishing line.
Photograph: Lukas Gorys

Behind them, Button brought the Honda home in fourth place, never having been lower than that once he'd passed Webber's Williams. The RA106 lacked the pace to run with the leaders but it was another solid performance and more points for the team, which gained another point after Rubens Barrichello made up for his qualifying performance with a fighting drive into eighth place.

The Honda duo was separated by Pedro de la Rosa, Giancarlo Fisichella and Ralf Schumacher. The Spaniard was McLaren's lone flag bearer after Räikkönen's early demise and was also delayed in the first-corner incident. It did not help him that he was on a one-stop refuelling strategy, but an intelligent drive enabled him to climb up to fifth and regain lost places after his stop on the 30th lap when Ralf Schumacher and Kubica made their pit calls.

Schumacher Jr and Fisichella both benefited from the intervention of the safety car after Liuzzi's spin and were able to make up a lot of the ground that was lost on the opening lap. When Fisichella pitted at the end of that lap, Renault switched him to a one-stop strategy and, having made up most of his deficit under the safety car, he was able to drive a strong race to

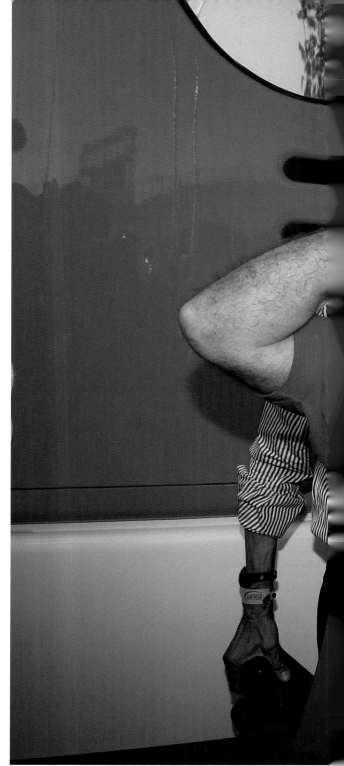

claim sixth. Toyota likewise refuelled Schumacher during his first-lap stop and switched him to a one-stop strategy, and he too was able to haul away and take seventh place ahead of Barrichello.

Team-mate Jarno Trulli was also involved in the opening-lap mêlée, albeit without a need to stop for repairs, and struggled home only ninth on Bridgestone's harder tyre.

After his great start Webber seemed on target for points, having stayed around seventh place, but eventually he lost out to single-stoppers Fisichella and Schumacher and could manage only tenth. David Coulthard and his Red Bull team-mate Christian Klien had another good scrap, which was resolved in the Austrian's favour after the Scot retired three laps from the finish with a gearbox problem.

Kubica's once-promising day – he ran as high as sixth early on – ended with a disappointing 12th place as he grappled with graining Michelins in the latter part of the race. He was followed home by Speed and team-mate Heidfeld – who found the balance and grip of his BMW-Sauber ruined after the first-lap bump with Fisichella – and Coulthard was classified 15th.

Christijan Albers drove a great race for Midland until succumbing to suspected engine problems after 46 laps; the other retirements were Nico Rosberg, whose Williams lost its water pressure after 41 laps, and Sakon Yamamoto, who spun in Turn One on lap 24.

Takuma Sato was in the pits for 23 minutes having a new floor and other components fitted to his damaged Super Aguri following the opening-lap collision with Monteiro. The undertray had to come from the spare SA06, so by the time he got going again he was too far behind to be classified.

Once again, then, Ferrari forced Renault into damage limitation mode, but at least this time Alonso was able to fight with the red cars and to beat Schumacher's. That left the gap between them at 12 points with four races to go but Ferrari had now closed to within two points of the *Régie* in the constructors' championship.

These, however, were academic points as far as Felipe Massa was concerned. He joined fellow countrymen Emerson Fittipaldi, Carlos Pace, Nelson Piquet, Ayrton Senna and Rubens Barrichello in the ranks of Brazilian drivers who have won grands prix and

became the 35th race winner for the Prancing Horse. If his voice got a little wavery at times, it was understandable – this was the greatest day of his racing life.

'It's just fantastic,' he said. 'When you've been working so hard your whole career to get to this moment, it's just amazing. Now I'm here, I'm really happy. It's been a fantastic day for me.

'I did a very good start and first lap, the car was well balanced during the whole race and even after the safety car I managed to pull away. But I was not too aggressive on the car. Every set of tyres, every single part of the race car, just responded in a fantastic way and I managed to keep the gap. It's difficult to say what I thought when I crossed the line but it was like a dream come true. Very special. It was always my dream to be a Ferrari driver and winning for the first time for Ferrari is definitely something special for me. It will take a while to sink in.'

Two races in a row with two new winners. It made you wonder what Monza could possibly hold in store as the dramatic championship race swept ever onwards.

David Tremayne

Above: **Another happy father. Luis Antonio Massa enjoys his boy's delight in the immediate aftermath of the race.**
Photograph: XPB.cc

Centre left: **David Coulthard locks a wheel as he struggles with the Red Bull RB2.**
Photograph: James Moy/www.crash.net

Bottom left: **Michael Schumacher offers his congratulations to Massa on joining the exclusive club of GP winners.**
Photograph: Russell Batchelor/XPB.cc

FIA F1 WORLD CHAMPIONSHIP • ROUND 14

PETROL OFISI
TURKISH GRAND PRIX

ISTANBUL 25–27 AUGUST 2006

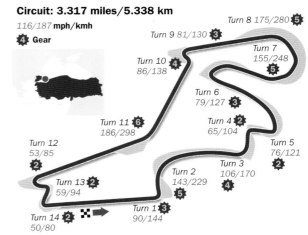

ISTANBUL KURTKOY INTERNATIONAL CIRCUIT

Circuit: 3.317 miles/5.338 km

116/187 mph/kmh

4 Gear

Turn 8 175/280 **5**
Turn 9 81/130 **3**
Turn 7 155/248 **5**
Turn 10 86/138 **4**
Turn 6 79/127 **3**
Turn 11 186/298 **6**
Turn 4 65/104 **2**
Turn 12 53/85 **2**
Turn 5 76/121 **2**
Turn 3 106/170 **4**
Turn 2 143/229 **4**
Turn 13 59/94 **2**
Turn 14 50/80 **2**
Turn 1 90/144 **3**

Photograph: James Moy/www.crashpa.net

RACE RESULTS

Pos.	Driver	Nat.	No.	Entrant	Car/Engine	Tyres	Laps	Time/Retirement	Speed (mph/km/h)	Gap to leader	Fastest race lap	
1	Felipe Massa	BR	6	Scuderia Ferrari Marlboro	Ferrari 248 F1-056 V8	B	58	1h 28m 51.082s	129.823/208.930		1m 28.123s	38
2	Fernando Alonso	E	1	Mild Seven Renault F1 Team	Renault R26-RS26 V8	M	58	1h 28m 56.657s	129.688/208.712	+5.575s	1m 28.245s	38
3	Michael Schumacher	D	5	Scuderia Ferrari Marlboro	Ferrari 248 F1-056 V8	B	58	1h 28m 56.738s	129.686/208.709	+5.656s	1m 28.005s	55
4	Jenson Button	GB	12	Lucky Strike Honda Racing F1 Team	Honda RA106-RA806E V8	M	58	1h 29m 03.416s	129.524/208.448	+12.334s	1m 28.474s	58
5	Pedro de la Rosa	E	4	Team McLaren Mercedes	McLaren MP4-21-Mercedes FO 108S V8	M	58	1h 29m 36.990s	128.715/207.146	+45.908s	1m 28.959s	54
6	Giancarlo Fisichella	I	2	Mild Seven Renault F1 Team	Renault R26-RS26 V8	M	58	1h 29m 37.676s	128.698/207.120	+46.594s	1m 28.546s	29
7	Ralf Schumacher	D	7	Panasonic Toyota Racing	Toyota TF106B-RVX-06 V8	B	58	1h 29m 50.419s	128.394/206.630	+59.337s	1m 29.084s	58
8	Rubens Barrichello	BR	11	Lucky Strike Honda Racing F1 Team	Honda RA106-RA806E V8	M	58	1h 29m 51.116s	128.377/206.603	+1m 0.034s	1m 28.733s	26
9	Jarno Trulli	I	8	Panasonic Toyota Racing	Toyota TF106B-RVX-06 V8	B	57			+1 lap	1m 30.048s	24
10	Mark Webber	AUS	9	WilliamsF1 Team	Williams FW28-Cosworth CA2006 V8	B	57			+1 lap	1m 30.088s	50
11	Christian Klien	A	15	Red Bull Racing	Red Bull RB2-Ferrari 056 V8	M	57			+1 lap	1m 30.025s	26
12	Robert Kubica	POL	17	BMW Sauber F1 Team	BMW Sauber F1.06-BMW P86 V8	M	57			+1 lap	1m 29.723s	34
13	Scott Speed	USA	21	Scuderia Toro Rosso	Toro Rosso STR01-Cosworth TJ2005-2 V10	M	57			+1 lap	1m 29.933s	43
14	Nick Heidfeld	D	16	BMW Sauber F1 Team	BMW Sauber F1.06-BMW P86 V8	M	56			+2 laps	1m 30.335s	56
15	David Coulthard	GB	14	Red Bull Racing	Red Bull RB2-Ferrari 056 V8	M	55	Gearbox		+3 laps	1m 30.026s	24
	Christijan Albers	NL	19	MF1 Racing	Midland M16-Toyota RVX-06 V8	B	46	Accident			1m 30.403s	35
	Takuma Sato	J	22	Super Aguri F1 Team	Super Aguri SA06-Honda RA806E V8	B	41				1m 31.814s	33
	Nico Rosberg	D	10	WilliamsF1 Team	Williams FW28-Cosworth CA2006 V8	B	25	Water pressure loss			1m 30.071s	21
	Sakon Yamamoto	J	23	Super Aguri F1 Team	Super Aguri SA06-Honda RA806E V8	B	23	Spin			1m 32.337s	12
	Vitantonio Liuzzi	I	20	Scuderia Toro Rosso	Toro Rosso STR01-Cosworth TJ2005-2 V10	M	12	Spin			1m 32.148s	12
	Kimi Räikkönen	FIN	3	Team McLaren Mercedes	McLaren MP4-21-Mercedes FO 108S V8	M	1	Accident damage			No time	–
	Tiago Monteiro	P	18	MF1 Racing	Midland M16-Toyota RVX-06 V8	B	0	Accident			No time	–

All results and data © FOM 2006

Fastest lap: Michael Schumacher on lap 55, 1m 28.005s, 135.683 mph/218.360 km/h.

Lap record: Juan Pablo Montoya (McLaren MP4-20-Mercedes Benz V10), 1m 24.770s, 140.861 mph/226.693 km/h (2005)

22 ALBERS Midland — Engine penalty

20 YAMAMOTO Super Aguri

18 LIUZZI Toro Rosso

16 COULTHARD Red Bull

14 ROSBERG Williams

12 TRULLI Toyota

21 SATO Super Aguri

19 MONTEIRO Midland

17 SPEED Toro Rosso

15 R. SCHUMACHER Toyota — Engine penalty

13 BARRICHELLO Honda

11 DE LA ROSA McLaren

Grid order	1	2	3	4	5	6	7	8	9	10	11	12	13	14	15	16	17	18	19	20	21	22	23	24	25	26	27	28	29	30	31	32	33	34	35	36	37	38	39	40	41	42	43	44	45
6 MASSA	6	6	6	6	6	6	6	6	6	6	6	6	6	6	6	6	6	6	6	6	6	6	6	6	6	6	6	6	6	6	6	6	6	6	6	6	6	6	6	5	5	5	5	6	6
5 M. SCHUMACHER	5	5	5	5	5	5	5	5	5	5	5	5	5	5	5	1	1	1	1	1	1	1	1	1	1	1	1	1	1	1	1	1	1	1	1	1	1	1	1	6	6	6	6	1	1
1 ALONSO	1	1	1	1	1	1	1	1	1	1	1	1	1	1	1	5	5	5	5	5	5	5	5	5	5	5	5	5	5	5	5	5	5	5	5	5	5	5	5	1	1	1	1	5	5
2 FISICHELLA	9	12	12	12	12	12	12	12	12	12	12	12	12	12	12	12	12	12	12	12	12	12	12	12	12	12	12	12	12	12	12	12	12	12	12	12	12	12	12	12	12	12	12	12	12
16 HEIDFELD	12	9	9	9	9	9	9	9	9	9	9	9	9	9	9	10	10	10	10	10	10	10	10	10	4	4	4	4	4	4	7	7	17	17	4	4	4	4	4	4	4	4	4	4	4
12 BUTTON	10	10	10	17	17	17	17	17	17	17	17	17	17	17	17	15	15	15	15	15	15	4	4	4	15	15	11	2	2	2	17	17	4	9	9	9	11	11	11	11	11	11	11	2	2
3 RÄIKKÖNEN	20	17	17	10	10	10	10	10	10	10	10	10	10	10	10	4	4	4	4	4	4	15	15	15	8	11	2	7	7	7	4	4	9	9	11	11	9	9	2	2	2	2	2	9	9
17 KUBICA	17	15	15	15	15	15	15	15	15	15	15	15	15	15	8	8	8	8	8	8	8	8	8	8	11	2	17	17	17	9	9	9	11	2	2	2	2	8	8	8	8	8	8	3	14
9 WEBBER	15	20	20	20	4	4	4	4	4	4	4	4	4	4	4	11	11	11	11	11	11	11	11	14	7	17	9	9	9	11	2	2	19	19	19	8	7	7	7	7	7	7	7	14	
15 KLIEN	4	4	4	4	20	8	8	8	8	8	8	8	8	8	14	14	14	14	14	14	14	14	2	17	9	11	11	11	2	2	19	8	8	8	8	7	15	15	15	15	14	4			
4 DE LA ROSA	14	14	14	14	8	20	14	14	14	14	14	11	11	9	9	9	9	9	17	2	2	2	2	10	9	21	19	19	19	19	8	7	7	7	15	14	14	14	9						
8 TRULLI	8	11	8	8	14	14	20	11	11	11	11	14	14	17	17	17	17	2	17	17	7	7	7	21	19	8	8	8	8	8	15	15	15	14	21	21	21	15	15						
11 BARRICHELLO	23	8	11	11	11	11	11	20	20	20	20	19	19	7	7	7	2	7	7	7	17	17	21	19	15	15	15	15	15	15	14	14	14	21	14	9	9	9	17						
10 ROSBERG	11	23	23	19	19	19	19	19	19	19	19	23	23	2	2	2	7	17	2	19	19	21	19	16	8	14	14	14	14	14	21	21	21	15	17	17	17	17							
7 R. SCHUMACHER	19	19	19	23	23	23	23	23	23	23	23	7	7	19	19	19	19	19	19	21	21	19	16	2	14	19	21	21	21	21	17	19	19	19	19	19	19	19							
14 COULTHARD	7	7	7	7	7	7	7	7	7	7	7	2	2	23	23	23	21	21	21	19	19	16	16	16	16	16	16	16	16	16	16	16	16	16	16	16	16	16							
21 SPEED	2	2	2	2	2	2	2	2	2	2	2	21	21	21	21	21	23	23	23	16	16	22	22	20	22	22	22	22	22	22	22	22	22	22											
20 LIUZZI	16	21	21	21	21	21	21	21	21	21	21	16	16	16	16	16	16	16	16	22	22																								
18 MONTEIRO	21	16	16	16	16	16	16	16	16	16	16	22	22	22	22	22	22	22																											
23 YAMAMOTO	3	22	22	22	22	22	22	22	22	22	22																																		
22 SATO	22																																												
19 ALBERS																																													

TIME SHEETS

PRACTICE 1 (FRIDAY)

Sunny (track 39–43°C, air 30°C)

Pos.	Driver	Laps	Time
1	Kimi Räikkönen	5	1m 28.315s
2	Michael Schumacher	4	1m 28.777s
3	Jenson Button	5	1m 28.785s
4	Alexander Wurz	24	1m 28.959s
5	Anthony Davidson	19	1m 29.193s
6	Pedro de la Rosa	5	1m 29.376s
7	Nick Heidfeld	6	1m 29.780s
8	Sebastian Vettel	25	1m 29.964s
9	Robert Doornbos	16	1m 30.391s
10	Neel Jani	22	1m 30.576s
11	Rubens Barrichello	5	1m 30.838s
12	Giorgio Mondini	28	1m 30.846s
13	Scott Speed	5	1m 31.416s
14	Christijan Albers	10	1m 31.475s
15	Tiago Monteiro	10	1m 31.566s
16	Franck Montagny	13	1m 31.814s
17	Felipe Massa	5	1m 31.904s
18	Sakon Yamamoto	11	1m 32.212s
19	Vitantonio Liuzzi	6	1m 32.497s
20	Ralf Schumacher	5	No time
21	Jarno Trulli	2	No time
22	Giancarlo Fisichella	1	No time
23	Fernando Alonso	1	No time
24	Takuma Sato	1	No time
25	Robert Kubica	1	No time
26	Christian Klien	1	No time
27	David Coulthard	1	No time

PRACTICE 2 (FRIDAY)

Sunny (track 49–50°C, air 32–33°C)

Pos.	Driver	Laps	Time
1	Sebastian Vettel	29	1m 28.091s
2	Felipe Massa	18	1m 28.164s
3	Jenson Button	10	1m 28.506s
4	Anthony Davidson	31	1m 28.598s
5	Ralf Schumacher	21	1m 28.614s
6	Michael Schumacher	13	1m 28.819s
7	Robert Doornbos	15	1m 28.848s
8	Kimi Räikkönen	10	1m 29.042s
9	Pedro de la Rosa	16	1m 29.112s
10	Rubens Barrichello	16	1m 29.214s
11	Giorgio Mondini	27	1m 29.719s
12	Fernando Alonso	16	1m 29.741s
13	Neel Jani	30	1m 29.858s
14	Scott Speed	20	1m 29.890s
15	Jarno Trulli	18	1m 30.006s
16	Franck Montagny	25	1m 30.491s
17	Robert Kubica	9	1m 30.502s
18	Giancarlo Fisichella	16	1m 30.504s
19	Alexander Wurz	36	1m 30.509s
20	Vitantonio Liuzzi	17	1m 30.551s
21	Mark Webber	13	1m 30.775s
22	Christian Klien	16	1m 30.889s
23	Nico Rosberg	17	1m 31.015s
24	Takuma Sato	11	1m 31.091s
25	Sakon Yamamoto	21	1m 31.316s
26	Tiago Monteiro	15	1m 31.519s
27	Nick Heidfeld	10	1m 31.526s
28	David Coulthard	10	1m 31.540s
29	Christijan Albers	7	1m 32.102s

QUALIFYING (SATURDAY)

Sunny (track 45–46°C, air 33°C)

Pos.	Driver	First	Second	Third
1	Felipe Massa	1m 27.306s	1m 27.059s	1m 26.907s
2	Michael Schumacher	1m 27.385s	1m 25.850s	1m 27.284s
3	Fernando Alonso	1m 27.861s	1m 26.917s	1m 27.321s
4	Giancarlo Fisichella	1m 28.175s	1m 27.346s	1m 27.564s
5	Ralf Schumacher	1m 27.668s	1m 27.062s	1m 27.569s
6	Nick Heidfeld	1m 28.200s	1m 27.251s	1m 27.785s
7	Jenson Button	1m 28.222s	1m 26.872s	1m 27.790s
8	Kimi Räikkönen	1m 28.236s	1m 27.202s	1m 27.866s
9	Robert Kubica	1m 28.212s	1m 27.405s	1m 28.167s
10	Mark Webber	1m 28.307s	1m 27.608s	1m 29.436s
11	Christian Klien	1m 28.271s	1m 27.852s	
12	Pedro de la Rosa	1m 28.403s	1m 27.897s	
13	Jarno Trulli	1m 28.549s	1m 27.973s	
14	Rubens Barrichello	1m 28.411s	1m 28.257s	
15	Nico Rosberg	1m 28.889s	1m 28.386s	
16	Christijan Albers	1m 29.021s	1m 28.639s	
17	David Coulthard	1m 29.136s		
18	Scott Speed	1m 29.158s		
19	Vitantonio Liuzzi	1m 29.250s		
20	Tiago Monteiro	1m 29.901s		
21	Sakon Yamamoto	1m 30.607s		
22	Takuma Sato	1m 30.850s		

PRACTICE 3 (SATURDAY)

Sunny (track 43–45°C, air 32–33°C)

Pos.	Driver	Laps	Time
1	Michael Schumacher	12	1m 27.203s
2	Fernando Alonso	16	1m 27.924s
3	Giancarlo Fisichella	17	1m 27.963s
4	Robert Kubica	15	1m 27.964s
5	Nick Heidfeld	14	1m 28.151s
6	Jenson Button	17	1m 28.190s
7	Felipe Massa	14	1m 28.266s
8	Rubens Barrichello	15	1m 28.359s
9	Kimi Räikkönen	11	1m 28.368s
10	Christian Klien	9	1m 28.830s
11	Jarno Trulli	17	1m 28.861s
12	Scott Speed	14	1m 28.861s
13	Pedro de la Rosa	12	1m 29.034s
14	Mark Webber	10	1m 29.069s
15	Nico Rosberg	13	1m 29.176s
16	David Coulthard	12	1m 29.357s
17	Ralf Schumacher	18	1m 29.374s
18	Vitantonio Liuzzi	19	1m 29.426s
19	Christijan Albers	19	1m 29.668s
20	Sakon Yamamoto	17	1m 29.881s
21	Tiago Monteiro	17	1m 29.915s
22	Takuma Sato	21	1m 30.151s

CHASSIS LOG BOOK

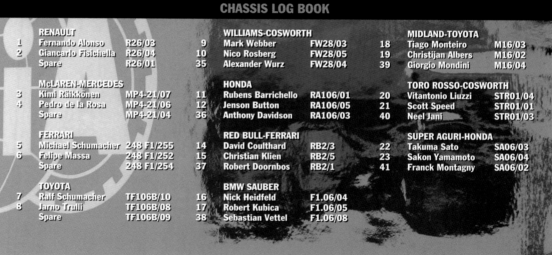

	RENAULT						
1	Fernando Alonso	R26/03	9	Mark Webber	FW28/03	18	Tiago Monteiro	M16/03
2	Giancarlo Fisichella	R26/04	10	Nico Rosberg	FW28/05	19	Christijan Albers	M16/02
	Spare	R26/01	35	Alexander Wurz	FW28/04	39	Giorgio Mondini	M16/04

WILLIAMS-COSWORTH
9 Mark Webber FW28/03
10 Nico Rosberg FW28/05
35 Alexander Wurz FW28/04

MIDLAND-TOYOTA
18 Tiago Monteiro M16/03
19 Christijan Albers M16/02
39 Giorgio Mondini M16/04

RENAULT
1 Fernando Alonso R26/03
2 Giancarlo Fisichella R26/04
Spare R26/01

McLAREN-MERCEDES
3 Kimi Räikkönen MP4-21/07
4 Pedro de la Rosa MP4-21/06
Spare MP4-21/04

HONDA
11 Rubens Barrichello RA106/01
12 Jenson Button RA106/05
36 Anthony Davidson RA106/03

TORO ROSSO-COSWORTH
20 Vitantonio Liuzzi STR01/04
21 Scott Speed STR01/01
40 Neel Jani STR01/03

FERRARI
5 Michael Schumacher 248 F1/255
6 Felipe Massa 248 F1/252
Spare 248 F1/254

RED BULL-FERRARI
14 David Coulthard RB2/3
15 Christian Klien RB2/5
37 Robert Doornbos RB2/1

SUPER AGURI-HONDA
22 Takuma Sato SA06/03
23 Sakon Yamamoto SA06/04
41 Franck Montagny SA06/02

TOYOTA
7 Ralf Schumacher TF106B/10
8 Jarno Trulli TF106B/08
Spare TF106B/09

BMW SAUBER
16 Nick Heidfeld F1.06/04
17 Robert Kubica F1.06/05
38 Sebastian Vettel F1.06/08

 **10** KLIEN Red Bull
 **8** KUBICA BMW-Sauber
 **6** BUTTON Honda
 **4** FISICHELLA Renault
 **2** M. SCHUMACHER Ferrari

 **9** WEBBER Williams
 **7** RÄIKKÖNEN McLaren
 **5** HEIDFELD BMW-Sauber
 **3** ALONSO Renault
 **1** MASSA Ferrari

RACE DISTANCE:
58 laps
192.250 miles/309.396 km

RACE WEATHER:
Sunny
track 51–52°C, air 35–36°C

Lap chart

46	47	48	49	50	51	52	53	54	55	56	57	58	•
6	6	6	6	6	6	6	6	6	6	6	6	6	1
1	1	1	1	1	1	1	1	1	1	1	1	1	2
5	5	5	5	5	5	5	5	5	5	5	5	5	3
12	12	12	12	12	12	12	12	12	12	12	12	12	4
4	4	4	4	4	4	4	4	4	4	4	4	5	5
2	2	2	2	2	2	2	2	2	2	2	2	2	6
7	7	7	7	7	7	7	7	7	7	7	7	7	7
11	11	11	11	11	11	11	11	11	11	11	11	11	8
8	8	8	8	8	8	8	8	8	8	8	8		
9	9	9	9	9	9	9	9	9	9	9	9		
14	14	14	14	14	14	14	14	14	15	15	15		
15	15	15	15	15	15	15	15	15	17	17	17		
17	17	17	17	17	17	17	17	17	21	21	21		
21	21	21	21	21	21	21	21	14	16				
19	16	16	16	16	16	16	16	16					
16													

Pit stop
One lap or more behind leader
13   Safety car deployed on laps shown

FOR THE RECORD

FIRST GRAND PRIX POLE POSITION AND WIN: Felipe Massa (above)
100th GRAND PRIX START: Kimi Räikkönen
200th POINT: Jenson Button

POINTS

	DRIVERS			CONSTRUCTORS	
1	Fernando Alonso	108	1	Renault	160
2	Michael Schumacher	96	2	Ferrari	158
3	Felipe Massa	62	3	McLaren	89
4	Giancarlo Fisichella	52	4	Honda	58
5	Kimi Räikkönen	49	5	Toyota	28
6	Jenson Button	36	6	BMW Sauber	26
7	Juan Pablo Montoya	26	7	Red Bull	16
8	Rubens Barrichello	22	8	Williams	10
9	Nick Heidfeld	19	9	Toro Rosso	1
10	Ralf Schumacher	18			
11	David Coulthard	14			
12	Pedro de la Rosa	14			
13	Jarno Trulli	10			
14	Jacques Villeneuve	7			
15	Mark Webber	6			
16	Nico Rosberg	4			
17	Christian Klien	2			
18	Vitantonio Liuzzi	1			

Photograph: James Moy/www.crashpa.net

Photographs: James Moy/www.crashpa.net

FIA F1 WORLD CHAMPIONSHIP/ROUND 15

ITALIAN GP
MONZA CIRCUIT

Kimi Räikkönen leads Michael Schumacher's Ferrari and the two BMW-Saubers through the first chicane immediately after the start, with the entire pack following on in well-disciplined pursuit.

Photograph: James Moy/www.crashpa.net

MONZA QUALIFYING

TO begin with, the build-up to the Italian Grand Prix was all about Michael Schumacher's impending announcement of retirement. Throughout practice and qualifying, it dominated conversations. It was thus utterly apposite that the man appeared to have wrapped up pole position – and that literally at the last moment it should be snatched from him by Kimi Räikkönen. Interestingly, it was the increasingly confident Felipe Massa, the winner in Turkey, who generally set the pace, once Sebastian Vettel had completed his Friday running for BMW. But in the dying seconds of qualifying the old Schumacher emerged and his 1m 21.486s appeared sufficient. But then Räikkönen came streaking out of the sun in his silver arrow to post a 1m 21.484s. Pole was his by two thousandths of a second.

It was the Finn's third pole of a season in which he had yet to win a race. 'It was very close but the car has been pretty good all weekend,' Räikkönen muttered. 'And the lap was not clean. I had quite a big moment twice in Ascari, but it was good enough for pole. I think I have quite a good car for the race. It's all going to be down to which tyre lasts longer in the race. But I'm confident.'

Schumacher did not look amused. 'The car is going very well,' he said, his voice clipped. 'The team was quite strong and consistent in the test here last week, so it is a comfortable position to be in. Obviously, two thousandths of a second is a tight battle and it would have been nice to be on pole for our home GP but what's important is what we achieve tomorrow.'

Once again Ferrari had been dominant, because Bridgestone had done its homework carefully and knew better than Michelin prior to the previous week's test that sections of the track had been resurfaced. By Saturday morning Michelin had found more grip and things looked more even again, but everything would depend on how much fuel Räikkönen and Schumacher were carrying and it transpired that the German had two laps' more.

'It was quite a clean lap,' Schumacher said when asked if he had made similar errors to Räikkönen's. And he brightened as he learned that arch-rival Fernando Alonso was only fifth – the Spaniard went over the first chicane after picking up a puncture and only squeaked into his final qualifying lap less than two seconds before the flag.

'It was a day when I was lucky and unlucky,' the championship leader said. 'Obviously, the puncture cost me a chance to fight for the pole, but equally I had this problem at a circuit where the car is competitive.'

Schumacher was informed of Alonso's problem and, in response to being asked his feelings about losing the pole, said, 'It's better than having Fernando alongside or in front of me.' He added, 'I'm happy that Nick is up here with us today, another German fellow,' in reference to third-fastest Nick Heidfeld of BMW Sauber. 'I am second on the grid; look where Fernando is. It's not bad for me. I'm feeling pretty confident.'

Massa, in all this, was only fourth, on 1m 21.704s, behind the surprised Heidfeld, who lapped in 1m 21.653s in a BMW that looked threateningly competitive.

Jenson Button took sixth for Honda with 1m 22.011s, heading BMW Sauber's Robert Kubica (1m 22.258s), McLaren's Pedro de la Rosa (1m 22.280s), Honda's Rubens Barrichello (1m 22.787s) and Renault's Giancarlo Fisichella (1m 23.175s, on a single-stop strategy).

Button's best lap in second qualifying bumped Jarno Trulli out of the top ten and you had to feel sorry for the Italian. He was only seven-tenths of a second off fastest man Felipe Massa (1m 21.924s to 1m 21.225s) in that session, such was the closeness of the times, but there were nine cars between them so he was left 11th ahead of Nico Rosberg (1m 22.203s), Ralf Schumacher (1m 22.280s), David Coulthard (1m 22.589s), Scott Speed (1m 23.165s) and Christian Klien, whose Red Bull was *hors de combat* for the session. Klien had bumped Tonio Liuzzi right at the end of first qualifying and then killed the Italian's chance of doing better than 17th place and 1m 23.043s by spinning on the exit to the second chicane and bringing out yellow flags.

Behind the Toro Rosso pilot, Christijan Albers lapped his Midland in 1m 23.116s to beat Mark Webber (1m 23.341s), Tiago Monteiro (1m 23.920s), Takuma Sato (1m 24.289s) and Sakon Yamamoto, whose Super Aguri threw the tread of its left-rear Bridgestone just after he had lapped it in 1m 26.001s. The session was red-flagged for ten minutes as the debris was cleaned up.

It was only later in the evening that the bombshell exploded and the stewards docked Alonso's three best laps times for impeding Massa on his last run, dropping him from fifth to tenth on the grid (see sidebar opposite).

THE 2006 Italian Grand Prix will be remembered for many things, but least of all for what happened on the track. The weekend on which Michael Schumacher announced that he would be bringing the curtain down on a dramatic era of F1 was characterised by acrimony and controversy surrounding Renault and Ferrari at a time when fans' perceptions of their sport were, according to surveys, less than wholly benign.

For Schumacher, his 90th grand prix victory was thus a bitter-sweet affair. Its tale is easily told. Beaten away at the start by poleman Kimi Räikkönen, he followed the McLaren for 15 laps until the Finn pitted for the first time. Schumacher ran two crucial laps farther and was able to rejoin ahead of the man who will replace him at Ferrari in 2007. Both refuelled again, on laps 38 and 39 respectively, but by then Schumacher was almost three seconds ahead. In the remaining laps he pulled farther away, aided a little here and there by lapped traffic, and concluded his 246th race with an easy win.

'I was hoping Kimi would be stopping a little bit earlier [than me], and so it happened,' he reported, somewhere in his post-race announcement of imminent retirement. 'If you stop early

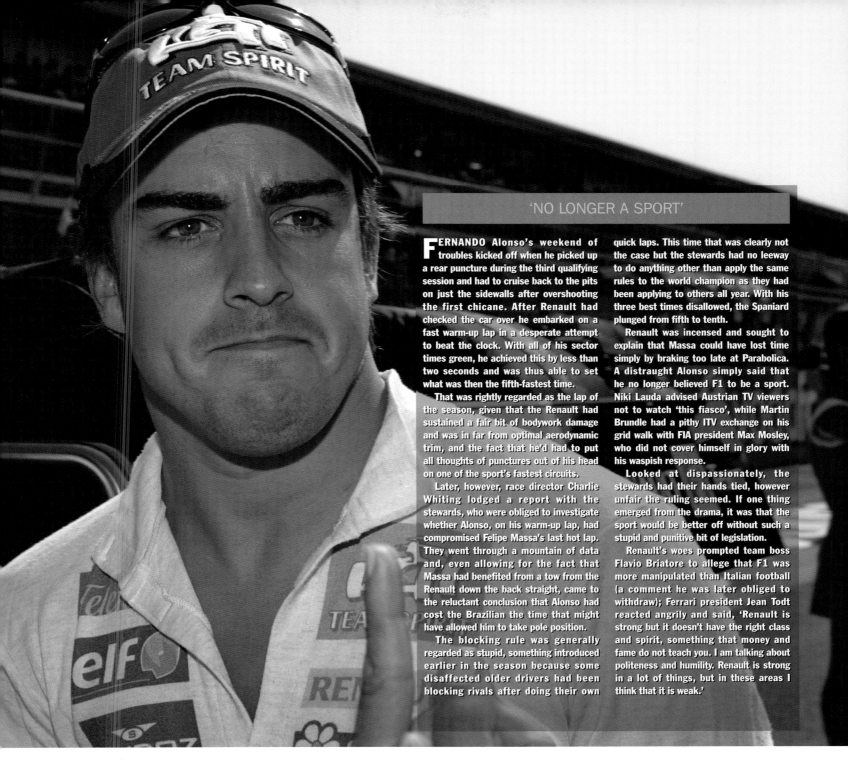

FERNANDO Alonso's weekend of troubles kicked off when he picked up a rear puncture during the third qualifying session and had to cruise back to the pits on just the sidewalls after overshooting the first chicane. After Renault had checked the car over he embarked on a fast warm-up lap in a desperate attempt to beat the clock. With all of his sector times green, he achieved this by less than two seconds and was thus able to set what was then the fifth-fastest time.

That was rightly regarded as the lap of the season, given that the Renault had sustained a fair bit of bodywork damage and was in far from optimal aerodynamic trim, and the fact that he'd had to put all thoughts of punctures out of his head on one of the sport's fastest circuits.

Later, however, race director Charlie Whiting lodged a report with the stewards, who were obliged to investigate whether Alonso, on his warm-up lap, had compromised Felipe Massa's last hot lap. They went through a mountain of data and, even allowing for the fact that Massa had benefited from a tow from the Renault down the back straight, came to the reluctant conclusion that Alonso had cost the Brazilian the time that might have allowed him to take pole position.

The blocking rule was generally regarded as stupid, something introduced earlier in the season because some disaffected older drivers had been blocking rivals after doing their own quick laps. This time that was clearly not the case but the stewards had no leeway to do anything other than apply the same rules to the world champion as they had been applying to others all year. With his three best times disallowed, the Spaniard plunged from fifth to tenth.

Renault was incensed and sought to explain that Massa could have lost time simply by braking too late at Parabolica. A distraught Alonso simply said that he no longer believed F1 to be a sport. Niki Lauda advised Austrian TV viewers not to watch 'this fiasco', while Martin Brundle had a pithy ITV exchange on his grid walk with FIA president Max Mosley, who did not cover himself in glory with his waspish response.

Looked at dispassionately, the stewards had their hands tied, however unfair the ruling seemed. If one thing emerged from the drama, it was that the sport would be better off without such a stupid and punitive bit of legislation.

Renault's woes prompted team boss Flavio Briatore to allege that F1 was more manipulated than Italian football (a comment he was later obliged to withdraw); Ferrari president Jean Todt reacted angrily and said, 'Renault is strong but it doesn't have the right class and spirit, something that money and fame do not teach you. I am talking about politeness and humility. Renault is strong in a lot of things, but in these areas I think that it is weak.'

---

it is the nature of this track that you then run heavy against a car that is light. I had a moment lapping Scott Speed in the first chicane, but otherwise it was trouble free.'

Räikkönen could afford to be philosophical, given what he will be driving next year. 'The start worked very well,' he said. 'I was a bit concerned about our starts but the guys did an excellent job to fix the start system. I got a good one and tried to go as fast as I could before my first stop but it turned out that we were not quick enough today. But it was quite an easy second. A good weekend.'

Behind them, the troubled Fernando Alonso drove his heart out for nothing. After the controversial ruling that put him back from fifth on the grid to tenth on Saturday evening, for impeding Felipe Massa's qualifying lap, the Spaniard ended the first lap seventh, chasing Räikkönen, Schumacher, Robert Kubica, Massa, Jenson Button and Nick Heidfeld, who made a less than brilliant getaway from third place on the grid.

Alonso jumped Heidfeld in a questionable move going into the first chicane, which went unpenalised (possibly because even the race management felt that he'd had enough for one weekend). Thereafter he chased Button without ever quite being able to find a way past, just as Massa a little farther up the road was being similarly stalemated by the mature driving of the increasingly impressive rookie Kubica.

In fact, the BMW Sauber drivers were on excellent form, for both Kubica and Heidfeld were running a decent amount of fuel. Nick refuelled on the 21st lap, Robert the 22nd, and for one glorious moment on lap 21 Mario Theissen and Peter Sauber saw their cars running first and second, the Pole ahead.

Alonso's stop on lap 19 dropped him back to tenth momentarily, but gradually he hauled in Massa and Kubica until they were running nose to tail for third. Massa stopped on lap 39, Kubica and Alonso on 41 – and rejoined side by side in the pit lane; Kubica was obliged to concede.

So now Alonso was on track for third place and some solid damage limitation after his bruising weekend – and that was when he suffered a rare Renault engine failure going down to the first chicane on the 43rd lap. Just as the loose wheel nut had in Hungary, this one looked like one of those moments

Above: A stony-faced Fernando Alonso tries to take in the magnitude of his penalty for inadvertently impeding Felipe Massa's Ferrari.

Photograph: Paul-Henri Cahier

Above: Robert Kubica delivered a simply stellar performance to take third place at Monza in the BMW-Sauber. Here he leads Felipe Massa's Ferrari.

Photograph: Jean-François Galeron/WRI

Right: Under new ownership. Victor R. Muller, chief executive officer of Spyker Cars N.V. and Spyker MF1 Racing; Michiel Mol, future director of Formula 1 racing of Spyker and Spyker MF1 Racing; and Colin Kolles, Spyker MF1 Racing team principal, pose for the cameras at Monza.

Photograph: James Moy/www.crashpa.net

when a championship is lost.

'I tried my best for my championship fight and for all the fans who came here today like they do in Spain. I am a sportsman and I never deliberately blocked anyone. I don't consider any more that F1 is a sport.' That was what he'd said that morning after his penalty.

Now he said, 'You have to push everything to the limit when you start from tenth. Yourself, the car, the tyres and the engine. Without the penalty, this car had the pace to fight for the victory.'

Incredibly, what had once seemed an unassailable championship lead was now down to only two points with three races to go.

Alonso's misfortune was Kubica's gain and the Pole wiped away the disappointment of Hungary by taking his first podium after only three races. It was well deserved. 'I'm really surprised,' he admitted. 'The team and I knew we had good tyres for qualifying and the race. We were concerned about qualifying after the tyre choice we made, but we were competitive and got through to qualifying three and knew

we would have a quite consistent car for the race. I made a good start but unfortunately I locked the fronts and flat-spotted my first set of tyres, so I had a lot of vibration.

'I had a tough fight with Felipe and Fernando, and being the first guy [of that group] to be lapping people I always lost a second. I was side by side with Fernando in the pits, then it was risky with the oil when he blew up. Then Felipe had a tyre problem, so the end of the race was quite easy.'

Massa flat-spotted his right-front tyre braking for Alonso's oil cloud in the chicane, which dropped him back to an eventual ninth-placed finish in his own version of a bad weekend.

Giancarlo Fisichella shored up some of the damage for Renault, which lost its lead in the constructors' championship to Ferrari. The Italian's one-stop refuelling strategy brought him home fourth, ahead of Button. The Englishman had a strong run for Honda and his team-mate Rubens Barrichello was sixth after a one-stop run.

Jarno Trulli brought his Toyota home seventh ahead of Nick Heidfeld, who could have been a podium contender but for a

step today towards that.

'We are only two points down, so the mindset is very easy. It's difficult to say that I am more focused than ever because I am always focused once I am in the car. The championship started off difficult but we returned after another tough mid-season and now we are two points behind with just three races to go. Nobody would have thought we could be in that position, but now we focus 100 percent on the constructors' and drivers' championships.'

The following day, Schumacher might not have been feeling quite so cheerful, however. Renault's Flavio Briatore found himself busily retracting comments he had made alleging that F1 was more manipulated than Italian football. He had told Italy's RAI television network, 'This is a world championship that has already been decided at the table. We have understood how things go – it has all been decided. They [F1's authorities] have decided to give the world championship to Schumacher and that is what will be.'

Meanwhile, a bitter Alonso accused Michael of being the most unsporting driver in world championship history as he paid him an unusual back-handed tribute. Comparing Schumacher's departure with the dramatic retirement of French footballer Zinedine Zidane in the World Cup final in June (he was sent off for head-butting Italian player Marco Materazzi), the Spaniard said, 'Zidane retired with more glory than Michael Schumacher. Michael is the most unsporting driver with the largest number of sanctions in the history of F1.

'But that doesn't take away from the fact that he has been the best driver and it has been an honour to battle against him. Everyone has their time and things will be more equal now.'

Alonso then launched an attack on what he perceived to be institutional bias in favour of Schumacher and Ferrari. 'In F1 there are commercial and political interests,' he said. 'We are talking about the most successful driver in history and a little bit of help has never gone amiss. Quite often they go over the line of what is acceptable.'

Speaking of his penalty, he fired a final broadside. 'He who laughs last, laughs longest. If we get things right in two of the three races left, the world title will be ours.'

One way and another, Monza was quite some weekend.

David Tremayne

DIARY

It is confirmed in the Monza paddock on Saturday evening that Alex Shnaider has sold his interest in Midland to a Dutch consortium headed by entrepreneur Michiel Mol and the Spyker car company. The team is renamed Spyker MF1 and former Toyota technical director Mike Gascoyne is named as the new chief technical officer.

Red Bull Racing announces after the Italian Grand Prix that Christian Klien has been released from his contract with immediate effect. The Austrian's race seat will be taken for the rest of the year by test driver Robert Doornbos, with German GP2 racer Michael Ammermüller taking over Doornbos's role.

The week after the Italian Grand Prix, Renault confirms speculation that it will supply its engines to Red Bull GmbH for 2007 and 2008. The energy drinks company does not identify which of its teams – Red Bull Racing or Scuderia Toro Rosso – will run the French engines.

The GPDA issues a statement at Monza saying that it is extremely concerned about safety issues in the second chicane. The FIA counters by announcing that Monza had had the first trials of a revolutionary type of safety barrier.

drive-through penalty for speeding in the pit lane. He just held off Massa. Mark Webber in the Williams was tenth. Christian Klien and David Coulthard one-stopped their Red Bulls to 11th and 12th places after a race-long fight, heading home Scott Speed and Tonio Liuzzi in their Toro Rossos.

Ralf Schumacher, Takuma Sato and Christijan Albers' Spyker (*née* Midland) completed the finishers as Tiago Monteiro had to retire his Spyker (*née* Midland) with a random brake problem, Nico Rosberg broke a driveshaft over the kerb in the second chicane, Sakon Yamamoto encountered hydraulic problems and Pedro de la Rosa's Mercedes engine lost its oil pressure.

Figuratively and literally, it was Michael Schumacher's day and there were emotional scenes on the podium as he was fêted by the adoring *tifosi*. 'Monza is just unbelievable,' he said. 'It has always been very special.'

He savoured the prospect of the fight for a record eighth title as he chose his words carefully. 'Now I'd like to concentrate on these last three wins,' he added – wins, not races, note – 'to finish it in style with the championship, and we made a big

Main: Michael Schumacher goes through that familiar ritual of spraying the champagne yet one more time.
Photograph: James Moy/www.crashpa.net

Centre: Ninety wins and still counting.
Photograph: Jad Sherif/WRI

Bottom: Arm raised aloft, Michael Schumacher takes the chequered flag at Monza for the final time in his career.
Photograph: Jean-François Galeron/WRI

WITHIN 15 minutes of Michael Schumacher's 90th grand prix victory, Ferrari kept its promise and announced that the German would indeed be retiring and would be replaced by Kimi Räikkönen as Felipe Massa's partner.

Schumacher made a lengthy post-victory speech in which he admitted, 'It was obviously pretty emotional on the in-lap after the race, informing everybody of my decision. That and being on the podium knowing it was the last opportunity here with such a crowd. They gave me so much in terms of their feelings to me. It just overwhelmed me. Monza is just unbelievable. It has always been very special, particularly after a race when all the fans are around. Due to the nature of the circumstances, obviously it was an unbelievable feeling I had out there today.

'This is a very special day and it is great to finish this in this style, looking at the championship as well but much more at what is going to happen sometime in the future. All the fans and motor sport-interested people had a right to be explained what's going to happen. I'm sorry it took longer than you would have wanted. But this is the right moment. It's been an exceptional time, a really exceptional time, what motor sport in more than 30 years has given to me. I have really loved every single moment – the good and the bad ones, they are what make life so special.

'I particularly want to thank my family, starting with my dad and my passed-away mum, my wife and my kids, who at all times supported what I was doing. Without their strength to survive in this business and sport, to perform would have been impossible. I cannot be thankful enough. And to all my mates in the Benetton time and especially in the Ferrari days, when I made so many friends, met so many great guys. It was really tough to decide to not work at this level again with all of them. But one day it has to come and I felt that this is the moment.'

Yet the question remained: was he put into a position by Ferrari where he was effectively obliged to retire? Insiders suggested that Ferrari chairman Luca di Montezemolo insisted on signing Räikkönen to secure the team's future, leaving Schumacher either to accept a team-mate of equal stature for the first time or to withdraw with dignity.

Perhaps the real clue lay in one sentence, when Schumacher said, 'I decided with the team that I'm going to retire.'

GRAN PREMIO VODAFONE D'ITALIA

MONZA 8–10 SEPTEMBER 2006

AUTODROMO NAZIONALE DI MONZA

Circuit: 3.600 miles/ 5.793 km

Lesmo 2 99/160

Lesmo 1 71/114

Variante della Roggia 72/115

211/340

Variante Ascari 90/145

Curva Parabolica 109/176

Primo Variante 72/115

Curva Biassono 109/176 · 218/350

116/187 **mph/kmh** · **Gear**

Photograph: James Moy/www.crashpa.net

RACE RESULTS

Pos.	Driver	Nat.	No.	Entrant	Car/Engine	Tyres	Laps	Time/Retirement	Speed (mph/km/h)	Gap to leader	Fastest race lap	
1	Michael Schumacher	D	5	Scuderia Ferrari Marlboro	Ferrari 248 F1-056 V8	B	53	1h 14m 51.975s	152.742/245.814		1m 22.575s	14
2	Kimi Räikkönen	FIN	3	Team McLaren Mercedes	McLaren MP4-21-Mercedes FO 108S V8	M	53	1h 15m 00.021s	152.468/245.374	+8.046s	1m 22.559s	13
3	Robert Kubica	POL	17	BMW Sauber F1 Team	BMW Sauber F1.06-BMW P86 V8	M	53	1h 15m 18.389s	151.849/244.377	+26.414s	1m 23.111s	21
4	Giancarlo Fisichella	I	2	Mild Seven Renault F1 Team	Renault R26-RS26 V8	M	53	1h 15m 24.020s	151.660/244.073	+32.045s	1m 23.617s	25
5	Jenson Button	GB	12	Lucky Strike Honda Racing F1 Team	Honda RA106-RA806E V8	M	53	1h 15m 24.660s	151.638/244.038	+32.685s	1m 23.518s	51
6	Rubens Barrichello	BR	11	Lucky Strike Honda Racing F1 Team	Honda RA106-RA806E V8	M	53	1h 15m 34.384s	151.638/244.038	+42.409s	1m 23.794s	27
7	Jarno Trulli	I	8	Panasonic Toyota Racing	Toyota TF106B-RVX-06 V8	B	53	1h 15m 36.637s	151.238/243.394	+44.662s	1m 23.869s	25
8	Nick Heidfeld	D	16	BMW Sauber F1 Team	BMW Sauber F1.06-BMW P86 V8	M	53	1h 15m 37.284s	151.216/243.359	+45.309s	1m 23.294s	20
9	Felipe Massa	BR	6	Scuderia Ferrari Marlboro	Ferrari 248 F1-056 V8	B	53	1h 15m 37.930s	151.195/243.325	+45.955s	1m 23.003s	41
10	Mark Webber	AUS	9	WilliamsF1 Team	Williams FW28-Cosworth CA2006 V8	B	53	1h 16m 04.577s	150.312/241.904	+1m 12.602s	1m 24.197s	27
11	Christian Klien	A	15	Red Bull Racing	Red Bull RB2-Ferrari 056 V8	M	52			+1 lap	1m 24.571s	37
12	David Coulthard	GB	14	Red Bull Racing	Red Bull RB2-Ferrari 056 V8	M	52			+1 lap	1m 24.984s	51
13	Scott Speed	USA	21	Scuderia Toro Rosso	Toro Rosso STR01-Cosworth TJ2005-2 V10	M	52			+1 lap	1m 25.094s	50
14	Vitantonio Liuzzi	I	20	Scuderia Toro Rosso	Toro Rosso STR01-Cosworth TJ2005-2 V10	M	52			+1 lap	1m 24.764s	52
15	Ralf Schumacher	D	7	Panasonic Toyota Racing	Toyota TF106B-RVX-06 V8	B	52			+1 lap	1m 24.837s	41
16	Takuma Sato	J	22	Super Aguri F1 Team	Super Aguri SA06-Honda RA806E V8	B	51			+2 laps	1m 25.676s	15
17	Christijan Albers	NL	19	Spyker MF1 Team	Spyker M16-Toyota RVX-06 V8	B	51			+2 laps	1m 25.494s	17
	Tiago Monteiro	P	18	Spyker MF1 Team	Spyker M16-Toyota RVX-06 V8	B	44	Brakes			1m 24.822s	27
	Fernando Alonso	E	1	Mild Seven Renault F1 Team	Renault R26-RS26 V8	M	43	Engine			1m 23.121s	38
	Pedro de la Rosa	E	4	Team McLaren Mercedes	McLaren MP4-21-Mercedes FO 108S V8	M	20	Engine			1m 23.702s	8
	Sakon Yamamoto	J	23	Super Aguri F1 Team	Super Aguri SA06-Honda RA806E V8	B	18	Hydraulics			1m 26.548s	15
	Nico Rosberg	D	10	WilliamsF1 Team	Williams FW28-Cosworth CA2006 V8	B	9	Driveshaft			1m 25.362s	8

Fastest lap: Kimi Räikkönen on lap 13, 1m 22.559s, 156.961 mph/252.604 km/h.

Lap record: Rubens Barrichello (Ferrari F2004 V10), 1m 21.046s, 159.892 mph/257.320 km/h (2004).

All results and data © FOM 2006

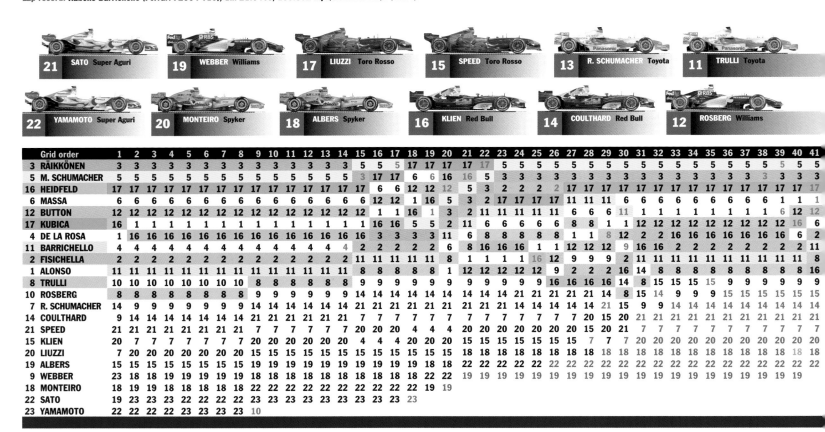

21 SATO Super Aguri	19 WEBBER Williams	17 LIUZZI Toro Rosso	15 SPEED Toro Rosso	13 R. SCHUMACHER Toyota	11 TRULLI Toyota

22 YAMAMOTO Super Aguri	20 MONTEIRO Spyker	18 ALBERS Spyker	16 KLIEN Red Bull	14 COULTHARD Red Bull	12 ROSBERG Williams

Grid order	1	2	3	4	5	6	7	8	9	10	11	12	13	14	15	16	17	18	19	20	21	22	23	24	25	26	27	28	29	30	31	32	33	34	35	36	37	38	39	40	41
3 RÄIKKÖNEN	3	3	3	3	3	3	3	3	3	3	3	3	3	3	5	5	5	17	17	17	17	17	5	5	5	5	5	5	5	5	5	5	5	5	5	5	5	5	5	5	5
5 M. SCHUMACHER	5	5	5	5	5	5	5	5	5	5	5	5	5	5	3	17	17	6	6	16	16	5	3	3	3	3	3	3	3	3	3	3	3	3	3	3	3	3	3	3	3
16 HEIDFELD	17	17	17	17	17	17	17	17	17	17	17	17	17	17	6	6	12	12	12	12	5	3	2	2	2	17	17	17	17	17	17	17	17	17	17	17	17	17	17	17	17
6 MASSA	6	6	6	6	6	6	6	6	6	6	6	6	6	6	12	12	1	16	5	2	17	17	17	11	11	11	6	6	6	6	6	6	6	6	6	1	1				
12 BUTTON	12	12	12	12	12	12	12	12	12	12	12	12	12	12	1	1	16	1	3	2	11	11	11	11	11	6	6	6	11	1	1	1	1	1	1	6	12	12			
17 KUBICA	16	1	1	1	1	1	1	1	1	1	1	1	1	1	16	16	5	5	2	11	6	6	6	6	8	8	1	1	12	12	12	12	12	12	12	12	16	6			
4 DE LA ROSA	1	16	16	16	16	16	16	16	16	16	16	16	16	16	3	3	3	3	11	6	8	8	8	8	8	1	1	8	12	2	16	16	16	16	16	16	6	2			
11 BARRICHELLO	4	4	4	4	4	4	4	4	4	4	4	4	4	4	2	2	2	2	6	8	16	16	16	1	1	12	12	12	9	16	16	2	2	2	2	2	2	11			
2 FISICHELLA	2	2	2	2	2	2	2	2	2	2	2	2	2	2	11	11	11	11	8	1	1	1	16	12	9	2	2	2	9	11	11	11	11	11	11	11	11	8			
1 ALONSO	11	11	11	11	11	11	11	11	11	11	11	11	11	11	8	8	8	8	1	12	12	12	12	2	2	9	2	2	16	14	8	8	8	8	8	8	8	16			
8 TRULLI	10	10	10	10	10	10	10	10	8	8	8	8	8	8	9	9	9	9	9	9	9	9	9	16	16	16	16	14	2	15	15	15	15	9	9	9	9	9			
10 ROSBERG	8	8	8	8	8	8	8	8	9	9	9	9	9	9	14	14	14	14	14	14	21	21	21	21	21	8	15	14	9	9	15	15	15	15	15				
7 R. SCHUMACHER	14	9	9	9	9	9	9	9	14	14	14	14	14	14	21	21	21	21	21	21	14	14	14	14	14	21	14	9	14	14	14	14	14	14	14	14	14				
14 COULTHARD	9	14	14	14	14	14	14	14	21	21	21	21	21	21	7	7	7	7	20	7	7	7	20	15	20	20	7	7	7	7	7	7	7	7	7	7	7				
21 SPEED	21	21	21	21	21	21	21	21	7	7	7	7	7	7	20	20	20	20	4	4	20	20	20	20	20	20	20	20	20	20	20	20	20	20	20	20					
15 KLIEN	20	7	7	7	7	7	7	7	20	20	20	20	20	20	4	4	4	20	20	15	15	15	15	7	7	7	20	20	20	20	20	20	20	20	20	20					
20 LIUZZI	7	20	20	20	20	20	20	20	15	15	15	15	15	15	15	15	15	18	18	18	18	18	18	18	18	18	18	18	18	18	18	18	18	18	18	18	18	18			
19 ALBERS	15	15	15	15	15	15	15	15	19	19	19	19	19	19	18	18	18	22	22	22	22	22	22	22	22	22	22	22	22	22	22	22	22	22	22	22	22	22			
9 WEBBER	23	18	18	18	18	18	18	18	18	18	18	18	18	18	19	19	19	19	19	19	19	19	19	19	19	19	19	19	19	19	19	19	19	19	19	19	19	19			
18 MONTEIRO	18	19	19	19	19	19	19	22	22	22	22	22	22	22	22	22	22	19																							
22 SATO	19	23	23	23	22	22	22	23	23	23	23	23	23	23	23			23																							
23 YAMAMOTO	22	22	22	22	23	23	23	23	23	10																															

PRACTICE 1 (FRIDAY)

Hazy sunshine (track 32–36ºC, air 27–29ºC)

Pos.	Driver	Laps	Time
1	Sebastian Vettel	22	1m 23.263s
2	Robert Kubica	5	1m 23.745s
3	Alexander Wurz	19	1m 23.868s
4	Kimi Räikkönen	5	1m 24.037s
5	Neel Jani	24	1m 24.196s
6	Tiago Monteiro	7	1m 25.413s
7	Robert Doornbos	19	1m 25.578s
8	Christijan Albers	7	1m 25.766s
9	Takuma Sato	20	1m 26.708s
10	Sakon Yamamoto	20	1m 27.310s
11	Franck Montagny	7	1m 27.597s
12	Giorgio Mondini	7	1m 28.444s
13	Anthony Davidson	2	No time
14	Pedro de la Rosa	1	No time
15	Felipe Massa	1	No time
16	Jarno Trulli	2	No time
17	Nick Heidfeld	1	No time
18	Ralf Schumacher	2	No time
19	Vitantonio Liuzzi	3	No time
20	Scott Speed	1	No time
21	Nico Rosberg	1	No time
22	Mark Webber	1	No time
23	Christian Klien	1	No time
24	David Coulthard	1	No time

PRACTICE 2 (FRIDAY)

Sunny (track 36–39ºC, air 30–31ºC)

Pos.	Driver	Laps	Time
1	Sebastian Vettel	29	1m 22.631s
2	Michael Schumacher	11	1m 23.138s
3	Felipe Massa	12	1m 23.182s
4	Alexander Wurz	26	1m 23.414s
5	Pedro de la Rosa	12	1m 23.970s
6	Kimi Räikkönen	11	1m 24.034s
7	Nick Heidfeld	9	1m 24.330s
8	Fernando Alonso	15	1m 24.577s
9	Robert Kubica	5	1m 24.813s
10	Franck Montagny	24	1m 24.943s
11	Christijan Albers	11	1m 24.985s
12	Jarno Trulli	12	1m 25.027s
13	Nico Rosberg	9	1m 25.040s
14	Christian Klien	11	1m 25.108s
15	Giancarlo Fisichella	16	1m 25.160s
16	Tiago Monteiro	12	1m 25.277s
17	Ralf Schumacher	22	1m 25.316s
18	David Coulthard	11	1m 25.318s
19	Anthony Davidson	8	1m 25.356s
20	Mark Webber	11	1m 25.500s
21	Giorgio Mondini	29	1m 25.586s
22	Vitantonio Liuzzi	19	1m 25.707s
23	Scott Speed	21	1m 25.755s
24	Neel Jani	32	1m 25.878s
25	Robert Doornbos	31	1m 26.058s
26	Takuma Sato	21	1m 26.118s
27	Sakon Yamamoto	14	1m 26.705s

QUALIFYING (SATURDAY)

Sunny (track 40–41ºC, air 28ºC)

Pos.	Driver	First	Second	Third
1	Kimi Räikkönen	1m 21.994s	1m 21.349s	1m 21.484s
2	Michael Schumacher	1m 21.711s	1m 21.353s	1m 21.486s
3	Nick Heidfeld	1m 21.764s	1m 21.425s	1m 21.653s
4	Felipe Massa	1m 22.028s	1m 21.225s	1m 21.704s
5	Jenson Button	1m 22.512s	1m 21.572s	1m 22.011s
6	Robert Kubica	1m 22.437s	1m 21.270s	1m 22.258s
7	Pedro de la Rosa	1m 22.422s	1m 21.878s	1m 22.280s
8	Rubens Barrichello	1m 22.640s	1m 21.688s	1m 22.787s
9	Giancarlo Fisichella	1m 22.486s	1m 21.722s	1m 23.175s
10	Fernando Alonso	1m 21.747s	1m 21.526s	1m 25.688s*
11	Jarno Trulli	1m 22.093s	1m 21.924s	
12	Nico Rosberg	1m 22.581s	1m 22.203s	
13	Ralf Schumacher	1m 22.622s	1m 22.280s	
14	David Coulthard	1m 22.618s	1m 22.589s	
15	Scott Speed	1m 22.943s	1m 23.165s	
16	Christian Klien	1m 22.898s	No time	
17	Vitantonio Liuzzi	1m 23.043s		
18	Christijan Albers	1m 23.116s		
19	Mark Webber	1m 23.341s		
20	Tiago Monteiro	1m 23.920s		
21	Takuma Sato	1m 24.289s		
22	Sakon Yamamoto	1m 26.001s		

* Fastest three times disallowed for impeding Massa

PRACTICE 3 (SATURDAY)

Sunny (track 31–36ºC, air 24–25ºC)

Pos.	Driver	Laps	Time
1	Felipe Massa	12	1m 21.665s
2	Nick Heidfeld	13	1m 22.052s
3	Michael Schumacher	14	1m 22.257s
4	Robert Kubica	12	1m 22.280s
5	Fernando Alonso	15	1m 22.371s
6	Giancarlo Fisichella	15	1m 22.412s
7	Kimi Räikkönen	11	1m 22.682s
8	Rubens Barrichello	18	1m 22.835s
9	Pedro de la Rosa	11	1m 22.915s
10	Christian Klien	11	1m 23.081s
11	Ralf Schumacher	17	1m 23.244s
12	Jenson Button	15	1m 23.295s
13	Nico Rosberg	8	1m 23.334s
14	Jarno Trulli	15	1m 23.467s
15	David Coulthard	9	1m 23.536s
16	Mark Webber	8	1m 23.599s
17	Scott Speed	20	1m 23.659s
18	Vitantonio Liuzzi	20	1m 23.777s
19	Christijan Albers	17	1m 24.186s
20	Tiago Monteiro	14	1m 24.541s
21	Takuma Sato	25	1m 24.549s
22	Sakon Yamamoto	19	1m 24.717s

CHASSIS LOG BOOK

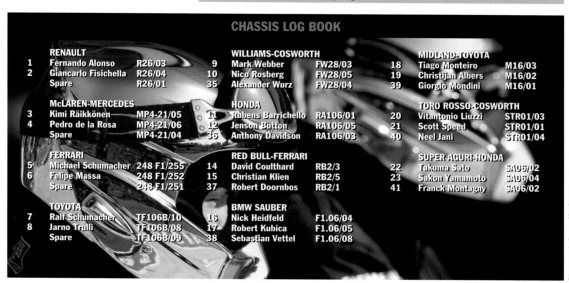

RENAULT
1 Fernando Alonso — R26/03 — 9
2 Giancarlo Fisichella — R26/04 — 10
Spare — R26/01 — 35

McLAREN-MERCEDES
3 Kimi Räikkönen — MP4-21/05 — 11
4 Pedro de la Rosa — MP4-21/06 — 12
Spare — MP4-21/04 — 36

FERRARI
5 Michael Schumacher — 248 F1/255 — 14
6 Felipe Massa — 248 F1/252 — 15
Spare — 248 F1/251 — 37

TOYOTA
7 Ralf Schumacher — TF106B/10 — 16
8 Jarno Trulli — TF106B/08 — 17
Spare — TF106B/09 — 38

WILLIAMS-COSWORTH
18 Mark Webber — FW28/03
19 Nico Rosberg — FW28/05
35 Alexander Wurz — FW28/04

HONDA
Rubens Barrichello — RA106/01 — 20
Jenson Button — RA106/05 — 21
Anthony Davidson — RA106/03 — 40

RED BULL-FERRARI
David Coulthard — RB2/3 — 22
Christian Klien — RB2/5 — 23
Robert Doornbos — RB2/1 — 41

BMW SAUBER
Nick Heidfeld — F1.06/04
Robert Kubica — F1.06/05
Sebastian Vettel — F1.06/08

MIDLAND-TOYOTA
18 Tiago Monteiro — M16/03
19 Christijan Albers — M16/02
39 Giorgio Mondini — M16/01

TORO ROSSO-COSWORTH
20 Vitantonio Liuzzi — STR01/03
21 Scott Speed — STR01/01
40 Neel Jani — STR01/04

SUPER AGURI-HONDA
22 Takuma Sato — SA06/02
23 Sakon Yamamoto — SA06/04
41 Franck Montagny — SA06/02

Photograph: James Moy/www.crashpa.net

9 FISICHELLA Renault

7 DE LA ROSA McLaren

5 BUTTON Honda

3 HEIDFELD BMW-Sauber

1 RÄIKKÖNEN McLaren

10 ALONSO Renault
Misdemeanour penalty

8 BARRICHELLO Honda

6 KUBICA BMW-Sauber

4 MASSA Ferrari

2 M. SCHUMACHER Ferrari

RACE DISTANCE:
53 laps
190.587 miles/306.720 km

RACE WEATHER:
Sunny
track 40–41ºC, air 26–27ºC

Lap chart

42	43	44	45	46	47	48	49	50	51	52	53	*
5	5	5	5	5	5	5	5	5	5	5	5	1
3	3	3	3	3	3	3	3	3	3	3	3	2
1	1	17	17	17	17	17	17	17	17	17	17	3
17	17	6	2	2	2	2	2	2	2	2	2	4
6	6	2	12	12	12	12	12	12	12	12	12	5
2	2	12	11	11	11	11	11	11	11	11	11	6
12	12	11	8	8	8	8	8	8	8	8	8	7
11	11	8	16	16	16	16	16	16	16	16	16	8
8	8	16	6	6	6	6	6	6	6	6	6	
16	16	9	9	9	9	9	9	9	9	9	9	
9	9	15	15	15	15	15	15	15	15			
15	15	14	14	14	14	14	14	14	14			
14	14	21	21	21	21	21	21	21	21			
21	21	7	7	7	20	20	20	20				
7	7	20	20	20	20	7	7	7				
20	20	22	22	22	22	22	22					
18	18	19	19	19	19	19	19	19				
22	22	18										

Pit stop
One lap or more behind leader
Drive-through penalty

FOR THE RECORD

90th GRAND PRIX WIN:
Michael Schumacher

50th GRAND PRIX START: Honda

FIRST PODIUM & FIRST LAP LED:
Robert Kubica (above)

POINTS

DRIVERS
1	Fernando Alonso	108
2	Michael Schumacher	106
3	Felipe Massa	62
4	Giancarlo Fisichella	57
5	Kimi Räikkönen	57
6	Jenson Button	40
7	Juan Pablo Montoya	26
8	Rubens Barrichello	25
9	Nick Heidfeld	20
10	Ralf Schumacher	18
11	Pedro de la Rosa	14
12	David Coulthard	14
13	Jarno Trulli	12
14	Jacques Villeneuve	7
15	Robert Kubica	6
16	Mark Webber	6
17	Nico Rosberg	4
18	Christian Klien	2
19	Vitantonio Liuzzi	1

CONSTRUCTORS
1	Ferrari	168
2	Renault	165
3	McLaren	97
4	Honda	65
5	BMW Sauber	33
6	Toyota	30
7	Red Bull	16
8	Williams	10
9	Toro Rosso	1

Photographs: James Moy/www.crashpa.net

FIA F1 WORLD CHAMPIONSHIP/ROUND 16

CHINESE GP
SHANGHAI CIRCUIT

Above: Michael Schumacher's irrepressible
grin again beams out from an F1
podium, this time after he wins at
Shanghai. Second- and third-placed
Fernando Alonso and Giancarlo
Fisichella look distinctly pensive.
Photograph: James Moy/www.crashpa.net

Main photograph: Michael Schumacher's Bridgestone tyres may look a little careworn in this shot, but he maximised their potential in the changing conditions to great effect and came home to score his 91st career victory even though Fernando Alonso was closing fast by the chequered flag.
Photograph: Paul-Henri Cahier

SHANGHAI QUALIFYING

THE rain at Shanghai was kind to the Michelin runners – and Renault in particular – as it exposed the weakness in Ferrari's Bridgestone armour.

While Michael Schumacher slithered around, unable to muster the grip to do anything better than sixth place, Fernando Alonso, Giancarlo Fisichella, Rubens Barrichello, Jenson Button and Kimi Räikkönen all upstaged him.

It was an altogether dreary weekend, weather-wise, though on Saturday morning Schumacher had been able to pip Alonso for fastest time in overcast and damp conditions. It was the rain in the afternoon that did for him, however, when Michelin had a clear advantage.

Alonso and Fisichella were unbeatable in first qualifying, half a second ahead of the McLarens of Pedro de la Rosa and Kimi Räikkönen and more than a second faster than Tonio Liuzzi's Toro Rosso. Felipe Massa was only 13th and Schumacher 14th as Ralf Schumacher and Jarno Trulli in their Toyotas (1m 48.894s and 1m 49.098s respectively), Christijan Albers and Tiago Monteiro in their Spykers (1m 49.542s and 1m 49.903s) and Takuma Sato and Sakon Yamamoto in their Super Aguris (1m 50.326s and 1m 55.560s) were all eliminated.

Monteiro briefly brought out the red flag when his car ran out of fuel after a radio problem and a misunderstanding unsettled the Spyker team. Yamamoto didn't help himself by spinning in slippery Turn 14, but he was in good company as Räikkönen, Barrichello, Mark Webber and Nico Rosberg all had similar moments.

Ferrari continued to struggle in second qualifying as Jenson Button and Nick Heidfeld moved up to chase the Renaults. Schumacher was only ninth after improving from the relegation zone in the closing minutes and Massa (1m 45.970s) was eliminated together with Scott Speed (1m 45.851s), David Coulthard (1m 45.968s), Liuzzi (1m 46.172s), Webber (1m 46.413s) and Rosberg (1m 47.419s).

Thus Alonso, Fisichella, Button, Heidfeld, De la Rosa, Barrichello, Robert Kubica, Räikkönen, Schumacher and Robert Doornbos – making an impressive début for Red Bull as Christian Klien's replacement – were left to fight out the top ten positions. It was a foregone conclusion that Renault would continue to dominate because track conditions did not improve. Alonso gave himself and his team a much-needed fillip by taking pole with 1m 44.360s and Fisichella backed him up with 1m 44.992s, despite running over a wing mirror that had vibrated loose from Räikkönen's McLaren.

The outcome gave Renault its first full front row since Canada and Alonso his sixth pole of the season, and it looked just like old times.

'It looked okay from the beginning of qualifying,' Alonso said cheerfully. 'There's nothing to say, really. The car and the team have been fantastic in these conditions and I was really comfortable. Turn One was very difficult on intermediates, though. As soon as you went off-line and touched big water, you were off. But with the fuel we had in the car there were more possibilities than normal to be able to repeat laps.'

He was unsure what to expect from the race, however. 'To be honest, who knows? We have no information for the dry but we are very competitive then, so if it's a normal race I think we will be really, really strong. And we'll be strong if it's wet like this, but it's always dangerous then and difficult to finish races. Whatever, we have to finish the job tomorrow. It's a surprise, the pace of the car today and how comfortable we were. We were really competitive.'

Besides his problem with debris, Fisichella was feeling slightly chastened after nearly getting stuck in the gravel trap in Turn One in the second session. He admitted that he was cautious after that, but added, 'The car balance was very good, so I felt comfortable in the last session.'

Barrichello and Button shared exactly the same time, 1m 45.503s, third place going to the Brazilian because he set the time earlier.

'I'm very impressed to have the same time as Jenson,' Barrichello smiled. 'That's the best a team can expect! But I was lucky to do that. After that spin in the second session, recovering pumped me up so much. Turn One was so difficult; it was impossible to push. I completely lost the car, but it was all positive from there as the engine was still running. It looks like we are competitive in the wet, we are faster than some of the guys, so it's quite good.'

Räikkönen's 1m 45.754s was good enough for fifth. After changes to his car, Schumacher screwed himself up for a lap of 1m 45.775s, which gave him sixth, ahead of spinner De la Rosa (1m 45.877s), Heidfeld and Kubica (1m 46.053s and 1m 46.632s) and Doornbos (1m 48.021s).

An engine change on Friday morning dropped Massa from 13th to 21st; Sato also needed one and moved from 21st to 22nd. With more rain forecast for Sunday, Renault retired for the night feeling a lot more optimistic than it had for some time.

F Fernando Alonso was feeling bruised and hard-done-by after the Italian GP, the Chinese race was sufficient to tip him over the edge into paranoia.

In wet conditions, the Spaniard owned the Shanghai circuit for the first 22 laps as he started from pole and headed Renault team-mate Giancarlo Fisichella. But by the chequered flag, another 34 laps later, he had become the victim of one of Michael Schumacher's greatest conjuring tricks. He left the track even further demoralised as his arch-rival finally caught up with his points tally in their fight for the world championship.

It all unravelled thus. As Alonso shot into the lead at the start, Fisichella dutifully slotted in behind and fended off an attack by fast-starting Kimi Räikkönen on a track made treacherous by standing water and heavy spray. Farther back, Jenson Button got the drop on Honda team-mate Rubens Barrichello, and Schumacher maintained his starting position – sixth – to keep Pedro de la Rosa at bay.

That was how things stayed until lap eight, when Schumacher out-fumbled Barrichello, and by then it was clear that the Ferrari-Bridgestone alliance wasn't at quite such a disadvantage on intermediate tyres as it had been during qualifying. Nevertheless, Alonso was headed for the tall timber and Michael was 22.7s in arrears by lap 11.

By then, Räikkönen was becoming increasingly frustrated behind Fisichella, finally forcing his way by two laps later.

Alonso had a 16.4s lead over the Finn, but Schumacher had slipped past Button and was up to fourth. Button had been going well until his rear Michelins began losing grip and this was the point at which the slightly drying conditions began to favour the Bridgestones.

Räikkönen made a little ground on Alonso before refuelling on lap 16, a lap after Button. When Barrichello and De la Rosa refuelled on lap 17, Kimi moved back up to fourth. But that was as far as he went. On the 19th lap the McLaren expired yet again, this time with a throttle problem.

'I think we might have won today,' Räikkönen said and indeed he might have had a shot at it. Instead, things were beginning to go Schumacher's way for the 91st time.

Michael pitted for fuel on lap 21 while running third behind the Renaults. Alonso came in a lap later, Fisi a lap later still. But what was this? When Alonso restarted, having had a new pair of front tyres fitted, he was suddenly up to four seconds a lap slower than either Fisichella or Schumacher, who hadn't changed tyres. Alonso had been concerned about the wear rate on his left-front and now his replacements were refusing to come in soon enough.

'I had a good start and everything was fine for the first 15 or 20 laps,' he explained. 'In the pit stop I decided to change only the front tyres, because they were nearly slicks, and suddenly there was not a thing I could do as Giancarlo and Michael

Left: The mechanic's work is never done. Lights burn late into the night in the Toyota garage as the TF106Bs are fettled for the weekend's action.

Below: Fernando Alonso takes the lead in heavy rain ahead of Renault team-mate Giancarlo Fisichella with the Hondas of Rubens Barrichello and Jenson Button leading the rest of the sodden pack.
Photographs: James Moy/www.crashpa.net

DIARY

Briton Anthony Davidson is said to be 99 percent sure of a race drive with Super Aguri. Honda Racing chief executive Nick Fry says, 'That's what Anthony deserves.'

Scuderia Toro Rosso announces that former Cosworth development chief Alex Hitzinger will be its new technical director and that he will also be head of advanced technologies for Red Bull F1.

Baran Asena, head of the beleaguered Turkish Grand Prix, describes the fine of $5 million levied by the FIA as 'devastating' to the economy of the Istanbul Circuit.

The Spyker MF1 team confirms that it will run Ferrari engines in 2007. Besides revealing that it has also re-signed Dutchman Christijan Albers, it admits that Johnny Herbert's contract as sporting relations director has not been renewed.

kept their original tyres and came to me really quickly. The gap just disappeared.'

By lap 28 what had been a 10.6s advantage only four laps earlier was now 0.4s and Fisi had a dilemma. He had Michael right on his gearbox and his team-mate holding him up. What was he to do? Alonso was clearly blocking him, and on lap 29 Fisi overtook, only to run wide and be repassed as Michael was poised waiting to pounce. Fisichella made a move stick on lap 30 and led past the pits, with Schumacher right next to Alonso. The inevitable happened a lap later as the Ferrari screamed past the Renault and, hand over fist, Alonso began to lose further time.

Now the race seemed Fisichella's to lose. Initially he kept his head, teasing a 1.9s advantage on lap 32 out to 2.6s by lap 34, until Schumacher began charging at him again.

Alonso stopped again on lap 35, for dry tyres, losing further time – at least 13s – when the right-rear wheel nut fell out of the airgun as his mechanic went to refit it.

Fisichella came under even greater pressure from Schumacher now, with the Ferrari never more than a second behind. There was respite as Schumacher pitted on the 40th lap and when Fisi came in a lap later he rejoined comfortably in the lead. Renault, it seemed, still had it in the bag.

But no!

There was Fisichella, exiting the pits before Schumacher crossed the finish line, suddenly slithering wide on to the wet in Turn One. The corner was still treacherous (indeed, Tiago Monteiro had just gone off there and beached his Spyker), but

the Italian's error was unforgivable even if Schumacher did allow later that he'd had a moment there himself.

As Fisichella sorted himself out, Schumacher said thanks very much and snatched the inside line and the lead. Fisi, gentleman that he is, offered zero resistance as he pulled back to the right. The game was over.

'It was clear that Turn One was going to be difficult,' Schumacher said. 'I took it reasonably easy but still almost went in too fast. So I was thinking it could be an issue with Giancarlo and there it was: he went wide, I took my opportunity and I was able to turn down the revs and drive safely home.'

Now Michael romped away, his Ferrari rejuvenated by a set of dry Bridgestones after his original set had worn themselves down to slicks. His lead was 7.6s on lap 42, 11.8s by 45, 13.7s by 49.

In his wake, Alonso had started to fly again and set a string of fastest laps as he hauled in his hapless team-mate, who either had gone to pieces as he did in Japan in 2005 or was simply waiting to do the decent thing and let Alonso catch him.

By lap 49 the Spaniard had scythed past him into second place. Michael was at this stage 13.7s ahead but Alonso was still flying and, thanks to a two-second gain on lap 52 alone, he had the gap down to 6.6s going into the last lap. It was a forlorn cause, of course, and even though it was only 3.1s by the flag Schumacher was in control. But what might have happened had Fisi been able to contain him?

The 91st victory of Schumacher's career – his seventh of the season – drew him exactly equal with Alonso in the points table

with two races to run: 116 points apiece. Hollywood couldn't have scripted it better. Shanghai had never smiled upon Schumacher before but now it had given him a very nice going-away present.

'It was quite an exciting and extreme weekend,' Schumacher smiled. 'It was a gamble to stay on the original set of tyres but it paid out. Now we are on equal points. If we look back some while ago it is a miracle we are here, but thanks to great work from everyone [in the Ferrari team] we've managed it and go to the last two races fighting. I believe we will have to wait until the last one for a decision to be reached, so it's an interesting couple of weeks we face. I really look forward to that.'

Alonso tried hard to keep his spirits up. 'When I stopped again I changed early to dry tyres and hoped to find a miracle. But I think that the weekend has been fantastic and we [the team and I] have to focus on the positive thing: that the middle stint was the only part of the race when we weren't

Left: The spectacular vista from the Shanghai circuit's main grandstand as the entire field lines up on the spacious starting grid prior to the off.

Below left: Sakon Yamamoto brought the Super Aguri SA06 home to his first race finish.
Photographs: James Moy/www.crashpa.net

Bottom: Scuderia Toro Rosso driver Scott Speed is framed in a haze of exhaust fumes at the end of his day's work.
Photograph: Jad Sherif/WRI

quick. I am very confident for the last two races but this was one opportunity lost.'

An opportunity that he didn't lose was the chance to criticise his team. In his angst Alonso, normally a placid fellow, hit out at anyone and everyone, including the Renault team and driving partner Giancarlo Fisichella. Alonso was once regarded as the calm young man who was rattling Schumacher's cage, but his hitherto hidden emotional streak surfaced as the pressure of the battle mounted.

'I fought Fisichella in the last corner, I overtook him once, he overtook me and I overtook him again,' he complained. 'These risky moments, with three races to go in the championship, and with your team-mate... it's not good enough.

'I think the team does the maximum it can. The guys have given me a fantastic car, winning the championship last year and fighting this year. So therefore what the team does in every race is unbelievable, to be equal in the drivers' championship and almost equal in the constructors'.

'For sure the team is giving me a fantastic car, but for sure on some occasions I have felt a little alone. I had difficult moments at Indy, when I was not competitive, and in China I was off the pace for about ten laps and losing four seconds a lap. In these two moments, my opinion is that maybe I should have had more help from the team.'

He told Sport-Informations-Dienst: 'I don't believe that Felipe Massa would have driven past Schumacher in the same situation.'

Fisichella was bemused by all this. 'I'm very surprised; I don't know why he said it,' he said at Suzuka the following week. 'Obviously I race for myself and I don't race for Fernando. If there is a possibility to help, that is okay, but I cannot stop my car on the track to let him past.'

He denied Alonso's assertion that their clash risked Alonso's championship aspirations – especially because Alonso was losing four seconds a lap at the time.

'Absolutely not,' Fisichella said. 'I was on the wet side and we both braked quite late because behind us there was Michael, so that is the reason why the first time I lost control of the car. But it wasn't dangerous.'

Alonso wasn't the only unhappy man after the race. Nick Heidfeld was livid with backmarkers Christijan Albers and Takuma Sato, whose insistence on racing him when being lapped in the closing stages led to a situation in which the German lost his seven-second cushion to a recovering Button.

It had begun to rain quite heavily and the two Bridgestone-shod drivers were quicker – Albers did not help matters by later suggesting Heidfeld should 'wear one of those red thongs and go play beach volleyball' – but that did not excuse their behaviour. Sato was subsequently disqualified and Albers penalised 25s.

What happened was that six cars came into the final corner together: Sato, against whom Button managed to wipe off Heidfeld; Barrichello; Albers; and De la Rosa. As Button slid inside Heidfeld, Barrichello screwed up his braking and took out the BMW. The hapless German thus fell from fourth to an eventual seventh, behind Button, De la Rosa and Barrichello, and was not amused.

Farther back, Mark Webber scored the final point after David Coulthard half spun out of eighth place on lap 48, three laps after a contretemps between Felipe Massa and Coulthard in the final corner had left the Brazilian to retire with suspension damage.

Robert Kubica was up to fifth place before half distance

despite a brief bump from Robert Doornbos's Red Bull, but then lost any chances of a good finish by gambling too much on the change to dry tyres. After another stop to go back to intermediates he matched the pace of Fisichella, Schumacher and Alonso but could not better 13th at the finish.

Doornbos needed a new nose after a lap but passed 11 cars on his way to 12th behind Tonio Liuzzi, who refuelled only once, and Nico Rosberg, who was trapped in traffic for much of his race. Scott Speed brought the other Toro Rosso home 15th, behind Sato and ahead of Sakon Yamamoto, who thus achieved his first GP finish.

The race proved a disaster for Toyota, with neither Jarno Trulli nor Ralf Schumacher doing much before retiring with loss of pneumatic pressure and oil pressure respectively. But at one stage, as conditions improved towards the end, it was interesting to note that Ralf twice set the fastest lap before Alonso hit his stride.

David Tremayne

Left: Nick Heidfeld battles with Takuma Sato. The Japanese driver was disqualified after a collision with the German.
Photograph: Jad Sherif/WRI

Below: Cosworth's Bernard Ferguson (centre) in conversation with Simon Arkless of Champion and Frank Dernie of Williams.
Photograph: James Moy/www.crashpa.net

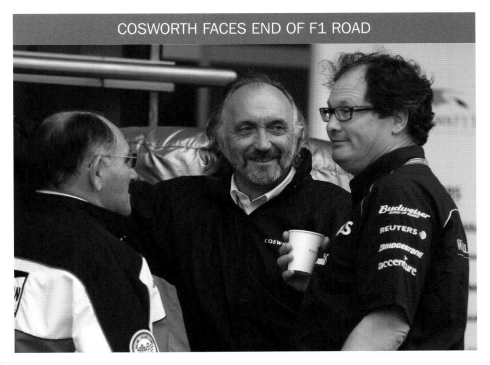

COSWORTH FACES END OF F1 ROAD

The Spyker MF1 team confirmed at Shanghai that it had done an engine supply deal with Ferrari for 2007. With Williams switching to Toyota, Spyker had been Cosworth's last hope of remaining in the top-most echelon of the sport, to which it had contributed the most successful engine in history and a slew of race wins and world championships. The bleak news came as Cosworth approached the anniversary of its legendary DFV V8's introduction in June 1967.

Cosworth's managing director Bernard Ferguson said, 'I think the facts speak for themselves. I don't think Cosworth will be in F1 next year. Obviously we have got to go back and look at the options and there are perhaps opportunities with all the legislation on engines that the FIA is putting together, so maybe we could help with policing that, but we are a bit numb.

'It is very disappointing,' he continued. 'We thought that we had a pretty strong product, a pretty reliable product and pretty good staff. I believe that the rear end of Spyker's 2007 car was designed for a Cosworth installation. There was a lot of interaction between our engineers and theirs, so we were pretty confident. But after the change in the purchase structure, when Spyker became part of the mechanism, there seemed to be considerably more enthusiasm for the Ferrari deal than there had been. The thing that swung it was the opportunity in the future for Spyker to work on a road car engine collaboration with Ferrari.'

Ferguson indicated that Cosworth Racing was some way down the road on a review of its products and a diversification programme, away from motor racing. 'The trouble with racing is that it is binary – you are either in or you are out of it. But the diversification will really come in the longer term; we could have done with another couple of years in F1.'

FIA F1 WORLD CHAMPIONSHIP • ROUND 16
SINOPEC
CHINESE GRAND PRIX
SHANGHAI 29 SEPTEMBER–1 OCTOBER 2006

SHANGHAI INTERNATIONAL CIRCUIT

Circuit: 3.387 miles / 5.451 km

116/187 mph/kmh

⚙ Gear

Turn 1 145/234
Turn 2 57/91
Turn 3 57/91
Turn 5 180/290
Turn 4 93/150
Turn 7 165/266
Turn 6 63/102
Turn 16 113/181
Turn 8 109/174
Turn 12 65/104
Turn 9 112/181
Turn 11 57/91
Turn 15 120/192
Turn 10 122/195
Turn 14 55/88
Turn 13 156/250

Photograph: James Moy/www.crashpa.net

RACE RESULTS

Pos.	Driver	Nat.	No.	Entrant	Car/Engine	Tyres	Laps	Time/Retirement	Speed (mph/km/h)	Gap to leader	Fastest race lap	
1	Michael Schumacher	D	5	Scuderia Ferrari Marlboro	Ferrari 248 F1-056 V8	B	56	1h 37m 32.747s	116.597/187.644		1m 38.553s	50
2	Fernando Alonso	E	1	Mild Seven Renault F1 Team	Renault R26-RS26 V8	M	56	1h 37m 35.868s	116.534/187.544	+3.121s	1m 37.586s	49
3	Giancarlo Fisichella	I	2	Mild Seven Renault F1 Team	Renault R26-RS26 V8	M	56	1h 38m 16.944s	115.723/186.238	+44.197s	1m 39.332s	53
4	Jenson Button	GB	12	Lucky Strike Honda Racing F1 Team	Honda RA106-RA806E V8	M	56	1h 38m 44.803s	115.179/185.362	+1m 12.056s	1m 39.206s	51
5	Pedro de la Rosa	E	4	Team McLaren Mercedes	McLaren MP4-21-Mercedes FO 108S V8	M	56	1h 38m 49.884s	115.080/185.203	+1m 17.137s	1m 39.149s	45
6	Rubens Barrichello	BR	11	Lucky Strike Honda Racing F1 Team	Honda RA106-RA806E V8	M	56	1h 38m 51.878s	115.041/185.141	+1m 19.131s	1m 39.749s	52
7	Nick Heidfeld	D	16	BMW Sauber F1 Team	BMW Sauber F1.06-BMW P86 V8	M	56	1h 39m 04.726s	114.793/184.741	+1m 31.979s	1m 39.164s	53
8	Mark Webber	AUS	9	WilliamsF1 Team	Williams FW28-Cosworth CA2006 V8	B	56	1h 39m 16.335s	114.569/184.381	+1m 43.588s	1m 39.907s	44
9	David Coulthard	GB	14	Red Bull Racing	Red Bull RB2-Ferrari 056 V8	M	56	1h 39m 16.543s	114.565/184.374	+1m 43.796s	1m 40.549s	52
10	Vitantonio Liuzzi	I	20	Scuderia Toro Rosso	Toro Rosso STR01-Cosworth TJ2005-2 V10	M	55			+1 lap	1m 41.710s	53
11	Nico Rosberg	D	10	WilliamsF1 Team	Williams FW28-Cosworth CA2006 V8	B	55			+1 lap	1m 40.471s	52
12	Robert Doornbos	NL	15	Red Bull Racing	Red Bull RB2-Ferrari 056 V8	M	55			+1 lap	1m 39.801s	52
13	Robert Kubica	POL	17	BMW Sauber F1 Team	BMW Sauber F1.06-BMW P86 V8	M	55			+1 lap	1m 40.193s	51
14	Scott Speed	USA	21	Scuderia Toro Rosso	Toro Rosso STR01-Cosworth TJ2005-2 V10	M	55			+1 lap	1m 39.681s	49
15	Christijan Albers	NL	19	Spyker MF1 Team	Midland M16-Toyota RVX-06 V8	B	53			+3 laps	1m 41.483s	50
16	Sakon Yamamoto	J	23	Super Aguri F1 Team	Super Aguri SA06-Honda RA806E V8	B	52			+4 laps	1m 41.847s	42
	Ralf Schumacher	D	7	Panasonic Toyota Racing	Toyota TF106B-RVX-06 V8	B	49	Oil pressure			1m 39.823s	47
	Felipe Massa	BR	6	Scuderia Ferrari Marlboro	Ferrari 248 F1-056 V8	B	44	Accident/front suspension			1m 39.397s	42
	Jarno Trulli	I	8	Panasonic Toyota Racing	Toyota TF106B-RVX-06 V8	B	38	Pneumatic pressure loss			1m 44.787s	24
	Tiago Monteiro	P	18	Spyker MF1 Team	Midland M16-Toyota RVX-06 V8	B	37	Spin			1m 45.356s	35
	Kimi Räikkönen	FIN	3	Team McLaren Mercedes	McLaren MP4-21-Mercedes FO 108S V8	M	18	Throttle			1m 44.094s	14
	Takuma Sato	J	22	Super Aguri F1 Team	Super Aguri SA06-Honda RA806E V8	B	55	Disqualified for blocking faster drivers		+1 lap	1m 40.856s	48

Fastest lap: Fernando Alonso on lap 49, 1m 37.586s, 124.952 mph/201.090 km/h.

Lap record: Michael Schumacher (Ferrari F2004 V10), 1m 32.238s, 132.196 mph/212.749 km/h (2004).

All results and data © FOM 2006

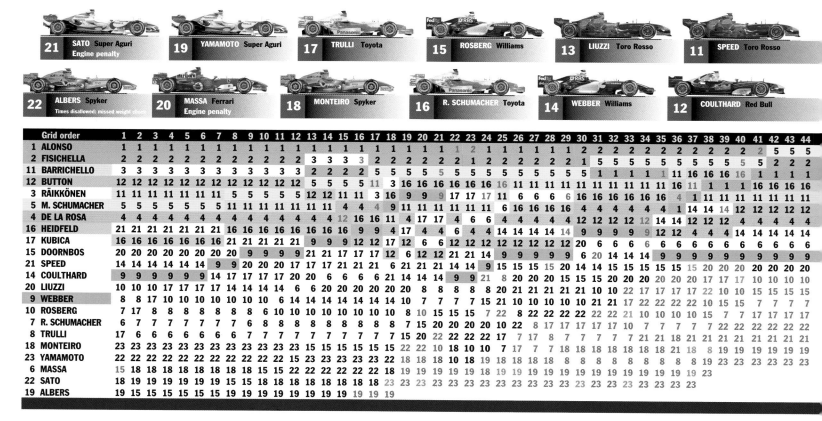

	Grid order	1	2	3	4	5	6	7	8	9	10	11	12	13	14	15	16	17	18	19	20	21	22	23	24	25	26	27	28	29	30	31	32	33	34	35	36	37	38	39	40	41	42	43	44
1	ALONSO	1	1	1	1	1	1	1	1	1	1	1	1	1	1	1	1	1	1	1	1	1	2	1	1	1	1	1	2	2	2	2	2	2	2	2	2	2	2	2	2	5	5	5	
2	FISICHELLA	2	2	2	2	2	2	2	2	2	2	3	3	3	3	2	2	2	2	2	2	1	2	2	2	2	1	5	5	5	5	5	5	5	5	5	5	5	5	2	2	2	
11	BARRICHELLO	3	3	3	3	3	3	3	3	3	3	2	2	5	5	5	5	5	5	5	5	5	1	5	5	5	5	1	1	1	1	1	11	16	16	16	16	1	1	1	1		
12	BUTTON	12	12	12	12	12	12	12	12	12	12	5	5	5	12	3	16	16	16	16	16	16	11	11	11	11	11	11	11	11	11	16	1	1	1	1	16	16	16				
3	RÄIKKÖNEN	11	11	11	11	11	11	11	5	5	5	5	12	12	11	11	3	9	9	9	17	17	6	6	16	16	16	16	4	11	11	11	11	11	11								
5	M. SCHUMACHER	5	5	5	5	5	5	5	11	11	11	11	11	11	4	4	9	11	11	11	6	16	16	16	4	4	4	4	14	14	14	12	12	12	12								
4	DE LA ROSA	4	4	4	4	4	4	4	4	4	4	4	4	4	12	16	16	11	4	17	17	4	6	4	4	4	12	12	12	12	12	14	14	12	12	4	4	4					
16	HEIDFELD	21	21	21	21	21	21	21	16	16	16	16	16	16	16	9	4	17	4	4	4	14	14	14	14	9	9	9	9	12	4	4	14	14	14	14							
17	KUBICA	16	16	16	16	16	16	16	21	21	21	21	21	6	12	12	12	12	6	12	12	12	12	20	6	6	6	6	6	6	6	6	6	6									
15	DOORNBOS	20	20	20	20	20	20	20	9	9	9	9	21	21	17	17	17	6	12	12	21	21	21	14	20	14	14	14	9	9	9	9	9	9									
21	SPEED	14	14	14	14	14	14	9	9	20	20	20	17	17	21	21	21	6	21	21	14	14	9	15	15	15	20	14	14	15	15	15	20	20	20	20	20	20					
14	COULTHARD	9	9	9	9	9	9	14	17	17	17	17	20	20	6	6	6	21	14	14	9	9	21	8	8	20	20	15	15	20	20	20	17	17	17	10	10	10					
20	LIUZZI	10	10	10	10	17	17	17	14	14	14	14	6	6	20	20	8	8	8	8	8	8	20	21	21	21	15	20	20	17	17	17	22	10	10	15	15	15					
9	WEBBER	8	8	17	10	10	10	10	10	10	10	10	14	14	14	14	14	14	15	15	7	7	7	7	15	10	10	10	10	22	15	15	10	15	15	7	7	7					
10	ROSBERG	7	17	8	8	8	8	8	8	8	8	6	10	10	9	15	15	15	7	22	22	22	22	22	10	22	22	22	17	17	7	7	17	17	7	7							
7	R. SCHUMACHER	6	7	7	7	7	7	7	6	6	6	8	8	15	20	20	22	8	17	17	17	17	17	17	7	17	7	17	17	17	17	17											
8	TRULLI	17	6	6	6	6	6	6	7	7	7	7	7	7	8	8	22	22	22	22	17	7	17	8	7	17	17	7	21	21	18	21	21	21	21	21							
18	MONTEIRO	23	23	23	23	23	23	23	23	23	23	15	15	18	15	15	10	10	10	7	7	7	18	18	18	18	18	18	18	8	19	19	19	19	19	19							
23	YAMAMOTO	22	22	22	22	22	22	22	22	15	15	22	18	19	18	18	10	18	18	19	19	18	18	18	18	18	18	8	8	23	23	23	23	23									
6	MASSA	15	18	18	18	18	15	15	15	22	22	18	22	22	19	19	19	19	19	19	19	19	19	19	23	23	23	23	23	23	23												
22	SATO	18	15	19	19	15	18	18	18	18	18	19	19	23	23	23	23	23	23	23	23	23	23																				
19	ALBERS	19	15	15	15	19	19	19	19	19	19	19	19																														

21 SATO Super Aguri — Engine penalty
19 YAMAMOTO Super Aguri
17 TRULLI Toyota
15 ROSBERG Williams
13 LIUZZI Toro Rosso
11 SPEED Toro Rosso
22 ALBERS Spyker — Times disallowed: missed weight check
20 MASSA Ferrari — Engine penalty
18 MONTEIRO Spyker
16 R. SCHUMACHER Toyota
14 WEBBER Williams
12 COULTHARD Red Bull

PRACTICE 1 (FRIDAY)

Overcast, breezy (track 31–32°C, air 26–27°C)

Pos.	Driver	Laps	Time
1	Alexander Wurz	21	1m 35.574s
2	Anthony Davidson	26	1m 35.591s
3	Jenson Button	4	1m 37.291s
4	Michael Schumacher	4	1m 37.712s
5	Neel Jani	21	1m 37.734s
6	Alexandre Prémat	24	1m 37.787s
7	Sebastian Vettel	24	1m 37.913s
8	Robert Kubica	6	1m 38.062s
9	Michael Ammermüller	18	1m 38.460s
10	Franck Montagny	19	1m 38.464s
11	Vitantonio Liuzzi	6	1m 39.000s
12	Rubens Barrichello	4	1m 39.217s
13	Scott Speed	7	1m 39.428s
14	Christijan Albers	6	1m 39.494s
15	Takuma Sato	8	1m 39.887s
16	Tiago Monteiro	7	1m 39.947s
17	Sakon Yamamoto	10	1m 41.415s
18	Kimi Räikkönen	4	1m 45.890s
19	Nick Heidfeld	1	No time
20	Jarno Trulli	2	No time
21	Ralf Schumacher	2	No time
22	David Coulthard	1	No time
23	Robert Doornbos	2	No time

PRACTICE 2 (FRIDAY)

Overcast, light rain (track 27–30°C, air 24–25°C)

Pos.	Driver	Laps	Time
1	Alexander Wurz	26	1m 35.539s
2	Sebastian Vettel	23	1m 35.579s
3	Anthony Davidson	30	1m 35.714s
4	Felipe Massa	8	1m 36.599s
5	Michael Schumacher	12	1m 36.641s
6	Fernando Alonso	10	1m 36.739s
7	Franck Montagny	26	1m 37.278s
8	Michael Ammermüller	26	1m 37.678s
9	Tiago Monteiro	13	1m 37.698s
10	Giancarlo Fisichella	12	1m 37.718s
11	Jenson Button	10	1m 37.861s
12	Pedro de la Rosa	9	1m 38.022s
13	Mark Webber	6	1m 38.045s
14	Nick Heidfeld	11	1m 38.062s
15	Alexandre Prémat	26	1m 38.098s
16	Rubens Barrichello	16	1m 38.276s
17	Ralf Schumacher	14	1m 38.888s
18	Jarno Trulli	11	1m 38.959s
19	Scott Speed	18	1m 39.080s
20	Neel Jani	28	1m 39.118s
21	Kimi Räikkönen	4	1m 39.179s
22	Robert Kubica	5	1m 39.217s
23	Nico Rosberg	15	1m 39.522s
24	Vitantonio Liuzzi	20	1m 39.570s
25	Sakon Yamamoto	22	1m 39.636s
26	David Coulthard	15	1m 40.155s
27	Robert Doornbos	15	1m 40.214s
28	Christijan Albers	14	1m 40.319s
29	Takuma Sato	9	1m 41.315s

QUALIFYING (SATURDAY)

Rain, overcast (track 23°C, air 22°C)

Pos.	Driver	First	Second	Third
1	Fernando Alonso	1m 44.128s	1m 43.951s	1m 44.360s
2	Giancarlo Fisichella	1m 44.378s	1m 44.336s	1m 44.992s
3	Rubens Barrichello	1m 47.072s	1m 45.288s	1m 45.503s
4	Jenson Button	1m 45.809s	1m 44.662s	1m 45.503s
5	Kimi Räikkönen	1m 44.909s	1m 45.622s	1m 45.754s
6	Michael Schumacher	1m 47.366s	1m 45.660s	1m 45.775s
7	Pedro de la Rosa	1m 44.808s	1m 45.095s	1m 45.877s
8	Nick Heidfeld	1m 46.249s	1m 45.055s	1m 46.053s
9	Robert Kubica	1m 46.049s	1m 45.576s	1m 46.632s
10	Robert Doornbos	1m 46.387s	1m 45.747s	1m 48.021s
11	Scott Speed	1m 46.222s	1m 45.851s	
12	David Coulthard	1m 45.931s	1m 45.968s	
13	Felipe Massa	1m 47.231s	1m 45.970s	
14	Vitantonio Liuzzi	1m 45.564s	1m 46.172s	
15	Mark Webber	1m 48.560s	1m 46.413s	
16	Nico Rosberg	1m 47.535s	1m 47.419s	
17	Ralf Schumacher	1m 48.894s		
18	Jarno Trulli	1m 49.098s		
19	Christijan Albers	1m 49.542s		
20	Tiago Monteiro	1m 49.903s		
21	Takuma Sato	1m 50.326s		
22	Sakon Yamamoto	1m 55.560s		

PRACTICE 3 (SATURDAY)

Overcast, damp (track 26°C, air 23°C)

Pos.	Driver	Laps	Time
1	Michael Schumacher	8	1m 40.193s
2	Fernando Alonso	7	1m 40.365s
3	Jenson Button	12	1m 40.590s
4	Vitantonio Liuzzi	9	1m 40.795s
5	Scott Speed	11	1m 41.150s
6	Mark Webber	10	1m 41.287s
7	Christijan Albers	11	1m 41.463s
8	Giancarlo Fisichella	6	1m 41.691s
9	Pedro de la Rosa	7	1m 41.823s
10	David Coulthard	18	1m 41.836s
11	Nico Rosberg	11	1m 42.588s
12	Tiago Monteiro	14	1m 42.612s
13	Nick Heidfeld	5	1m 43.216s
14	Rubens Barrichello	9	1m 43.448s
15	Felipe Massa	10	1m 43.500s
16	Takuma Sato	12	1m 43.722s
17	Jarno Trulli	14	1m 44.027s
18	Robert Doornbos	12	1m 45.434s
19	Ralf Schumacher	12	1m 46.023s
20	Sakon Yamamoto	10	1m 46.850s
21	Robert Kubica	1	No time
22	Kimi Räikkönen	2	No time

CHASSIS LOG BOOK

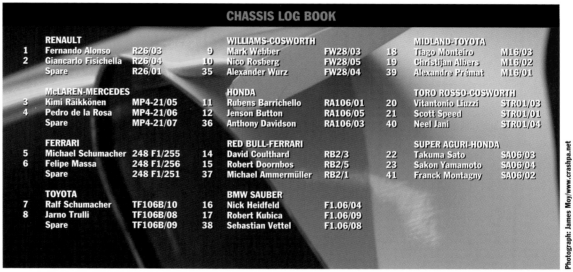

RENAULT
1	Fernando Alonso	R26/03
2	Giancarlo Fisichella	R26/04
	Spare	R26/01

McLAREN-MERCEDES
3	Kimi Räikkönen	MP4-21/05
4	Pedro de la Rosa	MP4-21/06
	Spare	MP4-21/07

FERRARI
5	Michael Schumacher	248 F1/255
6	Felipe Massa	248 F1/256
	Spare	248 F1/251

TOYOTA
7	Ralf Schumacher	TF106B/10
8	Jarno Trulli	TF106B/08
	Spare	TF106B/09

WILLIAMS-COSWORTH
9	Mark Webber	FW28/03
10	Nico Rosberg	FW28/05
35	Alexander Wurz	FW28/04

HONDA
11	Rubens Barrichello	RA106/01
12	Jenson Button	RA106/05
36	Anthony Davidson	RA106/03

RED BULL-FERRARI
14	David Coulthard	RB2/3
15	Robert Doornbos	RB2/5
37	Michael Ammermüller	RB2/1

BMW SAUBER
16	Nick Heidfeld	F1.06/04
17	Robert Kubica	F1.06/09
38	Sebastian Vettel	F1.06/08

MIDLAND-TOYOTA
18	Tiago Monteiro	M16/03
19	Christijan Albers	M16/02
39	Alexandre Prémat	M16/01

TORO ROSSO-COSWORTH
20	Vitantonio Liuzzi	STR01/03
21	Scott Speed	STR01/01
40	Neel Jani	STR01/04

SUPER AGURI-HONDA
22	Takuma Sato	SA06/03
23	Sakon Yamamoto	SA06/04
41	Franck Montagny	SA06/02

Photograph: James Moy/www.crashpa.net

9 KUBICA BMW-Sauber

7 DE LA ROSA McLaren

5 RÄIKKÖNEN McLaren

3 BARRICHELLO Honda

1 ALONSO Renault

10 DOORNBOS Red Bull

8 HEIDFELD BMW-Sauber

6 M. SCHUMACHER Ferrari

4 BUTTON Honda

2 FISICHELLA Renault

RACE DISTANCE:
56 laps
189.559 miles/305.066 km

RACE WEATHER:
Rain, cloudy, drying, scattered cloud
track 23°C, air 22°C

45	46	47	48	49	50	51	52	53	54	55	56	
5	5	5	5	5	5	5	5	5	5	5	5	1
2	2	2	1	1	1	1	1	1	1	1	1	2
1	1	1	2	2	2	2	2	2	2	2	2	3
16	16	16	16	16	16	16	16	16	16	16	12	4
11	11	11	11	11	11	11	11	11	11	11	4	5
12	12	12	12	4	4	4	4	4	12	12	11	6
4	4	4	12	12	12	12	12	4	4	4	16	7
14	14	14		9	9	9	9	9	9	9	9	8
9	9	9	14	14	14	14	14	14	14	14	14	
20	20	20	20	20	20	20	20	20	20	20		
10	10	10	10	10	10	10	10	10	10	10		
15	15	15	7	15	15	15	15	15	15	15		
7	7	7	15	7	17	17	17	17	17	17		
17	17	17	17	7	22	22	22	22	22	22		
22	22	22	22	22	21	21	21	21	21	21		
21	21	21	21	21	19	19	19	19				
19	19	19	19	19	23	23	23					
23	23	23	23	23								

Pit stop
One lap or more behind leader

FOR THE RECORD

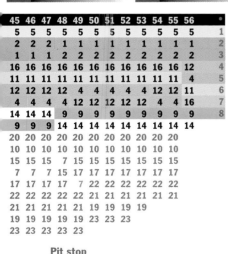

50th POLE POSITION: Renault

POINTS

	DRIVERS	
1	Michael Schumacher	116
2	Fernando Alonso	116
3	Giancarlo Fisichella	63
4	Felipe Massa	62
5	Kimi Räikkönen	57
6	Jenson Button	45
7	Rubens Barrichello	28
8	Juan Pablo Montoya	26
9	Nick Heidfeld	22
10	Pedro de la Rosa	13
11	Ralf Schumacher	13
12	David Coulthard	14
13	Jarno Trulli	12
14	Mark Webber	7
15	Jacques Villeneuve	7
16	Robert Kubica	6
17	Nico Rosberg	4
18	Christian Klien	2
19	Vitantonio Liuzzi	1

RENAULT F1 Team
MILD SEVEN
RENAULT F1 Team

	CONSTRUCTORS	
1	Renault	179
2	Ferrari	178
3	McLaren	101
4	Honda	73
5	BMW Sauber	35
6	Toyota	30
7	Red Bull	16
8	Williams	11
9	Toro Rosso	1

You don't bring a knife to a gunfight Michael...

Photographs: James Moy/www.crashpa.net

JAPANESE GP

SUZUKA

Main: Fernando Alonso finally ends a run of seven races without a win by posting a commanding victory at Suzuka after championship rival Michael Schumacher retires with engine failure in his Ferrari.

Inset: Alonso celebrates this long-overdue success with his elated Renault pit crew.
Photographs: Paul-Henri Cahier

SUZUKA QUALIFYING

WHEN poor weather on Friday morning in Suzuka had cleared for the afternoon and Giancarlo Fisichella headed Felipe Massa at the end of the second practice session, the times were evenly matched: 1m 34.337s for the Renault, 1m 34.408 for the Ferrari. Their team leaders were just behind, Michael Schumacher on 1m 34.565s and Fernando Alonso on 1m 34.863s.

That was why the sheer speed of the Ferraris on Saturday morning, and again in qualifying, left the Michelin runners not just stunned, but pole-axed.

The first sign of what lay in store emerged when Schumacher lapped in 1m 30.653s in the final practice session, with Jenson Button the fastest Michelin runner in 1m 32.310s. Bridgestone, it seemed, had made another jump. And so it proved, as the red cars went on to annex the front row of the grid. There were no prizes for guessing who occupied the second row either, for if it's Japan it's Toyota playing games.

As Massa just edged Schumacher to take the second pole position of his career, with 1m 29.599s to the German's 1m 29.711s, Ralf Schumacher and Jarno Trulli were third and fourth on 1m 29.989s to 1m 30.039s. That immediately prompted a rash of betting on just how soon the red-and-white cars would be stopping for fuel.

The Toyotas' presence ahead of its pair of drivers was the last thing that Renault wanted. Alonso and Fisichella closed the gap to Ferrari with sterling efforts, but respective laps of 1m 30.371s and 1m 30.599s left them only fifth and sixth. This was particularly bad news for Alonso, who desperately needed to get ahead of Schumacher, rather than having to fight his way by rivals who were not in the title hunt just to catch a glimpse of him.

Worse still, in second qualifying Schumacher had been fastest with a dramatic lap of 1m 28.954s, which may now stand as the fastest F1 lap that was ever recorded at Suzuka. 'There is so much grip and they fly through the Esses!' the German said. 'It's funny when you think we are running only V8 engines...'

Ferrari thus started exactly where it wanted to and with Renault where it would have liked its cars to be, had there been a choice. Schumacher was all smiles afterwards, as befitted a man who seemed on the verge of winning his eighth world championship. 'We are on the first row, Renaults the third,' he grinned. 'That's a very good start for us. Felipe did a great job and I'm pretty happy where I am. Having Alonso behind me is more important than being behind my team-mate.'

Not surprisingly, the increasingly impressive Massa was also pretty happy. 'This is a fantastic circuit and I really enjoy driving here,' he said. 'I managed a good lap and the car is behaving very well at the moment.'

On this long and challenging circuit, which most of the drivers love, the lap times were similar team by team. As the animals came in two by two, Jenson Button took seventh for Honda with 1m 30.992s, ahead of Rubens Barrichello on 1m 31.478s.

The first break in that pattern came with Nick Heidfeld, who made it through from the second session for BMW Sauber to take ninth place with 1m 31.513s. Instead of team-mate Robert Kubica sitting alongside him on the fifth row, he had Nico Rosberg, who staged a bit of a resurgence and made full use of his Bridgestones to lap his Williams-Cosworth in 1m 31.856s.

Kimi Räikkönen's chances of getting into the third session had evaporated when he slid wide pushing too hard in the Spoon Curve. He had been only 15th after the first session, and thus dangerously close to elimination, and now he was left only 11th for McLaren on 1m 30.827s at the track on which he had won so brilliantly the previous year.

Robert Kubica duly lined up alongside him, having similarly lost control of his BMW-Sauber and very nearly brushed the bridge wall on the exit to Degner Two on his final attempt. He thus had to fall back on a lap of 1m 31.094s. Pedro de la Rosa failed to get his McLaren through to the final session, lapping it in 1m 31.254s, which was just enough to stay ahead of Mark Webber. The Australian was another to survive a scare at Degner Two and his previous 1m 31.276s left him 14th.

Tonio Liuzzi did a fine job as the only one of the four Red Bull drivers to escape from the first session, pushing his recalcitrant Toro Rosso to 1m 31.943s. Christijan Albers also made it through, for Spyker, to take an eventual 16th place on 1m 33.750s.

David Coulthard was the first of the first-session failures on 1m 32.252s for Red Bull, with team-mate Robert Doornbos alongside him on the grid on 1m 32.402s. Scott Speed was next up on 1m 32.867s, after an off in Spoon Curve. Takuma Sato beat Tiago Monteiro, Super Aguri versus Spyker, with 1m 33.666s to 1m 33.709s, and Sakon Yamamoto failed to get a lap after setting the fastest sector-one time and then half spinning and stalling at the Spoon Curve early on.

FOR 36 laps of the Japanese Grand Prix, Michael Schumacher seemed implacably on course to securing an eighth world championship title. From his place on the front row of the grid, Schumacher gave immediate chase to pole-sitting team-mate Felipe Massa, who got away faster on the cleaner side of the road. But on a day when the title was at stake nobody expected the Brazilian to stay in front and, sure enough, he subtly surrendered the lead as they went into the start of the third lap.

Thereafter the race seemed Schumacher's to lose rather than Fernando Alonso's to win.

The Spaniard was on feisty form. Knowing that he had to get at least one of the Toyotas that started ahead of him before the end of the opening lap, he took a significant risk in overtaking Jarno Trulli's going into the first corner, before settling down to chase Ralf Schumacher's.

Already the lap times revealed that whatever advantage Bridgestone had enjoyed in qualifying had now been equalised, but where Schumacher had a clear road ahead of him, Alonso's was full of red and white. Nevertheless, Schumacher was not dropping Massa and nor was he extending by much the 3.5s gap the Ferraris had opened up over the Toyota.

The first sign that things might be going Alonso's way came on the 13th lap. That was when he made a major effort going into Turn One and squeezed by Schumacher Jr and when Massa suddenly swept into the pits for what seemed like an early fuel stop.

It transpired that the Brazilian was three laps ahead of his intended schedule, having picked up a punctured rear tyre, so that left the two title protagonists going at it *mano a mano.* Schumacher, of course, had the advantage. Alonso refuelled on lap 15, the Ferrari running three laps more, but Massa's

problems made him history as far as the Renault driver was concerned and all Alonso had to concentrate on was keeping up the pressure on Schumacher.

This he did. The gap between the two leaders was never less than 4.2s (on lap 28) or greater than 5.9s (on lap 34), fluctuating as they ran through traffic, but if anything the Renault was fractionally faster. If only it had been able to qualify faster on its Michelins, we would have had a wheel-to-wheel battle.

'In the second stint the gap was more or less the same, depending on traffic, and I was thinking it was possible to win. Why not?' Alonso said. 'We were only halfway through the race.'

Everything became academic on the 37th lap, however, when the unthinkable happened. Going through the Degner corners, Schumacher's Ferrari suddenly trailed a wisp, then a plume, of oil smoke as its engine exploded under the strain, just as Alonso's had at Monza. It was so unexpected that onlookers had to make mental checks: one of the Spykers? No. Massa? No. It's Schumacher!

When he came across the stricken Ferrari, Alonso admitted to similar thoughts and that initially he had thought it was one of the Dutch cars. 'From a distance it looked more orange than red, so immediately I braked, thinking there might be oil on the track.' He had already survived a moment there earlier on while chasing Ralf Schumacher. 'I didn't realise until we were side by side that it was Michael…'

He also confessed that he had permitted himself a smile of satisfaction. 'I have had so many problems these last couple of races and I needed to recover these unlucky moments. But Michael was leading the race and I just didn't believe what I was seeing. A mechanical problem for a Ferrari car doesn't happen often. So after the pace of my car, that was the second surprise – the biggest one of the race, for sure.'

As Renault immediately instructed its man to wind down the revs, Schumacher was remarkably philosophical and bore the crushing disappointment with great dignity. There was no throwing of the helmet or balaclava as he removed them track-side, nor even any real outward sign of emotion. When he got back to the pits it was he who consoled his heartbroken mechanics. One minute they had been headed for triumph; the next the great dream was all but over.

'We are a great team,' Michael said, suddenly a man mellowed and made greater by failure. 'Our guys are the best and I have a great affection for everyone at Ferrari and am always more than satisfied in the way we work. Incidents like today's can happen and they are part of racing. You win together but you also lose together. Today we did our best. I was leading the race and then my engine broke. That's the simplest way to sum it up. That is Formula 1.'

From then on it was just a matter for Alonso of keeping it all tidy and avoiding mistakes because Massa was some 16s adrift, doubtless warned by Ferrari to turn down his own engine just in case. In the closing stages Giancarlo Fisichella began to catch him, but Massa was equally safe.

Fisichella had not made a great start, dropping a place to Jenson Button, whom he was not able to pass until the fifth lap. Then he had to chase after Trulli's Toyota until it refuelled on lap 12. He gained another place when Schumacher Jr refuelled on 13, and then stopped himself on 14, dropping all the way back to ninth. His second stop finally put him ahead of the Toyotas for good but still behind Kimi Räikkönen and the pesky Button, until they stopped on the 41st and 37th laps

respectively. That finally settled the last podium place in his favour, much to the delight of Renault, which regained its advantage in the constructors' championship.

Button was a distant fourth, well ahead of Räikkönen, by the flag. And he was reasonably pleased with the Honda's performance because the result continued the team's run of consecutive points finishes, Jenson taking his sixth in succession. Only Michael Schumacher had scored more points than him since Hockenheim. What a contrast the second half of the Englishman's season was to the first.

'We had a solid race and I think we did the best job possible given the fight going on for the championship,' he said. 'We just haven't quite got enough to beat the two contenders right now, but we will get there, trust me!'

Interestingly, the RA106 was good enough for fifth-fastest lap in 1m 33.451s, which put it in the same territory as Massa's Ferrari (1m 33.296s), Räikkönen's McLaren (1m 33.344s), Robert Kubica's BMW (1m 33.509s), Fisichella's Renault (1m 33.564s), and the Toyotas of Ralf Schumacher (1m 33.607s) and Jarno Trulli (1m 33.866s).

The final points went to Räikkönen, Trulli, Schumacher Jr and BMW Sauber's Nick Heidfeld.

Räikkönen drove a hard race for McLaren, but the MP4-21 was a mere shadow of the previous year's car and the team rued its choice of Michelin's softer tyre. Like the Renaults and Hondas, the silver cars were better over long runs, but they still lacked the pace to challenge for the win.

There was unhappiness in the Toyota camp, where team principal Tsutomu Tomita made no bones about things and

DIARY

It is announced that former Michelin sporting director Pierre Dupasquier will be awarded France's *Légion d'Honneur* by sports minister Jean-François Lamour.

As the F1 circus bids a fond farewell to Suzuka after 20 great years, headed for Toyota-owned Fuji Speedway in 2007, there is talk of a Pacific GP at Suzuka. However, a Toyota vice president says that his company has no intention of letting Suzuka back into the grand prix game during the duration of its five-year contract.

Following the incidents during wheel changes in Hungary and China, Renault alters its pit crew in Japan, with the right-rear wheel-man assigned to different duties.

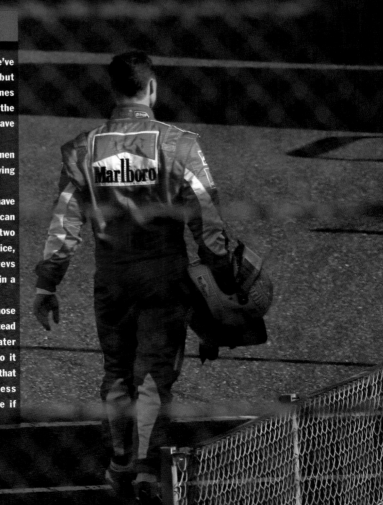

SO WHY DID MICHAEL'S ENGINE BREAK?

THERE was, it must be said, a great deal of talk in the paddock and the press room after the race of 'natural justice' following Michael Schumacher's engine problem. And also talk that such things lay beyond the control of anyone with an interest in nudging the championship in any particular direction.

But what went wrong? Where Cosworth's FA-2006 V8 was able to run over 20,000 rpm right from the start of the season, Ferrari had a lot of trouble running anywhere close to 19,000 during testing and lost several engines in the final test in Bahrain. For the first three or four races its V8 accordingly ran in a detuned state just so it would live.

Almost certainly, given the way the pace of the Ferraris and Renaults evened out in the race, Michael was having to push his engine hard to maintain his lead over Alonso, and therein lay his undoing.

'The Suzuka problem was a one-off, we hope,' technical boss Ross Brawn said. 'It was a failure of the top end of a valve where it connects to the collets around the pneumatic piston; nothing we've seen before, so we've been super-vigilant – we always are – but super-vigilant on the build of these engines to try and make sure that we can avoid the problem occurring again, but we don't have a complete explanation for what happened.'

Brawn went on to explain Ferrari's regimen with two-race engines in practice, qualifying and the race.

'Over the life of two-race engines, we have a certain number of higher-rev laps we can do and they are generally spread over two races. I think all of us run low revs in practice, medium revs in a race and then high revs in qualifying, and occasionally higher revs in a race if you need them.

'Of course, having a one-race engine, those higher revs are available over one race instead of two, so if we need to, there's a greater opportunity to run revs, but we won't do it unless we have to and we've always taken that approach: you don't use the revs unless you have to but we know they're there if we need them.'

frankly described sixth and seventh places as 'hugely disappointing' after the team had expected a podium finish.

Ralf compounded things when he complained that he had been faster but that his team-mate had not let him past and, curiously, Toyota seemed to support this argument with a little public criticism of its better-placed driver.

Trulli, who complained of an unspecified problem that affected his car's handling – tyre graining, it subsequently emerged – took what seemed a reasonable view: that an overtaking move would have proved Schumacher's point. But many cynical observers took all of this to be something of a smokescreen to obscure the fact that the qualifying performance had been another publicity stunt, with the drivers' argument a product of their near collision in the first corner.

As things would transpire in Brazil, Heidfeld's point here for BMW-Sauber would be crucial, for Toyota's five-point haul had brought it dangerously close to fifth place overall in the constructors' stakes. But the point might just as easily have gone to Robert Kubica, who drove a very feisty race in an F1.06 that proved surprisingly competitive.

Heidfeld had struggled for much of his final stint with graining on Michelin's softer tyre, whereas Kubica had opted for the harder option. He had a major moment at Degner Two on the 31st lap, losing 10s to his team-mate, but was able to regain all of it as he set the race's sixth-fastest lap and was right on Heidfeld's tail for the remaining laps.

For BMW Sauber and Toyota, Brazil would be as critical a race as it was for Renault and Ferrari.

Nico Rosberg's resurgence continued with a forceful drive to tenth for Williams but team-mate Mark Webber, after complaining of 'massive' power understeer, ran wide exiting the chicane on the 39th lap, couldn't get it back and crashed heavily into the outside wall.

The Australian's new team, Red Bull, also had a miserable race. Its two RB2s were embroiled in a great scrap for 14th with the Toro Rossos of Tonio Liuzzi and Scott Speed and Christijan Albers' Spyker, but David Coulthard had to retire when he lost fourth gear and team-mate Robert Doornbos ended up 'winning' the quintet scrap by placing 13th. Liuzzi had a brush with Webber on the opening lap that upset the handling of his STR01, spun through 360 degrees exiting the chicane on the third because of a graining problem and lost four places, and then fought back for the rest of the afternoon to finish 14th. Speed had the upper hand on all of them for some time, but dropped it at the Degner Curve and eventually retired with power steering failure.

Super Aguri was delighted to bring both of its SA06s to the finish in front of the huge home crowd. Interestingly, those spectators who had not opted for Honda garb had chosen to back Super Aguri; Toyota-clad fans were few and far between.

Spyker had mixed fortunes. Albers' strong run ended spectacularly on the 20th lap when his rear suspension broke in an explosion of parts that tore off the rear wing and the right-rear wheel. The Dutchman was extremely lucky the incident happened exiting the chicane, where he could pull his three-wheeler straight into the pits. Had it occurred farther around the track – say, at the back of the pits, in the Degner Curves or in 130R (even though these days the latter is easy flat for pretty much everyone and not the great challenge it used to be) – it could have been a lot worse. Tiago Monteiro's crew changed him from a single-stop strategy to a two-stopper as the race progressed, but tyre and balance problems prevented him from really getting up with the fight in which his team-mate was embroiled.

So now Alonso needed only to finish eighth in Brazil, regardless of what Schumacher and Ferrari might achieve, to retain his crown. But he did not accept that things were over.

'I don't say that I have one hand on the trophy, not at all,' he insisted. 'It's a bit too early to realise what happened today and for sure the same thing can happen in Brazil and you can lose everything. We [the team and I] always thought the title would be decided there and for sure now we are in a much better position than before. When we were equal on points we needed to beat Michael and Ferrari, and it was not easy to approach this race with that pressure. Now we only need a few points, but we need to finish the race and sometimes that is not the case. You never know what's gonna happen. We need to have our maximum concentration and professionalism, and see what happens.'

For Michael, however, things were a lot clearer. He had accepted that it was over. 'We are nine points behind in the constructors' classification and we will do all we can to win this title in Brazil. As for the drivers', it is lost. I don't want to head off for a race hoping that my rival has to retire. That is not the way in which I want to win the title.'

David Tremayne

Below: The sense of relief on Alonso's face is obvious as he clutches his trophy.

Bottom: Nick Heidfeld took a crucial point to put BMW Sauber into fifth place in the constructors' championship.
Photographs: James Moy/www.crashpa.net

FUJI TELEVISION
JAPANESE GRAND PRIX

SUZUKA 6–8 OCTOBER 2006

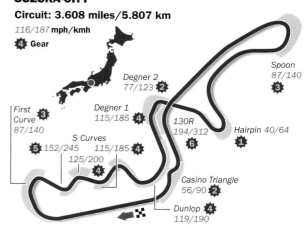

SUZUKA INTERNATIONAL RACING COURSE, SUZUKA-CITY

Circuit: 3.608 miles/5.807 km

116/187 mph/kmh

🔧 Gear

Spoon 87/140 ③

Degner 2 77/123 ②

Degner 1 115/185 ④

First Curve 87/140 ③

130R 194/312 ⑥

Hairpin 40/64 ①

S Curves 152/245 ⑤ 115/185 ④
125/200 ④

Casino Triangle 56/90 ②

Dunlop 119/190 ④

Photograph: James Moy/www.crashpa.net

RACE RESULTS

Pos.	Driver	Nat.	No.	Entrant	Car/Engine	Tyres	Laps	Time/Retirement	Speed (mph/km/h)	Gap to leader	Fastest race lap	
1	Fernando Alonso	E	1	Mild Seven Renault F1 Team	Renault R26-RS26 V8	M	53	1h 23m 53.413s	136.690/219.982		1m 32.676s	14
2	Felipe Massa	BR	6	Scuderia Ferrari Marlboro	Ferrari 248 F1-056 V8	B	53	1h 24m 09.564s	136.253/219.278	+16.151s	1m 33.296s	37
3	Giancarlo Fisichella	I	2	Mild Seven Renault F1 Team	Renault R26-RS26 V8	M	53	1h 24m 17.366s	136.043/218.940	+23.953s	1m 33.451s	35
4	Jenson Button	GB	12	Lucky Strike Honda Racing F1 Team	Honda RA106-RA806E V8	M	53	1h 24m 27.514s	135.771/218.502	+34.101s	1m 33.451s	35
5	Kimi Räikkönen	FIN	3	Team McLaren Mercedes	McLaren MP4-21-Mercedes FO 108S V8	M	53	1h 24m 37.009s	135.517/218.093	+43.596s	1m 33.344s	24
6	Jarno Trulli	I	8	Panasonic Toyota Racing	Toyota TF106B-RVX-06 V8	B	53	1h 24m 40.130s	135.433/217.959	+46.717s	1m 33.866s	2
7	Ralf Schumacher	D	7	Panasonic Toyota Racing	Toyota TF106B-RVX-06 V8	B	53	1h 24m 42.282s	135.376/217.867	+48.869s	1m 33.607s	2
8	Nick Heidfeld	D	16	BMW Sauber F1 Team	BMW Sauber F1.06-BMW P86 V8	M	53	1h 25m 09.508s	134.655/216.706	+1m 16.095s	1m 34.525s	31
9	Robert Kubica	POL	17	BMW Sauber F1 Team	BMW Sauber F1.06-BMW P86 V8	M	53	1h 25m 10.345s	134.632/216.670	+1m 16.932s	1m 33.509s	39
10	Nico Rosberg	D	10	WilliamsF1 Team	Williams FW28-Cosworth CA2006 V8	B	52			+1 lap	1m 34.802s	33
11	Pedro de la Rosa	E	4	Team McLaren Mercedes	McLaren MP4-21-Mercedes FO 108S V8	M	52			+1 lap	1m 34.120s	22
12	Rubens Barrichello	BR	11	Lucky Strike Honda Racing F1 Team	Honda RA106-RA806E V8	M	52			+1 lap	1m 34.071s	40
13	Robert Doornbos	NL	15	Red Bull Racing	Red Bull RB2-Ferrari 056 V8	M	52			+1 lap	1m 35.099s	37
14	Vitantonio Liuzzi	I	20	Scuderia Toro Rosso	Toro Rosso STR01-Cosworth TJ2005-2 V10	M	52			+1 lap	1m 34.131s	22
15	Takuma Sato	J	22	Super Aguri F1 Team	Super Aguri SA06-Honda RA806E V8	B	52			+1 lap	1m 35.082s	26
16	Tiago Monteiro	P	18	Spyker MF1 Team	Spyker M16-Toyota RVX-06 V8	B	51			+2 laps	1m 35.260s	27
17	Sakon Yamamoto	J	23	Super Aguri F1 Team	Super Aguri SA06-Honda RA806E V8	B	50			+3 laps	1m 35.594s	22
18	Scott Speed	USA	21	Scuderia Toro Rosso	Toro Rosso STR01-Cosworth TJ2005-2 V10	M	48	Steering		+5 laps	1m 34.560s	37
	Mark Webber	AUS	9	WilliamsF1 Team	Williams FW28-Cosworth CA2006 V8	B	39	Accident			1m 35.092s	19
	Michael Schumacher	D	5	Scuderia Ferrari Marlboro	Ferrari 248 F1-056 V8	B	36	Engine			1m 32.792s	32
	David Coulthard	GB	14	Red Bull Racing	Red Bull RB2-Ferrari 056 V8	M	35	Gearbox			1m 35.052s	20
	Christijan Albers	NL	19	Spyker MF1 Team	Spyker M16-Toyota RVX-06 V8	B	20	Driveshaft/rear suspension			1m 36.036s	19

Fastest lap: Fernando Alonso on lap 14, 1m 32.676s, 140.165 mph/225.572 km/h.

Lap record: Kimi Räikkönen (McLaren MP4-20-Mercedes Benz V10) on lap 44, 1m 31.540s, 141.904 mph/228.376 km/h (2005).

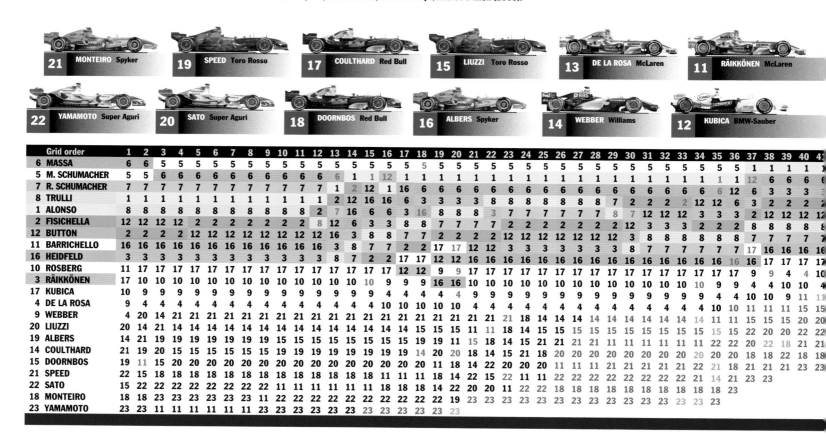

Grid order	1	2	3	4	5	6	7	8	9	10	11	12	13	14	15	16	17	18	19	20	21	22	23	24	25	26	27	28	29	30	31	32	33	34	35	36	37	38	39	40	41
6 MASSA	6	6	5	5	5	5	5	5	5	5	5	5	5	5	5	5	5	5	5	5	5	5	5	5	5	5	5	5	5	5	5	5	5	5	5	5	1	1	1	1	
5 M. SCHUMACHER	5	5	6	6	6	6	6	6	6	6	6	6	1	1	12	1	1	1	1	1	1	1	1	1	1	1	1	1	1	1	1	1	1	1	1	1	12	6	6	6	
7 R. SCHUMACHER	7	7	7	7	7	7	7	7	7	7	1	2	12	1	16	6	6	6	6	6	6	6	6	6	6	6	6	6	6	6	6	12	6	12	6	3	3	3		
8 TRULLI	1	1	1	1	1	1	1	1	1	1	2	12	16	16	3	3	3	3	8	8	8	2	2	2	2	12	12	6	2	2	2	2									
1 ALONSO	8	8	8	8	8	8	8	8	8	8	2	7	16	6	6	3	16		3	7	7	7	7	7	7	8	7	12	12	12	3	3	3	2	12	12	12	12			
2 FISICHELLA	12	12	12	12	2	2	2	2	2	2	8	12	6	3	3	16	8	7	7	7	2	2	2	2	2	12	3	3	3	2	2	2	8	12	12	12					
12 BUTTON	2	2	2	12	12	12	12	12	12	12	16	3	8	8	7	7	2	2	2	2	12	12	12	12	12	3	8	8	8	8	8	7	7	7	7						
11 BARRICHELLO	16	16	16	16	16	16	16	16	16	16	3	8	7	7	2	2	17	17	12	12	3	3	3	3	3	3	7	7	7	7	7	17	16	16	16						
16 HEIDFELD	3	3	3	3	3	3	3	3	3	3	7	2	2	17	12	12	16	16	16	16	16	16	16	16	16	16	16	16	16	16	16	16	17	17	17						
10 ROSBERG	11	17	17	17	17	17	17	17	17	17	17	17	17	12	9	17	17	17	17	17	17	17	17	17	17	17	17	17	17	17	9	9	4	10							
3 RÄIKKÖNEN	17	10	10	10	10	10	10	10	10	10	10	10	10	10	10	9	9	16	16	10	10	10	10	10	10	10	10	10	10	10	9	9	4	4							
17 KUBICA	10	9	9	9	9	9	9	9	9	9	9	4	4	4	4	4	4	9	9	9	9	9	9	9	9	9	9	9	9	9	4	10	10	11							
4 DE LA ROSA	9	4	4	4	4	4	4	4	4	4	4	10	10	10	10	10	4	4	4	4	4	4	4	4	4	4	4	4	10	10	11	11	11	15							
9 WEBBER	4	20	14	21	21	21	21	21	21	21	21	21	21	21	21	21	18	14	14	14	14	14	14	11	11	15	15	15	20	20											
20 LIUZZI	20	14	21	14	14	14	14	14	14	14	14	14	14	14	11	18	14	14	14	14	14	14	14	11	11	15	15	15	22	20	20	22									
19 ALBERS	14	19	19	19	19	19	19	19	19	15	15	15	15	15	15	14	21	21	21	11	11	11	11	15	15	15	22	20	22	22											
14 COULTHARD	21	19	20	15	15	15	15	15	15	19	19	19	19	14	20	20	14	14	21	20	20	20	20	20	20	22	20	18	21	21											
15 DOORNBOS	19	11	15	20	20	20	20	20	20	20	20	20	20	20	11	11	20	20	20	20	11	11	11	21	21	21	21	21	21	23											
21 SPEED	22	15	18	18	18	18	18	18	18	18	18	11	11	11	14	15	22	11	11	22	22	22	22	22	22	22	23	23	23												
22 SATO	15	22	22	22	22	22	11	11	11	11	11	18	18	18	18	22	11	22	22	22	20	11	21	23	23	23	14	21	23												
18 MONTEIRO	18	18	11	11	11	11	22	22	22	22	11	23	23	23	23	23	18	18	18	18	18	18	18	18	18	18	23														
23 YAMAMOTO	23	23	11	11	11	11	11	11	23	23	23	23	23	23	23	23	23	23	23	23	23	23	23	23	23	23															

258

PRACTICE 1 (FRIDAY)

Heavy, light rain (track 21–23ºC, air 21–22ºC)

Pos.	Driver	Laps	Time
1	Anthony Davidson	18	1m 45.349s
2	Neel Jani	21	1m 46.138s
3	Sebastian Vettel	20	1m 46.585s
4	Michael Ammermüller	21	1m 47.162s
5	Adrian Sutil	21	1m 47.773s
6	Scott Speed	7	1m 47.814s
7	Christijan Albers	6	1m 47.838s
8	Franck Montagny	13	1m 47.918s
9	Alexander Wurz	19	1m 47.919s
10	Takuma Sato	11	1m 48.042s
11	Sakon Yamamoto	9	1m 50.479s
12	Mark Webber	1	No time
13	Nico Rosberg	1	No time
14	Kimi Räikkönen	1	No time
15	Vitantonio Liuzzi	2	No time
16	Robert Doornbos	1	No time
17	Robert Kubica	1	No time
18	David Coulthard	1	No time
19	Fernando Alonso	1	No time
20	Nick Heidfeld	1	No time
21	Giancarlo Fisichella	1	No time
22	Tiago Monteiro	4	No time
23	Pedro de la Rosa	1	No time
24	Rubens Barrichello	1	No time
25	Jarno Trulli	1	No time
26	Ralf Schumacher	1	No time
27	Jenson Button	1	No time

PRACTICE 2 (FRIDAY)

Wet, drying (track 24–25ºC, air 23–24ºC)

Pos.	Driver	Laps	Time
1	Giancarlo Fisichella	8	1m 34.337s
2	Felipe Massa	10	1m 34.408s
3	Michael Schumacher	10	1m 34.565s
4	Fernando Alonso	5	1m 34.863s
5	Anthony Davidson	23	1m 34.906s
6	Sebastian Vettel	30	1m 34.912s
7	Jenson Button	6	1m 35.002s
8	Pedro de la Rosa	6	1m 35.064s
9	Jarno Trulli	12	1m 35.343s
10	Kimi Räikkönen	5	1m 35.367s
11	Ralf Schumacher	12	1m 35.375s
12	Michael Ammermüller	25	1m 35.433s
13	Rubens Barrichello	10	1m 35.528s
14	Mark Webber	5	1m 35.866s
15	Nico Rosberg	10	1m 36.176s
16	Christijan Albers	4	1m 36.180s
17	Alexander Wurz	25	1m 36.234s
18	Robert Kubica	5	1m 36.299s
19	Franck Montagny	20	1m 37.354s
20	Vitantonio Liuzzi	15	1m 37.441s
21	Scott Speed	16	1m 37.501s
22	David Coulthard	6	1m 37.596s
23	Tiago Monteiro	9	1m 37.702s
24	Neel Jani	26	1m 37.741s
25	Robert Doornbos	9	1m 37.788s
26	Takuma Sato	18	1m 38.533s
27	Nick Heidfeld	5	1m 38.779s
28	Sakon Yamamoto	14	1m 38.955s
29	Adrian Sutil	14	1m 43.914s

QUALIFYING (SATURDAY)

Cloudy, windy (track 31–33ºC, air 23–24ºC)

Pos.	Driver	First	Second	Third
1	Felipe Massa	1m 30.112s	1m 29.830s	1m 29.599s
2	Michael Schumacher	1m 31.279s	1m 28.954s	1m 29.711s
3	Ralf Schumacher	1m 30.595s	1m 30.299s	1m 29.989s
4	Jarno Trulli	1m 30.420s	1m 30.204s	1m 30.039s
5	Fernando Alonso	1m 30.976s	1m 30.357s	1m 30.371s
6	Giancarlo Fisichella	1m 31.696s	1m 30.306s	1m 30.599s
7	Jenson Button	1m 30.847s	1m 30.268s	1m 30.992s
8	Rubens Barrichello	1m 31.972s	1m 30.598s	1m 31.478s
9	Nick Heidfeld	1m 31.811s	1m 30.470s	1m 31.513s
10	Nico Rosberg	1m 30.585s	1m 30.321s	1m 31.856s
11	Kimi Räikkönen	1m 32.080s	1m 30.827s	
12	Robert Kubica	1m 31.204s	1m 31.094s	
13	Pedro de la Rosa	1m 31.581s	1m 31.254s	
14	Mark Webber	1m 31.647s	1m 31.276s	
15	Vitantonio Liuzzi	1m 31.741s	1m 31.943s	
16	Christijan Albers	1m 32.221s	1m 33.750s	
17	David Coulthard	1m 32.252s		
18	Robert Doornbos	1m 32.402s		
19	Scott Speed	1m 32.867s		
20	Takuma Sato	1m 33.666s		
21	Tiago Monteiro	1m 33.709s		
22	Sakon Yamamoto	No time		

PRACTICE 3 (SATURDAY)

Sunny, cloudy, windy (track 32–34ºC, air 23–24ºC)

Pos.	Driver	Laps	Time
1	Michael Schumacher	13	1m 30.653s
2	Ralf Schumacher	15	1m 31.863s
3	Jenson Button	12	1m 32.310s
4	Giancarlo Fisichella	13	1m 32.527s
5	Fernando Alonso	14	1m 32.555s
6	Nick Heidfeld	15	1m 32.590s
7	Nico Rosberg	18	1m 32.730s
8	Kimi Räikkönen	12	1m 32.730s
9	Robert Kubica	17	1m 32.787s
10	Felipe Massa	15	1m 32.790s
11	Vitantonio Liuzzi	20	1m 32.977s
12	Pedro de la Rosa	12	1m 33.163s
13	Scott Speed	20	1m 33.213s
14	Christijan Albers	23	1m 33.270s
15	Mark Webber	17	1m 33.339s
16	David Coulthard	16	1m 33.451s
17	Robert Doornbos	12	1m 33.663s
18	Rubens Barrichello	16	1m 33.748s
19	Tiago Monteiro	19	1m 33.824s
20	Jarno Trulli	15	1m 34.118s
21	Sakon Yamamoto	10	1m 34.646s
22	Takuma Sato	20	1m 34.727s

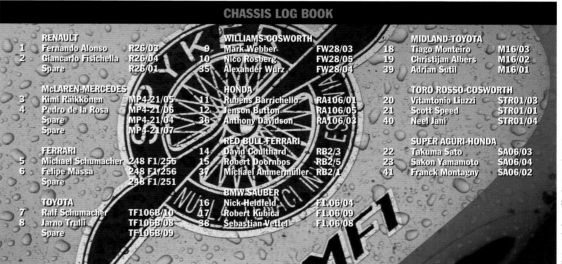

CHASSIS LOG BOOK

RENAULT
1 Fernando Alonso — R26/03
2 Giancarlo Fisichella — R26/04
Spare — R26/01

McLAREN-MERCEDES
3 Kimi Räikkönen — MP4-21/05
4 Pedro de la Rosa — MP4-21/06
Spare — MP4-21/04
Spare — MP4-21/07

FERRARI
5 Michael Schumacher — 248 F1/256
6 Felipe Massa — 248 F1/256
Spare — 248 F1/251

TOYOTA
7 Ralf Schumacher — TF106B/10
8 Jarno Trulli — TF106B/08
Spare — TF106B/09

WILLIAMS-COSWORTH
9 Mark Webber — FW28/03
10 Nico Rosberg — FW28/05
35 Alexander Wurz — FW28/04

HONDA
11 Rubens Barrichello — RA106/01
12 Jenson Button — RA106/05
36 Anthony Davidson — RA106/03

RED BULL-FERRARI
14 David Coulthard — RB2/3
15 Robert Doornbos — RB2/5
37 Michael Ammermüller — RB2/1

BMW SAUBER
16 Nick Heidfeld — F1.06/04
17 Robert Kubica — F1.06/09
38 Sebastian Vettel — F1.06/08

MIDLAND-TOYOTA
18 Tiago Monteiro — M16/03
19 Christijan Albers — M16/02
39 Adrian Sutil — M16/01

TORO ROSSO-COSWORTH
20 Vitantonio Liuzzi — STR01/03
21 Scott Speed — STR01/01
40 Neel Jani — STR01/04

SUPER AGURI-HONDA
22 Takuma Sato — SA06/03
23 Sakon Yamamoto — SA06/04
41 Franck Montagny — SA06/02

Photograph: James Moy/www.crashpa.net

9 HEIDFELD BMW-Sauber

7 BUTTON Honda

5 ALONSO Renault

3 R. SCHUMACHER Toyota

1 MASSA Ferrari

10 ROSBERG Williams

8 BARRICHELLO Honda

6 FISICHELLA Renault

4 TRULLI Toyota

2 M. SCHUMACHER Ferrari

RACE DISTANCE:
53 laps
191.117 miles/307.573 km

RACE WEATHER:
Sunny, windy, cloudy
track 31–33ºC, air 22–24ºC

42	43	44	45	46	47	48	49	50	51	52	53	º
1	1	1	1	1	1	1	1	1	1	1	1	1
6	6	6	6	6	6	6	6	6	6	6	6	2
2	2	2	2	2	2	2	2	2	2	2	2	3
12	12	12	12	12	12	12	12	12	12	12	12	4
3	3	3	3	3	3	3	3	3	3	3	3	5
8	8	8	8	8	8	8	8	8	8	8	8	6
7	7	7	7	7	7	7	7	7	7	7	7	7
16	16	16	16	16	16	16	16	16	16	16	16	8
17	17	17	17	17	17	17	17	17	17	17	17	
10	10	10	10	10	10	10	10	10	10	10		
4	4	4	4	4	4	4	4	4	4			
11	11	11	11	11	11	11	11	11	11	11		
15	15	15	15	15	15	15	15	15	15	15		
20	20	20	20	20	20	20	20	20	20	20		
22	22	22	22	22	22	22	22	22	22	22		
21	21	21	21	21	21	18	18	18	18			
18	18	18	18	18	18	21	23	23				
23	23	23	23	23	23	23						

Pit stop
One lap or more behind leader

FOR THE RECORD

T-Car

150th POINT: Toyota

POINTS

DRIVERS

1	Fernando Alonso	126
2	Michael Schumacher	116
3	Felipe Massa	70
4	Giancarlo Fisichella	69
5	Kimi Räikkönen	61
6	Jenson Button	50
7	Rubens Barrichello	28
8	Juan Pablo Montoya	26
9	Nick Heidfeld	23
10	Ralf Schumacher	20
11	Pedro de la Rosa	18
12	Jarno Trulli	15
13	David Coulthard	14
14	Mark Webber	7
15	Jacques Villeneuve	7
16	Robert Kubica	6
17	Nico Rosberg	4
18	Christian Klien	2
19	Vitantonio Liuzzi	1

CONSTRUCTORS

1	Renault	195
2	Ferrari	186
3	McLaren	105
4	Honda	78
5	BMW Sauber	36
6	Toyota	35
7	Red Bull	16
8	Williams	11
9	Toro Rosso	1

Photographs: James Moy/www.crashpa.net

BRAZILIAN GP

INTERLAGOS

Main: Wearing the serenely confident smile of a double world champion, Fernando Alonso tosses his Renault team cap into the admiring crowd after clinching his second title crown at the legendary Interlagos circuit.
Photograph: James Moy/www.crashpa.net

Left: Renault and Michelin personnel delight in their mutual championship success. Sadly Michelin will not be back to defend its crown in 2007.
Photograph: Jad Sherif/WRI

Right: The roadside advertising hoarding on the route out of São Paulo to Interlagos says it all.

Photograph: Jean-François Galeron/WRI

Below: McLaren majority shareholders Mansour Ojjeh and Ron Dennis reflect on a disappointing season.

Photograph: Paul-Henri Cahier

Centre: Possibly the final grand prix for Cosworth, stalwart of F1 for the past 39 years.

Photograph: Paul-Henri Cahier

Above: Goodbye as well to Lucky Strike, original bankroller of the British American Racing Team, now Honda Racing.

Right: Michael Schumacher prepares to race. But for the last time?

Photographs: James Moy/www.crashpa.net

INTERLAGOS QUALIFYING

Bitter-sweet. That's the best way to describe qualifying for Ferrari for Michael Schumacher's last-ever grand prix.

All through the first and second sessions the two Ferraris had been quick, swapping fastest lap. At the start of the third session, as is their habit, Schumacher and Felipe Massa had headed the field out of the pits. But as the Brazilian surged onto the back straight, Schumacher's car faltered, then stuttered its way back to the pits, where it remained for the rest of the 15 minutes.

There was a problem in the fuel system; clearly it couldn't have been the mechanical pump, because that would have stopped him straight away, but something was restricting the feed and the Ferrari mechanics were unable to do anything about it in the time available.

For the German, this was the knock-out qualifying format at its most excruciating. In his 249th and final grand prix he desperately needed to win to have the remotest chance of beating Fernando Alonso and now he had a new mountain to scale come the race.

While the former champ would thus start tenth on the grid, regardless of what anyone else did, Massa was in a world of his own as he stormed around his home track to take pole easily with a lap of 1m 10.680s. 'I was lucky to get a tow from Nick [Heidfeld],' he said cheerfully, 'but in any case it was a great lap and it's fantastic to be on pole at my home GP. The car is just fantastic and the tyres were working really well with the sunshine. It was fantastic to see people around waving their hands, to hear them screaming. The Brazilian people are very hot about F1!'

The eight cars sat between the two Ferraris showed varying degrees of speed. Kimi Räikkönen said he was very pleased with the way his McLaren had got better with each qualifying session, after taking the other front row slot, but his lap of 1m 11.299s was a long way from Massa's, even if Michelin, in its final outing, expected to be quicker in the race than in qualifying. In that respect it was Suzuka all over again, albeit with a smaller gap between the French manufacturer and dominant Bridgestone.

Jarno Trulli's third place on the grid, with 1m 11.328s, was another indication of Bridgestone's superiority, given that nobody believed that the red-and-white car was genuinely a match for McLaren and Renault, which had champion-elect Fernando Alonso in fourth place after a lap of 1m 11.567s on Michelin tyres that had been selected with relatively low ambient and track temperatures in mind.

The Spaniard said he was very happy with his lap and well he might have been given that all he needed from the weekend was a single point for eighth place — and that assuming that Michael managed to win...

Qualifying was also bitter-sweet for Honda. Jenson Button had generally shown local boy Rubens Barrichello the way around in practice, but in second qualifying his RA106 had an electronic problem as the traction control activated itself too often. As Button failed to make the cut, Barrichello rose to the occasion with 1m 11.619s for fifth place, just ahead of Giancarlo Fisichella in the second Renault, who did not particularly impress with 1m 11.629s. Several observers felt he should have helped his team-mate by qualifying better than that.

The presence of Ralf Schumacher in seventh place in the second Toyota on 1m 11.695s, with the BMW-Saubers of Nick Heidfeld (1m 11.882s) and Robert Kubica (1m 12.131s) right behind, augured well for the battle over fifth place in the constructors' table, which BMW led by a single point after Suzuka.

Behind the front five rows, Mark Webber shared row six with Pedro de la Rosa. The Williams driver lapped in 1m 11.650s; the McLaren pilot in 1m 11.658s. Nico Rosberg backed Webber with 13th place on 1m 11.679s and the unhappy Button lined up 14th on 1m 11.742s.

Robert Doornbos was faster than David Coulthard for Red Bull, but lost his 15th place on the grid for a lap of 1m 12.591s when his RB2 was consigned to the back row following an engine change. That elevated Tonio Liuzzi a place, the Italian having taken his Toro Rosso around in 1m 12.861s. Team-mate Scott Speed lined up alongside him, which was only just. The improving American had had the upper hand through most of first qualifying but lost out to Liuzzi at the very end by a mere 0.001s.

Behind them came Christijan Albers in the faster Spyker on 1m 13.138s, his team-mate Tiago Monteiro sharing the back row with Doornbos after the Portuguese spun on his first flying lap and failed to record a time. Coulthard was an unimpressive 18th in his Red Bull on 1m 13.249s, ahead of the Super Aguris of Takuma Sato, on 1m 13.269s, and the improving Sakon Yamamoto, who lapped in 1m 13.357s.

The scene was thus set for a potentially epic race, with Massa perhaps torn between an understandable desire for victory on his home ground and a wish to help his team-mate to retire with yet another championship crown. Alonso, meanwhile, needed to play it cool and keep clear of a hungry Schumacher. It was a promising scenario.

AND so an era came to a glorious end. No, the retiring Michael Schumacher did not win his 249th and final race; nor did he prevent Fernando Alonso from retaining the championship. But as the Spaniard finished second to local star Felipe Massa, and thus scored seven more points than he needed, Schumacher drove heroically to overcome qualifying problems and then a puncture during the race to snatch a valiant fourth place and set the fastest lap.

The race belonged to Massa right from the start and he thus became the first Brazilian to win his home race since an emotional Ayrton Senna did so back in 1993. Massa was just a schoolboy as his compatriot took that historic success.

Massa led fellow front-row man Kimi Räikkönen into the first corner, with Alonso slotting into fourth behind Jarno Trulli's Toyota. Farther back, Schumacher immediately got into a heady scrap with brother Ralf, who was being ganged up on by the two BMW-Saubers of Robert Kubica and Nick Heidfeld.

All of this was brought to a temporary end, however, when Nico Rosberg crashed his Williams heavily in the penultimate corner, necessitating deployment of the safety car. Earlier in that opening lap he had already rammed the back of team-mate Mark Webber's FW28, the third time that the Australian had suffered at a team-mate's hands in this race. Webber lost his rear wing, Rosberg his front, but whereas Webber made it back to the pits to retire, Rosberg had his accident.

'Such a waste,' Webber said of his last race for the team and Cosworth's last F1 outing for the foreseeable future. 'It was an interesting first few corners. I was fighting with Jenson [Button] and Pedro [de la Rosa] going into the first one and putting a bit of pressure on Pedro. It was shaping up to be quite fun, but I braked a bit later going into Turn Four and then I was hit from behind. I lost the diffuser and that was that. It looks like Nico lost his braking point. He was very deep going into the corner and I didn't think he was going to make it.'

Rosberg had a contrary view, at least about braking points.

'I was trying to get out of traffic, gain some ground and get back the place I had just lost to Jenson so I was close behind Mark going into the corner. I think he braked hard and maybe an extra metre too early, perhaps because something had happened next to him, and I hit him.'

There was a suggestion that Rosberg had sustained a puncture, which led to his subsequent shunt.

The safety car went in at the end of lap six, so racing resumed at the start of seven. Räikkönen clung to Massa for a lap, but in the course of the ninth Massa opened a massive 2.4s and that was that. That lap, and the next, brought the end of Toyota's challenge. First Ralf Schumacher pulled into the pits; a lap later, in came Trulli. Both had suffered rear suspension failures.

The ninth lap was also the beginning of the end for Schumacher's waning title hopes. He had just pulled off a great overtaking move for fifth place around the outside of Giancarlo Fisichella in the final corner when his new-found jinx struck yet again. The Ferrari twitched alarmingly in the right-hand section

DIARY

Even before Michael Schumacher drives his last grand prix, Audi reportedly offers him $12.5 million to race either at Le Mans or in the DTM.

In a ceremony in New York on 23 October, former world champion Mario Andretti is made a *Commendatore* by Italy's Consul General Antonio Bandini. The title ranks with the Order of the British Empire or France's *Légion d'Honneur*.

Though the San Marino Grand Prix is not listed on the official 2007 calendar released by the FIA's World Motor Sport Council the week before the Brazilian Grand Prix, race officials remain hopeful that financial issues can be resolved, and modification work be completed, in time for the race to go ahead.

In conjunction with new title sponsorship from AT&T, Williams announces an aggressive revamp of its technical department, including the return of Patrick Head to a full-time role.

of the Senna-Ess, the first corner, and he was forced to crawl into the pits at the end of lap nine with his left-rear Bridgestone tyre in shreds. It transpired that the damage had been caused by Fisichella's front-wing end-plate.

Schumacher said that he had felt nothing, but Ferrari's Jean Todt was adamant after the race. 'It's definitely in the overtaking manoeuvre that Michael got the puncture,' he said. 'We have to see in slow motion. It's definitely a racing incident, but let's say that the overtaking manoeuvre wasn't very much helped, which I can understand. It wasn't very well supported and probably it did not help Michael.'

Massa by now was easily opening up his lead over Räikkönen, and Alonso was stroking along quite happily in third place with Fisichella riding shotgun. Already, Renault had instructed Alonso to wind down the revs. Schumacher was way down in 17th place. The 71-lap encounter was only ten laps old and all the excitement had gone out of the championship fight.

Even if Alonso retired, Schumacher's title hopes had evaporated. But he wasn't about to give up. Instead, he got his head down and started setting some very quick laps. By the 40th lap he was back in the points – and he kept climbing. True, he was slightly out of kilter on pit stops, having refuelled on the ninth as his new tyre was fitted, but this was a wonderful drive, reminiscent of Jackie Stewart's race at Monza in 1973 when he too recovered to fourth after a pit stop to replace a puncture, though on that occasion the drive was sufficient to clinch the Scot his third and final world championship.

On lap 51 Schumacher sliced by the unimpressive Barrichello for sixth place and, incredibly, that brought him back up to Fisichella, another man who did not appear to be overtaxing himself. Twice Schumacher closed in, only to drop back momentarily, but going into the Senna-Ess on the 63rd lap Fisichella cracked and slid on to the grass, to cheers in the

press room, and Schumacher was widely applauded as he sped through into fifth. But even then his great charge was not over.

Räikkönen was also within reach. He had lost second place to Alonso during the first pit stops, as the Spaniard ran five laps longer, and then had Button pull off a great passing move into Senna on the 29th lap. Now he had Michael thirsting after him.

For several laps Räikkönen held the much quicker Ferrari at bay, driving like an ace himself, but at the end of the 68th lap Schumacher continued to go to the left on the pit straight after Räikkönen had made his one legal blocking move. The Ferrari squeezed alongside the McLaren and as they entered the Senna-Ess for the 69th time Michael slipped ahead into fourth place.

'I ran wide once towards the end of the race, which allowed Michael to close in,' the Finn said of his final race for McLaren, 'and despite all my efforts I couldn't keep him behind.'

'The race was rather chaotic – I guess that's the right word for it,' Schumacher said. 'I had an insanely quick car today. I probably had enough speed to lap everyone, to be honest. I did that sort of, anyhow.

'All in all, I'd have to say it was a class finale with the car, with the speed we've got. But it just wasn't meant to be, today, for me.'

Another star was Button, who climbed from 14th to the front, on a dry road this time, in a Honda that was beginning to look the business. In particular, his move on Räikkönen must surely have laid to rest the old suggestion that he lacks aggression or the ability to overtake. Nobody passes Kimi easily, as Michael discovered.

Over the closing laps, Button hounded Alonso to the flag. 'A massive well done to both Felipe and Fernando,' he said afterwards. 'After yesterday's problems it's a great result to come from 14th to third, a great way to end the year and one of most enjoyable races I've had, fighting through the field.'

Behind the vanquished Fisichella and Barrichello, De la Rosa made the most of a single-stop strategy to take the final point for eighth. For much of the race he had resisted attack from Heidfeld, who had a series of adventures.

Early in the race, a late overtaking move by team-mate Robert Kubica had damaged his front wing. That cost the German a lot of ground and later a brush overtaking Tonio Liuzzi in the Senna-Ess damaged the front suspension on both cars. When Heidfeld crashed heavily with eight laps to go, he suspected it was a legacy of that clash. Kubica had to settle for ninth, just out of the points, complaining that there was just no more speed to be squeezed from the F1.06. But with the Toyotas failing, the point that Heidfeld had scored in Japan proved conclusive for BMW as it held on to fifth place in the constructors' stakes ahead of the Japanese motor giant.

On this occasion Takuma Sato was also a star, making full use of his Bridgestone tyres to set ninth-fastest lap on his way to tenth overall, having featured early on in a fabulous scrap with Liuzzi, Scott Speed, David Coulthard, Robert Doornbos, Christijan Albers and his own team-mate, Sakon Yamamoto. The latter actually set seventh-fastest lap, albeit after a late pit stop to fit his Super Aguri with fresh rubber.

Left: Felipe Massa makes a perfect start from pole position to lead into Turn One with his Ferrari 248.
Photograph: XPB.cc/Photo4

Centre left: Nico Rosberg takes a breather after his particularly violent first-lap shunt.

Below: Oh no! Michael Schumacher looks in his mirror to see his left-rear tyre has been deflated by fleeting contact with Giancarlo Fisichella's front wing.

Main: Jenson Button drives splendidly to climb through the field to finish third in his Honda after traction control problems ruined his qualifying.
Photographs: James Moy/www.crashpa.net

Speed beat Liuzzi this time and they thrashed their Red Bull stablemates. Coulthard retired with gearbox failure and Doornbos took 12th between the Toro Rossos as Liuzzi slowed after the brush with Heidfeld.

Spyker had little to write home about, Albers leading Tiago Monteiro home in 14th place.

Up front, Felipe Massa completed his 71st lap and picked up a Brazilian flag on his slow-down tour to celebrate the greatest day of his racing life. The authority of his drive made him a genuine contender for the 2007 title.

'It's just amazing, isn't it?' he beamed. 'For 13 years a Brazilian has not won here; now here I am in front of my people. I had a fantastic car and maybe this was the easiest race of my life! I was just controlling everything. This is a dream come true, to see people bringing me the Brazilian flag, screaming my name, dancing... All drivers would love to be in my position; those who have been know just how special it is'

Emotions flowed after the race. Schumacher, ready to depart with honour and dignity, said, 'I'm really happy for Felipe that he could be the next Brazilian after Senna to win here. And naturally I congratulate Fernando as well.'

The Spaniard wore the biggest smile of them all. Renault had had concerns about its tyre choice on the grid as the track temperature momentarily soared to 51°C but, in its last race, Michelin's rubber behaved perfectly.

Flavio Briatore said of his driver that he made fewer mistakes than Schumacher. Renault president Alain Dassas said, 'As for our departing champion, Fernando deserves the second title like no other. He has been an extraordinary part of our team and we will miss him.'

Alonso himself said, 'It has been a fantastic weekend and now I probably need some time to believe that I'm champion again. I'm 25 years old, two championships now, and two constructors' as well. Last race for Renault after five years, fantastic way to finish the relationship with this success.

'I will have these memories with them all my life and to finish the last race like this is something that you never dream of, you never even try to dream of, because it's always more than what you expected.

'It was a very long race, obviously, for us because I only needed one point to become champion and, for sure, if I could help the team become constructors' champion as well, I was ready to do it. And, you know, everything was as planned. Ferrari were too quick but we managed to overtake Kimi in the first pit stop and then there was a lot of pressure from Jenson, but we managed to finish second. But it didn't matter the position, the important thing today was to become champion for the second consecutive time and we did it. Nothing more to say – it's an unbelievable feeling.'

He also felt it apposite to pay tribute to Schumacher. 'It's been very close between us and it's been good to fight with him. I have always said to become champion when Michael is still on the track made it more valuable. I was extremely lucky to win these two championships and we all wish him the best for his new life with his family. It's been a pleasure to race with him.'

And so, on his final day, Michael Schumacher lost yet won, his fighting fourth place among the young lions he leaves to scrap over his mantle bringing down the curtain on a fabulous career and one of the sport's most dramatic eras. He had his moments of brilliance and his moments of controversy, and opinion will forever be divided over his place in the pantheon. But in his last race there was no doubt that he went out a hero.

David Tremayne

FERRARI MAKES CHANGES

FERRARI was always going to be a different place without Michael Schumacher and, days after the Brazilian Grand Prix brought the 2006 season to its conclusion, the team revealed some of the revisions that had been expected – and some that hadn't.

Philosophical in defeat, Jean Todt conceded, 'We were far behind at a certain period of the championship and we came back two races before the end of the championship. We were not reliable enough in the two last races and it has been paid at a high cost, which is fair. So no complaint and now we have to close that chapter and open another one and that's part of the Ferrari history.'

Besides Schumacher, his long-time friend and colleague Ross Brawn, 51, Ferrari's technical director, is also stepping aside. The Englishman had, of course, masterminded Schumacher's successes at Benetton in 1994 with Cosworth power and again in 1995 with Renault before both switched to Ferrari. Now he confirmed the season-long suggestions that he would be taking a sabbatical in 2007 as Kimi Räikkönen took Schumacher's place alongside Felipe Massa.

Ferrari revealed that Brawn's place will be taken by little-known Ferrari industrial director Mario Almondo and that current team manager Stefano Domenicali will take over the role of sporting director from Todt. The previous day Todt, Ferrari's newly promoted chief executive officer, had agreed to take on the interim role of managing director of the company's Gestione Sportiva. Almondo and Domenicali will both report to him.

On other technical fronts, Aldo Costa will continue to head the chassis department but Paolo Martinelli, the father of Ferrari's successful V10 and V8 engines, is leaving the engine department for a position within the Fiat Group. His deputy Gilles Simon is his successor.

Over the Brazilian GP weekend, former chief designer Rory Byrne, 62, had also confirmed that he would retain his connections with Ferrari at least until 2009. Byrne said he would continue to act as a consultant to the team, having handed over the design reins to Costa in 2005.

Speculation continued, however, that Todt had wanted to retire at the same time as Schumacher after they had collectively written such an extraordinary chapter in motor sport history with 11 world titles (six constructors' and five drivers') and close to 100 grand prix victories. But he was persuaded to stay on for one more year by president Luca di Montezemolo, who wanted to maintain a measure of consistency.

Further speculation suggested that Todt planned to retire at the end of 2007 and that Brawn might then return to take over Todt's role in overall charge of the Ferrari race team.

GRANDE PRÉMIO DO BRASIL

INTERLAGOS 20–22 OCTOBER 2006

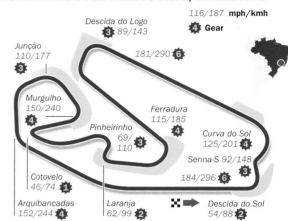

AUTODROMO JOSÉ CARLOS PACE, INTERLAGOS

116/187 mph/kmh
4 Gear

Descida do Logo 3 89/143
Junção 110/177 3
181/290 6
Murgulho 150/240 4
Ferradura 115/185 4
Pinheirinho 69/110 3
Curva do Sol 125/201 4
Senna-S 92/148 3
Cotovelo 46/74 1
184/296 6
Arquibancadas 152/244 4
Laranja 62/99 2
Descida do Sol 54/88 2

Photograph: James Moy/www.crashpa.net

Circuit: 2.677 miles/4.309 km

RACE RESULTS

Pos.	Driver	Nat.	No.	Entrant	Car/Engine	Tyres	Laps	Time/Retirement	Speed (mph/km/h)	Gap to leader	Fastest race lap	
1	Felipe Massa	BR	6	Scuderia Ferrari Marlboro	Ferrari 248 F1-056 V8	B	71	1h 31m 53.751s	124.107/199.731		1m 12.877s	23
2	Fernando Alonso	E	1	Mild Seven Renault F1 Team	Renault R26-RS26 V8	M	71	1h 32m 12.409s	123.689/199.058	+18.658s	1m 12.961s	70
3	Jenson Button	GB	12	Lucky Strike Honda Racing F1 Team	Honda RA106-RA806E V8	M	71	1h 32m 13.145s	123.672/199.031	+19.394s	1m 13.053s	71
4	Michael Schumacher	D	5	Scuderia Ferrari Marlboro	Ferrari 248 F1-056 V8	B	71	1h 32m 17.845s	123.567/198.862	+24.094s	1m 12.162s	70
5	Kimi Räikkönen	FIN	3	Team McLaren Mercedes	McLaren MP4-21-Mercedes FO 108S V8	M	71	1h 32m 22.254s	123.469/198.704	+28.503s	1m 13.281s	18
6	Giancarlo Fisichella	I	2	Mild Seven Renault F1 Team	Renault R26-RS26 V8	M	71	1h 32m 24.038s	123.429/198.640	+30.287s	1m 13.121s	70
7	Rubens Barrichello	BR	11	Lucky Strike Honda Racing F1 Team	Honda RA106-RA806E V8	M	71	1h 32m 34.045s	123.207/198.282	+40.294s	1m 13.391s	48
8	Pedro de la Rosa	E	4	Team McLaren Mercedes	McLaren MP4-21-Mercedes FO 108S V8	M	71	1h 32m 45.819s	122.946/197.863	+52.068s	1m 13.817s	63
9	Robert Kubica	POL	17	BMW Sauber F1 Team	BMW Sauber F1.06-BMW P86 V8	M	71	1h 33m 01.393s	122.603/197.311	+1m 07.642s	1m 14.117s	25
10	Takuma Sato	J	22	Super Aguri F1 Team	Super Aguri SA06-Honda RA806E V8	B	70			+1 lap	1m 13.401s	47
11	Scott Speed	USA	21	Scuderia Toro Rosso	Toro Rosso STR01-Cosworth TJ2005-2 V10	M	70			+1 lap	1m 13.862s	69
12	Robert Doornbos	NL	15	Red Bull Racing	Red Bull RB2-Ferrari 056 V8	M	70			+1 lap	1m 13.700s	62
13	Vitantonio Liuzzi	I	20	Scuderia Toro Rosso	Toro Rosso STR01-Cosworth TJ2005-2 V10	M	70			+1 lap	1m 13.687s	69
14	Christijan Albers	NL	19	Spyker MF1 Team	Spyker M16-Toyota RVX-06 V8	B	70			+ 1 lap	1m 14.591s	61
15	Tiago Monteiro	P	18	Spyker MF1 Team	Spyker M16-Toyota RVX-06 V8	B	69			+2 laps	1m 14.410s	38
16	Sakon Yamamoto	J	23	Super Aguri F1 Team	Super Aguri SA06-Honda RA806E V8	B	69			+2 laps	1m 13.379s	67
17	Nick Heidfeld	D	16	BMW Sauber F1 Team	BMW Sauber F1.06-BMW P86 V8	M	63	Rear suspension/accident		+8 laps	1m 14.163s	18
	David Coulthard	GB	14	Red Bull Racing	Red Bull RB2-Ferrari 056 V8	M	14	Gearbox			1m 16.045s	12
	Jarno Trulli	I	8	Panasonic Toyota Racing	Toyota TF106B-RVX-06 V8	B	10	Rear suspension			1m 14.882s	9
	Ralf Schumacher	D	7	Panasonic Toyota Racing	Toyota TF106B-RVX-06 V8	B	9	Rear suspension			1m 16.835s	8
	Mark Webber	AUS	9	WilliamsF1 Team	Williams FW28-Cosworth CA2006 V8	B	1	Accident			No time	–
	Nico Rosberg	D	10	WilliamsF1 Team	Williams FW28-Cosworth CA2006 V8	B	0	Puncture/accident			No time	–

All results and data © FOM 2006

Fastest lap: Michael Schumacher on lap 70, 1m 12.162s, 133.574 mph/214.966 km/h.

Lap record: Juan Pablo Montoya (Williams FW26-BMW V10), 1m 11.473s, 134.862 mph/217.038 km/h (2004)

22 DOORNBOS Red Bull — Engine penalty
20 YAMAMOTO Super Aguri
18 COULTHARD Red Bull
16 SPEED Toro Rosso
14 BUTTON Honda
12 DE LA ROSA McLaren
21 MONTEIRO Spyker
19 SATO Super Aguri
17 ALBERS Spyker
15 LIUZZI Toro Rosso
13 ROSBERG Williams
11 WEBBER Williams

Grid order	1	2	3	4	5	6	7	8	9	10	11	12	13	14	15	16	17	18	19	20	21	22	23	24	25	26	27	28	29	30	31	32	33	34	35	36	37	38	39	40	41	42	43	44	45	46	47	48	49	50	51	52	53	54	55
6 MASSA	6	6	6	6	6	6	6	6	6	6	6	6	6	6	6	6	6	6	6	6	6	6	6	6	6	1	1	6	6	6	6	6	6	6	6	6	6	6	6	6	6	6	6	6	6	6	6	6	6	6	6	6	6	6	6
3 RÄIKKÖNEN	3	3	3	3	3	3	3	3	3	3	3	3	3	3	3	3	3	3	3	3	3	12	1	6	17		4	4	4	4	4	1	1	1	1	1	1	1	1	1	1	1	1	1	1	1	1	1	1	1	1	1	1	1	1
8 TRULLI	8	8	8	8	8	8	8	8	1	1	1	1	1	1	1	1	1	1	1	1	3	12	12	12	6	17	4	1	1	1	1	1	12	12	12	12	12	12	12	12	12	12	12	3	12	12	12	12	12	12	12	12	12	12	12
1 ALONSO	1	1	1	1	1	1	1	1	2	2	2	2	2	2	2	2	2	2	2	2	12	17	17	17	4	16	3	12	12	12	12	12	3	3	3	3	3	3	3	3	3	3	3	12	12	3	3	3	3
11 BARRICHELLO	11	2	2	2	2	2	5	2	11	11	11	11	11	11	11	11	11	11	11	11	2	4	4	4	16	1	12	3	3	3	3	3	4	2	2	2	2	2	2	2	2	2	2	2	2	2	2	2	2	2	2	2	2	2	2
2 FISICHELLA	2	5	5	5	5	5	2	11	12	12	12	12	12	12	12	12	12	11	16	16	16	3	3	16	2	2	2	2	2	11	11	11	11	11	11	11	11	11	5	17	11	5	5	5	5	5
7 R. SCHUMACHER	5	11	11	11	11	11	12	17	17	17	17	17	17	17	17	17	3	3	12	2	11	11	11	11	11	11	17	17	5	5	5	5	17	11	5	11	11	11	11	11
16 HEIDFELD	7	7	7	7	7	12	12	17	4	4	4	4	4	4	4	4	2	2	11	17	17	17	17	16	11	11	11	11	17	17	5	5	5	5	17	11	5	4	4	4	4
17 KUBICA	17	17	17	17	17	7	7	4	16	16	16	16	16	16	16	16	16	11	11	11	11	11	21	16	16	16	16	16	4	4	4	4	4	4	4	4	17	17	17	17	17
5 M. SCHUMACHER	12	12	12	12	12	17	17	16	21	21	21	21	21	21	21	21	21	16	16	16	21	5	5	4	4	22	22	22	22	22	22	22	21	21	21	21	21	22
9 WEBBER	4	4	4	4	4	4	20	20	20	20	20	20	20	20	20	20	20	20	20	16	20	20	5	5	15	15	18	18	18	21	21	21	21	21	22	22	22	21	15
4 DE LA ROSA	16	16	16	16	16	16	16	21	24	14	14	14	4	4	4	4	22	22	22	22	22	22	15	15	20	18	18	22	22	21	16	16	16	16	16	16	16	16	16
10 ROSBERG	10	10	10	19	19	19	19	14	14	23	23	23	23	23	23	23	23	15	18	5	15	15	21	21	15	15	20	20	20	20	20	20	20	20	20	20
12 BUTTON	21	21	21	21	21	14	14	23	23	15	15	15	15	15	23	5	18	18	20	20	21	15	15	20	20	20	20	20	20	20	20	20
20 LIUZZI	22	22	22	22	22	21	21	14	14	15	15	15	15	15	19	23	20	20	22	20	20	20	19	19	19	19	19	19	19	19	19	19
21 SPEED	14	14	14	14	14	14	14	15	15	18	18	18	18	18	5	19	19	19	23	23	23	23	23	18	18	18	18	18	18
19 ALBERS	19	19	19	19	19	19	15	18	18	18	5	5	5	5	5	5	19	23	23	23	23	18	18	18	18	23	23	23	23	23
14 COULTHARD	23	23	23	23	23	23	23	7	8	5	5	5	14
22 SATO	15	15	15	15	15	15	15	15	5
23 YAMAMOTO	18	18	18	18	18	18	18	18	5
18 MONTEIRO	9
15 DOORNBOS	

PRACTICE 1 (FRIDAY)

Overcast, scattered cloud (track 25–31°C, air 19–22°C)

Pos.	Driver	Laps	Time
1	Kimi Räikkönen	5	1m 13.764s
2	Anthony Davidson	32	1m 13.902s
3	Alexander Wurz	25	1m 13.922s
4	Sebastian Vettel	29	1m 14.204s
5	Pedro de la Rosa	5	1m 14.237s
6	Jenson Button	4	1m 14.487s
7	Jarno Trulli	8	1m 14.888s
8	Neel Jani	25	1m 15.159s
9	Rubens Barrichello	6	1m 15.661s
10	Michael Ammermüller	22	1m 15.711s
11	Ralf Schumacher	6	1m 16.168s
12	Takuma Sato	16	1m 16.534s
13	Ernesto Viso	32	1m 16.737s
14	Scott Speed	14	1m 17.047s
15	Vitantonio Liuzzi	8	1m 17.311s
16	Sakon Yamamoto	14	1m 17.388s
17	Franck Montagny	6	1m 17.744s
18	Nick Heidfeld	1	No time
19	Robert Kubica	1	No time
20	Christijan Albers	1	No time
21	Tiago Monteiro	1	No time
22	David Coulthard	1	No time
23	Robert Doornbos	1	No time
24	Giancarlo Fisichella	1	No time
25	Fernando Alonso	1	No time

PRACTICE 2 (FRIDAY)

Overcast (track 27–30°C, air 20°C)

Pos.	Driver	Laps	Time
1	Alexander Wurz	33	1m 12.547s
2	Anthony Davidson	37	1m 12.653s
3	Sebastian Vettel	33	1m 12.870s
4	Jarno Trulli	21	1m 13.483s
5	Jenson Button	13	1m 13.485s
6	Michael Schumacher	15	1m 13.713s
7	Ralf Schumacher	22	1m 13.765s
8	Franck Montagny	20	1m 13.792s
9	Kimi Räikkönen	8	1m 13.803s
10	Fernando Alonso	16	1m 13.820s
11	Pedro de la Rosa	16	1m 13.926s
12	Giancarlo Fisichella	17	1m 14.053s
13	Rubens Barrichello	17	1m 14.434s
14	Michael Ammermüller	31	1m 14.436s
15	Tiago Monteiro	18	1m 14.468s
16	Robert Kubica	15	1m 14.510s
17	Felipe Massa	15	1m 14.561s
18	Nick Heidfeld	13	1m 14.793s
19	Mark Webber	15	1m 14.839s
20	Ernesto Viso	26	1m 14.972s
21	Takuma Sato	27	1m 15.023s
22	Christijan Albers	21	1m 15.086s
23	Nico Rosberg	14	1m 15.124s
24	David Coulthard	21	1m 15.214s
25	Vitantonio Liuzzi	22	1m 15.737s
26	Scott Speed	28	1m 15.855s
27	Neel Jani	22	1m 15.868s
28	Robert Doornbos	8	1m 16.251s
29	Sakon Yamamoto	9	1m 18.321s

QUALIFYING (SATURDAY)

Scattered cloud (track 31–34°C, air 20–21°C)

Pos.	Driver	First	Second	Third
1	Felipe Massa	1m 10.643s	1m 10.775s	1m 10.680s
2	Kimi Räikkönen	1m 12.035s	1m 11.386s	1m 11.299s
3	Jarno Trulli	1m 11.885s	1m 11.343s	1m 11.328s
4	Fernando Alonso	1m 11.791s	1m 11.148s	1m 11.567s
5	Rubens Barrichello	1m 12.017s	1m 11.578s	1m 11.619s
6	Giancarlo Fisichella	1m 12.042s	1m 11.461s	1m 11.629s
7	Ralf Schumacher	1m 11.713s	1m 11.550s	1m 11.695s
8	Nick Heidfeld	1m 12.307s	1m 11.648s	1m 11.882s
9	Robert Kubica	1m 12.040s	1m 11.589s	1m 12.131s
10	Michael Schumacher	1m 11.565s	1m 10.313s	No time
11	Mark Webber	1m 11.973s	1m 11.650s	
12	Pedro de la Rosa	1m 11.825s	1m 11.658s	
13	Nico Rosberg	1m 11.974s	1m 11.679s	
14	Jenson Button	1m 12.085s	1m 11.742s	
15	Robert Doornbos	1m 12.530s	1m 12.591s	
16	Vitantonio Liuzzi	1m 12.855s	1m 12.861s	
17	Scott Speed	1m 12.856s		
18	Christijan Albers	1m 13.138s		
19	David Coulthard	1m 13.249s		
20	Takuma Sato	1m 13.269s		
21	Sakon Yamamoto	1m 13.357s		
22	Tiago Monteiro	No time		

PRACTICE 3 (SATURDAY)

Overcast, scattered cloud (track 28–31°C, air 19°C)

Pos.	Driver	Laps	Time
1	Felipe Massa	17	1m 11.443s
2	Michael Schumacher	15	1m 11.631s
3	Jenson Button	15	1m 12.306s
4	Robert Kubica	20	1m 12.535s
5	Giancarlo Fisichella	15	1m 12.567s
6	Rubens Barrichello	18	1m 12.697s
7	Fernando Alonso	14	1m 12.721s
8	Kimi Räikkönen	12	1m 12.723s
9	Pedro de la Rosa	15	1m 12.780s
10	Nick Heidfeld	15	1m 13.037s
11	Mark Webber	16	1m 13.205s
12	Nico Rosberg	13	1m 13.380s
13	Scott Speed	18	1m 13.455s
14	Vitantonio Liuzzi	20	1m 13.530s
15	Robert Doornbos	21	1m 13.564s
16	Ralf Schumacher	20	1m 13.642s
17	Takuma Sato	21	1m 13.814s
18	Tiago Monteiro	15	1m 13.832s
19	David Coulthard	20	1m 13.944s
20	Jarno Trulli	19	1m 14.051s
21	Christijan Albers	19	1m 14.108s
22	Sakon Yamamoto	21	1m 14.875s

CHASSIS LOG BOOK

Photograph: Jad Sherif/WRI

RENAULT
1	Fernando Alonso	R26/03
2	Giancarlo Fisichella	R26/04
	Spare	R26/01

McLAREN-MERCEDES
3	Kimi Räikkönen	MP4-21/05
4	Pedro de la Rosa	MP4-21/04
	Spare	MP4-21/07
	Spare	MP4-21/06

FERRARI
5	Michael Schumacher	248 F1/255
6	Felipe Massa	248 F1/256
	Spare	248 F1/251

TOYOTA
7	Ralf Schumacher	TF106B/10
8	Jarno Trulli	TF106B/08
	Spare	TF106B/09

WILLIAMS-COSWORTH
9	Mark Webber	FW28/03
10	Nico Rosberg	FW28/05
35	Alexander Wurz	FW28/04

HONDA
11	Rubens Barrichello	RA106/01
12	Jenson Button	RA106/05
36	Anthony Davidson	RA106/03

RED BULL-FERRARI
14	David Coulthard	RB2/3
15	Robert Doornbos	RB2/5
37	Michael Ammermüller	RB2/1

BMW SAUBER
16	Nick Heidfeld	F1.06/04
17	Robert Kubica	F1.06/09
38	Sebastian Vettel	F1.06/08

MIDLAND-TOYOTA
18	Tiago Monteiro	M16/03
19	Christijan Albers	M16/02
39	Ernesto Viso	M16/01

TORO ROSSO-COSWORTH
20	Vitantonio Liuzzi	STR01/03
21	Scott Speed	STR01/01
40	Neel Jani	STR01/04

SUPER AGURI-HONDA
22	Takuma Sato	SA06/03
23	Sakon Yamamoto	SA06/04
41	Franck Montagny	SA06/02

10 M. SCHUMACHER Ferrari

8 HEIDFELD BMW-Sauber

6 FISICHELLA Renault

4 ALONSO Renault

2 RÄIKKÖNEN McLaren

9 KUBICA BMW-Sauber

7 R. SCHUMACHER Toyota

5 BARRICHELLO Honda

3 TRULLI Toyota

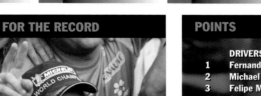
1 MASSA Ferrari

RACE DISTANCE:
71 laps
190.083 miles/305.909 km

RACE WEATHER:
Sun and scattered cloud
track 40–42°C, air 23–25°C

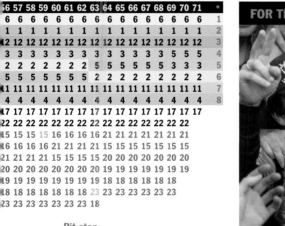

56	57	58	59	60	61	62	63	64	65	66	67	68	69	70	71	•
6	6	6	6	6	6	6	6	6	6	6	6	6	6	6	6	1
1	1	1	1	1	1	1	1	1	1	1	1	1	1	1	1	2
12	12	12	12	12	12	12	12	12	12	12	12	12	12	12	12	3
3	3	3	3	3	3	3	3	3	3	3	3	3	5	5	5	4
2	2	2	2	2	2	2	5	5	5	5	5	5	3	3	3	5
5	5	5	5	5	5	5	2	2	2	2	2	2	2	2	2	6
11	11	11	11	11	11	11	11	11	11	11	11	11	11	11	11	7
4	4	4	4	4	4	4	4	4	4	4	4	4	4	4	4	8
17	17	17	17	17	17	17	17	17	17	17	17	17	17	17	17	9
22	22	22	22	22	22	22	22	22	22	22	22	22	22	22	22	10
15	15	15	15	16	16	16	16	21	21	21	21	21	21	21	21	11
16	16	16	16	21	21	21	21	15	15	15	15	15	15	15		12
21	21	21	21	15	15	15	15	15	15	15	15	15	15			13
20	20	20	20	20	20	20	20	19	19	19	19	19	19			14
19	19	19	19	19	19	19	19	18	18	18	18	18	18			15
18	18	18	18	18	18	23	23	23	23	23	23	23				16
23	23	23	23	23	23	18										17

Pit stop

One lap or more behind leader

1 **Safety car deployed on laps shown**

FOR THE RECORD

Photographs: James Moy/www.crash.net

SECOND WORLD CHAMPIONSHIP:
Fernando Alonso

POINTS

	DRIVERS				CONSTRUCTORS	
1	Fernando Alonso	134		1	Renault	206
2	Michael Schumacher	121		2	Ferrari	201
3	Felipe Massa	80		3	McLaren	110
4	Giancarlo Fisichella	72		4	Honda	86
5	Kimi Räikkönen	65		5	BMW Sauber	36
6	Jenson Button	56		6	Toyota	35
7	Rubens Barrichello	30		7	Red Bull	16
8	Juan Pablo Montoya	26		8	Williams	11
9	Nick Heidfeld	23		9	Toro Rosso	1
10	Ralf Schumacher	20				
11	Pedro de la Rosa	19				
12	Jarno Trulli	15				
13	David Coulthard	14				
14	Mark Webber	7				
15	Jacques Villeneuve	7				
16	Robert Kubica	6				
17	Nico Rosberg	4				
18	Christian Klien	2				
19	Vitantonio Liuzzi	1				

GRANDE PRÊMIO DO BRASIL — SÃO PAULO 2006 — FIA Formula 1 WORLD CHAMPIONSHIP

STATISTICS: 2006 DRIVERS' POINTS TABLE Compiled by DAVID HAYHOE

Place	Driver	Nationality	Date of birth	Car	Bahrain	Malaysia	Australia	San Marino	Europe	Spain	Monaco	Britain	Canada	USA	France	Germany	Hungary	Turkey	Italy	China	Japan	Brazil	Points total
1	Fernando ALONSO	E	29/7/81	Renault	1	2f	1	2f	2p	1p	1p	1pf	1p	5	2	5	R	2	R	2pf	1f	2	134
2	Michael SCHUMACHER	D	3/1/69	Ferrari	2p	6	R	1p	1f	2	5f	2	2	1pf	1pf	1f	8*	3f	1	1	R	4f	121
3	Felipe MASSA	BR	25/4/81	Ferrari	9	5	R	4	3	4f	9	5	5	2	3	2	7f	1p	9	R	2p	1p	80
4	Giancarlo FISICHELLA	I	14/1/73	Renault	R	1p	5	8	6	3	6	4	4	3	6	6	R	6	4	3	3	6	72
5	Kimi RÄIKKÖNEN	FIN	17/10/79	McLaren-Mercedes	3	R	2f	5	4	5	R	3	3f	R	5	3p	Rp	R	2pf	R	5	5	65
6	Jenson BUTTON	GB	19/1/80	Honda	4	3	10*p	7	R	6	11	R	9	R	R	4	1	4	5	4	4	3	56
7	Rubens BARRICHELLO	BR	23/5/72	Honda	15	10	7	10	5	7	4	10	R	6	R	R	4	8	6	6	12	7	30
8	Juan Pablo MONTOYA	COL	20/9/75	McLaren-Mercedes	5	4	R	3	R	R	2	6	R	R	-	-	-	-	-	-	-	-	26
9	Nick HEIDFELD	D	10/5/77	BMW-Sauber	12	R	4	13	10	8	7	7	7	R	8	R	3	14	8	7	8	17*	23
10	Ralf SCHUMACHER	D	30/6/75	Toyota	14	8	3	9	R	8	R	8	R	R	4	9	6	7	15	R	7	R	20
11	Pedro DE LA ROSA	E	24/2/71	McLaren-Mercedes	-	-	-	-	-	-	-	-	-	-	7	R	2	5	R	5	11	8	19
12	Jarno TRULLI	I	13/7/74	Toyota	16	9	R	R	9	10	17*	11	6	4	R	7	12*	9	7	R	6	R	15
13	David COULTHARD	GB	27/3/71	Red Bull-Ferrari	10	R	8	R	R	14	3	12	8	7	9	11	5	15*	12	9	R	R	14
14	Mark WEBBER	AUS	27/8/76	Williams-Cosworth	6	R	6	R	6	9	R	R	12	R	R	R	R	10	10	8	R	R	7
15	Jacques VILLENEUVE	CDN	9/4/71	BMW-Sauber	R	7	6	12	8	12	14	8	R	11	R	-	-	-	-	-	-	-	7
16	Robert KUBICA	POL	7/12/84	BMW-Sauber	-	-	-	-	-	-	-	-	-	-	-	-	DQ	12	3	13	9	9	6
17	Nico ROSBERG	D	27/6/85	Williams-Cosworth	7f	R	R	11	7	11	R	9	R	9	14	R	R	R	11	10	R	R	4
18	Christian KLIEN	A	7/2/83	Red Bull-Ferrari	8	R	R	R	R	13	R	14	11	R	12	8	R	11	11	-	-	-	2
19	Vitantonio LIUZZI	I	6/8/80	Toro Rosso-Cosworth	11	11	R	14	R	15*	10	13	13	8	13	10	R	14	10	14	13	R	1
20	Scott SPEED	USA	24/1/83	Toro Rosso-Cosworth	13	R	9	15	11	R	13	R	10	R	10	12	11	13	13	14	18*	11	
21	Tiago MONTEIRO	P	24/7/76	Midland/Spyker-Toyota	17	13	R	16	12	16	15	16	14	R	15	DQ	9	R	R	16	R	15	
22	Christijan ALBERS	NL	16/4/79	Midland/Spyker-Toyota	R	12	11	R	13	R	12	15	R	R	15	DQ	10	R	17	15	R	14	
23	Takuma SATO	J	28/1/77	Super Aguri-Honda	18	14	12	R	R	R	R	17	R	15*	R	R	13	NC	16	DQ	15	10	
24	Robert DOORNBOS	NL	23/9/81	Red Bull-Ferrari	-	-	-	-	-	-	-	-	-	-	-	-	-	-	-	12	13	12	
25	Yuji IDE	J	21/1/77	Super Aguri-Honda	R	R	13	R	-	-	-	-	-	-	-	-	-	-	-	-	-	-	
26	Sakon YAMAMOTO	J	9/7/82	Super Aguri-Honda	-	-	-	-	-	-	-	-	-	-	-	R	R	R	16	R	17	16	
27	Franck MONTAGNY	F	5/1/78	Super Aguri-Honda	-	-	-	-	R	R	16	18	R	R	16	-	-	-	-	-	-	-	

The following drivers took part in Friday practice sessions at grand prix meetings but not in official qualifying or the race:

Michael AMMERMÜLLER	D	17/2/86	Red Bull-Ferrari
Anthony DAVIDSON	GB	18/4/79	Honda
Neel JANI	CH	8/12/83	Toro Rosso-Cosworth
Gorgio MONDINI	CH	19/7/80	Midland-Toyota
Alexandre PRÉMAT	F	5/4/82	Midland/Spyker-Toyota
Adrian SUTIL	D	11/1/83	Midland/Spyker-Toyota
Sebastian VETTEL	D	3/7/87	BMW-Sauber
Ernesto VISO	YV	19/3/85	Midland/Spyker-Toyota
Markus WINKELHOCK	D	13/6/80	Midland-Toyota
Alexander WURZ	A	15/2/74	Williams-Cosworth

KEY

p	pole position	f	fastest lap
R	retired	DQ	disqualified
*	classified, but not running at the finish		
NC	not classified		

These drivers took part in test sessions and also in grands prix:
Robert Doornbos, Robert Kubica, Franck Montagny, Sakon Yamamoto

POINTS & PERCENTAGES
Compiled by DAVID HAYHOE

Photograph: James Moy/www.crashpa.net

Photograph: James Moy/www.crashpa.net

GRID POSITIONS: 2006

Pos.	Driver	Starts	Best	Worst	Average
1	Fernando Alonso	18	1	15	4.28
2	Michael Schumacher	18	1	22	5.44
3	Giancarlo Fisichella	18	1	11	5.61
4	Kimi Räikkönen	18	1	22	5.83
5	Felipe Massa	18	1	21	6.67
6	Juan Pablo Montoya	10	4	12	7.20
7	Rubens Barrichello	18	3	20	7.61
8	Jenson Button	18	1	19	7.78
9	Robert Kubica	6	6	12	8.83
10	Pedro de la Rosa	8	4	13	8.87
11	Ralf Schumacher	18	3	22	9.94
12	Nick Heidfeld	18	3	15	10.17
13	Jarno Trulli	18	3	22	10.44
14	Mark Webber	18	2	19	11.00
15	Christian Klien	15	8	17	12.73
16	Jacques Villeneuve	12	6	22	12.75
17	Nico Rosberg	18	3	22	13.28
18	David Coulthard	18	7	22	14.17
19	Vitantonio Liuzzi	18	12	22	15.44
20	Scott Speed	18	11	20	16.17
21	Robert Doornbos	3	10	22	16.67
22	Christijan Albers	18	14	22	18.00
23	Tiago Monteiro	18	15	21	18.11
24	Takuma Sato	18	17	21	19.72
25	Franck Montagny	7	19	21	20.14
26	Yuji Ide	4	18	22	20.75
27	Sakon Yamamoto	7	19	22	20.86

CAREER PERFORMANCES: 2006 DRIVERS

Driver	Nationality	Races	Championships	Wins	2nd places	3rd places	4th places	5th places	6th places	7th places	8th places	Pole positions	Fastest laps	Points
Christijan Albers	NL	37	-	-	-	-	-	1	-	-	-	-	-	4
Fernando Alonso	E	87	2	15	14	8	8	5	2	2	1	15	8	381
Rubens Barrichello	BR	233	-	9	26	26	17	15	9	10	5	13	15	519
Jenson Button	GB	118	-	1	4	10	12	15	5	7	8	3	-	223
David Coulthard	GB	211	-	13	26	22	11	17	13	15	6	12	18	513
Pedro de la Rosa	E	72	-	-	1	-	-	4	4	1	5	-	1	29
Robert Doornbos	NL	11	-	-	-	-	-	-	-	-	-	-	-	-
Giancarlo Fisichella	I	177	-	3	6	9	13	12	15	11	11	3	2	246
Nick Heidfeld	D	115	-	-	2	3	3	2	9	9	9	1	-	79
Yuji Ide	J	4	-	-	-	-	-	-	-	-	-	-	-	-
Christian Klien	A	46	-	-	-	-	-	1	1	1	5	-	-	14
Robert Kubica	POL	6	-	-	-	1	-	-	-	-	-	-	-	6
Vitantonio Liuzzi	I	22	-	-	-	-	-	-	-	-	2	-	-	2
Felipe Massa	BR	70	-	2	3	2	4	5	3	4	5	3	2	107
Franck Montagny	F	7	-	-	-	-	-	-	-	-	-	-	-	-
Tiago Monteiro	P	37	-	-	-	1	-	-	-	-	1	-	-	7
Juan Pablo Montoya	COL	94	-	7	15	8	10	8	3	4	3	13	12	307
Kimi Räikkönen	FIN	104	-	9	15	12	8	7	4	4	3	11	19	346
Nico Rosberg	D	18	-	-	-	-	-	-	-	2	-	-	1	4
Takuma Sato	J	69	-	-	-	1	2	3	4	-	3	-	-	40
Michael Schumacher	D	249	7	91	43	20	11	10	7	6	4	68	76	1369
Ralf Schumacher	D	163	-	6	6	15	19	17	11	11	7	6	8	324
Scott Speed	USA	18	-	-	-	-	-	-	-	-	-	-	-	-
Jarno Trulli	I	164	-	1	3	3	13	12	11	9	9	3	-	175
Jacques Villeneuve	CDN	163	1	11	5	7	10	6	10	9	11	13	9	235
Mark Webber	AUS	86	-	-	1	2	3	8	8	4	-	-	-	69
Sakon Yamamoto	J	7	-	-	-	-	-	-	-	-	-	-	-	-

Note: As is now common practice, drivers retiring on the formation lap are not counted as having started. Where races have been subject to a restart, those retiring during an initial race are included as having started.

UNLAPPED: 2006
Number of cars on same lap as leader

Grand Prix	Starters	at 1/4 distance	at 1/2 distance	at 3/4 distance	at full distance
Bahrain	22	20	17	13	11
Malaysia	22	16	12	10	8
Australia	22	18	14	11	9
San Marino	22	19	16	14	12
Europe	22	19	13	12	8
Spain	22	18	10	8	6
Monaco	22	18	9	5	6
Britain	22	18	15	11	9
Canada	22	14	10	7	5
USA	22	12	10	7	6
France	22	19	11	6	7
Germany	22	17	11	9	9
Hungary	22	14	7	6	4
Turkey	22	17	15	13	8
Italy	22	21	17	14	10
China	22	22	15	11	9
Japan	22	22	16	11	9
Brazil	22	17	15	11	9

LAP LEADERS: 2006

Grand Prix	Fernando Alonso	Michael Schumacher	Felipe Massa	Giancarlo Fisichella	Kimi Räikkönen	Jenson Button	Juan Pablo Montoya	Robert Kubica	Mark Webber	Ralf Schumacher	Jarno Trulli	Total
Bahrain	25	27	-	-	-	1	4	-	-	-	-	57
Malaysia	12	-	-	42	-	2	-	-	-	-	-	56
Australia	51	-	-	-	1	3	-	2	-	-	-	57
San Marino	5	55	-	-	-	-	2	-	-	-	-	62
Europe	30	22	-	-	8	-	-	-	-	-	-	60
Spain	54	11	-	1	-	-	-	-	-	-	-	66
Monaco	77	-	-	-	-	-	-	1	-	-	-	78
Britain	59	-	-	1	-	-	-	-	-	-	-	60
Canada	65	-	-	-	5	-	-	-	-	-	-	70
USA	1	43	29	-	-	-	-	-	-	-	-	73
France	3	63	-	-	-	-	-	-	2	2	-	70
Germany	-	58	-	-	9	-	-	-	-	-	-	67
Hungary	34	-	-	-	17	19	-	-	-	-	-	70
Turkey	-	4	54	-	-	-	-	-	-	-	-	58
Italy	-	34	-	-	14	-	-	5	-	-	-	53
China	28	15	-	13	-	-	-	-	-	-	-	56
Japan	17	34	2	-	-	-	-	-	-	-	-	53
Brazil	2	-	69	-	-	-	-	-	-	-	-	71
Total	463	366	154	57	54	25	6	5	3	2	2	1137
(Percent)	40.7	32.2	13.5	5.0	4.7	2.2	0.5	0.4	0.3	0.2	0.2	100.0

RETIREMENTS: 2006
Number of cars that retired

Grand Prix	Starters	at 1/4 distance	at 1/2 distance	at 3/4 distance	at full distance	% of finishers
Bahrain	22	1	2	4	4	81.8
Malaysia	22	3	5	7	8	63.6
Australia	22	4	5	8	10	54.5
San Marino	22	2	3	5	6	72.7
Europe	22	3	6	7	9	59.1
Spain	22	1	3	5	6	72.7
Monaco	22	0	0	5	6	72.7
Britain	22	4	4	4	4	81.8
Canada	22	5	5	5	8	63.6
USA	22	10	11	12	13	40.9
France	22	2	3	4	6	72.7
Germany	22	4	6	7	8	63.6
Hungary	22	5	7	9	10	54.5
Turkey	22	3	5	6	7	68.2
Italy	22	1	3	3	5	77.3
China	22	0	1	3	5	77.3
Japan	22	0	1	4	5	77.3
Brazil	22	5	5	5	6	72.7

LEWIS, AND THE ART OF WINNING

by ANDREW VAN DE BURGT, Editor, *Autosport*

Main: Lewis Hamilton scored five wins and put in some brilliant drives to take the GP2 title at his first attempt.

Below: Lewis now has his sights set firmly on an F1 future, but realises that planning the timing of his graduation to the sport's senior category is absolutely crucial.

Photographs: GP2 Media Service

Above: In his second season of GP2 competition Alexandre Prémat found himself playing a supporting role to Lewis Hamilton in the ART squad.

Right: Piquet Sports provided both the personnel and the machinery for the young Nelson Piquet to mount a serious title challenge. Next year he has an F1 test driver role with Renault.

Photographs: James Moy/www.crashpa.net

THE second season of GP2 more than lived up to its billing following its stunning impact as F1's new support series in 2005. If anything, the racing was even more action-packed and exhilarating, which was the perfect sub-plot to a tense two-way fight for the title that went right down to the wire.

That the championship was ultimately decided in the distinctly underwhelming fashion of a stewards' ruling over a yellow flag decision was just about the only blot on a captivating year of great racing.

Over the winter, GP2 decided to ditch its F1-style grooved tyres in favour of more conventional slicks. Initial testing by 2005 vice-champion Heikki Kovalainen suggested the increase in grip had made the car too easy to drive, so one of the three rear-wing elements was removed to make the 600-bhp Dallara-Renault a slightly more tricky beast to handle.

The result was a car with much greater front-end grip than rear and finding a balance in an inherently oversteering car was the magic bullet each team strove for all season. First out of the blocks was Piquet Sports. A great win in the wet at Spa aside, 2005 had been a disappointing year for the team and its highly rated lead driver Nelson Piquet Jr. But winter testing had gone well and it was no surprise when the son of triple F1 world champion Piquet Sr won the season-opening race at Valencia from pole.

Valencia was GP2's only stand-alone event and the series celebrated the start of its second season with a lavish pyrotechnically illuminated opening bash in the downtown district of Spain's third city.

GP2 stuck with its two-race format, with a longer 'feature' race taking place first and a short 'sprint' following. The grid for the sprint was decided by the finishing order of the feature, but with the top eight reversed.

On his GP2 début, Red Bull-backed Michael Ammermüller won the sprint at Valencia, but it was to be his – and Arden International's – only win of the year.

In Formula 3000, the forerunner to GP2, Arden had been the team to beat. But that was then; the new order in GP2 has brought a French team run under the name of ART Grand Prix to prominence. After wrapping up the first GP2 title with Nico Rosberg, ART brought in another highly rated youngster, called Lewis Hamilton, to pair up with team favourite Alex Prémat.

It took a while for the combination to gel, although Hamilton had shone in winter testing and gave a hint of what was to come with a charging drive to second at Valencia.

Next time out, at Imola, it was GP2's impressive newcomer Trident Racing that stole the headlines as ex-Minardi F1 driver Gianmaria Bruni raced away from pole to victory in the feature race. The sprint race win fell to Ernesto Viso, the likeable Venezuelan claiming his maiden win following a switch to iSport from BCN over the winter.

It was not until the third round of the season, at the Nürburgring, that Hamilton really sprang to life, but when he did it was truly worth waiting for. His win in the feature was so dominant that he was even able to pick up a drive-through penalty for speeding in the pit lane and still resume in the lead. Without the penalty his winning margin would have exceeded 40 seconds.

The win meant he started eighth on the grid for the sprint but, in an extraordinary demonstration of sublime racecraft, he scythed his way through the pack. His ability to brake harder and later than any of his rivals would be the ace in his hand throughout the season.

His weakest link, though, was qualifying and another average starting position forced ART to bring him in early for his mandatory pit stop at the next race, held at Barcelona, in the hope of leapfrogging him up the order. It worked, too, and he assumed the lead following the stops. But team-mate Prémat was next up and catching fast. The Frenchman was on much newer rubber and had a clear speed advantage.

There are no team orders at ART, but the team doesn't expect its drivers to hit each other, either – but that's exactly what happened. Prémat clipped the rear of Hamilton's car as they exited the hairpin. Hamilton was able to continue to claim second, but those two lost points could have been crucial.

Centre left: Timo Glock did a great job consolidating his reputation as a potential F1 talent. Here he effusively celebrates his win at Hockenheim.

Left: Prémat enjoys the trappings of victory at Barcelona, where he tipped team-mate Lewis Hamilton into a spin.

Below: Gianmaria Bruni celebrates a crushing win at Imola.
Photographs: James Moy/www.crashpa.net

Above: First-lap action in Turkey. Andreas Zuber leads from Xandinho Negrão (car 12) and Adam Carroll (car 9).
Photograph: James Moy/www.crashpa.net

Right: Venezuelan rising star Ernesto Viso notched up a good win at Imola. Later in the year he took on the role of third driver for the newly rebranded Spyker F1 team at the Brazilian GP.
Photographs: Mike Weston/www.crashpa.net

Centre right: Nicolas Lapierre had a tough season with Arden.

Below right: Giorgio Pantano scored an emotional double win at the Monza season finale.
Photographs: James Moy/www.crashpa.net

Viso showed Imola was no fluke by taking sprint race honours, while Piquet kept his early title lead with a strong second.

During his demolition of the F3 Euro Series opposition in 2005, Hamilton took two imperious wins at Monaco – and GP2 was no different. Only Franck Perera, in by far his best drive of the season, was close – and even he was out of sight at the end.

But good as Hamilton's drive was in Monaco, it was nothing compared with his performances at Silverstone.

Piquet took pole, as he did more times than the rest of the field put together in 2006, but lost this one after a yellow flag infringement. Not that it made any difference, for Hamilton was unstoppable in front of his home fans and swept to his fourth win of the year. In the sprint he was simply inspired, passing Piquet and Clivio Piccione in a stunning three-abreast move through Becketts.

Hamilton's drive rightly took all the plaudits but, farther back, Timo Glock, in his first drive for iSport after a mid-season switch from BCN, recovered from stalling on the grid to nick the final point. It was a drive as good as Hamilton's and from now on the German would be a constant threat.

The final mid-season test took place ahead of the next round (at Magny-Cours) and somewhere during the Paul Ricard test runs ART lost its way. Hamilton was nowhere in the feature as Glock grabbed a commanding win, and a typical charging drive in the sprint netted Hamilton fifth as Giorgio Pantano celebrated his first GP2 success, transforming the fortunes of Giancarlo Fisichella's team following his mid-season call-up.

Hamilton may not have been setting the pace but, when Piquet failed to score in Germany after his car broke in race one, Hamilton assumed a seemingly impregnable 26-point lead. For the record, Bruni and Glock snaffled up the Hockenheim wins.

But things turned about abruptly in Hungary. Hamilton made his first driving error of the season when he crashed in free practice and then amazingly followed it up with his second in qualifying, meaning he started right at the back. Typically Piquet was on pole and he drove into the distance in the feature. For the sprint race the track was sodden but Piquet was again imperious and two wins, both fastest laps and pole gave him the first ever GP2 maximum points haul. Suddenly it was game on!

Piquet followed this up with another easy win from pole in Turkey, leaving Hamilton's once-huge lead dangling by a thread. But the Briton produced a virtuoso display in the sprint, recovering from an early spin to scythe through from 18th to second in what he admitted was his finest performance in a racing car. The win went to Trident's Andreas Zuber, but the Austrian's great performance was totally overshadowed by Hamilton's effort.

The season finale played out at Monza, a fitting venue for an exhilarating title showdown. Hamilton held a ten-point lead, so needed to beat Piquet and score fastest lap in the feature to wrap up the title. Piquet was on pole as expected but Pantano separated the title protagonists and the Italian was on inspired form all weekend, leaving Piquet and Hamilton in his dust. Second for Piquet and third for Hamilton meant there were six points between them with seven still to play for.

But as the sun set over the historic Monza park, the stewards pored over the data for Pantano's fastest lap and decided it had been set while yellow flags waved for Perera's stricken DAMS machine. The lap was annulled and the fastest lap point went to Hamilton instead – who became the 2006 GP2 champion.

With one of the best starts ever to go unpenalised, Pantano shot from eighth to lead into the first corner of the sprint and the season ended with an emotional Italian savouring an amazing home double.

His wins lifted Pantano to fifth overall in the standings behind Hamilton and Piquet, who were head and shoulders above the rest, and Prémat, who secured third from Glock after the German hurt his wrist in a feature race shunt with Spaniard Adrian Valles.

Viso took sixth, Bruni seventh. Adam Carroll had a frustrating season with Racing Engineering and took eighth; the spectacular Brit was on pole at Silverstone and could have won the sprint in Hungary before he spun off while leading. Nicolas Lapierre took ninth despite missing two rounds after a back-breaking pile-up in Monaco, while José María López – probably the best qualifier after Piquet – took tenth following a frustrating year at Super Nova that promised much but delivered little.

GP2 again showed that one-make single seater racing can be exciting, that overtaking is possible almost everywhere expect Barcelona and that in Hamilton and Piquet there are two bright stars waiting in the wings for a centre-stage role in F1.

Below: Red Bull protégé Michael Ammermüller took a single victory, in the sprint race at Valencia.
Photograph: Mike Weston/www.crashpa.net

Bottom: Nelson Piquet Jr was edged out in the title race by Hamilton, but enjoyed plenty of podiums throughout the year.
Photograph: GP2 Media Service

A1 GP 'WORLD CUP OF MOTORSPORT' REVIEW

FRANCE *'FORMIDABLE'*

by OLLIE BARSTOW

The pack thunders away at the start of the race at Shanghai. Malaysia's Alex Yoong, Alexandre Prémat of France and GB's Darren Manning head the field, followed by Indonesia's Ananda Mikola and Portugal's Cesar Campaniço.
Photograph: A1 GP Media Service

WITH a reach of up to ten million viewers around the world and a grid representing 80 percent of the global population, the A1 Grand Prix 'World Cup of Motorsport' was an intriguing concept.

After two years of preparation and months of publicity, and with a dose of the cynicism that goes with any alien motor racing series threatening to upset the established order, A1 Grand Prix went live at Brands Hatch on 25 September, 2005 in front of a healthy crowd of patriotic, if curious, fans. Seven months and 22 races later, the curtain closed on the inaugural season and, although spectator levels were occasionally suspect, the concept and close racing had nonetheless invigorated several careers and done enough for the series to merit a second season.

The compelling format led to an impressive 26-strong cosmopolitan field that lined up in Kent for the fruition of Sheikh Maktoum's ambitious brainchild, with usual suspects such as Great Britain, France, Brazil and Germany joined by lesser heralded nations, including Lebanon, Pakistan and Indonesia. The varied line-up brought former F1 personalities together with up-and-coming GP2 drivers and the odd touring car, sports car, IndyCar, ChampCar and national formula star.

Still, it did not take long for an order to be established and it was the tricolore of France that marked itself out as the one to beat, the formidable combination of Alex Prémat and Nicolas Lapierre proving dominant over the first half of the season.

However, France wasn't the first country to feature on the list of race winners: that honour instead went to Brazil, the French duo's GP2 rival Nelson Piquet Jr giving A1 GP the cachet of a renowned name storming to wins in both races at Brands.

The next round, at the Lausitzring in Germany, kick-started a devastating run of eight victories for France. Indeed, following a weekend of falling foul to the frustrating teething problems that come with any new car, Lapierre took over from Prémat to hit back with two lights-to-flag wins. Taking advantage of a feature race grid decided by the outcome of the sprint event, Prémat repeated Lapierre's feat at Estoril, Portugal, with Lapierre returning to double up yet again in the series' first foray outside Europe, at Australia's Eastern Creek circuit.

Victories seven and eight followed at Sepang with Prémat at the wheel – although only after a fierce fight in both races that showcased just how close the racing in identical 550-bhp Zytek-engined Lola chassis could become. With liberal use of the 'power boost' button, which offered an extra 30 bhp for a short amount of time to help with overtaking, France embarked

on an afternoon of tussling with both Switzerland and Great Britain, who, together with Brazil, were fast emerging as the biggest competition for the runaway leaders.

Indeed, it was Switzerland, run by the DAMS team that was overseeing the French project and armed with driver Neel Jani, that was arguably providing the sternest challenge, having appeared on the podium once in Germany, twice in Portugal and again in Australia. Nonetheless, despite Jani's best efforts in a pair of races that were, at times, heart-stopping as he battled for the lead, it was Prémat who came away with two wins, while Jani had to settle for two more second places.

Still, Switzerland would not have to wait much longer to break its duck and end the French streak, with Jani triumphing from pole at the very next round, in a hot and dusty Dubai. With Lapierre struggling for once, France did not even make the podium, allowing a pair of unfamiliar faces – Enrico Toccacelo for Italy and Tomas Enge for the Czech Republic – to join Jani.

While the French domination had somewhat taken the spectacle away from the championship fight, battles farther down the field were still intensely fought, with New Zealand, Australia, Mexico, Britain, Canada, Ireland and Portugal all tasting champagne in the first five meetings.

The respite was short-lived, however, for, despite stumbling in the first Dubai race, Lapierre put France back where it was used to being in the feature event after Jani hit problems. The British entry of former F3 champion Robbie Kerr took second, having had a mixed season to that point, with four podiums between various incidents, some self-inflicted, some merely unlucky. Stephen Simpson, meanwhile, made South Africa the 13th nation from the 26 competing to score a podium.

With half the season down and France in a commanding position, South Africa and the streets of Durban beckoned for a field reduced to 24 after Russia called it quits and Japan briefly sat out in a bid to come back stronger later in the season.

Prémat delivered France its tenth win from 13 starts, Kerr and Jani again joining him on the podium. It was very nearly the Netherlands, and Jos Verstappen, that celebrated, but the former F1 star spun after making a daring final-lap move on Prémat.

Undeterred by starting 16th for the second race, Verstappen proved that his street-fighting form was no fluke, using several safety car periods and slick pit work, and some opportunistic racing, to make the most of Jani's mechanical woes on the final lap of the feature race to claim a stunning victory.

Rounds 15 and 16 took the championship to Indonesia and the little-known Sentul circuit, further evidence of A1 GP's determination to take motor sport to untouched markets. A healthy crowd turned up to see Lapierre put France even farther out of reach. Second place allowed Kerr to keep the pressure on Switzerland and Brazil – which had now switched to former F1 driver, and son of team boss Emerson, Christian Fittipaldi following Piquet's decision to concentrate on his GP2 campaign.

If the sprint race was predictable, however, the feature rewarded the Indonesian spectators for their attendance, as Sean McIntosh give Canada a surprise victory after a thrilling run from last on the grid – with a drive-through penalty to boot.

During a physical race, McIntosh made the most of numerous safety car periods to hit the front with five laps remaining and continued for a stunning win. Alex Yoong gave Malaysia reason to celebrate with second, its first podium, and Marcus Marshall took third for Australia on his A1 début.

The next round, at Curitiba in Brazil, was cancelled, giving the championship a short break before it visited Mexico's Monterrey circuit. France redressed the balance with another double victory, Prémat upholding the team's record for having won at least one race each weekend since the second round. It was a victory that set the team well on the way to confirming the inevitable during the following round, at Laguna Seca, California, with second place from Lapierre enough to confirm France as the first winner of the 'World Cup of Motorsport'.

The spoils on the day, though, were claimed by Mexico, with Salvador Duran annexing the top of the podium in both races. The British F3 driver had proved to be one of the surprise packages over the course of the season, with two earlier visits to the podium, and looked set to be a thorn in the sides of those chasing the higher points positions towards its close.

The title decided, the inaugural season came to a close at Shanghai, China, with exciting races and two new names on the winners' list as France split the races between its drivers for the first time. Taking advantage of the misguided strategy, Malaysia and the Czech Republic – with former F1 drivers Yoong and Enge – brought their seasons to an end on a high.

France was crowned champion with a comprehensive 51-point margin over nearest rival Switzerland, the gap having widened as the latter switched from the F1-committed Jani to Giorgio Mondini for the final rounds. Great Britain – which had to replace Kerr with Darren Manning in China – was a lonely third overall, ahead of surprise package New Zealand, whose

consistent scoring disguised the fact that it had managed only a single podium all season. Malaysia's late flourish put it in fifth overall, ahead of Brazil, the early frontrunner struggling towards the end of the season without Piquet at the wheel.

In all, a total of 54 drivers appeared over the 22 races, with eight winners and 18 visitors to the podium. A1 GP may have lost two nations by the finale and struggled to combat mid-season rumours of financial difficulties, but most people were in agreement that it was a concept that was here to stay.

With the creases from the first season having been ironed out, and the series proving less of an unknown quantity, A1 GP returned for a second campaign with a field of 23, having lost Portugal, Russia, Austria and Japan, and gained Greece and Singapore, and a calendar eager to exploit the more popular nations on the grid. Indeed, no country has taken A1 Grand Prix to its heart more than the Netherlands and the series rewarded its supporters' enthusiasm with a season-opener at Zandvoort.

In front of a crowd that would rival that of any Formula 1 GP, several new faces adorned the familiar teams, none more so than Adrian Zaugg, who pulled off a surprise maiden win for South Africa in race one, heading podium stalwarts Mexico and France, which fielded recognised pilots Duran and Lapierre.

It was the second race, though, that got the fans' hearts pumping with a thrilling drive from new national hero Jeroen Bleekemolen. He stepped in after Verstappen pulled out of his drive just days before the race, following financial qualms, and – making the most of his local knowledge in tricky weather conditions – scythed his way to the front of the field. However, local joy proved short-lived as the circuit began drying rapidly and the ensuing pit stops for dry-weather tyres allowed Nico Hülkenberg to catch and pass Bleekemolen for Germany's first-ever win. Bleekemolen finished fourth, behind the USA – Philip Giebler delivered its first podium – and Australia's Ryan Briscoe.

Just a week later the series headed east to another new venue, Brno in the Czech Republic, where, despite the hype surrounding Enge's appearance in his homeland, it was all about Malaysia as Yoong stormed to a superb double win, holding off the advances of Canada's James Hinchcliffe.

With two exciting rounds down and a calendar that includes races in Beijing, China, and Taupo in New Zealand for the first time, and stronger financial backing, A1 Grand Prix looks in rude health. It has a dedicated field of teams and ever-increasing awareness, and the series' unique selling point may just be enough for it to become a permanent motor sport fixture.

A1GP™
World Cup of Motorsport™

Netherlands
1 October 06

Czech Republic
8 October 06

China
12 November 06

Malaysia
26 November 06

Indonesia
10 December 06

New Zealand
21 January 07

Australia
4 February 07

South Africa
25 February 07

Brazil
18 March 07

Mexico
25 March 07

China
15 April 07

Great Britain
29 April 07

RAB CAPITAL

SKY SPORTS

GET YOUR HEART RACING

FORMULA 3 REVIEW
BRIT'S TOP OF THE CROP
by CRAIG LLEWELLYN

Above: Paul di Resta emerged triumphant in the F3 Euro Series at the wheel of his ASM team Dallara-Mercedes.

Centre right: Echoes of Ayrton. Bruno Senna looks uncannily like his late uncle as he dons his balaclava.

Centre far right: Rookie Oliver Jarvis attracted a lot of attention for his excellent performances in his Carlin Motorsport Dallara.
Photographs: Jakob Ebrey Motorsports Photography

Bottom right: Sebastian Vettel may have been edged out by Di Resta but his graduation to Formula 1 with BMW Sauber is more than adequate compensation.
Photograph: XPB.cc

IF BOTH major F3 competitions – the Euro Series and British International Championship – were dominated by just one driver each in 2005, 2006 at least provided closer rivalries and title races that went close, if not all the way, to the wire.

Lewis Hamilton's 2005 Euro Series campaign has become the stuff of F3 legend, with 16 race wins in 20 outings, setting him up for an equally laudable season in GP2. Several other leading lights joined Hamilton in progressing from the Euro Series, leaving the way open for a fresh face to emerge.

With a crop of talented youngsters, including Jonathan Summerton and Kamui Kobayashi, joining the battle against established Euro 'veterans' Paul di Resta, Richard Antinucci, Sebastian Vettel, Kohei Hirate, Esteban Guerrieri and Giedo van der Garde, and some with prior F3 experience, such as Charlie Kimball and Kazuki Nakajima, switching from other series, it appeared that something special would be required for one man to break away.

Unsurprisingly, Vettel and Brit Di Resta, fifth and tenth in 2005, emerged as the frontrunners, even though it took five races for Di Resta to reach the top step of the podium, at Oschersleben. Vettel had already opened his account, in race two of the opening round at Hockenheim. Di Resta, however, went on to win four more times, adding a home success at Brands Hatch (England) and victories at the Norisring (Germany), Zandvoort (Holland) – in a repeat of his Ultimate Masters triumph – and Le Mans (France), while Vettel kept up the pressure by taking top spot twice at the Nürburgring (Germany) in August – some five rounds after his maiden success – and once more at Barcelona (Spain) to keep the title race alive into its closing stages.

Neither man could establish a meaningful advantage, however, for both were prone to mistakes and bad results, allowing no fewer than nine other drivers to take the top step and a grand total of 15 to make the podium.

Due to the introduction of reverse grids for the second race of each weekend, the list of winners took on a slightly unusual appearance, with Antinucci and Guerrieri taking 'best of the rest' honours with triumphs at Barcelona and Le Mans (France),

and Lausitz (Germany) and Hockenheim respectively. They were joined in the 'top step club' by Hirate, Nakajima, Van der Garde, Kimball, Sébastien Buemi – who had graduated from Formula BMW – Summerton and reigning Recaro F3 Cup champion Peter Elkmann, the latter benefiting from the Brands Hatch Indy circuit's lack of overtaking opportunities to win from the equally unfancied Michael Herck and Kobayashi.

Di Resta eventually claimed the title, making it three British champions in a row, on the opening day of the final meeting. Despite Hockenheim's being a favourite of rival Vettel's, Di Resta was able to secure the crown with tenth place in race one. He had started from pole, adding a decisive point to his tally, but a jump-start penalty after a hasty getaway meant that he had a nerve-wracking afternoon as Vettel pursued the win that would have taken the title race into the next day. As it was, Vettel finished third, handing the crown to his ASM team-mate.

Vettel's future, however, looks the more assured: he has already made his Formula 1 début with BMW Sauber. Backed by drinks giant Red Bull, he appears to have everything going for him and is confirmed as BMW's test and reserve driver for 2007. Di Resta, by contrast, ends the year struck by the usual British affliction of lacking sponsorship. ASM and Mercedes appear keen that he try the German touring car championship DTM, following in 2004 champion Jamie Green's wheeltracks rather than predecessor Hamilton's.

Hirate made the most of his move to Manor Motorsport to claim third overall, edging Guerrieri by three points. He spearheaded a renewed Far Eastern threat to the Euro Series, with Nakajima joining him in John Booth's potent squad and claiming seventh in the table in his first Euro foray. ASM's Kobayashi, meanwhile, claimed ninth in his first F3 campaign and comfortably took rookie honours ahead of Summerton.

Behind them, Guerrieri was fourth and Antinucci fifth. Van der Garde was sixth but will feel that, given his F3 experience, he should have challenged his team-mates up front. His sole win came at the tricky Norisring street circuit, but he was inconsistent elsewhere, scoring less than half of Di Resta's tally.

Moreau and Summerton completed the top ten, the latter

improving all the time and netting his first F3 win as he made the most of the last reverse grid of the year. Moreau, however, was disappointing, taking just one podium with Signature-Plus, at the opening meeting. Kimball and Romain Grosjean claimed 12th and 13th, Kimball on the same points tally as Buemi.

Unsurprisingly, ASM cruised to the teams' title, 50 points clear of Manor, with Signature-Plus taking third, all benefiting from running more than the average two cars.

The main topic of conversation before the British series kicked off was not so much who would win, but what. The introduction of the all-conquering Mercedes-Benz engine from the Euro Series caused consternation among those not being granted access to it, but the questions died down just as soon as the venerable Mugen-Honda unit proved capable of holding its own.

Second-year driver Mike Conway was the pre-season favourite, joining 2005 newcomer Räikkönen Robertson Racing and the Merc engine. His closest rivals were reckoned to be team-mate Bruno Senna, reigning national class (for older cars) king Salvador Duran and Hitech colleague James Walker, leaving rookies Oliver Jarvis, Maro Engel and Yelmer Buurman with less pressure on their young shoulders.

Some 23 years after his uncle Ayrton won the British title, Senna was quickest out of the traps, claiming a double win at Oulton Park, while Conway languished in fifth and third. Double R's third driver Stephen Jelley and the equally unfancied Christian Bakkerud grabbed early moments in the limelight.

By the end of the second meeting, however, it was apparent that Conway's pre-season popularity was well judged as he embarked on a run of seven straight podium finishes – including wins at Donington and Snetterton (two). A rogue fourth place in race one at Spa (Belgium) proved a minor interruption and the victories continued to flow at Silverstone GP (two) and Brands Hatch GP to give him a commanding advantage by late August.

Wins seven and eight followed on the series' return to Silverstone, before Conway's sole retirement, in race one of the Thruxton finale, added a blip to his record. That aside, seventh in

Oulton was followed by generally strong results, especially for a rookie, culminating in a first win at Mondello Park in the fourth round. Only one more win followed, at Brands Hatch GP in August, but Jarvis proved the closest to matching Conway's all-round talent, taking the runner-up spot in the end-of-season standings after a brace of podiums at the Thruxton finale.

Next season could provide a difficult choice for the Briton who, having tested World Series by Renault (WSbR) machinery in December 2005, has gone on to add A1 Grand Prix to his CV. A pair of race outings in WSbR's Barcelona 2006 finale showed that he has the recognition to step up, but taking the F3 title in year two could be a better career move. He wouldn't have to face Senna, who is already eyeing a move to GP2.

Should Jarvis opt to stay put, his most likely opposition could come from fellow second-year pilots Buurman and Engel, who proved almost as surprising in their rookie seasons.

Buurman was the only driver to break the duopoly of Double R and Carlin, taking the honours on the final laps at Spa and Thruxton, but it was his wet-weather prowess that really caught attention as he claimed fourth in the points.

Engel, meanwhile, stepped up to the series with backing from ambitious Monaco-based, Japanese-funded F1 wannabe Direxiv. While the company's grand prix ambitions faded and died, however, Engel continued to flourish, taking a mid-season win – and two poles – at Spa and adding second places there and at Donington and Brands Hatch GP for good measure. His season ended quietly, with a string of ninth places, but he is one to watch should he be back for more in 2007.

Bakkerud was the only other driver to win in 2006, success in the first race at Mugello going some way to erasing the mix of bad luck and bad mistakes that had dogged him since his graduation in 2005. He took sixth in the championship and is another man looking to move up next season.

Bakkerud edged Jelley for P6, the Briton having surpassed expectation, and previous results, following his surprise move to Räikkönen Robertson. Meanwhile, fellow Briton James Walker

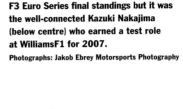

Below: Kohei Hirate finished third in the F3 Euro Series final standings but it was the well-connected Kazuki Nakajima (below centre) who earned a test role at WilliamsF1 for 2007.

Photographs: Jakob Ebrey Motorsports Photography

race three of the season at Donington Park proved his worst result as he cruised to an eventual 71-point winning margin.

A taste of things to come was provided mid-season when Conway was called up to DPR's GP2 Series team to stand in for the injured Olivier Pla at the British Grand Prix. Eleventh and 12th places without pre-race testing showed that the Briton would not be out of his depth in the higher class and he has already tested with stronger outfits with a view to 2007.

Senna's winning start continued in the opening race of round two, at Donington, but he then embarked on an erratic few months, with 11th and tenth next time out at Pau (France) followed by a win in the first race at Mondello Park. A massive shunt in the first race at Snetterton, in which it is believed that his Dallara brushed the underside of the bridge on Revett Straight, precluded his participation in the second event, but did not appear to dent his confidence: he stayed in the fight with a string of podiums, including a win at Mugello. However, those results were again interspersed with lesser scores and Senna quickly found himself embroiled in a battle for second overall.

His rival in that scrap was none other than Jarvis, the reigning Formula Renault champion armed with a Mugen engine and the experience of Carlin Motorsport. A podium first time out at

soil, but the Dutchman fluffed his lines at the lights and, with overtaking at a premium on the seaside track, could only get back into second after passing Buemi early on.

Di Resta, who had started on the front row, was away and gone and the race in his wake proved to be largely processional, with Hirate, Romain Grosjean and Vettel running line astern more or less from the start to complete the top six.

With the event running on similar Kumho tyres to the Euro Series', it was not surprising that the continental series annexed the top positions, but the leading UK-based runner managed just seventh, as was the case in 2005. This time, Senna proved to have the beating of team-mate Conway – who crashed out after five laps of the final – and Jarvis, who followed the Brazilian across the line, with Engel next up, in a distant 15th.

The 'British is best' theme continued on the opposite side of the globe, with Ben Clucas and James Winslow to the fore in the Australian and Asian series respectively.

Unable to find the budget to build on a successful sporadic national class campaign in the UK, Clucas took up the opportunity to join Team BRM in Australia and impressed from the outset. He began as he meant to go on, winning all but one of those races he started. With the crown all but in his hand luggage, the Briton took the liberty of missing the final couple of rounds, indulging in a successful V8 test with FPR.

Tim Macrow snatched runners-up honours with double top in the final meeting, relegating Michael Trimble to third. Chris Gilmour and Leanne Tander rounded out the top five, the female racer taking a historic pole for the final weekend.

Winslow is another talent lost to his native series, but has shown what the UK is missing by coming good late in his second Asian campaign. He was third overall in 2005 and a string of solid finishes early in 2006 led to eight wins and the championship, ahead of Tyson Sy and Ali Jackson. Winslow also made headlines around the world for his dramatic rescue of rival Moreno Soeprapto from a fiery accident at Sentul (Indonesia).

Jackson, too, enjoyed a run of success, taking four wins in five races mid-season to establish a temporary European one-two at the head of the standings, with the Asian pursuit headed by Tyson Sy of the Philippines, who opened the year with a hat-trick of victories. Another Brit, Dillon Battistini finished fourth overall, ahead of Soeprapto and Dado Pena.

Britain could also have claimed success in the Germany-based Recaro F3 Cup, but Joey Foster suffered serious back injuries at the seventh round at Lausitz, ruling him out for the rest of the year. Another unable to find the funds for a UK campaign, Foster linked up with Lola and HS Technik Motorsport, taking four wins in the opening eight races, but his accident allowed JB Motorsport's Ho-Pin Tung to ease to the title, ahead of Ferdinand Kool and Harald Schlegelmilch.

One driver who would certainly have challenged Di Resta and Vettel in the Euro Series instead took top honours in Japan, driving for TOM'S. Adrian Sutil played the back-up role to Lewis Hamilton at ASM in 2005 and his departure for the Far East left the way open for the 2006 title rivals to slot in to the all-conquering French squad.

Like Clucas in Australia, Sutil defied a lack of familiarity to win the opening round and took four further victories to emerge on top of the points ahead of Brazilian Roberto Streit (Inglng) and TOM'S team-mate Kazuya Oshima. Controversy clouded the final round, from which the TOM'S duo was excluded for technical irregularities, allowing first-time winners Hiroaki Ishiura and British F3 refugee Marko Asmer to join Takuya Izawa, Kodai Tsukakoshi, category veteran Fabio Carbone, Oshima, Streit and Sutil on the victor list.

The Spanish F3 series remains undecided as AUTOCOURSE goes to press, with Ricardo Risatti holding a decent 16-point advantage over nearest rivals Roldan Rodriguez and Máximo Cortés with the final Barcelona double-header to run. The rest of the field, headed by Nicolas Prost, son of Alain, is a fair way behind but, after the shenanigans of 2005 – when the unfancied Andy Soucek came through first-lap final-race mayhem to claim the title – no one is taking anything for granted.

Finally, the Sud-Am series has two rounds to run, but is headed by Mario Moraes, who holds a tenuous three-point advantage over the highly rated Luiz Razia.

Top: Mike Conway in action on the superb Pau street circuit, which hosted a round of the British championship. Conway (above centre left), did a very good job winning the British F3 crown for Räikkönen Robertson Racing.
Photographs: Jakob Ebrey Motorsports Photography

Centre right: Di Resta gained kudos from seeing off BMW Sauber protégé Sebastian Vettel to win the Euro Series crown.
Photograph: XPB.cc

Above: Venezuelan Rodolfo Gonzalez took the national class honours in the British F3 Championship.
Photograph: Jakob Ebrey Motorsports Photography

– a pre-season tip, remember – struggled to make an impact, claiming ninth overall, behind rookie James Jakes, after just three podium appearances, all before mid-season. Duran, likewise, struggled against expectations, his best being fourth at Silverstone before ducking out of the final round to return to A1 Grand Prix with Team Mexico.

The national class, however, continued to be a successful hunting ground for the South Americans, with Rodolfo Gonzalez cruising to a comfortable title by winning at least one race at almost every round. Only the second Silverstone meeting slipped through the Venezuelan's grasp, but it was already too late for his rivals to make up the ground lost early on.

South Africa's Cristiano Morgado claimed second spot 55 points shy of the title winner, while Juha Annala was unable to make the most of a year's F3 experience and finished third. Morgado took his four wins in the final four meetings with Fluid Motorsport's rare Lola, while Annala lucked into his trio when Gonzalez faltered at Pau, Snetterton and Silverstone.

This year Zandvoort provided the in-season blue-riband event in which British F3 meets Euro Series. Once again, the Euro Series came out on top, this time with Di Resta heading the field. He should have had to take second best behind ASM team-mate Van der Garde, who excelled in qualifying on home

FORMULA 3
EURO SERIES

KONI Official Partner of the Formula 3 Euro Series

ITT
Engineered for life

SPORTS & GT REVIEW by GARY WATKINS

AUDI'S DIESEL DOMINATION

Main: The victorious Audi R10 TDI relentlessly chasing down its opposition en route to a historic Le Mans victory.

Left: Race winners Emanuele Pirro, Frank Biela and Marco Werner with team boss, Dr Wolfgang Ullrich.

Top right: The two Audi Sport Team Joest cars cross the line together at the end of the race, with the winning car of Biela, Pirro and Werner on the right.

Photographs: Mike Weston/www.crashpa.net

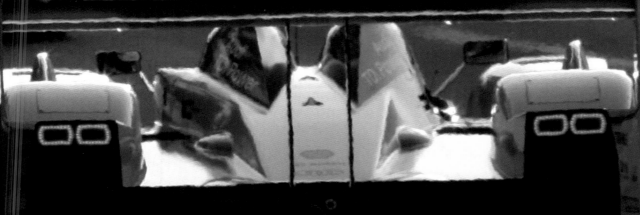

HISTORY was made at Le Mans in 2006. And not because Tom Kristensen failed to win the 24 Hours for the first time this millennium. The story of the 74th running of the great event was more about technology than human spirit, which is why it will find a prominent place in the annals of the sport in years to come. That is a pity for race winners Emanuele Pirro, Frank Biela and Marco Werner because they drove a near-faultless race.

Yet their achievements paled into insignificance alongside those of Audi. Domination by the German manufacturer at La Sarthe is nothing new but doing it with a car powered by diesel made headlines around the world.

Which, of course, was Audi's intention when it decided to go back to La Sarthe with a full factory team in place of the importer-backed squads that had won the race in 2004 and 2005. The chances are that it wouldn't have returned at all had not the opportunity to go with diesel power arisen courtesy of a rule change in which it almost certainly had a hand back in 2003.

Audi likes to promote a message when it goes racing and the top LMP1 prototype class is now open to 5.5-litre turbo-diesels, presenting just such an opportunity. Would the Ingolstadt marque have returned but for that chance? No one could tell, but Audi Sport boss Dr Wolfgang Ullrich offered some indication at the official launch of its diesel-powered R10 in Paris in December 2005.

'I went to the board with the idea of a diesel, so I can't say how they would have reacted if I came with another idea,' he said. 'Whenever we do a new project we want to bring a message, just as we did with FSI [direct fuel injection] on the R8. If we had come back using the same technology as before, there would have been no message.'

Work – hard work and lots of it – was something that Audi faced when it took the decision to go racing with a diesel. There were several technology barriers to be overcome on the way to producing the world's first purpose-designed diesel racing engine and a car into which to shoehorn it.

'The biggest challenge of going to Le Mans with diesel power is that no one had built such an engine in the past,' said Dr Ulrich Baretzky, the man behind the new V12 powerplant and also the conventionally fuelled twin-turbo V8 that powered the R10's predecessor, the R8, and the Bentley Speed 8.

'There was no experience to build on, so we were starting from zero.' The demands faced by Baretzky and Audi Sport's engine technology department included producing an engine light enough for an open-top LMP1 prototype.

'Weight is everything in a race car,' he said. 'We couldn't compromise the behaviour of the car with a massive weight at the rear. That is why we made the engine in aluminium and worked hard to keep it as light as possible.'

The 5.5-litre V12 still had to be phenomenally strong – stronger than a petrol engine. Baretzky pointed out that the cylinder pressures inside a road-going diesel were already significantly higher than those in the R8 powerplant. How that strength was engineered into the R10 TDI race engine was something he wouldn't disclose.

'We do this in a very clever way,' was all he would say.

Audi successfully overcame the technical problems associated with running a diesel. The R10 didn't have the kind of test programme enjoyed by the R8 six years previously. Yet by the time of its race début at the Sebring 12 Hours, the opening round of the American Le Mans Series, in March, it was already a reliable racing machine.

The technical brains at Audi Sport, led by Baretzky and technical director Wolfgang Apel, had done their jobs well.

Some would argue that Ullrich had done an even better job during his negotiations with the men in blazers at the Automobile Club de l'Ouest (ACO), the organisers of Le Mans. Audi and Ullrich clearly held all the aces when they went into the smoke-filled room with the ACO. The race organisers needed Audi's continued participation at a time when no other car makers were queuing up to join the LMP1 grid.

That explains why those running conventional, petrol-engined machinery in the LMP1 class cried foul long before the R10 had even seen the light of day. The calculations of the engine specialists providing power to the rest of the prototype field – the likes of Judd, Zytek and AER – reckoned the rules favoured the diesels.

Left: Emanuele Pirro sits calmly through a scheduled pit stop for the winning Audi R10 TDI at Le Mans.

Bottom: The Le Mans GT1 class-winning Chevrolet Corvette C6R was shared by Oliver Gavin, Olivier Beretta and Jan Magnussen in the epic French event.
Photographs: Mike Weston/www.crashpa.net

Below: Audi's roll of honours needs a revamp after its highly successful 2006 campaign.
Photograph: Richard Dole/LAT Photographic

That gave them a clear advantage in terms of power. Not just a few horses and not even a few tens of horsepower, but perhaps as much as 100 bhp.

Factor in the massive torque offered by a turbo-diesel and the advantages in terms of fuel economy and it was easy to understand why the best of the privateers ranged against Audi and the crack Joest Racing team at Le Mans was talking down its chances long before the race began.

'There is no way we can win unless Audi has problems,' said Emmanuel Collard, lead driver at the Pescarolo Sport squad. The Frenchman qualified third, two seconds behind the Audis, and fell away at a similar rate over the opening laps. His opinion didn't change after the first couple of stints.

'The Audi was just too fast,' said Collard, who shared his Judd-engined C60 with Erik Comas and Nicolas Minassian. 'I was really trying in the opening laps, taking kerbs and pushing hard, but I was still two seconds a lap slower. They were faster than us under acceleration, under braking, everywhere.'

Pescarolo could only hope for those problems, technical or otherwise. Audi did have its troubles, but they were largely restricted to one car. Pirro, Biela and Werner ran through the race with only one technical glitch on the way to a four-lap victory.

Seven-times Le Mans winner Kristensen had to relinquish his crown because it was his R10, the number 7 or 'yellow', after the colour of its roll structure, that hit the lion's share of Audi's problems. The car he shared with Allan McNish and Rinaldo Capello required prolonged stops to change its fuel injectors, repair a bent corner after a clash with a slower car and replace one of the V12 TDI powerplant's turbochargers. There was never going to be any way back from those kinds of delays.

Or, as Kristensen put it, 'You don't win Le Mans if you keep parking the car in the night.'

The first of those trips into the garage occurred as early as the fourth hour. Capello had reported that the engine wasn't running cleanly and Kristensen was back in the pits just seven laps after taking over the car. The entire bank of fuel injectors on the right side of the V12 TDI engine required changing at the cost of 20 minutes.

Kristensen resumed in 11th place, six laps behind the sister car. The race may not have been four hours old, yet it had had its last change at the top of the leader board.

The best of the Pescarolos, which Comas had taken over from Collard, was already the best part of a lap behind. The team's worst-case scenario was playing out in front of its eyes. Its Judd-powered C60 hadn't proved to be anywhere a match for the all-new Audi.

What's more, the more fancied of the two Pescarolos encountered the kind of problems Collard had hoped would hit the Audis. It lost the best part of 30 laps during the night with an electrical problem that took four prolonged pit stops to cure. A distant fifth was all Collard and co could manage at the finish.

Biela, Pirro and Werner encountered their one delay of any consequence approaching the 11-hour mark, when fifth gear broke. Even though replacing the entire rear-end, gearbox, rear suspension *et al* is now outlawed at Le Mans, the Joest mechanics were able to replace the internals of the R10's Xtrac gearbox in under ten minutes.

The lost time halved the leaders' advantage at the front of the field. The second-string Pescarolo, driven by Franck Montagny, Eric Hélary and World Rally champion Sébastien Loeb, had slipped to four laps behind at the ten-hour mark, but the Audi's pace ensured that there would need to be further problems if it was to get any closer. And those never came.

Pescarolo did hang on to the runner-up spot, finishing 'best of the rest' for the second year in a row. The Kristensen Audi was just too far behind after its multitude of delays and ended up third, a further nine laps back.

Corvette drivers Oliver Gavin, Olivier Beretta and Jan Magnussen claimed a hat-trick of GT1 class victories for the Pratt & Miller Chevy team after a thrilling battle with the best of the Prodrive Aston Martins, driven by Stéphane Sarrazin, Stéphane Ortelli and Pedro Lamy. They were separated by just a handful of seconds for the first quarter of the race. The Aston DBR9 had built up a lead of just over a lap when clutch failure brought it into the pits with a shade under three hours to go.

That allowed the Corvette to notch up its fifth class victory in six years at Le Mans and claim an impressive fourth overall. The second Prodrive Aston, driven by Tomas Enge, Andrea Piccini and Darren Turner, came through to second after losing six laps early on when Turner jumped a kerb coming into the pits and split an oil line.

It was another classic confrontation between the Pratt & Miller and Prodrive teams, but one that was always going to be overshadowed by Audi's overall victory. It was the same over in the American Le Mans Series (ALMS).

The R10 had an impressive maiden season, even by Audi standards. It won first time out at Sebring, with McNish, Capello and Kristensen, and took the laurels every time it appeared. Those with long memories will remember that the all-conquering R8 was beaten third time out.

The R10s didn't re-cross the Atlantic again until after Le Mans. In between times McNish and Capello relied on the trusty R8, notching up two more victories from three starts. It was fitting that the car should end its career on a round 50 ALMS victories at Lime Rock, New England, in July.

Two R10s, run by the US Champion squad, were back on the ALMS grid for the final six races. They were pushed hard by the US Dyson team's pair of AER-engined Lola B06/10s and, for the final two races, the Zytek 06s, but the Audi was too good an all-round package to be beaten even when the series organisers started handing out weight breaks to its competitors.

McNish and Capello were the class act in the ALMS and claimed the drivers' crown with ease. Team mates Pirro and Biela beat them only twice and their only other defeat came when they were still at the wheel of the R8. Porsche's new LMP2 class RS Spyder, run by Penske, won overall at Mid-Ohio with Timo Bernhard and Romain Dumas.

Lucas Luhr and Sascha Maassen claimed the LMP2 title and GT1 honours went to Chevrolet and the Gavin-Beretta pairing. The American marque and Aston Martin each won five races, but the British manufacturer needed help from the organisers in the form of 'performance balancing'. A series of rule adjustments through the year undoubtedly helped the DBR9's competitiveness, but did little for the credibility of the series.

There was no such tinkering of the rules over in the Le Mans Series in Europe even though one team managed to do what Audi couldn't in America. Pescarolo drivers Collard and Jean-Christophe Boullion, who missed Le Mans with a wrist injury, won all five races in the lone C60 in which they were joined by Eric Hélary in one race and Didier Andre in the final two.

That Andre finished runner-up in the championship courtesy of his wins at Donington Park, England, and Jarama, Spain, said everything about the level of competition faced by Pescarolo. None of its rivals managed to string together anything approaching a coherent championship challenge.

Pescarolo may have dominated the championship, but it would be incorrect to say it had things entirely its own way. There were lots of cars that could take the fight to the French team, at least early on. Take the Donington round in August, for example. No fewer than six cars led the race, but only the Pescarolo and the works Zytek 06S topped the lap charts after the halfway stage.

The factory Courage-Mugen LC70, the Judd-engined example run by Serge Saulnier's Swiss Spirit squad and Creation Autosportif's new CA06/H all had the pace to challenge for an hour or possibly two. The moment the lead driver climbed out, however, any chance of victory disappeared. The only real exception came when Zytek paired Stefan Johansson with Hideki Noda in its new 06S for two races.

Aston Martin claimed GT1 honours with the Larbre Competition team in the LMS to give the DBR9 its first title. That was something a flotilla of four Astons couldn't do in the FIA GT Championship. Factory-blessed cars from Scuderia Italia, plus privately entered DBR9s run by DTM refugees Phoenix Racing and the new RaceAlliance team, couldn't stop Maserati from winning both drivers' and teams' titles.

The Vitaphone Racing squad, run by long-time sports car and touring car driver Michael Bartels, was the most professional in the series, had the best car in the ever-controversial MC12 super car, arguably the two best driver line-ups and, unlike in 2005, luck on its side. Bartels fittingly took the drivers' crown together with Andrea Bertolini after a championship challenge built around victory in the double-points Spa 24 Hours round.

Honours in the GT2 division went to Ferrari. Jaime Melo and Matteo Bobbi claimed the title aboard the best of the new 430 GTs entered by the works-backed AF Corse team.

FIA GTs had a difficult year after its split from the World Touring Car Championship. Grand-Am over in the US, on the other hand, went from strength to strength. Grids continued to grow and the level of the teams improved, as well.

That makes Jörg Bergmeister's title with Krohn Racing all the more remarkable. The Atlanta-based team barely existed a couple of months prior to the season opener at Daytona in January yet, once it fitted Ford engines into its Riley chassis, it became the class act in the championship.

Class is a word that can also be used to describe the R10. The book closed on one great Audi prototype in 2006; there was evidence to suggest it opened on an even greater car.

Above: Audi's sports car racing success had a global reach, the German marque taking the honours in the American Le Mans Series. Here Allan McNish raises the sparks as he rushes through the famous corkscrew at Laguna Seca.
Photograph: ALMS Media

Below: Michael Bartels and Andrea Bertolini were the class of the field in the FIA GT Championship with their beautifully prepared Maserati.
Photograph: Mike Weston/www.crashpa.net

TOURING CAR REVIEW

THRILLS GALORE
by MATT SALISBURY

Main: Bruno Spengler takes the chequered flag to win the Hockenheim DTM finale for Mercedes-Benz. The German series continues to sustain great interest from its broad and loyal fan base.
Photograph: Manzoni/XPB.cc

Right: Door-to-door combat is the order of the day in the BTCC. Here, the two main championship protagonists Matt Neal and Jason Plato dispute the same piece of track.
Photograph: Jakob Ebrey Motorsport Photography

Far right: The WTCC turned out to be an equally hard-edged affair. Here Alex Zanardi's BMW finds itself the unwilling contents of a SEAT sandwich.
Photograph: Photo 4/XPB.cc

IT has been a somewhat historic year for touring car fans, the tin-top brigade again having provided some of the most exciting racing on the motor sport calendar.

Andy Priaulx came through a titanic battle to successfully defend his World Touring Car Championship crown, while Matt Neal became the first man to successfully defend the title in the modern era of the British Touring Car Championship (BTCC). Elsewhere, Bernd Schneider secured a record-breaking fifth championship in the German DTM series and, down under, the recent Holden domination of the famous Bathurst 1000 race has finally come to an end.

As was the case 12 months ago, in its first season, the WTCC title was decided on the streets of Macau. However, while the title fight was a three-way affair going into the 2005 finale – with Priaulx, Dirk Müller and Fabrizio Giovanardi all in with a shout of lifting the inaugural world crown – nine drivers were still in contention for the title.

Despite the withdrawal of Alfa Romeo as a works entry for the 2006 season, it was the Italian marque that led the way going to Macau, with Augusto Farfus proudly on top of the championship pile. The Brazilian moved to the head of the field at Valencia and he held a single-point lead over defending champion Priaulx and his fellow BMW ace Jorg Müller – with Gabriele Tarquini, Rickard Rydell, Dirk Müller, James Thompson, Yvan Muller and Peter Terting all mathematically capable of lifting the crown.

Victory for Priaulx in the opening race put him in the driving seat for the final race of the season and, despite victory for Jorg Müller, fifth place ensured that the Briton who ended the season on top of the world by just a single point – allowing him to match Roberto Ravaglia in winning three titles in a row.

'I'm numb with emotion,' said Priaulx, who also won the European Touring Car Championship in 2004. 'Winning three titles in a row is almost too much to take. To be honest, the pressure in the second race was unbearable and I couldn't have taken another lap of it. The only other person still in the title hunt, Jorg, was getting away in front and I was constantly under pressure from Fabrizio Giovanardi - he was hitting me every lap. But I knew I needed to finish sixth or better and we did it. It's a fantastic feeling.

'Lot of factors have come into play this season and I can't forget that in the penultimate race meeting, I came from almost last to score a single point – how important that proved to be…'

The fact that so many drivers could have claimed the title in Macau is an indication of how the season panned out, with no one able to stamp his authority on one of the most wide-open championships seen anywhere in recent memory. The 20 race wins were split between 11 drivers, with Priaulx taking five wins, Jorg Müller four and Farfus three. Eight other drivers took one victory each, including Rob Huff and Salvatore Tavano, two of the more unlikely winners. Despite SEAT's fielding as many as seven cars in some races, the rear-wheel-drive BMWs took more than half of the race wins, with Alfa Romeo on four, SEAT on three and Chevrolet on two – the Chevrolet Lacetti claiming its maiden WTCC victory in wet conditions at Brands Hatch in the hands of Alain Menu.

The 2007 WTCC season will have to go a long way to match the 2006 campaign in terms of drama, with the rumours already starting on who will be the front-runners for the new season. Only one thing is for sure, Priaulx and BMW remain the combination to beat.

At the start of the 2005 BTCC season, just 12 cars lined up on the grid at Donington Park. More than double that figure were present for the 2006 season finale – an indication of the continuing resurgence of the series.

As was the case last season, Team Halfords, with its Team Dynamics-built and run Honda Integras, was the team to beat: Steve Neal's privately run squad successfully defended the four titles it claimed in 2005. By far the most important of those was a second successive drivers' crown for son Matt, who

Far left: SEAT's WTCC championship contender Gabriele Tarquini leads team-mate Peter Terting at Valencia.
Photograph: Photo 4/XPB.cc

Far left centre: BMW's Jörg Müller consolidated his reputation as a seasoned touring car campaigner.
Photograph: Mike Weston/www.crashpa.net

Centre right: SEAT's James Thompson is now one of the most experienced and versatile of all the contemporary touring car competitors.

Bottom centre: Alfa Romeo's Augustus Farfus at Magny-Cours.

Bottom left: Chevrolet's Alain Menu all kitted up, strapped in and prepared for action.
Photographs: Photo 4/XPB.cc

Below: Britain's Andy Priaulx retained his crown for BMW at the season's finale in Macau.
Photograph: Malcolm Griffiths/LAT Photographic

become the first man since Chris Hodgetts in 1987 to win back-to-back BTCC titles and the first to successfully defend the crown in the 2-litre era.

It was another campaign built on consistency for the man known as 'the people's champ': he failed to finish just three of the 30 races and claimed points in all of the others. Neal took victories at Mondello Park (twice), Oulton Park, Thruxton, Croft, Snetterton, Knockhill and Silverstone en route to the title and the seemingly bullet-proof Integra scored points on more than one occasion when it really shouldn't have done – most notably at Snetterton and Knockhill after heavy contact. Aided by the impressive débutant Gordon Shedden and Gareth Howell – who won six races between them – Neal also helped Team Halfords to the teams' title.

'It's unbelievable and I'm over the moon,' Neal said on clinching the crown, 'not for me but for the guys here in the team. There are a lot of people who have helped us over the year, who have shown faith in us and invested in the programme and it is great to do it for them.'

With 2005 nemesis Yvan Muller having moved on to the WTCC, it was left to Jason Plato, at the wheel of the new SEAT Leon, to emerge as Neal's closest rival. His car was quick from the off and carried Plato to eight wins over the course of the season, but an equal number of retirements told its own story. The fact that the 2001 champion was able to keep the championship alive until the season finale at Silverstone was an indication of how strong the SEAT package was on its day, but he ended the season 48 points shy of Neal's tally. Plato was the man SEAT pinned its hopes on for the drivers' title; three-times race winner James Thompson and Darren Turner shared the second car and strong performances from both meant that SEAT was able to take a first manufacturers' title.

That ended a five-year winning streak for Vauxhall, which endured a trying second season with the Astra Sport Hatch. The loss of two of its three drivers at the end of 2005 meant new faces were brought in – young gun Tom Chilton and experienced multiple touring car champion Fabrizio Giovanardi – with both taking time to become truly comfortable in the car. Despite a double podium for Chilton in the season opener at Brands

Hatch, the campaign failed to hit the heights of recent seasons and it wasn't until the 23rd race that Giovanardi claimed the teams' first win of the year – and Vauxhall's 100th in BTCC competition. Another win came in the following meeting at Brands Hatch but two victories from the season wasn't what the team had expected at the start of the year.

Once again, the MG ZS was the car of choice for West Surrey Racing, now running under the Team RAC banner and welcoming Colin Turkington back into the fold alongside Rob Collard. Although Collard would endure a trying second season with the car, Dick Bennetts' team managed to find more pace than ever from the ageing MG to allow Turkington to fight for the title, eventually settling for third – just a point behind Plato in the final reckoning. The team also became the most high-profile entrant to switch to alternative fuel at Knockhill, as bioethanol continues to be embraced by the BTCC.

A raft of newcomers enlivened the grid, with Mike Jordan in particular impressing as he secured a popular win at Mondello Park in the car that Neal used to claim his first title. Two Alfa Romeos competed in the hands of Mark Smith and Eoin Murray, and BMW was also back – the distinctive wail of an ex-Schnitzer 320i securing a cult following for multiple BMW champion Martyn Bell.

With new teams joining throughout the year, bumper crowds and a TV deal better than ever, the BTCC is in good shape heading into 2007, when it adopts the Super 2000 rules (for modified production cars) used in the WTCC. With SEAT the only leading team that already has S2000 machinery, Team Halfords and the rest have work to do to take the fight to the Spanish marque next season.

In the DTM it was an old hand who emerged on top of the pile as Bernd Schneider secured his fifth title. Defending champion Gary Paffett had moved on to F1 after taking up the chance of a test drive with McLaren and Schneider quickly set about reclaiming the title he had last won in 2003 with victories in the opening two rounds at Hockenheim and Lausitz. A fifth place next time out, at Oschersleben, was followed by a run of five podium finishes before the championship was secured at Le Mans – fifth place good enough to put Schneider out of

Far left: Matt Neal took back-to-back titles in his Team Dynamics Honda.

Left: Gordon Shedden assumed the supporting role as team-mate to Matt Neal with admirable aplomb.

Below: Fabrizio Giovanardi struggled to maintain a front-running pace in his Vauxhall Astra.

Photographs: Jakob Ebrey Motorsport Photography

Opposite: Craig Lowndes' no. 888 Betta Ford Falcon bounces the kerbing at the Barbagallo Raceway in Perth.
Photograph: Graphic Dak/Dirk Klynsmith

Right: Mika Häkkinen's Mercedes spits flames at the Norisring. The double F1 champion failed to win a race during his second season contesting the DTM.
Photograph: XPB.cc

Below right: Bernd Schneider took a remarkable fifth DTM title for Mercedes.
Photograph: Miltenberg/XPB.cc

Centre: After five seasons with Mercedes in the DTM, Jean Alesi decided to look for a new challenge for 2007.

Bottom: Mattias Ekström spearheaded Audi's challenge.
Photographs: Mike Weston/www.crashpa.net

reach of Bruno Spengler and Tom Kristensen.

'I am very excited about my fifth championship title; it is a really special one for me,' Schneider said. 'This is a great day in my life.'

Spengler in particular impressed in taking the fight to Schneider in only his second season in the championship, taking his maiden victory at the Norisring and then winning again at the Nürburging, Le Mans and in the season finale at Hockenheim to secure the runner-up slot. Kristensen took wins at Oschersleben and Zandvoort with Mattias Ekström and Martin Tomczyk settling for a victory apiece – the latter finally making it to the top step of the podium in his sixth season of racing.

The fact that only two manufacturers were represented didn't detract from the racing action, with some of the older 2005 machines running well – most notably at the Nürburging when Jean Alesi stormed through the field from 14th on the grid and just missed out on a podium finish. Vanina Ickx and Susie Stoddart became the first women to compete in the DTM since Ellen Lohr departed in 1995, racing in 2004-spec machinery alongside Mattias Lauda.

In the Australian V8 Supercar Series, Russell Ingall secured the 2005 championship, his maiden title, but, as this edition of AUTOCOURSE goes to press, the Stone Brothers Racing driver is fourth in the 2006 table, which is headed by Team Betta Electrical driver Craig Lowndes. Should Lowndes go on to secure the title, it will be his fourth V8 Supercar crown and first as a Ford driver, although Holden driver Rick Kelly is only 30 points behind.

Alongside Jamie Whincup, Lowndes helped Ford end a seven-year drought in the Bathurst 1000, the victory made all the more emotional as it made Lowndes the first winner of the Peter Brock Trophy, his late mentor and friend having been killed while competing in the Targa West Rally a month before the big race. On what was already a difficult weekend following Brock's death, development driver Mark Porter lost his life in an accident on the Mountain.

Having raced at Shanghai in 2005, the V8s have a round in Bahrain still to come in 2006 as they continue to expand and appeal to a wider audience. This effort is reflected in the announcement of a 14-round schedule for 2007, with every event counting towards the championship.---

PETER BROCK

PETER BROCK might at first glance be considered little more than a very successful touring car driver, so regular readers of AUTOCOURSE may wonder why his obituary is within the covers of an annual that devotes itself primarily to happenings within the F1 business.

Yet race fans throughout Australia and New Zealand will know that Brock, who was killed in an accident during an asphalt historic rally in Western Australia on 8 September, was probably better known there than many F1 competitors. It is no understatement to describe him as a motor sport legend and the fact that he received a state funeral at Melbourne's St Paul's Cathedral testifies to his remarkable status within his country's motor sports community.

Brock's exploits were legend. Nine victories in the Bathurst 1000 touring car race at Mount Panorama earned him the nickname 'King of the Mountain'. He also won the 1974, '78 and '80 Australian Touring Car Championships.

The 61-year-old was known for driving for the official Holden team, originally for the famous Holden Dealer Team and then for HRT in a span from '94 to '97. Brock had his last drive in the famous Bathurst 1000 with HRT in 2004.

'I remember the very first touring car race I had and I lined up alongside him on the grid,' said five-times Bathurst winner Mark Skaife. 'When I looked across and saw that I was on the grid next to Peter Brock, I knew I had made it.

'I was fortunate to race with and against him and learned an immense amount from his approach to motor sport. He was the guy whom all the young guys aimed at emulating.'

UNITED STATES RACING REVIEW
CHASING AN AUDIENCE
by GORDON KIRBY

NASCAR's emergence over the past ten years as a major-league sport in America has reached the point where the Daytona-based stock car racing organisation likes to claim it is the USA's number-two sport behind only the National Football League. NASCAR argues that it has 75 million regular domestic viewers, including bums on seats in the grandstands and those watching on TV, and that it therefore ranks ahead of traditional major American sports such as baseball, basketball, college football (huge in America), golf, tennis and ice hockey.

Whether NASCAR's lofty claim is true may be open to question but the fact is that NASCAR is bigger than ever and the collectables – or 'trinkets and trash' – business of the individual drivers and NASCAR itself is massive to the point of sometimes being rudely obtrusive. The latest boom for example, has been NASCAR branding on a dizzying array of children's toys. As the old theory goes, catch them when they're young and keep them forever.

As big as it has become and as undiminished as NASCAR's momentum is, there are however some signs that all is not perfect. Many tracks are no longer selling out, TV ratings were down seven percent this year across the board for most races and some teams are beginning to complain about runaway costs. Ray Evernham's factory Dodge team is conspicuous for its lack of major commercial sponsorship and Evernham has talked openly about how he needs to find a billionaire partner if he's to stay in business for the long run. Yet Evernham is expected to run four cars in 2007 and more than 50 cars are expected to try to qualify for the 42 starting places in most of next year's 36 Nextel Cup races.

Another area of concern is the second division Busch series. For many years, more and more people have complained that the series has been 'Buschwhacked' by the first division Cup drivers and teams, who use it as a development and testing series. In recent years, the Cup drivers and teams have seriously taken over the Busch series and the 2006 Busch championship was a no-contest with Richard Childress's number-one Cup driver Kevin Harvick running away with the title driving his own cars. Clearly, the Busch series has lost its role as the primary stepping-stone to the top level Cup series and is losing fan interest, both at the track and on TV. Nor have any serious solutions been proposed for its problems.

Then there's the 'car of tomorrow', the 'universal car' that arrives in 2007. A strictly defined 'spec' car that's taller and wider than the existing one, the new Nextel Cup car will make its début at the half-mile Bristol bullring (Tennessee) in March and will be required wear for 16 races next year on tracks shorter than 1.5 miles and for the two road courses and the autumn Talladega (Alabama) race. In 2008, the car of tomorrow will also run at the superspeedways and two-mile tracks. In 2009, it will run everywhere.

NASCAR's leaders believe the chunkier car of tomorrow will substantially improve safety and reduce costs, at least for the smaller teams. Most of the teams worry that it will cost a lot of money to scrap their current fleet – the big teams have 15 or more cars per driver – and to build and develop all-new cars. It will probably be ranked as the biggest change in NASCAR's long history, so it will be interesting to see how the new, identity-free spec car works out.

In search of market growth, NASCAR has put a lot of time and effort in recent years into expanding south and north of the border into Mexico and Canada. In 2005, a second-tier Busch race was inaugurated on the Autodromo Hermanos Rodriguez road circuit in Mexico City and late this summer NASCAR announced that it had acquired the Canadian stock car organisation CASCAR. The group has been renamed NASCAR Canada and major Canadian retailer the Canadian Tire Corporation has signed on as

NASCAR's continuing propensity for pulling in capacity crowds – as evidenced by this view of Martinsville – ensures that the category thrives as the commercial centrepiece of the US racing scene.
Photograph: LAT South/LAT Photographic

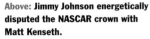

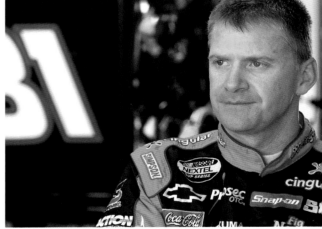

Above: Jimmy Johnson energetically disputed the NASCAR crown with Matt Kenseth.
Photograph: Autostock/LAT Photographic

Centre: Kevin Harvick took a firm grasp on proceedings in the Busch series and pretty much dominated the contest.
Photograph: LAT South/LAT Photographic

Above right: Veteran contender Jeff Burton continued to be a competitive force driving for Richard Childress.
Photograph: F. Peirce Williams/LAT Photographic

Top: Bank Of America 500 race winner Kasey Kahne and Matt Kenseth lead a restart under the lights at Charlotte.
Photograph: LAT South/LAT Photographic

sponsor of the new series. Also, NASCAR has replaced ChampCar (Championship Auto Racing Teams; CART open-wheel racing) as the second event at Le Circuit Gilles Villeneuve in Montreal, with a Busch race planned for August, 2007.

Another area of growth is NASCAR's diversity programme, which has been devised to attract women and drivers of differing ethnic backgrounds. A well-funded diversity division has been created, complete with its own vice-president and marketing budget. For some years a number of women and non-white drivers have been working their ways up through NASCAR's lower, grass-roots ranks, but thus far none of these aspirants has arrived on a full-time basis in NASCAR's top Nextel Cup division.

Veteran black driver Bill Lester has raced in the truck series and made one Cup series start last year, but the diversity programme was struggling for credibility until, wonder of wonders, Juan Pablo Montoya decided he'd had enough of Formula 1 and announced that he was going to join former CART employer Chip Ganassi's NASCAR team in 2007. With that, McLaren F1 team boss Ron Dennis fired Montoya and, in early October, the Columbian made his stock car début in one of Ganassi's cars in an ARCA race at Talladega. Montoya qualified on the front row and finished third in the race, and

then ran a number of other ARCA and Busch races before planning to make his expected Cup début in the season-closer at Homestead in November.

Other big changes to NASCAR's long-standing character and identity are also arriving. After sweeping a path through off-road racing, IMSA (International Motorsports Association, which sanctions the American Le Mans series), CART and IRL (Indy Racing League), Toyota entered NASCAR in the past year, competing first in the truck series. But in 2007, Toyota will make its Nextel Cup début, signing up NASCAR veterans Darrell and Michael Waltrip among others as team owners. It will be interesting to watch Toyota's influence on NASCAR, particularly because it comes at a time when NASCAR's traditional American manufacturers – General Motors, Ford and Dodge – are facing massive problems with steadily dwindling sales, huge layoffs and plant closures. This is a critical stage in America's industrial and car-making history, with the domestic car builders facing profoundly fundamental problems.

In every other form of racing in which it's competed, in the United States, at least – although not at this point in F1 – Toyota has out-spent, out-powered, out-politicked and eventually steamrollered the opposition; and in F1 today, of course, Toyota has established new standards for spending and enormity of operation. It will be interesting to see which NASCAR teams join the Toyota bandwagon as it gathers strength. Most people believe Roger Penske and Chip Ganassi will be key Toyota players. Penske's dealerships sell more Toyotas (and more Hondas) than anyone else's in the United States and nobody is more aware of Toyota's resources and capability than Roger Penske. Very aware of it, too, is Ganassi, who has won with Toyota in CART and IRL and who won races this past year in the GrandAm sports car series with Lexus-powered cars.

Nor is it likely to be long before questions will be asked by the directors and bean counters at General Motors, Ford and Dodge. If Toyota kicks them in the butt as many people believe it will, how long will the cash-strapped Detroit dinosaurs keep spending on a losing proposition? Many NASCAR diehards can't imagine their favourite form of racing without Chevy and Ford, but by 2010 that question may become a real issue.

And, too, it's expected that over the next few years Toyota Racing Development (TRD) will build motors, parts and probably chassis, too, for the entire stock car industry. Over the next few years TRD will move its operations from Southern California to Charlotte (North Carolina) and Toyota's expansive embrace of stock car racing will help TRD to become a serious profit centre over time, as well as pushing Chevrolet, Ford and Dodge to the margins of grass-roots American racing. Toyota has already arrived in midget racing, winning its début USAC (United States Auto Club) race this winter, and has also embarked on an NHRA (National Hot Rod Association drag racing) Funny Car programme for 2007. To many observers, it appears that history is on Toyota's side in all this, given that many of GM's and Ford's UAW (a workplace union) employees or their children will inevitably end up working in non-union shops for Toyota and Honda, a trend that is already taking place.

NASCAR: BIG IS BEAUTIFUL

Meanwhile, NASCAR's much-hyped, ten-race, end-of-season 'chase' for the Cup came in for a lot of criticism in 2006. Invented three years ago by NASCAR's third-generation boss Brian France, the chase is a play-off system in which only the top ten drivers in the points after 26 of the year's 36 races are eligible to fight for the championship. The idea was to try to infuse some new drama into the final months of the season but, as the play-off system wound down this year, it seemed to be more about luck and plodding consistency than performance.

This year's chase turned fairly quickly into a foggy muddle with first Kevin Harvick then Jeff Burton surging to the top of the points table. Bad luck, accidents and mechanical failures cost early chase favourites Jimmie Johnson, Jeff Gordon and Dale Earnhardt Jr valuable points when it counted, while veteran Mark Martin and rookie Denny Hamlin hung in there as championship contenders during the year's closing races.

By most measures the year's most competitive driver was 2003 champion Matt Kenseth, who shared the championship lead with Johnson for most of the year and enjoyed the best statistical record. He had more top-five finishes and more top tens than anyone else, and also won a handful of races. In fact, using NASCAR's traditional system of counting all races down to the bitter end, rather than reordering the top ten for the chase, Kenseth would have enjoyed an almost unbeatable 200-point advantage with five races to go. But the vagaries of the play-off system meant otherwise.

As AUTOCOURSE goes press, with two races to run, the title chase is close. Most of the top ten are in with a chance but it looks to be a duel between Matt Kenseth and Jimmie Johnson.

NASCAR is dominated these days by seven or eight multi-car teams. Among these are Jack Roush's five-car Ford team with Kenseth and Martin among its drivers; Richard Childress Racing's resurgent three-car Chevrolet team, which includes Burton and Harvick; Rick Hendrick's four Chevrolets with Johnson and Gordon; Dale Earnhardt Inc's three Chevies (Dale Jr included); Joe Gibbs Racing's trio of Chevrolets (including 2005 champion Tony Stewart and this year's rookie sensation Denny Hamlin); and Ray Evernham's Dodge team led by the

fast, popular Kasey Kahne. Indeed, in only his third season, Kahne, 26, was NASCAR's winningest Cup driver and was especially strong on medium-speed, 1.5-mile superspeedways.

Two notable big teams missed the top ten cut for this year's championship chase. None of Chip Ganassi's three drivers made it; nor did Roger Penske's two superstars Kurt Busch and Ryan Newman. Busch joined Penske a year ago after winning the 2004 championship with Jack Roush's team, but had a tough first year in which neither Penske driver featured in many races. Busch won one race and recorded another half a dozen top-five finishes and Newman's results were even more dismal.

Then there are long-time NASCAR teams such as Robert Yates Racing, the Wood Brothers and Petty Enterprises, who are reduced today to mid- and even back-field roles. It seems that if you can't run three or more cars, there's not much point in trying.

Below left: Matt Kenseth is heading the scrap for overall NASCAR honours with just two rounds remaining.
Photograph: LAT South/LAT Photographic

Centre: Despite missing out on a place in the chase, the front-running Tony Stewart continued to be a feisty competitor.
Photograph: Autostock/LAT Photographic

Bottom: The familiar DuPont colours of Jeff Gordon's number 24 Chevrolet Monte Carlo.
Photograph: LAT South/LAT Photographic

Above: In one of the most thrilling finishes ever seen at the Brickyard, Sam Hornish Jr takes the chequered flag to win the Indianapolis 500 just feet ahead of 19-year-old rookie Marco Andretti, whose father Michael is watching the fun from third place.
Photograph: Phillip Abbott/LAT Photographic

Bottom right: Target Chip Ganassi's Dan Wheldon and Scott Dixon lead Sam Hornish in a nail-biting finale to the IRL season at Chicagoland.
Photograph: Dan Streck/LAT Photographic

IRL: GOING ITS OWN WAY

For a few months from late winter through spring there was talk – as there has been almost regularly in recent years – of a ChampCar-IRL reunification. ChampCar co-owner Kevin Kalkhoven put a lot of time and effort into trying to build a working relationship with Indianapolis Motor Speedway boss and IRL founder Tony George. Everyone, it seemed, including the *Indianapolis Star*'s editorial page, clamoured for the two series to come together, but George proved as intransigent as ever. Near the end of the summer, George protested that a story in the *Star* about impending plans for a merger was totally wrong and that no such plans were on the table. So ended the latest reunification talks.

'I like Kevin and admire what he's trying to do,' remarked former CART and current IRL team owner Bobby Rahal at one point during the proceedings. 'But it's not about him. It's about somebody else.' Indeed, as four-times Indy 500 winner Rick Mears used to say, 'It's all about one man.' And as Al Unser Jr said to me last spring, 'You have to accept that Tony [George] is the new, young emperor of IndyCar racing.'

The IRL is apparently trying to bring sponsor value and media interest to its series by adding street or road races, most of them retreads of failed CART races such as St Petersburg (Florida) and Belle Isle (Detroit). Everybody in the IRL seems to want the series to be just like CART used to be –

a mix of ovals, road and street circuits – as the IRL tries to morph into a further version of what many fans call 'CART Light'.

The championship went down to the wire and Sam Hornish took his third IRL title – his first with Roger Penske's team. Hornish also won the Indy 500, nosing past rookie Marco Andretti at the chequered flag to win by a whisker, and added three more wins and a string of other useful results. Hornish had won the IRL championship twice with Panther Racing, but this was Penske's first IRL trophy since joining the series in 2002 and adds to its record of 11 CART championships and 14 Indy 500 wins.

Team-mate Helio Castroneves battled with Hornish all year for the title, also winning four races, but in the end he was beaten to second in the points by Dan Wheldon. On an equal footing with everyone else this past year – all Honda-powered – Penske's cars were the ones to beat in most races.

There's no question that Hornish is a very good oval racer, but he's been less impressive in the IRL's few road and street races. It would be great for the sport to see how good Hornish really is by testing him on all types of tracks against ChampCar drivers Sébastien Bourdais, Paul Tracy, Justin Wilson *et al* and until that happens Hornish will remain an unquantifiable element of Tony George's dystopian vision.

The season marked the end of a couple of eras for Penske. It was the last for Marlboro as Penske's primary sponsor after 17 years and the end of a 22-year run for the cigarette maker as a

AGR's Tony Kanaan, Marco Andretti and Dario Franchitti finished sixth, seventh and eighth in the points. The team was nowhere near as strong as in previous years, with 2004 champion Kanaan winning just once and rookie Marco Andretti taking the team's only other win. Marco, just 19, won a mid-season road race at Sears Point (California) after coming awfully close to scooping an Indy 500 win on his first try, only to be foiled at the line by Hornish. Marco is clearly an impressive talent and continues in the IRL with the family team in 2007. Will he move to Europe in 2008? At this point, it seems unlikely.

All the rage last year, Danica Patrick had a disappointing second season in the IRL. She was steady but unspectacular, with a pair of fourths her best results. She finished ninth in the points ahead of Tomas Scheckter and Bryan Herta and decided in mid-summer to leave Bobby Rahal's team for greener pastures at Andretti-Green for next year. Danica and her supporters hope the move will re-ignite the spark and gain her that elusive first win.

At the Homestead season-opener an accident in the race-day morning warm-up cost Paul Dana his life. Dana crashed heavily into Ed Carpenter's car, which had clipped the wall and spun, and was killed instantly. An IRL rookie, Dana had made his way through F2000 and the IRL's Indy Pro Series (IPS) before putting together a sponsorship deal to race in the IRL with Bobby Rahal's team.

The 2006 IPS championship was taken by Brit Jay Howard.

Finally, the IRL is switching to ethanol fuel in 2007. Honda is building a 3.5-litre engine (up from last year's 3.0-litre V8) to suit the Midwest-produced corn-based fuel. IndyCars have run on methanol for more than 40 years. Fuel consumption will be less voracious, so the tank size has been cut to 25 gallons.

Left: Big man from the Lone Star state. Sam Hornish Jr follows in the Indy 500-winning wheel tracks of fellow Texans A.J. Foyt and Johnny Rutherford.

Top: Chip off the old block? Marco Andretti continued his family's respected US racing tradition into a third generation.
Photographs: Dan Streck/LAT Photographic

Above: Paul Dana was killed in a tragic accident during the opening race weekend at Homestead.
Photograph: Mike Levitt/LAT Photographic

sponsor in CART and IRL. And, too, it was the last year for Team Penske as a resident of Reading, Pennsylvania. Penske has been based in Reading for 40 years, going back to his team's formative years in the CanAm, TransAm and long-distance sports car racing, but the team has now moved down to North Carolina to be part of what had been the Penske South operation. All of Penske's race teams – NASCAR, IRL and ALMS organisations – are being consolidated in Mooresville, North Carolina, under former IRL team boss Tim Cindric's overall direction.

Dan Wheldon, Scott Dixon and Chip Ganassi's team kept some serious championship pressure on Penske's pair. Wheldon is probably the IRL's most aggressive driver and he showed that he had made the right move in departing the Andretti-Green operation for Ganassi after winning both the Indy 500 and the championship with AGR in 2005. Wheldon didn't have the best of luck with Ganassi in 2006 but he won the year's first and last races and finished only two points behind Hornish. After a couple of glum years with Toyota engines, team-mate Dixon also enjoyed a good year, winning a couple of races and finishing a competitive fourth in the championship.

Brazilian Vitor Meira did a great job with the Panther team to finish fifth in the points. Meira is a good tester and racer who did well to out-point all of Andretti-Green's fleet of four drivers and Bobby Rahal's trio of cars. He twice finished second in 2006 and is entirely capable of winning a race.

BOURDAIS EQUALS A LEGENDARY RECORD

Meanwhile, ChampCar is pushing on, minus oval races but with new venues both domestic and worldwide as well as an interesting new Panoz spec car, new teams and a proven new Atlantic series. New events on ChampCar's 2007 schedule include the season-opener at a new street race in Las Vegas (Nevada) and the closer in another new street race in downtown Phoenix (Arizona). Other new races include a long-sought event on the permanent road course in Zuhai, China, in May – ChampCar will become America's first major-league sporting organisation to hold a regular event in mainland China. Also on the 2007 schedule is a visit to the refurbished and extremely challenging Mt Tremblant-St Jovite road course in the Laurentian mountains 90 minutes north of Montreal (Canada) and two races in Europe in September – Assen in Holland and Oserschleben in Germany.

In company with the top-rated Newman/Haas team, Sébastien Bourdais swept to his third straight ChampCar Vanderbilt Cup title. Bourdais won seven of 14 races, including the first four of the year. He usually qualified on the front row, missing only three times, and, if he finished, he was almost invariably on the podium.

Bourdais is a superb driver, ridiculously spurned by F1, and with Newman/Haas he has been the man to beat in ChampCar for the past three or four years. By winning his third consecutive championship this year he goes down in history as the first man to equal Ted Horne's rare achievement from nearly 60 years ago – Horne was AAA champion in 1946, '47 and '48.

Whatever he might say, Bourdais is broken-hearted that his F1 chance has passed him by so he stoically pushes on with his career in America with Newman/Haas. It will be

interesting to see if Bourdais and Newman/Haas will continue to set the pace with next year's new Panoz DP01 'spec' car.

ChampCar's second most successful driver in 2006 was A.J. Allmendinger, who enjoyed a Cinderella season after he was fired by RuSPORT and hired by Forsythe over the course of a week in June. After a promising but win-free year and a half with RuSPORT, Allmendinger showed what he can do with Forsythe, winning three races in a row after his début with the team and winning again at Road America in September. In the end, Allmendinger was the only man to offer any kind of championship challenge to Bourdais, although it came to nothing when A.J. crashed in the year's penultimate race at Surfers Paradise (Australia).

But as the season came to an end Allmendinger joined a growing trend by making the jump to NASCAR. He entered a couple of NASCAR truck races in the autumn and signed a lucrative contract to drive in the Nextel Cup series in 2007 for a new Red Bull-Toyota team. A sad loss for ChampCar and American open-wheel racing as a whole.

Paul Tracy felt the heat from Allmendinger's searing pace during the latter's brief tenure with Forsythe. Tracy has been Forsythe's team leader for the past four years and, after considering and then rejecting a move to NASCAR last year, Paul signed a new five-year contract with Forsythe. At 37, Tracy is entering a new phase of his career and it will be interesting to see how he adjusts and performs as he approaches his 40th birthday. He did not have a good year in 2006, failing to win a race and finishing a distant seventh in the championship after many incidents and accidents.

With RuSPORT the past two years, Briton Justin Wilson has established himself as one of ChampCar's top drivers. He scored an excellent win at Edmonton (Canada) in July, hunting down Bourdais and cleanly out-braking the Frenchman for the lead before motoring away on his own. But there were too few days like that and, after Allmendinger's surprisingly successful move to Forsythe, more and more questions were asked about RuSPORT's ability to get the job done. Then, in practice at Surfers Paradise at the end of the year, Wilson broke his wrist in a relatively minor accident. It was that kind of season.

Cristiano da Matta was brought in to replace Allmendinger as Wilson's team-mate at RuSPORT and, after a few middling races, enjoyed a strong run at San José (California) at the end of July, beating Wilson into second behind Bourdais. But in testing at Road America (Wisconsin) a week later Da Matta was seriously injured when he struck a deer, taking the blow squarely on the helmet. The prognosis did not look good initially, but after a month and a half in a Wisconsin hospital with his family by his side, Da Matta flew home first to Miami then to Brazil to continue a long recuperation process. It's unlikely that he will ever race again but he is expected to recover most of his physical and mental capabilities.

Nobody else made much of a mark in ChampCar this year. The most impressive of the rest were CTE-HVM Racing's Nelson Philippe and rookie Dan Clarke, both showing impressive bursts of speed in some races. Frenchman Philippe became the youngest winner in ChampCar history when he came through to win a messy race at Surfers Paradise – he was 20 years and three months old. Team-mate Clarke may also develop into a race winner over the next year or two.

Canadian Andrew Ranger and Mexican Mario Dominguez also did well to wring speed and results out of tightly budgeted machinery. Australian Will Power was ChampCar's rookie of the year, driving for Derrick Walker's Team Australia operation, and put in a great show to take pole and lead a good deal of the race at Surfers Paradise.

Katherine Legge did not disgrace herself in her rookie ChampCar season with Kevin Kalkhoven's PKV team. She drove well, if not fiendishly fast, and put in a number of good races. Her big moment came at Road America in September when her car lost a rear wing flap and she crashed heavily, cartwheeling along the guard-rail and fencing. Incredibly, she emerged from the wreckage unscathed and with her good humour intact.

ChampCar enters a new 'spec car' era in 2007 with the arrival of the Panoz DP01. This is powered by the turbo Ford-

Above: Australian Will Power emerged as ChampCar's rookie of the year.
Photograph: Lesley-Ann Miller/LAT Photographic

Above right: The Panoz chassis, the new shape of ChampCar for 2007.
Photograph: Mike Levitt/LAT Photographic

Top: Justin Wilson leads the field at San José.
Photograph: Phillip Abbot/LAT Photographic

Opposite: Allan McNish in the winning Audi leads the pack at the Mazda Raceway, Laguna Seca.
Photograph: Richard Dole/LAT Photographic

Cosworth XFE engine used in recent years and, although it's a spec car, development of specific areas – most likely only mechanical items – will be allowed in 2008 and 2009. The primary goals are to reduce costs and encourage closer racing and more overtaking. Following specifications laid down by ChampCar's technology director Scot Elkins and operations boss Tony Cotman, the new car produces much of its downforce from its underwing so that it carries much smaller external wings than the Lola B2/00 ChampCar of recent years. The theory is that this will make it less aerodynamically sensitive and more capable of racing in close quarters.

The new car generates around 5,500 lb of downforce at 200 mph, with the underwing accounting for nearly 50 percent of that. It will substantially reduce the cost of at least entering the ChampCar World Series. The cost of most major components is close to half the cost of similar parts for the recent Lola chassis and that should make it possible for more teams to enter the series.

The prototype DP01 completed 13 days and more than 2,000 miles of testing at Sebring (Florida) in August and September driven by ChampCar and F1 veteran Roberto Moreno. The first cars will be delivered to teams at the end of November and pre-season testing with it will be permitted only in three official test sessions. There will be just a single,

two- or three-day test in each of January, February and March prior to the season-opening races at Las Vegas and Long Beach (California) next April.

The new ChampCar has attracted some new teams and drivers into the series, starting with Bob Gelles, whose existing Atlantic and Formula BMW operations are being expanded to include a ChampCar team. Pacific Motorsports also announced that it will join ChampCar next year, with rookies Ryan Dalziel and Alex Figge. The team raced in Atlantic for a few years and in the GrandAm sports car series over the past two years. Dalziel finished second in the 2003 and 2004 Atlantic championships. This year's Atlantic stand-outs Simon Pagenaud and Graham Rahal are also expected to move up to ChampCar next year and, near the end of the season, Kalkhoven and Forsythe were confidently predicting a full field of 24 cars for 2007. If so, the pendulum in American open-wheel racing will swing in ChampCar's direction.

ATLANTIC REVIVAL AND OTHER SERIES

ChampCar's revitalised Mazda-Cosworth Atlantic series was a pleasure to watch this past year with full, competitive fields and plenty of talented young drivers. The key ingredients were a combination of a new cheaper spec car from Swift, a similarly less expensive 300-bhp Mazda four-cylinder engine developed by Cosworth, and a $2-million prize for the champion dedicated to his rookie season in ChampCar. French rookie Simon Pagenaud, a protégé of Bourdais's, won the championship and the prize. Pagenaud, 22, was competitive everywhere, edging young Rahal for the title and proving himself a tough racer as well as a very fast, clean driver.

Bobby Rahal's 17-year-old son Graham demonstrated speed, poise, aggression and maturity as he took four poles and won five races – more than anyone else – and was the most impressive Atlantic driver of the year. Rahal tested a Newman/Haas Lola ChampCar in September and is expected to drive for the team in 2007. German Andreas Wirth, 21, won two races and hopes to graduate to ChampCar; other youngsters who looked good were Brazilian Raphael Matos, who usually ran up front and who won a race, and American Jonathan Bomarito, who came through to win the season finale at Road America. Canadian James Hinchcliffe also impressed.

Formula BMW and Star Mazda are separate entry-level open-wheel series that run as support races to a variety of different categories. Both series are sanctioned by IMSA. The 2006 Formula BMW USA championship was won by 17-year-old Canadian Robert Wickens, who is expected to race in Europe soon. The Star-Mazda championship was taken by Adrian Carrio.

In sports car racing the Audi R10 turbo diesel, winner at Sebring and Le Mans, was all the rage in the American Le Mans Series. Allan McNish and Rinaldo Capello dominated for Audi, winning eight of ten races with team-mates Emanuele Pirro and Frank Biela winning the other two. The ALMS series also took pride in the arrival of Penske's LMP2 Porsches, which swept the smaller prototype category with primary drivers Sascha Maassen and Lucas Luhr, who shared the championship. The Penske Porsches will be challenged in 2007 by Honda, which enters the LMP2 category with its Acura brand, and teams from Andretti-Green, Adrian Fernandez and Highcroft Racing (owned by historic and sports car racer Duncan Dayton).

Bill France Jr's brother Jimmy France is the godfather of the Rolex GrandAm sports car series, which plugs along, growing steadily with full fields but few fans. Even 'name' drivers such as Scott Pruett and Max Papis and teams such as Chip Ganassi's have done little to raise much interest in the series, which is based on NASCAR's low-tech principles, but France's commitment means the GrandAm will be around for many years to come. Of course, sports car racing needs a pair of duelling series even less than open-wheel racing does but, as with the ChampCar-IRL split, there seems little or no chance of any unification.

Above: A perennial racer. At 67 years of age, Dieter Quester continues to race with the enthusiasm he has shown for more than 40 years.

Above left: Graham Rahal, son of 1986 Indy 500 winner Bobby, and Simon Pagenaud emerged as stars of the Toyota Atlantic series.

Left: Brit Jay Howard is the Infiniti Pro champion.
Photographs: LAT Photographic

Main photograph: Stars of Tomorrow record-breaker Sam Jenkins on familiar turf – leading the pack. The young Bristol ace is tipped as hot property in the future, and based on his form throughout 2006, it's not hard to see why.
Photographs: Mike Weston/www.crashpa.net

Insets far right: A trio of youngsters aiming for the top. Tom Ingam (top left), Max McGuire (far right) and Jack Harvey.

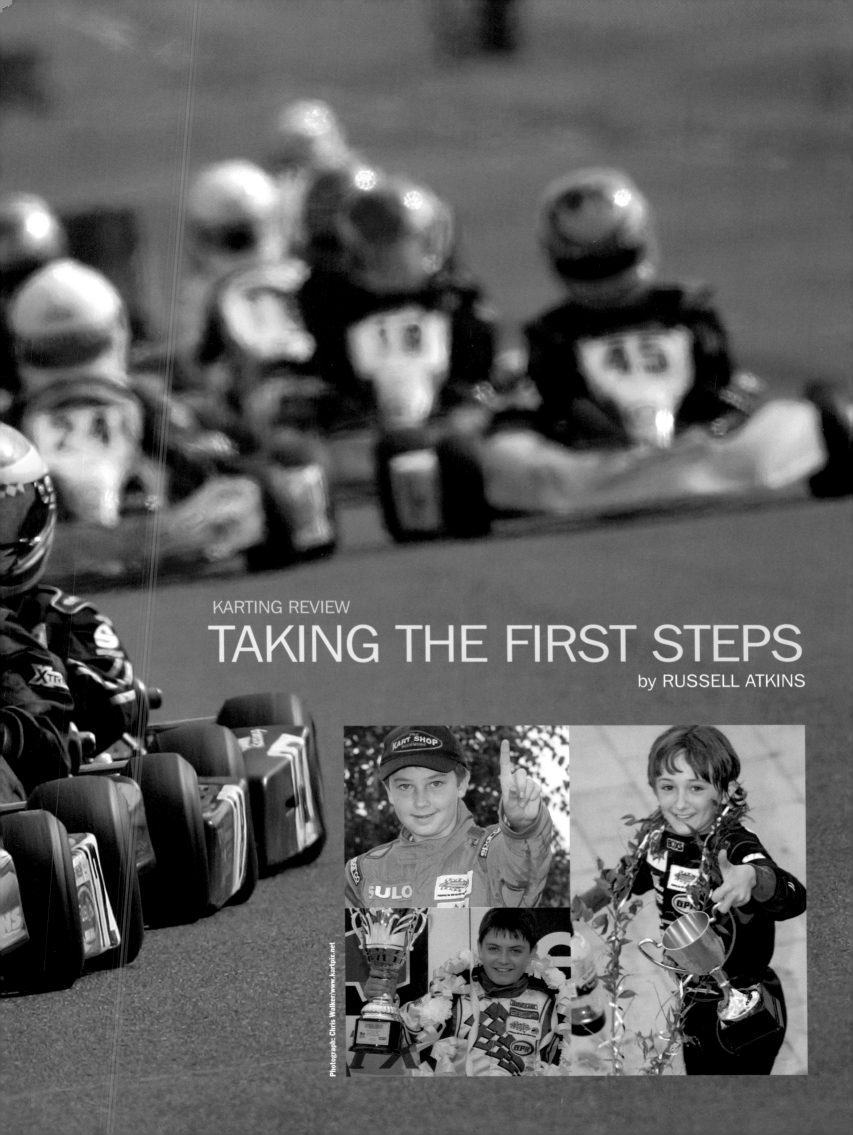

KARTING REVIEW

TAKING THE FIRST STEPS

by RUSSELL ATKINS

Photograph: Chris Walker/www.kartpix.net

KARTING may in essence be the bottom rung of the motor racing ladder but it is also the perfect forming ground for the careers of thousands of young Formula 1 hopefuls, all eager to follow in the wheel tracks of their grand prix heroes. Michael Schumacher, Fernando Alonso and Jenson Button all took their tentative first steps in the lowest formula, after all...

The UK's premier karting series, BRDC Stars of Tomorrow, enjoyed a superbly competitive year in 2006 with frenetically paced spills and thrills from beginning to end and a whole raft of exciting talent for the future, all of which was captured and broadcast on SkySports TV.

Sam Jenkins made the cadet class (for drivers over nine years old) his own, becoming the first driver ever to win the title twice in back-to-back seasons. The young Bristol ace began the year at a lightning pace, storming to victory after victory, which meant that by the time his rivals had finally caught up in terms of speed, it was already too late. Of his pursuers, Alexander Albon made perhaps the greatest impression, triumphing at Silverstone, Genk (Belgium) and Buckmore Park, and there were also victories and notable performances from Max McGuire – who separately clinched the prestigious British Open Championship 'O' plate at Rye House – Callum Bowyer, Abigail Gerry, James Appleton and Jacob Stilp.

In the Mini Max category (for 11- to 16-year-olds), Tom Ingram and his family-run Ingram Racing outfit fought off the might of a number of better-backed drivers to lift the crown. Although claiming but a sole victory, the young High Wycombe ace was a model of consistency season long and his triumph in the final round at Buckmore was as popular as it was well deserved. Ingram's chief competitors for the honours were long-time championship leader Max Hawkins – who finished with the honour of having registered the most victories – Christopher Smiley and triple winner Max Goff, with Lewis Hall and Brad Smith also making it onto the top step of the rostrum over the course of the year.

Stepping up again to Junior Max (for 13- to 16-year-olds), fans were treated to a season-long duel between David Sutton and Jack Hawksworth, the former winning each of the first eight rounds and his Bradford rival tracking him every inch of the way. Hawksworth finally got his revenge at Genk in August with a double victory, but although it was enough to guarantee him second in the standings, Sutton was already home and dry. In their wake a four-way scrap for third in the title race was decided in favour of Daniel Lloyd Junior ahead of Devon Modell, Daniel Payne and feisty young lady racer Amanda Lassu.

The JICA class (a European and worldwide class for 12- to 16-year-olds) – although running with a smaller field after the opening two rounds at Rowrah and Shenington following the departure of front-runners such as Jack Harvey and Oliver Rowland to concentrate on other programmes – was perhaps the most closely contested of all. Early runaway championship leader Nigel Moore was gradually reeled in by James Godbehere as the season progressed, the two taking their duel into the final meeting at Buckmore. Despite Godbehere's doing all that was asked of him, Moore's advantage – courtesy of six wins – was just enough for him to hold on and clinch his second consecutive JICA title by the narrowest of margins. Jordan Lennox-Lamb – unbeatable on his day, with triumphs at both Shenington and Buckmore but unfortunately suffering too many 'off' days – Alice Powell, Nick Cristofaro and Craig Stirling completed the top six.

Stars' only gearbox class, Super ICC (for over-16s), was also a highly disputed campaign, with no fewer than six drivers sharing the victory spoils and four of them heading into the final meeting still with a shout at clinching the championship. With the added kudos of having the title settled on European soil at Genk, it was Frank Wrathall who claimed a double victory to seal a frustrating injury-plagued season on a high and send out a calling card for 2007. Courtesy of a second place in the weekend's first final, though, Silverstone and Larkhall winner Dean Stoneman did just enough to take the overall honours ahead of fellow double victors Nick Smith, Wrathall and Tom Hibbert. Sam Moore and Scott Allen also triumphed during the year.

Many of the same faces could be found competing in the Super One Championship, most prominently in cadets (eight to 13 years), where leading Stars protagonists Jenkins, Gerry and Bowyer tussled it out for overall honours. Jenkins again proved unbeatable in the end-of-season rankings, though this time the margin of his dominance was nowhere near as marked. Leading lady Gerry eventually prevailed in the battle for the runner-up slot ahead of Bowyer, with Samuel Blake, Jake Dennis, McGuire, Appleton, Brett Wykes and Stilp all enjoying moments in the sun. Albon was another title contender, but a disqualification from victory in the final round scuppered his championship dreams and left him down in an unrepresentative 17th place in the end-of-year standings.

In Mini Max, meanwhile, double round winner Ryan Singleton just managed to hold off namesake Ryan Denton to lift the trophy, with Ashley Sutton and Alex Jeffrey not far behind in third and fourth. The leading Stars contender was champion Ingram in tenth, some way ahead of Hawkins, Hall and Goff. Junior Rotax Max also had a healthy influx of Stars participants, with Mitchell Bayer-Goldman just fending off a season-long onslaught from Sutton and Hawksworth – renewing their Stars rivalry – Lloyd Jr, Modell and Lassu in her first year in the category. The fact that five Stars drivers made it into the top six of the championship is testament to the strength not only of the series, but also of young home-grown karting talent.

Michael Simpson prevailed in the Formula Rotax Max class – contested by an incredible 72 drivers – with consecutive triumphs in rounds two and three proving enough to clinch the crown ahead of Iain Inglis, Dan Holland and Benjy Russell. In Formula Rotax Max 177 it was Stephen Cobb who dominated.

Right: Jack Hawksworth had a busy time of it in 2006. Aside from his British exploits – finishing second in Stars of the Future and third in Super One – the Junior Max front-runner even found time to claim the Euro Challenge trophy on foreign soil. One to watch in the future without a doubt.

Below right and below: Amanda Lassu impressed many in her maiden campaign in Junior Max. The Barnsley ace – one of the leading ladies on the British karting scene – drove well all season, and her feisty manner on track and personable nature off it look set to serve her well in years to come.

Bottom left: Nigel Moore and the pursuing James Godbehere duelled season-long in Stars of Tomorrow's JICA category, with the former just holding on to claim his second successive class title from his dogged opponent.

Photographs: Mike Weston/www.crashpa.net

The only one of the top four drivers to compete in all five rounds – winning four of them – Cobb took the honours by 27 points from Dave Wooder, Florent Lambert and Chris Bone. With five victories, Ollie Millroy claimed the ICA trophy by staving off the challenge of Lee Bell, Matt Truelove and Jonathan Walker, while Mark Litchfield sealed Formula A success at the end of a season-long battle with Jason Parrott, Chris Rogers and Jamie Croxford.

In JICA, finally, Harvey's defection from Stars paid off as the promising young Lincolnshire ace lifted the laurels following a superb début campaign, the key to which was a stunning run of four consecutive wins mid-season. Rowland chased him all the way but, despite two dominant victories in the final round at Rowrah, he fell agonisingly short, missing out on the title by just a single point. Stars runner-up Godbehere – although never quite making it onto the top step of the podium over the year – was consistency personified on his way to third in the end-of-season rankings ahead of Jordan Chamberlain, with Scott Jenkins – elder brother of Sam – fifth.

Jenkins, though, gained his revenge on the European stage, most notably with a triumphant performance in the prestigious Monaco Kart Cup at the end of the year, leading home a British one-two-three around the streets of the Principality as Rowland and Moore came home second and third. Jenkins' superb Monaco success was another feather in his cap after he had already clinched the Italian series title and been crowned vice-champion of Europe at Mariembourg (Belgium) earlier in the campaign.

His triumph in the Italian Open Masters was truly the performance of a star in the making, dominating half the rounds he contested to lift the laurels in the 100 ICA Junior category by a comfortable 24-point margin over Flavio Camponeschi, Antonio da Costa and Kazeem Manzur. In the 100 ICA class, meanwhile, home favourite Antonio Piccioni almost matched Jenkins, claiming four victories on his way to sealing the title, easily ahead of closest rivals Marco Wittmann and Daniel Mancinelli, who divided up five of the remaining six wins between them.

The 125 ICC class had a driver with an even more dominant showing: Alessandro Manetti – with an amazing 75 percent win ratio – swept all before him to lift the laurels well clear of Davide Fore, Francesco Laudato and Roberto Toninelli. The final class to make up the Masters, 100 Formula A, was rather more hotly disputed, with four drivers finishing within just 21 points of each other, and the eventual champion – Nikolaj Bollingtoft – prevailing by the tiniest margin of two points. Each of the top three drivers – Bollingtoft, Cesetti Sauro and highly rated Frenchman Jules Bianchi – won only once, but their consistency was enough to keep them in front of fourth-placed Marco Ardigo, whose two victories at Muro Leccese and in the San Egidio finale were let down by a number of low scores that ultimately destroyed his title chances.

Elsewhere on the continent, the four-round Euro Challenge brought together more than 150 competitors from 24 countries for races in France, Italy, Austria and Belgium, in the process attracting some of the very best young drivers in the world.

In Junior Rotax it was Jack Hawksworth who ended the season on top, claiming a well-deserved crown after his consistency, fighting spirit and all-round ability shone through. With more than 50 entries, the battle for supremacy was always going to be tight and Hawksworth would face no sterner rival than Australian Steel Guiliana, who matured considerably from a hot-headed youngster in 2005 to become one of the most improved drivers over the year. Mats Vanderbrand was always up at the sharp end of proceedings, too, taking third in the final standings, while a special mention must go to Stars of Tomorrow Junior Max champion David Sutton, who joined the series late but proved to be the form driver of the last two rounds to show just what might have been.

In Senior Max, Wesleigh Orr – no stranger to the championship – overcame a tricky start to his campaign by jumping ship from Swiss Hutless to a works CRG-backed seat that helped propel him to title success ahead of more than 60 competitors. The South African's ability to hustle his equipment through from low grid positions was matchless: he knew just when to be aggressive and when to back off, and his calculated ruthlessness achieved its desired goal. Hard-charging Dutch ace Mike Joosens missed out on his chance to lift the laurels with a poor final round at Genk, but his characteristic never-say-die approach ensured the runner-up spot was safely his, with Englishman Martin Pearce third. The winner of the last race – Scot John Boyd – also showed great potential and is likely to be a championship challenger in 2007.

The newly formed WSK International Series, meanwhile, was fought out over four rounds, at La Conca and Lonato in Italy, Mariembourg in Belgium and Jesolo in Italy (once a happy hunting ground of Ayrton Senna, no less). The four classes provided spectacular racing and hotly disputed title battles, with plenty of names worth keeping an eye on in the future.

Will Stevens emerged victorious in 100 ICA Jr, claiming two victories from the seven races contested to see off the challenges of fellow double-race-winner Antonio da Costa and Kazeem Manzur. Stevens stamped his authority on the series from the off with a convincing victory in round one, though it would be Manzur's turn to stake his claim by triumphing at Lonato. Stevens swapped his Birel chassis for an Intrepid at Mariembourg, where Da Costa and Spaniard Miki Monras shared the honours, and as the karters headed into the final round at Jesolo just 20 points separated the top three, with any one of ten drivers still mathematically capable of lifting the trophy. The heavens also played their part, leaving the Venetian circuit practically waterlogged, so the action was reduced to just one winner-takes-all final, and though Manzur threw everything

he had at Stevens, it was not enough. The Team Zanardi pilot had nevertheless done enough to guarantee himself third position in the title chase, just behind a disappointed Da Costa.

In 100 ICA Spaniard Miquel Julia Perello sealed the honours, though he was pushed hard towards the end of the season by young Adrien Tambay, son of former grand prix ace Patrick, with two wins to his name. Perello's sole triumph came at Lonato, where Czech lady racer Lucie Panackova set a blistering pace throughout practice, having already finished a superb second at La Conca. Others to shine included Finn Matias Laine and 2004 Italian ICA Junior champion Simone Brenna, who would clinch the second final of the weekend.

Sicily-born local star Maurizio Pignato – a late entrant into the championship due to budgetary restrictions but wasting little time in making his mark – also inscribed his name among the winners' circle after overcoming Perello and compatriot Roberto Merhi at Mariembourg to celebrate his 18th birthday in style. Tambay – who struggled on used tyres in final number one – later made amends with his début success at international level. Perello seemed to suffer from the conditions more than most in the Jesolo finale, as Kevin Engmann seized pole position for the all-important race and made all the early running. Tambay's spectacular charge through the field left the Swede powerless to resist, however, as his French rival swept through into a lead he would hold all the way to the flag. Merhi ultimately relieved Engmann of the runner-up position, but Perello's seventh place was enough for the CRG ace to hold on and clinch the crown by just two points over his countryman. Tambay's late-season spurt earned him third a mere two points farther back, with Laine and Engmann taking fourth and fifth.

The 100 Formula A category developed into a two-horse race between Valtteri Bottas and Jonathan Thonon, the pair accounting for five of the seven race victories between them. Ultimately it was flying Finn Bottas who prevailed, by a solid margin, scoring in every round and proving to be the very model of consistency as Thonon chose to switch his attention to 125 ICC from Mariembourg and beyond. Others to register wins were Nigel Melker and Alessandro Bressan, and it was Kiwi Mitchell Cunningham who took third in the standings, just three points adrift of second-placed Thonon.

In 125 ICC it was the turn of Jules Bianchi to impose his authority, narrowly edging out Italian Riccardo Nalon courtesy of a late-season flourish, having missed the opening meeting. Nalon failed to win a final all year and though the wheels threatened to come permanently off his wagon following a poor round at Mariembourg, a run of strong results elsewhere kept the Jesolo Race star in the hunt right to the end. Late-starter

Below: European star Scott Jenkins – elder brother of Sam – had a strong season in 2006, with victory in the Italian Open Masters and Monaco Kart Cup against serious opposition.

Bottom: Formula A European champion Marco Ardigo, who survived a scare in the final round at Ampfing in Germany to seal the honours following a season-long challenge from leading British ace Riki Christodoulou.

Photographs: Chris Walker/www.kartpix.net

Anthony Puppo, who like Bianchi missed La Conca, also briefly threatened with a dominant performance at Lonato. The Frenchman, though, slipped back to fifth in the eventual standings after skipping the Belgian round, allowing Jesolo winner Thomas Knopper and compatriot Kevin Leijtens to leapfrog him into third and fourth.

The ICA European Championship – held at Ampfing in Germany in August – produced victory for Italian Nicola Nole from a 70-kart field, after on-the-road winner Anthony Abbasse was penalised five seconds by officials for what was deemed to be a rash last-lap passing manoeuvre. This dropped the Frenchman back to second, pending an appeal from his Sodikart team, with Johan Jokinen coming through the pack strongly to nick the final podium spot and Rick Dreezen fourth in front of Marco Zipoli, Kevin Engmann and Mike Courquin. The luckless Ollie Millroy – the fastest of the eight-strong Brit pack – and Matt Truelove did not even make it past the first lap following a multi-kart fracas.

The dénouement of the Formula A European Championship – taking place at the same meeting – was filled with tension and

uncertainty, as reigning champion and long-time series leader Marco Ardigo found himself worryingly off the pace in his efforts to stave off the attentions of Briton Riki Christodoulou. A disappointing seventh-quickest in timed qualifying, the Italian's weekend went from bad to worse as he continued to struggle throughout the heats and could register only lowly 20th and tenth-placed finishes in the all-important finals.

Dane Michael Christensen had dominated qualifying, a full quarter of a second faster than anyone else, with Christo fifth and Jules Bianchi sixth. It was the Frenchman who went on to ace the heats, setting a pace that not even Christensen was able to live with, and the WSK 125 ICC champion won the opening final with some ease. With Christo fighting his way through the pack into second, things were looking bleak for the beleaguered Ardigo as Gary Catt, Mark Litchfield, Davide Fore and Jonathan Thonon filled out the top six.

After slipping back to seventh, Christensen made amends in final number two with a superb victory, just ahead of Jérémy Iglesias, who had made an electric start from the eighth row of the grid. Bianchi took third to round off an excellent weekend and secure fifth in the end-of-season standings, but all eyes were on Christo, as began the chain reaction of events that would guarantee Ardigo's title. Running closely behind his countryman, Litchfield accidentally gave him a nudge with just four laps to go, tipping him into a spin. As if that were not bad enough, one lap later Christo's engine went bang to seal Ardigo's triumph. Fore and Litchfield were deprived of third and fourth places with similarly blown engines, allowing Bianchi through and onto the rostrum ahead of Arnaud Kozlinski and Brits Alexander Sims and Jason Parrott. Ardigo's eventual margin over Christo in the title chase was eight points, with Kozlinski moving up to third ahead of Catt, Bianchi, Fore, Thonon and Christensen.

Many of the same names were in evidence in the CIK-FIA Formula A World Cup and World Championship, held at Suzuka in Japan and Angerville in France respectively. The former was won by Kozlinski, on the pace from the word go and signalling his intent with victory in the pre-final. The 2005 Asia-Pacific winner Bianchi was close behind in second, with Christodoulou an excellent third, having begun the pre-final down in 27th place. European title-holder Ardigo took fourth ahead of Fore, with Thonon demoted seven places to 11th following a last-lap collision with Christodoulou. The ICA Asia-Pacific Championship produced victory for German Marco Wittmann, with Kristaps Meters and Matt Truelove completing the podium.

It was surprise package Francesco Antonucci who triumphed in a rain-interrupted World Championship four months later, dashing triple title-holder Fore's hopes of adding a fourth crown to his laurels. The early advantage was held by Bianchi, but the Frenchman's joy was to be short-lived as water in his airbox put him out of the race, the same fate that befell pre-final victor Sims. Antonucci charged through the field to overhaul Fore nine laps from the flag, with Thonon coming home third ahead of Christensen, Sauro Cesetti and Valtteri Bottas. Mike Courquin clinched the ICA World Cup after withstanding sustained pressure from pursuers Giacomo Patrono and Rick Dreezen.

Across the Pond, meanwhile, the élite North American championship Stars of Karting continued its growth, having come a long way towards unifying top-level American karting under the CIK format. Record entry numbers, televised races and continued sponsor support have boosted the young championship and given it a bright outlook as it heads into 2007 and beyond.

In North America ICC shifter karts are king, and this year Gary Carlton fought through tragic adversity to lift the crown in the Cytomax ICC class. The 20-year-old began the season with Trackmagic and showed well in the opening round at Oklahoma. During round two in Arizona, however, Carlton received word on Saturday night that his team owner and mentor, Fausto Vitello, had suffered a fatal heart attack. The next day, Carlton and his team decided to do what their team owner would have wanted, channelling their emotions and energies to take victory.

Soon after, with the future of the squad up in the air, Carlton decided to switch to the factory CRG outfit of PCH Motorsports, with the highly regarded Mike Speed – father of Formula 1 ace

Scott – tuning for him. Carlton didn't miss a beat, securing three additional victories as he sped to the title and the $25,000 Jim Trueman Memorial Career Enhancement Award that accompanies it, seeing off the threats of A1GP star Phil Giebler and ultra-quick Canadian Jordy Vorrath along the way.

The direct-drive ICA class has also grown in recent years to hold sizable prestige on the North American scene. In 2006 the shining star of that category was 18-year-old Tony Kart USA driver Joel Miller, who capped off a successful season with a dominant victory at the series finals in Toronto over Tyler Dueck, Caleb Loniewski and Nick Tonkin. Miller was also awarded the Skip Barber Snap-on Stars of Karting Scholarship, which will provide him with a free season of racing in the Skip Barber National Championship.

The Spec Racer category was created this year to take advantage of the popular TaG concept that has been sweeping the globe. The class came down to a straight fight between Canadian Devon Sandeen and Brandon Adkins. Even though Sandeen solidly won the finals in Toronto, Adkins' points advantage built up over the course of the season allowed him to hold on for the title.

As always, one of the hardest-fought divisions featured the young lions in the PCH Motorsports JICA category, a class that has seen many of its pilots graduate directly to Skip Barber, Formula BMW and oval track racing in recent years. The season boiled down to a fraught battle between Brett Smrz and Carlos Munoz. The Colombian walked away with the crown following a solid performance in Toronto, while other young talents worth keeping an eye on include Garrison Masters, Jacob Neal, Conor Daly – son of former grand prix star Derek (see below) – and Gustavo Menezes.

The King Taco Cadet class, finally, often provided the closest racing of all. Sage Karam returned to the fold looking to defend his 2005 crown, but he received strong competition from Oscar Tunjo and Gabriel Chaves. After some bad luck mid-season, Karam was able to return to winning ways but it was too little too late as Tunjo's season-long consistency was enough for the Colombian to seal the championship.

Left: Joel Miller clinched the US Stars of Karting ICA category in 2006, and his reward is a fully paid-for drive in the single-seater Skip Barber National Championship for 2007.

Below: Gary Carlton overcame tragedy to triumph in this year's Stars of Karting Cytomax ICC class across the Pond. The 20-year-old drew on the extensive knowledge and experience of Mike Speed – father of Formula One star Scott – as he sped his way towards title success.

Photograph: David Cole/eKartingNews.com

THE CLIMB TO THE TOP

US-domiciled former grand prix ace Derek Daly is a passionate supporter of karting. Here he chronicles his son Conor's early steps on a career path that, with a lot of talent and a bit of luck, could just enable him to follow his father all the way to the dizzy heights of Formula 1...

Halfway through his first full season of racing it became obvious to me that my 12-year-old son Conor would benefit from an additional challenge to that which his Yamaha Junior package could provide. Margay karts owner Keith Freber suggested he should test with a JICA engine.

Doing this, Conor quickly found that the physical requirements were far more that those with Yamaha horsepower. The higher horsepower made him think and react quicker and that was the type of environment I wanted – to stretch him both physically and mentally. We decided to race the JICA in the 250 unlimited class at our local track, Whiteland Raceway. It was a night race under the lights and Conor really enjoyed the experience... and wanted more.

That led to multiple phone calls to Stars of Karting organiser Paul Zalud and [team owner] Jonathan Nevoso. I had known Jonathan since he

ran Marco Andretti and was impressed by the results his drivers attained. Although it was a little late to put a deal together, John had a CRG chassis available and some Maxter engines... but we had to be our own mechanics. Conor's mechanic for the weekend would be his best friend Brandon Merrell.

During my Indycar career I spent many a day with Al Unser Sr, better known as 'Big Al'. On Thursday morning in Orlando we met Jonathan Nevoso's dad, another 'Big Al' and a real character who could weld, assemble and shout with the best of them. Big Al supplied us with all the bits to assemble a running kart bit by bit. The engine came from one box, the carb from somewhere else, the pipe

from another box and then bits like air box, wheels, throttle cable, gear, chain et al all appeared over a period of time. Eventually we had a fully operational JICA-engined CRG Road Rebel that Conor was really looking forward to driving.

We didn't really know what to expect from our first Stars of Karting weekend. The paddock was relatively small with a variety of teams housed under large tents, and the track a temporary 'street' circuit constructed in a parking lot. It was a mixture of hay bales, cones and water-filled plastic barriers, and provided the drivers with different challenges from those found on a purpose-built track.

After gradually getting accustomed to the track and closer to the pace throughout practice, in the final Conor got a great start and slotted into 12th place at the end of the first lap. He was able to hang on to the front pack until lap three, when an engine gremlin appeared and the engine would not rev above 14,200 rpm. He eventually finished 21st.

He had just finished the longest, fastest race he had ever competed in. He had also finished every lap of every session and gained an enormous amount of experience. Despite the disappointment of having to deal with an imbalance that he knew was costing him time, there was an inner smile I could see that said he was happy with his weekend's work and his step up to the JICA class.

My wife Rhonda's impression of the weekend was that it was easy to be there and easy to compete. It all ran on time and seemed to be well organised. The main reason for this might be that the Stars events, even the nationals, are still relatively small events. The organisational challenges will come when this series grows in stature.

Derek Daly

MAJOR RESULTS

OTHER CHAMPIONSHIP RACING SERIES WORLDWIDE

Compiled by DAVID HAYHOE

GP2 Series

All cars are Dallara-Renault.

GP2 SERIES, Circuit de la Comunitat Valenciana Ricardo Tormo, Cheste, Valencia, Spain, 8/9 April. Round 1. 45 and 28 laps of the 2.489-mile/4.005-km circuit.

Race 1 (112.005 miles/180.225 km).

1 Nelson Angelo Piquet, BR, 1h 03m 15.360s, 106.222 mph/170.948 km/h; **2** Lewis Hamilton, GB, 1h 03m 32.015s; **3** Adrián Vallés, E, 1h 03m 34.850s; **4** Nicolas Lapierre, F, 1h 03m 46.669s; **5** José Maria López, RA, 1h 03m 48.886s; **6** Gianmaria Bruni, I, 1h 03m 49.354s; **7** Michael Ammermüller, D, 1h 03m 50.747s; **8** Ernesto Viso, YV, 1h 04m 03.635s; **9** Alexandre Prémat, F, 1h 04m 08.388s; **10** Olivier Pla, F, 1h 04m 14.400s; **11** Franck Perera, F, 1h 04m 20.589s; **12** Ferdinando Monfardini, I, 1h 04m 26.787s; **13** Alexandre (Xandinho) Negrão, BR, 1h 04m 27.079s; **14** Adam Carroll, GB, 1h 04m 29.621s; **15** Fairuz Fauzy, MAL, 44 laps; **16** Timo Glock, D, 44; **17** Lucas di Grassi, BR, 44; **18** Javier Villa, E, 43; **19** Hiroki Yoshimoto, J, 27 (DNF-engine); **20** Andreas Zuber, A, 23 (DNF-accident); **21** Luca Filippi, I, 15 (DNF-gearbox); **22** Felix Porteiro, E, 7 (DNF-engine); **23** Sergio Hernández, E, 4 (DNF-gearbox); **24** Tristan Gommendy, F, 2 (DNF-engine); **25** Clivio Piccione, MC, 7 (DNF-accident).

Did not start: Jason Tahinci, TR (gearbox).

Fastest race lap: Lapierre, 1m 22.168s, 109.032 mph/175.469 km/h.

Fastest qualifying lap: Piquet, 1m 17.886s, 115.026 mph/185.116 km/h.

Race 2 (69.681 miles/112.140 km).

1 Michael Ammermüller, D, 38m 44.066s, 107.936 mph/173.705 km/h; **2** Ernesto Viso, YV, 38m 53.822s; **3** Nicolas Lapierre, F, 38m 54.279s; **4** Nelson Angelo Piquet, BR, 38m 55.041s; **5** Gianmaria Bruni, I, 39m 00.603s; **6** Lewis Hamilton, GB, 39m 02.576s; **7** Alexandre (Xandinho) Negrão, BR, 39m 16.812s; **8** Timo Glock, D, 39m 21.457s; **9** Javier Villa, E, 39m 28.150s; **10** Fairuz Fauzy, MAL, 39m 39.191s; **11** Tristan Gommendy, F, 39m 44.468s; **12** Hiroki Yoshimoto, J, 39m 47.770s; **13** Andreas Zuber, A, 39m 50.340s; **14** Franck Perera, F, 39m 53.838s; **15** Olivier Pla, F, 39m 53.838s; **16** Lucas di Grassi, BR, 27 laps; **17** Clivio Piccione, MC, 24 (DNF-spin); **18** Adrián Vallés, E, 23 (DNF-accident); **19** Adam Carroll, GB, 22 (DNF-accident); **20** José Maria López, RA, 22 (DNF-accident); **21** Ferdinando Monfardini, I, 5 (DNF-engine); **22** Alexandre Prémat, F, 3 (DNF-suspension); **23** Luca Filippi, I, 0 (DNF-gearbox); **24** Felix Porteiro, E, 0 (DNF-engine); **25** Jason Tahinci, TR, 0 (DNF-gearbox).

Did not start: Sergio Hernández, E (clutch).

Fastest lap: Zuber, 1m 21.244s, 110.272 mph/177.465 km/h.

Pole position: Viso.

Championship points.

Drivers: 1 Piquet, 16; **2** Lapierre, 10; **3** Hamilton, 9; **4** Ammermüller, 8; **5=** Viso, 6; **5=** Vallés, 6.

Teams: 1 Arden International, 18; **2** Piquet Sports, 16; **3** ART Grand Prix, 9.

GP2 SERIES, Autodromo Enzo e Dino Ferrari, Imola, Italy, 22/23 April. Round 2. 37 and 25 laps of the 3.081-mile/4.959-km circuit.

Race 1 (113.864 miles/183.246 km).

1 Gianmaria Bruni, I, 1h 01m 13.889s, 111.574 mph/179.560 km/h; **2** Michael Ammermüller, D, 1h 01m 24.796s; **3** Nicolas Lapierre, F, 1h 01m 28.403s; **4** Alexandre Prémat, F, 1h 01m 29.602s; **5** Nelson Angelo Piquet, BR, 1h 01m 30.661s; **6** Ernesto Viso, YV, 1h 01m 33.588s; **7** Timo Glock, D, 1h 02m 01.695s; **8** Hiroki Yoshimoto, J, 1h 02m 02.097s; **9** Adrián Vallés, E, 1h 02m 06.204s; **10** Felix Porteiro, E, 1h 02m 23.436s; **11** Luca Filippi, I, 1h 02m 37.337s; **12** Ferdinando Monfardini, I, 1h 02m 37.592s; **13** Javier Villa, E, 1h 02m 40.959s; **14** Andreas Zuber, A, 30 laps (DNF-engine); **15** Tristan Gommendy, F, 30 (DNF-accident); **16** Fairuz Fauzy, MAL, 29 (DNF-accident); **17** Adam Carroll, GB, 26 (DNF-spin); **18** Jason Tahinci, TR, 25 (DNF-engine); **19** Sergio Hernández, E, 25; **20** Alexandre (Xandinho) Negrão, BR, 13 (DNF-accident); **21** Franck Perera, F, 13 (DNF-accident); **22** Lucas di Grassi, BR, 7 (DNF-accident); **23** Olivier Pla, F, 7 (DNF-accident); **24** José Maria López, RA, 1 (DNF-gearbox); **25** Clivio Piccione, MC, 0 (DNF-engine).

Disqualified: Lewis Hamilton, GB (passed the safety car).

Fastest race lap: Vallés, 1m 35.261s, 116.448 mph/187.405 km/h.

Fastest qualifying lap: Bruni, 1m 32.691s, 119.677 mph/192.601 km/h.

Race 2 (76.887 miles/123.738 km).

1 Ernesto Viso, YV, 45m 17.116s, 101.871 mph/163.944 km/h; **2** Nelson Angelo Piquet, BR, 45m 17.712s; **3** Hiroki Yoshimoto, J, 45m 42.117s; **4** Timo Glock, D, 45m 46.017s; **5** Luca Filippi, I, 45m 46.394s; **6** Felix Porteiro, E, 45m 47.467s; **7** Nicolas Lapierre, F, 45m 48.618s; **8** Andreas Zuber, A, 45m 48.925s; **9** Ferdinando Monfardini, I, 45m 49.565s; **10** Lewis Hamilton, GB, 45m 50.482s; **11** Alexandre (Xandinho) Negrão, BR, 45m 52.942s; **12** Adam Carroll, GB, 45m 56.770s; **13** Sergio Hernández, E, 45m 57.205s; **14** Franck Perera, F, 45m 57.515s; **15** Fairuz Fauzy, MAL, 45m 58.869s; **16** Clivio Piccione, MC, 46m 00.322s; **17** Tristan Gommendy, F, 46m 06.254s; **18** Javier Villa, E, 46m 22.420s; **19** José Maria López, RA, 23 laps; **20** Olivier Pla, F, 23; **21** Jason Tahinci, TR, 19 (DNF-spin); **22** Gianmaria Bruni, I, 12 (DNF-brakes); **23** Michael Ammermüller, D, 1 (DNF-accident damage); **24** Alexandre Prémat, F, 0 (DNF-accident); **25** Adrián Vallés, E, 0 (DNF-accident); **26** Lucas di Grassi, BR, 0 (DNF-accident).

Fastest race lap: Viso, 1m 34.431s, 117.472 mph/189.052 km/h.

Pole position: Yoshimoto.

Championship points.

Drivers: 1 Piquet, 25; **2** Bruni, 18; **3=** Viso, 16; **3=** Ammermüller, 16; **3=** Lapierre, 16; **6** Hamilton, 9.

Teams: 1 Arden International, 32; **2** Piquet Sports, 25; **3** Trident Racing, 18.

GP2 SERIES, Nürburgring Grand Prix Circuit, Nürburg/Eifel, Germany, 6/7 May. Round 3. 35 and 24 laps of the 3.199-mile/5.148-km circuit.

Race 1 (111.948 miles/180.163 km).

1 Lewis Hamilton, GB, 1h 01m 26.097s, 109.333 mph/175.954 km/h; **2** Alexandre Prémat, F, 1h 01m 45.739s; **3** Adam Carroll, GB, 1h 01m 54.853s; **4** José Maria López, RA, 1h 01m 55.879s; **5** Nicolas Lapierre, F, 1h 01m 56.170s; **6** Ernesto Viso, YV, 1h 02m 01.881s; **7** Alexandre (Xandinho) Negrão, BR, 1h 02m 02.523s; **8** Hiroki Yoshimoto, J, 1h 02m 06.294s; **9** Javier Villa, E, 1h 02m 21.845s; **10** Michael Ammermüller, D, 1h 02m 22.735s; **11** Clivio Piccione, MC, 1h 02m 23.276s; **12** Sergio Hernández, E, 1h 02m 30.616s; **13** Tristan Gommendy, F, 1h 02m 31.103s; **14** Andreas Zuber, A, 1h 02m 42.606s; **15** Olivier Pla, F, 1h 02m 43.315s; **16** Felix Porteiro, E, 1h 02m 55.638s; **17** Timo Glock, D, 1h 03m 04.601s; **18** Lucas di Grassi, BR, 34 laps; **19** Fairuz Fauzy, MAL, 34; **20** Nelson Angelo Piquet, BR, 30 (DNF-puncture); **21** Ferdinando Monfardini, I, 29 (DNF-spin); **22** Gianmaria Bruni, I, 18 (DNF-accident); **23** Adrián Vallés, E, 18 (DNF-accident); **24** Luca Filippi, I, 11 (DNF-gearbox); **25** Franck Perera, F, 0 (DNF-engine).

Disqualified: Jason Tahinci, TR (completed 17 laps).

Fastest race lap: Hamilton, 1m 42.782s, 112.041 mph/180.311 km/h.

Fastest qualifying lap: Piquet, 1m 40.799s, 114.245 mph/183.858 km/h.

Race 2 (76.761 miles/123.535 km).

1 Lewis Hamilton, GB, 41m 18.772s, 111.483 mph/179.413 km/h; **2** Nicolas Lapierre, F, 41m 19.806s; **3** José Maria López, RA, 41m 22.593s; **4** Hiroki Yoshimoto, J, 41m 29.454s; **5** Adam Carroll, GB, 41m 30.418s; **6** Michael Ammermüller, D, 41m 32.965s; **7** Alexandre (Xandinho) Negrão, BR, 41m 38.383s; **8** Clivio Piccione, MC, 41m 40.250s; **9** Fairuz Fauzy, MAL, 41m 56.082s; **10** Ferdinando Monfardini, I, 41m 56.373s; **11** Ernesto Viso, YV, 41m 57.038s; **12** Tristan Gommendy, F, 41m 57.671s; **13** Lucas di Grassi, BR, 42m 00.898s; **14** Adrián Vallés, E, 42m 04.889s; **15** Franck Perera, F, 42m 09.680s; **16** Gianmaria Bruni, I, 42m 36.727s; **17** Alexandre Prémat, F, 42m 46.284s; **18** Jason Tahinci, TR, 42m 54.516s; **19** Nelson Angelo Piquet, BR, 23 laps (DNF-tyres); **20** Javier Villa, E, 23; **21** Timo Glock, D, 13 (DNF-electrics); **22** Felix Porteiro, E, 11 (DNF-gearbox); **23** Luca Filippi, I, 6 (DNF-gearbox); **24** Olivier Pla, F, 5 (DNF-suspension); **25** Sergio Hernández, E, 0 (DNF-engine); **26** Andreas Zuber, A, 0 (DNF-accident).

Fastest race lap: Prémat, 1m 40.983s, 114.037 mph/183.523 km/h.

Pole position: Yoshimoto.

Championship points.

Drivers: 1 Piquet, 27; **2** Hamilton, 26; **3** Lapierre, 25; **4=** Viso, 19; **4=** Bruni, 19; **6** Ammermüller, 17.

Teams: 1 Arden International, 42; **2** ART Grand Prix, 39; **3** Piquet Sports, 29.

GP2 SERIES, Circuit de Catalunya, Montmeló, Barcelona, Spain, 13/14 May. Round 4. 39 and 26 laps of the 2.875-mile/4.627-km circuit.

Race 1 (112.050 miles/180.327 km).

1 Alexandre Prémat, F, 57m 24.150s, 117.120 mph/188.486 km/h; **2** Lewis Hamilton, GB, 57m 26.337s; **3** Michael Ammermüller, D, 57m 35.113s; **4** Nelson Angelo Piquet, BR, 57m 35.870s; **5** Tristan Gommendy, F, 57m 37.155s; **6** Ferdinando Monfardini, I, 57m 38.998s; **7** Alexandre (Xandinho) Negrão, BR, 57m 44.263s; **8** Ernesto Viso, YV, 57m 55.892s; **9** Giorgio Pantano, I, 57m 57.863s; **10** Adam Carroll, GB, 58m 02.323s; **11** Timo Glock, D, 58m 12.810s; **12** Lucas di Grassi, BR, 58m 17.453s; **13** Franck Perera, F, 58m 26.740s; **14** Javier Villa, E, 58m 31.369s; **15** Jason Tahinci, TR, 58m 31.689s; **16** Clivio Piccione, MC, 38 laps; **17** Felix Porteiro, E, 38; **18** Adrián Vallés, E, 37; **19** Nicolas Lapierre, F, 34 (DNF-puncture); **20** José Maria López, RA, 22 (DNF-accident); **21** Gianmaria Bruni, I, 22 (DNF-accident); **22** Hiroki Yoshimoto, J, 20 (DNF-gearbox); **23** Andreas Zuber, A, 16 (DNF-wheel); **24** Sergio Hernández, E, 16 (DNF-puncture); **25** Fairuz Fauzy, MAL, 15 (DNF-spin).

Disqualified: Olivier Pla, F (car under the minimum weight limit).

Fastest race lap: Vallés, 1m 25.550s, 120.985 mph/194.707 km/h.

Fastest qualifying lap: Piquet, 1m 23.704s, mph/199.001 km/h.

Race 2 (74.674 miles/120.176 km).

1 Ernesto Viso, YV, 37m 37.277s, 119.093 mph/191.661 km/h; **2** Nelson Angelo Piquet, BR, 37m 38.007s; **3** Alexandre Prémat, F, 37m 38.858s; **4** Lewis Hamilton, GB, 37m 39.720s; **5** Tristan Gommendy, F, 37m 41.264s; **6** Ferdinando Monfardini, I, 37m 53.156s; **7** Giorgio Pantano, I, 37m 58.803s; **8** Michael Ammermüller, D, 38m 07.988s; **9** Lucas di Grassi, BR, 38m 08.310s; **10** Timo Glock, D, 38m 11.286s; **11** Andreas Zuber, A, 38m 11.992s; **12** Adam Carroll, GB, 38m 13.604s; **13** Sergio Hernández, E, 38m 17.041s; **14** Fairuz Fauzy, MAL, 38m 27.756s; **15** Javier Villa, E, 38m 28.350s; **16** Adrián Vallés, E, 38m 47.922s; **17** Gianmaria Bruni, I, 38m 53.524s; **18** Alexandre (Xandinho) Negrão, BR, 38m 59.504s; **19** Jason Tahinci, TR, 25 laps; **20** Olivier Pla, F, 25; **21** Nicolas Lapierre, F, 20 (DNF-engine); **22** Hiroki Yoshimoto, J, 16 (DNF-gearbox); **23** Felix Porteiro, E, 12 (DNF-engine); **24** José Maria López, RA, 8 (DNF-spin); **25** Franck Perera, F, 0 (DNF-accident); **26** Clivio Piccione, MC, 0 (DNF-accident).

Fastest race lap: Bruni, 1m 25.970s, 120.394 mph/193.755 km/h.

Pole position: Viso.

Championship points.

Drivers: 1 Piquet, 39; **2** Hamilton, 37; **3** Prémat, 27; **4** Viso, 26; **5** Lapierre, 25; **6** Ammermüller, 23.

Teams: 1 ART Grand Prix, 64; **2** Arden International, 48; **3** Piquet Sports, 43.

GP2 SERIES, Monte-Carlo street circuit, Monaco, 27 May. Round 5. 45 laps of the 2.075-mile/3.340-km circuit, 93.392 miles/150.300 km.

1 Lewis Hamilton, GB, 1h 03m 50.768s, 87.766 mph/141.245 km/h; **2** Franck Perera, F, 1h 03m 59.213s; **3** Alexandre Prémat, F, 1h 04m 27.080s; **4** Clivio Piccione, MC, 1h 04m 28.023s; **5** Andreas Zuber, A, 1h 05m 16.378s; **6** Felix Porteiro, E, 44 laps; **7** Michael Ammermüller, D, 44; **8** Sergio Hernández, E, 44; **9** Ferdinando Monfardini, I, 43; **10** Fairuz Fauzy, MAL, 43; **11** Lucas di Grassi, BR, 42; **12** Nelson Angelo Piquet, BR, 40; **13** Adrián Vallés, E, 39 (DNF-brakes); **14** Timo Glock, D, 36 (DNF-gearbox); **15** José Maria López, RA, 36; **16** Hiroki Yoshimoto, J, 23 (DNF-accident); **17** Ernesto Viso, YV, 23 (DNF-accident damage); **18** Jason Tahinci, TR, 12 (DNF-accident); **19** Giorgio Pantano, I, 11 (DNF-accident); **20** Olivier Pla, F, 2 (DNF-accident); **21** Javier Villa, E, 0 (DNF-accident); **22** Tristan Gommendy, F, 0 (DNF-engine); **23** Nicolas Lapierre, F, 0 (DNF-accident); **24** Gianmaria Bruni, I, 0 (DNF-accident); **25** Adam Carroll, GB, 0 (DNF-engine); **26** Alexandre (Xandinho) Negrão, BR, 0 (DNF-accident).

Fastest race lap: Di Grassi, 1m 22.563s, 90.493 mph/145.634 km/h.

Fastest qualifying lap: Hamilton, 1m 20.430s, 92.893 mph/149.496 km/h.

Championship points.

Drivers: 1 Hamilton, 49; **2** Piquet, 39; **3** Prémat, 33; **4** Viso, 26; **5=** Ammermüller, 25; **5=** Lapierre, 25.

Teams: 1 ART Grand Prix, 82; **2** Arden International, 50; **3** Piquet Sports, 43.

GP2 SERIES, Silverstone Grand Prix Circuit, Towcester, Northamptonshire, Great Britain, 10/11 June. Round 6. 36 and 23 laps of the 3.194-mile/5.141-km circuit.

Race 1 (114.936 miles/184.971 km).

1 Lewis Hamilton, GB, 1h 00m 53.888s, 113.241 mph/182.243 km/h; **2** Timo Glock, D, 1h 00m 58.902s; **3** Adam Carroll, GB, 1h 01m 00.033s; **4** Nelson Angelo Piquet, BR, 1h 01m 00.324s; **5** Giorgio Pantano, I, 1h 01m 02.616s; **6** Alexandre Prémat, F, 1h 01m 06.873s; **7** Clivio Piccione, MC, 1h 01m 09.034s; **8** Felix Porteiro, E, 1h 01m 10.976s; **9** Adrián Vallés, E, 1h 01m 11.847s; **10** Mike Conway, GB, 1h 01m 16.949s; **11** Fairuz Fauzy, MAL, 1h 01m 19.062s; **12** Jason Tahinci, TR, 1h 01m 30.221s; **13** Javier Villa, E, 1h 01m 48.918s; **14** Andreas Zuber, A, 30 laps; **15** Luca Filippi, I, 29 (DNF-gearbox); **16** Neel Jani, CH, 28; **17** Gianmaria Bruni, I, 26 (DNF-gearbox); **18** Hiroki Yoshimoto, J, 24 (DNF-gearbox); **19** Ferdinando Monfardini, I, 20 (DNF-accident); **20** Ernesto Viso, YV, 18 (DNF-gearbox); **21** Lucas di Grassi, BR, 16 (DNF-wing); **22** Michael Ammermüller, D, 7 (DNF-radiator); **23** Alexandre (Xandinho) Negrão, BR, 1 (DNF-accident damage); **24** Franck Perera, F, 0 (DNF-spin); **25** José Maria López, RA, 0 (DNF-accident).

Disqualified: Sergio Hernández, E, finished 10th in 1h 01m 16.426s, but was disqualified for illegal rear wing.

Fastest race lap: Hamilton, 1m 32.505s, 124.319 mph/200.071 km/h.

Fastest qualifying lap: Carroll, 1m 29.104s, 129.064 mph/207.707 km/h.

Race 2 (73.408 miles/118.138 km).

1 Lewis Hamilton, GB, 37m 27.225s, 117.597 mph/189.254 km/h; **2** Adam Carroll, GB, 37m 37.265s; **3** Clivio Piccione, MC, 37m 38.250s; **4** Giorgio Pantano, I, 37m 39.121s; **5** Nelson Angelo Piquet, BR, 37m 39.331s; **6** Timo Glock, D, 37m 42.358s; **7** Fairuz Fauzy, MAL, 37m 46.797s; **8** Ernesto Viso, YV, 37m 48.493s; **9** Luca Filippi, I, 37m 49.805s; **10** Franck Perera, F, 37m 50.113s; **11** Mike Conway, GB, 37m 51.003s; **12** Alexandre (Xandinho) Negrão, BR, 37m 52.110s; **13** Javier Villa, E, 37m 56.936s; **14** José Maria López, RA, 37m 59.207s; **15** Gianmaria Bruni, I, 38m 03.637s; **16** Jason Tahinci, TR, 38m 22.088s; **17** Hiroki Yoshimoto, J, 21 laps; **18** Adrián Vallés, E, 13 (DNF-gearbox); **19** Neel Jani, CH, 5 (DNF-accident); **20** Michael Ammermüller, D, 5 (DNF-accident); **21** Alexandre Prémat, F, 2 (DNF-driver gave up); **22** Andreas Zuber, A, 0 (DNF-accident).

Disqualified: Felix Porteiro, E, finished 2nd in 37m 36.285s but was disqualified for illegal position of the steering rack.

Did not start: Ferdinando Monfardini, I (injured in race 1 accident); Sergio Hernández, E and Lucas di Grassi, BR (team barred from race due to illegal rear wing in race 1).

Fastest race lap: Hamilton, 1m 31.313s, 125.941 mph/202.683 km/h.

Pole position: Porteiro.

Championship points.

Drivers: 1 Hamilton, 67; **2** Piquet, 46; **3** Prémat, 36; **4** Viso, 26; **5=** Ammermüller, 25; **5=** Lapierre, 25.

Teams: 1 ART Grand Prix, 103; **2=** Arden International, 50; **2=** Piquet Sports, 50.

GP2 SERIES, Circuit de Nevers, Magny-Cours, France, 15/16 July. Round 7. 41 and 28 laps of the 2.741-mile/4.411-km circuit.

Race 1 (112.261 miles/180.667 km).

1 Timo Glock, D, 1h 01m 14.385s, 109.989 mph/177.009 km/h; **2** Alexandre Prémat, F, 1h 01m 20.373s; **3** José Maria López, RA, 1h 01m 31.485s; **4** Nelson Angelo Piquet, BR, 1h 01m 38.611s; **5** Alexandre (Xandinho) Negrão, BR, 1h 01m 42.379s; **6** Giorgio Pantano, I, 1h 01m 45.971s; **7** Lucas di Grassi, BR, 1h 01m 48.662s; **8** Ferdinando Monfardini, I, 1h 02m 00.515s; **9** Hiroki Yoshimoto, J, 1h 02m 08.056s; **10** Ernesto Viso, YV, 1h 02m 08.536s; **11** Neel Jani, CH, 1h 02m 12.303s; **12** Michael Ammermüller, D, 1h 02m 16.543s; **13** Clivio Piccione, MC, 1h 02m 17.004s; **14** Sergio Hernández, E, 1h 02m 17.543s; **15** Adrián Vallés, E, 1h 02m 20.138s; **16** Olivier Pla, F, 1h 02m 29.706s; **17** Javier Villa, E, 1h 02m 35.623s; **18** Felix Porteiro, E, 1h 02m 36.396s; **19** Lewis Hamilton, GB, 40 laps; **20** Adam Carroll, GB, 40; **21** Franck Perera, F, 34 (DNF-engine); **22** Jason Tahinci, TR, 16 (DNF-gearbox); **23** Fairuz Fauzy, MAL, 4 (DNF-gearbox); **24** Gianmaria Bruni, I, 1 (DNF-clutch); **25** Andreas Zuber, A, 1 (DNF-accident); **26** Luca Filippi, I, 0 (DNF-accident).

Fastest race lap: Hamilton, 1m 27.418s, 112.873 mph/181.651 km/h.

Fastest qualifying lap: López, 1m 23.911s, 117.590 mph/189.243 km/h.

Race 2 (76.630 miles/123.324 km).

1 Giorgio Pantano, I, 40m 55.810s, 112.333 mph/180.782 km/h; **2** Nelson Angelo Piquet, BR, 40m 56.310s; **3** Alexandre Prémat, F, 41m 05.477s; **4** Timo Glock, D, 41m 06.710s; **5** Lewis Hamilton, GB, 41m 08.009s; **6** Lucas di Grassi, BR, 41m 13.225s; **7** Neel Jani, CH, 41m 13.694s; **8** Michael Ammermüller, D, 41m 24.964s; **9** Olivier Pla, F, 41m 36.538s; **10** Felix Porteiro, E, 41m 38.324s; **11** Sergio Hernández, E, 41m 39.778s; **12** Franck Perera, F, 41m 40.710s; **13** Adrián Vallés, E, 41m 41.151s; **14** Adam Carroll, GB, 41m 41.665s; **15** Fairuz Fauzy, MAL, 41m 42.365s; **16** Javier Villa, E, 41m 44.592s; **17** Jason Tahinci, TR, 42m 06.748s; **18** Andreas Zuber, A, 27 laps; **19** Gianmaria Bruni, I, 23 (DNF-gearbox); **20** Luca Filippi, I, 18 (DNF-spin); **21** Clivio Piccione, MC, 16 (DNF-suspension); **22** José Maria López, RA, 3 (DNF-engine); **23** Alexandre (Xandinho) Negrão, BR, 2 (DNF-accident damage); **24** Ferdinando Monfardini, I, 0 (DNF-accident); **25** Hiroki Yoshimoto, J, 0 (DNF-accident); **26** Ernesto Viso, YV, 0 (DNF-accident).

Fastest race lap: López, 1m 26.513s, 114.054 mph/183.551 km/h.

Pole position: Monfardini.

Championship points.

Drivers: 1 Hamilton, 70; **2** Piquet, 56; **3** Prémat, 48; **4** Glock, 28; **5** Viso, 26; **6=** Ammermüller, 25; **6=** Lapierre, 25.

Teams: 1 ART Grand Prix, 118; **2** Piquet Sports, 64; **3** iSport International, 55.

GP2 SERIES, Hockenheimring Grand Prix Circuit, Heidelberg, Germany, 29/30 July. Round 8. 40 and 27 laps of the 2.842-mile/4.574-km circuit.

Race 1 (113.686 miles/182.960 km).

1 Gianmaria Bruni, I, 57m 40.763s, 118.260 mph/190.321 km/h; **2** Lewis Hamilton, GB, 57m 42.001s; **3** Timo Glock, D, 57m 57.082s; **4** Ernesto Viso, YV, 58m 14.577s; **5** Giorgio Pantano, I, 58m 17.597s; **6** Adam Carroll, GB, 58m 32.911s; **7** José Maria López, RA, 58m 33.753s; **8** Clivio Piccione, MC, 58m 34.682s; **9** Michael Ammermüller, D, 58m 40.241s; **10** Sergio Hernández, E, 58m 54.169s; **11** Javier Villa, E, 58m 58.238s; **12** Felix Porteiro, E, 59m 02.499s; **13** Nelson Angelo Piquet, BR, 39 laps (DNF-fuel); **14** Franck Perera, F, 39; **15** Vitaly Petrov, RUS, 39; **16** Alexandre (Xandinho) Negrão, BR, 39; **17** Jason Tahinci, TR, 39; **18** Adrián Vallés, E, 39; **19** Alexandre Prémat, F, 38; **20** Nicolas Lapierre, F, 38; **21** Luca Filippi, I, 38; **22** Fairuz Fauzy, MAL, 37; **23** Hiroki Yoshimoto, J, 36; **24** Andreas Zuber, A, 8 (DNF-steering); **25** Ferdinando Monfardini, I, 0 (DNF-spin); **26** Lucas di Grassi, BR, 0 (DNF-engine).

Fastest race lap: Prémat, 1m 23.774s, 122.135 mph/196.557 km/h.

Fastest qualifying lap: Bruni, 1m 22.588s, 123.889 mph/199.380 km/h.

Race 2 (76.738 miles/123.498 km).

1 Timo Glock, D, 38m 36.598s, 119.251 mph/191.916 km/h; **2** José Maria López, RA, 38m 37.920s; **3** Lewis Hamilton, GB, 38m 49.208s; **4** Ernesto Viso, YV, 38m 51.278s; **5** Giorgio Pantano, I, 38m 57.949s; **6** Gianmaria Bruni, I, 38m 58.512s; **7** Nicolas Lapierre, F, 38m 58.751s; **8** Adam Carroll, GB, 39m 08.764s; **9** Alexandre (Xandinho) Negrão, BR, 39m 09.000s; **10** Fairuz Fauzy, MAL, 39m 11.968s; **11** Franck Perera, F, 39m 17.555s; **12** Ferdinando Monfardini, I, 39m 20.940s; **13** Javier Villa, E, 39m 21.184s; **14** Andreas Zuber, A, 39m 26.981s; **15** Vitaly Petrov, RUS, 39m 33.700s; **16** Luca Filippi, I, 39m 44.020s; **17** Jason Tahinci, TR, 39m 48.757s; **18** Felix Porteiro, E, 39m 49.168s; **19** Sergio Hernández, E, 22 (DNF-engine); **20** Michael Ammermüller, D, 20 (DNF-accident); **21** Adrián Vallés, E, 20 (DNF-accident); **22** Lucas di Grassi, BR, 14 (DNF-engine); **23** Hiroki Yoshimoto, J, 9 (DNF-accident); **24** Alexandre Prémat, F, 9 (DNF-accident). **25** Clivio Piccione, MC, 0 (DNF-accident); **26** Nelson Angelo Piquet, BR, 0 (DNF-throttle).

Fastest race lap: Di Grassi, 1m 24.477s, 121.119 mph/194.921 km/h.

Pole position: Piccione.

Championship points.

Drivers: 1 Hamilton, 82; **2** Piquet, 56; **3** Prémat, 49; **4** Glock, 40; **5** Viso, 34; **6** Bruni, 33.

Teams: 1 ART Grand Prix, 131; **2** iSport International, 75; **3** Piquet Sports, 64.

GP2 SERIES, Hungaroring, Mogyorod, Budapest, Hungary, 5/6 August. Round 9. 42 and 23 laps of the 2.722-mile/4.381-km circuit.

Race 1 (114.329 miles/183.995 km).

1 Nelson Angelo Piquet, BR, 1h 05m 13.884s, 105.160 mph/169.239 km/h; **2** Timo Glock, D, 1h 05m 46.679s; **3** Giorgio Pantano, I, 1h 05m 47.903s; **4** Ernesto Viso, YV, 1h 05m 53.767s; **5** Alexandre (Xandinho) Negrão, BR, 1h 05m 54.393s; **6** Alexandre Prémat, F, 1h 06m 08.679s; **7** Adam Carroll, GB, 1h 06m 09.959s; **8** José Maria López, RA, 1h 06m 11.974s; **9** Franck Perera, F, 1h 06m 12.550s; **10** Lewis Hamilton, GB, 1h 06m 27.702s; **11** Ferdinando Monfardini, I, 1h 06m 34.145s; **12** Luca Filippi, I, 41 laps; **13** Andreas Zuber, A, 41; **14** Lucas di Grassi, BR, 41; **15** Vitaly Petrov, RUS, 41; **16** Fairuz Fauzy, MAL, 41; **17** Adrián Vallés, E, 26 (DNF-accident); **18** Gianmaria Bruni, I, 25 (DNF-suspension); **19** Sergio Hernández, E, 25 (DNF-spin); **20** Jason Tahinci, TR, 22 (DNF-accident); **21** Hiroki Yoshimoto, J, 17 (DNF-accident); **22** Nicolas Lapierre, F, 17 (DNF-accident); **23** Javier Villa, E, 16 (DNF-accident); **24** Felix Porteiro, E, 16 (DNF-accident); **25** Clivio Piccione, MC, 7 (DNF-engine); **26** Michael Ammermüller, D, 0 (DNF-engine).

Fastest race lap: Piquet, 1m 30.711s, 108.036 mph/173.866 km/h.

Fastest qualifying lap: Piquet, 1m 29.464s, 109.541 mph/176.289 km/h.

Race 2 (62.067 miles/100.756 km).

1 Nelson Angelo Piquet, BR, 45m 59.804s, 81.667 mph/131.430 km/h; **2** Lewis Hamilton, GB, 46m 12.921s; **3** Alexandre Prémat, F, 46m 26.006s; **4** Ernesto Viso, YV, 46m 26.676s; **5** Timo Glock, D, 46m 27.035s; **6** Ferdinando Monfardini, I, 46m 40.918s; **7** Adrián Vallés, E, 46m 47.312s; **8** Gianmaria Bruni, I, 46m 50.118s; **9** Andreas Zuber, A, 46m 55.722s; **10** Vitaly Petrov, RUS, 47m 03.515s; **11** Michael Ammermüller, D, 47m 06.238s; **12** Felix Porteiro, E, 47m 34.879s; **13** Giorgio Pantano, I, 47m 50.121s; **14** Jason Tahinci, TR, 22 laps; **15** Javier Villa, E, 21 (DNF-accident); **16** Hiroki Yoshimoto, J, 18 (DNF-accident); **17** Sergio Hernández, E, 17 (DNF-accident); **18** Nicolas Lapierre, F, 12 (DNF-spin); **19** Adam Carroll, GB, 12 (DNF-accident damage); **20** Lucas di Grassi, BR, 10 (DNF-accident); **21** Franck Perera, F, 8 (DNF-accident); **22** Fairuz Fauzy, MAL, 7 (DNF-accident); **23** Clivio Piccione, MC, 5 (DNF-accident); **24** Alexandre (Xandinho) Negrão, BR, 4 (DNF-accident); **25** Luca Filippi, I, 4 (DNF-accident); **26** José Maria López, RA, 4 (DNF-throttle).

Fastest race lap: Piquet, 1m 51.716s, 87.723 mph/141.175 km/h.

Pole position: López.

Championship points.
Drivers: 1 Hamilton, 87; **2** Piquet, 76; **3** Prémat, 56; **4** Glock, 50; **5** Viso, 42; **6** Bruni, 33.
Teams: 1 ART Grand Prix, 143; **2** iSport International, 93; **3** Piquet Sports, 88.

GP2 SERIES, Istanbul Speed Park, Tuzla, Turkey, 26/27 August. Round 10. 34 and 23 laps of the 3.317-mile/5.338-km circuit.
Race 1 (112.620 miles/181.244 km).
1 Nelson Angelo Piquet, BR, 55m 59.398s, 120.686 mph/194.224 km/h; **2** Lewis Hamilton, GB, 56m 17.277s; **3** Alexandre Prémat, F, 56m 23.362s; **4** Timo Glock, D, 56m 23.988s; **5** Lucas di Grassi, BR, 56m 36.280s; **6** Adam Carroll, GB, 56m 41.104s; **7** Andreas Zuber, A, 56m 41.569s; **8** Alexandre (Xandinho) Negrão, BR, 56m 48.568s; **9** José Maria López, RA, 56m 56.344s; **10** Luca Filippi, I, 57m 03.075s; **11** Sergio Hernández, E, 57m 08.913s; **12** Franck Perera, F, 57m 09.776s; **13** Michael Ammermüller, D, 57m 11.676s; **14** Nicolas Lapierre, F, 57m 11.825s; **15** Javier Villa, E, 57m 16.781s; **16** Vitaly Petrov, RUS, 57m 23.261s; **17** Jason Tahinci, TR, 57m 33.215s; **18** Ferdinando Monfardini, I, 32 laps (DNF-gearbox); **19** Felix Porteiro, E, 30 (DNF-gearbox); **20** Hiroki Yoshimoto, J, 27 (DNF-engine); **21** Giorgio Pantano, I, 13 (DNF-gearbox); **22** Clivio Piccione, MC, 11 (DNF-brakes); **23** Adrián Vallés, E, 9 (DNF-gearbox); **24** Ernesto Viso, YV, 9 (DNF-spin); **25** Fairuz Fauzy, MAL, 8 (DNF-brakes); **26** Gianmaria Bruni, I, 6 (DNF-wheel).
Fastest race lap: Piquet, 1m 36.334s, 123.952 mph/199.480 km/h.
Fastest qualifying lap: Piquet, 1m 34.741s, 126.036 mph/202.835 km/h.

Race 2 (76.159 miles/122.566 km).
1 Andreas Zuber, A, 37m 54.990s, 120.516 mph/193.951 km/h; **2** Lewis Hamilton, GB, 37m 57.928s; **3** Adam Carroll, GB, 37m 58.816s; **4** Timo Glock, D, 38m 00.797s; **5** Nelson Angelo Piquet, BR, 38m 01.739s; **6** Nicolas Lapierre, F, 38m 05.337s; **7** Alexandre Prémat, F, 38m 11.683s; **8** Franck Perera, F, 38m 12.372s; **9** Lucas di Grassi, BR, 38m 12.990s; **10** Sergio Hernández, E, 38m 15.348s; **11** José Maria López, RA, 38m 15.600s; **12** Ferdinando Monfardini, I, 38m 15.967s; **13** Ernesto Viso, YV, 38m 18.000s; **14** Adrián Vallés, E, 38m 18.575s; **15** Gianmaria Bruni, I, 38m 21.350s; **16** Javier Villa, E, 38m 33.048s; **17** Jason Tahinci, TR, 38m 39.889s; **18** Vitaly Petrov, RUS, 38m 40.878s; **19** Hiroki Yoshimoto, J, 38m 55.613s; **20** Felix Porteiro, E, 4 laps (DNF-engine); **21** Alexandre (Xandinho) Negrão, BR, 2 (DNF-steering); **22** Fairuz Fauzy, MAL, 2 (DNF-engine); **23** Luca Filippi, I, 1 (DNF-accident); **24** Clivio Piccione, MC, 1 (DNF-accident); **25** Giorgio Pantano, I, 1 (DNF-accident); **26** Michael Ammermüller, D, 0 (DNF-engine).
Fastest race lap: Hamilton, 1m 36.822s, 123.327 mph/198.475 km/h
Pole position: Negrão.
Championship points.
Drivers: 1 Hamilton, 101; **2** Piquet, 91; **3** Prémat, 62; **4** Glock, 58; **5** Viso, 42; **6=** Bruni, 33; **6=** Carroll, 33.
Teams: 1 ART Grand Prix, 163; **2** Piquet Sports, 104; **3** iSport International, 101.

GP2 SERIES, Autodromo Nazionale di Monza, Milan, Italy, 9/10 September. Round 11. 32 and 21 laps of the 3.600-mile/5.793-km circuit.
Race 1 (114.995 miles/185.067 km).
1 Giorgio Pantano, I, 51m 31.171s, 133.924 mph/215.530 km/h; **2** Nelson Angelo Piquet, BR, 51m 36.225s; **3** Lewis Hamilton, GB, 51m 38.058s; **4** Luca Filippi, I, 51m 59.801s; **5** Alexandre Prémat, F, 52m 04.053s; **6** Nicolas Lapierre, F, 52m 10.456s; **7** Clivio Piccione, MC, 52m 11.827s; **8** Hiroki Yoshimoto, J, 52m 14.532s; **9** Javier Villa, E, 52m 28.175s; **10** Lucas di Grassi, BR, 52m 58.211s; **11** Jason Tahinci, TR, 31 laps; **12** Michael Ammermüller, D, 31; **13** Sergio Hernández, E, 31; **14** Fairuz Fauzy, MAL, 31; **15** Franck Perera, F, 30 (DNF-gearbox); **16** José Maria López, RA, 19 (DNF-accident damage); **17** Vitaly Petrov, RUS, 18 (DNF-lost water); **18** Timo Glock, D, 17 (DNF-accident); **19** Adrián Vallés, E, 17 (DNF-accident); **20** Gianmaria Bruni, I, 15 (DNF-accident); **21** Ferdinando Monfardini, I, 15 (DNF-accident); **22** Adam Carroll, GB, 10 (DNF-wheel lost); **23** Felix Porteiro, E, 8 (DNF-accident); **24** Andreas Zuber, A, 0 (DNF-accident); **25** Alexandre (Xandinho) Negrão, BR, 0 (DNF-accident); **26** Ernesto Viso, YV, 0 (DNF-accident).
Fastest race lap: Hamilton, 1m 31.038s, 142.342 mph/229.077 km/h (Pantano's fastest lap of 1m 30.976s, 142.439 mph/229.234 km/h was disallowed because he failed to slow down under yellow flags).
Fastest qualifying lap: Piquet, 1m 30.161s, 143.727 mph/231.306 km/h.

Race 2 (75.400 miles/121.344 km).
1 Giorgio Pantano, I, 32m 08.597s, 140.744 mph/226.505 km/h; **2** Lewis Hamilton, GB, 32m 09.008s; **3** Clivio Piccione, MC, 32m 22672s; **4** Nicolas Lapierre, F, 32m 29.803s; **5** Hiroki Yoshimoto, J, 32m 30.277s; **6** Nelson Angelo Piquet, BR, 32m 30.626s; **7** Luca Filippi, I, 32m 31.145s; **8** Ernesto Viso, YV, 32m 37.104s; **9** Gianmaria Bruni, I, 32m 52.564s; **10** Fairuz Fauzy, MAL, 32m 53.442s; **11** Adrián Vallés, E, 32m 54.120s; **12** Vitaly Petrov, RUS, 32m 54.378s; **13** Jason Tahinci, TR, 33m 09.871s; **14** Lucas di Grassi, BR, 33m 16.811s; **15** Franck Perera, F, 19 laps (DNF-steering); **16** José Maria López, RA, 17 (DNF-accident); **17** Andreas Zuber, A, 17; **18** Felix Porteiro, E, 16; **19** Alexandre Prémat, F, 15 (DNF-gearbox); **20** Sergio Hernández, E, 12 (DNF-gearbox); **21** Adam Carroll, GB, 5 (DNF-accident); **22** Alexandre (Xandinho) Negrão, BR, 4 (DNF-accident); **23** Ferdinando Monfardini, I, 4 (DNF-accident); **24** Michael Ammermüller, D, 2 (DNF-accident); **25** Javier Villa, E, 1 (DNF-throttle).
Did not start: Timo Glock, D (injured).
Fastest race lap: Hamilton, 1m 30.528s, 143.144 mph/230.368 km/h.
Pole position: Yoshimoto.

Final championship points
Drivers
1 Lewis Hamilton, GB, 114; **2** Nelson Angelo Piquet, BR, 102; **3** Alexandre Prémat, F, 66; **4** Timo Glock, D, 58; **5** Giorgio Pantano, I, 44; **6** Ernesto Viso, YV, 42; **7** Gianmaria Bruni, I, 33; **8** Adam Carroll, GB, 33; **9** Nicolas Lapierre, F, 32; **10** José Maria López, RA, 30; **11** Michael Ammermüller, D, 25; **12** Clivio Piccione, MC, 18; **13** Alexandre (Xandinho) Negrão, BR, 13; **14** Andreas Zuber, A, 12; **15** Hiroki Yoshimoto, J, 12; **16** Franck Perera, F, 8; **17** Lucas di Grassi, BR, 8; **18** Adrián Vallés, E, 7; **19** Luca Filippi, I, 7; **20** Tristan Gommendy, F, 6; **21** Ferdinando Monfardini, I, 6; **22** Felix Porteiro, E, 5; Sergio Hernández, E, 1.
Teams
1 ART Grand Prix, 180; **2** Piquet Sports, 115; **3** iSport International, 101; **4** Arden International, 57; **5** Petrol Ofisi FMS International, 46; **6** Trident Racing, 45; **7** Racing Engineering, 33; **8** Super Nova International, 30; **9** BCN Competición, 22; **10** DPR, 18; **11** DAMS, 14; **12** Campos Racing, 12; **13** Durango, 9.

Euro 3000 Championship

All cars are Lola B02/50-Zytek KV, unless stated.

EURO 3000 CHAMPIONSHIP, Autodromo Adria International Raceway, Adria, Italy, 8/9 April. 23 and 30 laps of the 1.679-mile/2.702-km circuit.
Round 1 (38.616 miles/62.146 km).
1 Marco Bonanomi, I, 26m 51.537s, 86.263 mph/138.827 km/h; **2** Tuka Rocha, BR (Lola Light), 27m 09.677s; **3** Paolo Nocera, I, 27m 10.395s; **4** Juan Cáceres, ROU, 27m 23.878s; **5** Giacomo Ricci, I, 27m 24.064s; **6** Vitaly Petrov, RUS, 27m 28.580s; **7** Oliver Martini, I, 27m 32.776s; **8** Stefano Gattuso, I, 27m 33.950s; **9** Matteo Cressoni, I, 27m 34.550s; **10** Marcello Puglisi, I, 27m 50.218s.
Fastest race lap: Bonanomi, 1m 05.608s, 92.126 mph/148.262 km/h.
Fastest qualifying lap: Bonanomi, 1m 07.806s, 89.140 mph/143.456 km/h.

Round 2 (50.368 miles/81.060 km).
1 Giacomo Ricci, I, 34m 53.011s, 86.634 mph/139.424 km/h; **2** Paolo Nocera, I, 35m 00.726s; **3** Stefano Gattuso, I, 35m 09.197s; **4** Juan Cáceres, ROU, 35m 12.355s; **5** Marco Bonanomi, I, 35m 12.478s; **6** Tuka Rocha, BR, 35m 13.655s; **7** Gavin Cronje, ZA, 35m 23.643s; **8** Marcello Puglisi, I, 35m 43.956s; **9** Francesco Dracone, I, 29 laps; **10** Glauco Solieri, I (Lola Light), 29.
Fastest race lap: Ricci, 1m 09.105s, 87.464 mph/140.759 km/h.
Pole position: Gattuso.

EURO 3000 CHAMPIONSHIP, Autodromo Enzo e Dino Ferrari, Imola, Italy, 6/7 May. 14 and 18 laps of the 3.081-mile/4.959-km circuit.
Round 3 (42.994 miles/69.192 km).
1 Giacomo Ricci, I, 23m 49.125s, 108.303 mph/174.296 km/h; **2** Marco Bonanomi, I, 23m 51.970s; **3** Oliver Martini, I, 24m 02.230s; **4** Roldán Rodríguez, E, 24m 19.680s; **5** Gavin Cronje, ZA, 24m 27.380s; **6** Matteo Cressoni, I, 24m 28.966s; **7** Tuka Rocha, BR (Lola Light), 25m 10.115s; **8** Glauco Solieri, I (Lola Light), 25m 15.380s; **9** Marcello Puglisi, I, 13 laps; **10** Fausto Ippoliti, I, 9 (DNF).
Fastest race lap: Ricci, 1m 40.909s, 109.930 mph/176.915 km/h.
Fastest qualifying lap: Bonanomi, 1m 39.965s, 110.969 mph/178.586 km/h.

Round 4 (55.319 miles/89.028 km).
1 Giacomo Ricci, I, 30m 55.771s, 107.314 mph/172.704 km/h; **2** Marco Bonanomi, I, 31m 05.497s; **3** Vitaly Petrov, RUS, 31m 22.717s; **4** Fausto Ippoliti, I, 31m 25.005s; **5** Roldán Rodríguez, E, 31m 25.742s; **6** Paolo Nocera, I, 31m 39.504s; **7** Juan Cáceres, ROU, 31m 41.065s; **8** Oliver Martini, I, 31m 41.991s; **9** Gavin Cronje, ZA, 31m 46.721s; **10** Ivan Bellarosa, I, 31m 48.927s.
Fastest race lap: Ricci, 1m 41.326s, 109.478 mph/176.187 km/h.
Pole position: Solieri.

EURO 3000 CHAMPIONSHIP, Circuit de Spa-Francorchamps, Stavelot, Belgium, 3/4 June. 10 and 14 laps of the 2.875-mile/4.627-km circuit.
Round 5 (28.751 miles/46.270 km).
1 Marco Bonanomi, I, 25m 06.229s, 68.717 mph/110.589 km/h; **2** Giacomo Ricci, I, 25m 06.791s; **3** Roldán Rodríguez, E, 25m 12.476s; **4** Stefano Gattuso, I, 25m 14.983s; **5** Jason Tahinci, TR, 25m 22.420s; **6** Gavin Cronje, ZA, 25m 35.804s; **7** Matteo Cressoni, I, 8 laps; **8** Juan Cáceres, ROU, 8; **9** Vitaly Petrov, RUS, 4 (DNF); **10** Tuka Rocha, BR (Lola Light), 2 (DNF).
Fastest race lap: Bonanomi, 2m 08.457s, 80.574 mph/129.671 km/h.
Fastest qualifying lap: Bonanomi, 2m 06.127s, 82.063 mph/132.067 km/h.

Round 6 (40.251 miles/64.778 km).
1 Giacomo Ricci, I, 34m 09.536s, 104.282 mph/167.826 km/h; **2** Juan Cáceres, ROU, 34m 11.297s; **3** Stefano Gattuso, I, 34m 12.220s; **4** Vitaly Petrov, RUS, 34m 12.833s; **5** Matteo Cressoni, I, 34m 12.949s; **6** Roldán Rodríguez, E, 34m 13.379s; **7** Paolo Nocera, I, 34m 14.781s; **8** Gavin Cronje, ZA, 34m 16.322s; **9** Ivan Bellarosa, I, 34m 22.548s; **10** Marcello Puglisi, I, 34m 23.201s.
Fastest race lap: Rodríguez, 2m 09.040s, 80.210 mph/129.086 km/h.
Pole position: Cáceres.

EURO 3000 CHAMPIONSHIP, Hungaroring, Mogyorod, Budapest, Hungary, 17/18 June. 15 and 18 laps of the 2.722-mile/4.381-km circuit.
Round 7 (40.833 miles/65.715 km).
1 Marco Bonanomi, I, 24m 27.460s, 100.173 mph/161.213 km/h; **2** Giacomo Ricci, I, 24m 38.757s; **3** Tuka Rocha, BR (Lola Light), 24m 55.402s; **4** Juan Cáceres, ROU, 24m 58.148s; **5** Stefano Gattuso, I, 24m 59.142s; **6** Matteo Cressoni, I, 24m 59.608s; **7** Vitaly Petrov, RUS, 25m 00.183s; **8** Gavin Cronje, ZA, 25m 09.051s; **9** Paolo Nocera, I, 25m 15.802s; **10** Ivan Bellarosa, I, 25m 17.695s.
Fastest qualifying lap: Bonanomi, 1m 36.101s, 101.976 mph/164.115 km/h.

Round 8 (49.000 miles/78.858 km).
1 Vitaly Petrov, RUS, 29m 51.466s, 98.467 mph/158.467 km/h; **2** Gavin Cronje, ZA, 30m 01.706s; **3** Tuka Rocha, BR (Lola Light), 30m 02.605s; **4** Giacomo Ricci, I, 30m 03.153s; **5** Roldán Rodríguez, E, 30m 03.691s; **6** Juan Cáceres, ROU, 30m 04.083s; **7** Stefano Gattuso, I, 30m 14.860s; **8** Oliver Martini, I, 30m 14.983s; **9** Paolo Nocera, I, 30m 21.152s; **10** Ivan Bellarosa, I, 30m 25.261s.
Pole position: Cronje.

EURO 3000 CHAMPIONSHIP, Autodromo Internazionale del Mugello, Scarperia, Firenze (Florence), Italy, 22/23 July. 13 and 16 laps of the 3.259-mile/5.245-km circuit.
Round 9 (42.368 miles/68.185 km).
1 Marco Bonanomi, I, 22m 24.922s, 113.408 mph/182.513 km/h; **2** Oliver Martini, I, 22m 27.505s; **3** Giacomo Ricci, I, 22m 27.981s; **4** Tuka Rocha, BR, 22m 34.845s; **5** Jérôme d'Ambrosio, B, 22m 35.104s; **6** Matteo Cressoni, I, 22m 39.633s; **7** Vitaly Petrov, RUS, 22m 40.457s; **8** Juan Cáceres, ROU, 22m 43.066s; **9** Paolo Nocera, I, 22m 46.759s; **10** Gavin Cronje, ZA, 22m 47.304s.
Fastest race lap: Bonanomi, 1m 41.929s, 115.107 mph/185.246 km/h.
Fastest qualifying lap: Bonanomi, 1m 39.989s, 117.340 mph/188.840 km/h.

Round 10 (52.145 miles/83.920 km).
1 Vitaly Petrov, RUS, 27m 58.324s, 111.852 mph/180.008 km/h; **2** Matteo Cressoni, I, 27m 01.876s; **3** Giacomo Ricci, I, 28m 11.118s; **4** Oliver Martini, I, 28m 18.006s; **5** Juan Cáceres, ROU, 28m 21.989s; **6** Tuka Rocha, BR, 28m 29.528s; **7** Paolo Nocera, I, 28m 29.577s; **8** Marco Bonanomi, I, 28m 31.322s; **9** Roldán Rodríguez, E, 28m 33.614s; **10** Stefano Gattuso, I, 28m 34.496s.
Fastest race lap: Ricci, 1m 41.491s, 115.604 mph/186.046 km/h.
Pole position: Cáceres.

EURO 3000 CHAMPIONSHIP, Silverstone Grand Prix Circuit, Towcester, Northamptonshire, Great Britain, 13 August. 15 and 19 laps of the 3.194-mile/5.141-km circuit.
Round 11 (47.917 miles/77.115 km).
1 Vitaly Petrov, RUS, 33m 03.009s, 86.990 mph/139.996 km/h; **2** Jérôme d'Ambrosio, B, 33m 06.322s; **3** Giacomo Ricci, I, 33m 35.469s; **4** Roldán Rodríguez, E, 35m 36.673s; **5** Marco Bonanomi, I, 35m 43.848s; **6** Matteo Cressoni, I, 35m 44.352s; **7** Tuka Rocha, BR, 35m 49.715s; **8** Paolo Nocera, I, 35m 55.952s; **9** Juan Cáceres, ROU, 35m 56.627s; **10** Gavin Cronje, ZA, 35m 57.555s.
Fastest race lap: Petrov, 2m 01.058s, 94.997 mph/152.882 km/h.
Fastest qualifying lap: Bonanomi, 1m 37.272s, 118.266 mph/190.266 km/h.

Round 12 (60.695 miles/97.679 km).
1 Tuka Rocha, BR, 31m 50.305s, 114.381 mph/184.078 km/h; **2** Juan Cáceres, ROU, 32m 06.113s; **3** Oliver Martini, I, 32m 07.254s; **4** Marco Bonanomi, I, 32m 09.564s; **5** Jérôme d'Ambrosio, B, 32m 10.991s; **6** Stefano Gattuso, I, 32m 13.144s; **7** Matteo Cressoni, I, 32m 13.496s; **8** Alex Ciompi, I, 32m 16.873s; **9** Ivan Bellarosa, I, 32m 43.175s; **10** Francesco Dracone, I, 33m 15.894s.
Fastest race lap: Ricci, 1m 38.752s, 116.454 mph/187.415 km/h.
Pole position: Nocera.

EURO 3000 CHAMPIONSHIP, Circuit de Catalunya, Montmeló, Barcelona, Spain, 23/24 September. 23 and 28 laps of the 1.832-mile/2.949-km circuit.
Round 13 (42.146 miles/67.827 km).
1 Roldán Rodríguez, E, 30m 30.945s, 82.867 mph/133.361 km/h; **2** Giacomo Ricci, I, 30m 38.503s; **3** Vitaly Petrov, RUS, 30m 40.214s; **4** Jérôme d'Ambrosio, B, 30m 42.479s; **5** Tuka Rocha, BR, 30m 48.952s; **6** Davide Rigon, I, 31m 00.203s; **7** Alex Ciompi, I, 31m 03.246s; **8** Gavin Cronje, ZA, 31m 03.956s; **9** Stefano Gattuso, I, 31m 04.885s; **10** Matteo Cressoni, I, 31m 19.972s.
Fastest race lap: Petrov, 1m 11.781s, 91.901 mph/147.899 km/h.
Fastest qualifying lap: Rodríguez, 1m 11.506s, 92.254 mph/148.468 km/h.

Round 14 (51.308 miles/82.572 km).
1 Vitaly Petrov, RUS, 28m 57.774s, 106.290 mph/171.057 km/h; **2** Davide Rigon, I, 29m 01.033s; **3** Matteo Cressoni, I, 29m 11.729s; **4** Tuka Rocha, BR, 29m 14.455s; **5** Johnny Cecotto Jr., YV, 29m 27.564s; **6** Gavin Cronje, ZA, 29m 51.008s; **7** Ivan Bellarosa, I, 29m 56.900s; **8** Francesco Dracone, I, 27 laps; **9** Stefano Gattuso, I, 23; **10** Roldán Rodríguez, E, 23.
Fastest race lap: d'Ambrosio, 1m 01.017s, 108.113 mph/173.990 km/h.
Pole position: Cronje.

EURO 3000 CHAMPIONSHIP, Autodromo di Vallelunga, Campagnano di Roma, Italy, 15 October. 16 and 20 laps of the 2.538-mile/4.085-km circuit.
Round 15 (40.613 miles/65.359 km).
1 Marco Bonanomi, I, 22m 57.253s, 106.158 mph/170.844 km/h; **2** Jérôme d'Ambrosio, B, 23m 06.234s; **3** Tuka Rocha, BR, 23m 06.865s; **4** Vitaly Petrov, RUS, 23m 09.973s; **5** Giacomo Ricci, I, 23m 11.547s; **6** Fausto Ippoliti, I, 23m 19.822s; **7** Matteo Cressoni, I, 23m 22.512s; **8** Gavin Cronje, ZA, 23m 31.793s; **9** Ivan Bellarosa, I, 23m 32.383s; **10** Francesco Provenzano, I, 23m 40.854s.
Fastest race lap: Roldán Rodríguez, E, 1m 25.062s, 107.426 mph/172.885 km/h.
Fastest qualifying lap: Rodríguez, 1m 24.256s, 108.454 mph/174.539 km/h.

Round 16 (50.766 miles/81.700 km).
1 Fausto Ippoliti, I, 29m 01.410s, 104.948 mph/168.897 km/h; **2** Vitaly Petrov, RUS, 29m 03.936s; **3** Giacomo Ricci, I, 29m 05.119s; **4** Tuka Rocha, BR, 29m 06.524s; **5** Jérôme d'Ambrosio, B, 29m 09.879s; **6** Roldán Rodríguez, E, 29m 10.937s; **7** Matteo Cressoni, I, 29m 17.324s; **8** Ivan Bellarosa, I, 29m 45.335s; **9** Francesco Dracone, I, 30m 10.406s; **10** Marco Bonanomi, I, 19 laps.
Fastest race lap: Bonanomi, 1m 25.512s, 106.861 mph/171.975 km/h.
Pole position: Cronje.

EURO 3000 CHAMPIONSHIP, Autodromo Internazionale di Misano, Misano Adriatico, Rimini, Italy, 22 October. 16 and 20 laps of the 2.523-mile/4.060-km circuit.
Round 17 (40.364 miles/64.960 km).
1 Giacomo Ricci, I, 23m 00.165s, 105.286 mph/169.440 km/h; **2** Vitaly Petrov, RUS, 23m 01.141s; **3** Jérôme d'Ambrosio, B, 23m 10.923s; **4** Diego Nunes, BR, 23m 11.347s; **5** Marco Bonanomi, I, 23m 12.722s; **6** Fausto Ippoliti, I, 23m 16.195s; **7** Gavin Cronje, ZA, 23m 22.964s; **8** Marco Mocci, I, 23m 42.875s; **9** Ivan Bellarosa, I, 23m 44.926s; **10** Bianca Steiner, A, 24m 15.287s.
Fastest race lap: Bonanomi, 1m 23.691s, 108.518 mph/174.642 km/h.
Fastest qualifying lap: Ricci, 1m 39.014s, 117.724 mph/147.615 km/h.

Round 18 (50.455 miles/81.200 km).
1 Marco Bonanomi, I, 28m 03.020s, 107.925 mph/173.687 km/h; **2** Giacomo Ricci, I, 28m 03.447s; **3** Vitaly Petrov, RUS, 28m 15.717s; **4** Jérôme d'Ambrosio, B, 28m 16.413s; **5** Gavin Cronje, ZA, 28m 20.915s; **6** Diego Nunes, BR, 28m 32.880s; **7** Marco Mocci, I, 28m 47.550s; **8** Ivan Bellarosa, I, 28m 47.746s; **9** Bianca Steiner, A, 29m 10.552s; **10** Leandro Romano, I, 19 laps.
Fastest race lap: Ricci, 1m 22.185s, 110.506 mph/177.842 km/h.
Pole position: Mocci.

Final championship points
1 Giacomo Ricci, I, 106; **2** Marco Bonanomi, I, 94; **3** Vitaly Petrov, RUS, 72; **4** Tuka Rocha, BR, 51; **5** Jérôme d'Ambrosio, B, 39; **6** Roldán Rodríguez, E, 36; **7** Juan Cáceres, ROU, 28; **8** Matteo Cressoni, I, 27; **9** Oliver Martini, I, 23; **10** Gavin Cronje, ZA, 20; **11** Stefano Gattuso, I, 19; **12** Fausto Ippoliti, I, 15; **13** Paolo Nocera, I, 13; **14** Davide Rigon, I, 8; **15** Diego Nunes, BR, 6; **16** Jason Tahinci, TR, 4; **17** Alex Ciompi, I, 2; **18** Johnny Cecotto Jr, YV, 2; **19** Glauco Solieri, I, 1; **20** Marco Mocci, I, 1.

F3000 International Masters

All cars are Lola B99/50-Zytek KV, unless stated.

F3000 INTERNATIONAL MASTERS, Autodromo Nazionale di Monza, Milan, Italy, 1/2 April. Round 1. 2 x 15 laps of the 3.600-mile/5.793-km circuit.
Race 1 (53.802 miles/86.586 km).
1 Jaroslav 'Jarek' Janis, CZ (Lola B2/50-Zytek KV), 30m 46.630s, 104.887 mph/168.799 km/h; **2** Jan Charouz, CZ (Lola B2/50-Zytek KV), 30m 47.522s; **3** Davide di Benedetto, I, 30m 48.464s; **4** Ignazio Belluardo, I, 30m 49.306s; **5** Fausto Ippoliti, I, 30m 50.818s; **6** Timo Lienemann, D, 30m 51.615s; **7** Michele Merendino, I, 30m 53.968s; **8** Massimo Torre, I, 14 laps; **9** Gianmaria Gabbiani, I, 14; **10** Giovanni Tedeschi, I, 7 (DNF).
Fastest race lap: Janis, 1m 41.573s, 127.579 mph/205.318 km/h.
Fastest qualifying lap: Massimiliano 'Max' Busnelli, I, 1m 40.376s, 129.100 mph/207.766 km/h.

Race 2 (53.802 miles/86.586 km).
1 Jaroslav 'Jarek' Janis, CZ (Lola B2/50-Zytek KV), 25m 50.683s, 124.905 mph/201.014 km/h; **2** Ignazio Belluardo, I, 25m 50.723s; **3** Jan Charouz, CZ (Lola B2/50-Zytek KV), 25m 53.365s; **4** Davide di Benedetto, I, 25m 59.492s; **5** Luca Persiani, I, 26m 04.013s; **6** Timo Lienemann, D, 26m 08.263s; **7** Fausto Ippoliti, I, 26m 13.739s; **8** Massimo Torre, I, 26m 28.904s; **9** Gianmaria Gabbiani, I, 26m 44.995s; **10** Massimiliano 'Max' Busnelli, I, 14 laps.
Fastest race lap: Lienemann, 1m 41.978s, 127.072 mph/204.502 km/h.
Pole position: Torre.

F3000 INTERNATIONAL MASTERS, Circuit de Nevers, Magny-Cours, France, 29/30 April. Round 2. 2 x 19 laps of the 2.741-mile/4.411-km circuit.
Race 1 (51.959 miles/83.620 km).
1 Jaroslav 'Jarek' Janis, CZ (Lola B2/50-Zytek KV), 29m 40.423s, 105.061 mph/169.078 km/h; **2** Matteo Bobbi, I, 29m 52.069s; **3** Alessandro Pierguidi, I, 30m 03.515s; **4** Daniel Move, RUS, 30m 04.712s; **5** Giovanni Tedeschi, I, 30m 11.263s; **6** Marco Mocci, I, 30m 13.536s; **7** Jan Charouz, CZ (Lola B2/50-Zytek KV), 30m 16.597s; **8** Ignazio Belluardo, I, 30m 19.226s; **9** Luca Persiani, I, 30m 22.223s; **10** Davide di Benedetto, I, 30m 31.534s.
Fastest race lap: Janis, 1m 32.360s, 106.833 mph/171.931 km/h.
Fastest qualifying lap: Janis, 1m 30.520s, 109.005 mph/175.426 km/h.

Race 2 (51.959 miles/83.620 km).
1 Ignazio Belluardo, I, 29m 34.444s, 105.415 mph/169.648 km/h; **2** Jaroslav 'Jarek' Janis, CZ (Lola B2/50-Zytek KV), 29m 34.736s; **3** Marco Mocci, I, 29m 54.680s; **4** Giovanni Tedeschi, I, 29m 59.446s; **5** Luca Persiani, I, 30m 06.094s; **6** Massimo Torre, I, 30m 08.287s; **7** Alessandro Pierguidi, I, 30m 10.737s; **8** Davide di Benedetto, I, 30m 28.781s; **9** Jan Charouz, CZ (Lola B2/50-Zytek KV), 30m 29.414s; **10** Emilio de Villota Jr., E, 30m 43.439s.
Fastest race lap: Janis, 1m 31.856s, 107.420 mph/172.874 km/h.
Pole position: Belluardo.

F3000 INTERNATIONAL MASTERS, Brands Hatch Indy Circuit, West Kingsdown, Dartford, Kent, Great Britain, 20/21 May, Round 3. 13 and 19 laps of the 2.301-mile/3.703-km circuit.
Race 1 (29.894 miles/48.109 km).
1 Jaroslav 'Jarek' Janis, CZ (Lola B2/50-Zytek KV), 25m 20.828s, 70.762 mph/113.880 km/h; **2** Emilio de Villota Jr., E, 25m 21.501s; **3** Jan Charouz, CZ (Lola B2/50-Zytek KV), 25m 22.253s; **4** Davide di Benedetto, I, 25m 24.227s; **5** Luca Persiani, I, 25m 26.626s; **6** Marcello Puglisi, I, 25m 28.589s; **7** Tor Graves, GB, 25m 34.620s; **8** Giovanni Tedeschi, I, 25m 35.209s; **9** Gianmaria Gabbiani, I, 25m 39.306s; **10** Kristian Ghedina, I, 25m 42.201s.
Fastest race lap: De Villota Jr, 1m 19.855s, 103.730 mph/166.937 km/h.
Fastest qualifying lap: Janis, 1m 29.702s, 92.343 mph/148.612 km/h.

Race 2 (43.699 miles/70.327 km).
1 Luca Persiani, I, 30m 08.792s, 86.974 mph/139.970 km/h; **2** Jan Charouz, CZ (Lola B2/50-Zytek KV), 30m 09.012s; **3** Jaroslav 'Jarek' Janis, CZ (Lola B2/50-Zytek KV), 30m 09.536s; **4** Ignazio Belluardo, I, 30m 16.979s; **5** Giovanni Tedeschi, I, 30m 23.109s; **6** Marco Mocci, I, 30m 31.850s; **7** Jean de Pourtales, F, 30m 32.598s; **8** Davide di Benedetto, I, 30m 39.511s; **9** Emilio de Villota Jr, E, 30m 39.938s; **10** Gianmaria Gabbiani, I, 30m 49.276s.
Fastest race lap: Janis, 1m 18.305s, 105.783 mph/170.242 km/h.
Pole position: Tedeschi.

F3000 INTERNATIONAL MASTERS, Motorsport Arena Oschersleben, Germany, 3/4 June. Round 4. 17 and 23 laps of the 2.279-mile/3.667-km circuit.
Race 1 (38.376 miles/62.339 km).
1 Massimo Torre, I, 30m 09.262s, 77.075 mph/124.039 km/h; **2** Filip Salaquarda, CZ, 30m 13.913s; **3** Daniel Move, RUS, 30m 33.546s; **4** Alessandro Pierguidi, I, 30m 39.782s; **5** Jan Charouz, CZ (Lola B2/50-Zytek KV), 30m 45.872s; **6** Marco Mocci, I, 30m 48.012s; **7** Ignazio Belluardo, I, 31m 00.453s; **8** Luca Persiani, I, 31m 06.016s; **9** Giovanni Tedeschi, I, 31m 15.912s; **10** Emilio de Villota Jr., E, 31m 20.628s.
Fastest race lap: Salaquarda, 1m 43.787s, 79.035 mph/127.195 km/h.
Fastest qualifying lap: Pierguidi, 1m 23.647s, 98.065 mph/157.820 km/h.

Race 2 (52.407 miles/84.341 km).
1 Ignazio Belluardo, I, 31m 15.215s, 100.610 mph/161.916 km/h; **2** Filip Salaquarda, CZ, 31m 15.866s; **3** Marco Mocci, I, 31m 22.567s; **4** Jan Charouz, CZ (Lola B2/50-Zytek KV), 31m 22.776s; **5** Davide di Benedetto, I, 31m 24.531s; **6** Emilio de Villota Jr., E, 31m 26.512s; **7** Kristian Ghedina, I, 31m 26.997s; **8** Massimo Torre, I, 31m 36.162s; **9** Michele Merendino, I, 31m 51.610s; **10** Glauco Solieri, I, 32m 20.121s.
Fastest race lap: Persiani, 1m 19.038s, 103.784 mph/167.023 km/h.
Pole position: Persiani.

F3000 INTERNATIONAL MASTERS, Automotodrom Brno Masaryk Circuit, Brno, Czech Republic, 2/3 September. Round 5. 16 and 15 laps of the 3.357-mile/5.403-km circuit.
Race 1 (53.716 miles/86.448 km).
1 Davide di Benedetto, I, 30m 38.312s, 105.194 mph/169.292 km/h; **2** Jan Charouz, CZ (Lola B2/50-Zytek KV), 30m 40.218s; **3** Marcello Puglisi, I, 30m 53.658s; **4** Luca Persiani, I, 30m 54.003s; **5** Emilio de Villota Jr., E, 30m 54.134s; **6** Ignazio Belluardo, I, 31m 05.993s; **7** Giovanni Tedeschi, I, 31m 07.897s; **8** Marco Mocci, I, 31m 08.494s; **9** Jean de Pourtales, F, 31m

09.496s; **10** Tor Graves, GB, 31m 15.814s.
Fastest race lap: De Benedetto, 1m 51.897s, 108.012 mph/173.827 km/h.
Fastest qualifying lap: Vitaly Petrov, RUS, 1m 50.796s, 109.085 mph/175.555 km/h.

Race 2 (50.359 miles/81.045 km).
1 Jan Charouz, CZ (Lola B2/50-Zytek KV), 28m 51.918s, 104.677 mph/168.461 km/h; **2** Luca Persiani, I, 29m 03.063s; **3** Davide di Benedetto, I, 29m 05.477s; **4** Marco Mocci, I, 29m 06.982s; **5** Marcello Puglisi, I, 29m 07.309s; **6** Ignazio Belluardo, I, 29m 14.593s; **7** Massimo Torre, I, 29m 14.818s; **8** Jean de Pourtales, F, 29m 14.939s; **9** Emilio de Villota Jr., E, 29m 15.428s; **10** Kristian Ghedina, I, 29m 20.677s.
Petrov finished 2nd in 28m 52.237s, but was given a 30-second penalty for overtaking under yellow flags.
Fastest race lap: Petrov, 1m 53.173s, 106.794 mph/171.867 km/h.
Pole position: Mocci.

F3000 INTERNATIONAL MASTERS, Istanbul Speed Park, Tuzla, Turkey, 23/24 September. Round 6. 14 and 16 laps of the 3.317-mile/5.338-km circuit.
Race 1 (46.310 miles/74.529 km).
1 Tomas Kostka, CZ (Lola B2/50-Zytek KV), 30m 23.286s, 91.437 mph/147.154 km/h; **2** Massimo Torre, I, 30m 28.289s; **3** Giovanni Tedeschi, I, 30m 58.639s; **4** Michele Merendino, I, 31m 14.814s; **5** Jean de Pourtales, F, 31m 20.505s; **6** Giovanni Faraonio, I, 31m 38.722s; **7** Jan Charouz, CZ (Lola B2/50-Zytek KV), 31m 52.374s; **8** Kristian Ghedina, I, 8 laps (DNF); **9** Luca Persiani, I, 5 (DNF); **10** Davide di Benedetto, I, 5 (DNF).
Fastest race lap: Torre, 2m 02.873s, 97.180 mph/156.395 km/h.
Fastest qualifying lap: Kostka, 1m 44.657s, 114.094 mph/183.616 km/h.

Race 2 (52.944 miles/85.205 km).
1 Jan Charouz, CZ (Lola B2/50-Zytek KV), 29m 06.117s, 109.155 mph/175.668 km/h; **2** Luca Persiani, I, 29m 10.293s; **3** Giovanni Tedeschi, I, 29m 10.541s; **4** Tor Graves, GB, 29m 36.973s; **5** Davide di Benedetto, I, 29m 59.061s; **6** Kristian Ghedina, I, 29m 59.840s; **7** Marcello Puglisi, I, 30m 29.937s; **8** Tomas Kostka, CZ (Lola B2/50-Zytek KV), 14 laps; **9** Jean de Pourtales, F, 13 (DNF); **10** Ignazio Belluardo, I, 12 (DNF).
Fastest race lap: Kostka, 1m 45.708s, 112.960 mph/181.791 km/h.
Pole position: Ghedina.

F3000 INTERNATIONAL MASTERS, Autódromo Fernanda Pires da Silva, Alcabideche, Estoril, Portugal, 21/22 October. Round 7. 17, 16 and 15 laps of the 2.599-mile/4.182-km circuit.
Race 1 (44.135 miles/71.028 km).
1 Luiz Razia, BR (Lola B2/50-Zytek KV), 31m 21.989s, 84.424 mph/135.867 km/h; **2** Giovanni Tedeschi, I, 31m 23.244s; **3** Marcello Puglisi, I, 31m 29.603s; **4** Tor Graves, GB, 31m 36.540s; **5** Davide di Benedetto, I, 31m 36.849s; **6** Luca Persiani, I, 31m 36.998s; **7** Michele Merendino, I, 31m 42.890s; **8** Giandomenico Sposito, I, 32m 15.003s; **9** Jean de Pourtales, F, 16 laps; **10** Emilio de Villota Jr., E, 15.
Fastest race lap: Tedeschi, 1m 40.531s, 93.055 mph/149.756 km/h.
Fastest qualifying lap: Tedeschi, 1m 33.046s, 100.540 mph/161.803 km/h.

Race 2 (41.536 miles/66.846 km).
1 Luiz Razia, BR (Lola B2/50-Zytek KV), 31m 16.290s, 79.695 mph/128.256 km/h **2** Davide di Benedetto, I, 31m 27.353s; **3** Massimo Torre, I, 31m 35.111s; **4** Jean de Pourtales, F, 31m 48.321s; **5** Luca Persiani, I, 31m 50.193s; **6** Dominik Schrami, D, 31m 51.596s; **7** Giandomenico Sposito, I, 31m 53.238s; **8** Michele Merendino, I, 31m 59.627s; **9** Giovanni Tedeschi, I, 32m 04.685s; **10** Emilio de Villota Jr., E, 32m 47.689s.
Fastest race lap: Razia, 1m 51.234s, 84.101 mph/135.347 km/h.
Pole position: Sposito.

Race 3 (38.938 miles/62.664 km).
1 Luiz Razia, BR (Lola B2/50-Zytek KV), 31m 14.749s, 74.770 mph/120.331 km/h **2** Davide di Benedetto, I, 31m 19.986s; **3** Jan Charouz, CZ (Lola B2/50-Zytek KV), 31m 20.957s; **4** Dominik Schrami, D, 31m 21.749s; **5** Emilio de Villota Jr., E, 31m 24.280s; **6** Tor Graves, GB, 31m 34.180s; **7** Giovanni Faraonio, I, 31m 34.313s; **8** Luca Persiani, I, 31m 54.010s; **9** Giovanni Tedeschi, I, 8 (DNF); **10** Massimo Torre, I, 8 (DNF).
Fastest race lap: Razia, 1m 54.181s, 81.930 mph/131.853 km/h.
Fastest qualifying lap: Persiani, 1m 31.609s, 102.117 mph/164.341 km/h.

Race 4: Cancelled due to bad condition of circuit.

Final championship points
Drivers
1 Jan Charouz, CZ, 75; **2** Davide di Benedetto, I, 62; **3** Jaroslav 'Jarek' Janis, CZ, 54; **4** Luca Persiani, I, 52; **5** Ignazio Belluardo, I, 47; **6** Giovanni Tedeschi, I, 36; **7** Massimo Torre, I, 32; **8** Luiz Razia, BR, 30; **9** Marco Mocci, I, 27; **10** Marcello Puglisi, I, 21; **11** Emilio de Villota Jr., E, 19; **12** Filip Salaquarda, CZ, 16; **13** Tor Graves, GB, 15; **14** Alessandro Pierguidi, I, 13; **15** Jean de Pourtales, F, 12; **16** Tomas Kostka, CZ, 11; **17** Daniel Move, RUS, 11; **18** Michele Merendino, I, 10; **19** Matteo Bobbi, I, 8; **20** Dominik Schrami, D, 8.
Teams
1 Charouz Racing, 186; **2** Pro Motorsport, 116; **3** ADM Motorsport, 100; **4** Scuderia Bigazzi, 37; **5** Fortuna Motorsport, 33; **6** Alan Racing, 32.

All-Japan Formula Nippon Championship

All cars are Lola B3/51-Mugen Honda.

2005

The following race was run after AUTOCOURSE 2005–2006 went to press.

ALL-JAPAN FORMULA NIPPON CHAMPIONSHIP, Suzuka International Racing Course, Suzuka-shi, Mie Prefecture, Japan, 27 November. Round 9. 51 laps of the 3.608-mile/5.807-km circuit, 184.023 miles/296.157 km.
1 Andre Lotterer, D, 1h 34m 23.413s, 116.976 mph/188.254 km/h; **2** Satoshi Motoyama, J, 1h 34m 23.739s; **3** Yuji Ide, J, 1h 34m 32.088s; **4** Benoît Tréluyer, F, 1h 34m 32.915s; **5** Richard Lyons, GB, 1h 35m 02.406s; **6** Takashi Kogure, J, 1h 35m 02.730s; **7** Tatsuya Kataoka, J, 1h 35m 05.311s; **8** Tsugio Matsuda, J, 1h 35m 05.331s; **9** Katsuyuki Hiranaka, J, 1h 35m 16.009s; **10** Ronnie Quintarelli, I, 1h 35m 23.533s.
Fastest race lap: Tréluyer, 1m 48.216s, 120.037 mph/193.180 km/h.
Fastest qualifying lap: Matsuda 1m 44.822s, 123.923 mph/199.435 km/h.

Final championship points
1 Satoshi Motoyama, J, 52; **2** Yuji Ide, J, 39; **3** Richard Lyons, GB, 30; **4** Andre Lotterer, D, 20; **5** Takashi Kogure, J, 15; **6** Benoît Tréluyer, F, 14; **7** Tsugio Matsuda, J, 14; **8** Takeshi Tsuchiya, J, 13; **9** Ronnie Quintarelli, I, 12; **10** Sakon Yamamoto, J, 9; **11** Tatsuya Kataoka, J, 7; **12** Naoki Hattori, J, 7; **13** Katsuyuki Hiranaka, J, 2.

2006

ALL-JAPAN FORMULA NIPPON CHAMPIONSHIP, Fuji International Speedway, Sunto-gun, Shizuoka Prefecture, Japan, 2 April. Round 1. 2 laps of the 2.835-mile/4.563-km circuit, 5.671 miles/9.126 km.
Rain restricted the race with results being declared after 2 laps. Half points were awarded.
1 Benoît Tréluyer, F (Lola FN06-Toyota), 7m 40.450s, 44.335 mph/71.351 km/h; **2** Tsugio Matsuda, J (Lola FN06-Toyota), 7m 44.669s; **3** Satoshi Motoyama, J (Lola FN06-Toyota), 7m 46.019s; **4** Björn Wirdheim, S (Lola FN06-Honda), 7m 47.402s; **5** Ronnie Quintarelli, I (Lola FN06-Toyota), 7m 48.541s; **6** Sakon Yamamoto, J (Lola FN06-Toyota), 7m 50.721s; **7** Masataka Yanagida, J (Lola FN06-Toyota), 7m 52.247s; **8** Andre Lotterer, D (Lola FN06-Toyota), 7m 53.950s; **9** Takeshi Tsuchiya, J (Lola FN06-Toyota), 7m 57.230s; **10** Takashi Kogure, J (Lola FN06-Honda), 7m 57.795s.
Fastest race lap: Yanagida, 3m 52.321s, 43.936 mph/70.707 km/h.
Fastest qualifying lap: Tréluyer, 1m 26.265s, 118.323 mph/190.422 km/h.

ALL-JAPAN FORMULA NIPPON CHAMPIONSHIP, Suzuka International Racing Course, Suzuka-shi, Mie Prefecture, Japan, 16 April. Round 2. 51 laps of the 3.608-mile/5.807-km circuit, 184.023 miles/296.157 km.
1 Loïc Duval, F (Lola FN06-Honda), 1h 36m 47.366s, 114.077 mph/183.588 km/h; **2** Björn Wirdheim, S (Lola FN06-Honda), 1h 36m 49.538s; **3** Benoît Tréluyer, F (Lola FN06-Toyota), 1h 36m 58.883s; **4** Sakon Yamamoto, J (Lola FN06-Toyota), 1h 36m 59.586s; **5** Andre Lotterer, D (Lola FN06-Toyota), 1h 37m 04.123s; **6** Hideki Mutoh, J (Lola FN06-Honda), 1h 37m 11.052s; **7** Tatsuya Kataoka, J (Lola FN06-Toyota), 1h 37m 48.568s; **8** Satoshi Motoyama, J (Lola FN06-Toyota), 1h 38m 01.841s; **9** Tsugio Matsuda, J (Lola FN06-Toyota), 1h 38m 02.004s; **10** Takeshi Tsuchiya, J (Lola FN06-Toyota), 1h 38m 10.363s.
Fastest race lap: Tréluyer, 1m 47.749s, 120.557 mph/194.017 km/h.
Fastest qualifying lap: Tréluyer, 1m 45.697s, 122.897 mph/197.784 km/h.

ALL-JAPAN FORMULA NIPPON CHAMPIONSHIP, Twin Ring Motegi, Motegi-machi, Haga-gun, Tochigi Prefecture, Japan, 28 May. Round 3. 62 laps of the 2.983-mile/4.801-km circuit, 184.959 miles/297.662 km.
1 Andre Lotterer, D (Lola FN06-Toyota), 1h 53m 49.348s, 97.498 mph/156.908 km/h; **2** Benoît Tréluyer, F (Lola FN06-Toyota), 1h 53m 50.412s; **3** Satoshi Motoyama, J (Lola FN06-Toyota), 1h 54m 44.481s; **4** Björn Wirdheim, S (Lola FN06-Honda), 1h 54m 49.237s; **5** Tsugio Matsuda, J (Lola FN06-Toyota), 1h 55m 21.712s; **6** Loïc Duval, F (Lola FN06-Honda), 1h 55m 31.263s; **7** Ryo Michigami, J (Lola FN06-Honda), 61 laps; **8** Hideki Mutoh, J (Lola FN06-Honda), 61; **9** Masataka Yanagida, J (Lola FN06-Toyota), 61; **10** Yuji Tachikawa, J (Lola FN06-Toyota), 61.
Fastest race lap: Matsuda, 1m 41.200s, 106.122 mph/170.786 km/h.
Fastest qualifying lap: Takashi Kogure, J (Lola FN06-Honda), 1m 35.971s, 111.904 mph/180.091 km/h.

ALL-JAPAN FORMULA NIPPON CHAMPIONSHIP, Suzuka International Racing Course, Suzuka-shi, Mie Prefecture, Japan, 9 July. Round 4. 51 laps of the 3.608-mile/5.807-km circuit, 184.023 miles/296.157 km.
1 Benoît Tréluyer, F (Lola FN06-Toyota), 1h 34m 26.397s, 116.915 mph/188.155 km/h; **2** Tsugio Matsuda, J (Lola FN06-Toyota), 1h 34m 35.632s; **3** Satoshi Motoyama, J (Lola FN06-Toyota), 1h 35m 00.301s; **4** Yuji Tachikawa, J (Lola FN06-Toyota), 1h 35m 06.589s; **5** Andre Lotterer, D (Lola FN06-Toyota), 1h 35m 32.191s; **6** Tatsuya Kataoka, J (Lola FN06-Toyota), 1h 35m 42.185s; **7** Takeshi Tsuchiya, J (Lola FN06-Toyota), 1h 35m 48.689s; **8** Toranosuke Takagi, J (Lola FN06-Toyota), 1h 35m 54.759s; **9** Takashi Kogure, J (Lola FN06-Honda), 1h 35m 57.029s; **10** Seiji Ara, J (Lola FN06-Toyota), 1h 36m 05.954s.
Fastest race lap: Tréluyer, 1m 48.713s, 119.488 mph/192.297 km/h.
Fastest qualifying lap: Tréluyer, 1m 45.905s, 122.656 mph/197.395 km/h.

ALL-JAPAN FORMULA NIPPON CHAMPIONSHIP, Autopolis International Racing Course, Kamit-sue-mura, Hita-gun, Oita Prefecture, Japan, 6 August. Round 5. 64 laps of the 2.904-mile/4.674-km circuit, 185.874 miles/299.136 km.
1 Tsugio Matsuda, J (Lola FN06-Toyota), 1h 47m 15.726s, 103.974 mph/167.329 km/h; **2** Toshihiro Kaneishi, J (Lola FN06-Honda), 1h 47m 26.625s; **3** Tatsuya Kataoka, J (Lola FN06-Toyota), 1h 47m 35.045s; **4** Yuji Tachikawa, J (Lola FN06-Toyota), 1h 47m 35.792s; **5** Ronnie Quintarelli, I (Lola FN06-Toyota), 1h 47m 42.482s; **6** Björn Wirdheim, S (Lola FN06-Honda), 1h 47m 43.057s; **7** Benoît Tréluyer, F (Lola FN06-Toyota), 1h 47m 43.283s; **8** Andre Lotterer, D (Lola FN06-Toyota), 1h 47m 43.758s; **9** Takeshi Tsuchiya, J (Lola FN06-Toyota), 1h 48m 04.876s; **10** Seiji Ara, J (Lola FN06-Toyota), 1h 48m 18.929s.
Fastest race lap: Loïc Duval, F (Lola FN06-Honda), 1m 38.166s, 106.508 mph/171.407 km/h.
Fastest qualifying lap: Takashi Kogure, J (Lola FN06-Honda), 1m 33.424s, 111.914 mph/180.107 km/h.

ALL-JAPAN FORMULA NIPPON CHAMPIONSHIP, Fuji International Speedway, Sunto-gun, Shizuoka Prefecture, Japan, 27 August. Round 6. 65 laps of the 2.835-mile/4.563-km circuit, 184.296 miles/296.595 km.
1 Benoît Tréluyer, F (Lola FN06-Toyota), 1h 44m 21.905s, 105.952 mph/170.513 km/h; **2** Andre Lotterer, D (Lola FN06-Toyota), 1h 44m 36.415s; **3** Satoshi Motoyama, J (Lola FN06-Toyota), 1h 44m 44.002s; **4** Toshihiro Kaneishi, J (Lola FN06-Honda), 1h 44m 44.958s; **5** Yuji Tachikawa, J (Lola FN06-Toyota), 1h 44m 45.381s; **6** Björn Wirdheim, S (Lola FN06-Honda), 1h 45m 01.801s; **7** Tsugio Matsuda, J (Lola FN06-Toyota), 1h 45m 02.320s; **8** Toranosuke Takagi, J (Lola FN06-Toyota), 1h 45m 13.316s; **9** Loïc Duval, F (Lola FN06-Honda), 1h 45m 27.406s; **10** Ronnie Quintarelli, I (Lola FN06-Toyota), 1h 45m 30.454s.
Fastest race lap: Motoyama, 1m 29.946s, 113.481 mph/182.629 km/h.
Fastest qualifying lap: Takashi Kogure, J (Lola FN06-Honda), 1m 28.184s, 115.748 mph/186.278 km/h.

ALL-JAPAN FORMULA NIPPON CHAMPIONSHIP, Sportsland-SUGO International Course, Shibata-gun, Miyagi Prefecture, Japan, 17 September. Round 7. 80 laps of the 2.302-mile/3.704-km circuit, 184.125 miles/296.320 km.
1 Loïc Duval, F (Lola FN06-Honda), 1h 47m 02.500s, 103.207 mph/166.096 km/h; **2** Benoît Tréluyer, F (Lola FN06-Toyota), 1h 47m 05.146s; **3** Tsugio Matsuda, J (Lola FN06-Toyota), 1h 47m 05.414s; **4** Ronnie Quintarelli, I (Lola FN06-Toyota), 1h 47m 30.807s; **5** Satoshi Motoyama, J (Lola FN06-Toyota), 1h 47m 31.089s; **6** Björn Wirdheim, S (Lola FN06-Honda), 1h 47m 59.549s; **7** Yuji Tachikawa, J (Lola FN06-Toyota), 1h 48m 08.638s; **8** Takeshi Tsuchiya, J (Lola FN06-Toyota), 79 laps; **9** Tatsuya Kataoka, J (Lola FN06-Toyota), 79; **10** Hideki Mutoh, J (Lola FN06-Honda), 79.
Fastest race lap: Mutoh, 1m 12.418s, 114.414 mph/184.131 km/h.
Fastest qualifying lap: Toranosuke Takagi, J (Lola FN06-Toyota), 1m 09.907s, 118.523 mph/190.744 km/h.

ALL-JAPAN FORMULA NIPPON CHAMPIONSHIP, Twin Ring Motegi, Motegi-machi, Haga-gun, Tochigi Prefecture, Japan, 22 October. Round 8. 62 laps of the 2.983-mile/4.801-km circuit, 184.959 miles/297.662 km.
1 Benoît Tréluyer, F (Lola FN06-Toyota), 1h 42m 56.839s, 107.798 mph/173.484 km/h; **2** Tsugio Matsuda, J (Lola FN06-Toyota), 1h 43m 21.710s; **3** Tatsuya Kataoka, J (Lola FN06-Toyota), 1h 43m 35.680s; **4** Loïc Duval, F (Lola FN06-Honda), 1h 43m 48.367s; **5** Yuji Tachikawa, J (Lola FN06-Toyota), 1h 43m 59.035s; **6** Masataka Yanagida, J (Lola FN06-Toyota), 1h 44m 11.560s; **7** Naoki Yokomizo, J (Lola FN06-Toyota), 1h 44m 30.107s; **8** Takeshi Tsuchiya, J (Lola FN06-Toyota), 61 laps; **9** Ronnie Quintarelli, I (Lola FN06-Toyota), 61; **10** Hideki Mutoh, J (Lola FN06-Honda), 61.
Fastest race lap: Satoshi Motoyama, J (Lola FN06-Toyota), 1m 37.769s, 109.846 mph/176.779 km/h.
Fastest qualifying lap: Takashi Kogure, J (Lola FN06-Honda), 1m 33.954s, 114.306 mph/183.958 km/h.

Provisional championship points
Drivers
1 Benoît Tréluyer, F, 51; **2** Tsugio Matsuda, J, 31; **3** Loïc Duval, F, 24; **4** Andre Lotterer, D, 20; **5** Satoshi Motoyama, J, 16; **6** Björn Wirdheim, S, 13.5; **7** Yuji Tachikawa, J, 10; **8** Toshihiro Kaneishi, J, 9; **9** Tatsuya Kataoka, J, 9; **10** Ronnie Quintarelli, I, 6; **11** Sakon Yamamoto, J, 3.5; **12** Hideki Mutoh, J, 1; **13** Masataka Yanagida, J, 1.
Teams
1 mobilecast Team Impul, 82; **2** PIAA Nakajima Racing, 25; **3** DHG Tom's Racing, 20.

Result of the Suzuka race will be given in AUTOCOURSE 2007–2008.

British Formula 3 International Series

BRITISH FORMULA 3 INTERNATIONAL SERIES, Oulton Park Circuit, Tarporley, Cheshire, Great Britain, 17 April. 16 and 18 laps of the 2.692-mile/4.332-km circuit.
Round 1 (43.072 miles/69.318 km).
1 Bruno Senna, BR (Dallara F306-Mercedes Benz), 31m 00.537s, 83.341 mph/134.124 km/h; **2** Stephen Jelley, GB (Dallara F306-Mercedes Benz), 31m 02.091s; **3** Oliver Jarvis, GB (Dallara F306-Mugen Honda), 31m 11.106s; **4** Maro Engel, D (Dallara F306-Mercedes Benz), 31m 11.756s; **5** Mike Conway, GB (Dallara F306-Mercedes Benz), 31m 12.360s; **6** Yelmer Buurman, NL (Dallara F306-Mercedes Benz), 31m 12.832s; **7** Christian Bakkerud, DK (Dallara F306-Mugen Honda), 31m 13.188s; **8** James Jakes, GB (Dallara F306-Mercedes Benz), 31m 15.274s; **9** Stuart Hall, GB (Dallara F306-Mercedes Benz), 31m 15.618s; **10** Jonathan Kennard, GB (Dallara F306-Mugen Honda), 31m 17.077s.
National class winner: Rodolfo González, YV (Dallara F304-Mugen Honda), 31m 21.018s (11th).
Fastest race lap: Jelley, 1m 31.093s, 106.388 mph/171.215 km/h.
Fastest qualifying lap: Senna, 1m 30.109s, 107.550 mph/173.085 km/h.

Round 2 (48.456 miles/77.982 km).
1 Bruno Senna, BR (Dallara F306-Mercedes Benz), 27m 29.844s, 105.732 mph/170.159 km/h; **2** Christian Bakkerud, DK (Dallara F306-Mugen Honda), 27m 37.178s; **3** Mike Conway, GB (Dallara F306-Mercedes Benz), 27m 37.534s; **4** Oliver Jarvis, GB (Dallara F306-Mugen Honda), 27m 38.777s; **5** Maro Engel, D (Dallara F306-Mercedes Benz), 27m 45.398s; **6** Stuart Hall, GB (Dallara F306-Mercedes Benz), 27m 45.871s; **7** Alberto Valério, BR (Dallara F306-Mugen Honda), 27m 47.906s; **8** Rodolfo González, YV (Dallara F304-Mugen Honda), 27m 59.551s (1st national class); **9** Yelmer Buurman, NL (Dallara F306-Mercedes Benz), 28m 01.241s; **10** Charlie Hollings, GB (Dallara F306-Mercedes Benz), 28m 10.258s.
Fastest race lap: Senna, 1m 30.941s, 106.566 mph/171.501 km/h.
Fastest qualifying lap: Conway, 1m 30.394s, 107.211 mph/172.539 km/h.

BRITISH FORMULA 3 INTERNATIONAL SERIES, Donington Park National Circuit, Castle Donington, Great Britain, 21 May. 2 x 20 laps of the 1.9573-mile/3.150-km circuit.
Round 3 (39.112 miles/62.945 km).
1 Bruno Senna, BR (Dallara F306-Mercedes Benz), 25m 30.643s, 91.990 mph/148.043 km/h; **2** James Walker, GB (Dallara F306-Mercedes Benz), 25m 32.538s; **3** Stephen Jelley, GB (Dallara F306-Mercedes Benz), 25m 33.475s; **4** Oliver Jarvis, GB (Dallara F306-Mugen Honda), 25m 35.438s; **5** Yelmer Buurman, NL (Dallara F306-Mercedes Benz), 25m 35.729s; **6** Salvador Durán, MEX (Dallara F306-Mercedes Benz), 25m 45.748s; **7** Mike Conway, GB (Dallara F306-Mercedes Benz), 25m 46.281s; **8** Jonathan Kennard, GB (Dallara F306-Mugen Honda), 25m 50.694s; **9** Christian Bakkerud, DK (Dallara F306-Mugen Honda), 25m 50.928s; **10** Stuart Hall, GB (Dallara F306-Mercedes Benz), 25m 51.927s.
National class winner: Rodolfo González, YV (Dallara F304-Mugen Honda), 26m 08.015s (13th).
Fastest race lap: Jelley, 1m 14.716s, 94.308 mph/151.773 km/h.
Fastest qualifying lap: Conway, 1m 03.796s, 110.450 mph/177.752 km/h.

Round 4 (39.112 miles/62.945 km).
1 Mike Conway, GB (Dallara F306-Mercedes Benz), 27m 41.989s, 84.720 mph/136.343 km/h; **2** Maro Engel, D (Dallara F306-Mercedes Benz), 27m 43.779s; **3** Yelmer Buurman, NL (Dallara F306-Mercedes Benz), 27m 45.306s; **4** Bruno Senna, BR (Dallara F306-Mercedes Benz), 27m 45.660s; **5** Dennis Retera, GB (Dallara F306-Mugen Honda), 27m 56.111s; **6** Karl Reindler, AUS (Dallara F306-Mugen Honda), 28m 00.880s; **7** Rodolfo González, YV (Dallara F304-Mugen Honda), 28m 03.378s (1st national class); **8** Charlie Hollings, GB (Dallara F306-Mercedes Benz), 28m 07.040s; **9** James Jakes, GB (Dallara F306-Mercedes Benz), 28m 08.538s; **10** Jonathan Kennard, GB (Dallara F306-Mugen Honda), 28m 13.448s.
Fastest race lap: Senna, 1m 11.034s, 99.196 mph/159.640 km/h.
Fastest qualifying lap: Conway, 1m 03.205s, 111.483 mph/179.414 km/h.

66th GRAND PRIX DE PAU, FIA FORMULA 3 EUROPE CUP, Circuit de Pau Ville, France, 4/5 June. 20 and 22 laps of the 1.715-mile/2.760-km circuit.
Round 5 (34.300 miles/55.200 km).
1 Romain Grosjean, F (Dallara F305-Mercedes Benz), 30m 33.016s, 67.364 mph/108.411 km/h (1st invitational class); **2** Mike Conway, GB (Dallara F306-Mercedes Benz), 30m 37.420s (1st championship class); **3** Oliver Jarvis, GB (Dallara F306-Mugen Honda), 30m 49.908s; **4** Charlie Kimball, GB (Dallara F306-Mercedes Benz), 30m 50.290s; **5** Maro Engel, D (Dallara F306-Mugen Honda), 30m 57.763s; **6** Guillaume Moreau, F (Dallara F305-Mercedes Benz), 30m 58.219s*; **7** Yelmer Buurman, NL (Dallara F306-Mercedes Benz), 31m 01.851s; **8** James Jakes, GB (Dallara F306-Mercedes Benz), 31m 02.929s; **9** James Walker, GB (Dallara F306-Mercedes Benz), 31m 03.307s; **10** Jonathan Kennard, GB (Dallara F306-Mugen Honda), 31m 06.168s.
* Finished 3rd, but given a 12-second penalty due to incident with Engel.
National class winner: Rodolfo González, YV (Dallara F304-Mugen Honda), 31m 09.037s (12th).
Fastest race lap: Grosjean, 1m 13.168s, 84.380 mph/135.797 km/h.
Fastest qualifying lap: Grosjean, 1m 12.679s, 84.948 mph/136.711 km/h.

Round 6 (37.730 miles/60.720 km).
1 Romain Grosjean, F (Dallara F305-Mercedes Benz), 27m 18.507s, 82.897 mph/133.409 km/h (1st invitational class); **2** Guillaume Moreau, F (Dallara F305-Mercedes Benz), 27m 20.850s; **3** Mike Conway, GB (Dallara F306-Mercedes Benz), 27m 25.150s; **4** Yelmer Buurman, NL (Dallara F306-Mercedes Benz), 27m 55.673s; **5** Maro Engel, D (Dallara F306-Mugen Honda), 27m 55.857s; **6** Charlie Kimball, GB (Dallara F306-Mercedes Benz), 27m 56.267s; **7** Oliver Jarvis, GB (Dallara F306-Mugen Honda), 28m 01.056s; **8** Salvador Durán, MEX (Dallara F306-Mercedes Benz), 28m 02.075s; **9** Stephen Jelley, GB (Dallara F306-Mercedes Benz), 28m 02.574s; **10** Bruno Senna, BR (Dallara F306-Mercedes Benz), 28m 02.822s.
National class winner: Juho Annala, FIN (Dallara F304-Mugen Honda), 27m 33.639s (15th).
Fastest race lap: Grosjean, 1m 13.593s, 83.893 mph/135.012 km/h.
Fastest qualifying lap: Grosjean, 1m 12.414s, 85.259 mph/137.211 km/h.

BRITISH FORMULA 3 INTERNATIONAL SERIES, Mondello Park, Naas, County Kildare, Republic of Ireland, 25 June. 17 and 16 laps of the 2.177-mile/3.503-km circuit.
Round 7 (37.003 miles/59.551 km).
1 Bruno Senna, BR (Dallara F306-Mercedes Benz), 30m 09.913s, 73.601 mph/118.450 km/h; **2** Mike Conway, GB (Dallara F306-Mercedes Benz), 30m 10.450s; **3** Stephen Jelley, GB (Dallara F306-Mercedes Benz), 30m 12.533s; **4** Oliver Jarvis, GB (Dallara F306-Mugen Honda), 30m 13.633s; **5** Maro Engel, D (Dallara F306-Mugen Honda), 30m 18.919s; **6** Yelmer Buurman, NL (Dallara F306-Mercedes Benz), 30m 25.638s; **7** Jonathan Kennard, GB (Dallara F306-Mugen Honda), 30m 33.677s; **8** Alberto Valério, BR (Dallara F306-Mugen Honda), 30m 34.995s; **9** Karl Reindler, AUS (Dallara F306-Mugen Honda), 30m 35.382s; **10** James Jakes, GB (Dallara F306-Mercedes Benz), 30m 35.921s.
National class winner: Rodolfo González, YV (Dallara F304-Mugen Honda), 30m 45.138s (14th).
Fastest race lap: Senna, 1m 34.373s, 83.032 mph/133.627 km/h.
Fastest qualifying lap: Senna, 1m 41.513s, 77.192 mph/124.228 km/h.

Round 8 (34.827 miles/56.048 km).
1 Oliver Jarvis, GB (Dallara F306-Mugen Honda), 30m 04.338s, 69.486 mph/111.826 km/h; **2** James Walker, GB (Dallara F306-Mercedes Benz), 30m 08.772s; **3** Mike Conway, GB (Dallara F306-Mercedes Benz), 30m 09.659s; **4** Christian Bakkerud, DK (Dallara F306-Mugen Honda), 30m 10.978s; **5** Bruno Senna, BR (Dallara F306-Mercedes Benz), 30m 12.006s; **6** James Jakes, GB (Dallara F306-Mercedes Benz), 30m 19.597s; **7** Yelmer Buurman, NL (Dallara F306-Mercedes Benz), 30m 20.430s; **8** Maro Engel, D (Dallara F306-Mugen Honda), 30m 22.838s; **9** Stuart Hall, GB (Dallara F306-Mercedes Benz), 30m 23.423s; **10** Karl Reindler, AUS (Dallara F306-Mugen Honda), 30m 24.848s.
National class winner: Rodolfo González, YV (Dallara F304-Mugen Honda), 30m 27.972s (13th).
Fastest race lap: Jarvis, 1m 34.298s, 83.098 mph/133.733 km/h.
Fastest qualifying lap: Jarvis, 1m 31.519s, 85.621 mph/137.794 km/h.

BRITISH FORMULA 3 INTERNATIONAL SERIES, Snetterton Circuit, Thetford, Norfolk, Great Britain, 16 July. 2 x 27 laps of the 1.952-mile/3.141-km circuit.
Round 9 (52.704 miles/84.819 km).
1 Mike Conway, GB (Dallara F306-Mercedes Benz), 29m 59.324s, 105.448 mph/169.701 km/h; **2** James Jakes, GB (Dallara F306-Mercedes Benz), 30m 05.818s; **3** James Walker, GB (Dallara F306-Mercedes Benz), 30m 09.298s; **4** Oliver Jarvis, GB (Dallara F306-Mugen Honda), 30m 13.055s; **5** Yelmer Buurman, NL (Dallara F306-Mercedes Benz), 30m 13.727s; **6** Salvador Durán, MEX (Dallara F306-Mercedes Benz), 30m 14.593s; **7** Stephen Jelley, GB (Dallara F306-Mercedes Benz), 30m 15.015s; **8** Stuart Hall, GB (Dallara F306-Mercedes Benz), 30m 23.070s; **9** Alberto Valério, BR (Dallara F306-Mugen Honda), 30m 28.395s; **10** Karl Reindler, AUS (Dallara F306-Mugen Honda), 30m 40.263s.
National class winner: Rodolfo González, YV (Dallara F304-Mugen Honda), 30m 40.703s, (11th).
Fastest race lap: Conway, 1m 03.031s, 111.488 mph/179.423 km/h.
Fastest qualifying lap: Conway, 1m 02.088s, 113.181 mph/182.148 km/h.

Round 10 (52.704 miles/84.819 km).
1 Mike Conway, GB (Dallara F306-Mercedes Benz), 31m 01.047s, 101.950 mph/164.073 km/h; **2** Oliver Jarvis, GB (Dallara F306-Mugen Honda), 31m 02.304s; **3** Maro Engel, D (Dallara F306-Mugen Honda), 31m 07.798s; **4** Stephen Jelley, GB (Dallara F306-Mercedes Benz), 31m 08.431s; **5** James Jakes, GB (Dallara F306-Mercedes Benz), 31m 09.554s; **6** Yelmer Buurman, NL (Dallara F306-Mercedes Benz), 31m 10.064s; **7** Christian Bakkerud, DK (Dallara F306-Mugen Honda), 31m 16.354s; **8** James Walker, GB (Dallara F306-Mercedes Benz), 31m 19.795s; **9** Jonathan Kennard, GB (Dallara F306-Mugen Honda), 31m 20.275s; **10** Stuart Hall, GB (Dallara F306-Mercedes Benz), 31m 20.566s.
National class winner: Juho Annala, FIN (Dallara F304-Mugen Honda), 31m 33.104s (12th).
Fastest race lap: Jarvis, 1m 02.811s, 111.878 mph/180.051 km/h.
Fastest qualifying lap: Jarvis, 1m 02.040s, 113.269 mph/132.289 km/h.

BRITISH FORMULA 3 INTERNATIONAL SERIES, Circuit de Spa-Francorchamps, Stavelot, Belgium, 28/29 July. 2 x 12 laps of the 4.335-mile/6.976-km circuit.
Round 11 (52.016 miles/83.712 km).
1 Yelmer Buurman, NL (Dallara F306-Mercedes Benz), 31m 22.800s, 99.457 mph/160.061 km/h; **2** Maro Engel, D (Dallara F306-Mugen Honda), 31m 23.272s; **3** Bruno Senna, BR (Dallara F306-Mercedes Benz), 31m 29.738s; **4** Mike Conway, GB (Dallara F306-Mercedes Benz), 31m 31.198s; **5** Oliver Jarvis, GB (Dallara F306-Mugen Honda), 31m 32.447s; **6** James Walker, GB (Dallara F306-Mercedes Benz), 31m 35.614s; **7** Christian Bakkerud, DK (Dallara F306-Mugen Honda), 31m 41.563s; **8** James Jakes, GB (Dallara F306-Mercedes Benz), 31m 44.831s; **9** Jonathan Kennard, GB (Dallara F306-Mugen Honda), 31m 50.101s; **10** Karl Reindler, AUS (Dallara F306-Mugen Honda), 31m 57.739s.
National class winner: Rodolfo González, YV (Dallara F304-Mugen Honda), 32m 18.728s (14th).
Invitational class winner: Mário Moraes, BR (Dallara F304-Mugen Honda), 32m 29.073s (15th).
Fastest race lap: Jakes, 2m 25.633s, 107.152 mph/172.444 km/h.
Fastest qualifying lap: Engel, 2m 15.777s, 114.930 mph/184.962 km/h.

Round 12 (52.016 miles/83.712 km).
1 Maro Engel, D (Dallara F306-Mugen Honda), 30m 51.865s, 101.119 mph/162.734 km/h; **2** Mike Conway, GB (Dallara F306-Mercedes Benz), 30m 57.870s; **3** Bruno Senna, BR (Dallara F306-Mercedes Benz), 30m 59.329s; **4** Jonathan Kennard, GB (Dallara F306-Mugen Honda), 31m 02.915s; **5** Salvador Durán, MEX (Dallara F306-Mercedes Benz), 31m 05.004s; **6** Yelmer Buurman, NL (Dallara F306-Mercedes Benz), 31m 05.153s; **7** Karl Reindler, AUS (Dallara F306-Mugen Honda), 31m 07.884s; **8** Stephen Jelley, GB (Dallara F306-Mercedes Benz), 31m 08.991s; **9** Michael Herck, B (Dallara F306-Mercedes Benz), 31m 11.317s (1st invitational class); **10** James Walker, GB (Dallara F306-Mercedes Benz), 31m 11.743s.
National class winner: Rodolfo González, YV (Dallara F304-Mugen Honda), 31m 18.110s (13th).
Fastest race lap: Engel, 2m 17.316s, 113.642 mph/182.889 km/h.
Fastest qualifying lap: Engel, 2m 15.497s, 115.168 mph/185.344 km/h.

BRITISH FORMULA 3 INTERNATIONAL SERIES, Silverstone Grand Prix Circuit, Towcester, Northamptonshire, Great Britain, 13 August. 14 and 16 laps of the 3.194-mile/5.140-km circuit.
Round 13 (44.714 miles/71.960 km).
1 Mike Conway, GB (Dallara F306-Mercedes Benz), 31m 57.344s, 83.955 mph/135.112 km/h; **2** Bruno Senna, BR (Dallara F306-Mercedes Benz), 31m 59.017s; **3** Yelmer Buurman, NL (Dallara F306-Mercedes Benz), 32m 01.130s; **4** Oliver Jarvis, GB (Dallara F306-Mugen Honda), 32m 05.103s; **5** James Walker, GB (Dallara F306-Mercedes Benz), 32m 05.200s; **6** Salvador Durán, MEX (Dallara F306-Mercedes Benz), 32m 08.219s; **7** Stephen Jelley, GB (Dallara F306-Mercedes Benz), 32m 09.363s; **8** James Jakes, GB (Dallara F306-Mercedes Benz), 32m 10.031s; **9** Stuart Hall, GB (Dallara F306-Mugen Honda), 32m 10.331s; **10** Maro Engel, D (Dallara F306-Mugen Honda), 32m 12.845s.
Invitational class winner: Mário Moraes, BR (Dallara F304-Mugen Honda), 32m 29.132s (13th).
National class winner: Martin Kudzak, S (Lola-Dome F106/4-Mugen Honda), 32m 29.606s (14th).
Fastest race lap: Senna, 2m 02.531s, 93.836 mph/151.015 km/h.
Fastest qualifying lap: Senna, 1m 41.326s, 113.474 mph/182.618 km/h.

Round 14 (51.102 miles/82.240 km).
1 Mike Conway, GB (Dallara F306-Mercedes Benz), 28m 04.877s, 109.816 mph/175.718 km/h; **2** Christian Bakkerud, DK (Dallara F306-Mugen Honda), 28m 05.188s; **3** Oliver Jarvis, GB (Dallara F306-Mugen Honda), 28m 11.308s; **4** Salvador Durán, MEX (Dallara F306-Mercedes Benz), 28m 12.679s; **5** Maro Engel, D (Dallara F306-Mugen Honda), 28m 17.586s; **6** Jonathan Kennard, GB (Dallara F306-Mugen Honda), 28m 26.726s; **7** James Walker, GB (Dallara F306-Mercedes Benz), 28m 29.253s; **8** Bruno Senna, BR (Dallara F306-Mercedes Benz), 28m 29.354s; **9** Karl Reindler, AUS (Dallara F306-Mugen Honda), 28m 30.876s; **10** James Jakes, GB (Dallara F306-Mercedes Benz), 28m 32.647s.
National class winner: Rodolfo González, YV (Dallara F304-Mugen Honda), 28m 46.107s (14th).
Invitational class winner: Mário Moraes, BR (Dallara F304-Mugen Honda), 28m 54.980s (15th).
Fastest race lap: Bakkerud, 1m 43.491s, 111.100 mph/178.798 km/h.
Fastest qualifying lap: Conway, 1m 42.014s, 112.709 mph/181.387 km/h.

BRITISH FORMULA 3 INTERNATIONAL SERIES, Brands Hatch Grand Prix Circuit, West Kingsdown, Dartford, Kent, Great Britain, 27 August. 22 and 18 laps of the 2.301-mile/3.703-km circuit.
Round 15 (50.645 mph/81.505 km).
1 Mike Conway, GB (Dallara F306-Mercedes Benz), 29m 40.653s, 102.390 mph/164.782 km/h; **2** Maro Engel, D (Dallara F306-Mugen Honda), 29m 41.270s; **3** Yelmer Buurman, NL (Dallara F306-Mercedes Benz), 29m 51.527s; **4** Oliver Jarvis, GB (Dallara F306-Mugen Honda), 29m 54.331s; **5** Stephen Jelley, GB (Dallara F306-Mercedes Benz), 29m 59.240s; **6** James Jakes, GB (Dallara F306-Mercedes Benz), 30m 10.140s; **7** Bruno Senna, BR (Dallara F306-Mercedes Benz), 30m 10.620s; **8** Stuart Hall, GB (Dallara F306-Mugen Honda), 30m 11.151s; **9** James Walker, GB (Dallara F306-Mercedes Benz), 30m 11.686s; **10** Christian Bakkerud, DK (Dallara F306-Mugen Honda), 30m 12.148s.
National class winner: Rodolfo González, YV (Dallara F304-Mugen Honda), 30m 39.438s (13th).
Fastest race lap: Engel, 1m 19.923s, 103.645 mph/166.800 km/h.
Fastest qualifying lap: Conway, 1m 18.835s, 105.075 mph/169.102 km/h.

Round 16 (41.444 miles/66.698 km).
1 Oliver Jarvis, GB (Dallara F306-Mugen Honda), 26m 05.551s, 95.300 mph/153.372 km/h; **2** Maro Engel, D (Dallara F306-Mugen Honda), 26m 06.523s; **3** Mike Conway, GB (Dallara F306-Mercedes Benz), 26m 08.019s; **4** Yelmer Buurman, NL (Dallara F306-Mercedes Benz), 26m 08.784s; **5** Bruno Senna, BR (Dallara F306-Mercedes Benz), 26m 09.736s; **6** James Walker, GB (Dallara F306-Mercedes Benz), 26m 10.843s; **7** James Jakes, GB (Dallara F306-Mercedes Benz), 26m 12.487s; **8** Stephen Jelley, GB (Dallara F306-Mercedes Benz), 26m 12.951s; **9** Christian Bakkerud, DK (Dallara F306-Mugen Honda), 26m 13.513s; **10** Stuart Hall, GB (Dallara F306-Mugen Honda), 26m 14.258s.
National class winner: Cristiano Morgado, ZA (Lola-Dome F106/4-Mugen Honda), 26m 22.367s (14th).
Fastest race lap: Jarvis, 1m 20.229s, 103.249 mph/166.164 km/h.
Fastest qualifying lap: Jarvis, 1m 18.860s, 105.042 mph/169.048 km/h.

BRITISH FORMULA 3 INTERNATIONAL SERIES, Autodromo Internazionale del Mugello, Scarperia, Firenze (Florence), Italy, 16/17 September. 2 x 16 laps of the 3.259-mile/5.245-km circuit.
Round 17 (52.145 miles/83.920 km).
1 Christian Bakkerud, DK (Dallara F306-Mugen Honda), 28m 15.456s, 110.722 mph/178.189 km/h; **2** Stephen Jelley, GB (Dallara F306-Mercedes Benz), 28m 25.980s; **3** Alberto Valério, BR (Dallara F306-Mugen Honda), 28m 31.847s; **4** Yelmer Buurman, NL (Dallara F306-Mercedes Benz), 28m 32.334s; **5** James Jakes, GB (Dallara F306-Mercedes Benz), 28m 42.081s; **6** Mike Conway, GB (Dallara F306-Mercedes Benz), 28m 42.392s; **7** Salvador Durán, MEX (Dallara F306-Mercedes Benz), 28m 47.370s; **8** James Walker, GB (Dallara F306-Mercedes Benz), 29m 00.061s; **9** Rodolfo González, YV (Dallara F304-Mugen Honda), 29m 12.431s (1st national class); **10** Bruno Senna, BR (Dallara F306-Mercedes Benz), 29m 12.813s.
Invitational class winner: Mauro Massironi, I (Dallara F304-Opel), 29m 36.166s (14th).
Fastest race lap: Bakkerud, 1m 44.514s, 112.260 mph/180.664 km/h.
Fastest qualifying lap: Oliver Jarvis, GB (Dallara F306-Mugen Honda), 1m 42.658s, 114.289 mph/183.931 km/h.

Round 18 (52.145 miles/83.920 km).
1 Bruno Senna, BR (Dallara F306-Mercedes Benz), 31m 58.248s, 97.862 mph/157.493 km/h; **2** Oliver Jarvis, GB (Dallara F306-Mugen Honda), 32m 06.040s; **3** Mike Conway, GB (Dallara F306-Mercedes Benz), 32m 07.049s; **4** Maro Engel, D (Dallara F306-Mugen Honda), 32m 20.898s; **5** James Jakes, GB (Dallara F306-Mercedes Benz), 32m 30.472s; **6** Christian Bakkerud, DK (Dallara F306-Mugen Honda), 32m 31.144s; **7** Salvador Durán, MEX (Dallara F306-Mercedes Benz), 32m 32.189s; **8** Alberto Valério, BR (Dallara F306-Mugen Honda), 32m 47.051s; **9** Stephen Jelley, GB (Dallara F306-Mercedes Benz), 32m 50.294s; **10** Stuart Hall, GB (Dallara F306-Mugen Honda), 33m 00.265s.
National class winner: Cristiano Morgado, ZA (Lola-Dome F106/4-Mugen Honda), 33m 19.324s (11th).
Invitational class winner: Fabrizio Crestani, I (Dallara F304-Opel), 33m 23.207s (14th).
Fastest race lap: Senna, 1m 57.849s, 99.557 mph/160.221 km/h.
Fastest qualifying lap: Jarvis, 1m 59.997s, 97.775 mph/157.353 km/h.

BRITISH FORMULA 3 INTERNATIONAL SERIES, Silverstone International Circuit, Towcester, Northamptonshire, Great Britain, 24 September. 2 x 24 laps of the 2.249-mile/3.619-km circuit.
Round 19 (53.976 miles/86.866 km).
1 Mike Conway, GB (Dallara F306-Mercedes Benz), 30m 48.767s, 105.104 mph/169.149 / km/h; **2** Oliver Jarvis, GB (Dallara F306-Mugen Honda), 30m 53, 285s; **3** Christian Bakkerud, DK (Dallara F306-Mugen Honda), 31m 05.904s; **4** Bruno Senna, BR (Dallara F306-Mercedes Benz), 31m 06.658s; **5** Yelmer Buurman, NL (Dallara F306-Mercedes Benz), 31m 07.240s; **6** Stephen Jelley, GB (Dallara F306-Mercedes Benz), 31m 08.253s; **7** James Walker, GB (Dallara F306-Mercedes Benz), 31m 11.475s; **8** James Jakes, GB (Dallara F306-Mercedes Benz), 31m 12.809s; **9** Maro Engel, D (Dallara F306-Mugen Honda), 31m 13.500s; **10** Salvador Durán, MEX (Dallara F306-Mercedes Benz), 31m 20.796s.
National class winner: Cristiano Morgado, ZA (Lola-Dome F106/4-Mugen Honda), 31m 47.940s (15th).
Fastest race lap: Conway, 1m 16.282s, 106.138 mph/170.812 km/h.
Fastest qualifying lap: Conway, 1m 15.322s, 107.491 mph/172.989 km/h.

Round 20 (53.976 miles/86.866 km).
1 Mike Conway, GB (Dallara F306-Mercedes Benz), 30m 50.441s, 105.009 mph/168.996 / km/h; **2** Bruno Senna, BR (Dallara F306-Mercedes Benz), 30m 52.006s; **3** Oliver Jarvis, GB (Dallara F306-Mugen Honda), 30m 57.051s; **4** Yelmer Buurman, NL (Dallara F306-Mercedes Benz), 30m 58.200s; **5** James Jakes, GB (Dallara F306-Mercedes Benz), 31m 13.013s; **6** James Walker, GB (Dallara F306-Mercedes Benz), 31m 15.054s; **7** Christian Bakkerud, DK (Dallara F306-Mugen Honda), 31m 18.607s; **8** Stuart Hall, GB (Dallara F306-Mugen Honda), 31m 20.574s; **9** Maro Engel, D (Dallara F306-Mugen Honda), 31m 21.626s; **10** Salvador Durán, MEX (Dallara F306-Mercedes Benz), 31m 28.890s.
National class winner: Juho Annala, FIN (Dallara F304-Mugen Honda), 32m 06.818s (14th).
Fastest race lap: Conway, 1m 16.407s, 105.964 mph/170.533 km/h.
Fastest qualifying lap: Conway, 1m 15.313s, 107.503 mph/173.010 km/h.

BRITISH FORMULA 3 INTERNATIONAL SERIES, Thruxton Circuit, Andover, Hampshire, Great Britain, 1 October. 22 and 25 laps of the 2.356-mile/3.792-km circuit.
Round 21 (51.832 miles/83.416 km).
1 Danny Watts, GB (Dallara F306-Mercedes Benz), 30m 14.765s, 102.820 mph/165.474 km/h (1st invitational class); **2** Oliver Jarvis, GB (Dallara F306-Mugen Honda), 30m 16.668s (1st championship class); **3** Stephen Jelley, GB (Dallara F306-Mercedes Benz), 30m 18.108s; **4** Bruno Senna, BR (Dallara F306-Mercedes Benz), 30m 19.902s; **5** Christian Bakkerud, DK (Dallara F306-Mugen Honda), 30m 31.161s; **6** Alberto Valério, BR (Dallara F306-Mugen Honda), 30m 33.267s; **7** Stuart Hall, GB (Dallara F306-Mugen Honda), 30m 33.482s; **8** Greg Mansell, GB (Dallara F306-Mercedes Benz), 30m 34.311s; **9** Maro Engel, D (Dallara F306-Mugen Honda), 30m 35.058s; **10** Rodolfo González, YV (Dallara F304-Mugen Honda), 30m 51.798s (1st national class).
Fastest race lap: Bakkerud, 1m 13.883s, 114.798 mph/184.749 km/h.
Fastest qualifying lap: Watts, 1m 06.932s, 126.720 mph/203.936 km/h.

Round 22 (58.900 miles/94.790 km).
1 Yelmer Buurman, NL (Dallara F306-Mercedes Benz), 30m 46.132s, 114.856 mph/184.843 km/h; **2** Christian Bakkerud, DK (Dallara F306-Mugen Honda), 30m 47.327s; **3** Oliver Jarvis, GB (Dallara F306-Mugen Honda), 30m 47.437s; **4** Mike Conway, GB (Dallara F306-Mercedes Benz), 30m 53.472s; **5** Stephen Jelley, GB (Dallara F306-Mercedes Benz), 30m 56.034s; **6** Bruno Senna, BR (Dallara F306-Mercedes Benz), 30m 56.949s; **7** Alberto Valério, BR (Dallara F306-Mugen Honda), 31m 01.589s; **8** James Jakes, GB (Dallara F306-Mercedes Benz), 31m 04.341s; **9** Jonathan Kennard, GB (Dallara F306-Mugen Honda), 31m 04.629s; **10** Stuart Hall, GB (Dallara F306-Mugen Honda), 31m 05.907s.
National class winner: Cristiano Morgado, ZA (Lola-Dome F106/4-Mugen Honda), 31m 47.116s (12th).
Invitational class winner: Leo Mansell, GB (Dallara F306-Mercedes Benz), 31m 59.712s (13th).
Fastest race lap: Valério, 1m 11.292s, 118.970 mph/191.463 km/h.
Fastest qualifying lap: Engel, 1m 09.705s, 121.679 mph/195.823 km/h.

Final championship points
1 Mike Conway, GB, 321; **2** Oliver Jarvis, GB, 250; **3** Bruno Senna, BR, 229; **4** Yelmer Buurman, NL, 186; **5** Maro Engel, D, 174; **6** Christian Bakkerud, DK, 129; **7** Stephen Jelley, GB, 126; **8** James Jakes, GB, 96; **9** James Walker, GB, 92; **10** Salvador Durán, MEX, 54; **11** Alberto Valério, BR, 42; **12** Jonathan Kennard, GB, 36; **13** Stuart Hall, GB, 32; **14** Karl Reindler, AUS, 18; **15** Dennis Retera, GB, 8; **16** Charlie Hollings, GB, 6; **17** Keiko Ihara, J, 4.
National Class
1 Rodolfo González, YV, 355; **2** Cristiano Morgado, ZA, 300; **3** Juho Annala, FIN, 258; **4** Rodolfo Ávila, MAC, 182; **5** Martin Kudzak, S, 105.

Formula 3 Euro Series

FORMULA 3 EURO SERIES, Hockenheimring Grand Prix Circuit, Heidelberg, Germany, 8/9 April. 22 and 18 laps of the 2.842-mile/4.574-km circuit.
Round 1 (62.527 miles/100.628 km).
1 Kohei Hirate, J (Dallara F305-Mercedes Benz), 40m 27.868s, 92.714 mph/149.209 km/h; **2** Kazuki Nakajima, J (Dallara F305-Mercedes Benz), 40m 30.296s; **3** Paul di Resta, GB (Dallara F305-Mercedes Benz), 40m 35.520s; **4** Guillaume Moreau, F (Dallara F305-Mercedes Benz), 40m 39.973s; **5** Sebastian Vettel, D (Dallara F305-Mercedes Benz), 40m 40.696s; **6** Kamui Kobayashi, J (Dallara F305-Mercedes Benz), 40m 50.861s; **7** Richard Antinucci, USA (Dallara F305-Mercedes Benz), 40m 56.063s; **8** Yelmer Buurman, NL (Dallara F305-Mercedes Benz), 40m 58.825s; **9** James Jakes, GB. (Dallara F306-Mercedes Benz), 41m 15.336s; **10** Alejandro Núnez, E (Dallara F306-Mercedes Benz), 41m 19.777s.
Tim Sandtler, D (Dallara F305-Mercedes Benz) finished 10th in 41m 16.889s, but was given a 30-second penalty for pushing another car.
Fastest race lap: Nakajima, 1m 34.509s, 108.262 mph/174.231 km/h.
Fastest qualifying lap: Esteban Guerreri, RA (Dallara F305-Mercedes Benz), 1m 33.651s, 109.254 mph/175.827 km/h.

Round 2 (51.159 miles/82.332 km).
1 Sebastian Vettel, D (Dallara F305-Mercedes Benz), 28m 42.167s, 106.942 mph/172.106 km/h; **2** Guillaume Moreau, F (Dallara F305-Mercedes Benz), 28m 42.666s; **3** Esteban Guerreri, RA (Dallara F305-Mercedes Benz), 28m 43.119s; **4** Kohei Hirate, J (Dallara F305-Mercedes Benz), 28m 43.843s; **5** Kamui Kobayashi, J (Dallara F305-Mercedes Benz), 28m 45.733s; **6** Kazuki Nakajima, J (Dallara F305-Mercedes Benz), 28m 46.542s; **7** Giedo van der Garde, NL (Dallara F305-Mercedes Benz), 28m 47.150s; **8** James Jakes, GB (Dallara F306-Mercedes Benz), 29m 00.140s; **9** Joao Urbano, P (Dallara F306-Mercedes Benz), 29m 09.855s; **10** Alejandro Núnez, E (Dallara F306-Mercedes Benz), 29m 10.661s.
Fastest race lap: Hirate, 1m 33.987s, 108.863 mph/175.199 km/h.
Pole position: Buurman.

FORMULA 3 EURO SERIES, EuroSpeedway Lausitz, Klettwitz, Dresden, Germany, 29/30 April. 29 and 24 laps of the 2.139-mile/3.442 circuit.
Round 3 (62.024 miles/99.818 km).
1 Esteban Guerreri, RA (Dallara F305-Mercedes Benz), 40m 10.103s, 92.646 mph/149.099 km/h; **2** Paul di Resta, GB (Dallara F305-Mercedes Benz), 40m 16.626s; **3** Sebastian Vettel, D (Dallara F305-Mercedes Benz), 40m 22.258s; **4** Jonathan Summerton, USA (Dallara F305-Mercedes Benz), 40m 23.699s; **5** Richard Antinucci, USA (Dallara F305-Mercedes Benz), 40m 25.074s; **6** Romain Grosjean, F (Dallara F305-Mercedes Benz), 40m 27.307s; **7** Guillaume Moreau, F (Dallara F305-Mercedes Benz), 40m 27.672s; **8** Kazuki Nakajima, J (Dallara F305-Mercedes Benz), 40m 28.946s; **9** Charlie Kimball, USA (Dallara F306-Mercedes Benz), 40m 35.816s; **10** Joao Urbano, P (Dallara F306-Mercedes Benz), 40m 43.109s.
Fastest race lap: Guerrieri, 1m 15.672s, 101.749 mph/163.749 km/h.
Fastest qualifying lap: Di Resta, 1m 14.929s, 102.758 mph/165.373 km/h.

Round 4 (51.330 miles/82.608 km).
1 Kazuki Nakajima, J (Dallara F305-Mercedes Benz), 30m 39.592s, 100.451 mph/161.660 km/h; **2** Richard Antinucci, USA (Dallara F305-Mercedes Benz), 30m 47.015s; **3** Paul di Resta, GB (Dallara F305-Mercedes Benz), 30m 50.522s; **4** Romain Grosjean, F (Dallara F305-Mercedes Benz), 30m 52.041s; **5** Esteban Guerreri, RA (Dallara F305-Mercedes Benz), 30m 52.436s; **6** Sebastian Vettel, D (Dallara F305-Mercedes Benz), 30m 59.678s; **7** Jonathan Summerton, USA (Dallara F305-Mercedes Benz), 31m 00.372s; **8** Charlie Kimball, USA (Dallara F306-Mercedes Benz), 31m 09.790s; **9** Giedo van der Garde, NL (Dallara F305-Mercedes Benz), 31m 11.823s; **10** Kamui Kobayashi, J (Dallara F305-Mercedes Benz), 31m 12.073s.
Fastest race lap: Nakajima, 1m 15.576s, 101.878 mph/163.957 km/h.
Pole position: Nakajima.

FORMULA 3 EUROSERIES, Motorsport Arena Oschersleben, Germany, 20/21 May. 30 and 22 laps of the 2.279-mile/3.667-km circuit.
Round 5 (68.357 miles/110.010 km).
1 Paul di Resta, GB (Dallara F305-Mercedes Benz), 40m 30.860s, 101.234 mph/162.921 km/h; **2** Esteban Guerreri, RA (Dallara F305-Mercedes Benz), 40m 31.407s; **3** Romain Grosjean, F (Dallara F305-Mercedes Benz), 40m 31.905s; **4** Kohei Hirate, J (Dallara F305-Mercedes Benz), 40m 32.356s; **5** Sebastian Vettel, D (Dallara F305-Mercedes Benz), 40m 32.831s; **6** Kazuki Nakajima, J (Dallara F305-Mercedes Benz), 40m 34.366s; **7** Sébastien Buemi, CH (Dallara F305-Mercedes Benz), 40m 49.421s; **8** Guillaume Moreau, F (Dallara F305-Mercedes Benz), 40m 49.924s; **9** Richard Antinucci, USA (Dallara F305-Mercedes Benz), 40m 53.656s; **10** Charlie Kimball, USA (Dallara F306-Mercedes Benz), 41m 04.184s.
Fastest race lap: Peter Elkmann, D (Dallara F306-Opel), 1m 19.965s, 102.580 mph/165.087 km/h.
Fastest qualifying lap: Guerreri, 1m 18.445s, 104.568 mph/168.286 km/h.

Round 6 (50.128 miles/80.674 km).
1 Sébastien Buemi, CH (Dallara F305-Mercedes Benz), 29m 38.477s, 101.470 mph/163.300 km/h; **2** Kohei Hirate, J (Dallara F305-Mercedes Benz), 29m 45.392s; **3** Esteban Guerreri, RA (Dallara F305-Mercedes Benz), 29m 48.393s; **4** Guillaume Moreau, F (Dallara F305-Mercedes Benz), 29m 48.638s; **5** Kazuki Nakajima, J (Dallara F305-Mercedes Benz), 29m 49.831s; **6** Romain Grosjean, F (Dallara F305-Mercedes Benz), 29m 50.587s; **7** Kamui Kobayashi, J (Dallara F305-Mercedes Benz), 30m 01.430s; **8** Alejandro Núnez, E (Dallara F306-Mercedes Benz), 30m 08.105s; **9** Joao Urbano, P (Dallara F306-Mercedes Benz), 30m 08.635s; **10** Filip Salaquarda, CZ (Dallara F306-Opel), 30m 13.644s.
Fastest race lap: Buemi, 1m 19.626s, 103.017 mph/165.790 km/h.
Pole position: Moreau.

FORMULA 3 EUROSERIES, Brands Hatch Indy Circuit, West Kingsdown, Dartford, Kent, Great Britain, 1/2 July. 56 and 42 laps of the 1.199-mile/1.929-km circuit.
Round 7 (67.123 miles/108.024 km).
1 Paul di Resta, GB (Dallara F305-Mercedes Benz), 40m 22.460s, 99.751 mph/160.534 km/h; **2** Sebastian Vettel, D (Dallara F305-Mercedes Benz), 40m 23.029s; **3** Richard Antinucci, USA (Dallara F305-Mercedes Benz), 40m 33.355s*; **4** Giedo van der Garde, NL (Dallara F305-Mercedes Benz), 40m 33.970s; **5** James Jakes, GB (Dallara F306-Mercedes Benz), 40m 34.987s; **6** Kamui Kobayashi, J (Dallara F305-Mercedes Benz), 40m 44.308s; **7** Michael Herck, B (Dallara F306-Mercedes Benz), 40m 45.999s; **8** Peter Elkmann, D (Dallara F306-Opel), 40m 48.340s; **9** Romain Grosjean, F (Dallara F305-Mercedes Benz), 40m 49.116s; **10** James Walker, GB (Dallara F306-Mercedes Benz), 40m 49.682s.
* Originally disqualified but reinstated following an appeal.
Fastest race lap: Di Resta, 42.633s, 101.214 mph/162.888 km/h.
Fastest qualifying lap: Di Resta, 42.323s, 101.955 mph/164.081 km/h.

Round 8 (50.342 miles/81.018 km).
1 Peter Elkmann, D (Dallara F306-Opel), 30m 28.842s, 99.097 mph/159.481 km/h; **2** Michael Herck, B (Dallara F306-Mercedes Benz), 30m 29.810s; **3** Kamui Kobayashi, J (Dallara F305-Mercedes Benz), 30m 30.477s; **4** James Jakes, GB (Dallara F306-Mercedes Benz), 30m 33.059s; **5** Paul di Resta, GB (Dallara F305-Mercedes Benz), 30m 33.744s; **6** Romain Grosjean, F (Dallara F305-Mercedes Benz), 30m 34.805s; **7** Sebastian Vettel, D (Dallara F305-Mercedes Benz), 30m 34.998s; **8** James Walker, GB (Dallara F306-Mercedes Benz), 30m 35.969s; **9** Yelmer Buurman, NL (Dallara F305-Mercedes Benz), 30m 40.418s; **10** Jonathan Summerton, USA (Dallara F305-Mercedes Benz), 30m 40.879s.
Fastest race lap: Vettel, 42.717s, 101.015 mph/162.568 km/h.
Pole position: Elkmann.

FORMULA 3 EURO SERIES, Norisring, Nürnberg (Nuremberg), Germany, 22/23 July. 48 and 32 laps of the 1.429-mile/2.300-km circuit.
Round 9 (68.599 miles/110.400 km).
1 Paul di Resta, GB (Dallara F305-Mercedes Benz), 40m 09.638s, 102.487 mph/164.937 km/h; **2** Sebastian Vettel, D (Dallara F305-Mercedes Benz), 40m 11.639s; **3** Jonathan Summerton, USA (Dallara F305-Mercedes Benz), 40m 14.167s; **4** Kohei Hirate, J (Dallara F305-Mercedes Benz), 40m 20.025s; **5** Kamui Kobayashi, J (Dallara F305-Mercedes Benz), 40m 20.580s; **6** Giedo van der Garde, NL (Dallara F305-Mercedes Benz), 40m 25.427s; **7** Sébastien Buemi, CH (Dallara F305-Mercedes Benz), 40m 27.987s; **8** Joao Urbano, P (Dallara F306-Mercedes Benz), 40m 40.246s; **9** Peter Elkmann, D (Dallara F306-Opel), 40m 40.686s; **10** Esteban Guerreri, RA (Dallara F305-Mercedes Benz), 40m 43.327s.
Fastest race lap: Vettel, 49.421s, 104.105 mph/167.540 km/h.
Fastest qualifying lap: Van der Garde, 49.194s, 104.585 mph/168.313 km/h.

Round 10 (45.733 miles/73.600 km).
1 Giedo van der Garde, NL (Dallara F305-Mercedes Benz), 26m 44.440s, 102.614 mph/165.141 km/h; **2** Kamui Kobayashi, J (Dallara F305-Mercedes Benz), 26m 56.947s; **3** Peter Elkmann, D (Dallara F306-Opel), 26m 58.442s; **4** Charlie Kimball, USA (Dallara F306-Mercedes Benz), 27m 01.483s; **5** Kazuki Nakajima, J (Dallara F305-Mercedes Benz), 27m 03.449s; **6** Guillaume Moreau, F (Dallara F305-Mercedes Benz), 27m 06.855s; **7** Alejandro Nunez, E (Dallara F306-Mercedes Benz), 27m 07.488s; **8** Romain Grosjean, F (Dallara F305-Mercedes Benz), 27m 10.825s; **9** Tim Sandtler, D (Dallara F305-Mercedes Benz), 27m 12.920s; **10** Michael Herck, B (Dallara F306-Mercedes Benz), 27m 13.451s.
Fastest race lap: Buemi, 49.435s, 104.075 mph/167.493 km/h.
Pole position: Urbano.

FORMULA 3 EURO SERIES, Nürburgring Short Circuit, Nürburg/Eifel, Germany, 19/20 August. 29 and 18 laps of the 2.255-mile/3.629-km circuit.
Round 11 (65.394 miles/105.241 km).
1 Sebastian Vettel, D (Dallara F305-Mercedes Benz), 40m 59.630s, 95.713 mph/154.034 km/h; **2** Paul di Resta, GB (Dallara F305-Mercedes Benz), 41m 05.614s; **3** Giedo van der Garde, NL (Dallara F305-Mercedes Benz), 41m 07.795s; **4** Sébastien Buemi, CH (Dallara F305-Mercedes Benz), 41m 09.341s; **5** Kohei Hirate, J (Dallara F305-Mercedes Benz), 41m 13.993s; **6** Michael Herck, B (Dallara F306-Mercedes Benz), 41m 20.699s; **7** Richard Antinucci, USA (Dallara F305-Mercedes Benz), 41m 21.832s; **8** Kamui Kobayashi, J (Dallara F305-Mercedes Benz), 41m 22.858s; **9** Kazuki Nakajima, J (Dallara F305-Mercedes Benz), 41m 37.050s; **10** Charlie Kimball, USA (Dallara F306-Mercedes Benz), 41m 38.437s.
Fastest race lap: Vettel, 1m 23.917s, 96.737 mph/155.682 km/h.
Fastest qualifying lap: Vettel, 1m 23.104s, 97.683 mph/157.205 km/h.

Round 12 (40.589 miles/65.322 km).
1 Sebastian Vettel, D (Dallara F305-Mercedes Benz), 30m 12.489s, 80.619 mph/129.743 km/h; **2** Richard Antinucci, USA (Dallara F305-Mercedes Benz), 30m 12.924s; **3** Kamui Kobayashi, J (Dallara F305-Mercedes Benz), 30m 14.802s; **4** Peter Elkmann, D (Dallara F306-Opel), 30m 15.205s; **5** Esteban Guerreri, RA (Dallara F305-Mercedes Benz), 30m 15.588s; **6** Charlie Kimball, USA (Dallara F306-Mercedes Benz), 30m 16.267s; **7** Filip Salaquarda,

CZ (Dallara F306-Opel), 30m 18.882s; **8** Sébastien Buemi, CH (Dallara F305-Mercedes Benz), 30m 20.131s; **9** Tim Sandtler, D (Dallara F305-Mercedes Benz), 30m 22.920s; **10** Romain Grosjean, F (Dallara F305-Mercedes Benz), 30m 26.948s.
Fastest race lap: Kobayashi, 1m 23.842s, 96.823 mph/155.822 km/h.
Pole position: Kobayashi.

FORMULA 3 EURO SERIES, Circuit Park Zandvoort, Netherlands, 2/3 September. 26 and 18 laps of the 2.676-mile/4.307-km circuit.
Round 13 (69.582 miles/111.982 km).
1 Paul di Resta, GB (Dallara F305-Mercedes Benz), 41m 05.497s, 101.601 mph/163.510 km/h; **2** Giedo van der Garde, NL (Dallara F305-Mercedes Benz), 41m 07.267s; **3** Kohei Hirate, J (Dallara F305-Mercedes Benz), 41m 07.848s; **4** Romain Grosjean, F (Dallara F305-Mercedes Benz), 41m 08.372s; **5** Kamui Kobayashi, J (Dallara F305-Mercedes Benz), 41m 09.922s; **6** Jonathan Summerton, USA (Dallara F305-Mercedes Benz), 41m 11.433s; **7** Guillaume Moreau, F (Dallara F305-Mercedes Benz), 41m 12.729s; **8** Esteban Guerreri, RA (Dallara F305-Mercedes Benz), 41m 14.783s; **9** Michael Herck, B (Dallara F306-Mercedes Benz), 41m 22.062s; **10** Peter Elkmann, D (Dallara F306-Opel), 41m 23.507s.
Fastest race lap: Kazuki Nakajima, J (Dallara F305-Mercedes Benz), 1m 33.241s, 103.329 mph/166.292 km/h.
Fastest qualifying lap: Di Resta, 1m 31.955s, 104.774 mph/168.617 km/h.

Round 14 (48.172 miles/77.526 km).
1 Charlie Kimball, USA (Dallara F306-Mercedes Benz), 30m 33.295s, 94.595 mph/152.236 km/h; **2** Sebastian Vettel, D (Dallara F305-Mercedes Benz), 30m 33.972s; **3** Kazuki Nakajima, J (Dallara F305-Mercedes Benz), 30m 59.546s; **4** Esteban Guerreri, RA (Dallara F305-Mercedes Benz), 31m 14.446s; **5** Giedo van der Garde, NL (Dallara F305-Mercedes Benz), 31m 15.213s; **6** Tim Sandtler, D (Dallara F305-Mercedes Benz), 31m 15.998s; **7** Guillaume Moreau, F (Dallara F305-Mercedes Benz), 31m 16.022s; **8** Sébastien Buemi, CH (Dallara F305-Mercedes Benz), 31m 16.163s; **9** Peter Elkmann, D (Dallara F306-Opel), 31m 25.488s; **10** Filip Salaquarda, CZ (Dallara F306-Opel), 31m 29.635s.
Fastest race lap: Vettel, 1m 36.182s, 100.169 mph/161.207 km/h.
Pole position: Guerreri.

FORMULA 3 EURO SERIES, Circuit de Catalunya, Montmeló, Barcelona, Spain, 23/24 September. 2 x 26 laps of the 1.832-mile/2.949-km circuit.
Round 15 (47.643 miles/76.674 km).
1 Sebastian Vettel, D (Dallara F305-Mercedes Benz), 33m 28.008s, 85.415 mph/137.462 km/h; **2** Kohei Hirate, J (Dallara F305-Mercedes Benz), 33m 41.865s; **3** Esteban Guerreri, RA (Dallara F305-Mercedes Benz), 33m 50.241s; **4** Kazuki Nakajima, J (Dallara F305-Mercedes Benz), 33m 52.046s; **5** Kamui Kobayashi, J (Dallara F305-Mercedes Benz), 33m 52.963s; **6** Charlie Kimball, USA (Dallara F306-Mercedes Benz), 33m 54.560s; **7** Sébastien Buemi, CH (Dallara F305-Mercedes Benz), 33m 59.862s; **8** Richard Antinucci, USA (Dallara F305-Mercedes Benz), 34m 04.494s; **9** Guillaume Moreau, F (Dallara F305-Mercedes Benz), 34m 07.941s; **10** Paul di Resta, GB (Dallara F305-Mercedes Benz), 34m 12.343s.
Fastest race lap: Vettel, 1m 13.683s, 89.528 mph/144.082 km/h.
Fastest qualifying lap: Di Resta, 1m 01.299s, 107.616 mph/173.190 km/h.

Round 16 (47.643 miles/76.674 km).
1 Richard Antinucci, USA (Dallara F305-Mercedes Benz), 30m 01.471s, 95.208 mph/153.222 km/h; **2** Charlie Kimball, USA (Dallara F306-Mercedes Benz), 30m 05.442s; **3** Kazuki Nakajima, J (Dallara F305-Mercedes Benz), 30m 06.382s; **4** Kohei Hirate, J (Dallara F305-Mercedes Benz), 30m 07.227s; **5** Sébastien Buemi, CH (Dallara F305-Mercedes Benz), 30m 12.614s; **6** Paul di Resta, GB (Dallara F305-Mercedes Benz), 30m 13.209s; **7** Esteban Guerreri, RA (Dallara F305-Mercedes Benz), 30m 13.872s; **8** Giedo van der Garde, NL (Dallara F305-Mercedes Benz), 30m 21.389s; **9** Romain Grosjean, F (Dallara F305-Mercedes Benz), 30m 22.106s; **10** Guillaume Moreau, F (Dallara F305-Mercedes Benz), 30m 23.816s.
Fastest race lap: Hirate, 1m 01.876s, 106.612 mph/171.575 km/h.
Pole position: Antinucci.

FORMULA 3 EURO SERIES, Circuit Le Mans-Bugatti, France, 14/15 October. 26 and 18 laps of the 2.597-mile/4.180-km circuit.
Round 17 (67.531 miles/108.680 km).
1 Paul di Resta, GB (Dallara F305-Mercedes Benz), 39m 59.914s, 101.300 mph/163.025 km/h; **2** Jonathan Summerton, USA (Dallara F305-Mercedes Benz), 40m 00.939s; **3** Guillaume Moreau, F (Dallara F305-Mercedes Benz), 40m 07.533s; **4** Charlie Kimball, USA (Dallara F306-Mercedes Benz), 40m 10.076s; **5** Kohei Hirate, J (Dallara F305-Mercedes Benz), 40m 17.433s; **6** Esteban Guerreri, RA (Dallara F305-Mercedes Benz), 40m 18.315s; **7** Michael Herck, B (Dallara F306-Mercedes Benz), 40m 30.908s; **8** Richard Antinucci, USA (Dallara F305-Mercedes Benz), 40m 31.915s; **9** Sebastian Vettel, D (Dallara F305-Mercedes Benz), 40m 32.625s; **10** Tim Sandtler, D (Dallara F305-Mercedes Benz), 40m 33.192s.
Fastest race lap: Guerreri, 1m 31.373s, 102.332 mph/164.688 km/h.
Fastest qualifying lap: Giedo van der Garde, NL (Dallara F305-Mercedes Benz), 1m 30.144s, 103.727 mph/166.933 km/h.

Round 18 (46.752 miles/75.240 km).
1 Richard Antinucci, USA (Dallara F305-Mercedes Benz), 27m 42.137s, 101.259 mph/162.961 km/h; **2** Charlie Kimball, USA (Dallara F306-Mercedes Benz), 27m 42.779s; **3** Kohei Hirate, J (Dallara F305-Mercedes Benz), 27m 43.970s; **4** Jonathan Summerton, USA (Dallara F305-Mercedes Benz), 27m 44.740s; **5** Guillaume Moreau, F (Dallara F305-Mercedes Benz), 27m 46.292s; **6** Paul di Resta, GB (Dallara F305-Mercedes Benz), 27m 48.783s; **7** Kazuki Nakajima, J (Dallara F305-Mercedes Benz), 27m 49.808s; **8** Esteban Guerreri, RA (Dallara F305-Mercedes Benz), 27m 50.948s; **9** Sebastian Vettel, D (Dallara F305-Mercedes Benz), 27m 53.033s; **10** Romain Grosjean, F (Dallara F305-Mercedes Benz), 27m 55.004s.
Fastest race lap: Sébastien Buemi, CH (Dallara F305-Mercedes Benz), 1m 30.978s, 102.776 mph/165.403 km/h.
Pole position: Antinucci.

FORMULA 3 EURO SERIES, Hockenheimring Grand Prix Circuit, Heidelberg, Germany, 28/29 October. 22 and 18 laps of the 2.842-mile/4.574-km circuit.
Round 19 (62.527 miles/100.628 km).
1 Esteban Guerreri, RA (Dallara F305-Mercedes Benz), 35m 11.187s, 106.622 mph/171.591 km/h; **2** Sébastien Buemi, CH (Dallara F305-Mercedes Benz), 35m 12.015s; **3** Sebastian Vettel, D (Dallara F305-Mercedes Benz), 35m 13.794s; **4** Guillaume Moreau, F (Dallara F305-Mercedes Benz), 35m 15.445s; **5** Kohei Hirate, J (Dallara F305-Mercedes Benz), 35m 20.313s; **6** Charlie Kimball, USA (Dallara F306-Mercedes Benz), 35m 20.803s; **7** Roberto Streit, BR (Dallara F306-Mercedes Benz), 35m 23.852s; **8** Jonathan Summerton, USA (Dallara F305-Mercedes Benz), 35m 35.389s; **9** Giedo van der Garde, NL (Dallara F305-Mercedes Benz), 35m 36.176s; **10** Paul di Resta, GB (Dallara F305-Mercedes Benz), 35m 37.060s.
Fastest race lap: Buemi, 1m 34.995s, 107.708 mph/173.340 km/h.
Fastest qualifying lap: Di Resta, 1m 34.518s, 108.252 mph/174.214 km/h.

Round 20 (51.159 miles/82.332 km).
1 Jonathan Summerton, USA (Dallara F305-Mercedes Benz), 28m 47.189s, 106.631 mph/171.605 km/h; **2** Giedo van der Garde, NL (Dallara F305-Mercedes Benz), 28m 52.106s; **3** Sébastien Buemi, CH (Dallara F305-Mercedes Benz), 28m 53.083s; **4** Esteban Guerreri, RA (Dallara F305-Mercedes Benz), 28m 53.453s; **5** Roberto Streit, BR (Dallara F306-Mercedes Benz), 28m 58.940s; **6** Paul di Resta, GB (Dallara F305-Mercedes Benz), 29m 00.206s; **7** Kohei Hirate, J (Dallara F305-Mercedes Benz), 29m 06.909s; **8** Richard Antinucci, USA (Dallara F305-Mercedes Benz), 2m 07.701s; **9** Kamui Kobayashi, J (Dallara F305-Mercedes Benz), 29m 10.232s; **10** Natacha Gachnang, CH (Dallara F305-Mercedes Benz), 29m 25.383s.
Fastest race lap: Buemi, 1m 34.650s, 108.101 mph/173.971 km/h.
Pole position: Summerton.

Final championship points
Drivers
1 Paul di Resta, GB, 86; **2** Sebastian Vettel, D, 75; **3** Kohei Hirate, J, 61; **4** Esteban Guerreri, RA, 58; **5** Richard Antinucci, USA, 38; **6** Giedo van der Garde, NL, 37; **7** Kazuki Nakajima, J, 36; **8** Kamui Kobayashi, J, 34; **9** Guillaume Moreau, F, 32; **10** Jonathan Summerton, USA, 32; **11** Sébastien Buemi, CH, 31; **12** Charlie Kimball, USA, 31; **13** Romain Grosjean, F, 19; **14** Peter Elkmann, D, 14; **15** Michael Herck, B, 12; **16** James Jakes, GB, 7; **17** Roberto Streit, BR, 4; **18** Joao Urbano, P, 1; **19** Yelmer Buurman, NL, 1; **20** Tim Sandtler, D, 1.
Rookie-Cup
1 Kamui Kobayashi, J, 119; **2** Jonathan Summerton, USA, 107; **3** Tim Sandtler, D, 104.
Teams
1 ASM Formula 3, 197; **2** Manor Motorsport, 147; **3** Signature-Plus, 91.
Nations' Cup
1 Japan, 124; **2** USA, 100; **3** Great Britain, 90.

Recaro F3-Cup

RECARO F3-CUP, Motorsport Arena Oschersleben, Germany, 22/23 April. 13 and 18 laps of the 2.279-mile/3.667-km circuit.
Round 1 (29.621 miles/47.671 km).
1 Ho-Pin Tung, CHN (Lola B06/30-Opel), 25m 02.508s, 70.973 mph/114.219 km/h; **2** Renger van der Zande, NL (Dallara F306-Mercedes Benz), 25m 04.751s; **3** Dominik Schrami, D (Dallara F306-Opel), 25m 10.576s; **4** Riccardo Azzoli, I (SLC R1-006-Opel), 25m 11.566s; **5** Ferdinand Kool, NL (Lola B06/30-Opel), 25m 11.892s; **6** Récardo Bruins, ROK/NL (Dallara F306-Opel), 25m 12.206s; **7** Salvatore Gatto, I (SLC R1-006-Opel), 25m 14.946s; **8** Harald Schegelmilch, LV (Dallara F304-Opel), 25m 15.402s; **9** Hiroyuki Matsumura, J (Dallara F306-Opel), 25m 15.873s; **10** Ronny Wechselberger, D (Dallara F304-Opel), 25m 16.690s.
Fastest race lap: Joey Foster, GB (Lola B06/30-Opel), 1m 22.810s, 99.056 mph/159.416 km/h.
Fastest qualifying lap: Nico Hülkenberg, D (Dallara F306-Opel), 1m 42.451s, 80.066 mph/128.854 km/h.

Round 2 (41.014 miles/66.006 km).
1 Joey Foster, GB (Lola B06/30-Opel), 25m 16.490s, 97.364 mph/156.692 km/h; **2** Nico Hülkenberg, D (Dallara F306-Opel), 25m 16.976s; **3** Harald Schegelmilch, LV (Dallara F304-Opel), 25m 22.092s; **4** Riccardo Azzoli, I (SLC R1-006-Opel), 25m 26.405s; **5** Ferdinand Kool, NL (Lola B06/30-Opel), 25m 28.109s; **6** Ho-Pin Tung, CHN (Lola B06/30-Opel), 25m 31.345s; **7** Dominik Schrami, D (Dallara F306-Opel), 25m 42.722s; **8** Ronny Wechselberger, D (Dallara F304-Opel), 25m 49.941s; **9** Natacha Gachnang, CH (Dallara F304-Opel), 25m 50.480s; **10** Salvatore Gatto, I (SLC R1-006-Opel), 25m 51.124s.
Fastest race lap: Foster, 1m 21.926s, 100.125 mph/161.136 km/h.
Fastest qualifying lap: Hülkenberg, 1m 37.744s, 83.922 mph/135.059 km/h.

JIM CLARK REVIVAL, Hockenheimring Grand Prix Circuit, Heidelberg, Germany, 29/30 April. 2 x 16 laps of the 2.842-mile/4.574-km circuit.
Round 3 (45.474 miles/73.184 km).
1 Joey Foster, GB (Lola B06/30-Opel), 26m 15.747s, 103.892 mph/167.198 km/h; **2** Récardo Bruins, ROK/NL (Dallara F306-Opel), 26m 19.386s; **3** Ferdinand Kool, NL (Lola B06/30-Opel), 26m 23.029s; **4** Renger van der Zande, NL (Dallara F306-Mercedes Benz), 26m 23.813s; **5** Nico Hülkenberg, D (Dallara F306-Opel), 26m 25.998s; **6** Ho-Pin Tung, CHN (Lola B06/30-Opel), 26m 26.525s; **7** Harald Schegelmilch, LV (Dallara F304-Opel), 26m 27.443s; **8** Riccardo Azzoli, I (SLC R1-006-Opel), 26m 35.219s; **9** Johannes Theobald, D (Dallara F304-Mercedes Benz), 26m 39.389s; **10** Salvatore Gatto, I (SLC R1-006-Opel), 26m 40.182s.
Fastest race lap: Bruins, 1m 37.285s, 105.173 mph/169.259 km/h.
Fastest qualifying lap: Kool, 1m 36.714s, 105.794 mph/170.258 km/h.

Round 4 (45.474 miles/73.184 km).
1 Nico Hülkenberg, D (Dallara F306-Opel), 26m 23.468s, 105.173 mph/166.383 km/h; **2** Ferdinand Kool, NL (Lola B06/30-Opel), 26m 25.570s; **3** Renger van der Zande, NL (Dallara F306-Mercedes Benz), 26m 25.833s; **4** Joey Foster, GB (Lola B06/30-Opel), 26m 27.659s; **5** Ho-Pin Tung, CHN (Lola B06/30-Opel), 26m 29.177s; **6** Riccardo Azzoli, I (SLC R1-006-Opel), 26m 37.930s; **7** Salvatore Gatto, I (SLC R1-006-Opel), 26m 48.388s; **8** Johannes Theobald, D (Dallara F304-Mercedes Benz), 26m 51.713s; **9** Natacha Gachnang, CH (Dallara F304-Opel), 26m 53.689s; **10** Ronny Wechselberger, D (Dallara F304-Opel), 26m 57.726s.
Fastest race lap: Foster, 1m 37.439s, 105.007 mph/168.991 km/h.
Fastest qualifying lap: Hülkenberg, 1m 37.774s, 104.647 mph/168.412 km/h.

RECARO F3-CUP, EuroSpeedway Lausitz, Klettwitz, Dresden, Germany, 13/14 May. 17 and 18 laps of the 2.139-mile/3.442-km circuit.
Round 5 (36.359 miles/58.514 km).
1 Ho-Pin Tung, CHN (Lola B06/30-Opel), 25m 05.968s, 86.916 mph/139.877 km/h; **2** Joey Foster, GB (Lola B06/30-Opel), 25m 06.928s; **3** Renger van der Zande, NL (Dallara F306-Mercedes Benz), 25m 10.455s; **4** Nico Hülkenberg, D (Dallara F306-Opel), 25m 13.401s; **5** Harald Schegelmilch, LV (Dallara F304-Opel), 25m 13.422s; **6** Riccardo Azzoli, I (SLC R1-006-Opel), 25m 13.899s; **7** Marcello Thomaz, BR (Dallara F306-Opel), 25m 15.215s; **8** Cyndie Allemann, CH (Dallara F306-Mercedes Benz), 25m 15.355s; **9** Johannes Theobald, D (Dallara F304-Mercedes Benz), 25m 15.661s; **10** Hiroyuki Matsumura, J (Dallara F306-Opel), 25m 16.088s.
Fastest race lap: Foster, 1m 18.628s, 97.924 mph/157.593 km/h.
Fastest qualifying lap: Tung, 1m 17.722s, 99.065 mph/159.430 km/h.

Round 6 (38.498 miles/61.956 km).
1 Ho-Pin Tung, CHN (Lola B06/30-Opel), 23m 51.715s, 96.801 mph/155.786 kmh; **2** Nico Hülkenberg, D (Dallara F306-Opel), 23m 53.869s; **3** Ferdinand Kool, NL (Lola B06/30-Opel), 24m 01.615s; **4** Harald Schegelmilch, LV (Dallara F304-Opel), 24m 05.549s; **5** Riccardo Azzoli, I (SLC R1-006-Opel), 24m 06.488s; **6** Hiroyuki Matsumura, J (Dallara F306-Opel), 24m 14.031s; **7** Cyndie Allemann, CH (Dallara F306-Mercedes Benz), 24m 16.892s; **8** Salvatore Gatto, I (SLC R1-006-Opel), 24m 17.581s; **9** Ronny Wechselberger, D (Dallara F304-Opel), 24m 17.823s; **10** Natacha Gachnang, CH (Dallara F306-Opel), 24m 18.181s.
Fastest race lap: Hülkenberg, 1m 18.126s, 98.553 mph/158.605 km/h.
Fastest qualifying lap: Foster, 1m 17.225s, 99.703 mph/160.456 km/h.

RECARO F3-CUP, Nürburgring Short Circuit, Nürburg/Eifel, Germany, 27/28 May. 2 x 18 laps of the 2.248-mile/3.618-km circuit.
Round 7 (40.466 miles/65.124 km).
1 Joey Foster, GB (Lola B06/30-Opel), 25m 14.663s, 96.179 mph/154.785 km/h; **2** Riccardo Azzoli, I (SLC R1-006-Opel), 25m 20.137s; **3** Harald Schegelmilch, LV (Dallara F304-Opel), 25m 20.633s; **4** Ferdinand Kool, NL (Lola B06/30-Opel), 25m 22.137s; **5** Ho-Pin Tung, CHN (Lola B06/30-Opel), 25m 24.028s; **6** Cyndie Allemann, CH (Dallara F306-Mercedes Benz), 25m 46.842s; **7** Johannes Theobald, D (Dallara F304-Mercedes Benz), 25m 57.847s; **8** Norman Knop, D (Dallara F306-Opel), 25m 59.457s; **9** Natacha Gachnang, CH (Dallara F306-Opel), 26m 00.205s; **10** Rolf Biland, CH (Dallara F304-TOM's Toyota), 26m 05.973s.
Fastest race lap: Tung, 1m 22.524s, 98.071 mph/157.830 km/h.
Fastest qualifying lap: Azzoli, 1m 29.948s, 89.977 mph/144.804 km/h.

Round 8 (40.466 miles/65.124 km).
1 Joey Foster, GB (Lola B06/30-Opel), 25m 04.663s, 96.818 mph/155.813 km/h; **2** Ho-Pin Tung, CHN (Lola B06/30-Opel), 25m 10.667s; **3** Ferdinand Kool, NL (Lola B06/30-Opel), 25m 13.804s; **4** Renger van der Zande, NL (Dallara F306-Mercedes Benz), 25m 14.734s; **5** Récardo Bruins, ROK/NL (Dallara F306-Opel), 25m 22.508s; **6** Johannes Theobald, D (Dallara F304-Mercedes Benz), 25m 24.065s; **7** Riccardo Azzoli, I (SLC R1-006-Opel), 25m 24.408s; **8** Nico Hülkenberg, D (Dallara F306-Opel), 25m 26.420s; **9** Cyndie Allemann, CH (Dallara F306-Mercedes Benz), 25m 27.041s; **10** Natacha Gachnang, CH (Dallara F306-Opel), 25m 27.314s.
Fastest race lap: Foster, 1m 22.634s, 97.941 mph/157.620 km/h.
Fastest qualifying lap: Kool, 1m 24.829s, 95.406 mph/153.542 km/h.

RECARO F3-CUP, Nürburgring Grand Prix Circuit, Nürburg/Eifel, Germany, 17 June. 2 x 15 laps of the 2.882-mile/4.638-km circuit.
Round 9 (43.229 miles/69.570 km).
1 Ho-Pin Tung, CHN (Lola B06/30-Opel), 25m 07.203s, 103.253 mph/166.170 km/h; **2** Joey Foster, GB (Lola B06/30-Opel), 25m 09.023s; **3** Ferdinand Kool, NL (Lola B06/30-Opel), 25m 10.461s; **4** Harald Schegelmilch, LV (Dallara F304-Opel), 25m 22.367s; **5** Nico Hülkenberg, D (Ligier JS47/06-Opel), 25m 23.280s; **6** Marcello Thomaz, BR (Dallara F306-Opel), 25m 27.541s; **7** Renger van der Zande, NL (Dallara F306-Mercedes Benz), 25m 28.398s; **8** Natacha Gachnang, CH (Dallara F306-Opel), 25m 28.767s; **9** Cyndie Allemann, CH (Dallara F306-Mercedes Benz), 25m 35.606s; **10** Johannes Theobald, D (Dallara F304-Mercedes Benz), 25m 39.492s.
Fastest race lap: Tung, 1m 39.333s, 104.446 mph/168.089 km/h.
Fastest qualifying lap: Kool, 1m 39.651s, 104.112 mph/167.553 km/h.

Round 10 (43.229 miles/69.570 km).
1 Ho-Pin Tung, CHN (Lola B06/30-Opel), 25m 13.358s, 102.833 mph/165.494 km/h; **2** Marcello Thomaz, BR (Dallara F306-Opel), 25m 26.009s; **3** Natacha Gachnang, CH (Dallara F306-Opel), 25m 26.478s; **4** Récardo Bruins, ROK/NL (Dallara F306-Opel), 25m 28.674s; **5** Ferdinand Kool, NL (Lola B06/30-Opel), 25m 30.338s; **6** Salvatore Gatto, I (SLC R1-006-Opel), 25m 35.979s; **7** Cyndie Allemann, CH (Dallara F306-Mercedes Benz), 25m 37.598s; **8** Joey Foster, GB (Lola B06/30-Opel), 25m 41.253s; **9** Harald Schegelmilch, LV (Dallara F304-Opel), 25m 43.441s; **10** Dominick Muermans, NL (Dallara F306-Opel), 25m 48.463s.
Fastest race lap: Tung, 1m 39.707s, 104.054 mph/167.459 km/h.
Fastest qualifying lap: Tung, 1m 40.087s, 103.659 mph/166.823 km/h.

RECARO F3-CUP, Nationale Circuit Assen, Netherlands, 15/16 July. 2 x 16 laps of the 2.830-mile/4.555-km circuit.
Round 11 (45.286 miles/72.880 km).
1 Johnny Cecotto Jr, YV (Dallara F306-Mugen Honda), 25m 28.145s, 106.684 mph/171.690 km/h; **2** Nico Hülkenberg, D (Ligier JS47/06-Opel), 25m 29.452s; **3** Harald Schegelmilch, LV (Dallara F304-Opel), 25m 37.922s; **4** Joey Foster, GB (Lola B06/30-Opel), 25m 51.158s; **5** Renger van der Zande, NL (Dallara F306-Mercedes Benz), 25m 52.903s; **6** Ho-Pin Tung, CHN (Lola B06/30-Opel), 25m 53.796s; **7** Salvatore Gatto, I (SLC R1-006-Opel), 26m 00.451s; **8** Riccardo Azzoli, I (SLC R1-006-Opel), 26m 06.972s; **9** Christer Jöns, D (Dallara F304-Opel), 26m 15.105s; **10** Dominick Muermans, NL (Dallara F306-Opel), 26m 26.118s.
Fastest race lap: Foster, 1m 34.018s, 108.375 mph/174.413 km/h.
Fastest qualifying lap: Foster, 1m 33.128s, 109.411 mph/176.080 km/h.

Round 12 (45.286 miles/72.880 km).
1 Harald Schegelmilch, LV (Dallara F304-Opel), 25m 15.149s, 107.599 mph/173.163 km/h; **2** Nico Hülkenberg, D (Ligier JS47/06-Opel), 25m 15.627s; **3** Ferdinand Kool, NL (Lola B06/30-Opel), 25m 19.982s; **4** Johnny Cecotto Jr, YV (Dallara F306-Mugen Honda), 25m 20.791s; **5** Ho-Pin Tung, CHN (Lola B06/30-Opel), 25m 24.252s; **6** Renger van der Zande, NL (Dallara F306-Mercedes Benz), 25m 24.523s; **7** Récardo Bruins, ROK/NL (Dallara F306-Opel), 25m 46.439s; **8** Cyndie Allemann, CH (Dallara F306-Mercedes Benz), 25m 51.525s; **9** Salvatore Gatto, I (SLC R1-006-Opel), 25m 58.485s; **10** Riccardo Azzoli, I (SLC R1-006-Opel), 26m 05.783s.
Fastest race lap: Hülkenberg, 1m 33.132s, 109.406 mph/176.073 km/h.
Fastest qualifying lap: Foster, 1m 32.151s, 110.571 mph/177.947 km/h.

RECARO F3-CUP, EuroSpeedway Lausitz Eastside 100 Oval, Klettwitz, Dresden, Germany, 29/30 July. 31 and 30 laps of the 2.020-mile/3.251-km circuit.
Round 13 (62.622 miles/100.781 km).
1 Ho-Pin Tung, CHN (Lola B06/30-Opel), 24m 59.259s, 150.368 mph/241.993 km/h; **2** Cyndie Allemann, CH (Dallara F306-Mercedes Benz), 24m 59.367s; **3** Renger van der Zande, NL (Dallara F306-Mercedes Benz), 24m 59.476s; **4** Marcel Schuler, D (Dallara F304-TOM's Toyota), 24m 59.485s; **5** Rolf Biland, CH (Dallara F304-TOM's Toyota), 24m 59.711s; **6** Marko Nevalainen, FIN (Dallara F304-Opel), 25m 00.239s; **7** Martin Konrad, A (Dallara F304-Opel), 25m 02.097s; **8** Norman Knop, D (Dallara F306-Opel), 25m 03.774s; **9** Riccardo Azzoli, I (SLC R1-006-Opel), 25m 07.628s; **10** Urs Rüttimann, CH (Dallara F304-Opel), 25m 11.505s.
Fastest race lap: Leonardo Valois, SK (Dallara F304-Opel), 47.394s, 153.443 mph/246.943 km/h.
Fastest qualifying lap: Allemann, 47.330s, 153.651 mph/247.277 km/h.

Round 14 (60.602 miles/97.530 km).
1 Ferdinand Kool, NL (Lola B06/30-Opel), 25m 42.338s, 141.453 mph/227.646 km/h; **2** Harald Schegelmilch, LV (Dallara F304-Opel), 25m 42.355s; **3** Cyndie Allemann, CH (Dallara F306-Mercedes Benz), 25m 42.674s; **4** Renger van der Zande, NL (Dallara F306-Mercedes Benz), 25m 42.707s; **5** Leonardo Valois, SK (Dallara F304-Opel), 25m 42.818s; **6** Ronny Wechselberger, D (Dallara F304-Opel), 25m 42.901s; **7** Ho-Pin Tung, CHN (Lola B06/30-Opel), 25m 43.087s; **8** Nico Hülkenberg, D (Ligier JS47/06-Opel), 25m 43.424s; **9** Rolf Biland, CH (Dallara F304-TOM's Toyota), 25m 43.534s; **10** Riccardo Azzoli, I (SLC R1-006-Opel), 25m 43.730s.
Fastest race lap: Wechselberger, 47.296s, 153.761 mph/247.454 km/h.
Fastest qualifying lap: Kool, 47.105s, 154.384 mph/248.458 km/h.

RECARO F3-CUP, Nationale Circuit Assen, Netherlands, 12/13 August, 2 x 16 laps of the 2.830-mile/4.555-km circuit.
Round 15 (45.286 miles/72.880 km).
1 Harald Schegelmilch, LV (Dallara F304-Opel), 25m 41.426s, 105.764 mph/170.211 km/h; **2** Renger van der Zande, NL (Dallara F306-Mercedes Benz), 25m 51.360s; **3** Ferdinand Kool, NL (Lola B06/30-Opel), 25m 57.710s; **4** Nico Hülkenberg, D (Ligier JS47/06-Opel), 26m 00.501s; **5** Marcello Thomaz, BR (Dallara F306-Opel), 26m 04.687s; **6** Ho-Pin Tung, CHN (Lola B06/30-Opel), 26m 05.231s; **7** Natacha Gachnang, CH (Dallara F305-Opel), 26m 14.725s; **8** Nathan Antunes, AUS (Lola B06/30-Opel), 26m 17.443s; **9** Ronny Wechselberger, D (Dallara F304-Opel), 26m 24.473s; **10** Johannes Theobald, D (Dallara F304-Mercedes Benz), 26m 24.947s.
Fastest race lap: Hülkenberg, 1m 35.414s, 106.790 mph/171.862 km/h.
Fastest qualifying lap: Schlegelmilch, 1m 34.263s, 108.094 mph/ 173.960 km/h.

Round 16 (45.286 miles/72.880 km).
1 Harald Schegelmilch, LV (Dallara F304-Opel), 25m 35.116s, 106.199 mph/170.911 km/h; **2** Ferdinand Kool, NL (Lola B06/30-Opel), 25m 37.670s; **3** Nico Hülkenberg, D (Ligier JS47/06-Opel), 25m 38.529s; **4** Renger van der Zande, NL (Dallara F306-Mercedes Benz), 25m 44.881s; **5** Ho-Pin Tung, CHN (Lola B06/30-Opel), 25m 44.990s; **6** Nathan Antunes, AUS (Lola B06/30-Opel), 25m 55.751s; **7** Cyndie Allemann, CH (Dallara F306-Mercedes Benz), 26m 04.962s; **8** Johnny Cecotto Jr, YV (SLC R1-006-Opel), 26m 07.591s; **9** Johannes Theobald, D (Dallara F304-Mercedes Benz), 26m 18.780s; **10** Marcello Thomaz, BR (Dallara F306-Opel), 26m 21.688s.
Fastest race lap: Hülkenberg, 1m 35.034s, 107.217 mph/172.549 km/h.
Fastest qualifying lap: Schlegelmilch, 1m 33.719s, 108.721 mph/174.970 km/h.

RECARO F3-CUP, Salzburgring, Hof bei Salzburg, Austria, 16/17 September. 18 and 17 laps of the 2.644-mile/4.255-km circuit.
Round 17 (47.591 miles/76.590 km).
1 Nathan Antunes, AUS (Lola B06/30-Opel), 25m 39.185s, 111.310 mph/179.136 km/h; **2** Ho-Pin Tung, CHN (Lola B06/30-Opel), 25m 41.631s; **3** Renger van der Zande, NL (Dallara F306-Mercedes Benz), 25m 41.895s; **4** Riccardo Azzoli, I (SLC R1-006-Opel), 25m 43.039s; **5** Johnny Cecotto Jr, YV (SLC R1-006-Opel), 25m 49.431s; **6** Johannes Theobald, D (Dallara F304-Mercedes Benz), 25m 50.796s; **7** Nico Hülkenberg, D (Ligier JS47/06-Opel), 25m 51.152s; **8** Récardo Bruins, ROK/NL (Dallara F306-Opel), 25m 51.405s; **9** Ronny Wechselberger, D (Dallara F304-Opel), 25m 52.096s; **10** Mattia Pavoni, I (Dallara F306-Mugen Honda), 25m 54.561s.
Fastest race lap: Harald Schegelmilch, LV (Dallara F304-Opel), 1m 19.360s, 119.937 mph/193.019 km/h.
Fastest qualifying lap: Van der Zande, 1m 18.919s, 120.607 mph/194.098 km/h.

Round 18 (44.947 miles/72.335 km).
1 Ho-Pin Tung, CHN (Lola B06/30-Opel), 25m 27.969s, 105.898 mph/170.426 km/h; **2** Renger van der Zande, NL (Dallara F306-Mercedes Benz), 25m 28.281s; **3** Ferdinand Kool, NL (Lola B06/30-Opel), 25m 29.067s; **4** Harald Schegelmilch, LV (Dallara F304-Opel), 25m 29.679s; **5** Cyndie Allemann, CH (Dallara F306-Mercedes Benz), 25m 29.819s; **6** Récardo Bruins, ROK/NL (Dallara F306-Opel), 25m 29.868s; **7** Johannes Theobald, D (Dallara F304-Mercedes Benz), 25m 30.262s; **8** Ronny Wechselberger, D (Dallara F304-Opel), 25m 30.444s; **9** Riccardo Azzoli, I (SLC R1-006-Opel), 25m 30.946s; **10** Dominick Muermans, NL (Dallara F306-Opel), 25m 31.253s.
Fastest race lap: Hülkenberg, 1m 18.905s, 120.628 mph/194.132 km/h.
Fastest qualifying lap: Antunes, 1m 19.518s, 119.698 mph/192.636 km/h.

RECARO F3-CUP, Motorsport Arena Oschersleben, Germany, 30 September/1 October. 2 x 19 laps of the 2.279-mile/3.667-km circuit.
Round 19 (43.293 miles/69.673 km).
1 Ho-Pin Tung, CHN (Lola B06/30-Opel), 25m 57.556s, 100.063 mph/161.036 km/h; **2** Renger van der Zande, NL (Dallara F306-Mercedes Benz), 26m 00.585s; **3** Ferdinand Kool, NL (Lola B06/30-Opel), 26m 04.709s; **4** Harald Schegelmilch, LV (Lola B06/30-Opel), 26m 10.601s; **5** Nathan Antunes, AUS (Lola B06/30-Opel), 26m 15.769s; **6** Récardo Bruins, ROK/NL (Dallara F306-Opel), 26m 18.415s; **7** Natacha Gachnang, CH (Dallara F306-Opel), 26m 26.017s; **8** Dominick Muermans, NL (Dallara F306-Opel), 26m 30.622s; **9** Marcello Thomaz, BR (Dallara F306-Opel), 26m 31.784s; **10** Riccardo Azzoli, I (SLC R1-006-Opel), 26m 38.543s.
Fastest race lap: Tung, 1m 21.086s, 101.162 mph/162.085 km/h.
Fastest qualifying lap: Tung, 1m 19.867s, 102.706 mph/165.290 km/h.

Round 20 (43.293 miles/69.673 km).
1 Ho-Pin Tung, CHN (Lola B06/30-Opel), 25m 45.599s, 100.837 mph/162.282 km/h; **2** Récardo Bruins, ROK/NL (Dallara F306-Opel), 25m 53.236s; **3** Nathan Antunes, AUS (Lola B06/30-Opel), 26m 09.631s; **4** Harald Schegelmilch, LV (Lola B06/30-Opel), 26m 09.985s; **5** Ferdinand Kool, NL (Lola B06/30-Opel), 26m 10.612s; **6** Renger van der Zande, NL (Dallara F306-Mercedes Benz), 26m 11.713s; **7** Dominick Muermans, NL (Dallara F306-Opel), 26m 12.577s; **8** Ronny Wechselberger, D (Dallara F304-Opel), 26m 33.268s; **9** Benjamin Leuchter, D (Dallara F306-Opel), 26m 35.711s; **10** Cyndie Allemann, CH (Dallara F306-Mercedes Benz), 26m 35.935s.
Fastest race lap: Tung, 1m 20.560s, 101.823 mph/163.868 km/h.
Fastest qualifying lap: Tung, 1m 20.130s, 102.369 mph/164.747 km/h.

Final championship points
Formel 3-Cup
1 Ho-Pin Tung, CHN, 145; **2** Ferdinand Kool, NL, 99; **3** Harald Schegelmilch, LV, 91; **4** Renger van der Zande, NL, 89; **5** Nico Hülkenberg, D, 78; **6** Joey Foster, GB, 76; **7** Récardo Bruins, ROK/NL, 38; **8** Riccardo Azzoli, I, 38; **9** Cyndie Allemann, CH, 30; **10** Nathan Antunes, AUS, 25; **11** Johnny Cecotto Jr, YV, 20; **12** Marcello Thomaz, BR, 17; **13** Natacha Gachnang, CH, 11; **14** Johannes Theobald, D, 11; **15** Salvatore Gatto, I, 10; **16** Dominik Schrami, D, 8; **17** Ronny Wechselberger, D, 7; **18** Marcel Schuler, D, 5; **19** Leonardo Valois, SK, 5; **20** Rolf Biland, CH, 4; **21** Hiroyuki Matsumura, J, 3; **22** Marko Nevalainen, FIN, 3; **23** Dominick Muermans, NL, 3; **24** Martin Konrad, A, 2; **25** Norman Knop, D, 2.
Formel 3-Trophy
1 Harald Schegelmilch, LV, 152; **2** Johannes Theobald, D, 126; **3** Ronny Wechselberger, D, 118; **4** Rolf Biland, CH, 93; **5** Marcel Schuler, D, 50.
Rookie Cup
1 Harald Schlegelmilch, 117; **2** Renger van der Zande, 115; **3** Nico Hülkenberg, 90; **4** Joey Foster, 75; **5** Cyndie Allemann, 63.

Italian Formula 3 Championship

ITALIAN FORMULA 3 CHAMPIONSHIP, Autodromo Adria International Raceway, Adria, Italy, 9 April. Round 1. 2 x 23 laps of the 1.679-mile/2.702-km circuit.
Race 1 (38.616 miles/62.146 km).
1 Davide Rigon, I (Dallara F304-Opel), 29m 53.589s, 77.508 mph/124.736 km/h; **2** Michele Rugolo, I (Dallara F304-Mugen Honda), 29m 53.967s; **3** Mauro Massironi, I (Dallara F304-Opel), 29m 54.553s; **4** Alex Frassineti, I (Dallara F304-Opel), 29m 57.512s; **5** Efisio Marchese, I (Dallara F304-Opel), 29m 58.379s; **6** Federico Glorioso, I (Dallara F304-Opel), 29m 59.175s; **7** Giuseppe Terranova, I (Dallara F304-Opel), 29m 59.767s; **8** Imerio Brigliadori, I (Dallara F303-Opel), 30m 00.844s; **9** Manuele Gatto, I (Dallara F304-Mugen Honda), 30m 01.683s; **10** Jacopo Faccioni, I (Dallara F304-Opel), 30m 02.187s.
Fastest race lap: Rigoni, 1m 12.505s, 83.363 mph/134.159 km/h.
Fastest qualifying lap: Frassineti, 1m 11.885s, 84.082 mph/135.316 km/h.

Race 2 (38.616 miles/62.146 km).
1 Alex Frassineti, I (Dallara F304-Opel), 27m 54.846s, 83.003 mph/133.579 km/h; **2** Davide Rigon, I (Dallara F304-Opel), 27m 55.500s; **3** Mauro Massironi, I (Dallara F304-Opel), 28m 01.493s; **4** Fabrizio Crestani, I (Dallara F304-Opel), 28m 05.645s; **5** Giuseppe Terranova, I (Dallara F304-Opel), 28m 06.745s; **6** Efisio Marchese, I (Dallara F304-Opel), 28m 07.551s; **7** Michele Rugolo, I (Dallara F304-Mugen Honda), 28m 08.187s; **8** Imerio Brigliadori, I (Dallara F303-Opel), 28m 24.552s; **9** Manuele Gatto, I (Dallara F304-Mugen Honda), 28m 29.170s; **10** Jacopo Faccioni, I (Dallara F304-Opel), 28m 38.303s.
Fastest race lap: Massironi, 1m 12.001s, 83.946 mph/135.098 km/h.
Fastest qualifying lap: Frassineti, 1m 11.927s, 84.032 mph/135.237 km/h.

ITALIAN FORMULA 3 CHAMPIONSHIP, Autodromo Internazionale Enzo e Dino Ferrari, Imola, Italy, 7 May. Round 2. 2 x 13 laps of the 3.081-mile/4.959-km circuit.
Race 1 (39.913 miles/64.233 km).
1 Michele Rugolo, I (Dallara F304-Mugen Honda), 23m 42.102s, 101.037 mph/162.603 km/h; **2** Mauro Massironi, I (Dallara F304-Opel), 23m 42.988s; **3** Fabrizio Crestani, I (Dallara F304-Opel), 23m 45.315s; **4** Alex Frassineti, I (Dallara F304-Opel), 23m 49.436s; **5** Davide Rigon, I (Dallara F304-Opel), 23m 52.064s; **6** Efisio Marchese, I (Dallara F304-Opel), 24m 08.340s; **7** Imerio Brigliadori, I (Dallara F303-Opel), 24m 20.263s; **8** Federico Glorioso, I (Dallara F304-Opel), 24m 22.152s; **9** Manuele Gatto, I (Dallara F304-Mugen Honda), 24m 22.455s; **10** Jacopo Faccioni, I (Dallara F304-Opel), 24m 29.165s.
Fastest race lap: Crestani, 1m 48.282s, 102.445 mph/164.869 km/h.
Fastest qualifying lap: Rugolo, 1m 48.058s, 102.658 mph/165.211 km/h.

Race 2 (39.913 miles/64.233 km).
1 Michele Rugolo, I (Dallara F304-Mugen Honda), 23m 50.063s, 100.475 mph/161.698 km/h; **2** Mauro Massironi, I (Dallara F304-Opel), 23m 50.645s; **3** Alex Frassineti, I (Dallara F304-Opel), 23m 51.705s; **4** Fabrizio Crestani, I (Dallara F304-Opel), 23m 52.441s; **5** Davide Rigon, I (Dallara F304-Opel), 23m 56.564s; **6** Giuseppe Terranova, I (Dallara F304-Opel), 24m 04.995s; **7** Manuele Gatto, I (Dallara F304-Mugen Honda), 24m 07.442s; **8** Efisio Marchese, I (Dallara F304-Opel), 24m 07.697s; **9** Jacopo Faccioni, I (Dallara F304-Opel), 24m 26.727s; **10** Federico Glorioso, I (Dallara F304-Opel), 24m 27.182s.
Fastest race lap: Massironi, 1m 48.796s, 101.961 mph/164.090 km/h.
Fastest qualifying lap: Frassineti, 1m 48.222s, 102.502 mph/164.960 km/h.

ITALIAN FORMULA 3 CHAMPIONSHIP, Autodromo Mario Umberto Borzacchini, Magione, Perugia, Italy, 11 June. Round 3. 2 x 24 laps of the 1.558-mile/2.507-km circuit.
Race 1 (37.387 miles/60.168 km).
1 Mauro Massironi, I (Dallara F304-Opel), 27m 23.133s, 81.912 mph/131.824 km/h; **2** Alex Frassineti, I (Dallara F304-Opel), 27m 25.500s; **3** Giuseppe Terranova, I (Dallara F304-Opel), 27m 35.155s; **4** Michele Rugolo, I (Dallara F304-Mugen Honda), 27m 39.719s; **5** Manuele Gatto, I (Dallara F304-Mugen Honda), 27m 50.884s; **6** Fabrizio Crestani, I (Dallara F304-Opel), 27m 51.403s; **7** Federico Glorioso, I (Dallara F304-Opel), 27m 51.630s; **8** Sergio Ghiotto, I (Dallara F302-Opel), 28m 16.751s; **9** Dino Lusuardi, I (Dallara F394-FIAT), 28m 28.880s; **10** 'Gioga', I (Dallara F300-FIAT), 28m 34.608s.
Fastest race lap: Davide Rigon, I (Dallara F304-Opel), 1m 07.464s, 83.126 mph/133.778 km/h.
Fastest qualifying lap: Massironi, 1m 06.704s, 84.073 mph/135.302 km/h.

Race 2 (37.387 miles/60.168 km).
1 Davide Rigon, I (Dallara F304-Opel), 27m 17.874s, 83.126 mph/132.248 km/h; **2** Michele Rugolo, I (Dallara F304-Mugen Honda), 27m 20.848s; **3** Efisio Marchese, I (Dallara F304-Opel), 27m 25.314s; **4** Federico Glorioso, I (Dallara F304-Opel), 27m 30.156s; **5** Alex Frassineti, I (Dallara F304-Opel), 27m 31.345s; **6** Manuele Gatto, I (Dallara F304-Mugen Honda), 27m 41.923s; **7** Imerio Brigliadori, I (Dallara F303-Opel), 27m 42.794s; **8** Mauro Massironi, I (Dallara F304-Opel), 27m 46.055s; **9** Fabrizio Crestani, I (Dallara F304-Opel), 27m 49.882s; **10** Jacopo Faccioni, I (Dallara F304-Opel), 27m 55.815s.
Fastest race lap: Rigon, 1m 07.022s, 83.674 mph/134.660 km/h.
Fastest qualifying lap: Massironi, 1m 06.715s, 84.059 mph/135.279 km/h.

ITALIAN FORMULA 3 CHAMPIONSHIP, Autodromo di Vallelunga, Campagnano di Roma, Italy, 25 June. Round 4. 2 x 15 laps of the 2.538-mile/4.085-km circuit.
Race 1 (38.075 miles/61.275 km).
1 Mauro Massironi, I (Dallara F304-Opel), 23m 12.942s, 98.402 mph/158.362 km/h; **2** Fabrizio Crestani, I (Dallara F304-Opel), 23m 13.686s; **3** Michele Rugolo, I (Dallara F304-Mugen Honda), 23m 14.718s; **4** Davide Rigon, I (Dallara F304-Opel), 23m 15.703s; **5** Giuseppe Terranova, I (Dallara F304-Opel), 23m 19.004s; **6** Efisio Marchese, I (Dallara F304-Opel), 23m 21.517s; **7** Alex Frassineti, I (Dallara F304-Opel), 23m 23.574s; **8** Manuele Gatto, I (Dallara F304-Mugen Honda), 23m 24.964s; **9** Imerio Brigliadori, I (Dallara F303-Opel), 23m 35.822s; **10** Jacopo Faccioni, I (Dallara F304-Opel), 23m 44.388s.
Fastest race lap: Rugolo, 1m 31.789s, 99.553 mph/160.215 km/h.
Fastest qualifying lap: Crestani, 1m 31.172s, 100.227 mph/161.299 km/h.

Race 2 (38.075 miles/61.275 km).
1 Mauro Massironi, I (Dallara F304-Opel), 23m 26.642s, 97.444 mph/156.820 km/h; **2** Fabrizio Crestani, I (Dallara F304-Opel), 23m 27.223s; **3** Michele Rugolo, I (Dallara F304-Mugen Honda), 23m 28.500s; **4** Davide Rigon, I (Dallara F304-Opel), 23m 30.681s; **5** Manuele Gatto, I (Dallara F304-Mugen Honda), 23m 35.841s; **6** Alex Frassineti, I (Dallara F304-Opel), 23m 36.376s; **7** Efisio Marchese, I (Dallara F304-Opel), 23m 37.234s; **8** Giuseppe Terranova, I (Dallara F304-Opel), 23m 37.712s; **9** Imerio Brigliadori, I (Dallara F303-Opel), 23m 53.593s; **10** Jacopo Faccioni, I (Dallara F304-Opel), 23m 55.044s.
Fastest race lap: Frassineti, 1m 32.678s, 98.598 mph/158.678 km/h.
Fastest qualifying lap: Massironi, 1m 31.318s, 100.067 mph/161.041 km/h.

ITALIAN FORMULA 3 CHAMPIONSHIP, Autodromo Internazionale del Mugello, Scarperia, Firenze (Florence), Italy, 23 July. Round 5. 2 x 12 laps of the 3.259-mile/5.245-km circuit.
Race 1 (39.109 miles/62.940 km).
1 Mauro Massironi, I (Dallara F304-Opel), 21m 36.729s, 108.575 mph/174.735 km/h; **2** Fabrizio Crestani, I (Dallara F304-Opel), 21m 37.915s; **3** Michele Rugolo, I (Dallara F304-Mugen Honda), 21m 40.350s; **4** Manuele M. Gatto, I (Dallara F304-Mugen Honda), 21m 50.687s; **5** Alex Frassineti, I (Dallara F304-Opel), 21m 51.067s; **6** Giuseppe Terranova, I (Dallara F304-Opel), 21m 56.183s; **7** Federico Glorioso, I (Dallara F304-Opel), 21m 56.659s; **8** Imerio Brigliadori, I (Dallara F303-Opel), 21m 57.650s; **9** Efisio Marchese, I (Dallara F304-Opel), 21m 59.059s; **10** Sergio Ghiotto, I (Dallara F302-Opel), 22m 07.998s.
Fastest race lap: Rigon, 1m 46.206s, 110.471 mph/177.786 km/h.
Fastest qualifying lap: Rigon, 1m 46.167s, 110.512 mph/177.851 km/h.

Race 2 (39.109 miles/62.940 km).
1 Mauro Massironi, I (Dallara F304-Opel), 21m 35.612s, 108.669 mph/174.885 km/h; **2** Davide Rigon, I (Dallara F304-Opel), 21m 37.747s; **3** Alex Frassineti, I (Dallara F304-Opel), 21m 40.994s; **4** Michele Rugolo, I (Dallara F304-Mugen Honda), 21m 42.361s; **5** Fabrizio Crestani, I (Dallara F304-Opel), 21m 42.672s; **6** Giuseppe Terranova, I (Dallara F304-Opel), 21m 43.646s; **7** Manuele M. Gatto, I (Dallara F304-Mugen Honda), 21m 53.518s; **8** Efisio Marchese, I (Dallara F304-Opel), 21m 55.379s; **9** Jacopo Faccioni, I (Dallara F304-Opel), 22m 16.572s; **10** Vlado Arabadzhiev, RUS (Dallara F304-Opel), 22m 21.492s.
Fastest race lap: Terranova, 1m 46.526s, 110.140 mph/177.252 km/h.
Fastest qualifying lap: Massironi, 1m 46.202s, 110.476 mph/177.793 km/h.

ITALIAN FORMULA 3 CHAMPIONSHIP, Autodromo Riccardo Paletti, Varano dei Melegari, Parma, Italy, 3 September. Round 6. 2 x 26 laps of the 1.476-mile/2.375-km circuit.
Race 1 (38.370 miles/61.750 km).
1 Mauro Massironi, I (Dallara F304-Opel), 28m 09.914s, 81.738 mph/131.545 km/h; **2** Alex Frassineti, I (Dallara F304-Opel), 28m 11.121s; **3** Davide Rigon, I (Dallara F304-Opel), 28m 16.468s; **4** Efisio Marchese, I (Dallara F304-Opel), 28m 17.225s; **5** Imerio Brigliadori, I (Dallara F303-Opel), 28m 34.649s; **6** Federico Glorioso, I (Dallara F304-Opel), 28m 43.611s; **7** Jacopo Faccioni, I (Dallara F304-Opel), 28m 51.711s; **8** Fabrizio Crestani, I (Dallara F304-Opel), 28m 53.696s; **9** Sergio Ghiotto, I (Dallara F302-Opel), 29m 06.097s; **10** Vlado Arabadzhiev, RUS (Dallara F304-Opel), 25 laps.
Fastest race lap: Massironi, 1m 03.479s, 83.693 mph/134.690 km/h.
Fastest qualifying lap: Massironi, 1m 02.596s, 84873 mph/136.590 km/h.

Race 2 (38.370 miles/61.750 km).
1 Mauro Massironi, I (Dallara F304-Opel), 28m 03.252s, 82.062 mph/132.065 km/h; **2** Alex Frassineti, I (Dallara F304-Opel), 28m 03.787s; **3** Davide Rigon, I (Dallara F304-Opel), 28m 13.759s; **4** Fabrizio Crestani, I (Dallara F304-Opel), 28m 14.568s; **5** Giuseppe Terranova, I (Dallara F304-Opel), 28m 29.965s; **6** Imerio Brigliadori, I (Dallara F303-Opel), 28m 40.867s; **7** Manuele M. Gatto, I (Dallara F304-Mugen Honda), 28m 47.204s; **8** Jacopo Faccioni, I (Dallara F304-Opel), 28m 53.368s; **9** Vlado Arabadzhiev, RUS (Dallara F304-Opel), 25 laps; **10** Sergio Ghiotto, I (Dallara F302-Opel), 25.
Fastest race lap: Massironi, 1m 03.948s, 83.079 mph/133.702 km/h.
Fastest qualifying lap: Massironi, 1m 02.671s, 84.772 mph/136.426 km/h.

ITALIAN FORMULA 3 CHAMPIONSHIP, Autodromo di Vallelunga, Campagnano di Roma, Italy, 1 October. Round 7. 2 x 15 laps of the-mile/4.085-km circuit.
Race 1 (38.075 miles/61.275 km).
1 Mauro Massironi, I (Dallara F304-Opel), 23m 09.049s, 98.678 mph/158.806 km/h; **2** Davide Rigon, I (Dallara F304-Opel), 23m 09.473s; **3** Efisio Marchese, I (Dallara F304-Opel), 23m 18.567s; **4** Alex Frassineti, I (Dallara F304-Opel), 23m 20.076s; **5** Michele Rugolo, I (Dallara F304-Mugen Honda), 23m 21.953s; **6** Fabrizio Crestani, I (Dallara F304-Opel), 23m 23.516s; **7** Vlado Arabadzhiev, RUS (Dallara F304-Opel), 23m 39.598s; **8** Federico Glorioso, I (Dallara F304-Opel), 23m 41.432s; **9** Imerio Brigliadori, I (Dallara F303-Opel), 23m 42.356s; **10** Jacopo Faccioni, I (Dallara F304-Opel), 23m 54.209s.
Fastest race lap: Rigon, 1m 31.810s, 99.530 mph/160.178 km/h.
Fastest qualifying lap: Massironi, 1m 31.438s, 99.935 mph/160.830 km/h.

Race 2 (38.075 miles/61.275 km).
1 Mauro Massironi, I (Dallara F304-Opel), 23m 14.066s, 98.323 mph/158.234 km/h; **2** Davide Rigon, I (Dallara F304-Opel), 23m 14.497s; **3** Efisio Marchese, I (Dallara F304-Opel), 23m 15.822s; **4** Giuseppe Terranova, I (Dallara F304-Opel), 23m 18302s; **5** Alex Frassineti, I (Dallara F304-Opel), 23m 19.443s; **6** Fabrizio Crestani, I (Dallara F304-Opel), 23m 27.174s; **7** Federico Glorioso, I (Dallara F304-Opel), 23m 48.406s; **8** Imerio Brigliadori, I (Dallara F303-Opel), 23m 50.715s; **9** Vlado Arabadzhiev, RUS (Dallara F304-Opel), 23m 54.044s; **10** Paolo Bossini, I (Dallara F304-Opel), 24m 03.440s.
Fastest race lap: Rigon, 1m 32.092s, 99.226 mph/159.688 km/h.
Fastest qualifying lap: Massironi, 1m 31.529s, 99.836 mph/160.670 km/h.

ITALIAN FORMULA 3 CHAMPIONSHIP, Autodromo Internazionale di Misano, Misano Adriatico, Rimini, Italy, 22 October. Round 8. 2 x 16 laps of the 2.523-mile/4.060-km circuit.
Race 1 (40.364 miles/64.960 km).
1 Davide Rigon, I (Dallara F304-Opel), 29m 19.732s, 82.576 mph/132.893 km/h; **2** Alex Frassineti, I (Dallara F304-Opel), 29m 23.253s; **3** Efisio Marchese, I (Dallara F304-Opel), 29m 31.209s; **4** Giuseppe Terranova, I (Dallara F304-Opel), 29m 57.520s; **5** Fabrizio Crestani, I (Dallara F304-Opel), 30m 23.483s; **6** Jacopo Faccioni, I (Dallara F304-Opel), 30m 30.204s; **7** Mauro Massironi, I (Dallara F304-Opel), 30m 31.117s; **8** Manuele M. Gatto, I (Dallara F303-Opel), 30m 38.349s; **9** Imerio Brigliadori, I (Dallara F303-Opel), 15 laps; **10** Federico Glorioso, I (Dallara F304-Opel), 15.
Fastest race lap: Crestani, 1m 35.511s, 95.088 mph/153.029 km/h.
Fastest qualifying lap: Rigon, 1m 45.799s, 85.842 mph/138.148 km/h.

Race 2 (40.364 miles/64.960 km).
1 Davide Rigon, I (Dallara F304-Opel), 23m 38.274s, 102.456 mph/164.888 km/h; **2** Fabrizio Crestani, I (Dallara F304-Opel), 23m 38.688s; **3** Michele Rugolo, I (Dallara F304-Mugen Honda), 23m 41.170s; **4** Mauro Massironi, I (Dallara F304-Opel), 23m 41.255s; **5** Efisio Marchese, I (Dallara F304-Opel), 23m 41.773s; **6** Manuele M. Gatto, I (Dallara F303-Opel), 23m 42.966s; **7** Alex Frassineti, I (Dallara F303-Opel), 23m 52.217s; **8** Imerio Brigliadori, I (Dallara F303-Opel), 23m 58.139s; **9** Federico Glorioso, I (Dallara F304-Opel), 24m 30.262s; **10** Vlado Arabadzhiev, RUS (Dallara F304-Opel), 24m 44.975s.
Fastest race lap: Frassineti, 1m 27.329s, 103.997 mph/167.367 km/h.
Fastest qualifying lap: Terranova, 1m 46.099s, 85.599 mph/137.758 km/h.

Final championship points
1 Mauro Massironi, I, 139; **2** Davide Rigon, I, 111; **3** Alex Frassineti, I, 93; **4** Michele Rugolo, I, 78; **5** Fabrizio Crestani, I, 76; **6** Efisio Marchese, I, 51; **7** Giuseppe Terranova, I, 42; **8** Manuele M. Gatto, I, 31; **9** Federico Glorioso, I, 22; **10** Jacopo Faccioni, I, 8; **11** Vlado Arabadzhiev, RUS, 5.

All-Japan Formula 3 Championship

ALL-JAPAN FORMULA 3 CHAMPIONSHIP, Fuji International Speedway, Sunto-gun, Shizuoka Prefecture, Japan, 1/2 April. 15 and 16 laps of the 2.835-mile/4.563-km circuit.
Round 1 (42.530 miles/68.445 km).
1 Adrian Sutil, D (Dallara F305-Toyota), 24m 08.852s, 105.675 mph/170.067 km/h; **2** Koudai Tsukakoshi, J (Dome F107-Mugen Honda), 24m 13.964s; **3** Kazuya Oshima, J (Dallara F305-Toyota), 24m 16.766s; **4** Roberto Streit, BR (Dallara F306-Nissan), 24m 20.217s; **5** Marko Asmer, EE (Dallara F306-Nissan), 24m 37.718s; **6** Jonny Reid, NZ (Dallara F306-Toyota), 24m 37.972s; **7** Hideto Yasuoka, J (Dallara F305-Toyota), 24m 39.767s; **8** Takuya Izawa, J (Dome F107-Mugen Honda), 24m 40.685s; **9** Kouki Saga, J (Dallara F306-Toyota), 24m 45.857s; **10** Daisuke Ikeda, J (Dallara F305-Toyota), 24m 46.436s.
Fastest race lap: Oshima, 1m 36.054s, 106.265 mph/171.016 km/h.
Fastest qualifying lap: Oshima, 1m 35.870s, 106.469 mph/171.344 km/h.

Round 2 (45.365 miles/73.008 km).
1 Kazuya Oshima, J (Dallara F305-Toyota), 35m 08.369s, 77.460 mph/124.659 km/h; **2** Jonny Reid, NZ (Dallara F306-Toyota), 35m 34.026s; **3** Fabio Carbone, BR (Dallara F305-Nissan), 35m 39.172s; **4** Adrian Sutil, D (Dallara F305-Toyota), 35m 44.801s; **5** Koudai Tsukakoshi, J (Dome F107-Mugen Honda), 35m 50.857s; **6** Daisuke Ikeda, J (Dallara F305-Toyota), 35m 52.669s; **7** Satoru Okada, J (Dallara F305-Toyota), 36m 15.510s; **8** Marko Asmer, EE (Dallara F306-Nissan), 36m 29.089s; **9** Motohiko Isozaki, J (Dallara F305-Toyota), 36m 34.578s; **10** Takuya Izawa, J (Dome F107-Mugen Honda), 10 laps (DNF).
Fastest race lap: Oshima, 1m 48.814s, 93.804 mph/150.962 km/h.
Fastest qualifying lap: Oshima, 1m 35.766s, 106.584 mph/171.530 km/h.

ALL-JAPAN FORMULA 3 CHAMPIONSHIP, Suzuka International Racing Course, Suzuka-shi, Mie Prefecture, Japan, 15/16 April. 12 and 17 laps of the 3.608-mile/5.807-km circuit.
Round 3 (43.300 miles/69.684 km).
1 Roberto Streit, BR (Dallara F306-Toyota), 23m 50.429s, 108.973 mph/175.375 km/h; **2** Kazuya Oshima, J (Dallara F305-Toyota), 23m 54.407s; **3** Fabio Carbone, BR (Dallara F306-Nissan), 23m 57.605s; **4** Takuya Izawa, J (Dome F107-Mugen Honda), 23m 57.605s; **5** Adrian Sutil, D (Dallara F305-Toyota), 24m 06.551s; **6** Jonny Reid, NZ (Dallara F306-Toyota), 24m 07.784s; **7** Marko Asmer, EE (Dallara F306-Nissan), 24m 10.920s; **8** Hiroaki Ishiura, J (Dallara F305-Toyota), 24m 11.869s; **9** Daisuke Ikeda, J (Dallara F305-Toyota), 24m 14.323s; **10** Satoru Okada, J (Dallara F305-Toyota), 24m 32.202s.
Fastest race lap: Streit, 1m 56.738s, 111.274 mph/179.077 km/h.
Fastest qualifying lap: Streit, 2m 09.361s, 100.416 mph/161.603 km/h.

Round 4 (61.341 miles/98.719 km).
1 Takuya Izawa, J (Dome F107-Mugen Honda), 33m 19.346s, 110.450 mph/177.752 km/h; **2** Fabio Carbone, BR (Dallara F305-Nissan), 33m 21.895s; **3** Adrian Sutil, D (Dallara F305-Toyota), 33m 22.500s; **4** Marko Asmer, EE (Dallara F306-Nissan), 33m 29.139s; **5** Roberto Streit, BR (Dallara F306-Toyota), 33m 30.943s; **6** Kazuya Oshima, J (Dallara F305-Toyota), 33m 31.019s; **7** Hiroaki Ishiura, J (Dallara F305-Toyota), 33m 32.158s; **8** Hideto Yasuoka, J (Dallara F305-Toyota), 33m 35.168s; **9** Koudai Tsukakoshi, J (Dome F107-Mugen Honda), 33m 39.484s; **10** Jonny Reid, NZ (Dallara F306-Toyota), 33m 48.183s.
Fastest race lap: Tsukakoshi, 1m 56.180s, 111.808 mph/179.938 km/h.
Fastest qualifying lap: Carbone, 2m 07.285s, 102.054 mph/164.239 km/h.

ALL-JAPAN FORMULA 3 CHAMPIONSHIP, Twin Ring Motegi, Motegi-machi, Haga-gun, Tochigi Prefecture, Japan, 27/28 May. 14 and 20 laps of the 2.983-mile/4.801-km circuit.
Round 5 (41.765 miles/67.214 km).
1 Roberto Streit, BR (Dallara F306-Toyota), 28m 25.547s, 88.156 mph/141.872 km/h; **2** Jonny Reid, NZ (Dallara F306-Toyota), 28m 34.017s; **3** Adrian Sutil, D (Dallara F305-Toyota), 28m 49.463s; **4** Marko Asmer, EE (Dallara F306-Nissan), 28m 55.403s; **5** Kazuya Oshima, J (Dallara F305-Toyota), 28m 56.734s; **6** Daisuke Ikeda, J (Dallara F305-Toyota), 29m 00.843s; **7** Koudai Tsukakoshi, J (Dome F107-Mugen Honda), 29m 02.281s; **8** Hideto Yasuoka, J (Dallara F305-Toyota), 29m 10.183s; **9** Kouki Saga, J (Dallara F306-Toyota), 29m 16.067s; **10** Hiroaki Ishiura, J (Dallara F305-Toyota), 29m 33.322s.
Fastest race lap: Streit, 2m 00.163s, 89.375 mph/143.834 km/h.
Fastest qualifying lap: Tsukakoshi, 1m 46.006s, 101.311 mph/163.043 km/h.

Round 6 (59.664 miles/96.020 km).
1 Adrian Sutil, D (Dallara F305-Toyota), 40m 16.484s, 88.886 mph/143.047 km/h; **2** Fabio Carbone, BR (Dallara F305-Nissan), 40m 29.728s; **3** Koudai Tsukakoshi, J (Dome F107-Mugen Honda), 40m 35.337s; **4** Roberto Streit, BR (Dallara F306-Toyota), 40m 43.028s; **5** Takuya Izawa, J (Dome F107-Mugen Honda), 41m 00.430s; **6** Kazuya Oshima, J (Dallara F305-Toyota), 41m 04.799s; **7** Marko Asmer, EE (Dallara F306-Nissan), 41m 05.423s; **8** Hiroaki Ishiura, J (Dallara F305-Toyota), 41m 07.838s; **9** Hideto Yasuoka, J (Dallara F305-Toyota), 41m 13.444s; **10** Kouki Saga, J (Dallara F306-Toyota), 41m 27.899s.
Fastest race lap: Sutil, 1m 59.512s, 89.862 mph/144.618 km/h.
Fastest qualifying lap: Sutil, 1m 45.880s, 101.431 mph/163.237 km/h.

ALL-JAPAN FORMULA 3 CHAMPIONSHIP, Okayama International Circuit (TI Circuit Aida), Aida Gun, Okayama Prefecture, Japan, 17/18 June. 18 and 25 laps of the 2.301-mile/3.703-km circuit.
Round 7 (41.417 miles/66.654 km).
1 Adrian Sutil, D (Dallara F305-Toyota), 28m 59.910s, 85.695 mph/137.911 km/h; **2** Koudai Tsukakoshi, J (Dome F107-Mugen Honda), 29m 31.621s; **3** Takuya Izawa, J (Dome F107-Mugen Honda), 29m 38.575s; **4** Fabio Carbone, BR (Dallara F305-Nissan), 29m 41.436s; **5** Hiroaki Ishiura, J (Dallara F305-Toyota), 29m 42.223s; **6** Marko Asmer, EE (Dallara F306-Nissan), 29m 42.908s; **7** Daisuke Ikeda, J (Dallara F305-Toyota), 29m 54.572s; **8** Kazuya Oshima, J (Dallara F305-Toyota), 29m 54.931s; **9** Kouki Saga, J (Dallara F306-Toyota), 30m 03.101s; **10** Jonny Reid, NZ (Dallara F306-Toyota), 30m 03.357s.
Fastest race lap: Sutil, 1m 35.621s, 86.627 mph/139.412 km/h.
Fastest qualifying lap: Tsukakoshi, 1m 25.685s, 96.672 mph/155.579 km/h.

Round 8 (57.523 miles/92.575 km).
1 Adrian Sutil, D (Dallara F305-Toyota), 36m 54.164s, 93.527 mph/150.517 km/h; **2** Marko Asmer, EE (Dallara F306-Nissan), 37m 00.065s; **3** Fabio Carbone, BR (Dallara F305-Nissan), 37m 06.914s; **4** Koudai Tsukakoshi, J (Dome F107-Mugen Honda), 37m 07.557s; **5** Takuya Izawa, J (Dome F107-Mugen Honda), 37m 09.471s; **6** Daisuke Ikeda, J (Dallara F305-Toyota), 37m 27.885s; **7** Hiroaki Ishiura, J (Dallara F305-Toyota), 37m 28.765s; **8** Roberto Streit, BR (Dallara F306-Toyota), 37m 30.371s; **9** Satoru Okada, J (Dallara F305-Toyota), 37m 35.066s; **10** Kouki Saga, J (Dallara F306-Toyota), 37m 53.739s.
Fastest race lap: Sutil, 1m 27.903s, 94.233 mph/151.653 km/h.
Fastest qualifying lap: Sutil, 1m 25.627s, 96.738 mph/155.684 km/h.

ALL-JAPAN FORMULA 3 CHAMPIONSHIP, Suzuka International Racing Course, Suzuka City, Mie Prefecture, Japan, 8/9 July. 12 and 17 laps of the 3.608-mile/5.807-km circuit.
Round 9 (43.330 miles/69.684 km).
1 Koudai Tsukakoshi, J (Dome F107-Mugen Honda), 23m 48.965s, 109.085 mph/175.555 km/h; **2** Takuya Izawa, J (Dome F107-Mugen Honda), 23m 57.855s; **3** Adrian Sutil, D (Dallara F305-Toyota), 24m 00.892s; **4** Roberto Streit, BR(Dallara F306-Toyota), 24m 03.093s; **5** Hiroaki Ishiura, J (Dallara F305-Toyota), 24m 04.179s; **6** Fabio Carbone, BR (Dallara F305-Nissan), 24m 05.462s; **7** Jonny Reid, NZ (Dallara F306-Toyota), 24m 11.462s; **8** Hideto Yasuoka, J (Dallara F305-Toyota), 24m 12.396s; **9** Wataru Kobayakawa, J (Dallara F305-Toyota), 24m 20.214s; **10** Motohiko Isozaki, J (Dallara F305-Toyota), 24m 22.391s.
Fastest race lap: Tsukakoshi, 1m 58.562s, 109.562 mph/176.322 km/h.

Fastest qualifying lap: Tsukakoshi, 1m 58.197s, 109.900 mph/176.867 km/h.

Round 10 (61.341 miles/98.719 km).
1 Takuya Izawa, J (Dome F107-Mugen Honda), 34m 27.674s, 106.800 mph/171.878 km/h; **2** Koudai Tsukakoshi, J (Dome F107-Mugen Honda), 34m 30.820s; **3** Adrian Sutil, D (Dallara F305-Toyota), 34m 31.935s; **4** Kazuya Oshima, J (Dallara F305-Toyota), 34m 32.521s; **5** Marko Asmer, EE (Dallara F305-Nissan), 34m 32.799s; **6** Fabio Carbone, BR (Dallara F305-Nissan), 34m 34.666s; **7** Roberto Streit, BR (Dallara F306-Toyota), 34m 35.276s; **8** Daisuke Ikeda, J (Dallara F305-Toyota), 34m 43.707s; **9** Kouki Saga, J (Dallara F306-Toyota), 34m 52.447s; **10** Motohiko Isozaki, J (Dallara F305-Toyota), 35m 06.144s.
Fastest race lap: Tsukakoshi, 1m 58.208s, 109.890 mph/176.850 km/h.
Fastest qualifying lap: Tsukakoshi, 1m 57.424s, 110.624 mph/178.031 km/h.

ALL-JAPAN FORMULA 3 CHAMPIONSHIP, Autopolis International Racing Course, Kamit-sue-mura, Hita-gun, Oita Prefecture, Japan, 5/6 August. 14 and 20 laps of the 2.904-mile/4.674-km circuit.
Round 11 (40.660 miles/65.436 km).
1 Kazuya Oshima, J (Dallara F305-Toyota), 24m 18.943s, 100.330 mph/161.465 km/h; **2** Roberto Streit, BR (Dallara F306-Toyota), 24m 21.830s; **3** Takuya Izawa, J (Dome F107-Mugen Honda), 24m 31.773s; **4** Fabio Carbone, BR (Dallara F305-Nissan), 24m 33.445s; **5** Jonny Reid, NZ (Dallara F306-Toyota), 24m 37.494s; **6** Adrian Sutil, D (Dallara F305-Toyota), 24m 38.266s; **7** Koudai Tsukakoshi, J (Dome F107-Mugen Honda), 24m 39.194s; **8** Marko Asmer, EE (Dallara F305-Nissan), 24m 40.304s; **9** Daisuke Ikeda, J (Dallara F305-Toyota), 24m 45.733s; **10** Hiroaki Ishiura, J (Dallara F305-Toyota), 24m 46.718s.
Fastest race lap: Oshima, 1m 43.827s, 100.701 mph/162.061 km/h.
Fastest qualifying lap: Oshima, 1m 42.356s, 102.148 mph/164.390 km/h.

Round 12 (58.086 miles/93.480 km).
1 Roberto Streit, BR (Dallara F306-Toyota), 35m 10.230s, 99.093 mph/159.474 km/h; **2** Kazuya Oshima, J (Dallara F305-Toyota), 35m 17.149s; **3** Adrian Sutil, D (Dallara F305-Toyota), 35m 20.478s; **4** Koudai Tsukakoshi, J (Dome F107-Mugen Honda), 35m 25.059s; **5** Jonny Reid, NZ (Dallara F306-Toyota), 35m 31.094s; **6** Marko Asmer, EE (Dallara F305-Nissan), 35m 32.023s; **7** Takuya Izawa, J (Dome F107-Mugen Honda), 35m 42.473s; **8** Hiroaki Ishiura, J (Dallara F305-Toyota), 35m 43.302s; **9** Kouki Saga, J (Dallara F306-Toyota), 35m 53.372s; **10** Daisuke Ikeda, J (Dallara F305-Toyota), 35m 53.896s.
Fastest race lap: Oshima, 1m 44.883s, 99.687 mph/160.430 km/h.
Fastest qualifying lap: Oshima, 1m 43.257s, 101.256 mph/162.956 km/h.

ALL-JAPAN FORMULA 3 CHAMPIONSHIP, Fuji International Speedway, Sunto-gun, Shizuoka Prefecture, Japan, 26/27 August. 15 and 21 laps of the 2.835-mile/4.563-km circuit.
Round 13 (42.530 miles/68.445 km).
1 Kazuya Oshima, J (Dallara F305-Toyota), 24m 33.668s, 103.895 mph/167.203 km/h; **2** Marko Asmer, EE (Dallara F305-Nissan), 24m 43.264s; **3** Fabio Carbone, BR (Dallara F305-Nissan), 24m 49.594s; **4** Roberto Streit, BR (Dallara F306-Toyota), 24m 50.740s; **5** Jonny Reid, NZ (Dallara F306-Toyota), 24m 52.598s; **6** Takuya Izawa, J (Dome F107-Mugen Honda), 24m 57.893s; **7** Hiroaki Ishiura, J (Dallara F305-Toyota), 24m 58.646s; **8** Kouki Saga, J (Dallara F306-Toyota), 25m 00.756s; **9** Daisuke Ikeda, J (Dallara F305-Toyota), 25m 03.164s; **10** Hiroyuki Matsumura, J (Dallara F305-Toyota), 25m 14.288s.
Fastest race lap: Oshima, 1m 37.869s, 104.294 mph/167.844 km/h.
Fastest qualifying lap: Kodai Tsukakoshi, J (Dome F107-Mugen Honda), 1m 38.545s, 103.578 mph/166.693 km/h.

Round 14 (59.542 miles/95.823 km).
1 Adrian Sutil, D (Dallara F305-Toyota), 37m 19.500s, 95.713 mph/154.035 km/h; **2** Kazuya Oshima, J (Dallara F305-Toyota), 37m 21.991s; **3** Roberto Streit, BR (Dallara F306-Toyota), 37m 23.801s; **4** Takuya Izawa, J (Dome F107-Mugen Honda), 37m 36.281s; **5** Marko Asmer, EE (Dallara F305-Nissan), 37m 36.905s; **6** Fabio Carbone, BR (Dallara F305-Nissan), 37m 39.884s; **7** Jonny Reid, NZ (Dallara F306-Toyota), 37m 40.326s; **8** Hiroaki Ishiura, J (Dallara F305-Toyota), 37m 45.253s; **9** Daisuke Ikeda, J (Dallara F305-Toyota), 37m 48.192s; **10** Kouki Saga, J (Dallara F306-Toyota), 37m 56.657s.
Fastest race lap: Streit, 1m 45.585s, 96.672 mph/155.578 km/h.
Fastest qualifying lap: Oshima, 1m 38.155s, 103.990 mph/167.355 km/h.

ALL-JAPAN FORMULA 3 CHAMPIONSHIP, Sportsland-SUGO International Course, Shibata-gun, Miyagi Prefecture, Japan, 16/17 September. 18 and 25 laps of the 2.302-mile/3.704-km circuit.
Round 15 (41.428 miles/66.672 km).
1 Fabio Carbone, BR (Dallara F305-Nissan), 23m 16.058s, 106.830 mph/171.926 km/h; **2** Kazuya Oshima, J (Dallara F305-Toyota), 23m 18.591s; **3** Adrian Sutil, D (Dallara F305-Toyota), 23m 22.645s; **4** Roberto Streit, BR (Dallara F306-Toyota), 23m 27.629s; **5** Koudai Tsukakoshi, J (Dome F107-Mugen Honda), 23m 29.663s; **6** Takuya Izawa, J (Dome F107-Mugen Honda), 23m 35.624s; **7** Daisuke Ikeda, J (Dallara F305-Toyota), 23m 41.884s; **8** Marko Asmer, EE (Dallara F305-Nissan), 23m 43.006s; **9** Jonny Reid, NZ (Dallara F306-Toyota), 23m 46.425s; **10** Kouki Saga, J (Dallara F306-Toyota), 23m 48.295s.
Fastest race lap: Sutil, 1m 16.594s, 108.176 mph/174.091 km/h.
Fastest qualifying lap: Carbone, 1m 16.687s, 108.045 mph/173.880 km/h.

Round 16 (57.539 miles/92.600 km).
1 Fabio Carbone, BR (Dallara F305-Nissan), 42m 48.812s, 80.637 mph/129.772 km/h; **2** Adrian Sutil, D (Dallara F305-Toyota), 42m 53.706s; **3** Roberto Streit, BR (Dallara F306-Toyota), 43m 00.856s; **4** Kazuya Oshima, J (Dallara F305-Toyota), 43m 03.375s; **5** Koudai Tsukakoshi, J (Dome F107-Mugen Honda), 43m 05.067s; **6** Marko Asmer, EE (Dallara F305-Nissan), 43m 11.052s; **7** Takuya Izawa, J (Dome F107-Mugen Honda), 43m 35.741s; **8** Kouki Saga, J (Dallara F306-Toyota), 43m 36.175s; **9** Daisuke Ikeda, J (Dallara F305-Toyota), 43m 39.492s; **10** Hiroyuki Matsumura, J (Dallara F305-Toyota), 43m 39.668s.
Fastest race lap: Sutil, 1m 26.971s, 95.269 mph/153.320 km/h.
Fastest qualifying lap: Carbone, 1m 16.257s, 108.654 mph/174.861 km/h.

ALL-JAPAN FORMULA 3 CHAMPIONSHIP, Twin Ring Motegi, Motegi-machi, Haga-gun, Tochigi Prefecture, Japan, 21/22 October. 14 and 20 laps of the 2.983-mile/4.801-km circuit.
Round 17 (41.765 miles/67.214 km).
1 Hiroaki Ishiura, J (Dallara F305-Toyota), 25m 13.677s, 99.330 mph/159.856 km/h; **2** Koudai Tsukakoshi, J (Dome F107-Mugen Honda), 25m 15.195s; **3** Takuya Izawa, J (Dome F107-Mugen Honda), 25m 17.022s; **4** Fabio Carbone, BR (Dallara F305-Nissan), 25m 20.314s; **5** Roberto Streit, BR (Dallara F306-Toyota), 25m 22.365s; **6** Daisuke Ikeda, J (Dallara F305-Toyota), 25m 29.360s; **7** Kouki Saga, J (Dallara F306-Toyota), 25m 30.474s; **8** Satoru Okada, J (Dallara F305-Toyota), 25m 34.932s; **9** Hiroyuki Matsumura, J (Dallara F305-Toyota), 25m 37.223s; **10** Motohiko Isozaki, J (Dallara F305-Toyota), 25m 40.896s.
Fastest race lap: Streit, 1m 47.238s, 100.147 mph/161.170 km/h.
Fastest qualifying lap: Ishiura, 1m 46.421s, 100.916 mph/162.407 km/h.

Round 18 (59.664 miles/96.020 km).
1 Marko Asmer, EE (Dallara F305-Nissan), 36m 02.297s, 99.334 mph/159.863 km/h; **2** Kouki Saga, J (Dallara F306-Toyota), 36m 25.875s; **3** Roberto Streit, BR (Dallara F306-Toyota), 36m 26.036s; **4** Jonny Reid, NZ (Dallara F306-Toyota), 36m 27.727s; **5** Takuya Izawa, J (Dome F107-Mugen Honda), 36m 28.235s; **6** Hiroaki Ishiura, J (Dallara F305-Toyota), 36m 29.087s; **7** Daisuke Ikeda, J (Dallara F305-Toyota), 36m 34.500s; **8** Satoru Okada, J (Dallara F305-Toyota), 36m 42.885s; **9** Motohiko Isozaki, J (Dallara F305-Toyota), 36m 51.841s; **10** Hiroyuki Matsumura, J (Dallara F305-Toyota), 37m 03.137s.
Fastest race lap: Asmer, 1m 47.482s, 99.919 mph/160.804 km/h.
Fastest qualifying lap: Adrian Sutil, D (Dallara F305-Toyota), 1m 45.736s, 101.569 mph/163.459 km/h.

Final championship points (best 14 scores).
1 Adrian Sutil, D, 212; **2** Kazuya Oshima, J, 185; **3** Roberto Streit, BR, 182; **4** Fabio Carbone, BR, 169; **5** Koudai Tsukakoshi, J, 153; **6** Takuya Izawa, J, 151; **7** Marko Asmer, EE, 124; **8** Jonny Reid, NZ, 88; **9** Hiroaki Ishiura, J, 69; **10** Daisuke Ikeda, J, 50; **11** Kouki Saga, J, 39; **12** Hideto Yasuoka, J, 15; **13** Satoru Okada, J, 13; **14** Motohiko Isozaki, J, 7; **15** Hiroyuki Matsumura, J, 5; **16** Wataru Kobayakawa, J, 2.

Major Non-Championship Formula 3 2005

The following races were run after AUTOCOURSE 2005–2006 went to press.

FIA F3 WORLD CUP, 52nd MACAU GP, Circuito Da Guia, Macau, 20 November. 10 and 15 laps of the 3.803-mile/6.120-km circuit.
Qualification race (38.028 miles/61.200 km).
1 Loïc Duval, F (Dallara F305-Mercedes Benz), 22m 19.317s, 102.217 mph/164.502 km/h; **2** Robert Kubica, PL (Dallara F305-Mugen Honda), 22m 20.894s; **3** Lucas di Grassi, BR (Dallara F305-Mercedes Benz), 22m 26.708s; **4** Mike Conway, GB (Dallara F305-Mercedes Benz), 22m 27.497s; **5** Paolo Montin, I (Dallara F305-Mugen Honda), 22m 33.685s; **6** Joao de Oliveira, BR (Dallara F305-TOM's Toyota), 22m 34.358s; **7** Kazuki Nakajima, J (Dallara F305-TOM's Toyota), 22m 40.863s; **8** Sebastien Vettel, D (Dallara F305-Mercedes Benz), 22m 41.478s; **9** Charlie Kimball, GB (Dallara F305-Mugen Honda), 22m 47.021s; **10** Danny Watts, GB (Dallara F305-TOM's Toyota), 22m 48.092s.
Fastest race lap: Kubica, 2m 12.003s, 103.710 mph/166.905 km/h.
Fastest qualifying lap: Duval, 2m 11.348s, 104.227 mph/167.738 km/h.

Feature race (57.042 miles/91.800 km).
1 Lucas di Grassi, BR (Dallara F305-Mercedes Benz), 40m 49.730s, 83.826 mph/134.905 km/h; **2** Robert Kubica, PL (Dallara F305-Mugen Honda), 40m 50.389s; **3** Sebastien Vettel, D (Dallara F305-Mercedes Benz), 40m 53.654s; **4** Joao de Oliveira, BR (Dallara F305-TOM's Toyota), 40m 56.733s; **5** Kazuki Nakajima, J (Dallara F305-TOM's Toyota), 40m 58.349s; **6** Loïc Duval, F (Dallara F305-Mercedes Benz), 40m 58.435s; **7** Christian Bakkerud, DK (Dallara F305-Mugen Honda), 41m 00.915s; **8** Paolo Montin, I (Dallara F305-Mugen Honda), 41m 02.220s; **9** Romain Grosjean, CH (Dallara F305-Mugen Honda), 41m 02.737s; **10** Franck Perera, F (Dallara F305-Opel), 41m 03.020s.
Fastest race lap: Duval, 2m 11.929s, 103.768 mph/166.999 km/h.
Pole position: Duval.

2006

16th BP ULTIMATE MASTERS OF FORMULA 3, Circuit Park Zandvoort, Netherlands, 6 August. 25 laps of the 2.677-mile/4.30748-km circuit, 66.914 miles/107.687 km.
1 Paul di Resta, GB (Dallara F306-Mercedes Benz), 39m 47.771s, 100.884 mph/162.358 km/h; **2** Giedo van der Garde, NL (Dallara F306-Mercedes Benz), 39m 48.247s; **3** Sébastien Buemi, CH (Dallara F306-Mercedes Benz), 39m 52.338s; **4** Kohei Hirate, J (Dallara F306-Mercedes Benz), 39m 58.702s; **5** Romain Grosjean, F (Dallara F306-Mercedes Benz), 39m 59.629s; **6** Sebastien Vettel, D (Dallara F306-Mercedes Benz), 40m 00.152s; **7** Bruno Senna, BR (Dallara F306-Mercedes Benz), 40m 01.158s; **8** Oliver Jarvis, GB (Dallara F306-Mugen Honda), 40m 01.585s; **9** Charlie Kimball, USA (Dallara F306-Mercedes Benz), 40m 04.550s; **10** Jonathan Summerton, USA (Dallara F306-Mercedes Benz), 40m 05.256s.
Fastest race lap: Van der Garde, 1m 34.558s, 101.901 mph/163.994 km/h.
Fastest qualifying lap: Van der Garde, 1m 32.920s, 103.697 mph/166.885 km/h.

Results of the Macau races will be given in AUTOCOURSE 2007–2008.

FIA GT Championship 2005

The following races were run after AUTOCOURSE 2005–2006 went to press.

FIA GT CHAMPIONSHIP, Dubai Autodrome, United Arab Emirates, 18 November. Round 10. 89 laps of the 3.352-mile/5.394-km circuit, 298.299 miles/480.066 km.
1 Pedro Lamy/Gabriele Gardel, P/CH (Ferrari 550 Maranello), 3h 01m 07.031s, 98.820 mph/159.035 km/h (1st GT1 class); **2** Michael Bartels/Timo Scheider, D/D (Maserati MC12), 3h 01m 07.806s; **3** Bert Longin/Anthony Kumpen/Mike Hezemans, B/B/NL (Chevrolet Corvette C5-R), 3h 01m 15.059s; **4** Andrea Bertolini/Karl Wendlinger, I/A (Maserati MC12), 3h 01m 17.250s; **5** Fabio Babini/Thomas Biagi, I/I (Maserati MC12), 3h 01m 27.885s; **6** Andrea Piccini/Jean-Denis Deletraz/Stéphane Lemeret, I/CH/B (Ferrari 575 Maranello GTC), 3h 03m 15.739s; **7** Justin Keen/Liz Halliday, GB/USA (Lister Storm GT), 86 laps; **8** Emmanuel Collard/Tim Sugden, F/GB (Porsche 996 GT3-RSR), 86 (1st GT2 class); **9** Nikolai Fomenko/Alexei Vasiliev, RUS/RUS (Ferrari 550 Maranello), 85; **10** Steve Zacchia/JeanLuc Blanchemain/Vincent Vosse, CH/F/B (Ferrari 550 Maranello), 84.
Fastest race lap: Lamy/Gardel, 1m 56.015s, 104.004 mph/167.378 km/h.
Fastest qualifying lap: Christophe Bouchut/Stéphane Ortelli, F/MC (Aston Martin DBR9), 1m 55.215s, 104.726 mph/168.541 km/h.

FIA GT CHAMPIONSHIP, Bahrain International Circuit, Sakhir, Bahrain, 25 November. Round 11. 90 laps of the 3.363-mile/5.412 km circuit, 302.502 miles/486.834 km.
1 Christophe Bouchut/Antonio Gárcia, F/E (Aston Martin DBR9), 3h 01m 36.661s, 99.940 mph/160.838 km/h (1st GT1 class); **2** Philipp Peter/Jamie Davies, A/GB (Maserati MC12), 3h 02m 02.870s; **3** Bert Longin/Anthony Kumpen/Mike Hezemans, B/B/NL (Chevrolet Corvette C5-R), 3h 03m 10.084s; **4** Pedro Lamy/Gabriele Gardel, P/CH (Ferrari 550 Maranello), 3h 03m 30.643s*; **5** Michael Bartels/Timo Scheider, D/D (Maserati MC12), 89 laps; **6** Marco Cioci/Andrea Montermini, I/I (Ferrari 575GTC), 89; **7** Paolo Ruberti/Robert Lechner, I/A (Saleen S7R), 88; **8** Steve Zacchia/Raymond Narac/Roland Berville, CH/F/F (Ferrari 550 Maranello), 88; **9** Fabio Babini/Thomas Biagi, I/I (Maserati MC12), 87 (DNF-transmission); **10** Marc Lieb/Mike Rockenfeller, D/D (Porsche 996 GT3-RSR), 87 (1st GT2 class).
* Originally disqualified for not having the required 3 litres of fuel in the tank at the end of the race, but reinstated after appeal.
Fastest race lap: Peter/Davies, 1m 56.478s, 103.936 mph/167.269 km/h.
Fastest qualifying lap: Bouchut/Gárcia, 1m 54.184s, 106.024 mph/170.630 km/h.

Final championship points
GT1 Drivers
1 Gabriele Gardel, CH, 75; **2=** Timo Scheider, D, 74; **2=** Michael Bartels, D, 74; **3=** Karl Wendlinger, A, 71; **3=** Andrea Bertolini, I, 71; **4=** Thomas Biagi, I, 63; **4=** Fabio Babini, I, 63; **5** Pedro Lamy, P, 60; **6=** Anthony Kumpen, B, 52; **6=** Bert Longin, B, 52; **6=** Mike Hezemans, NL, 52; **7** Philipp Peter, A, 45; **8** Christophe Bouchut, F, 24; **9** Eric van de Poele, B, 20; **10=** Andrea Piccini, I, 18; **10=** Jean-Denis Deletraz, CH, 18; **11=** Chris Buncombe, GB, 17; **11=** Roman Rusinov, RUS, 17; **12=** Steve Zacchia, CH, 16; **12=** Jamie Davies, GB, 16.
GT1 Teams
1 Vitaphone Racing Team, 137; **2** JMB Racing, 103; **3** Labre Compétition, 91; **4** GLPK-Carsport, 52; **5** G.P.C. Sport, 33.5.
GT1 Manufacturers
1 Maserati, 239; **2** Ferrari, 125; **3** Corvette, 60.
GT2 Drivers
1= Marc Lieb, D, 102; **1=** Mike Rockenfeller, D, 102; **2=** Emmanuel Collard, F, 78; **2=** Tim Sugden, GB, 78; **3** Luigi Moccia, I, 55; **4** Gerold Ried, D, 45; **5** Christian Ried, D, 44; **6** Jan Vonka, CZ, 27.5; **7** Emanuele Busnelli, I, 27; **8=** Wolfgang Kaufmann, D, 23; **8=** Mauro Casadei, I, 23.
GT2 Teams
1 GruppeM Racing, 180; **2** Proton Competition, 45; **3** Ebimotors, 39.
GT2 Manufacturers
1 Porsche, 324; **2** Ferrari, 41; **3** Spyker, 12.

2006

SILVERSTONE SUPERCAR SHOWDOWN, Silverstone Grand Prix Circuit, Towcester, Northamptonshire, Great Britain, 7 May. Round 1. 95 laps of the 3.194-mile/5.140-km circuit, 303.555 miles/488.525 km.
1 Michael Bartels/Andrea Bertolini, D/I (Maserati MC12 GT1), 3h 00m 40.717s, 100.805 mph/162.230 km/h (1st GT1 class); **2** Jaroslav 'Jarek' Janis/Sascha Bert, CZ/D (Saleen S7R), 3h 00m 45.452s; **3** Fabio Babini/Fabrizio Gollin, I/I (Aston Martin DBR9), 3h 01m 44.736s; **4** Christophe Bouchut/David Brabham, F/AUS (Aston Martin DBR9), 3h 01m 46.587s; **5** Jamie Davies/Thomas Biagi, GB/I (Maserati MC12 GT1), 3h 02m 09.298s; **6** Andrea Piccini/Jean-Denis Deletraz, I/CH (Aston Martin DBR9), 94 Laps; **7** Christian Pescatori/Miguel Ramos, I/P (Aston Martin DBR9), 94; **8** Mike Hezemans/Anthony Kumpen/Bert Longin, NL/B/B (Chevrolet Corvette C6.R), 94; **9** Jaime Melo Jr/Matteo Bobbi, BR/I (Ferrari 430 GT2), 91 (1st GT2 class); **10** Emmanuel Collard/Luca Riccitelli, F/I (Porsche 996 GT3-RSR), 91.
Fastest race lap: Janis/Bert, 1m 46.532s, 107.929 mph/173.694 km/h.
Fastest qualifying lap: Hezemans/Kumpen/Longin, 1m 58.288s, 97.202 mph/156.432 km/h.

BRNO SUPERCAR 500, Automotodrom Brno Masaryk Circuit, Brno, Czech Republic, 28 May. Round 2. 88 laps of the 3.357-mile/5.403-km circuit, 295.440 miles/475.464 km.
1 Jaroslav 'Jarek' Janis/Sascha Bert, CZ/D (Saleen S7R), 3h 00m 22.759s, 98.273 mph/158.155 km/h (1st GT1 class); **2** Andrea Piccini/Jean-Denis Deletraz, I/CH (Aston Martin DBR9), 3h 00m 23.567s; **3** Fabio Babini/Fabrizio Gollin, I/I (Aston Martin DBR9), 3h 01m 25.381s; **4** Michael Bartels/Andrea Bertolini, D/I (Maserati MC12 GT1), 3h 01m 26.083s; **5** Christian Pescatori/Miguel Ramos, I/P (Aston Martin DBR9), 3h 02m 13.485s; **6** Christophe Bouchut/Peter Kox, F/NL (Lamborghini Murcielago GTR), 87 laps; **7** Jamie Davies/Thomas Biagi, GB/I (Maserati MC12 GT1), 87; **8** Tim Sugden/Iradj Alexander-David, GB/CH (Ferrari 430 GT2), 84 (1st GT2 class); **9** Emmanuel Collard/Luca Riccitelli, F/I (Porsche 996 GT3-RSR), 84; **10** Jaime Melo Jr/Matteo Bobbi, BR/I (Ferrari 430 GT2), 84.
Fastest race lap: Janis/Bert, 1m 57.584s, 102.788 mph/165.420 km/h.
Fastest qualifying lap: Janis/Bert, 1m 55.660s, 104.497 mph/168.172 km/h.

OSCHERSLEBEN SUPERCAR 500, Motorsport Arena Oschersleben, Germany, 2 July. Round 3. 125 laps of the 2.279-mile/3.667-km circuit, 284.704 miles/458.187 km.
1 Michael Bartels/Andrea Bertolini, D/I (Maserati MC12 GT1), 3h 01m 11.822s, 94.274 mph/151.720 km/h (1st GT1 class); **2** Jamie Davies/Thomas Biagi, GB/I (Maserati MC12 GT1), 3h 01m 26.185s; **3** Andrea Piccini/Jean-Denis Deletraz, I/CH (Aston Martin DBR9), 3h 01m 31.602s; **4** Jaroslav 'Jarek' Janis/Sascha Bert, CZ/D (Saleen S7R), 3h 01m 39.649s; **5** Fabio Babini/Fabrizio Gollin, I/I (Aston Martin DBR9), 3h 01m 13.336s; **6** Christian Pescatori/Miguel Ramos, I/P (Aston Martin DBR9), 124 laps; **7** Karl Wendlinger/Philipp Peter, A/A (Aston Martin DBR9), 124; **8** Shaun Balfe/Jamie Derbyshire, GB/GB (Saleen S7R), 122; **9** Andrew Kirkaldy/Nathan Kinch, GB/GB (Ferrari 430 GT2), 121 (1st GT2 class); **10** Mika Salo/Rui Aguas, FIN/P (Ferrari 430 GT2), 120.
Fastest race lap: Bert Longin/Anthony Kumpen/Mike Hezemans, B/B/NL (Chevrolet Corvette C6.R), 1m 23.527s, 98.026 mph/158.047 km/h.
Fastest qualifying lap: Bartels/Bertolini, 1m 21.520s, 100.624 mph/161.938 km/h.

SPA 24-HOURS, Circuit de Spa-Francorchamps, Stavelot, Belgium, 29–30 July. Round 4. 589 laps of the 4.335-mile/6.976-km circuit, 2553.130 miles/4108.864 km.
1 Michael Bartels/Andrea Bertolini/Eric van de Poele, D/I/B (Maserati MC12 GT1), 24h 01m 39.542s, 106.258 mph/171.006 km/h (1st GT1 class); **2** Andrea Piccini/Jean-Denis Deletraz/Stéphane Lemeret/Marcel Fässler, I/CH/B/CH (Aston Martin DBR9), 24h 03m 20.994s; **3** Mike Hezemans/Anthony Kumpen/Bert Longin/Kurt Mollekens, NL/B/B/B (Chevrolet Corvette C6.R), 580 laps; **4** Christian Pescatori/Fabio Babini/Tomás Enge/Peter Kox, I/I/CZ/NL (Aston Martin DBR9), 578; **5** Jos Menten/Jean-Philippe Belloc/Patrick Bornhauser/Fred Bouvy, NL/F/F/B (Chevrolet Corvette C6.R), 565; **6** Mika Salo/Rui Aguas/Timo Scheider, FIN/P/D (Ferrari 430 GT2), 560 (1st GT2 class); **7** Jaime Melo Jr/Matteo Bobbi/Stéphane Ortelli, BR/I/MC (Ferrari 430 GT2), 557; **8** Jaroslav 'Jarek' Janis/Sascha Bert/Andrea Montermini/Jan Charouz, CZ/D/I/CZ (Saleen S7R), 554; **9** Andrew Kirkaldy/Nathan Kinch/Marino Franchitti, GB/GB/GB (Ferrari 430 GT2), 548; **10** Jeroen Bleekemolen/Jonny Kane/Donny Crevels, NL/GB/NL (C8 Spyder GT2 R), 541.
Fastest race lap: Vincent Vosse/Jamie Davies/Thomas Biagi, B/GB/I (Maserati MC12 GT1), 2m 16.847s, 115.702 mph/183.516 km/h.
Fastest qualifying lap: Piccini/Deletraz/Lemeret/Fässler, 2m 14.871s, 115.702 mph/186.205 km/h.

PAUL RICARD SUPERCAR 500, Circuit ASA Paul Ricard, Le Beausset, France, 20 August. Round 5. 87 laps of the 3.598-mile/5.791-km circuit, 313.057 miles/503.817 km.
1 Mike Hezemans/Anthony Kumpen/Bert Longin, NL/B/B (Chevrolet Corvette C6.R), 2h 50m 04.129s, 110.446 mph/177.746 km/h (1st GT1 class); **2** Jean-Philippe Belloc/Jos Menten, F/NL (Chevrolet Corvette C6.R), 2h 50m 07.454s; **3** Jamie Davies/Thomas Biagi, GB/I (Maserati MC12 GT1), 2h 51m 22.645s; **4** Karl Wendlinger/Philipp Peter, A/A (Aston Martin DBR9), 2h 51m 34.269s; **5** Fabio Babini/Fabrizio Gollin, I/I (Aston Martin DBR9), 86 laps; **6** Andrea Piccini/Jean-Denis Deletraz, I/CH (Aston Martin DBR9), 86; **7** Michael Bartels/Andrea Bertolini, D/I (Maserati MC12 GT1), 86; **8** Andrea Montermini/Sascha Bert, I/D (Saleen S7R), 86; **9** Andrew Kirkaldy/Nathan Kinch, GB/GB (Ferrari 430 GT2), 83 (1st GT2 class); **10** Tim Mullen/Marino Franchitti, GB/GB (Ferrari 430 GT2), 83.
Fastest race lap: Belloc/Menten, 1m 53.343s, 114.291 mph/183.934 km/h.
Fastest qualifying lap: Belloc/Menten, 1m 52.841s, 114.800 mph/184.752 km/h.

DIJON SUPERCAR 500, Circuit de Dijon-Prenois, Fontaine-les-Dijon, France, 3 September. Round 6. 132 laps of the 2.361-mile/3.800-km circuit, 311.680 miles/501.600 km.
1 Jamie Davies/Thomas Biagi, GB/I (Maserati MC12 GT1), 2h 55m 10.533s, 106.755 mph/171.805 km/h (1st GT1 class); **2** Karl Wendlinger/Philipp Peter, A/A (Aston Martin DBR9), 2h 55m 30.466s; **3** Andrea Piccini/Jean-Denis Deletraz, I/CH (Aston Martin DBR9), 2h 55m 34.155s; **4** Jaroslav 'Jarek' Janis/Sascha Bert, CZ/D (Saleen S7R), 2h 55m 34.287s; **5** Michael Bartels/Andrea Bertolini, D/I (Maserati MC12 GT1), 2h 55m 57.997s; **6** Christian Pescatori/Fabio Babini, I/I (Aston Martin DBR9), 2h 56m 06.554s; **7** Fabrizio Gollin/Miguel Ramos, I/P (Aston Martin DBR9), 131 laps; **8** Christophe Bouchut/Benjamin Leuenberger, F/CH (Lamborghini Murcielago GTR), 127; **9** Jaime Melo Jr/Matteo Bobbi, BR/I (Ferrari 430 GT2), 127 (1st GT2 class); **10** Tim Mullen/Chris Niarchos, GB/CDN (Ferrari 430 GT2), 125.
Fastest race lap: Janis/Bert, 1m 15.119s, 113.159 mph/182.111 km/h.
Fastest qualifying lap: Janis/Bert, 1m 14.623s, 113.911 mph/183.321 km/h.

MUGELLO SUPERCAR 500, Autodromo Internazionale del Mugello, Scarperia, Firenze (Florence), Italy, 17 September. Round 7. 86 laps of the 3.259-mile/5.245-km circuit, 280.282 miles/451.070 km.
1 Karl Wendlinger/Philipp Peter, A/A (Aston Martin DBR9), 3h 00m 43.799s, 93.050 mph/149.749 km/h (1st GT1 class); **2** Michael Bartels/Andrea Bertolini, D/I (Maserati MC12 GT1), 3h 00m 48.522s; **3** Jamie Davies/Thomas Biagi, GB/I (Maserati MC12 GT1), 3h 00m 48.948s; **4** Andrea Montermini/Sascha Bert/Jaroslav 'Jarek' Janis, I/D/CZ (Saleen S7R), 3h 00m 49.309s; **5** Christian Pescatori/Fabio Babini, I/I (Aston Martin DBR9), 3h 01m 17.878s; **6** Andrea Piccini/Jean-Denis Deletraz, I/CH (Aston Martin DBR9), 3h 01m 47.401s; **7** Mike Hezemans/Anthony Kumpen/Bert Longin, NL/B/B (Chevrolet Corvette C6.R), 3h 02m 07.295s; **8** Emmanuel Collard/Luca Riccitelli, F/I (Porsche 996 GT3-RSR), 83 laps (1st GT2 class); **9** Jaime Melo Jr/Matteo Bobbi, BR/I (Ferrari 430 GT2), 83; **10** Tim Sugden/Iradj Alexander-David, GB/CH (Ferrari 430 GT2), 82.
Fastest race lap: Montermini/Bert/Janis, 1m 49.112s, 107.529 mph/173.052 km/h.
Fastest qualifying lap: Bartels/Bertolini, 1m 48.436s, 108.200 mph/174.130 km/h.

BUDAPEST SUPERCAR 500, Hungaroring, Mogyorod, Budapest, Hungary, 1 October. Round 8. 102 laps of the 2.722-mile/4.381-km circuit, 277.667 miles/446.862 km.
1 Jaroslav 'Jarek' Janis/Sascha Bert/Andrea Montermini, CZ/D/I (Saleen S7R), 3h 01m 38.944s, 91.715 mph/147.602 km/h (1st GT1 class); **2** Mike Hezemans/Anthony Kumpen/Bert Longin, NL/B/B (Chevrolet Corvette C6.R), 3h 01m 49.450s; **3** Fabio Babini/Matteo Malucelli, I/I (Aston Martin DBR9), 3h 02m 05.630s; **4** Andrea Piccini/Jean-Denis Deletraz, I/CH (Aston Martin DBR9), 3h 02m 57.374s; **5** Michael Bartels/Andrea Bertolini, D/I (Maserati MC12 GT1), 3h 03m 01.756s; **6** Fabrizio Gollin/Miguel Ramos, I/P (Aston Martin DBR9), 3h 03m 02.442s; **7** Jamie Davies/Thomas Biagi, GB/I (Maserati MC12 GT1), 101 laps; **8** Christophe Bouchut/Peter Kox/Benjamin Leuenberger, F/NL/CH (Lamborghini Murcielago GTR), 101; **9** João Barboza/Shaun Balfe, P/GB (Saleen S7R), 99; **10** Andrew Kirkaldy/Nathan Kinch, GB/GB (Ferrari 430 GT2), 98 (1st GT2 class).
Fastest race lap: Babini/Malucelli, 1m 43.076s, 95.076 mph/153.009 km/h.
Fastest qualifying lap: Janis/Bert/Montermini, 1m 42.034s, 96.047 mph/154.572 km/h.

ADRIA SUPERCAR 500, Autodromo Adria International Raceway, Adria, Italy, 15 October. Round 9. 144 laps of the 1.679-mile/2.702-km circuit, 241.768 miles/389.088 km.
1 Jamie Davies/Thomas Biagi, GB/I (Maserati MC12 GT1), 3h 00m

59.760s, 80.146 mph/128.982 km/h (1st GT1 class); **2** Michael Bartels/Andrea Bertolini, D/I (Maserati MC12 GT1), 3h 01m 08.852s; **3** Mike Hezemans/Anthony Kumpen/Bert Longin, NL/B/B (Chevrolet Corvette C6.R), 3h 01m 40.941s; **4** Christian Pescatori/Fabio Babini, I/I (Aston Martin DBR9), 3h 02m 00.150s; **5** Fabrizio Gollin/Miguel Ramos, I/P (Aston Martin DBR9), 143 laps; **6** Tim Mullen/Marino Franchitti, GB/GB (Ferrari 430 GT2), 139 (1st GT2 class); **7** Paolo Ruberti/Raffaele Giammaria, I/I (Ferrari 430 GT2), 139; **8** Tim Sugden/Iradj Alexander-David, GB/CH (Ferrari 430 GT2), 139; **9** Luigi Moccia/Emanuele Busnelli, I/I (Porsche 996 GT3 RSR), 136; **10** Bas Leinders/Renaud Kuppens, B/B (Gillet Vertigo), 128 (1st G2 class).

Mika Salo/Rui Aguas, FIN/P (Ferrari 430 GT2), finished 7th, 139 laps, but were disqualified for a ride height infringement.

Fastest race lap: Davies/Biagi, 1m 12.462s, 83.412 mph/134.239 km/h.

Fastest qualifying lap: Jaroslav 'Jarek' Janis/Andrea Montermini/Sascha Bert, CZ/I/D (Saleen S7R), 1m 11.304s, 84.767 mph/136.419 km/h.

Provisional championship points

GT1 Drivers

1= Michael Bartels, D, 69; **1=** Andrea Bertolini, I, 69; **2** Sascha Bert, D, 55; **3** Jaroslav 'Jarek' Janis, CZ, 54; **4=** Jean-Denis Deletraz, CH, 52; **4=** Andrea Piccini, I, 52; **5=** Jamie Davies, GB, 48; **5=** Thomas Biagi, I, 48; **6** Fabio Babini, I, 46; **7=** Bert Longin, B, 40; **7=** Anthony Kumpen, B, 40; **7=** Mike Hezemans, NL, 40; **8** Fabrizio Gollin, I, 30.5; **9** Christian Pescatori, I, 29; **10=** Karl Wendlinger, A, 28.5; **10=** Philipp Peter, A, 28.5; **11** Andrea Montermini, I, 24; **12** Miguel Ramos, P, 19.5; **13=** Eric van de Poele, B, 18; **13=** Stéphane Lemeret, B, 18; **13=** Marcel Fässler, CH, 18.

GT1 Teams

1 Vitaphone Racing Team, 117; **2** Aston Martin Racing BMS, 65.5; **3** Zakpeed Racing, 55; **4** Phoenix Racing, 52; **5** GLPK-Carsport, 40.

GT1 Manufacturers

1 Aston Martin, 151; **2** Maserati, 111; **3=** Saleen 57; **3=** Corvette, 57.

GT2 Drivers

1= Matteo Bobbi, I, 71; **1=** Jaime Melo Jr, BR, 71; **2=** Mika Salo, FIN, 55; **2=** Rui Aguas, P, 55; **3** Tim Mullen, GB, 50.5; **4=** Nathan Kinch, GB, 43; **4=** Andrew Kirkaldy, GB, 43; **5=** Tim Sugden, GB, 38; **5=** Iradj Alexander-David, CH, 38; **6** Luca Riccitelli, I, 33.

GT2 Teams

1 AF Corse, 126; **2** Scuderia Ecosse, 93.5; **3** Ebimotors, 54.

GT2 Manufacturers

1 Ferrari, 260; **2** Porsche, 86.5; **3** Spyker, 10.

Results of the Dubai race will be given in AUTOCOURSE 2007–2008.

Le Mans Series 2005

The following race was run after AUTOCOURSE 2005–2006 went to press.

1000 km of ISTANBUL, Istanbul Speed Park, Tuzla, Turkey, 13 November. Round 5. 173 laps of the 3.317-mile/5.338-km circuit, 573.820 miles/923.474 km.

1 Emmanuel Collard/Jean-Christophe Boullion, F/F (Pescarolo C60-Judd), 6h 01m 32.594s, 95.228 mph/153.255 km/h; **2** Stéphane Ortelli/Allan McNish, MC/GB (Audi R8), 6h 02m 42.469s; **3** Nicolas Minassian/Jamie Campbell-Walter/Jean-Denis Deletraz, F/GB/F (DBA 03S-Judd), 171 laps; **4** Hayanari Shimoda/Tom Chilton/Caspar Elgaard, J/GB/DK (Zytek 04S), 171; **5** Sam Hignett/Gregor Fisken/Jason Tahincioglu, GB/GB/TR (Zytek 04S), 169; **6** Thomas Erdos/Mike Newton, BR/GB (MG Lola EX264-AER), 164 (1st P2 class); **7** Gareth Evans/Peter Owen/Guy Smith, GB/GB/GB (Lola B05/40-Judd), 164; **8** Vanina Ickx/João Barbosa/Martin Short, B/P/GB (Dallara LMP-Judd), 164; **9** Didier Theys/Thed Bjork, B/S (Lola B05/40-Judd), 163; **10** Christian Pescatori/Michele Bartyan/Toni Seiler, I/I/CH (Ferrari 550 Maranello), 161 (1st GT1 class).

Fastest race lap: Collard/Boullion, 1m 51.813s, 106.792 mph/171.866 km/h.

Fastest qualifying lap: Collard/Boullion, 1m 39.359s, 120.178 mph/193.408 km/h.

Final championship points

P1 Drivers

1= Emmanuel Collard, F, 34; **1=** Jean-Christophe Boullion, F, 34; **2** Hayanari Shimoda, J, 32; **3=** Stéphane Ortelli, MC, 26; **3=** Allan McNish, GB, 26; **4=** Vanina Ickx, B, 25; **4=** Martin Short, GB, 25; **5=** Nicolas Minassian, F, 24; **5=** Jamie Campbell-Walter, GB, 24; **6** Tom Chilton, GB, 22; **7** João Barbosa, P, 19; **8=** Sam Hignett, GB, 16; **8=** John Stack, GB, 16; **9** Casper Elgaard, DK, 15; **10** Haruki Kurosawa, J, 13; **11** Alexander Frei, CH, 11; **12=** John Nielsen, DK, 10; **12=** Christian Vann, GB, 10; **13** Erik Comas, F, 8; **14** Gregor Fisken, GB, 7.

P2 Drivers

1= Gareth Evans, GB, 34; **2=** Thomas Erdos, BR, 33; **2=** Mike Newton, GB, 33; **3=** Claude-Yves Gosselin, F, 27; **3=** Vincent Vosse, B, 27; **4=** Peter Owen, GB, 26; **4=** Bob Berridge, GB, 26; **5** Didier Theys, B, 21; **6** Karim Ojjeh, ZA, 17; **7=** Michael Vergers, NL, 13; **7=** Juan Barazi, DK, 13.

GT1 Drivers

1= Michele Bartyan, I, 35; **1=** Christian Pescatori, I, 35; **1=** Toni Seiler, CH, 35; **1=** Matteo Cressoni, I, 35; **2=** Christophe Bouchut, F, 31; **2=** Alexei Vasiliev, RUS, 31.

GT2 Drivers

1= Xavier Pompidou, F, 30; **1=** Marc Lieb, D, 30; **2=** Andrew Kirkaldy, GB, 28; **2=** Nathan Kinch, GB, 28; **3=** Franco Groppi, I, 20; **3=** Luigi Moccia, I, 20; **3=** Yves Lambert, B, 20; **3=** Markus Palttala, FIN, 20.

P1 Teams

1 Pescarolo Sport, 34; **2** Zytek Motorsport, 32; **3** Audi Playstation Team ORECA, 26.

P2 Teams

1 Chamberlain Synergy Motorsport, 34; **2** RML, 33; **3** Paul Belmondo Racing, 27.

GT1 Teams

1 BMS Scuderia Italia (car no. 51), 27; **2** BMS Scuderia Italia (car no. 52), 35; **3** Convers Team, 31.

GT2 Teams

1 Sebah Automotive, 30; **2** Scuderia Ecosse, 28; **3** Autorlando Sport, 20.

2006

1000 km of ISTANBUL, Istanbul Speed Park, Tuzla, Turkey, 9 April. Round 1. 134 laps of the 3.317-mile/5.338-km circuit, 444.262 miles/715.292 km.

1 Emmanuel Collard/Jean-Christophe Boullion, F/F (Pescarolo C60-Judd), 4h 01m 42.625s, 110.329 mph/177.558 km/h (1st P1 class); **2** Michael Vergers/Juan Barazi/Jean-Philippe Belloc, NL/DK/F (Courage C65-AER), 128 laps (1st P2 class); **3** Nicolas Kiesa/Jens Moller/Justin Keen, DK/DK/GB (Lister Storm Hybrid-Chevrolet), 127; **4** Bob Berridge/Gareth Evans/Peter Owen, GB/GB/GB (Lola B06/10-AER), 127; **5** Marc Rostan/Pierre Bruneau, F/F (Pilbeam-Judd), 125; **6** Pedro Lamy/Gabriele Gardel/Vincent Vosse, P/CH/B (Aston Martin DBR9), 125 (1st GT1 class); **7** Ed Morris/Jean-Francois Leroch/Frank Hahn, GB/F/B (Courage C65-Judd), 125; **8** Paul Belmondo/Didier Adre/Yann Clairay, F/F/F (Courage C65-Ford), 124; **9** Peter Kox/Robert Pergl/Alexei Vasiliev, NL/CZ/RUS (Ferrari 550 Maranello), 124; **10** Jérôme Policand/Patrice Goueslard/Anthony Beltoise, F/F/F (Chevrolet Corvette C5-R), 123.

Fastest race lap: Collard/Boullion, 1m 41.281s, 117.897 mph/189.737 km/h.

Fastest qualifying lap: Collard/Boullion, 1m 40.266s, 119.091 mph/191.658 km/h.

1000 km of SPA, Circuit de Spa-Francorchamps, Stavelot, Belgium, 14 May. Round 2. 134 laps of the 4.335-mile/6.976-km circuit, 580.848 miles/934.784 km.

1 Emmanuel Collard/Jean-Christophe Boullion, F/F (Pescarolo C60-Judd), 6h 01m 35.407s, 96.382 mph/155.112 km/h (1st P1 class); **2** Harold Primat/Marcel Fässler, CH/CH (Courage LC70-Judd), 133 laps; **3** John Nielsen/Caspar Elgaard/Philip Andersen, DK/DK/DK (Zytek 06S), 132; **4** Miguel Amaral/Miguel Angel de Castro/Angel Burgueno, P/E/E (Lola B05/40-AER), 132 (1st P2 class); **5** Mike Newton/Thomas Erdos, GB/BR (MG Lola EX264), 131; **6** Bill Binnie/Allen Timpany/Sam Hancock, USA/GB/GB (Lola 05/42-Zytek), 129; **7** Stéphane Ortelli/Soheil Ayari, MC/F (Saleen S7R), 129 (1st GT1 class); **8** Michael Vergers/Juan Barazi/Davide Valsecchi, NL/DK/I (Courage C65-AER), 128; **9** Antonio Gárcia/Richard Lyons, E/GB (Aston Martin DBR9), 128; **10** Pertti Kuismanen/Jos Menten/Markus Palttala, FIN/NL/FIN (Chevrolet Corvette C6.R), 126.

Fastest race lap: Collard/Boullion, 2m 06.687s, 123.177 mph/198.233 km/h.

Fastest qualifying lap: Primat/Fässler, 2m 19.538s, 111.832 mph/179.977 km/h.

1000 km of NÜRBURGRING, Nürburgring Grand Prix Circuit, Nürburg/Eifel, Germany, 16 July. Round 3. 189 laps of the 3.192-mile/5.137-km circuit, 603.285 miles/970.893 km.

1 Emmanuel Collard/Jean-Christophe Boullion/Eric Hélary, F/F/F (Pescarolo C60-Judd), 6h 00m 26.030s, 100.426 mph/161.621 km/h (1st P1 class); **2** Nicolas Minassian/Felipe Ortiz/Beppe Gabbiani, F/CH/I (Creation CA06/H-Judd), 186 laps; **3** Jan Lammers/Alex Yoong, NL/MAL (Dome S101-Hb-Judd), 186; **4** Bob Berridge/Gareth Evans/Peter Owen, GB/GB/GB (Lola B06/10-AER), 184; **5** Miguel Amaral/Miguel Angel de Castro/Angel Burgueno, P/E/E (Lola B05/40-AER), 183 (1st P2 class); **6** Bill Binnie/Allen Timpany/Sam Hancock, USA/GB/GB (Lola 05/42-Zytek), 182; **7** Stefan Johansson/Hideki Noda, S/J (Zytek 06S), 181; **8** Martin Short/João Barbosa, GB/P (Radical SR9-Judd), 181; **9** Mike Newton/Thomas Erdos, GB/BR (MG Lola EX264), 180; **10** Pedro Lamy/Gabriele Gardel/Vincent Vosse, P/CH/B (Aston Martin DBR9), 177 (1st GT1 class).

Fastest race lap: Jean-Marc Gounon/Alexander Frei/Gregor Fisken, F/CH/GB (Courage LC70-Mugen Honda), 1m 47.247s, 107.147 mph/172.436 km/h.

Fastest qualifying lap: Minassian/Ortiz/Gabbiani, 1m 44.850s, 109.596 mph/176.378 km/h.

1000 km of DONINGTON, Donington Park Grand Prix Circuit, Castle Donington, Great Britain, 27 August. Round 4. 249 laps of the 2.500-mile/4.023-km circuit, 622.444 miles/1001.727 km.

1 Emmanuel Collard/Jean-Christophe Boullion/Didier Andre, F/F/F (Pescarolo C60-Judd), 5h 59m 26.921s, 103.900 mph/167.211 km/h (1st P1 class); **2** Nicolas Minassian/Kevin McGarrity, F/GB (Creation CA06/H-Judd), 247 laps; **3** Jamie Campbell-Walter/Felipe Ortiz/Beppe Gabbiani, GB/CH/I (Creation CA06/H-Judd), 245; **4** Mike Newton/Thomas Erdos, GB/BR (MG Lola EX264), 239 (1st P2 class); **5** Jean-Marc Gounon/Gregor Fisken/Alexander Frei, F/GB/CH (Courage LC70-Mugen Honda), 238; **6** Antonio Gárcia/Peter Hardman, E/GB (Aston Martin DBR9), 238 (1st GT1 class); **7** Jérôme Policand/Patrice Goueslard/Luc Alphand, F/F/F (Chevrolet Corvette C5-R), 238; **8** Peter Kox/Robert Pergl/Alexei Vasiliev, NL/CZ/RUS (Ferrari 550 Maranello), 231; **9** Pertti Kuismanen/Jos Menten/Markus Palttala, FIN/NL/FIN (Chevrolet Corvette C6.R), 228; **10** Marc Rostan/Pierre Bruneau, F/F (Pilbeam-Judd), 227.

Fastest race lap: Campbell-Walter/Ortiz/Gabbiani, 1m 21.527s, 110.383 mph/177.644 km/h.

Fastest qualifying lap: Gounon/Fisken/Frei, 1m 20.756s, 111.437 mph/179.340 km/h.

1000 km of JARAMA, Circuito del Jarama, San Sebastián de los Reyes, Madrid, Spain, 24 September. Round 5. 237 laps of the 2.392-mile/3.850-km circuit, 566.970 miles/912.450 km.

1 Emmanuel Collard/Jean-Christophe Boullion/Didier Andre, F/F/F (Pescarolo C60-Judd), 6h 01m 01.399s, 94.227 mph/151.644 km/h (1st P1 class); **2** Miguel Amaral/Miguel Angel de Castro/Angel Burgueno, P/E/E (Lola B05/40-AER), 233 laps (1st P2 class); **3** Harold Primat/Marcel Fässler, CH/CH (Courage LC70-Judd), 232; **4** Nicolas Minassian/Felipe Ortiz/Beppe Gabbiani, F/CH/I (Creation CA06/H-Judd), 230; **5** Bob Berridge/Gareth Evans/Peter Owen, GB/GB/GB (Lola B06/10-AER), 229; **6** Stéphane Ortelli/Soheil Ayari, MC/F (Saleen S7R), 226 (1st GT1 class); **7** Pedro Lamy/Gabriele Gardel/Vincent Vosse, P/CH/B (Aston Martin DBR9), 225; **8** Antonio Gárcia/David Brabham/Peter Hardman, E/AUS/GB (Aston Martin DBR9), 224; **9** Pertti Kuismanen/Jos Menten/Markus Palttala, FIN/NL/FIN (Chevrolet Corvette C6.R), 223; **10** Peter Kox/Robert Pergl/Alexei Vasiliev, NL/CZ/RUS (Ferrari 550 Maranello), 223.

Fastest race lap: Jean-Marc Gounon/Gregor Fisken/Alexander Frei, F/GB/CH (Courage LC70-Mugen Honda), 1m 24.570s, 101.835 mph/163.888 km/h.

Fastest qualifying lap: Collard/Boullion/Andre, 1m 23.242s, 103.460 mph/166.502 km/h.

Final championship points

P1 Drivers

1= Emmanuel Collard, F, 50; **1=** Jean-Christophe Boullion, F, 50; **2** Didier Andre, F, 20; **3=** Felipe Ortiz, CH, 20; **3=** Beppe Gabbiani, I, 20; **4=** Bob Berridge, GB, 20; **4=** Gareth Evans, GB, 20; **5=** Harold Primat, CH, 19; **5=** Marcel Fässler, CH, 19; **6** Nicolas Minassian (car no.9), F, 14; **7** Peter Owen, GB, 14; **8** Eric Hélary, F, 10; **9** Kevin McGarrity, GB, 9; **10=** Nicolas Kiesa, DK, 8; **10=** Jens Moller, DK, 8; **11** Nicolas Minassian (car no.10), F, 8; **12=** Gregor Fisken, GB, 7; **12=** Jean-Marc Gounon, F, 7; **12=** Alexander Frei, CH, 7; **13=** John Nielsen, DK, 6; **13=** Caspar Elgaard, DK, 6; **13=** Philip Andersen, DK, 6; **14=** Jan Lammers, NL, 6; **14=** Alex Yoong, MAL, 6; **15** Jamie Campbell-Walter, GB, 6.

P2 Drivers

1= Michael Vergers, NL, 28; **1=** Juan Barazi, DK, 28; **2=** Mike Newton, GB, 26; **2=** Thomas Erdos, BR, 26; **3=** Marc Rostan, F, 24; **3=** Pierre Bruneau, F, 24; **4=** Miguel Angel de Castro (car no.40), E, 30; **4=** Angel Burgueno (car no.40), E, 30; **4=** Miguel Amaral, P, 20; **5=** Sam Hancock, GB, 20; **5=** Allen Timpany, GB, 20.

GT1 Drivers

1= Pedro Lamy, P, 32; **1=** Gabriele Gardel, CH, 32; **1=** Vincent Vosse, B, 32; **2=** Peter Kox, NL, 28; **2=** Alexei Vasiliev, RUS, 28; **2=** Robert Pergl, CZ, 28.

GT2 Drivers

1= Joel Camathias, CH, 34; **1=** Marc Lieb, D, 34; **2=** Lawrence Tomlinson, GB, 21; **2=** Richard Dean, GB, 21.

P1 Teams

1 Pescarolo Sport, 50; **2** Creation Autosportif, 20; **3** Chamberlain Synergy Motorsport, 20.

P2 Teams

1 Barazi-Epsilon, 28; **2** RML, 26; **3** Pierre Bruneau, 24.

GT1 Teams

1 Aston Martin Racing Larbre, 32; **2** Convers Menx Team, 28; **3** Team Oreca, 25.

GT2 Teams

1 Autorlando Sport, 34; **2** Team LNT (car no.82), 21; **3** Team LNT (car no. 81), 20.

American Le Mans Series

MOBIL 1 TWELVE HOURS OF SEBRING, Sebring International Raceway Florida, USA, 18 March. Round 1. 349 laps of the 3.700-mile/5.955-km circuit, 1291.300 miles/2708.146 km.

1 Tom Kristensen/Rinaldo Capello/Allan McNish, DK/I/GB (Audi R10 TDI), 12h 01m 56.561s, 107.319 mph/172.713 km/h (1st P1 class); **2** Jon Field/Clint Field/Liz Halliday, USA/USA/USA (Lola B05/40-AER), 345 laps (1st P2 class); **3** Jan Magnussen/Oliver Gavin/Olivier Beretta, DK/GB/MC (Chevrolet Corvette C6.R), 338 (1st GT1 class); **4** Stéphane Sarrazin/Jason Bright/Pedro Lamy, F/AUS/P (Aston Martin DBR9), 337; **5** Andy Wallace/James Weaver/Butch Leitzinger, GB/GB/USA (Lola B06/10-AER), 336; **6** Darren Turner/Nicolas Kiesa/Tomás Enge, GB/DK/CZ (Aston Martin DBR9), 324; **7** Ron Fellows/Johnny O'Connell/Massimiliano 'Max' Papis, CDN/USA/I (Chevrolet Corvette C6.R), 324; **8** Emmanuel Collard/Lucas Luhr/Sascha Maassen, F/D/D (Porsche RS Spyder), 323 (DNF-driveshaft); **9** Sébastien Bourdais/David Brabham/Scott Maxwell, F/AUS/CDN (Panoz Esperante GTLM-Ford), 320 (1st GT2 class); **10** Marc Lieb/Johannes van Overbeek/Jon Fogarty, D/USA/USA (Porsche 911 GT3 RSR), 320.

Fastest race lap: McNish, 1m 48.373s, 122.909 mph/197.803 km/h.

Fastest qualifying lap: Kristensen/Capello/McNish, 1m 45.828s, 125.865 mph/202.559 km/h.

LONE STAR GRAND PRIX, Reliant Park Circuit, Houston, Texas, USA, 13 May. Round 2. 143 laps of the 1.690-mile/2.720-km circuit, 241.670 miles/388.930 km.

1 Rinaldo Capello/Allan McNish, I/GB (Audi R8), 2h 45m 16.938s, 87.730 mph/141.188 km/h (1st P1 class); **2** Oliver Gavin/Olivier Beretta, GB/MC (Chevrolet Corvette C6.R), 138 laps (1st GT1 class); **3** Ron Fellows/Johnny O'Connell, CDN/USA (Chevrolet Corvette C6.R), 137; **4** Darren Turner/Tomás Enge, GB/CZ (Aston Martin DBR9), 137; **5** Stéphane Sarrazin/Pedro Lamy, F/P (Aston Martin DBR9), 137; **6** James Weaver/Butch Leitzinger, GB/USA (Lola B06/10-AER), 134; **7** Mike Rockenfeller/Klaus Graf, D/D (Porsche 911 GT3-RSR), 134 (1st GT2 class); **8** Johannes van Overbeek/Wolf Henzler, USA/D (Porsche 911 GT3-RSR), 133; **9** Jaime Melo Jr/Mika Salo, BR/FIN (Ferrari 430GT Berlinetta), 132; **10** Jörg Bergmeister/Patrick Long, D/USA (Porsche 911 GT3-RSR), 131.

Fastest race lap: Capello, 1m 05.148s, 93.387 mph/150.292 km/h.

Fastest qualifying lap: Weaver, 1m 04.459s, 94.386 mph/151.899 km/h.

AMERICAN LE MANS AT MID-OHIO, Mid-Ohio Sports Car Course, Lexington, Ohio, USA, 21 May. Round 3. 119 laps of the 2.258-mile/3.634-km circuit, 269.993 miles/434.512 km.

1 Timo Bernhard/Romain Dumas, D/F (Porsche RS Spyder), 2h 45m 52.293s, 97.974 mph/ km/h (1st P2 class); **2** Sascha Maassen/Lucas Luhr, D/D (Porsche RS Spyder), 2h 45m 52.727s; **3** Rinaldo Capello/Allan McNish, I/GB (Audi R8), 2h 45m 59.596s (1st P1 class) **4** Liz Halliday/Clint Field, USA/USA (Lola B05/40-AER), 116 laps; **5** James Weaver/Butch Leitzinger, GB/USA (Lola B06/10-AER), 116; **6** Oliver Gavin/Olivier Beretta, GB/MC (Chevrolet Corvette C6.R), 116 (1st GT1 class); **7** Ron Fellows/Johnny O'Connell, CDN/USA (Chevrolet Corvette C6.R), 116; **8** Darren Turner/Tomás Enge, GB/CZ (Aston Martin DBR9), 115; **9** Stéphane Sarrazin/Pedro Lamy, F/P (Aston Martin DBR9), 115; **10** Jamie Bach/Guy Cosmo, USA/USA (Courage C65-Mazda), 112.

Fastest race lap: Luhr, 1m 13.774s, 110.185 mph/177.326 km/h.

Fastest qualifying lap: Maassen, 1m 12.815s, 111.636 mph/179.661 km/h.

NEW ENGLAND GRAND PRIX, Lime Rock Park, Lakeville, Connecticut, USA, 1 July. Round 4. 177 laps of the 1.540-mile/2.478-km circuit, 272.580 miles/438.675 km.

1 Rinaldo Capello/Allan McNish, I/GB (Audi R8), 2h 45m 46.554s, 98.656 mph/158.772 km/h (1st P1 class); **2** Timo Bernhard/Romain Dumas, D/F (Porsche RS Spyder), 2h 45m 58.366s (1st P2 class); **3** Sascha Maassen/Lucas Luhr, D/D (Porsche RS Spyder), 174 laps; **4** Stéphane Sarrazin/Pedro Lamy, F/P (Aston Martin DBR9), 166 (1st GT1 class); **5** Ron Fellows/Johnny O'Connell, CDN/USA (Chevrolet Corvette C6.R), 166; **6** Darren Turner/Tomás Enge, GB/CZ (Aston Martin DBR9), 166; **7** Jörg Bergmeister/Patrick Long, D/USA (Porsche 911 GT3-RSR), 162 (1st GT2 class); **8** Johannes van Overbeek/Wolf Henzler, USA/D (Porsche 911 GT3-RSR), 161; **9** Bill Auberlen/Joey Hand, USA/USA (BMW E46 M3), 160; **10** Justin Marks/Bryan Sellers, USA/USA (BMW E46 M3), 158.

Fastest race lap: Dumas, 47.074s, 117.772 mph/189.536 km/h.

Fastest qualifying lap: Bernhard/Dumas, 45.588s, 121.611 mph/195.714 km/h.

GRAND PRIX OF UTAH, Miller Motorsports Park, Tooele, Utah, USA, 15 July. Round 5. 65 laps of the 4.486–mile/7.722-km circuit, 291.590 miles/469.269 km.

1 Frank Biela/Emanuele Pirro, D/I (Audi R10), 2h 46m 00.377s, 105.390 mph/169.609 km/h (1st P1 class); **2** Sascha Maassen/Lucas Luhr, D/D (Porsche RS Spyder), 2h 46m 00.695s (1st P2 class) **3** James Weaver/Butch Leitzinger, GB/USA (Lola B06/10-AER), 2h 46m 45.560s; **4** Rinaldo Capello/Allan McNish, I/GB (Audi R10), 2h 47m 10.880s; **5** Guy Smith/Chris Dyson, GB/USA (Lola B06/10-AER), 64 laps; **6** Andy Wallace/Duncan Dayton, GB/USA (Lola EX257-AER), 62; **7** Darren Turner/Tomás Enge, GB/CZ (Aston Martin DBR9), 62 (1st GT1 class); **8** Stéphane Sarrazin/Andrea Piccini, F/I (Aston Martin DBR9), 61; **9** Liz Halliday/Clint Field/Jon Field, USA/USA/USA (Lola B05/40-AER), 61; **10** Ron Fellows/Johnny O'Connell, CDN/USA (Chevrolet Corvette C6.R), 61.

Fastest race lap: Maassen, 2m 23.665s, 112.412 mph/180.909 km/h.

Fastest qualifying lap: Biela/Pirro, 2m 21.554s, 114.088 mph/183.607 km/h.

AMERICAN LE MANS PORTLAND GRAND PRIX, Portland International Raceway, Oregon, USA, 22 July. Round 6. 142 laps of the 1.964-mile/3.161-km circuit, 278.888 miles/448.827 km.

1 Rinaldo Capello/Allan McNish, I/GB (Audi R10), 2h 45m 08.847s, 101.323 mph/163.064 km/h (1st P1 class) **2** Frank Biela/Emanuele Pirro, D/I (Audi R10), 2h 45m 50.898s; **3** Guy Smith/Chris Dyson, GB/USA (Lola B06/10-AER), 140 laps; **4** James Weaver/Butch Leitzinger, GB/USA (Lola B06/10-AER), 138; **5** Liz Halliday/Clint Field/Jon Field, USA/USA/USA (Lola B05/40-AER), 135 (1st P2 class); **6** Andy Wallace/Duncan Dayton, GB/USA (Lola EX257-AER), 134; **7** Oliver Gavin/Olivier Beretta, GB/MC (Chevrolet Corvette C6.R), 133 (1st GT1 class); **8** Bryan Willman/Chris McMurry, USA/USA (Lola EX257), 133; **9** Darren Turner/Tomás Enge/Andrea Piccini, GB/CZ/I (Aston Martin DBR9), 133; **10** Ron Fellows/Johnny O'Connell, CDN/USA (Chevrolet Corvette C6.R), 133.

Fastest race lap: McNish, 1m 04.313s, 109.937 mph/176.927 km/h.

Fastest qualifying lap: Weaver/Leitzinger, 1m 03.101s, 112.049 mph/180.325 km/h.

GENERAC 500 AT ROAD AMERICA, Road America Circuit, Elkhart Lake, Wisconsin, USA, 20 August. Round 7. 76 laps of the 4.048-mile/6.515-km circuit, 307.648 miles/495.111 km

1 Frank Biela/Emanuele Pirro, D/I (Audi R10), 2h 45m 32.115s, 111.510 mph/179.458 km/h (1st P1 class); **2** Rinaldo Capello/Allan McNish, I/GB (Audi R10), 2h 45m 32.515s; **3** James Weaver/Butch Leitzinger, GB/USA (Lola B06/10-AER), 2h 45m 32.828s; **4** Sascha Maassen/Timo Bernhard, D/D (Porsche RS Spyder), 2h 45m 59.489s (1st P2 class); **5** Lucas Luhr/Romain Dumas, D/F (Porsche RS Spyder), 2h 45m 59.639s; **6** Andy Wallace/Duncan Dayton, GB/USA (Lola EX257-AER), 2h 46m 00.176s; **7** Guy Smith/Chris Dyson, GB/USA (Lola B06/10-AER), 75 laps; **8** Liz Halliday/Clint Field/Jon Field, USA/USA/USA (Lola B05/40-AER), 75; **9** Ron Fellows/Johnny O'Connell, CDN/USA (Chevrolet Corvette C6.R), 74 (1st GT1 class); **10** Oliver Gavin/Olivier Beretta, GB/MC (Chevrolet Corvette C6.R), 73.

Fastest race lap: Smith, 1m 51.586s, 130.597 mph/210.176 km/h.

Fastest qualifying lap: Capello/McNish, 1m 49.181s, 133.474 mph/214.805 km/h.

THE LABOUR DAY WEEKEND GRAND PRIX OF MOSPORT, Mosport International Raceway, Bowmanvile, Ontario, Canada, 3 September. Round 8. 133 laps of the 2.459-mile/3.957-km circuit, 327.047 miles/526.331 km.

1 Rinaldo Capello/Allan McNish, I/GB (Audi R10), 2h 45m 00.142s, 118.924 mph/191.390 km/h (1st P1 class); **2** Guy Smith/Chris Dyson, GB/USA (Lola B06/10-AER), 2h 45m 02.936s; **3** James Weaver/Butch Leitzinger/Rob Dyson, GB/USA/USA (Lola B06/10-AER), 2h 45m 37.272s; **4** Frank Biela/Emanuele Pirro, D/I (Audi R10), 132 laps; **5** Lucas Luhr/Romain Dumas, D/F (Porsche RS Spyder), 131 (1st P2 class); **6** Sascha Maassen/Timo Bernhard, D/D (Porsche RS Spyder), 131; **7** Stéphane Sarrazin/Pedro Lamy, F/P (Aston Martin DBR9), 124 (1st GT1 class); **8** Oliver Gavin/Olivier Beretta, GB/MC (Chevrolet Corvette C6.R), 123; **9** Tomás Enge/Peter Kox, CZ/NL (Aston Martin DBR9), 123; **10** Ron Fellows/Johnny O'Connell, CDN/USA (Chevrolet Corvette C6.R), 122.

Fastest race lap: Smith, 1m 07.446s, 131.252 mph/211.229 km/h.

Fastest practice lap: Weaver/Leitzinger/Dyson (Rob), 1m 06.843s, 132.436 mph/213.135 km/h (qualifying cancelled due to bad weather).

PETITE LE MANS, Road Atlanta Motorsports Center, Braselton, Georgia, USA, 30 September. Round 9. 394 laps of the 2.540-mile/4.088-km circuit, 1000.760 miles/1610.567 km.

1 Rinaldo Capello/Allan McNish, I/GB (Audi R10), 9h 16m 49.835s, 107.835 mph/173.543 km/h (1st P1 class) **2** Stefan Johansson/Johnny Mowlem/Haruki Kurosawa, S/GB/J (Zytek 06S), 390 laps; **3** Duncan Dayton/Memo Gidley/Vitor Meira, USA/USA/BR (Lola B01/60-AER), 389; **4** Nicolas Minassian/Harold Primat/Jamie Campbell-Walter, F/CH/GB (Creation CA06/H-Judd), 388; **5** Sascha Maassen/Timo Bernhard/Emmanuel Collard, D/D/F (Porsche RS Spyder), 386; **6** Lucas Luhr/Romain Dumas/Mike Rockenfeller, D/F/D (Porsche RS Spyder), 385; **7** Frank Biela/Emanuele Pirro/Marco Werner, D/I/D (Audi R10), 383; **8** Tomás Enge/Darren Turner, CZ/GB (Aston Martin DBR9), 374; **9** Stéphane Sarrazin/Pedro Lamy, F/P (Aston Martin DBR9), 373; **10** Oliver Gavin/Olivier Beretta/Jan Magnussen, GB/MC/DK (Chevrolet Corvette C6.R), 372 (1st GT1 class).

Fastest race lap: James Weaver, GB (Lola B06/10-AER), 1m 12.374s, 126.344 mph/203.330 km/h.

Fastest qualifying lap: Minassian/Primat/Campbell-Walter, 1m 10.829s, 129.100 mph/207.766 km/h.

MONTEREY SPORTS CAR CHAMPIONSHIPS, Mazda Raceway Laguna Seca, Monterey, California, USA, 22 October. Round 10. 159 laps of the 2.238-mile/3.602-km circuit, 355.842 miles/572.672 km.

1 Rinaldo Capello/Allan McNish, I/GB (Audi R10), 4h 00m 45.954s, 88.678 mph/142.713 km/h (1st P1 class) **2** Frank Biela/Emanuele Pirro, D/I (Audi R10), 4h 01m 04.533s; **3** Nicolas Minassian/Harold Primat, F/CH (Creation CA06/H-Judd), 4h 01m 14.956s; **4** Lucas Luhr/Romain Dumas, D/F (Porsche RS Spyder), 4h 01m 49.922s (1st P2 class); **5** Sascha Maassen/Timo Bernhard, D/D (Porsche RS Spyder), 158 laps; **6** James Weaver/Chris Dyson, GB/USA (Lola B06/10-AER), 158; **7** Stefan Johansson/Johnny Mowlem, S/GB (Zytek 06S), 157; **8** Stéphane Sarrazin/Pedro Lamy, F/P (Aston Martin DBR9), 153 (1st GT1 class); **9** Oliver Gavin/Olivier Beretta, GB/MC (Chevrolet Corvette C6.R), 153; **10** Ron Fellows/Johnny O'Connell, CDN/USA (Chevrolet Corvette C6.R), 152.

Fastest race lap: Luhr, 1m 14.157s, 108.645 mph/174.847 km/h.

Fastest qualifying lap: Johansson/Mowlem, 1m 13.731s, 109.273 mph/175.858 km/h.

Final championship points

P1 Drivers

1= Rinaldo Capello, I, 204; **1=** Allan McNish, GB, 204; **2** James Weaver, GB, 119; **3** Butch Leitzinger, USA, 106; **4=** Frank Biela, D, 99; **4=** Emanuele Pirro, I, 99; **5** Chris Dyson, USA, 73; **6** Guy Smith, GB, 60; **7** Michael Lewis, USA, 50; **8** Andy Wallace, GB, 48; **9** Duncan Dayton, USA, 45; **10** Chris McMurry, USA, 41; **11=** Stefan Johansson, S, 33; **11=** Johnny Mowlem, GB, 33; **12=** Nicolas Minassian, F, 32; **12=** Harold Primat, CH, 32; **13** Tom Kristensen, DK, 26; **14** Haruki Kurosawa, J, 22; **15** Bryan Willman, USA, 21; **16=** Memo Gidley, USA, 19; **16=** Vitor Meira, BR, 19; **17** Jamie Campbell-Walter, GB, 16; **18** Marco Werner, D, 14; **19** John Graham, CDN, 9.

P2 Drivers

1= Sascha Maassen, D, 184; **1=** Lucas Luhr, D, 184; **2=** Clint Field, USA, 166; **2=** Liz Halliday, USA, 166; **3=** Timo Bernhard, D, 155; **3=** Romain Dumas, F, 155; **4** Jon Field, USA, 71; **5=** Guy Cosmo, USA, 67; **5=** Jamie Bach, USA, 67; **6** Emmanuel Collard, F, 48.

GT1 Drivers
1= Oliver Gavin, GB, 176; **1=** Olivier Beretta, MC, 176; **2** Stéphane Sarrazin, F, 163; **3** Tomâs Enge, CZ, 159; **4=** Ron Fellows, CDN, 152; **4=** Johnny O'Connell, USA, 152; **5** Pedro Lamy, P, 147; **6** Darren Turner, GB, 146.
GT2 Drivers
1 Jörg Bergmeister, D, 147; **2** Johannes van Overbeeck, USA, 141; **3** Patrick Long, USA, 137; **4** Wolf Henzler, D, 114; **5=** Scott Maxwell, CDN, 86; **5=** David Brabham, AUS, 86.
P1 Chassis Manufacturers
1 Audi, 215; **2** Lola, 160; **3** Zytek, 33; **4** Creation, 32.
P1 Engine Manufacturers
1 Audi, 215; **2** AER, 160; **3** Zytek, 33; **4** Judd, 32.
P1 Team Championship
1 Audi Sport North America, 215; **2** Dyson Racing Team, 125; **3** Autocon Motorsports, 60.
P2 Chassis Manufacturers
1 Porsche, 200; **2** Lola, 169; **3** Courage, 69.
P2 Engine Manufacturers
1 Porsche, 200; **2** AER, 166; **3** Mazda, 67.
P2 Team Championship
1 Penske Motorsports, 200; **2** Intersport Racing, 166; **3** B-K Motorsports, 67.
GT1 Automobile Manufacturers
1 Chevrolet, 189; **2** Aston Martin, 186.
GT1 Team Championship
1 Corvette Racing, 189; **2** Aston Martin Racing, 186.
GT2 Automobile Manufacturers
1 Porsche, 192; **2** Ferrari, 161; **3** Panoz, 111.
GT2 Team Championship
1 Risi Competizione, 161; **2** Petersen/White Lightning, 147; **3** Flying Lizard Motorsports, 145.

All-Japan (Super) GT Championship 2005

The following race was run after AUTOCOURSE 2005–2006 went to press.

SUZUKA GT, Suzuka International Racing Course, Ino-Cho, Suzuka-shi, Mie Prefecture, Japan, 6 November. Round 8. 39 laps of the 3.608-mile/5.807-km circuit, 140.724 miles/226.473 km.
1 Yuji Tachikawa/Toranosuke Takagi, J/J (Lexus SC430), 1h 41m 36.807s, 83.094 mph/133.726 km/h; **2** Satoshi Motoyama/Richard Lyons, J/GB (Nissan Fairlady Z), 1h 41m 38.345s; **3** Juichi Wakisaka/Akira Iida, J/J (Lexus SC430), 1h 42m 00.412s; **4** Toshihiro Kaneishi/Erik Comas, J/F (Nissan Fairlady Z), 1h 42m 08.579s; **5** Takeshi Tsuchiya/James Courtney, J/AUS (Lexus SC430), 1h 42m 09.732s; **6** Ryo Michigami/Takashi Kogure, J/J (Honda NSX), 1h 42m 10.611s; **7** Tatsuya Kataoka/Sakon Yamamoto, J/J (Lexus SC430), 1h 42m 16.585s; **8** Michael Krumm/Masataka Yanagida, D/J (Nissan Fairlady Z), 1h 42m 18.152s; **9** Benoît Tréluyer/Yuji Ide, F/J (Nissan Fairlady Z), 1h 42m 22.709s; **10** Tsugio Matsuda/Andre Lotterer, J/D (Honda NSX), 1h 42m 37.428s.
Fastest race lap: André Couto/Ronnie Quintarelli, P/I (Lexus SC430), 2m 11.081s, 99.098 mph/159.483 km/h.
Fastest qualifying lap: Tachiwaka/Takagi, 1m 53.801s, 114.146 mph/183.700 km/h.

Final championship points
1 Yuji Tachikawa, J, 67; **2** Toranosuke Takagi, J, 67; **3** Ralph Firman, GB, 61; **4** Daisuke Ito, J, 61; **5** James Courtney, AUS, 60; **6** Takeshi Tsuchiya, J, 60; **7** Satoshi Motoyama, J, 58; **8** Richard Lyons, GB, 58; **9** Masataka Yanagida, J, 57; **10** Michael Krumm, D, 57; **11** Akira Iida, J, 51; **12** Juichi Wakisaka, J, 51; **13** Sakon Yamamoto, J, 43; **14** Tatsuya Kataoka, J, 43; **15** Erik Comas, F, 42; **16** Toshihiro Kaneishi, J, 42; **17** Andre Lotterer, D, 38; **18** Tsugio Matsuda, J, 38; **19** Ryo Michigami, J, 36; **20** Takashi Kogure, J, 36.

2006

SUZUKA GT 300 km, Suzuka International Racing Course, Ino-Cho, Suzuka-shi, Mie Prefecture, Japan, 19 March. Round 1. 52 laps of the 3.608-mile/5.807-km circuit, 187.632 miles/301.964 km.
1 Juichi Wakisaka/Andre Lotterer, J/D (Lexus SC430), 1h 43m 40.197s, 108.594 mph/174.765 km/h; **2** Satoshi Motoyama/Tsugio Matsuda, J/J (Nissan Fairlady Z), 1h 43m 43.609s; **3** Daisuke Ito/Ralph Firman, J/GB (Honda NSX), 1h 43m 47.154s; **4** Ryo Michigami/Takashi Kogure, J/J (Honda NSX), 1h 43m 51.496s; **5** Yuji Tachikawa/Toranosuke Takagi, J/J (Lexus SC430), 1h 44m 08.541s; **6** Akira Iida/Tatsuya Kataoka, J/J (Lexus SC430), 1h 44m 24.783s; **7** Sébastien Philippe/Shinya Hosokawa, F/J (Honda NSX), 1h 44m 33.667s; **8** Manabu Orido/Takeshi Tsuchiya, J/J (Lexus SC430), 1h 44m 49.170s; **9** Naoki Yokomizo/Joâo Paulo de Oliveira, J/BR (Nissan Fairlady Z), 1h 44m 51.336s; **10** Erik Comas/Masataka Yanagida, F/J (Nissan Fairlady Z), 1h 44m 53.019s.
Fastest race lap: Benoît Tréluyer, F (Nissan Farlady Z), 1m 55.758s, 112.216 mph/180.594 km/h.
Fastest qualifying lap: Ito, 2m 06.533s, 102.660 mph/165.215 km/h.

OKAYAMA GT300 km, Okayama International Circuit (TI Circuit Aida), Aida Gun, Okayama Prefecture, Japan, 9 April. Round 2. 82 laps of the-mile/3.703-km circuit, 188.677 miles/303.646 kmm.
1 Ryo Michigami/Takashi Kogure, J/J (Honda NSX), 2h 01m 16.217s, 93.350 mph/150.233 km/h; **2** Sébastien Philippe/Shinya Hosokawa, F/J (Honda NSX), 2h 01m 56.268s; **3** Michael Krumm/Sakon Yamomoto, D/J (Nissan Fairlady Z), 2h 02m 02.524s; **4** Naoki Yokomizo/Joâo Paulo de Oliveira, J/BR (Nissan Fairlady Z), 2h 02m 17.594s; **5** Yuji Tachikawa/Toranosuke Takagi, J/J (Lexus SC430), 2h 02m 18.016s; **6** Benoît Tréluyer/Kazuki Hoshino, F/J (Nissan Fairlady Z), 2h 02m 22.935s; **7** Daisuke Ito/Ralph Firman, J/GB (Honda NSX), 2h 03m 00.392s; **8** Juichi Wakisaka/Andre Lotterer, J/D (Lexus SC430), 81 laps; **9** Manabu Orido/Takeshi Tsuchiya, J/J (Toyota Supra), 81; **10** Erik Comas/Masataka Yanagida, F/J (Nissan Fairlady Z), 81.
Fastest race lap: Michigami, 1m 25.632s, 96.732 mph/155.675 km/h.
Fastest qualifying lap: Michigami, 1m 24.043s, 98.561 mph/158.619 km/h.

FUJI GT 500 km, Fuji International Speedway, Sunto-gun, Shizuoka Prefecture, Japan, 4 May. Round 3. 110 laps of the 2.835-mile/4.563-km circuit, 311.885 miles/501.930 km.
1 Peter Dumbreck/Naoki Hattori, GB/J (Lexus SC430), 3h 02m 12.445s, 102.702 mph/165.283 km/h; **2** Akira Iida/Tatsuya Kataoka, J/J (Lexus SC430), 3h 02m 17.730s; **3** Satoshi Motoyama/Tsugio Matsuda, J/J (Nissan Fairlady Z), 3h 02m 43.409s; **4** Benoît Tréluyer/Kazuki Hoshino, F/J (Nissan Fairlady Z), 3h 02m 45.609s; **5** Manabu Orido/Takeshi Tsuchiya, J/J (Toyota Supra), 3h 02m 52.892s; **6** Loïc Duval/Hideki Mutoh, F/J (Honda NSX), 3h 02m 56.712s; **7** Daisuke Ito/Ralph Firman, J/GB (Honda NSX), 3h 03m 07.112s; **8** Juichi Wakisaka/Andre Lotterer, J/D (Lexus SC430), 3h 03m 12.881s; **9** Michael Krumm/Sakon Yamomoto, D/J (Nissan Fairlady Z), 3h 03m 26.248s; **10** Erik Comas/Masataka Yanagida, F/J (Nissan Fairlady Z), 109 laps.
Fastest race lap: Yuji Tachikawa, J (Lexus SC430), 1m 35.384s, 107.011 mph/172.218 km/h.
Fastest qualifying lap: Tachikawa, 1m 33.169s, 109.555 mph/176.312 km/h.

JAPAN GT CHAMPIONSHIP MALAYSIA, Sepang International Circuit, Selangor Darul Ehsan, Kuala Lumpur, Malaysia, 25 June. Round 4. 54 laps of the 3.444-mile/5.542-km circuit, 185.957 miles/299.268 km.
1 Daisuke Ito/Ralph Firman, J/GB (Honda NSX), 1h 51m 41.405s, 99.896 mph/160.767 km/h; **2** Richard Lyons/Michael Krumm, GB/D (Nissan Fairlady Z), 1h 51m 47.068s; **3** Benoît Tréluyer/Kazuki Hoshino, F/J (Nissan Fairlady Z), 1h 52m 06.525s; **4** Sébastien Philippe/Shinya Hosokawa, F/J (Honda NSX), 1h 52m 25.566s; **5** Satoshi Motoyama/Tsugio Matsuda, J/J (Nissan Fairlady Z), 1h 52m 33.042s; **6** Ryo Michigami/Takashi Kogure, J/J (Honda NSX), 1h 53m 01.859s; **7** Naoki Yokomizo/João Paulo de Oliveira, J/BR (Nissan Fairlady Z), 1h 53m 10.272s; **8** Erik Comas/Masataka Yanagida, F/J (Nissan Fairlady Z), 1h 53m 12.243s; **9** Loïc Duval/Hideki Mutoh, F/J (Honda NSX), 1h 53m 16.339s; **10** Manabu Orido/Takeshi Tsuchiya, J/J (Toyota Supra), 53 laps.
Fastest race lap: Firman, 2m 00.151s, 103.179 mph/166.051 km/h.
Fastest qualifying lap: Firman, 1m 57.866s, 105.180 mph/169.270 km/h.

SUGO GT 300 km, Sportsland-SUGO International Course, Shibata-gun, Miyagi Prefecture, Japan, 23 July. Round 5. 81 laps of the 2.302-mile/3.704-km circuit, 186.426 miles/300.024 km.
1 Yuji Tachikawa/Toranosuke Takagi, J/J (Lexus SC430), 1h 49m 19.104s, 102.321 mph/164.670 km/h; **2** Satoshi Motoyama/Tsugio Matsuda, J/J (Nissan Fairlady Z), 1h 49m 27.119s; **3** Richard Lyons/Michael Krumm, GB/D. (Nissan Fairlady Z), 1h 49m 48.270s; **4** Juichi Wakisaka/Andre Lotterer, J/D (Lexus SC430), 1h 50m 15.735s; **5** Loîc Duval/Hideki Mutoh, F/J (Honda NSX), 1h 50m 25.102s; **6** Benoît Tréluyer/Kazuki Hoshino, F/J (Nissan Fairlady Z), 1h 50m 30.513s; **7** Peter Dumbreck/Naoki Hattori, GB/J (Lexus SC430), 1h 50m 46.981s; **8** Daisuke Ito/Ralph Firman, J/GB (Honda NSX), 80 laps; **9** Akira Iida/Tatsuya Kataoka, J/J (Lexus SC430), 80; **10** Masataka Yanagida/Seji Ara, J/J (Nissan Fairlady Z), 80.
Fastest race lap: Takashi Kogure, J (Honda NSX), 1m 18.042s, 106.169 mph/170.862 km/h.
Fastest qualifying lap: Tachikawa, 1m 21.823s, 101.263 mph/162.966 km/h.

35th INTERNATIONAL POKKA 1000 km, Suzuka International Racing Course, Ino-Cho, Suzuka-shi, Mie Prefecture, Japan, 20 August. Round 6. 173 laps of the 3.608-mile/5.807-km circuit, 624.236 miles/1004.611 km.
1 Benoît Tréluyer/Kazuki Hoshino/Jérémie Dufour, F/J/F (Nissan Fairlady Z), 5h 57m 45.468s, 104.691 mph/168.485 km/h; **2** Richard Lyons/Michael Krumm/Fabio Carbone, GB/D/BR (Nissan Fairlady Z), 5h 59m 14.616s; **3** Peter Dumbreck/Naoki Hattori/Eiichi Tajima, GB/J/J (Lexus SC430), 172 laps; **4** Loîc Duval/Hideki Mutoh, F/J (Honda NSX), 172; **5** Erik Comas/Masataka Yanagida/Seji Ara, F/J/J (Nissan Fairlady Z), 172; **6** Daisuke Ito/Ralph Firman/Toshihiro Kaneishi, J/GB/J (Honda NSX), 172; **7** Yuji Tachikawa/Toranosuke Takagi/Ronnie Quintarelli, J/J/I (Lexus SC430), 171; **8** Naoki Yokomizo/João Paulo de Oliveira/Darren Manning, J/BR/GB (Nissan Fairlady Z), 171; **9** Sébastien Philippe/Shinya Hosokawa, F/J (Honda NSX), 168; **10** Juichi Wakisaka/Andre Lotterer/Adrian Sutil, J/D/D (Lexus SC430), 166.
Fastest race lap: Tréluyer, 1m 58.829s, 109.316 mph/175.927 km/h.
Fastest qualifying lap: Tréluyer, 1m 56.426s, 111.572 mph/179.558 km/h.

MOTEGI GT 300 km, Twin Ring Motegi, Motegi-machi, Haga-gun, Tochigi Prefecture, Japan, 10 September. Round 7. 63 laps of the 2.983-mile/4.801-km circuit, 187.942 miles/302.463 km.
1 Sébastien Philippe/Shinya Hosokawa, F/J (Honda NSX), 1h 56m 20.804s, 96.922 mph/155.980/km/h; **2** Juichi Wakisaka/Andre Lotterer, J/D (Lexus SC430), 1h 56m 38.471s; **3** Yuji Tachikawa/Toranosuke Takagi, J/J (Lexus SC430), 1h 57m 07.313s; **4** Akira Iida/Tatsuya Kataoka, J/J (Lexus SC430), 1h 57m 13.105s; **5** Ryo Michigami/Takashi Kogure, J/J (Honda NSX), 1h 57m 13.741s; **6** Masataka Yanagida/Seji Ara, J/J (Nissan Fairlady Z), 1h 57m 36.400s; **7** Peter Dumbreck/Naoki Hattori, GB/J (Lexus SC430), 1h 57m 44.438s; **8** Loîc Duval/Hideki Mutoh, F/J (Honda NSX), 1h 57m 44.509s; **9** André Couto/Katsuyuki Hiranaka, MAC/J (Toyota Supra), 1h 58m 05.558s; **10** Michael Krumm/Richard Lyons, D/GB (Nissan Fairlady Z), 1h 58m 07.381s.
Fastest race lap: Philippe, 1m 47.577s, 99.831 mph/160.663 km/h.
Fastest qualifying lap: Philippe, 1m 45.011s, 102.271 mph/164.588 km/h.

AUTOPOLIS GT 300 km, Autopolis International Racing Course, Kamit-sue-mura, Hita-gun, Oita Prefecture, Japan, 15 October. Round 8. 65 laps of the 2.904-mile/4.674-km circuit, 188.779 miles/303.810 km.
1 Satoshi Motoyama/Tsugio Matsuda, J/J (Nissan Fairlady Z), 1h 56m 15.613s, 97.426 mph/156.791 km/h; **2** Ryo Michigami/Takashi Kogure, J/J (Honda NSX), 1h 56m 23.538s; **3** Sébastien Philippe/Shinya Hosokawa, F/J (Honda NSX), 1h 56m 45.834s; **4** Benoît Tréluyer/Kazuki Hoshino, F/J (Nissan Fairlady Z), 1h 57m 18.097s; **5** Yuji Tachikawa/Toranosuke Takagi, J/J (Lexus SC430), 1h 57m 28.717s; **6** Michael Krumm/Richard Lyons, D/GB (Nissan Fairlady Z), 1h 57m 48.734s; **7** Juichi Wakisaka/Andre Lotterer, J/D (Lexus SC430), 1h 57m 50.298s; **8** Naoki Yokomizo/Joâo Paulo de Oliveira, J/BR (Nissan Fairlady Z), 1h 57m 50.468s; **9** Peter Dumbreck/Naoki Hattori, GB/J (Lexus SC430), 1h 58m 00.205s; **10** André Couto/Katsuyuki Hiranaka, MAC/J (Toyota Supra), 1h 58m 06.252s.
Fastest race lap: Motoyama, 1m 43.303s, 101.211 mph/162.884 km/h.
Fastest qualifying lap: Kogure, 1m 40.638s, 103.892 mph/167.197 km/h.

Provisional championship points
1 Sébastien Philippe, F, 79; **2** Shinya Hosokawa, J, 79; **3** Andre Lotterer, D, 73; **4** Yuji Tachikawa, J, 73; **5** Toranosuke Takagi, J, 73; **6** Juichi Wakisaka, J, 73; **7** Michael Krumm, D, 72; **8** Takashi Kogure, J, 72; **9** Ryo Michigami, J, 72; **10** Ralph Firman, GB, 71; **11** Daisuke Ito, J, 71; **12** Benoît Tréluyer, F, 70; **13** Kazuki Hoshino, J, 70; **14** Tsugio Matsuda, J, 69; **15** Satoshi Motoyama, J, 69; **16** Richard Lyons, GB, 57; **17** Peter Dumbreck, GB, 49; **18** Naoki Hattori, J, 49; **19** Akira Iida, J, 35; **20** Tatsuya Kataoka, J, 35.

Result of the Fuji race will be given in AUTOCOURSE 2007–2008.

Other Sports Car races

34th ADAC ZÜRICH 24h RENNEN, Nürburgring Nordschleife Circuit, Nürburg/Eifel, Germany, 17-18 June. 151 laps of the 15.769-mile/25.378-km circuit, 2381.143 miles/3832.078 km.
1 Lucas Luhr/Timo Bernhard/Mike Rockenfeller/Marcel Tiemann, (Porsche 911 GT3), 23h 59m 26.799s, 99.252 mph/159.731 km/h; **2** Jürgen Alzen/Uwe Alzen/Klaus Ludwig/Christian Abt, (Porsche GT3), 150 laps; **3** Hans-Peter Huppert-Nieder/Christopher Gerhard/Dirk Riebensahm/Werner Mohr, (Dodge Viper GTS-R), 142; **4** Bert Lambrecht/Jean-François Hemroulle/Dirk Schoysman, (Porsche 911 GT3), 140; **5** Claudia Hürtgen/Marc Hennerici/Johannes Stuck/Torsten Schubert, (BMW 120 d), 138; **6** Michael Schratz/Johannes Siegler/Arno Klasen/Jörg Viebahn, (Porsche 996 GT3-RS), 138; **7** Rudi Adams/Rainer Dörr/Marc Hennerici/Gregor Vogler, (BMW M3 CSL), 137; **8** Gary Williams/Julian Perry/Daniel Cooke/Trevor Reeves, (Porsche 911 GT3), 137; **9** Anthony Quinn/Klark Quinn/Craig Baird/Kevin Bell, (Porsche 996 GT3), 137; **10** Wolf Silverster/Thomas Dill/Matthew Marsh/Michael Bonk, (Porsche 996), 136.
Fastest qualifying lap: Luhr/Bernhard/Rockenfeller/Tiemann, 8m 38.136s, 109.564 mph/176.326 km/h.

74th 24 HEURES DU MANS, Circuit International Du Mans, Les Raineries, Le Mans, France, 17–18 June. 380 laps of the 8.482-mile/13.650-km circuit, 322.052 miles/518.000 km.
1 Frank Biela/Emanuele Pirro/Marco Werner, D/I/D (Audi R10 TDI), 24h 04m 47.325s, 133.849 mph/215.409 km/h (1st LMP1 class); **2** Franck Montagny/Eric Hélary/Sébastien Loeb, F/F/F (Pescarolo C60H-Judd), 376 laps; **3** Tom Kristensen/Rinado Capello/Allan McNish, DK/I/GB (Audi R10 TDI), 367; **4** Oliver Gavin/Olivier Beretta/Jan Magnussen, GB/MC/DK (Chevrolet Corvette C6.R), 355 (1st GT1 class); **5** Emmanuel Collard/Nicolas Minassian/Erik Comas, F/F/F (Pescarolo C60H-Judd), 352; **6** Darren Turner/Tomás Enge/Andrea Piccini, GB/CZ/I (Aston Martin DBR9), 350; **7** Luc Alphand/Jérôme Policand/Patrice Goueslard, F/F/F (Chevrolet Corvette C5-R), 346; **8** Thomas Erdos/Mike Newton/Andy Wallace, BR/GB/GB (MG Lola EX264-AER), 343 (1st LMP2 class); **9** David Brabham/Nelson Angelo Piquet/Antonio Gárcia, AUS/BR/E (Aston Martin DBR9), 343; **10** Stéphane Sarrazin/Pedro Lamy/Stéphane Ortelli, F/P/MC (Aston Martin DBR9), 342; **11** Johnny Mowlem/Terry Borcheller/Christian Fittipaldi, GB/USA/BR (Saleen S7R), 337; **12** Ron Fellows/Johnny O'Connell/Massimiliano 'Max' Papis, CDN/USA/I (Chevrolet Corvette C6.R), 327; **13** Bill Binnie/Yojiro Terada/Allen Timpany, USA/J/GB (Lola B05/40-Zytek), 326; **14** John Macaluso/Andy Lally/Gue/Ian James, USA/USA/GB (Courage C65-AER), 324; **15** Tom Kimber-Smith/Lawrence Tomlinson/Richard Dean, GB/GB/GB (Panoz Esperante GT-LM), 321 (1st GT2 class); **16** Lars-Erik Nielsen/Dominik Farnbacher/Pierre Ehret, DK/D/D (Porsche 911 GT3-RSR), 320; **17** Tim Mullen/Andrew Kirkaldy/Chris Niarchos, GB/GB/CDN (Ferrari F430 GT), 311; **18** Johannes van Overbeek/Patrick Long/Seth Neiman, USA/USA/USA (Porsche 911 GT3-RSR), 309; **19** Clint Field/Liz Halliday/Duncan Dayton, USA/USA/USA (Lola B05/40-AER), 297; **20** Martin Short/João Barbosa/Stuart Moseley, GB/P/GB (Radical SR9-Judd), 294; **21** Juan Barazi/Michael Vergers/Neil Cunningham, DK/NL/GB (Courage C65-AER), 294; **22** Kazuyuki Nishizawa/Shinichi Yamaji/Philip Collin, J/J/USA (Porsche 911 GT3-RSR), 291; **23** Yves Lambert/Christian Lefort/Romain Ianetta, B/B/F (Porsche 911 GT3-RSR), 282; **24** John Nielsen/Casper Elgaard/Philip Andersen, DK/DK/DK (Zytek 06S), 269; **25** Bob Berridge/Gareth Evans/Peter Owen, GB/GB/GB (Lola B06/10-AER), 267; **26** Marco Apicella/Yasutaka Hinoi/Koji Yamanishi, I/J/J (Lamborghini Murciélago R-GT), 283 (DNF-mechanical); **27** Xavier Pompidou/Christian Ried/Thorkild Thyrring, F/D/DK (Porsche 911 GT3-RSR), 256 (DNF-prop shaft); **28** Marc Rostan/Chris MacAllister/Simon Pullan, F/USA/GB (Pilbeam MP93-Judd), 244; **29** Jamie Campbell-Walter/Beppe Gabbiani/Felipe Ortiz, GB/I/CH (Creation CA06/H-Judd), 240 (DNF-engine); **30** Romain Dumas/Luca Riccitelli/Raymond Narac, F/I/F (Porsche 911 GT3-RSR), 211 (DNF-engine); **31** Jeroen Bleekemolen/Mike Hezemans/Jonny Kane, NL/NL/GB (Spyker C8 Spyder GT2-R), 202 (DNF-engine); **32** Gabriele Gardel/Patrick Bornhauser/Jean-Luc Blanchemain, CH/F/F (Ferrari 550 Maranello), 199 (DNF-clutch); **33** Peter Kox/Alexei Vasiliev/Robert Pergl, NL/RUS/CZ (Ferrari 550 Maranello), 196 (DNF-accident); **34** Yutaka Yamagishi/Jean-Rene de Fournoux/Miroslav Konopka, J/F/SK (Porsche 911 GT3-RS), 196 (DNF-fuel system); **35** Warren Hughes/Miguel Amaral/Miguel Angel De Castro, GB/P/E (Lola B05/40-AER), 193 (DNF-gearbox); **36** Jens Moller/Gavin Pickering/Nicolas Kiesa, DK/GB/DK (Lister Storm-Chevrolet), 192 (DNF-engine); **37** Jan Lammers/Alex Yoong/Stefan Johansson, NL/MAL/S (Dome S101-HB-Judd), 182 (DNF-accident); **38** Alexander Frei/Sam Hancock/Gregor Fisken, CH/GB/GB (Courage LC70-Mugen Honda), 171 (DNF-engine); **39** Jörg Bergmeister/Tracy Krohn/Niclas Jönsson, D/USA/S (Porsche 911 GT3-RSR), 148 (DNF-accident); **40** Julien Briche/Frédéric Hauchard/Patrice Roussel, F/F/F (WR-Peugeot), 134 (DNF-fire); **41** Harold Primat/Marcel Fässler/Philipp Peter, CH/CH/A (Courage LC70-Judd), 132 (DNF-gearbox); **42** Christian Vann/Tim Sugden/Nigel Smith, GB/GB/GB (Ferrari 550 Maranello), 124 (DNF-engine); **43** Patrick Bourdais/Tom Cloet/Adam Sharpe, F/B/GB (Porsche 911 GT3-RSR), 115 (DNF-accident); **44** Claude-Yves Gosselin/Karim Oijeh/Pierre Ragues, F/ZA/F (Courage C65-Mecachrome), 84 (DNF-gearbox); **45** Ed Morris/Frank Hahn/Jean-François Leroch, GB/B/F (Courage C65-Judd), 47 (DNF-gearbox); **46** Didier André/Yann Clairay/Jean-Pierre Bouvet, F/F/F (Courage C65-Mecachrome), 42 (DNF-accident); **47** Donny Crevels/Tom Coronel/Peter Dumbreck, NL/NL/GB (Spyker C8 Syder GT2-R), 40 (DNF-engine); **48** Shinji Nakano/Haruki Kurosawa/Jean-Marc Gounon, J/J/F (Courage LC70-Mugen Honda), 35 (DNF-power steering); **49** Scott Maxwell/Gunnar Jeanette/Tom Milner, CDN/USA/USA (Panoz Esperante GT-LM), 34 (DNF-fuel system); **50** Fabrizio Gollin/Fabio Babini/Christian Pescatori, I/I/I (Aston Martin DBR9), 3 (DNF-accident).
Fastest race lap: Kristensen, 3m 31.211s, 144.567 mph/232.658 km/h.
Fastest qualifying lap: Capello, 3m 30.466s, 145.079 mph/233.482 km/h.

V8 Supercar Championship Series 2005

The following races were run after AUTOCOURSE 2005–2006 went to press.

FERODO TRIPLE CHALLENGE, Symmons Plains Raceway, Launceston, Tasmania, Australia, 12/13 November. Round 12. 3 x 42 laps of the 2.778-mile/4.470-km circuit.
Race 1 (116.656 miles/187.740 km).
1 Garth Tander, AUS (Holden Commodore VZ), 37m 37.9265s, 185.995 mph/299.329 km/h; **2** Steven Richards, NZ (Holden Commodore VY), 37m 38.9493s; **3** Rick Kelly, AUS (Holden Commodore VZ), 37m 42.4512s; **4** Marcos Ambrose, AUS (Ford Falcon BA), 37m 43.2359s; **5** Craig Lowndes, AUS (Ford Falcon BA), 37m 50.1054s; **6** Paul Dumbrell, AUS (Holden Commodore VY), 37m 51.9739s; **7** Jason Bright, AUS (Ford Falcon BA), 37m 54.1833s; **8** Russell Ingall, AUS (Ford Falcon BA), 37m 55.0807s; **9** Steve Ellery, AUS (Ford Falcon BA), 37m 56.3272s; **10** Steven Johnson, AUS (Ford Falcon BA), 38m 06.2982s.
Fastest race lap: Tander, 52.1863, 191.604 mph/308.357 km/h.
Pole position: Richards (Steven), 52.0726s, 192.022 mph/309.030 km/h.

Race 2 (116.656 miles/187.740 km).
1 Garth Tander, AUS (Holden Commodore VZ), 42m 01.6956s, 166.540 mph/268.020 km/h; **2** Steven Richards, NZ (Holden Commodore VY), 42m 02.7158s; **3** Craig Lowndes, AUS (Ford Falcon BA), 42m 09.8762s; **4** Rick Kelly, AUS (Holden Commodore VZ), 42m 10.5926s; **5** Greg Murphy, NZ (Holden Commodore VZ), 42m 13.5152s; **6** Paul Dumbrell, AUS (Holden Commodore VY), 42m 15.2440s; **7** Steven Johnson, AUS (Ford Falcon BA), 42m 16.9741s; **8** Jason Richards, NZ (Holden Commodore VZ), 42m 17.2345s; **9** Russell Ingall, AUS (Ford Falcon BA), 42m 17.6409s; **10** Paul Radisich, NZ (Holden Commodore VZ), 42m 18.0503s.
Fastest race lap: Richards (Steven), 52m 3600s, 190.968 mph/307.334 km/h.

Race 3 (116.656 miles/187.740 km).
1 Garth Tander, AUS (Holden Commodore VZ), 37m 27.6869s, 186.842 mph/300.693 km/h; **2** Rick Kelly, AUS (Holden Commodore VZ), 37m 28.9664s; **3** Craig Lowndes, AUS (Ford Falcon BA), 37m 35.4204s; **4** Steven Richards, NZ (Holden Commodore VY), 37m 37.5607s; **5** Greg Murphy, NZ (Holden Commodore VZ), 37m 40.7427s; **6** Marcos Ambrose, AUS (Ford Falcon BA), 37m 41.2304s; **7** Todd Kelly, AUS (Holden Commodore VZ), 37m 43.3004s; **8** Steven Johnson, AUS (Ford Falcon BA), 37m 47.8380s; **9** Mark Skaife, AUS (Holden Commodore VZ), 37m 48.0143s; **10** Russell Ingall, AUS (Ford Falcon BA), 37m 48.6761s.
Fastest race lap: Richards (Steven), 52.0170s, 192.228 mph/309.360 km/h.

BIGPOND GRAND FINALE, Phillip Island Grand Prix Circuit, Cowes, Victoria, Australia, 26/27 November. Round 13. 23, 32 and 32 laps of the 2.771-mile/4.460-km circuit.
Race 1 (63.740 miles/102.580 km).
1 Craig Lowndes, AUS (Ford Falcon BA), 37m 30.4916s, 101.962 mph/164.092 km/h; **2** Garth Tander, AUS (Holden Commodore VZ), 37m 33.3138s; **3** Marcos Ambrose, AUS (Ford Falcon BA), 37m 39.1339s; **4** Rick Kelly, AUS (Holden Commodore VZ), 37m 42.1792s; **5** Russell Ingall, AUS (Ford Falcon BA), 37m 47.2869s; **6** Greg Murphy, NZ (Holden Commodore VZ), 37m 48.3437s; **7** Paul Radisich, NZ (Holden Commodore VZ), 37m 51.4189s; **8** Steve Ellery, AUS (Ford Falcon BA), 37m 51.9302s; **9** Paul Dumbrell, AUS (Holden Commodore VZ), 37m 53.4706s; **10** Paul Weel, AUS (Holden Commodore VZ), 37m 54.7884s.
Fastest race lap: Lowndes, 1m 34.6779s, 105.376 mph/169.586 km/h.
Pole position: Lowndes, 1m 33.2826s, 106.952 mph/172.122 km/h.

Race 2 (88.682 miles/142.720 km).
1 Marcos Ambrose, AUS (Ford Falcon BA), 51m 45.7816s, 102.794 mph/165.431 km/h; **2** Garth Tander, AUS (Holden Commodore VZ), 51m 52.1387s; **3** Craig Lowndes, AUS (Ford Falcon BA), 52m 03.0595s; **4** Rick Kelly, AUS (Holden Commodore VZ), 52m 05.7323s; **5** Russell Ingall, AUS (Ford Falcon BA), 52m 05.8683s; **6** Steve Ellery, AUS (Ford Falcon BA), 52m 06.6799s; **7** Greg Murphy, NZ (Holden Commodore VZ), 52m 06.9645s; **8** Paul Radisich, NZ (Holden Commodore VZ), 52m 12.4863s; **9** Paul Weel, AUS (Holden Commodore VZ), 52m 17.3569s; **10** Mark Skaife, AUS (Holden Commodore VZ), 52m 17.7944s.
Fastest race lap: Tander, 1m 34.0821s, 106.043 mph/170.659 km/h.

Race 3 (88.682 miles/142.720 km).
1 Marcos Ambrose, AUS (Ford Falcon BA), 54m 41.2786s, 97.296 mph/156.583 km/h; **2** Greg Murphy, NZ (Holden Commodore VZ), 54m 43.3522s; **3** Rick Kelly, AUS (Holden Commodore VZ), 54m 44.4252s; **4** Garth Tander, AUS (Holden Commodore VZ), 54m 45.4194s; **5** Russell Ingall, AUS (Ford Falcon BA), 54m 45.5484s; **6** Todd Kelly, AUS (Holden Commodore VZ), 54m 45.9631s; **7** Jason Bright, AUS (Ford Falcon BA), 54m 46.0926s; **8** Mark Skaife, AUS (Holden Commodore VZ), 54m 46.9760s; **9** Paul Weel, AUS (Holden Commodore VZ), 54m 49.5118s; **10** Steve Ellery, AUS (Ford Falcon BA), 54m 51.1540s.
Fastest race lap: Ambrose, 1m 34.9596s, 105.063 mph/169.082 km/h.

Final championship points
1 Russell Ingall, AUS, 1922; **2** Craig Lowndes, AUS, 1865; **3** Marcos Ambrose, AUS, 1856; **4** Todd Kelly, AUS, 1760; **5** Mark Skaife, AUS, 1754; **6** Garth Tander, AUS, 1734; **7** Steven Richards, NZ, 1669; **8** Rick Kelly, AUS, 1630; **9** Jason Bright, AUS, 1566; **10** Cameron McConville, AUS, 1501; **11** Greg Murphy, NZ, 1500; **12** Steven Johnson, AUS, 1460; **13** Steve Ellery, AUS, 1424; **14** Paul Radisich, NZ, 1384; **15** Glenn Seton, AUS, 1353; **16** Jamie Whincup, AUS, 1307; **17** Jason Richards, NZ, 1295; **18** John Bowe, AUS, 1235; **19** Paul Morris, AUS, 1059; **20** Paul Dumbrell, AUS, 1046.

2006

CLIPSAL 500, Adelaide street circuit, South Australia, Australia, 25/26 March. Round 1. 2 x 78 laps of the 2.001-mile/3.220-km circuit.
Race 1 (156.064 miles/251.160 km).
1 Craig Lowndes, AUS (Ford Falcon BA), 2h 04m 18.5229s, 75.327 mph/121.227 km/h; **2** Rick Kelly, AUS (Holden Commodore VZ), 2h 04m 19.7823s; **3** Jamie Whincup, AUS (Ford

Falcon BA), 2h 04m 20.1415s; **4** Cameron McConville, AUS (Holden Commodore VZ), 2h 04m 21.2972s; **5** Greg Murphy, NZ (Holden Commodore VZ), 2h 04m 23.8766s; **6** Todd Kelly, AUS (Holden Commodore VZ), 2h 04m 25.2570s; **7** Steven Richards, NZ (Holden Commodore VZ), 2h 04m 26.9040s; **8** Garth Tander, AUS (Holden Commodore VZ), 2h 04m 27.9997s; **9** Russell Ingall, AUS (Ford Falcon BA), 2h 04m 32.5528s; **10** Steven Johnson, AUS (Ford Falcon BA), 2h 04m 37.6592s.
Fastest race lap: Kelly (Todd), 1m 23.6018s, 86.158 mph/138.657 km/h.
Pole position: Mark Skaife, AUS (Holden Commodore VZ), 1m 21.6102s, 88.260 mph/142.041 km/h.

Race 2 (156.064 miles/251.160 km).
1 Jamie Whincup, AUS (Ford Falcon BA), 2h 01m 28.4014s, 77.085 mph/124.056 km/h; **2** Todd Kelly, AUS (Holden Commodore VZ), 2h 01m 30.3278s; **3** Rick Kelly, AUS (Holden Commodore VZ), 2h 01m 38.3490s; **4** Garth Tander, AUS (Holden Commodore VZ), 2h 01m 44.1111s; **5** Steven Richards, NZ (Holden Commodore VZ), 2h 01m 46.0367s; **6** Paul Dumbrell, AUS (Holden Commodore VZ), 2h 01m 47.2022s; **7** Russell Ingall, AUS (Ford Falcon BA), 2h 01m 47.7886s; **8** Max Wilson, BR (Ford Falcon BA), 2h 01m 48.7274s; **9** Steven Johnson, AUS (Ford Falcon BA), 2h 01m 49.2540s; **10** Jason Richards, NZ (Holden Commodore VZ), 2h 01m 49.8126s.
Fastest race lap: Richards (Jason), 1m 22.8244s, 86.966 mph/139.958 km/h.
Pole position: Lowndes.

PLACEMAKERS V8 SUPERCARS, Pukekohe Park Raceway, Auckland, New Zealand, 22/23 April. Round 2. 36, 47 and 50 laps of the 1.765-mile/2.841-km circuit.
Race 1 (miles/102.276 km).
1 Mark Skaife, AUS (Holden Commodore VZ), 39m 35.1429s, 96.325 mph/155.019 km/h; **2** Russell Ingall, AUS (Ford Falcon BA), 39m 36.5649s; **3** Jason Bright, AUS (Ford Falcon BA), 39m 42.3241s; **4** Mark Winterbottom, AUS (Ford Falcon BA), 39m 47.6921s; **5** Craig Lowndes, AUS (Ford Falcon BA), 39m 49.0231s; **6** Max Wilson, BR (Ford Falcon BA), 39m 57.8750s; **7** Steven Richards, NZ (Holden Commodore VZ), 39m 59.6275s; **8** James Courtney, AUS (Ford Falcon BA), 40m 00.5678s; **9** Steven Johnson, AUS (Ford Falcon BA), 40m 01.4029s; **10** Paul Dumbrell, AUS (Holden Commodore VZ), 40m 02.7717s.
Fastest race lap: Garth Tander, AUS (Holden Commodore VZ), 56.4767s, 112.527 mph/181.094 km/h.
Pole position: Tander, 55.7253s, 114.044 mph/183.536 km/h.

Race 2 (82.970 miles/133.527 km).
1 Garth Tander, AUS (Holden Commodore VZ), 1h 55m 39.7648s, 43.041 mph/69.267 km/h; **2** Jason Richards, NZ (Holden Commodore VZ), 1h 55m 42.4347s; **3** Mark Winterbottom, AUS (Ford Falcon BA), 1h 55m 47.0851s; **4** Cameron McConville, AUS (Holden Commodore VZ), 1h 55m 49.5107s; **5** Mark Skaife, AUS (Holden Commodore VZ), 1h 55m 56.1822s; **6** Russell Ingall, AUS (Ford Falcon BA), 1h 55m 57.8841s; **7** Paul Morris, AUS (Holden Commodore VZ), 1h 55m 59.5984s; **8** Will Davison, AUS (Ford Falcon BA), 1h 56m 00.1659s; **9** Steven Johnson, AUS (Ford Falcon BA), 1h 56m 00.3839s; **10** Rick Kelly, AUS (Holden Commodore VZ), 1h 56m 06.2581s.
Fastest race lap: Tander, 56.6930s, 112.097 mph/180.403 km/h.
Pole position: Greg Murphy, NZ (Holden Commodore VZ).

Race 3 (88.266 miles/142.050 km).
1 Mark Skaife, AUS (Holden Commodore VZ), 50m 57.1288s, 103.40 mph/167.274 km/h; **2** Craig Lowndes, AUS (Ford Falcon BA), 51m 00.7955s; **3** Mark Winterbottom, AUS (Ford Falcon BA), 51m 01.4869s; **4** Garth Tander, AUS (Holden Commodore VZ), 51m 03.2407s; **5** Russell Ingall, AUS (Ford Falcon BA), 51m 04.2638s; **6** Steven Richards, NZ (Holden Commodore VZ), 51m 04.9040s; **7** Rick Kelly, AUS (Holden Commodore VZ), 51m 15.0953s; **8** James Courtney, AUS (Ford Falcon BA), 51m 15.9045s; **9** Steven Johnson, AUS (Ford Falcon BA), 51m 17.0518s; **10** Jamie Whincup, AUS (Ford Falcon BA), 51m 17.3490s.
Fastest race lap: Ingall, 56.5219s, 112.437 mph/180.949 km/h.
Pole position: Tander.

PERTH V8 400, Barbagallo Raceway Wanneroo, Perth, Western Australia, Australia, 13/14 May. Round 3. 50, 58 and 58 laps of the 1.498-mile/2.410-km circuit.
Race 1 (174.875 miles/120.500 km).
1 Mark Skaife, AUS (Holden Commodore VZ), 49m 00.3114s, 91.674 mph/147.535 km/h; **2** Steven Richards, NZ (Holden Commodore VZ), 49m 00.7723s; **3** Craig Lowndes, AUS (Ford Falcon BA), 49m 00.9924s; **4** Garth Tander, AUS (Holden Commodore VZ), 49m 01.4237s; **5** Jason Bright, AUS (Ford Falcon BA), 49m 01.7900s; **6** Mark Winterbottom, AUS (Ford Falcon BA), 49m 06.5507s; **7** Rick Kelly, AUS (Holden Commodore VZ), 49m 07.7419s; **8** Max Wilson, BR (Ford Falcon BA), 49m 21.5113s; **9** Steven Johnson, AUS (Ford Falcon BA), 49m 21.7530s; **10** Russell Ingall, AUS (Ford Falcon BA), 49m 21.7676s.
Fastest race lap: Todd Kelly, AUS (Holden Commodore VZ), 57.5198s, 93.25 mph/150.835 km/h.
Pole position: Skaife, 55.8667s, 96.498 mph/155.298 km/h.

Race 2 (86.855 miles/139.780 km).
1 Dean Canto, AUS (Holden Commodore VZ), 57m 13.4263s, 1.069 mph/146.561 km/h; **2** Steven Richards, NZ (Holden Commodore VZ), 57m 14.8926s; **3** Greg Murphy, NZ (Holden Commodore VZ), 57m 16.0753s; **4** Jamie Whincup, AUS (Ford Falcon BA), 57m 16.1912s; **5** James Courtney, AUS (Ford Falcon BA), 57m 19.5969s; **6** Paul Radisich, NZ (Holden Commodore VZ), 57m 21.7307s; **7** Andrew Jones, AUS (Holden Commodore VZ), 57m 25.0429s; **8** Russell Ingall, AUS (Ford Falcon BA), 57m 26.3092s; **9** Jason Richards, NZ (Holden Commodore VZ), 57m 27.0953s; **10** Garth Tander, AUS (Holden Commodore VZ), 57m 27.7511s.
Fastest race lap: Kelly (Todd), 57.4096s, 93.904 mph/151.124 km/h.
Pole position: Radisich.

Race 3 (86.855 miles/139.780 km).
1 Mark Skaife, AUS (Holden Commodore VZ), 58m 24.7679s, 89.215 mph/143.578 km/h; **2** Craig Lowndes, AUS (Ford Falcon BA), 58m 25.4331s; **3** Mark Winterbottom, AUS (Ford Falcon BA), 58m 27.4734s; **4** Todd Kelly, AUS (Holden Commodore VZ), 58m 28.0506s; **5** Garth Tander, AUS (Holden Commodore VZ), 58m 28.3312s; **6** Russell Ingall, AUS (Ford Falcon BA), 58m 34.8207s; **7** Steven Richards, NZ (Holden Commodore VZ), 58m 35.2860s; **8** Jason Richards, NZ (Holden Commodore VZ), 58m 37.4045s; **9** Jamie Whincup, AUS (Ford Falcon BA), 58m 38.5404s; **10** Steven Johnson, AUS (Ford Falcon BA), 58m 39.3283s.
Fastest race lap: Tander, 57.2925s, 94.096 mph/151.433 km/h.
Pole position: Canto.

V8 SUPERCAR CHAMPIONSHIP SERIES, Winton Motor Raceway, Victoria, Australia, 3/4 June. Round 4. 34, 46 and 46 laps of the 1.864-mile/3.000-km circuit.
Race 1 (63.380 miles/102.000 km).
1 Jason Bright, AUS (Ford Falcon BA), 48m 58.1947s, 77.656 mph/124.974 km/h; **2** Craig Lowndes, AUS (Ford Falcon BA), 49m 04.3689s; **3** Paul Dumbrell, AUS (Holden Commodore VZ), 49m 07.4846s; **4** Todd Kelly, AUS (Holden Commodore VZ), 49m 13.1387s; **5** Mark Skaife, AUS (Holden Commodore VZ), 49m 16.2201s; **6** Garth Tander, AUS (Holden Commodore VZ), 49m 16.8950s; **7** Steven Richards, NZ (Holden Commodore VZ), 49m 17.3677s; **8** Mark Winterbottom, AUS (Ford Falcon BA), 49m 21.4159s; **9** Greg Murphy, NZ (Holden Commodore VZ), 49m 29.2665s; **10** Rick Kelly, AUS (Holden Commodore VZ), 49m 31.3390s.
Fastest race lap: Bright, 1m 24.2992s, 79.607 mph/128.115 km/h.
Pole position: Bright, 1m 23.6101s, 80.263 mph/129.170 km/h.

Race 2 (85.749 miles/138.000 km).
1 Jason Richards, NZ (Holden Commodore VZ), 1h 06m 28.8562s, 77.390 mph/124.546 km/h; **2** Jamie Whincup, AUS (Ford Falcon BA), 1h 06m 43.0595s; **3** Dean Canto, AUS (Holden Commodore VZ), 1h 06m 57.1376s; **4** Rick Kelly, AUS (Holden Commodore VZ), 1h 07m 01.3111s; **5** Russell Ingall, AUS (Ford Falcon BA), 1h 07m 01.6610s; **6** Max Wilson, BR (Ford Falcon BA), 1h 07m 06.3373s; **7** Steve Owen, AUS (Holden Commodore VZ), 1h 07m 06.6876s; **8** Craig Lowndes, AUS (Ford Falcon BA), 1h 07m 07.5835s; **9** Marcus Marshall, AUS (Ford Falcon BA), 1h 07m 12.1196s; **10** Garth Tander, AUS (Holden Commodore VZ), 1h 07m 15.2256s.
Warren Luff, AUS (Ford Falcon BA), finished 6th in 1h 07m 02.7612s, but was given a 27-second penalty.
Fastest race lap: Bright, 1m 24.8965s, 79.047 mph/127.213 km/h.
Pole position: Fabian Coulthard, NZ (Holden Commodore VZ).

Race 3 (85.749 miles/138.000 km).
1 Craig Lowndes, AUS (Ford Falcon BA), 1h 07m 17.6312s, 76.455 mph/123.042 km/h; **2** Jason Bright, AUS (Ford Falcon BA), 1h 07m 18.0225s; **3** Mark Skaife, AUS (Holden Commodore VZ), 1h 07m 37.2079s; **4** Rick Kelly, AUS (Holden Commodore VZ), 1h 07m 38.8260s; **5** Garth Tander, AUS (Holden Commodore VZ), 1h 07m 38.2255s; **6** Mark Winterbottom, AUS (Ford Falcon BA), 1h 07m 42.2733s; **7** Paul Dumbrell, AUS (Holden Commodore VZ), 1h 07m 45.7045s; **8** Jason Richards, NZ (Holden Commodore VZ), 1h 07m 46.7250s; **9** Jamie Whincup, AUS (Ford Falcon BA), 1h 07m 47.7902s; **10** Steven Richards, NZ (Holden Commodore VZ), 1h 07m 49.9949s.
Fastest race lap: Bright, 1m 24.1951s, 79.705 mph/128.273 km/h.
Pole position: Richards (Jason).

SKYCITY TRIPLE CROWN DARWIN, Hidden Valley Raceway, Darwin, Northern Territory, Australia, 1/2 July. Round 5. 34, 48 and 48 laps of the 1.783-mile/2.870-km circuit.
Race 1 (60.633 miles/97.580 km).
1 Mark Skaife, AUS (Holden Commodore VZ), 41m 07.5941s, 88.459 mph/142.360 km/h; **2** Rick Kelly, AUS (Holden Commodore VZ), 41m 08.3070s; **3** Mark Winterbottom, AUS (Ford Falcon BA), 41m 14.6906s; **4** Craig Lowndes, AUS (Ford Falcon BA), 41m 15.1266s; **5** Garth Tander, AUS (Holden Commodore VZ), 41m 15.6826s; **6** Jason Richards, NZ (Holden Commodore VZ), 41m 16.6770s; **7** Steven Richards, NZ (Holden Commodore VZ), 41m 23.4048s; **8** Paul Dumbrell, AUS (Holden Commodore VZ), 41m 27.7813s; **9** Jamie Whincup, AUS (Ford Falcon BA), 41m 27.9854s; **10** Russell Ingall, AUS (Ford Falcon BA), 41m 28.0041s.
Fastest race lap: Jason Bright, AUS (Ford Falcon BA), 1m 10.2958s, 91.328 mph/146.978 km/h.
Pole position: Bright, 1m 09.0322s, 93.000 mph/149.669 km/h.

Race 2 (85.600 miles/137.760 km).
1 Jason Bright, AUS (Ford Falcon BA), 1h 00m 37.8417s, 84.710 mph/136.326 km/h; **2** Steven Johnson, AUS (Ford Falcon BA), 1h 00m 42.1282s; **3** Craig Lowndes, AUS (Ford Falcon BA), 1h 00m 42.2795s; **4** Warren Luff, AUS (Ford Falcon BA), 1h 00m 46.6306s; **5** Jamie Whincup, AUS (Ford Falcon BA), 1h 00m 46.6962s; **6** James Courtney, AUS (Ford Falcon BA), 1h 00m 51.7571s; **7** Russell Ingall, AUS (Ford Falcon BA), 1h 00m 54.7262s; **8** Garth Tander, AUS (Holden Commodore VZ), 1h 00m 57.4402s; **9** Greg Murphy, NZ (Holden Commodore VZ), 1h 00m 58.9560s; **10** Rick Kelly, AUS (Holden Commodore VZ), 1h 01m 01.2093s.
Fastest race lap: Winterbottom, 1m 10.1260s, 91.550 mph/147.334 km/h.
Pole position: Luff.

Race 3 (85.600 miles/137.760 km).
1 Craig Lowndes, AUS (Ford Falcon BA), 57m 53.3776s, 88.721 mph/142.782 km/h; **2** Jason Richards, NZ (Holden Commodore VZ), 57m 57.1837s; **3** Garth Tander, AUS (Holden Commodore VZ), 58m 11.5271s; **4** Jason Bright, AUS (Ford Falcon BA), 58m 12.0281s; **5** Rick Kelly, AUS (Holden Commodore VZ), 58m 15.8068s; **6** Mark Skaife, AUS (Holden Commodore VZ), 58m 16.2951s; **7** Cameron McConville, AUS (Holden Commodore VZ), 58m 23.5980s; **8** Mark Winterbottom, AUS (Ford Falcon BA), 58m 25.0025s; **9** Russell Ingall, AUS (Ford Falcon BA), 58m 25.4393s; **10** Jason Bargwanna, AUS (Ford Falcon BA), 58m 46.5512s.
Max Wilson, BR (Ford Falcon BA), finished 10th in 58m 28.9404s, but was given a 27-second penalty.
Fastest race lap: Bright, 1m 10.2851s, 91.342 mph/147.001 km/h.
Pole position: Bright.

BIGPOND 300, Queensland Raceway, Ipswich, Queensland, Australia, 22/23 July. Round 6. 32, 45 and 45 laps of the 1.942-mile/3.126-km circuit.
Race 1 (62.157 miles/100.032 km).
1 Garth Tander, AUS (Holden Commodore VZ), 39m 57.9354s, 93.316 mph/150.177 km/h; **2** Jason Bright, AUS (Ford Falcon BA), 39m 59.5765s; **3** James Courtney, AUS (Ford Falcon BA), 40m 00.4475s; **4** Craig Lowndes, AUS (Ford Falcon BA), 40m 00.9525s; **5** Russell Ingall, AUS (Ford Falcon BA), 40m 01.4435s; **6** Steven Richards, NZ (Holden Commodore VZ), 40m 03.9194s; **7** Rick Kelly, AUS (Holden Commodore VZ), 40m 05.2286s; **8** Jamie Whincup, AUS (Ford Falcon BA), 40m 05.6051s; **9** Mark Winterbottom, AUS (Ford Falcon BA), 40m 05.8446s; **10** Max Wilson, BR (Ford Falcon BA), 40m 07.7044s.
Fastest race lap: Tander, 1m 11.4130s, 97.919 mph/157.584 km/h.
Pole position: Tander, 1m 10.3713s, 99.368 mph/159.917 km/h.

Race 2 (87.408 miles/140.670 km).
1 Mark Skaife, AUS (Holden Commodore VZ), 57m 49.9456s, 90.684 mph/145.942 km/h; **2** Garth Tander, AUS (Holden Commodore VZ), 57m 52.6080s; **3** James Courtney, AUS (Ford Falcon BA), 57m 53.9257s; **4** Rick Kelly, AUS (Holden Commodore VZ), 57m 54.8997s; **5** Craig Lowndes, AUS (Ford Falcon BA), 57m 56.5589s; **6** Paul Morris, AUS (Holden Commodore VZ), 57m 58.3991s; **7** Mark Winterbottom, AUS (Ford Falcon BA), 57m 59.3513s; **8** Jason Bright, AUS (Ford Falcon BA), 57m 59.8155s; **9** Russell Ingall, AUS (Ford Falcon BA), 58m 00.3002s; **10** Cameron McConville, AUS (Holden Commodore VZ), 58m 00.7142s.
Fastest race lap: Tander, 1m 11.9607s, mph/156.385 km/h.
Pole position: Todd Kelly, AUS (Holden Commodore VZ).

Race 3 (87.408 miles/140.670 km).
1 Garth Tander, AUS (Holden Commodore VZ), 56m 27.2356s, 92.899 mph/149.505 km/h; **2** Rick Kelly, AUS (Holden Commodore VZ), 56m 31.9486s; **3** Jason Bright, AUS (Ford Falcon BA), 56m 32.3848s; **4** Craig Lowndes, AUS (Ford Falcon BA), 56m 32.7280s; **5** Russell Ingall, AUS (Ford Falcon BA), 56m 33.2109s; **6** Steven Richards, NZ (Holden Commodore VZ), 56m 39.0807s; **7** Paul Radisich, NZ (Holden Commodore VZ), 56m 43.8866s; **8** Jamie Whincup, AUS (Ford Falcon BA), 56m 44.1400s; **9** Mark Winterbottom, AUS (Ford Falcon BA), 56m 44.5806s; **10** Greg Murphy, NZ (Holden Commodore VZ), 56m 45.6445s.
Fastest race lap: Courtney, 1m 11.7040s, 97.521 mph/156.945 km/h.
Pole position: Skaife.

V8 SUPERCAR CHAMPIONSHIP SERIES, Oran Park Raceway, Narellan, New South Wales, Australia, 12/13 August. Round 7. 38, 53 and 53 laps of the 1.628-mile/2.620-km circuit.
Race 1 (61.864 miles/99.560 km).
1 Todd Kelly, AUS (Holden Commodore VZ), 47m 30.4899s, 78.130 mph/125.738 km/h; **2** Craig Lowndes, AUS (Ford Falcon BA), 47m 30.8716s; **3** Rick Kelly, AUS (Holden Commodore VZ), 47m 31.9595s; **4** Jason Bright, AUS (Ford Falcon BA), 47m 34.2824s; **5** Jamie Whincup, AUS (Ford Falcon BA), 47m 35.4227s; **6** Jason Richards, NZ (Holden Commodore VZ), 47m 36.4667s; **7** Mark Winterbottom, AUS (Ford Falcon BA), 47m 39.9245s; **8** Steven Richards, NZ (Holden Commodore VZ), 47m 41.4296s; **9** James Courtney, AUS (Ford Falcon BA), 47m 42.5203s; **10** Steven Johnson, AUS (Ford Falcon BA), 47m 43.0986s.
Fastest race lap: Mark Skaife, AUS (Holden Commodore VZ), 1m 09.9019s, 83.843 mph/134.931 km/h.
Pole position: Bright, 1m 08.4191s, 85.660 mph/137.856 km/h.

Race 2 (86.284 miles/138.860 km).
1 Mark Skaife, AUS (Holden Commodore VZ), 1h 06m 52.5299s, 77.413 mph/124.583 km/h; **2** Craig Lowndes, AUS (Ford Falcon BA), 1h 06m 52.8781s; **3** Lee Holdsworth, AUS (Holden Commodore VZ), 1h 06m 58.2407s; **4** Steven Johnson, AUS (Ford Falcon BA), 1h 07m 01.8951s; **5** Russell Ingall, AUS (Ford Falcon BA), 1h 07m 02.9554s; **6** Jamie Whincup, AUS (Ford Falcon BA), 1h 07m 04.2371s; **7** Fabian Coulthard, NZ (Holden Commodore VZ), 1h 07m 06.4182s; **8** James Courtney, AUS (Ford Falcon BA), 1h 07m 14.5181s; **9** Jason Bargwanna, AUS (Ford Falcon BA), 1h 07m 18.7826s; **10** Todd Kelly, AUS (Holden Commodore VZ), 1h 07m 19.0675s.
Fastest race lap: Lowndes, 1m 10.5728s, 83.046 mph/133.649 km/h.
Pole position: Radisich.

Race 3 (86.284 miles/138.860 km).
1 Craig Lowndes, AUS (Ford Falcon BA), 1h 13m 53.5865s, 70.061 mph/112.752 km/h; **2** Rick Kelly, AUS (Holden Commodore VZ), 1h 14m 05.1698s; **3** James Courtney, AUS (Ford Falcon BA), 1h 14m 07.3498s; **4** Steven Johnson, AUS (Ford Falcon BA), 1h 14m 16.7385s; **5** Garth Tander, AUS (Holden Commodore VZ), 1h 14m 17.1208s; **6** Lee Holdsworth, AUS (Holden Commodore VZ), 1h 14m 17.5793s; **7** Cameron McConville, AUS (Holden Commodore VZ), 1h 14m 183611s; **8** Will Davison, AUS (Ford Falcon BA), 1h 14m 19.0249s; **9** Brad Jones, AUS (Ford Falcon BA), 1h 14m 21.8044s; **10** Greg Murphy, NZ (Holden Commodore VZ), 1h 14m 22.2360s.
Fastest race lap: Kelly (Rick), 1m 10.1845s, 83.505 mph/134.388 km/h.
Pole position: Skaife.

BETTA ELECTRICAL 500 MELBOURNE Sandown International Motor Raceway, Melbourne, Victoria, Australia, 3 September. Round 8. 161 laps of the 1.926-mile/3.100-km circuit, 310.126mile/499.100 km.
1 Jason Bright/Mark Winterbottom, AUS/AUS (Ford Falcon BA), 3h 22m 16.2945s, 91.933 mph/148.048 km/h; **2** Rick Kelly/Todd Kelly, AUS/AUS (Holden Commodore VZ), 3h 22m 16.4540s; **3** Craig Lowndes/Jamie Whincup, AUS/AUS (Ford Falcon BA), 3h 22m 34.0142s; **4** Will Davison/Steven Johnson, AUS/AUS (Ford Falcon BA), 3h 22m 39.1147s; **5** John Bowe/Brad Jones, AUS/AUS (Ford Falcon BA), 3h 22m 39.8524s; **6** Dean Canto/Lee Holdsworth, AUS/AUS (Holden Commodore VZ), 3h 22m 52.3777s; **7** Craig Baird/Jason Bargwanna, AUS/AUS (Ford Falcon BA), 160 laps; **8** Steve Ellery/Paul Morris, AUS/AUS (Holden Commodore VZ), 160; **9** James Courtney/Glenn Seton, AUS/AUS (Ford Falcon BA), 160; **10** Nathan Pretty/Paul Weel, AUS/AUS (Holden Commodore VZ), 160.
Fastest race lap: Mark Skaife/Garth Tander, AUS/AUS (Holden Commodore VZ), 1m 11.7104s, 96.701 mph/155.625 km/h.
Pole position: Tander, 1m 10.6102s, 98.208 mph/158.050 km/h.

SUPERCHEAP AUTO BATHURST 1000, Mount Panorama, Bathurst, New South Wales, Australia, 8 October. Round 9. 161 laps of the 3.861-mile/6.213-km circuit, 621.553 miles/1000.293 km.
1 Craig Lowndes/Jamie Whincup, AUS/AUS (Ford Falcon BA), 6h 59m 53.5852s, 88.816 mph/142.935 km/h; **2** Rick Kelly/Todd Kelly, AUS/AUS (Holden Commodore VZ), 6h 59m 54.1720s; **3** James Courtney/Glenn Seton, AUS/AUS (Ford Falcon BA), 7h 00m 03.1256s; **4** Russell Ingall/Luke Youlden, AUS/AUS (Ford Falcon BA), 7h 00m 03.1312s; **5** Paul Dumbrell/Steven Richards, AUS/AUS (Holden Commodore VZ), 7h 00m 04.3759s; **6** Steve Ellery/Paul Morris, AUS/AUS (Holden Commodore VZ), 7h 00m 07.9750s; **7** Tony Longhurst/Steve Owen, AUS/AUS (Holden Commodore VZ), 7h 00m 11.3233s; **8** Nathan Pretty/Paul Weel, AUS/AUS (Holden Commodore VZ), 7h 00m 13.1540s; **9** Alex Davison/Grant Denyer, AUS/AUS (Ford Falcon BA), 7h 00m 13.6298s; **10** Craig Baird/Jason Bargwanna, AUS/AUS (Ford Falcon BA), 7h 00m 16.0367s.
Fastest race lap: Lowndes/Whincup, 2m 08.6571s, 108.024 mph/173.848 km/h.
Pole position: Mark Skaife, AUS (Holden Commodore VZ), 2m 07.4221s, 109.071 mph/175.533 km/h.

GILLETTE V8 SUPERCAR CHALLENGE, Surfer's Paradise street circuit, Queensland, Australia, 21/22 October. Round 10. 3 x 22 laps of the 2.794-mile/4.496-km circuit.
Race 1 (61.461 miles/98.912 km).
1 Todd Kelly, AUS (Holden Commodore VZ), 43m 18.0998s, 85.162 mph/137.055 km/h; **2** Garth Tander, AUS (Holden Commodore VZ), 43m 19.4477s; **3** Mark Winterbottom, AUS (Ford Falcon BA), 43m 21.7285s; **4** Jason Richards, NZ (Holden Commodore VZ), 43m 30.7986s; **5** Steven Richards, NZ (Holden Commodore VZ), 43m 38.8250s; **6** Rick Kelly, AUS (Holden Commodore VZ), 43m 39.4297s; **7** Jason Bright, AUS (Ford Falcon BA), 43m 40.5582s; **8** Russell Ingall, AUS (Ford Falcon BA), 43m 42.1742s; **9** Jason Bargwanna, AUS (Ford Falcon BA), 43m 57.2771s; **10** Steven Johnson, AUS (Ford Falcon BA), 44m 00.1655s.
Fastest race lap: Winterbottom, 1m 51.4576s, 90.234 mph/145.217 km/h.
Pole position: Kelly (Todd), 1m 51.5522s, 90.157 mph/145.094 km/h.

Race 2 (61.461 miles/98.912 km).
1 Garth Tander, AUS (Holden Commodore VZ), 46m 22.3973s, 79.521 mph/127.977 km/h; **2** Todd Kelly, AUS (Holden Commodore VZ), 46m 22.9077s; **3** Mark Winterbottom, AUS (Ford Falcon BA), 46m 27.9748s; **4** Rick Kelly, AUS (Holden Commodore VZ), 46m 29.1431s; **5** Jason Richards, NZ (Holden Commodore VZ), 46m 29.9339s; **6** Jason Bright, AUS (Ford Falcon BA), 46m 30.3934s; **7** Craig Lowndes, AUS (Ford Falcon BA), 46m 32.0218s; **8** Russell Ingall, AUS (Ford Falcon BA), 46m 32.6141s; **9** Jason Bargwanna, AUS (Ford Falcon BA), 46m 49.0976s; **10** Steven Johnson, AUS (Ford Falcon BA), 46m 49.7313s.
Fastest race lap: Kelly (Todd), 1m 50.8518s, 90.727 mph/146.011 km/h.
Pole position: Jamie Whincup, AUS (Ford Falcon BA).

Race 3 (61.461 miles/98.912 km).
1 Rick Kelly, AUS (Holden Commodore VZ), 43m 30.3641s, 84.762 mph/136.411 km/h; **2** Todd Kelly, AUS (Holden Commodore VZ), 43m 30.8899s; **3** Mark Winterbottom, AUS (Ford Falcon BA), 43m 34.4258s; **4** Jason Bright, AUS (Ford Falcon BA), 43m 42.0566s; **5** Russell Ingall, AUS (Ford Falcon BA), 43m 42.6381s; **6** James Courtney, AUS (Ford Falcon BA), 43m 44.0438s; **7** Cameron McConville, AUS (Holden Commodore VZ), 43m 46.2740s; **8** Jamie Whincup, AUS (Ford Falcon BA), 43m 55.9684s; **9** Steven Johnson, AUS (Ford Falcon BA), 44m 01.3627s; **10** Steven Richards, NZ (Holden Commodore VZ), 44m 05.0852s.
Fastest race lap: Tander, 1m 50.6432s, 90.898 mph/146.286 km/h.
Pole position: Tander.

Provisional championship points
Drivers
1 Craig Lowndes, AUS, 2601; **2** Rick Kelly, AUS, 2571; **3** Mark Winterbottom, AUS, 2283; **4** Russell Ingall, AUS, 2211; **5** Garth Tander, AUS, 2105; **6** Jamie Whincup, AUS, 2000; **7** Jason Bright, AUS, 1988; **8** Steven Richards, NZ, 1982; **9** Todd Kelly, AUS, 1927; **10** Steven Johnson, AUS, 1927; **11** James Courtney, AUS, 1827; **12** Paul Dumbrell, AUS, 1716; **13** Jason Bargwanna, AUS, 1639; **14** Max Wilson, BR, 1541; **15** Will Davison, AUS, 1526; **16** Dean Canto, AUS, 1494; **17** Mark Skaife, AUS, 1485; **18** Jason Richards, NZ, 1469; **19** Paul Morris, AUS, 1467; **20** Cameron McConville, AUS, 1456.
Teams
1 Toll HSV Dealer Team, 5000; **2** Team Betta Electrical, 4675; **3** Ford Performance Racing, 4131.

Results of the Symmons Plains, Bahrain and Phillip Island races will be given in AUTOCOURSE 2007–2008.

Non-Championship Australian V8 Supercar Race

PANASONIC V8 SUPERCAR EVENT, Albert Park Lake Circuit, Melbourne, Victoria, Australia, 30 March/1/2 April. 10, 19 and 10 laps of the 3.295-mile/5.303-km circuit.
Race 1 (32.951 miles/53.030 km).
1 Todd Kelly, AUS (Holden Commodore VZ), 23m 08.8215s, 85.414 mph/137.460 km/h; **2** Mark Skaife, AUS (Holden Commodore VZ), 23m 09.4224s; **3** Craig Lowndes, AUS (Ford Falcon BA), 23m 10.8510s; **4** Paul Dumbrell, AUS (Holden Commodore VZ), 23m 11.6702s; **5** Cameron McConville, AUS (Holden Commodore VZ), 23m 12.6035s; **6** Mark Winterbottom, AUS (Ford Falcon BA), 23m 13.4025s; **7** Will Davison, AUS (Ford Falcon BA), 23m 14.1836s; **8** Jason Bright, AUS (Ford Falcon BA), 23m 14.4731s; **9** Steven Richards, NZ (Holden Commodore VZ), 23m 14.7086s; **10** Steven Johnson, AUS (Ford Falcon BA), 23m 15.4456s.
Jason Richards, NZ (Holden Commodore VZ), finished 3rd in 23m 10.2821s, but was given a 30-second penalty.
Fastest race lap: Jamie Whincup, AUS (Ford Falcon BA), 1m 58.6698s, 99.962 mph/160.873 km/h.
Fastest qualifying lap: Kelly (Todd).

Race 2 (62.607 miles/100.757 km).
1 Steven Richards, NZ (Holden Commodore VZ), 44m 37.0487s, 84.912 mph/135.494 km/h; **2** Mark Skaife, AUS (Holden Commodore VZ), 44m 37.7543s; **3** Todd Kelly, AUS (Holden Commodore VZ), 44m 38.2999s; **4** Craig Lowndes, AUS (Ford Falcon BA), 44m 38.3177s; **5** Garth Tander, AUS (Holden Commodore VZ), 44m 41.5468s; **6** Mark Winterbottom, AUS (Ford Falcon BA), 44m 43.7103s; **7** Will Davison, AUS (Ford Falcon BA), 44m 45.1959s; **8** Paul Dumbrell, AUS (Holden Commodore VZ), 44m 45.4244s; **9** Jamie Whincup, AUS (Ford Falcon BA), 44m 48.2314s; **10** Russell Ingall, AUS (Ford Falcon BA), 44m 51.2455s.
Cameron McConville finished 6th in 44m 42.5623s, but was given a 30-second penalty.
Fastest race lap: Kelly (Todd), 1m 59.3294s, 99.409 mph/159.984 km/h.

Race 3 (32.951 miles/53.030 km).
1 Steven Richards, NZ (Holden Commodore VZ), 20m 06.3894s, 98.330 mph/158.247 km/h; **2** Mark Skaife, AUS (Holden Commodore VZ), 20m 08.1457s; **3** Todd Kelly, AUS (Holden Commodore VZ), 20m 08.7899s; **4** Garth Tander, AUS (Holden Commodore VZ), 20m 10.5983s; **5** Craig Lowndes, AUS (Ford Falcon BA), 20m 10.8858s; **6** Will Davison, AUS (Ford Falcon BA), 20m 11.3872s; **7** Mark Winterbottom, AUS (Ford Falcon BA), 20m 12.2437s; **8** Paul Dumbrell, AUS (Holden Commodore VZ), 20m 12.9911s; **9** Jamie Whincup, AUS (Ford Falcon BA), 20m 15.5350s; **10** Paul Radisich, NZ (Holden Commodore VZ), 20m 19.1182s.
Fastest race lap: Kelly (Todd), 1m 59.0669s, 99.629 mph/160.337 km/h.

FIA World Touring Car Championship 2005

The following races were run after AUTOCOURSE 20052006 went to press.

FIA WORLD TOURING CAR CHAMPIONSHIP, Circuito Da Guia, Macau, 20 November. 10 and 11 laps of the 3.803-mile/6.120-km circuit.
Round 19 (38.028 miles/61.200 km).
1 Augusto Farfus Jr, BR (Alfa Romeo 156), 42m 11.373s, 54.082 mph/87.035 km/h; **2** Andy Priaulx, GB (BMW 320i), 42m 11.869s; **3** Rickard Rydell, S (SEAT Toledo Cupra), 42m 13.071s; **4** Nicola Larini, I (Chevrolet Lacetti), 42m 15.800s; **5** Alain Menu, CH (Chevrolet Lacetti), 42m 25.079s; **6** Duncan Huisman, D (BMW 320i), 42m 25.660s; **7** James Thompson, GB (Alfa Romeo 156), 42m 25.813s; **8** Peter Terting, D (SEAT Leon), 42m 26.545s; **9** Antonio Gárcia, E (BMW 320i), 42m 28.129s; **10** Dirk Müller, D (BMW 320i), 42m 32.255s.
Fastest race lap: Priaulx, 2m 33.903s, 88.952 mph/143.155 km/h.
Fastest qualifying lap: Priaulx, 2m 31.712s, 90.237 mph/145.222 km/h.

Round 20 (41.831 miles/67.320 km).
1 Duncan Huisman, NL (BMW 320i), 37m 51.579s, 66.293 mph/106.688 km/h; **2** Andy Priaulx, GB (BMW 320i), 37m 51.836s; **3** Alain Menu, CH (Chevrolet Lacetti), 37m 52.832s; **4** Augusto Farfus Jr, BR (Alfa Romeo 156), 37m 54.007s; **5** Alessandro 'Alex' Zanardi, I (BMW 320i), 37m 54.758s; **6** Jordi Gené, E (SEAT Leon), 37m 55.154s; **7** Peter Terting, D (SEAT Leon), 37m 55.772s; **8** Rickard Rydell, S (SEAT Toledo Cupra), 37m 56.548s; **9** Giuseppe Cirò, I (BMW 320i), 38m 28.161s; **10** Patrick Bernhardt, D (Ford Focus), 39m 13.061s.
Fastest race lap: Priaulx, 2m 33.757s, 89.037 mph/143.291 km/h.
Pole position: Terting.

Final championship points
Drivers
1 Andy Priaulx, GB, 101; **2** Dirk Müller, D, 86; **3** Fabrizio Giovanardi, I, 81; **4** Augusto Farfus Jr, BR, 65; **5** Jörg Müller, D, 59; **6** Rickard Rydell, S, 57; **7** Gabriele Tarquini, I, 55; **8** James Thompson, GB, 53; **9** Antonio Gárcia, E, 51; **10** Alessandro 'Alex' Zanardi, I, 36; **11** Jordi Gené, E, 33; **12** Peter Terting, D, 31; **13** Duncan Huisman, NL, 13; **14** Tom Coronel, NL, 11; **15** Jason Plato, GB, 10; **16** Nicola Larini, I, 9; **17** Alain Menu, CH, 9; **18** Stefano d'Aste, I, 8; **19** Roberto Colciago, I, 4; **20** Robert Huff, GB, 3.
Independents' Trophy
1 Marc Hennerici, D, 114; **2** Giuseppe Cirò, I, 107; **3** Stefano d'Aste, I, 96; **4** Carl Rosenblad, S, 94; **5** Tom Coronel, NL, 85.
Manufacturers
1 BMW, 273; **2** Alfa Romeo, 236; **3** SEAT, 183; **4** Chevrolet, 73; **5** Ford, 13.
Teams
1 Proteam Motorsport, 203; **2** GR Asia, 142; **3** Wiechers-Sport, 114; **4** Crawford Racing, 94; **5** JAS Motorsport, 89.

2006

FIA WORLD TOURING CAR CHAMPIONSHIP, Autodromo Nazionale di Monza, Milan, Italy, 2 April. 11 and 9 laps of the 3.600-mile/5.793-km circuit.
Round 1 (39.404 miles/63.414 km).
1 Andy Priaulx, GB (BMW 320si), 25m 44.220s, 91.861 mph/147.835 km/h; **2** Yvan Muller, F (SEAT Leon), 25m 47.754s; **3** James Thompson, GB (SEAT Leon), 25m 48.598s; **4** Dirk Müller, D (BMW 320si), 25m 48.887s; **5** Gabriele Tarquini, I (SEAT Leon), 25m 51.552s; **6** Rickard Rydell, S (SEAT Leon), 25m 51.859s; **7** Alessandro 'Alex' Zanardi, I (BMW 320si), 25m 52.559s; **8** Augusto Farfus Jr, BR (Alfa Romeo 156), 25m 57.128s; **9** Alessandro Balzan, I (Alfa Romeo 156), 25m 58.700s; **10** Alain Menu, CH (Chevrolet Lacetti), 25m 59.091s.
Fastest race lap: Tarquini, 2m 02.176s, 106.065 mph/170.694 km/h.
Fastest qualifying lap: Priaulx, 2m 00.254s, 107.760 mph/173.422 km/h.

Round 2 (32.204 miles/51.828 km).
1 Augusto Farfus Jr, BR (Alfa Romeo 156), 18m 37.438s, 103.752 mph/166.971 km/h; **2** Yvan Muller, F (SEAT Leon), 18m 38.389s; **3** Alain Menu, CH (Chevrolet Lacetti), 18m 40.018s; **4** Alessandro Balzan, I (Alfa Romeo 156), 18m 41.362s; **5** Jordi Gené, E (SEAT Leon), 18m 43.159s; **6** Gabriele Tarquini, I (SEAT Leon), 18m 44.365s; **7** Nicola Larini, I (Chevrolet Lacetti), 18m 45.333s; **8** Peter Terting, D (SEAT Leon), 18m 45.941s; **9** James Thompson, GB (SEAT Leon), 18m 46.165s; **10** Gianni Morbidelli, I (Alfa Romeo 156), 18m 46.852s.
Fastest race lap: Thompson, 2m 02.337s, 105.925 mph/170.470 km/h.
Pole position: Farfus Jr.

FIA WORLD TOURING CAR CHAMPIONSHIP, Circuit de Nevers, Magny-Cours, France, 30 April. 2 x 12 laps of the 2.741-mile/4.411-km circuit.
Round 3 (32.890 miles/52.932 km).
1 Dirk Müller, D (BMW 320si), 22m 22.141s, 88.221 mph/141.978 km/h; **2** Jörg Müller, D (BMW 320si), 22m 22.577s; **3** Rickard Rydell, S (SEAT Leon), 22m 23.219s; **4** Gabriele Tarquini, I (SEAT Leon), 22m 23.655s; **5** Jordi Gené, E (SEAT Leon), 22m 26.216s; **6** Peter Terting, D (SEAT Leon), 22m 26.814s; **7** James Thompson, GB (SEAT Leon), 22m 29.674s; **8** Andy Priaulx, GB (BMW 320si), 22m 30.081s; **9** Robert Huff, GB (Chevrolet Lacetti), 22m 36.586s; **10** Tom Coronel, NL (SEAT Toledo Cupra), 22m 37.587s.
Fastest race lap: Müller (Dirk), 1m 50.650s, 89.174 mph/143.511 km/h.
Fastest qualifying lap: Tarquini, 1m 49.306s, 90.271 mph/145.276 km/h.

Round 4 (32.890 miles/52.932 km).
1 Andy Priaulx, GB (BMW 320si), 22m 19.166s, 88.417 mph/142.293 km/h; **2** Jörg Müller, D (BMW 320si), 22m 20.072s; **3** Jordi Gené, E (SEAT Leon), 22m 22.769s; **4** James Thompson, GB (SEAT Leon), 22m 27.246s; **5** Gabriele Tarquini, I (SEAT Leon), 22m 30.866s; **6** Peter Terting, D (SEAT Leon), 22m 34.363s; **7** Yvan Muller, F (SEAT Leon), 22m 36.067s; **8** Nicola Larini, I (Chevrolet Lacetti), 22m 36.607s; **9** Robert Huff, GB (Chevrolet Lacetti), 22m 40.433s; **10** Stefano d'Aste, I (BMW 320si), 22m 41.042s.
Fastest race lap: Priaulx, 1m 50.859s, 89.006 mph/143.241 km/h.
Pole position: Prialux.

FIA WORLD TOURING CAR CHAMPIONSHIP, Brands Hatch Grand Prix Circuit, West Kingsdown, Dartford, Kent, Great Britain, 21 May. 14 and 16 laps of the 2.301-mile/3.703-km circuit.
Round 5 (32.194 miles/51.812 km).
1 Yvan Muller, F (SEAT Leon), 24m 04.470s, 80.237 mph/129.129 km/h; **2** Peter Terting, D (SEAT Leon), 24m 04.682s; **3** James Thompson, GB (SEAT Leon), 24m 04.980s; **4** Robert Huff, GB (Chevrolet Lacetti), 24m 05.147s; **5** Rickard Rydell, S (SEAT Leon), 24m 05.871s; **6** Gabriele Tarquini, I (SEAT Leon), 24m 11.086s; **7** Alain Menu, CH (Chevrolet Lacetti), 24m 11.960s; **8** Andy Priaulx, GB (BMW 320si), 24m 13.609s; **9** Dirk Müller, D (BMW 320si), 24m 21.932s; **10** Alessandro 'Alex' Zanardi, I (BMW 320si), 24m 28.659s.
Fastest race lap: Terting, 1m 41.572s, 81.552 mph/131.244 km/h.
Fastest qualifying lap: Rydell, 1m 34.493s, 87.661 mph/141.077 km/h.

Round 6 (36.796 miles/59.218 km).
1 Alain Menu, CH (Chevrolet Lacetti), 30m 02.722s, 73.482 mph/118.257 km/h; **2** Rickard Rydell, S (SEAT Leon), 30m 05.132s; **3** James Thompson, GB (SEAT Leon), 30m 06.273s; **4** Gabriele Tarquini, I (SEAT Leon), 30m 08.243s; **5** Yvan Muller, F (SEAT Leon), 30m 12.110s; **6** Dirk Müller, D (BMW 320si), 30m 12.490s; **7** Gianni Morbidelli, I (Alfa Romeo 156), 30m 13.128s; **8** Andy Priaulx, GB (BMW 320si), 30m 16.211s; **9** Alessandro 'Alex' Zanardi, I (BMW 320si), 30m 17.039s; **10** Jordi Gené, E (SEAT Leon), 30m 17.558s.
Fastest race lap: Menu, 1m 43.211s, 80.257 mph/129.160 km/h.
Pole position: Priaulx.

FIA WORLD TOURING CAR CHAMPIONSHIP, Motorsport Arena Oschersleben, Germany, 4 June. 2 x 14 laps of the 2.279-mile/3.667-km circuit.
Round 7 (31.900 miles/51.338 km).
1 Andy Priaulx, GB (BMW 320si), 22m 12.805s, 86.164 mph/138.667 km/h; **2** Dirk Müller, D (BMW 320si), 22m 13.274s; **3** Rickard Rydell, S (SEAT Leon), 22m 19.366s; **4** Gabriele Tarquini, I (SEAT Leon), 22m 20.342s; **5** James Thompson, GB (SEAT Leon), 22m 24.047s; **6** Augusto Farfus Jr, BR (Alfa Romeo 156), 22m 24.402s; **7** Jörg Müller, D (BMW 320si), 22m 24.730s; **8** Peter Terting, D (SEAT Leon), 22m 25.221s; **9** Gianni Morbidelli, I (Alfa Romeo 156), 22m 25.866s; **10** Tom Coronel, NL (SEAT Leon), 22m 26.248s.
Fastest race lap: Rydell, 1m 34.048s, 87.220 mph/140.366 km/h.
Fastest qualifying lap: Priaulx, 1m 35.661s, 85.749 mph/137.999 km/h.

Round 8 (31.900 miles/51.338 km).
1 Jörg Müller, D (BMW 320si), 22m 11.321s, 86.260 mph/138.822 km/h; **2** Augusto Farfus Jr, BR (Alfa Romeo 156), 22m 12.720s; **3** Dirk Müller, D (BMW 320si), 22m 13.028s; **4** Peter Terting, D (SEAT Leon), 22m 14.234s; **5** Rickard Rydell, S (SEAT Leon), 22m 17.050s; **6** James Thompson, GB (SEAT Leon), 22m 17.794s; **7** Gabriele Tarquini, I (SEAT Leon), 22m 18.718s; **8** Yvan Muller, F (SEAT Leon), 22m 20.808s; **9** Robert Huff, GB (Chevrolet Lacetti), 22m 20.971s; **10** Andy Priaulx, GB (BMW 320si), 22m 21.172s.
Fastest race lap: Farfus Jr, 1m 33.749s, 87.498 mph/140.814 km/h.
Pole position: Terting.

FIA WORLD TOURING CAR CHAMPIONSHIP, Autódromo Internacional de Curitiba, Brazil, 2 July. 16 and 14 laps of the 2.291-mile/3.6865-km circuit.
Round 9 (36.651 miles/58.984 km).
1 Jordi Gené, E (SEAT Leon), 26m 02.194s, 84.460 mph/135.925 km/h; **2** Peter Terting, D (SEAT Leon), 26m 03.869s; **3** Augusto Farfus Jr, BR (Alfa Romeo 156), 26m 05.180s; **4** Gabriele Tarquini, I (SEAT Leon), 26m 05.900s; **5** James Thompson, GB (SEAT Leon), 26m 06.532s; **6** Rickard Rydell, S (SEAT Leon), 26m 07.327s; **7** Gianni Morbidelli, I (Alfa Romeo 156), 26m 07.974s; **8** Andy Priaulx, GB (BMW 320si), 26m 08.601s; **9** Jörg Müller, D (BMW 320si), 26m 09.070s; **10** Alessandro 'Alex' Zanardi, I (BMW 320si), 26m 10.912s.
Fastest race lap: Gené, 1m 25.604s, 96.333 mph/155.032 km/h.
Fastest qualifying lap: Farfus Jr, 1m 24, 761s, 97.291 mph/156.574 km/h.

Round 10 (32.070 miles/51.611 km).
1 Andy Priaulx, GB (BMW 320si), 25m 42.910s, 74.826 mph/120.421 km/h; **2** Gianni Morbidelli, I (Alfa Romeo 156), 25m 43.704s; **3** Alessandro 'Alex' Zanardi, I (BMW 320si), 25m 43.932s; **4** James Thompson, GB (SEAT Leon), 25m 45.186s; **5** Gabriele Tarquini, I (SEAT Leon), 25m 45.951s; **6** Peter Terting, D (SEAT Leon), 25m 46.164s; **7** Jörg Müller, D (BMW 320si), 25m 46.904s; **8** Robert Huff, GB (Chevrolet Lacetti), 25m 47.672s; **9** Salvatore Tavano, I (Alfa Romeo 156), 25m 48.495s; **10** Alain Menu, CH (Chevrolet Lacetti), 25m 49.218s.
Fastest race lap: Zanardi, 1m 26.069s, 95.812 mph/154.194 km/h.
Pole position: Priaulx.

FIA WORLD TOURING CAR CHAMPIONSHIP, Miguel E. Abed International Racetrack, Puebla, Mexico, 30 July. 18 and 16 laps of the 2.013-mile/3.240-km circuit.
Round 11 (36.238 miles/58.320 km).
1 Salvatore Tavano, I (Alfa Romeo 156), 57m 38.172s, 37.725 mph/60.711 km/h; **2** Augusto Farfus Jr, BR (Alfa Romeo 156), 57m 38.482s; **3** Ryan Sharp, GB (Honda Accord Euro R), 57m 43.155s; **4** Tom Coronel, NL (SEAT Leon), 57m 43.583s; **5** James Thompson, GB (SEAT Leon), 57m 57.973s; **6** Dirk Müller, D (BMW 320si), 57m 59.788s; **7** Gianni Morbidelli, I (Alfa Romeo 156), 58m 01.440s; **8** Rickard Rydell, S (SEAT Leon), 58m 03.412s; **9** Peter Terting, D (SEAT Leon), 58m 03.754s; **10** Gabriele Tarquini, I (SEAT Leon), 58m 05.405s.
Fastest race lap: Sharp, 1m 44.994s, 69.029 mph/111.092 km/h.
Fastest qualifying lap: Tavano, 1m 41.309s, 71.540 mph/115.132 km/h.
Rydell achieved the fastest qualifying lap in 1m 41.259s (71.576 mph/115.190 km/h) but was given a 10-place grid penalty.

Round 12 (32.212 miles/51.840 km).
1 Augusto Farfus Jr, BR (Alfa Romeo 156), 28m 42.876s, 67.308 mph/108.321 km/h; **2** Gianni Morbidelli, I (Alfa Romeo 156), 28m 44.279s; **3** Rickard Rydell, S (SEAT Leon), 28m 53.176s; **4** Dirk Müller, D (BMW 320si), 28m 57.205s; **5** James Thompson, GB (SEAT Leon), 29m 04.313s; **6** Tom Coronel, NL (SEAT Leon), 29m 06.720s; **7** Andy Priaulx, GB (BMW 320si), 29m 06.834s; **8** Gabriele Tarquini, I (SEAT Leon), 29m 09.342s; **9** Jordi Gené, E (SEAT Leon), 29m 12.169s; **10** Pierre-Yves Corthals, B (Honda Accord Euro R), 29m 12.442s.
Fastest race lap: Farfus Jr, 1m 46.076s, 68.325 mph/109.958 km/h.
Pole position: Rydell.

FIA WORLD TOURING CAR CHAMPIONSHIP, Automotodrom Brno Masaryk Circuit, Brno, Czech Republic, 3 September. 2 x 10 laps of the 3.357-mile/5.403-km circuit.
Round 13 (33.573 miles/54.030 km).
1 Jörg Müller, D (BMW 320si), 22m 39.066s, 88.930 mph/143.118 km/h; **2** Alessandro 'Alex' Zanardi, I (BMW 320si), 22m 40.795s; **3** Yvan Muller, F (SEAT Leon), 22m 41.831s; **4** Jordi Gené, E (SEAT Leon), 22m 45.406s; **5** Andy Priaulx, GB (BMW 320si), 22m 45.854s; **6** Tom Coronel, NL (SEAT Leon), 22m 50.437s; **7** Alain Menu, CH (Chevrolet Lacetti), 22m 50.854s; **8** Robert Huff, GB (Chevrolet Lacetti), 22m 52.092s; **9** Dirk Müller, D (BMW 320si), 22m 54.842s; **10** Peter Terting, D (SEAT Leon), 22m 55.784s.
Fastest race lap: Muller (Yvan), 2m 14.183s, 90.072 mph/144.957 km/h.
Fastest qualifying lap: Gabriele Tarquini, I (SEAT Leon), 2m 12.286s, 91.364 mph/147.035 km/h.

Round 14 (33.573 miles/54.030 km).
1 Robert Huff, GB (Chevrolet Lacetti), 22m 36.004s, 89.131 mph/143.442 km/h; **2** Andy Priaulx, GB (BMW 320si), 22m 36.635s; **3** Yvan Muller, F (SEAT Leon), 22m 43.587s; **4** Jörg Müller, D (BMW 320si), 22m 43.778s; **5** Dirk Müller, D (BMW 320si), 22m 45.803s; **6** Jordi Gené, E (SEAT Leon), 22m 46.710s; **7** Nicola Larini, I (Chevrolet Lacetti), 22m 46.977s; **8** Peter Terting, D (SEAT Leon), 22m 48.517s; **9** Duncan Huisman, NL (BMW 320si), 22m 48.884s; **10** Gabriele Tarquini, I (SEAT Leon), 22m 54.662s.
Fastest race lap: Huff, 2m 13.809s, 90.324 mph/145.362 km/h.
Pole position: Huff.

FIA WORLD TOURING CAR CHAMPIONSHIP, Istanbul Speed Park, Tuzla, Turkey, 24 September. 2 x 10 laps of the 3.317-mile/5.338-km circuit.
Round 15 (33.043 miles/53.177 km).
1 Alessandro 'Alex' Zanardi, I (BMW 320si), 21m 19.910s, 92.939 mph/149.570 km/h; **2** Rickard Rydell, S (SEAT Leon), 21m 20.912s; **3** Gabriele Tarquini, I (SEAT Leon), 21m 23.847s; **4** Dirk Müller, D (BMW 320si), 21m 31.595s; **5** Duncan Huisman, NL (BMW 320si), 21m 31.915s; **6** Peter Terting, D (SEAT Leon), 21m 34.846s; **7** Nicola Larini, I (Chevrolet Lacetti), 21m 36.540s; **8** Tom Coronel, NL (SEAT Leon), 21m 43.328s; **9** Augusto Farfus Jr, BR (Alfa Romeo 156), 21m 45.007s; **10** Gianni Morbidelli, I (Alfa Romeo 156), 21m 45.838s.
Fastest race lap: Huisman, 2m 06.959s, 94.052 mph/151.362 km/h.
Fastest qualifying lap: Rydell, 2m 06.289s, 94.551 mph/152.165 km/h.

Round 16 (33.043 miles/53.177 km).
1 Gabriele Tarquini, I (SEAT Leon), 23m 06.124s, 85.817 mph/138.109 km/h; **2** Peter Terting, D (SEAT Leon), 23m 06.776s; **3** Nicola Larini, I (Chevrolet Lacetti), 23m 14.263s; **4** Rickard Rydell, S (SEAT Leon), 23m 14.400s; **5** Jordi Gené, E (SEAT Leon), 23m 14.603s; **6** Robert Huff, GB (Chevrolet Lacetti), 23m 15.637s; **7** Dirk Müller, D (BMW 320si), 23m 16.589s; **8** Jörg Müller, D (BMW 320si), 23m 19.049s; **9** Alessandro 'Alex' Zanardi, I (BMW 320si), 23m 25.812s; **10** Duncan Huisman, NL (BMW 320si), 23m 27.638s.
Fastest race lap: Tarquini, 2m 15.830s, 87.910 mph/141.476 km/h.
Pole position: Coronel.

FIA WORLD TOURING CAR CHAMPIONSHIP, Circuit de la Comunitat Valenciana Ricardo Tormo, Cheste, Valencia, Spain, 8 October. 15 and 13 laps of the 2.489-mile/4.005-km circuit.
Round 17 (37.329 miles/60.075 km).
1 Augusto Farfus Jr, BR (Alfa Romeo 156), 28m 20.311s, 79.035 mph/127.194 km/h; **2** Luca Rangoni, I (BMW 320si), 28m 21.054s; **3** Nicola Larini, I (Chevrolet Lacetti), 28m 22.605s; **4** Salvatore Tavano, I (Alfa Romeo 156), 28m 26.708s; **5** Peter Terting, D (SEAT Leon), 28m 28.009s; **6** Jörg Müller, D (BMW 320si), 28m 28.904s; **7** Duncan Huisman, NL (BMW 320si), 28m 34.725s; **8** Alain Menu, CH (Chevrolet Lacetti), 28m 35.049s; **9** James Thompson, GB (SEAT Leon), 28m 35.449s; **10** Yvan Muller, F (SEAT Leon), 28m 35.942s.
Fastest race lap: Jordi Gené, E (SEAT Leon), 1m 45.024s, 85.304 mph/137.282 km/h.
Fastest qualifying lap: Farfus Jr, 1m 44.534s, 85.704 mph/137.926 km/h.

Round 18 (32.352 miles/52.065 km).
1 Jörg Müller, D (BMW 320si), 23m 15.498s, 83.458 mph/134.313 km/h; **2** Duncan Huisman, NL (BMW 320si), 23m 16.359s; **3** Luca Rangoni, I (BMW 320si), 23m 16.983s; **4** Nicola Larini, I (Chevrolet Lacetti), 23m 17.893s; **5** Augusto Farfus Jr, BR (Alfa Romeo 156), 23m 19.933s; **6** Yvan Muller, F (SEAT Leon), 23m 26.822s; **7** Dirk Müller, D (BMW 320si), 23m 27.727s; **8** Andy Priaulx, GB (BMW 320si), 23m 27.881s; **9** Alain Menu, CH (Chevrolet Lacetti), 23m 28.736s; **10** Salvatore Tavano, I (Alfa Romeo 156), 23m 30.315s.
Fastest race lap: Müller (Jörg), 1m 45.819s, 84.663 mph/136.251 km/h.
Pole position: Menu.

FIA WORLD TOURING CAR CHAMPIONSHIP, Circuito Da Guia, Macau, 19 November. 9 and 11 laps of the 3.801-mile/6.120-km circuit.
Round 19 (34.225 miles/55.080 km).
1 Andy Priaulx, GB (BMW 320si), 23m 44.490s, 86.494 mph/139.199 km/h; **2** Duncan Huisman, NL (BMW 320si), 23m 45.510s; **3** Yvan Muller, F (SEAT Leon), 23m 45.875s; **4** Fabrizio Giovanardi, I (Honda Accord Euro R), 23m 47.151s; **5** Augusto Farfus Jr., BR (Alfa Romeo 156), 23m 54.086s; **6** Jörg Müller, D (BMW 320si), 23m 54.985s; **7** Tom Coronel, NL (SEAT Leon), 23m 55.579s; **8** Peter Terting, D (SEAT Leon), 24m 04.267s; **9** Robert Huff, GB (Chevrolet Lacetti), 24m 11.121s; **10** James Thompson, GB (SEAT Leon), 24m 14.549s.
Fastest race lap: Alain Menu, CH (Chevrolet Lacetti), 2m 34.249s, 88.753 mph/142.833 km/h.
Fastest qualifying lap: Priaulx, 2m 33.318s, 89.292 mph/143.701 km/h.

Round 20 (41.831 miles/67.320 km).
1 Jörg Müller, D (BMW 320si), 36m 01.074s, 69.683 mph/112.144 km/h; **2** Yvan Muller, F (SEAT Leon), 36m 03.176s; **3** Tom Coronel, NL (SEAT Leon), 36m 03.771s; **4** James Thompson, GB (SEAT Leon), 36m 05.547s; **5** Andy Priaulx, GB (BMW 320si), 36m 06.347s; **6** Fabrizio Giovanardi, I (Honda Accord Euro R), 36m 07.198s; **7** André Couto, MAC (SEAT Leon), 36m 11.418s ; **8** Dirk Müller, D (BMW 320si), 36m 12.482s; **9** Alessandro 'Alex' Zanardi, I (BMW 320si), 36m 12.908s; **10** Alain Menu, CH (Chevrolet Lacetti), 36m 20.450s.
Fastest race lap: Muller (Yvan), 2m 34.394s, 88.670 mph/142.699 km/
Pole position: Terting.

Final championship points
Drivers
1 Andy Priaulx, GB, 73; **2** Jörg Müller, D, 72; **3** Augusto Farfus Jr, BR, 64; **4** Yvan Muller, F, 62; **5** Gabriele Tarquini, I, 57; **6** Dirk Müller, D, 54; **7** Rickard Rydell, S, 54; **8** James Thompson, GB, 54; **9** Peter Terting, D, 49; **10** Jordi Gené, E, 36; **11** Alessandro 'Alex' Zanardi, I, 26; **12** Nicola Larini, I, 24; **13** Duncan Huisman, NL, 22; **14** Gianni Morbidelli, I, 22; **15** Alain Menu, CH, 21; **16** Robert Huff, GB, 20; **17** Tom Coronel, NL, 20; **18** Salvatore Tavano, I, 15; **19** Luca Rangoni, I, 14; **20** Fabrizio Giovanardi, I, 8; **21** Ryan Sharp, GB, 6; **22** Alessandro Balzan, I, 5; **23** André Coutu, MAC, 2.
Independents' Trophy
1 Tom Coronel, NL, 178; **2** Luca Rangoni, I, 100; **3** Stefano d'Aste, I, 93; **4** Ryan Sharp, GB, 75; **5** Maurizio Ceresoli, I, 69.
Manufacturers
1 BMW, 254; **2** SEAT, 235; **3** Alfa Romeo, 154; **4** Chevrolet, 128.
Teams
1 GR Asia, 247; **2** Proteam Motorsport, 192; **3** JAS Motorsport, 132; **4** Wiechers-Sport, 90; **5=** DB Motorsport, 25; **5=** Maurer Motorsport, 25.

German Touring Car Championship (DTM)

GERMAN TOURING CAR CHAMPIONSHIP, Hockenheimring Grand Prix Circuit, Heidelberg, Germany, 9 April. Round 1. 37 laps of the 2.842-mile/4.574-km circuit, 105.160 miles/169.238 km.
1 Bernd Schneider, D (Mercedes C-klasse), 59m 51.850s, 105.398 mph/169.622 km/h; **2** Tom Kristensen, DK (Audi A4), 59m 56.136s; **3** Heinz-Harald Frentzen, D (Audi A4), 59m 58.129s; **4** Mika Häkkinen, FIN (Mercedes C-klasse), 59m 58.917s; **5** Alexandros 'Alex' Margaritis, GR (Mercedes C-klasse), 1h 00m 03.126s; **6** Jean Alesi, F (Mercedes C-klasse), 1h 00m 09.249s; **7** Martin Tomczyk, D (Audi A4), 1h 00m 11.247s; **8** Timo Scheider, D (Audi A4), 1h 00m 15.332s; **9** Bruno Spengler, CDN (Mercedes C-klasse), 1h 00m 32.476s; **10** Susie Stoddart, GB (Mercedes C-klasse), 1h 00m 36.768s.
Fastest race lap: Spengler, 1m 34.726s, mph/173.831 km/h.
Fastest qualifying lap: Jamie Green, GB (Mercedes C-klasse), 1m 33.473s, 109.462 mph/176.162 km/h.

GERMAN TOURING CAR CHAMPIONSHIP, EuroSpeedway Lausitz, Klettwitz, Dresden, Germany, 30 April. Round 2. 48 laps of the 2.139-mile/3.442-km circuit, 102.660 miles/165.216 km.
1 Bernd Schneider, D (Mercedes C-klasse), 1h 03m 35.042s, 96.874 mph/155.903 km/h; **2** Tom Kristensen, DK (Audi A4), 1h 03m 36.470s; **3** Mika Häkkinen, FIN (Mercedes C-klasse), 1h 03m 38.791s; **4** Jamie Green, GB (Mercedes C-klasse), 1h 03m 38.931s; **5** Bruno Spengler, CDN (Mercedes C-klasse), 1h 03m 39.452s; **6** Alexandros 'Alex' Margaritis, GR (Mercedes C-klasse), 1h 03m 43.966s; **7** Jean Alesi, F (Mercedes C-klasse), 1h 03m 58.951s; **8** Martin Tomczyk, D (Audi A4), 1h 04m 01.510s; **9** Timo Scheider, D (Audi A4), 1h 04m 02.643s; **10** Pierre Kaffer, D (Audi A4), 1h 04m 05.045s.
Fastest race lap: Spengler, 1m 17.717s, 99.071 mph/159.440 km/h.
Fastest qualifying lap: Green, 1m 19.390s, 96.984 mph/156.080 km/h.

GERMAN TOURING CAR CHAMPIONSHIP, Motorsport Arena Oschersleben, Germany, 21 May. Round 3. 44 laps of the 2.279-mile/3.667-km circuit, 100.257 miles/161.348 km.
1 Tom Kristensen, DK (Audi A4), 1h 01m 29.257s, 97.831 mph/157.444 km/h; **2** Bruno Spengler, CDN (Mercedes C-klasse), 1h 01m 32.756s; **3** Jamie Green, GB (Mercedes C-klasse), 1h 01m 34.125s; **4** Heinz-Harald Frentzen, D (Audi A4), 1h 01m 53.879s; **5** Bernd Schneider, D (Mercedes C-klasse), 1h 01m 54.249s; **6** Martin Tomczyk, D (Audi A4), 1h 01m 56.617s; **7** Mattias Ekström, S (Audi A4), 1h 01m 56.985s; **8** Jean Alesi, F (Mercedes C-klasse), 1h 01m 59.901s; **9** Mika Häkkinen, FIN (Mercedes C-klasse), 1h 02m 04.122s; **10** Pierre Kaffer, D (Audi A4), 1h 02m 04.427s.
Fastest race lap: Kristensen, 1m 21.121s, 101.119 mph/162.734 km/h.
Fastest qualifying lap: Kristensen, 1m 19.264s, 103.488 mph/166.547 km/h.

GERMAN TOURING CAR CHAMPIONSHIP, Brands Hatch Indy Circuit, West Kingsdown, Dartford, Kent, Great Britain, 2 July. Round 4. 85 laps of the 1.199-mile/1.929-km circuit, 101.883 miles/163.965 km.
1 Mattias Ekström, S (Audi A4), 1h 03m 31.829s, 96.221 mph/154.853 km/h; **2** Jamie Green, GB (Mercedes C-klasse), 1h 03m 37.786s; **3** Bernd Schneider, D (Mercedes C-klasse), 1h 03m 45.666s; **4** Martin Tomczyk, D (Audi A4), 1h 03m 49.663s; **5** Christian Abt, D (Audi A4), 1h 03m 51.396s; **6** Jean Alesi, F (Mercedes C-klasse), 1h 03m 53.587s; **7** Bruno Spengler, CDN (Mercedes C-klasse), 1h 03m 57.842s; **8** Alexandros 'Alex' Margaritis, GR (Mercedes C-klasse), 1h 04m 07.012s; **9** Pierre Kaffer, D (Audi A4), 1h 04m 07.863s; **10** Timo Scheider, D (Audi A4), 1h 04m 08.101s.
Fastest race lap: Schneider, 43.408s, 99.407 mph/159.979 km/h.
Fastest qualifying lap: Tom Kristensen, DK (Audi A4), 42.406s, 101.756 mph/163.759 km/h.

GERMAN TOURING CAR CHAMPIONSHIP, Norisring, Nürnberg (Nuremberg), Germany, 23 July. Round 5. 69 laps of the 1.429-mile/2.300-km circuit, 98.612 miles/158.700 km.
1 Bruno Spengler, CDN (Mercedes C-klasse), 1h 00m 25.693s, 97.913 mph/157.575 km/h; **2** Bernd Schneider, D (Mercedes C-klasse), 1h 00m 26.544s; **3** Mika Häkkinen, FIN (Mercedes C-klasse), 1h 00m 33.401s; **4** Stefan Mücke, D (Mercedes C-klasse), 1h 00m 34.767s; **5** Tom Kristensen, DK (Audi A4), 1h 00m 36.761s; **6** Mattias Ekström, S (Audi A4), 1h 00m 37.146s; **7** Timo Scheider, D (Audi A4), 1h 00m 37.663s; **8** Pierre Kaffer, D (Audi A4), 1h 00m 39.699s; **9** Frank Stippler, D (Audi A4), 1h 00m 41.547s; **10** Christian Abt, D (Audi A4), 1h 00m 41.778s.
Fastest race lap: Spengler, 48.811s, 105.406 mph/169.633 km/h.
Fastest qualifying lap: Jamie Green, GB (Mercedes C-klasse), 48.489s, 106.106 mph/170.760 km/h.

GERMAN TOURING CAR CHAMPIONSHIP, Nürburgring Short Circuit, Nürburg/Eifel, Germany, 20 August. Round 6. 43 laps of the 2.255-mile/3.629-km circuit, 96.963 miles/156.047 km.

1 Bruno Spengler, CDN (Mercedes C-klasse), 1h 06m 28.696s, 87.514 mph/140.840 km/h; **2** Bernd Schneider, D (Mercedes C-klasse), 1h 06m 39.439s; **3** Martin Tomczyk, D (Audi A4), 1h 06m 41.200s; **4** Jean Alesi, F (Mercedes C-klasse), 1h 06m 49.082s; **5** Tom Kristensen, DK (Audi A4), 1h 06m 54.439s; **6** Heinz-Harald Frentzen, D (Audi A4), 1h 06m 56.175s; **7** Timo Scheider, D (Audi A4), 1h 07m 01.076s; **8** Mattias Ekström, S (Audi A4), 1h 07m 01.182s; **9** Jamie Green, GB (Mercedes C-klasse), 1h 07m 01.562s; **10** Christian Abt, D (Audi A4), 1h 07m 17.175s.
Fastest race lap: Spengler, 1m 24.699s, 95.843 mph/154.245 km/h.
Fastest qualifying lap: Spengler, 1m 23.462s, 97.264 mph/156.531 km/h.

GERMAN TOURING CAR CHAMPIONSHIP, Circuit Park Zandvoort, Netherlands, 3 September. Round 7. 38 laps of the 2.676-mile/4.307-km circuit, 101.697 miles/163.666 km.
1 Tom Kristensen, DK (Audi A4), 1h 02m 16.493s, 97.982 mph/157.687 km/h; **2** Bernd Schneider, D (Mercedes C-klasse), 1h 02m 17.278s; **3** Martin Tomczyk, D (Audi A4), 1h 02m 21.470s; **4** Bruno Spengler, CDN (Mercedes C-klasse), 1h 02m 26.282s; **5** Heinz-Harald Frentzen, D (Audi A4), 1h 02m 29.967s; **6** Timo Scheider, D (Audi A4), 1h 02m 31.400s; **7** Stefan Mücke, D (Mercedes C-klasse), 1h 02m 49.997s; **8** Jamie Green, GB (Mercedes C-klasse), 1h 02m 54.337s; **9** Pierre Kaffer, D (Audi A4), 1h 02m 55.456s; **10** Daniel la Rosa, D (Mercedes C-klasse), 1h 02m 55.913s.
Fastest race lap: Mika Häkkinen, FIN (Mercedes C-klasse), 1m 34.888s, 101.535 mph/163.405 km/h.
Fastest qualifying lap: Green, 1m 32.189s, 104.508 mph/168.189 km/h.

GERMAN TOURING CAR CHAMPIONSHIP, Circuit de Catalunya, Montmeló, Barcelona, Spain, 24 September. Round 8. 58 laps of the 1.832-mile/2.949-km circuit, 106.281 miles/171.042 km.
1 Martin Tomczyk, D (Audi A4), 1h 06m 07.496s, 96.436 mph/155.198 km/h; **2** Bernd Schneider, D (Mercedes C-klasse), 1h 06m 10.394s; **3** Heinz-Harald Frentzen, D (Audi A4), 1h 06m 10.965s; **4** Mattias Ekström, S (Audi A4), 1h 06m 18.458s; **5** Bruno Spengler, CDN (Mercedes C-klasse), 1h 06m 20.682s; **6** Frank Stippler, D (Audi A4), 1h 06m 21.825s; **7** Daniel la Rosa, D (Mercedes C-klasse), 1h 06m 22.553s; **8** Alexandros 'Alex' Margaritis, GR (Mercedes C-klasse), 1h 06m 26.308s; **9** Tom Kristensen, DK (Audi A4), 1h 06m 26.875s; **10** Christian Abt, D (Audi A4), 1h 06m 27.731s.
Fastest race lap: Schneider, 1m 03.919s, 103.204 mph/166.091 km/h.
Fastest qualifying lap: Tomczyk, 1m 13.900s, 89.266 mph/143.658 km/h.

GERMAN TOURING CAR CHAMPIONSHIP, Circuit Le Mans-Bugatti, France, 15 October. Round 9. 39 laps of the 2.597-mile/4.180-km circuit, 101.296 miles/163.020 km.
1 Bruno Spengler, CDN (Mercedes C-klasse), 1h 03m 09.292s, 96.236 mph/154.876 km/h **2** Mika Häkkinen, FIN (Mercedes C-klasse), 1h 03m 09.690s; **3** Tom Kristensen, DK (Audi A4), 1h 03m 22.062s; **4** Martin Tomczyk, D (Audi A4), 1h 03m 33.001s; **5** Bernd Schneider, D (Mercedes C-klasse), 1h 03m 33.336s; **6** Jamie Green, GB (Mercedes C-klasse), 1h 03m 33.802s; **7** Alexandros 'Alex' Margaritis, GR (Mercedes C-klasse), 1h 03m 37.994s; **8** Timo Scheider, D (Audi A4), 1h 03m 38.495s; **9** Christian Abt, D (Audi A4), 1h 03m 49.472s; **10** Heinz-Harald Frentzen, D (Audi A4), 1h 03m 51.569s.
Fastest race lap: Häkkinen, 1m 30.713s, 103.077 mph/165.885 km/h.
Fastest qualifying lap: Spengler, 1m 30.486s, 103.335 mph/166.301 km/h.

GERMAN TOURING CAR CHAMPIONSHIP, Hockenheimring Grand Prix Circuit, Heidelberg, Germany, 29 October. Round 10. 37 laps of the 2.842-mile/4.574-km circuit, 105.160 miles/169.238 km.
1 Bruno Spengler, CDN (Mercedes C-klasse), 1h 00m 13.459s, 104.768 mph/168.607 km/h; **2** Jamie Green, GB (Mercedes C-klasse), 1h 00m 14.962s; **3** Tom Kristensen, DK (Audi A4), 1h 00m 23.949s; **4** Bernd Schneider, D (Mercedes C-klasse), 1h 00m 24.966s; **5** Martin Tomczyk, D (Audi A4), 1h 00m 25.485s; **6** Timo Scheider, D (Audi A4), 1h 00m 32.985s; **7** Christian Abt, D (Audi A4), 1h 00m 34.818s; **8** Jean Alesi, F (Mercedes C-klasse), 1h 00m 49.739s; **9** Susie Stoddart, GB (Mercedes C-klasse), 1h 00m 51.934s; **10** Mathias Lauda, A (Mercedes C-klasse), 1h 01m 16.953s.
Fastest race lap: Green, 1m 34.954s, 107.755 mph/173.414 km/h.
Fastest qualifying lap: Frentzen, 1m 33.518s, 109.409 mph/176.077 km/h.

Final championship points
Drivers
1 Bernd Schneider, D, 71; **2** Bruno Spengler, CDN, 63; **3** Tom Kristensen, DK, 56; **4** Martin Tomczyk, D, 42; **5** Jamie Green, GB, 31; **6** Mika Häkkinen, FIN, 25; **7** Heinz-Harald Frentzen, D, 24; **8** Mattias Ekström, S, 21; **9** Jean Alesi, F, 15; **10** Timo Scheider, D, 12; **11** Alexandros 'Alex' Margaritis, GR, 11; **12** Stefan Mücke, D, 7; **13** Christian Abt, D, 6; **14** Frank Stippler, D, 3; **15** Daniel la Rosa, D, 2; **16** Pierre Kaffer, D, 1.
Teams
1 Vodafone/Salzgitter AMG-Mercedes, 102; **2** DaimlerChrysler Bank AMG-Mercedes, 88; **3** Audi Sport Team Abt, 80; **4** Audi Sport Team Abt Sportsline, 63; **5** stern/Easy Rent AMG-Mercedes, 26; **6** Audi Sport Team Rosberg, 15.

British Touring Car Championship

BRITISH TOURING CAR CHAMPIONSHIP, Brands Hatch Indy Circuit, West Kingsdown, Dartford, Kent, Great Britain, 9 April. 27, 24 and 20 laps of the 1.2262-mile/1.973-km circuit.
Round 1 (33.126 miles/53.311 km).
1 James Thompson, GB (SEAT Leon), 23m 49.571s, 83.419 mph/134.250 km/h; **2** Tom Chilton, GB (Vauxhall Astra Sport Hatch), 23m 50.891s; **3** Matt Neal, GB (Honda Integra), 23m 51.591s; **4** Colin Turkington, GB (MG ZS), 23m 52.217s; **5** Mike Jordan, GB (Honda Integra), 23m 53.342s; **6** Gavin Smith, IRL (Vauxhall Astra Sport Hatch), 23m 56.238s; **7** Rob Collard, GB (MG ZS), 23m 58.782s; **8** James Kaye, GB (Honda Civic Type-R), 24m 02.319s; **9** Jason Hughes, GB (MG ZS), 24m 09.807s; **10** Martyn Bell, GB (BMW 320i), 26 laps.
Fastest race lap: Chilton, 49.190s, 89.740 mph/144.423 km/h.
Fastest qualifying lap: Chilton, 48.975s, 90.134 mph/145.057 km/h.

Round 2 (29.446 miles/47.389 km).
1 James Thompson, GB (SEAT Leon), 20m 04.481s, 88.009 mph/141.637 km/h; **2** Colin Turkington, GB (MG ZS), 20m 05.024s; **3** Matt Neal, GB (Honda Integra), 20m 05.520s; **4** Gavin Smith, IRL (Vauxhall Astra Sport Hatch), 20m 14.728s; **5** Jason Plato, GB (SEAT Leon), 20m 15.493s; **6** Rob Collard, GB (MG ZS), 20m 17.377s; **7** Tom Chilton, GB (Vauxhall Astra Sport Hatch), 20m 17.710s; **8** Fabrizio Giovanardi, I (Vauxhall Astra Sport Hatch), 20m 19.334s; **9** James Kaye, GB (Honda Civic Type-R), 20m 19.602s; **10** David Pinkney, GB (Honda Integra), 20m 19.877s.
Fastest race lap: Plato, 49.289s, 89.560 mph/144.133 km/h.
Pole position: Thompson.

Round 3 (24.541 miles/39.495 km).
1 Jason Plato, GB (SEAT Leon), 16m 43.263s, 88.060 mph/141.719 km/h; **2** Colin Turkington, GB (MG ZS), 16m 47.275s; **3** Tom Chilton, GB (Vauxhall Astra Sport Hatch), 16m 49.143s; **4** Gordon Shedden, GB (Honda Integra), 16m 50.300s; **5** James Thompson, GB (SEAT Leon), 16m 50.599s; **6** Fabrizio Giovanardi, I (Vauxhall Astra Sport Hatch), 16m 52.165s; **7** Gavin Smith, IRL (Vauxhall Astra Sport Hatch), 16m 52.814s; **8** David Pinkney, GB (Honda Integra), 16m 53.188s; **9** Jason Hughes, GB (MG ZS), 17m 06.851s; **10** Fiona Leggate, GB (Vauxhall Astra Coupé), 17m 20.160s.
Disqualified: Collard finished 2nd in 16m 46.094s, but was disqualified for causing the accident with Neal.
Did not start: Mark Proctor, GB (Honda Civic Type-R) – electrics; Mark Smith, GB (Alfa Romeo 156) – gearbox.
Fastest race lap: Shedden, 49.281s, 89.574 mph/144.156 km/h.
Pole position: Chilton.

BRITISH TOURING CAR CHAMPIONSHIP, Mondello Park, Naas, County Kildare, Republic of Ireland, 23 April. 14, 17 and 14 laps of the 2.177-mile/3.503-km circuit.
Round 4 (30.473 miles/49.042 km).
1 Matt Neal, GB (Honda Integra), 25m 04.534s, 72.915 mph/117.346 km/h; **2** Jason Plato, GB (SEAT Leon), 25m 05.034s; **3** James Thompson, GB (SEAT Leon), 25m 14.212s; **4** Colin Turkington, GB (MG ZS), 25m 14.764s; **5** Gordon Shedden, GB (Honda Integra), 25m 19.819s; **6** Tom Chilton, GB (Vauxhall Astra Sport Hatch), 25m 23.331s; **7** Fabrizio Giovanardi, I (Vauxhall Astra Sport Hatch), 25m 25.835s; **8** Gavin Smith, IRL (Vauxhall Astra Sport Hatch), 25m 26.326s; **9** Mike Jordan, GB (Honda Integra), 25m 32.987s; **10** James Kaye, GB (Honda Civic Type-R), 25m 33.329s.
Fastest race lap: Neal, 1m 46.094s, 73.859 mph/118.864 km/h.
Fastest qualifying lap: Neal, 1m 45.333s, 74.393 mph/119.723 km/h.

Round 5 (37.003 miles/59.551 km).
1 Matt Neal, GB (Honda Integra), 34m 09.627s, 65.280 mph/105.058 km/h; **2** Jason Plato, GB (SEAT Leon), 34m 10.625s; **3** Colin Turkington, GB (MG ZS), 34m 11.308s; **4** David Pinkney, GB (Honda Integra), 34m 26.331s; **5** Gavin Smith, IRL (Vauxhall Astra Sport Hatch), 34m 28.348s; **6** James Kaye, GB (Honda Civic Type-R), 34m 30.469s; **7** Mike Jordan, GB (Honda Integra), 34m 31.304s; **8** Mark Proctor, GB (Honda Civic Type-R), 34m 45.977s; **9** Martyn Bell, GB (BMW 320i), 34m 48.381s; **10** Rob Collard, GB (MG ZS), 35m 11.476s.
Disqualified: Shedden finished 4th in 34m 20.871s, but was disqualified for incident with Thompson.
Fastest race lap: Plato, 1m 46.544s, 73.547 mph/118.362 km/h.
Pole position: Neal.

Round 6 (30.473 miles/49.042 km).
1 Mike Jordan, GB (Honda Integra), 25m 12.335s, 72.539 mph/116.741 km/h; **2** Colin Turkington, GB (MG ZS), 25m 13.391s; **3** Matt Neal, GB (Honda Integra), 25m 24.939s; **4** James Thompson, GB (SEAT Leon), 25m 25.413s; **5** Fabrizio Giovanardi, I (Vauxhall Astra Sport Hatch), 25m 27.898s; **6** Gordon Shedden, GB (Honda Integra), 25m 30.315s; **7** Mark Smith, GB (Alfa Romeo 156), 25m 32.219s; **8** Jason Plato, GB (SEAT Leon), 25m 32.419s; **9** Tom Chilton, GB (Vauxhall Astra Sport Hatch), 25m 33.835s; **10** David Pinkney, GB (Honda Integra), 25m 34.280s.
Fastest race lap: Collard, 1m 46.535s, 73.553 mph/118.372 km/h.
Pole position: Proctor.

BRITISH TOURING CAR CHAMPIONSHIP, Oulton Park Circuit, Tarporley, Cheshire, Great Britain, 14 May. 15, 15 and 17 laps of the 2.226-mile/3.582-km circuit.
Round 7 (33.390 miles/53.736 km).
1 Gordon Shedden, GB (Honda Integra), 22m 40.431s, 88.357 mph/142.197 km/h; **2** Mike Jordan, GB (Honda Integra), 22m 41.608s; **3** James Kaye, GB (Honda Civic Type-R), 22m 45.688s; **4** Matt Neal, GB (Honda Integra), 22m 45.860s; **5** Fabrizio Giovanardi, I (Vauxhall Astra Sport Hatch), 22m 52.206s; **6** Rob Collard, GB (MG ZS), 22m 52.416s; **7** Colin Turkington, GB (MG ZS), 22m 52.769s; **8** Gavin Smith, IRL (Vauxhall Astra Sport Hatch), 22m 53.044s; **9** Tom Chilton, GB (Vauxhall Astra Sport Hatch), 22m 54.201s; **10** David Pinkney, GB (Honda Integra), 22m 56.154s.
Fastest race lap: Jason Plato, GB (SEAT Leon), 1m 29.140s, 89.899 mph/144.678 km/h.
Fastest qualifying lap: Plato, 1m 35.063s, 95.072 mph/153.003 km/h.

Round 8 (33.390 miles/53.736 km).
1 Matt Neal, GB (Honda Integra), 22m 36.444s, 88.617 mph/142.615 km/h; **2** Fabrizio Giovanardi, I (Vauxhall Astra Sport Hatch), 22m 37.755s; **3** Gordon Shedden, GB (Honda Integra), 22m 42.176s; **4** James Thompson, GB (SEAT Leon), 22m 42.838s; **5** Rob Collard, GB (MG ZS), 22m 45.875s; **6** Jason Plato, GB (SEAT Leon), 22m 47.079s; **7** Tom Chilton, GB (Vauxhall Astra Sport Hatch), 22m 50.120s; **8** David Pinkney, GB (Honda Integra), 22m 54.757s; **9** James Kaye, GB (Honda Civic Type-R), 22m 59.167s; **10** Gavin Smith, IRL (Vauxhall Astra Sport Hatch), 22m 59.355s.
Fastest race lap: Turkington, 1m 28.403s, 90.649 mph/145.885 km/h.
Pole position: Shedden.

Round 9 (37.842 miles/60.901 km).
1 Jason Plato, GB (SEAT Leon), 26m 31.186s, 85.616 mph/137.786 km/h; **2** James Thompson, GB (SEAT Leon), 26m 31.702s; **3** Tom Chilton, GB (Vauxhall Astra Sport Hatch), 26m 33.841s; **4** Rob Collard, GB (MG ZS), 26m 34.325s; **5** Colin Turkington, GB (MG ZS), 26m 37.197s; **6** Gavin Smith, IRL (Vauxhall Astra Sport Hatch), 26m 38.854s; **7** Mike Jordan, GB (Honda Integra), 26m 39.279s; **8** Matt Neal, GB (Honda Integra), 26m 40.863s; **9** Fabrizio Giovanardi, I (Vauxhall Astra Sport Hatch), 26m 42.391s; **10** Jason Hughes, GB (MG ZS), 26m 46.104s.
Fastest race lap: Plato, 1m 28.603s, 90.444 mph/145.555 km/h.
Pole position: Chilton.

BRITISH TOURING CAR CHAMPIONSHIP, Thruxton Circuit, Andover, Hampshire, Great Britain, 4 June. 16, 18 and 19 laps of the 2.356-mile/3.792-km circuit.
Round 10 (37.696 miles/60.666 km).
1 Gordon Shedden, GB (Honda Integra), 21m 27.943s, 105.366 mph/169.570 km/h; **2** Matt Neal, GB (Honda Integra), 21m 34.641s; **3** Darren Turner, GB (SEAT Leon), 21m 39.257s; **4** Tom Chilton, GB (Vauxhall Astra Sport Hatch), 21m 41.017s; **5** Rob Collard, GB (MG ZS), 21m 46.506s; **6** Gavin Smith, IRL (Vauxhall Astra Sport Hatch), 21m 49.255s; **7** James Kaye, GB (Honda Civic Type-R), 21m 54.297s; **8** Colin Turkington, GB (MG ZS), 21m 59.708s; **9** Jason Hughes, GB (MG ZS), 22m 23.175s; **10** Fiona Leggate, GB (Vauxhall Astra Coupé), 15 laps.
Fastest race lap: Shedden, 1m 18.709s, 107.759 mph/173.421 km/h.
Fastest qualifying lap: Shedden, 1m 17.833s, 108.972 mph/175.373 km/h.

Round 11 (42.408 miles/68.249 km).
1 Matt Neal, GB (Honda Integra), 25m 19.868s, 100.449 mph/161.657 km/h; **2** Gordon Shedden, GB (Honda Integra), 25m 20.196s; **3** Rob Collard, GB (MG ZS), 25m 20.888s; **4** David Pinkney, GB (Honda Integra), 25m 22.292s; **5** Darren Turner, GB (SEAT Leon), 25m 23.480s; **6** Colin Turkington, GB (MG ZS), 25m 24.489s; **7** James Kaye, GB (Honda Civic Type-R), 25m 30.075s; **8** Fabrizio Giovanardi, I (Vauxhall Astra Sport Hatch), 25m 31.853s; **9** Tom Chilton, GB (Vauxhall Astra Sport Hatch), 25m 32.445s; **10** Jason Hughes, GB (MG ZS), 25m 32.728s.
Fastest race lap: Pinkney, 1m 19.728s, 106.382 mph/171.205 km/h.
Pole position: Shedden.

Round 12 (44.764 miles/72.041 km).
1 Colin Turkington, GB (MG ZS), 26m 45.270s, 100.388 mph/161.559 km/h; **2** Matt Neal, GB (Honda Integra), 26m 56.861s; **3** Jason Plato, GB (SEAT Leon), 26m 9.981s; **4** James Kaye, GB (Honda Civic Type-R), 27m 02.179s; **5** David Pinkney, GB (Honda Integra), 27m 03.647s; **6** Rob Collard, GB (MG ZS), 27m 03.841s; **7** Gavin Smith, IRL (Vauxhall Astra Sport Hatch), 27m 04.669s; **8** Tom Chilton, GB (Vauxhall Astra Sport Hatch), 27m 05.533s; **9** Jason Hughes, GB (MG ZS), 27m 18.199s; **10** Fiona Leggate, GB (Vauxhall Astra Coupé), 27m 18.393s.
Fastest race lap: Turkington, 1m 18.799s, 107.636 mph/173.223 km/h.
Pole position: Kaye.

BRITISH TOURING CAR CHAMPIONSHIP, Croft Racing Circuit, Croft-on-Tees, North Yorkshire, Great Britain, 16 July. 15, 15 and 14 laps of the 2.127-mile/3.423-km circuit.
Round 13 (31.905 miles/51.346 km).
1 Jason Plato, GB (SEAT Leon), 22m 08.206s, 86.475 mph/139.170 km/h; **2** James Thompson, GB (SEAT Leon), 22m 09.001s; **3** Matt Neal, GB (Honda Integra), 22m 13.251s; **4** Colin Turkington, GB (MG ZS), 22m 14.200s; **5** Rob Collard, GB (MG ZS), 22m 16.005s; **6** Fabrizio Giovanardi, I (Vauxhall Astra Sport Hatch), 22m 17.451s; **7** David Pinkney, GB (Honda Integra), 22m 18.291s; **8** James Kaye, GB (Honda Civic Type-R), 22m 27.491s; **9** Gavin Smith, IRL (Vauxhall Astra Sport Hatch), 22m 29.668s; **10** Eoin Murray, IRL (Alfa Romeo 156), 22m 31.627s.
Fastest race lap: Thompson, 1m 26.332s, 88.695 mph/142.740 km/h.
Fastest qualifying lap: Thompson, 1m 26.213s, 88.817 mph/142.937 km/h.

Round 14 (31.905 miles/51.346 km).
1 Matt Neal, GB (Honda Integra), 22m 10.791s, 86.308 mph/138.899 km/h; **2** Jason Plato, GB (SEAT Leon), 22m 11.757s; **3** Colin Turkington, GB (MG ZS), 22m 16.846s; **4** Gordon Shedden, GB (Honda Integra), 22m 17.538s; **5** James Thompson, GB (SEAT Leon), 22m 18.677s; **6** Gavin Smith, IRL (Vauxhall Astra Sport Hatch), 22m 18.689s; **7** James Kaye, GB (Honda Civic Type-R), 22m 24.173s; **8** Tom Chilton, GB (Vauxhall Astra Sport Hatch), 22m 26.875s; **9** David Pinkney, GB (Honda Integra), 22m 31.117s; **10** Mike Jordan, GB (Honda Integra), 22m 33.765s.
Fastest race lap: Shedden, 1m 26.930s, 88.085 mph/141.759 km/h.
Pole position: Plato.

Round 15 (29.778 miles/47.923 km).
1 James Thompson, GB (SEAT Leon), 20m 42.518s, 86.277 mph/138.849 km/h; **2** Colin Turkington, GB (MG ZS), 20m 45.470s; **3** Jason Plato, GB (SEAT Leon), 20m 47.934s; **4** Matt Neal, GB (Honda Integra), 20m 47.926s*; **5** Fabrizio Giovanardi, I (Vauxhall Astra Sport Hatch), 20m 51.207s; **6** Tom Chilton, GB (Vauxhall Astra Sport Hatch), 20m 52.811s; **7** Mike Jordan, GB (Honda Integra), 20m 58.302s; **8** Gavin Smith, IRL (Vauxhall Astra Sport Hatch), 20m 59.743s; **9** James Kaye, GB (Honda Civic Type-R), 21m 05.491s; **10** Rob Collard, GB (MG ZS), 21m 05.751s.
* Finished 3rd but was judged to have gained an unfair advantage when he passed Plato with all four wheels off the track, so demoted.
Fastest race lap: Shedden, 1m 26.898s, 88.117 mph/141.811 km/h.
Pole position: Smith (Gavin).

BRITISH TOURING CAR CHAMPIONSHIP, Donington Park National Circuit, Castle Donington, Great Britain, 30 July. 16, 19 and 17 laps of the 1.9573-mile/3.150-km circuit.
Round 16 (31.287 miles/50.352 km).
1 Gordon Shedden, GB (Honda Integra), 19m 48.048s, 94.804 mph/152.574 km/h; **2** Colin Turkington, GB (MG ZS), 19m 49.538s; **3** Fabrizio Giovanardi, I (Vauxhall Astra Sport Hatch), 19m 52.042s; **4** Matt Neal, GB (Honda Integra), 19m 52.328s; **5** Tom Chilton, GB (Vauxhall Astra Sport Hatch), 19m 54.036s; **6** Gavin Smith, IRL (Vauxhall Astra Sport Hatch), 19m 54.543s; **7** Jason Plato, GB (SEAT Leon), 19m 57.730s; **8** Mike Jordan, GB (Honda Integra), 20m 00.476s; **9** Rob Collard, GB (MG ZS), 20m 02.191s; **10** James Kaye, GB (Honda Civic Type-R), 20m 02.895s.
Fastest race lap: Shedden, 1m 12.970s, 96.563 mph/155.405 km/h.
Fastest qualifying lap: Shedden, 1m 12.548s, 97.126 mph/156.309 km/h.

Round 17 (37.159 miles/59.802 km).
1 Gordon Shedden, GB (Honda Integra), 27m 19.499s, 81.593 mph/131.312 km/h; **2** Gavin Smith, IRL (Vauxhall Astra Sport Hatch), 27m 20.627s; **3** Mike Jordan, GB (Honda Integra), 27m 24.731s; **4** Fabrizio Giovanardi, I (Vauxhall Astra Sport Hatch), 27m 25.992s; **5** Matt Neal, GB (Honda Integra), 27m 26.162s; **6** Eoin Murray, IRL (Alfa Romeo 156), 27m 26.889s; **7** James Kaye, GB (Honda Civic Type-R), 27m 31.497s; **8** Colin Turkington, GB (MG ZS), 27m 34.743s; **9** Darren Turner, GB (SEAT Leon), 27m 36.371s; **10** Adam Jones, GB (Lexus IS200), 27m 44.887s.
Fastest race lap: Collard, 1m 13.523s, 95.838 mph/154.236 km/h.
Pole position: Shedden.

Round 18 (33.244 miles/53.501 km).
1 Colin Turkington, GB (MG ZS), 24m 44.034s, 80.644 mph/129.784 km/h; **2** Fabrizio Giovanardi, I (Vauxhall Astra Sport Hatch), 24m 44.417s; **3** Gordon Shedden, GB (Honda Integra), 24m 48.902s; **4** Darren Turner, GB (SEAT Leon), 24m 49.602s; **5** Gavin Smith, IRL (Vauxhall Astra Sport Hatch), 24m 49.720s; **6** Tom Chilton, GB (Vauxhall Astra Sport Hatch), 24m 50.311s; **7** Matt Neal, GB (Honda Integra), 24m 50.327s; **8** James Kaye, GB (Honda Civic Type-R), 24m 56.670s; **9** David Pinkney, GB (Honda Integra), 24m 57.423s; **10** Martyn Bell, GB (BMW 320i), 25m 47.066s.
Fastest race lap: Turkington, 1m 13.351s, 96.062 mph/154.598 km/h.
Pole position: Turner.

BRITISH TOURING CAR CHAMPIONSHIP, Snetterton Circuit, Thetford, Norfolk, Great Britain, 13 August. 18, 21 and 18 laps of the 1.952-mile/3.141-km circuit.
Round 19 (35.136 miles/56.546 km).
1 Jason Plato, GB (SEAT Leon), 23m 48.514s, 88.546 mph/142.501 km/h; **2** James Thompson, GB (SEAT Leon), 23m 48.897s; **3** Fabrizio Giovanardi, I (Vauxhall Astra Sport Hatch), 24m 05.906s; **4** Gavin Smith, IRL (Vauxhall Astra Sport Hatch), 24m 09.026s; **5** Mike Jordan, GB (Honda Integra), 24m 09.135s; **6** Matt Neal, GB (Honda Integra), 24m 37.294s; **7** Gareth Howell, GB (Honda Integra), 24m 37.799s; **8** Mark Proctor, GB (Honda Civic Type-R), 24m 47.150s; **9** James Kaye, GB (Honda Civic Type-R), 24m 47.539s; **10** Jason Hughes, GB (MG ZS), 24m 53.456s.
Fastest race lap: Smith (Gavin), 1m 17.568s, 90.594 mph/145.797 km/h.
Fastest qualifying lap: Plato, 1m 11.793s, 97.881 mph/157.525 km/h.

Round 20 (40.992 miles/65.970 km).
1 Jason Plato, GB (SEAT Leon), 28m 22.073s, 86.701 mph/139.532 km/h; **2** James Thompson, GB (SEAT Leon), 28m 23.723s; **3** Colin Turkington, GB (MG ZS), 28m 25.479s; **4** Mike Jordan, GB (Honda Integra), 28m 28.954s; **5** Rob Collard, GB (MG ZS), 28m 29.191s; **6** Gordon Shedden, GB (Honda Integra), 28m 30.273s; **7** Tom Chilton, GB (Vauxhall Astra Sport Hatch), 28m 31.247s; **8** Matt Neal, GB (Honda Integra), 28m 37.065s; **9** Gareth Howell, GB (Honda Integra), 28m 37.980s; **10** Eoin Murray, IRL (Alfa Romeo 156), 28m 39.922s.
Fastest race lap: Turkington, 1m 13.252s, 95.932 mph/154.387 km/h.
Pole position: Plato.

Round 21 (35.136 miles/56.546 km).
1 Matt Neal, GB (Honda Integra), 22m 09.291s, 95.156 mph/153.138 km/h; **2** James Thompson, GB (SEAT Leon), 22m 09.948s; **3** Tom Chilton, GB (Vauxhall Astra Sport Hatch), 22m 13.972s; **4** Colin Turkington, GB (MG ZS), 22m 15.658s; **5** Gordon Shedden, GB (Honda Integra), 22m 21.716s; **6** Jason Plato, GB (SEAT Leon), 22m 23.380s; **7** Gavin Smith, IRL (Vauxhall Astra Sport Hatch), 22m 25.506s; **8** James Kaye, GB (Honda Civic Type-R), 22m 30.556s; **9** Mark Proctor, GB (Honda Civic Type-R), 22m 32.337s; **10** Eoin Murray, IRL (Alfa Romeo 156), 22m 36.281s.
Fastest race lap: Shedden, 1m 12.679s, 96.682s, 96.688 mph/155.605 km/h.
Pole position: Howell.

BRITISH TOURING CAR CHAMPIONSHIP, Knockhill Racing Circuit, Dunfermline, Fife, Scotland, Great Britain, 3 September. 27, 26 and 27 laps of the 1.2713-mile/2.046-km circuit.
Round 22 (34.263 miles/55.141 km).
1 Jason Plato, GB (SEAT Leon), 29m 34.436s, 69.513 mph/111.871 km/h; **2** Matt Neal, GB (Honda Integra), 29m 36.301s; **3** Gareth Howell, GB (Honda Integra), 29m 36.990s; **4** Fabrizio Giovanardi, I (Vauxhall Astra Sport Hatch), 29m 39.796s; **5** Mike Jordan, GB (Honda Integra), 29m 42.305s; **6** Gordon Shedden, GB (Honda Integra), 29m 42.739s; **7** Colin Turkington, GB (MG ZS), 29m 43.877s; **8** Jason Hughes, GB (MG ZS), 29m 45.799s; **9** Mark Proctor, GB (Honda Civic Type-R), 29m 48.777s; **10** Darren Turner, GB (SEAT Leon), 29m 55.629s.
Fastest race lap: Shedden, 57.966s, 78.955 mph/127.065 km/h.
Fastest qualifying lap: Plato, 57.467s, 79.640 mph/128168 km/h.

Round 23 (32.992 miles/53.095 km).
1 Fabrizio Giovanardi, I (Vauxhall Astra Sport Hatch), 24m 39.414s, 80.283 mph/129.202 km/h; **2** Gavin Smith, IRL (Vauxhall Astra Sport Hatch), 24m 43.720s; **3** David Pinkney, GB (Honda Integra), 24m 45.030s; **4** Jason Hughes, GB (MG ZS), 24m 47.539s; **5** Matt Neal, GB (Honda Integra), 24m 48.054s; **6** Mark Proctor, GB (Honda Civic Type-R), 24m 50.800s; **7** Gareth Howell, GB (Honda Integra), 24m 51.225s; **8** Martyn Bell, GB (BMW 320i), 25m 14.950s; **9** Colin Turkington, GB (MG ZS), 25 laps; **10** Jason Plato, GB (SEAT Leon), 25 (DNF).
Turner finished 2nd in 24m 40.051s, but was disqualified because his car was underweight.
Fastest race lap: Turkington, 53.745s, 85.155 mph/137.044 km/h.
Pole position: Plato.

Round 24 (34.263 miles/55.141 km).
1 Matt Neal, GB (Honda Integra), 25m 34.880s, 80.363 mph/129.371 km/h; **2** Gordon Shedden, GB (Honda Integra), 25m 35.024s; **3** Gareth Howell, GB (Honda Integra), 25m 35.526s; **4** Darren Turner, GB (SEAT Leon), 25m 40.148s; **5** Gavin Smith, IRL (Vauxhall Astra Sport Hatch), 25m 43.244s; **6** Fabrizio Giovanardi, I (Vauxhall Astra Sport Hatch), 25m 52.941s; **7** Rob Collard, GB (MG ZS), 25m 53.542s; **8** Mark Proctor, GB (Honda Civic Type-R), 26m 00.251s; **9** David Pinkney, GB (Honda Integra), 26m 08.018s; **10** Martyn Bell, GB (BMW 320i), 26m 13.571s.
Fastest race lap: Shedden, 53.311s, 85.849 mph/138.160 km/h.
Pole position: Proctor.

BRITISH TOURING CAR CHAMPIONSHIP, Brands Hatch Indy Circuit, West Kingsdown, Dartford, Kent, Great Britain, 24 September. 3 x 27 laps of the 1.1986-mile/1.929-km circuit.
Round 25 (32.380 miles/52.111 km).
1 Jason Plato, GB (SEAT Leon), 24m 04.158s, 80.717 mph/12.901 km/h; **2** Matt Neal, GB (Honda Integra), 24m 07.521s; **3** Colin Turkington, GB (MG ZS), 24m 11.010s; **4** Tom Chilton, GB (Vauxhall Astra Sport Hatch), 24m 13.449s; **5** Rob Collard, GB (MG ZS), 24m 18.124s; **6** Fabrizio Giovanardi, I (Vauxhall Astra Sport Hatch), 24m 21.443s; **7** Gordon Shedden, GB (Honda Integra), 24m 23.174s; **8** Mike Jordan, GB (Honda Integra), 24m 26.800s; **9** David Pinkney, GB (Honda Integra), 24m 28.033s; **10** Paul O'Neill, GB (Vauxhall Astra Coupé), 24m 28.212s.
Fastest race lap: Plato, 49.483s, 87.201 mph/140.336 km/h.
Fastest qualifying lap: Plato, 49.368s, 87.404 mph/140.663 km/h.

Round 26 (32.380 miles/52.111 km).
1 Jason Plato, GB (SEAT Leon), 23m 50.523s, 81.486 mph/131.139 / km/h; **2** Matt Neal, GB (Honda Integra), 23m 52.909s; **3** Colin Turkington, GB (MG ZS), 23m 53.469s; **4** Gordon Shedden, GB (Honda Integra), 23m 53.727s; **5** Fabrizio Giovanardi, I (Vauxhall Astra Sport Hatch), 23m 57.870s; **6** Tom Chilton, GB (Vauxhall Astra Sport Hatch), 23m 58.363s; **7** Rob Collard, GB (MG ZS), 23m 58.938s; **8** Gareth Howell, GB (Honda Integra), 23m 59.140s; **9** David Pinkney, GB (Honda Integra), 24m 01.580s; **10** Jason Hughes, GB (MG ZS), 24m 02.587s.
Fastest race lap: Plato, 49.780s, 86.681 mph/139.499 km/h.
Pole position: Plato.

Round 27 (32.380 miles/52.111 km).
1 Fabrizio Giovanardi, I (Vauxhall Astra Sport Hatch), 25m 26.598s, 76.358 mph/122.886 km/h; **2** Gordon Shedden, GB (Honda Integra), 25m 26.956s; **3** Jason Plato, GB (SEAT Leon), 25m 27.207s; **4** Colin Turkington, GB (MG ZS), 25m 27.571s; **5** Gareth Howell, GB (Honda Integra), 25m 29.261s; **6** Rob Collard, GB (MG ZS), 25m 30.222s; **7** Mike Jordan, GB (Honda Integra), 25m 30.756s; **8** Tom Chilton, GB (Vauxhall Astra Sport Hatch), 25m 31.660s; **9** Jason Hughes, GB (MG ZS), 25m 34.441s; **10** Gavin Smith, IRL (Vauxhall Astra Coupé), 25m 40.025s.
Fastest race lap: Chilton, 49.852s, 86.555 mph/139.297 km/h.
Pole position: Chilton.

BRITISH TOURING CAR CHAMPIONSHIP, Silverstone National Circuit, Towcester, Northamptonshire, Great Britain, 15 October. 22, 14 and 25 laps of the 1.639-mile/2.638-km circuit. Round 28 (36.104 miles/58.104 km).
1 Gareth Howell, GB (Honda Integra), 22m 40.400s, 95.541 mph/153.759 km/h; **2** Colin Turkington, GB (MG ZS), 22m 42.500s; **3** Tom Chilton, GB (Vauxhall Astra Sport Hatch), 22m 43.498s; **4** Matt Neal, GB (Honda Integra), 2m 44.691s; **5** James Thompson, GB (SEAT Leon), 22m 45.185s; **6** Gordon Shedden, GB (Honda Integra), 22m 45.673s; **7** Fabrizio Giovanardi, I (Vauxhall Astra Sport Hatch), 2m 46.380s; **8** Jason Plato, GB (SEAT Leon), 22m 50.309s; **9** Mike Jordan, GB (Honda Integra), 22m 50.507s; **10** Rob Collard, GB (MG ZS), 22m 53.113s.
Fastest race lap: Howell, 1m 00.866s, 96.941 mph/156.011 km/h.
Fastest qualifying lap: Howell, 1m 00.411s, 97.671 mph/157.186 km/h.

Round 29 (22.992 miles/37.002 km).
1 Matt Neal, GB (Honda Integra), 14m 27.047s, 95.463 mph/153.633 km/h; **2** Gordon Shedden, GB (Honda Integra), 14m 27.499s; **3** Fabrizio Giovanardi, I (Vauxhall Astra Sport Hatch), 14m 27.747s; **4** Gavin Smith, IRL (Vauxhall Astra Coupé), 14m 29.752s; **5** Rob Collard, GB (MG ZS), 14m 29.930s; **6** Gareth Howell, GB (Honda Integra), 14m 30.410s; **7** Tom Ferrier, GB (SEAT Toledo Cupra), 14m 35.941s; **8** Paul O'Neill, GB (Vauxhall Astra Coupé), 14m 42.232s; **9** Jason Hughes, GB (MG ZS), 14m 43.930s; **10** Darren Turner, GB (SEAT Leon), 14m 44.071s.
Fastest race lap: Shedden, 1m 00.859s, 96.952 mph/156.029 km/h.
Pole position: Howell.

Round 30 (41.021 miles/66.017 km).
1 Gareth Howell, GB (Honda Integra), 28m 09.575s, 87.404 mph/140.663 km/h; **2** Colin Turkington, GB (MG ZS), 28m 10.541s; **3** Tom Chilton, GB (Vauxhall Astra Sport Hatch), 28m 14.704s; **4** Jason Plato, GB (SEAT Leon), 28m 15.296s; **5** James Thompson, GB (SEAT Leon), 28m 15.679s; **6** Darren Turner, GB (SEAT Leon), 28m 16.202s; **7** Rob Collard, GB (MG ZS), 28m 18.769s; **8** Tom Ferrier, GB (SEAT Toledo Cupra), 28m 21.629s; **9** Paul O'Neill, GB (Vauxhall Astra Coupé), 28m 24.584s; **10** Gavin Smith, IRL (Vauxhall Astra Coupé), 28m 24.719s.
Fastest race lap: Howell, 1m 01.070s, 96.617 mph/155.490 km/h.
Pole position: Hughes.

Final championship points
Drivers
1 Matt Neal, GB, 289; **2** Jason Plato, GB, 241; **3** Colin Turkington, GB, 240; **4** Gordon Shedden, GB, 204; **5** Fabrizio Giovanardi, I, 163; **6** James Thompson, GB, 162; **7** Tom Chilton, GB, 139; **8** Gavin Smith, IRL, 123; **9** Rob Collard, GB, 117; **10** Mike Jordan, GB, 91; **11** Gareth Howell, GB, 80; **12** James Kaye, GB, 61; **13** David Pinkney, GB, 56; **14** Darren Turner, GB, 41; **15** Jason Hughes, GB, 27; **16** Mark Proctor, GB, 18; **17** Martyn Bell, GB, 8; **18** Eoin Murray, IRL, 8; **19** Tom Ferrier, GB, 7; **20** Paul O'Neill, GB, 7; **21** Fiona Leggate, GB, 3; **22** Adam Jones, GB, 1.
Independent Drivers
1 Matt Neal, GB, 337; **2** Colin Turkington, GB, 290; **3** Gordon Shedden, GB, 233; **4** Rob Collard, GB, 174; **5** Mike Jordan, GB, 162.
Manufacturers
1 SEAT, 572; **2** Vauxhall, 528.
Teams
1 Team Halfords, 512; **2** SEAT Sport UK, 418; **3** VX Racing, 386; **4** Team RAC, 332; **5** Team Eurotech Racing, 93.
Independent Teams
1 Team Halfords, 622; **2** Team RAC, 469; **3** Team Eurotech Racing, 164.

Indy Racing League (IRL) IndyCar Series

All cars are Dallara IR4-Honda, unless stated.

TOYOTA INDY 300, Homestead-Miami Speedway, Florida, USA, 26 March. Round 1. 200 laps of the 1.485-mile/2.390-km circuit, 297.000 miles/477.975 km.
1 Dan Wheldon, GB, 1h 46m 14.5286s, 167.730 mph/269.935 km/h; **2** Hélio Castroneves, BR, 1h 46m 14.5433s; **3** Sam Hornish Jr, USA, 1h 46m 15.0030s; **4** Dario Franchitti, GB, 1h 46m 15.4687s; **5** Scott Dixon, NZ, 1h 46m 15.7275s; **6** Kosuke Matsuura, J, 198 laps; **7** Scott Sharp, USA, 198; **8** Felipe Giaffone, BR, 198; **9** Tomas Scheckter, ZA, 197; **10** Eddie Cheever, USA, 196; **11** Tony Kanaan, BR, 159 (DNF-accident); **12** PJ Chesson, USA, 152 (DNF-gearbox); **13** Bryan Herta, USA, 140 (DNF-accident); **14** Buddy Lazier, USA, 12 (DNF-electrics); **15** Marco Andretti, GB, 12 (DNF-halfshaft); **16** Vitor Meira, BR, 10 (DNF-mechanical).
Did not start: Danica Patrick, USA (Panoz G Force 09B-Honda) and Buddy Rice, USA (Panoz G Force 09B-Honda) – withdrew following their team-mate's fatal accident; Paul Dana, USA (Panoz G Force 09B-Honda) – fatal accident in morning warm-up session; Ed Carpenter, USA – accident in morning warm-up session.
Most laps led: Hornish Jr, 145.
Fastest race lap: Dixon, 24.7198s, 216.264 mph/348.043 km/h.
Fastest qualifying lap: Hornish Jr, 24.4625s, 218.539 mph/351.704 km/h.

Championship points: **1** Wheldon, 50; **2** Castroneves, 40; **3** Hornish Jr, 38; **4** Franchitti, 32; **5** Dixon, 30; **6** Matsuura, 28.

HONDA GRAND PRIX OF ST. PETERSBURG, Streets of St. Petersburg, Florida, USA, 2 April. Round 2. 100 laps of the 1.800-mile/2.897-km circuit, 180.000 miles/289.682 km.
1 Hélio Castroneves, BR, 1h 56m 57.5172s, 92.340 mph/148.607 km/h (under caution); **2** Scott Dixon, NZ (Panoz G Force 09B-Honda), 1h 56m 57.6558s; **3** Tony Kanaan, BR, 1h 56m 58.1456s; **4** Bryan Herta, USA, 1h 56m 58.2985s; **5** Vitor Meira, BR, 1h 57m 00.1167s; **6** Danica Patrick, USA (Panoz G Force 09B-Honda), 1h 57m 00.5605s; **7** Kosuke Matsuura, J, 1h 57m 50.2344s; **8** Sam Hornish Jr, USA, 99 laps; **9** Felipe Giaffone, BR, 99; **10** Scott Sharp, USA (Panoz G Force 09B-Honda), 99; **11** Eddie Cheever, USA, 99; **12** Tomas Scheckter, ZA, 96 (DNF-accident); **13** Buddy Rice, USA (Panoz G Force 09B-Honda), 96 (DNF-accident); **14** Buddy Lazier, USA, 59 (DNF-mechanical); **15** Marco Andretti, GB, 58 (DNF-halfshaft); **16** Dan Wheldon, GB (Panoz G Force 09B-Honda), 57 (DNF-accident); **17** PJ Chesson, USA, 55 (DNF-suspension); **18** Roberto Moreno, BR, 32 (DNF-steering); **19** Dario Franchitti, GB, 15 (DNF-handling).
Most laps led: Castroneves, 40.
Fastest race lap: Kanaan, 1m 03.5842s, 101.912 mph/164.012 km/h.
Fastest qualifying lap: Franchitti, 1m 02.2753s, 104.054 mph/167.459 km/h.
Championship points: **1** Castroneves, 93; **2** Dixon, 70; **3** Wheldon, 64; **4** Hornish Jr, 62; **5=** Matsuura, 54; **5=** Kanaan, 54.

INDY JAPAN 300, Twin Ring Motegi, Motegi-machi, Haga-gun, Tochigi Prefecture, Japan, 22 April. Round 3. 200 laps of the 1.520-mile/2.446-km circuit, 304.000 miles/489.241 km.
1 Hélio Castroneves, BR, 1h 59m 01.3704s, 153.248 mph/246.629 km/h; **2** Dan Wheldon, GB, 1h 59m 07.7555s; **3** Tony Kanaan, BR, 1h 59m 09.9867s; **4** Sam Hornish Jr, USA, 1h 59m 10.3715s; **5** Buddy Rice, USA (Panoz G Force 09B-Honda), 1h 59m 11.1195s; **6** Bryan Herta, USA, 1h 59m 15.2676s; **7** Kosuke Matsuura, J, 1h 59m 16.1337s; **8** Danica Patrick, USA (Panoz G Force 09B-Honda), 1h 59m 16.8160s; **9** Scott Dixon, NZ, 199 laps; **10** Vitor Meira, BR, 199; **11** Dario Franchitti, GB, 199; Marco Andretti, GB, 199; **13** Tomas Scheckter, ZA, 196; **14** Buddy Lazier, USA, 195; **15** Felipe Giaffone, BR, 155 (DNF-accident); **16** Scott Sharp, USA, 42 (DNF-accident); **17** PJ Chesson, USA, 40 (DNF-accident); **18** Jeff Simmons, USA (Panoz G Force 09B-Honda), 40 (DNF-accident); **19** Tomás Enge, CZ, 25 (DNF-accident); **20** Ed Carpenter, USA, 25 (DNF-accident).
Most laps led: Castroneves, 184.
Fastest race lap: Dixon, 27.2804s, 200.584 mph/322.808 km/h.
Pole position: Castroneves *(qualifying rained out, so grid determined by driver points)*.
Championship points: **1** Castroneves, 146; **2** Wheldon, 104; **3** Hornish Jr, 94; **4** Dixon, 92; **5** Kanaan, 89; **6** Matsuura, 80.

90TH INDIANAPOLIS 500, Indianapolis Motor Speedway, Speedway, Indiana, USA, 28 May. Round 4. 200 laps of the 2.500-mile/4.023-km circuit, 500.000 miles/804.672 km.
1 Sam Hornish Jr, USA, 3h 10m 58.7590s, 157.085 mph/252.804 km/h; **2** Marco Andretti, USA, 3h 10m 58.8225s; **3** Michael Andretti, USA, 3h 10m 59.7677s; **4** Dan Wheldon, GB, 3h 11m 00.0282s; **5** Tony Kanaan, BR, 3h 11m 00.4046s; **6** Scott Dixon, NZ, 3h 11m 01.8156s; **7** Dario Franchitti, GB, 3h 11m 04.3839s; **8** Danica Patrick, USA (Panoz G Force 09B-Honda), 3h 11m 04.4853s; **9** Scott Sharp, USA, 3h 11m 09.8842s; **10** Vitor Meira, BR, 3h 11m 16.7144s; **11** Ed Carpenter, USA, 199 laps; **12** Buddy Lazier, USA, 199; **13** Eddie Cheever, USA, 198; **14** Massimiliano 'Max' Papis, I, 197; **15** Kosuke Matsuura, J, 196; **16** Roger Yasukawa, USA (Panoz G Force 09B-Honda), 194; **17** Jaques Lazier, USA (Panoz G Force 09B-Honda), 193; **18** Airton Dare, BR (Panoz G Force 09B-Honda), 193; **19** PJ Jones, USA (Panoz G Force 09B-Honda), 189; **20** Bryan Herta, USA, 188; **21** Felipe Giaffone, BR, 177 (DNF-accident); **22** Townsend Bell, USA, 161 (DNF-suspension); **23** Jeff Simmons, USA (Panoz G Force 09B-Honda), 152 (DNF-accident); **24** Al Unser Jr, USA, 145 (DNF-accident); **25** Hélio Castroneves, BR, 109 (DNF-accident); **26** Buddy Rice, USA (Panoz G Force 09B-Honda), 108 (DNF-accident); **27** Tomas Scheckter, ZA, 65 (DNF-accident); **28** Arie Luyendyk Jr, NL (Panoz G Force 09B-Honda), 54 (DNF-handling); **29** Stéphane Gregoire, F (Panoz G Force 09B-Honda), 49 (DNF-handling); **30** Larry Foyt, USA, 43 (DNF-handling); **31** Thiago Medeiros, BR (Panoz G Force 09B-Honda), 24 (DNF-electrics); **32** Jeff Bucknum, USA, 1 (DNF-accident); **33** PJ Chesson, USA, 1 (DNF-accident).
Did not qualify: Jon Herb, USA (Panoz G Force 09B-Honda); Marty Roth, CDN.
Most laps led: Wheldon, 148.
Fastest race lap: Dixon, 40.6777s, 221.251 mph/356.070 km/h.
Fastest leading lap: Hornish Jr, 40.9211s, 219.935 mph/353.952 km/h.
Pole position/Fastest qualifying lap: Hornish Jr, 2m 37.2155s, 228.985 mph/368.516 km/h (over four laps).
Championship points: **1** Castroneves, 156; **2** Hornish Jr, 144; **3** Wheldon, 139; **4** Dixon, 120; **5** Kanaan, 119; **6** Matsuura, 95.

WATKINS GLEN INDY GRAND PRIX, Watkins Glen International, Watkins Glen, New York, USA, 4 June. Round 5. 55 laps of the 3.370-mile/5.423-km circuit, 185.350 miles/298.292 km Race scheduled for 60 laps, but stopped after 2 hours.
1 Scott Dixon, NZ (Panoz G Force 09B-Honda), 2h 00m 20.0224s, 92.418 mph/148.732 km/h; **2** Vitor Meira, BR, 2h 00m 22.3535s; **3** Ryan Briscoe, AUS, 2h 00m 22.8223s; **4** Buddy Rice, USA (Panoz G Force 09B-Honda), 2h 00m 29.2508s; **5** Felipe Giaffone, BR, 2h 00m 31.5035s; **6** Ed Carpenter, USA, 2h 00m 32.4651s; **7** Hélio Castroneves, BR, 2h 00m 33.0679s; **8** Danica Patrick, USA (Panoz G Force 09B-Honda), 2h 00m 33.3513s; **9** Scott Sharp, USA (Panoz G Force 09B-Honda), 2h 00m 36.6686s; **10** Tomas Scheckter, ZA, 2h 01m 08.5096s; **11** Tony Kanaan, BR, 54 laps; **12** Sam Hornish Jr, USA, 54; **13** Bryan Herta, USA, 54; **14** Dario Franchitti, GB, 44; **15** Dan Wheldon, GB (Panoz G Force 09B-Honda), 41 (DNF-mechanical); **16** Marco Andretti, GB, 38 (DNF-accident); **17** Eddie Cheever, USA, 37 (DNF-accident); **18** Kosuke Matsuura, J, 19 (DNF-accident); **19** Jeff Simmons, USA (Panoz G Force 09B-Honda), 18 (DNF-accident).
Most laps led: Wheldon, 13.
Fastest race lap: Andretti, 1m 34.8752s, 127.873 mph/205.792 km/h.
Fastest qualifying lap: Castroneves, 1m 30.6783s, 133.792 mph/215.317 km/h.
Championship points: **1** Castroneves, 182; **2** Dixon, 170; **3** Hornish Jr, 162; **4** Wheldon, 157; **5** Kanaan, 138; **6** Meira, 124.

BOMBARDIER LEARJET 500, Texas Motor Speedway, Fort Worth, Texas, USA, 10 June. Round 6. 200 laps of the 1.455-mile/2.342-km circuit, 291.000 miles/468.319 km.
1 Hélio Castroneves, BR, 1h 34m 01.0482s, 185.710 mph/298.872 km/h; **2** Scott Dixon, NZ, 1h 34m 01.2884s; **3** Dan Wheldon, GB, 1h 34m 01.3463s; **4** Sam Hornish Jr, USA, 1h 34m 15.5871s; **5** Scott Sharp, USA, 1h 34m 15.6377s; **6** Vitor Meira, BR, 1h 34m 16.9776s; **7** Tony Kanaan, BR, 1h 34m 17.1880s; **8** Kosuke Matsuura, J, 1h 34m 23.3809s; **9** Ed Carpenter, USA, 1h 34m 24.0207s; **10** Tomas Scheckter, ZA, 199 laps; **11** Bryan Herta, USA, 199; **12** Danica Patrick, USA, 199; **13** Dario Franchitti, GB, 199; **14** Marco Andretti, GB, 199; **15** Jeff Simmons, USA, 199; **16** Felipe Giaffone, BR, 197; **17** Eddie Cheever, USA, 197; **18** Buddy Rice, USA, 70 (DNF-mechanical); **19** Buddy Lazier, USA, 56 (DNF-fuel pump).
Most laps led: Wheldon, 171.
Fastest race lap: Wheldon, 24.4535s, 214.202 mph/344.725 km/h.
Fastest qualifying lap: Hornish Jr, 24.5197s, 213.624 mph/343.795 km/h.
Championship points: **1** Castroneves, 232; **2** Dixon, 210; **3** Wheldon, 195; **4** Hornish Jr, 194; **5** Kanaan, 164; **6** Meira, 152.

SUN TRUST INDY CHALLENGE, Richmond International Raceway, Virginia, USA, 24 June. Round 7. 250 laps of the 0.750-mile/1.207-km circuit, 187.500 miles/301.752 km.
1 Sam Hornish Jr, USA, 1h 26m 49.4669s, 129.572 mph/208.526 km/h; **2** Vitor Meira, BR, 1h 26m 49.8576s; **3** Dario Franchitti, GB, 1h 26m 51.0564s; **4** Marco Andretti, GB, 1h 26m 56.0069s; **5** Scott Sharp, USA, 1h 26m 55.1346s*; **6** Bryan Herta, USA, 1h 27m 00.3886s; **7** Tomas Scheckter, ZA, 249 laps; **8** Ed Carpenter, USA, 249; **9** Dan Wheldon, GB, 249; **10** Hélio Castroneves, BR, 249; **11** Scott Dixon, NZ, 249; **12** Kosuke Matsuura, J, 247; **13** Buddy Rice, USA, 247; **14** Eddie Cheever, USA, 246; **15** Danica Patrick, USA, 246; **16** Buddy Lazier, USA, 245; **17** Felipe Giaffone, BR, 244; **18** Tony Kanaan, BR, 109 (DNF-gearbox); **19** Jeff Simmons, USA, 59 (DNF-accident).
*4th on timing - official positions taken at start of final yellow flag period.
Most laps led: Hornish Jr, 212.
Fastest race lap: Castroneves, 16.7234s, 161.450 mph/259.829 km/h.
Fastest qualifying lap: Castroneves, 15.5645s, 173.472 mph/279.176 km/h.
Championship points: **1** Castroneves, 252; **2** Hornish Jr, 247; **3** Dixon, 229; **4** Wheldon, 217; **5** Meira, 192; **6** Kanaan, 176.

KANSAS LOTTERY INDY 300, Kansas Speedway, Kansas City, Kansas, USA, 2 July. Round 8. 200 laps of the 1.520-mile/2.446-km circuit, 304.000 miles/489.241 km.
1 Sam Hornish Jr, USA, 1h 49m 00.3423s, 167.331 mph/269.293 km/h; **2** Dan Wheldon, GB, 1h 49m 00.4216s; **3** Vitor Meira, BR, 1h 49m 05.7315s; **4** Scott Dixon, NZ, 1h 49m 05.8581s; **5** Tony Kanaan, BR, 1h 49m 06.1185s; **6** Hélio Castroneves, BR, 1h 49m 07.3855s; **7** Tomas Scheckter, ZA, 1h 49m 10.0348s; **8** Kosuke Matsuura, J, 1h 49m 10.3304s; **9** Marco Andretti, GB, 199 laps; **10** Jeff Simmons, USA, 199; **11** Danica Patrick, USA, 198; **12** Dario Franchitti, GB, 198; **13** Bryan Herta, USA, 197; **14** Eddie Cheever, USA, 196; **15** Buddy Lazier, USA, 194; **16** Ed Carpenter, USA, 184; **17** Buddy Rice, USA, 174 (DNF-accident); **18** Scott Sharp, USA, 165 (DNF-accident); **19** Felipe Giaffone, BR, 66 (DNF-mechanical).
Most laps led: Hornish Jr, 149.
Fastest race lap: Castroneves, 25.9847s, 210.585 mph/338.904 km/h.
Fastest qualifying lap: Wheldon, 25.6257s, 213.536 mph/343.652 km/h.
Championship points: **1** Hornish Jr, 300; **2** Castroneves, 280; **3** Dixon, 261; **4** Wheldon, 257; **5** Meira, 227; **6** Kanaan, 206.

FIRESTONE INDY 200, Nashville Superspeedway, Lebanon, Tennessee, USA, 15 July. Round 9. 200 laps of the 1.300-mile/2.092-km circuit, 260.000 miles/418.429 km.
1 Scott Dixon, NZ, 1h 36m 46.2751s, 161.205 mph/259.434 km/h; **2** Dan Wheldon, GB, 1h 36m 46.3927s; **3** Vitor Meira, BR, 1h 36m 47.5507s; **4** Danica Patrick, USA, 1h 36m 48.7770s; **5** Hélio Castroneves, BR, 1h 36m 49.8398s; **6** Dario Franchitti, GB, 1h 36m 58.2200s; **7** Jeff Simmons, USA, 199 laps; **8** Marco Andretti, GB, 199; **9** Ryan Briscoe, AUS, 199; **10** Ed Carpenter, USA, 198; **11** Bryan Herta, USA, 198; **12** Tony Kanaan, BR, 170; **13** Kosuke Matsuura, J, 162 (DNF-accident); **14** Sam Hornish Jr, USA, 128 (DNF-accident); **15** Tomas Scheckter, ZA, 121 (DNF-mechanical); **16** Buddy Rice, USA, 61 (DNF-electrics); **17** Scott Sharp, USA, 58 (DNF-electrics); **18** Jeff Bucknum, USA, 36 (DNF-handling).
Most laps led: Wheldon, 115.
Fastest race lap: Wheldon, 23.1401s, 202.246 mph/325.484 km/h.
Fastest qualifying lap: Wheldon, 23.0210s, 203.293 mph/327.168 km/h.
Championship points: **1** Hornish Jr, 316; **2** Dixon, 311; **3** Castroneves, 310; **4** Wheldon, 300; **5** Meira, 262; **6** Kanaan, 224.

ABC SUPPLY/A.J. FOYT INDY 225, The Milwaukee Mile, Wisconsin State Fair Park, West Allis, Wisconsin, USA, 23 July. Round 10. 225 laps of the 1.015-mile/1.633-km circuit, 228.375 miles/367.534 km.
1 Tony Kanaan, BR, 1h 42m 37.8319s, 133.513 mph/214.868 kmh; **2** Sam Hornish Jr, USA, 1h 42m 39.6595s; **3** Tomas Scheckter, ZA, 1h 42m 39.8433s; **4** Danica Patrick, USA, 1h 42m 46.3027s; **5** Marco Andretti, GB, 1h 42m 48.0930s; **6** Dario Franchitti, GB, 1h 42m 49.0692s; **7** Bryan Herta, USA, 1h 42m 51.9514s; **8** Dan Wheldon, GB, 224 laps; **9** Jeff Simmons, USA, 223; **10** Scott Dixon, NZ, 223; **11** Buddy Rice, USA, 221; **12** Scott Sharp, USA, 219; 13 Jeff Bucknum, USA, 194 (DNF-accident); **14** Hélio Castroneves, BR, 170; **15** Vitor Meira, BR, 136 (DNF-accident); **16** Ed Carpenter, USA, 109 (DNF-suspension); **17** Kosuke Matsuura, J, 85 (DNF-mechanical); **18** Ryan Briscoe, AUS, 13 (DNF-handling).
Most laps led: Kanaan, 127.
Fastest race lap: Scheckter, 22.2961s, 163.885 mph/263.748 km/h.
Fastest qualifying lap: Castroneves, 21.1854s, 172.477 mph/277.575 km/h.
Championship: **1** Hornish Jr, 356; **2** Dixon, 331; **3** Castroneves, 326; **4** Wheldon, 324; **5=** Meira, 277; **5=** Kanaan, 277.

FIRESTONE INDY 400, Michigan International Speedway, Brooklyn, Michigan, USA, 30 July. Round 11. 200 laps of the 2.000-mile/3.219-km circuit, 400.000 miles/643.738 km.
1 Hélio Castroneves, BR, 2h 03m 43.7441s, 193.972 mph/312.168 km/h; **2** Vitor Meira, BR, 2h 03m 45.3670s; **3** Dan Wheldon, GB, 2h 03m 49.9700s; **4** Tony Kanaan, BR, 2h 03m 50.7315s; **5** Tomas Scheckter, ZA, 2h 04m 11.6446s; **6** Scott Sharp, USA, 2h 04m 12.3001s; **7** Ed Carpenter, USA, 199 laps; **8** Marco Andretti, GB, 199; **9** Kosuke Matsuura, J, 199; **10** Jeff Simmons, USA, 199; **11** Bryan Herta, USA, 199; **12** Dario Franchitti, GB, 199; **13** Buddy Rice, USA, 199; **14** Jeff Bucknum, USA, 198; **15** Buddy Lazier, USA, 198; **16** Scott Dixon, NZ, 197; **17** Danica Patrick, USA, 197 (DNF-mechanical); **18** Marty Roth, USA, 192; **19** Sam Hornish Jr, USA, 61 (DNF-mechanical).

Most laps led: Meira, 75.
Fastest race lap: Matsuura, 33.2737s, 216.387 mph/348.241 km/h.
Fastest qualifying lap: Castroneves, 33.2138s, 216.777 mph/348.869 km/h.
Championship points: **1** Castroneves, 376; **2** Hornish Jr, 368; **3** Wheldon, 359; **4** Dixon, 345; **5** Meira, 320; **6** Kanaan, 309.

MEIJER INDY 300, Kentucky Speedway, Florence, Kentucky, USA. 13 August. Round 12. 200 laps of the 1.480-mile/2.382-km circuit, 296.000 miles/476.366 km.
1 Sam Hornish Jr, USA, 1h 44m 03.4120s, 170.676 mph/274.676 km/h; **2** Scott Dixon, NZ, 1h 44m 03.9986s; **3** Hélio Castroneves, BR, 1h 44m 04.0631s; **4** Dan Wheldon, GB, 1h 44m 05.3033s; **5** Tony Kanaan, BR, 1h 44m 05.7169s; **6** Vitor Meira, BR, 1h 44m 05.9311s; **7** Tomas Scheckter, ZA, 1h 44m 06.2244s; **8** Danica Patrick, USA, 1h 44m 06.6528s; **9** Dario Franchitti, GB, 1h 44m 08.1190s; **10** Bryan Herta, USA, 1h 44m 08.2086s; **11** Ed Carpenter, USA, 199 laps; **12** Sarah Fisher, USA, 199; **13** Jeff Bucknum, USA, 199; **14** Jeff Simmons, USA, 199; **15** Buddy Rice, USA, 198; **16** Scott Sharp, USA, 198; **17** Marco Andretti, GB, 197; **18** Marty Roth, USA, 196; **19** Kosuke Matsuura, J, 118 (DNF-accident).
Most laps led: Wheldon, 66.
Fastest race lap: Herta, 24.3154s, 219.120 mph/352.640 km/h.
Fastest qualifying lap: Castroneves, 24.4037s, 218.328 mph/351.364 km/h.
Championship points: **1** Hornish Jr, 418; **2** Castroneves, 411; **3** Wheldon, 394; **4** Dixon, 385; **5** Meira, 348; **6** Kanaan, 339.

INDY GRAND PRIX OF SONOMA, Infineon Raceway, Sears Point, Sonoma, California, USA, 27 August. Round 13. 80 laps of the 2.300-mile/3.701-km circuit, 184.000 miles/296.119 km.
1 Marco Andretti, GB, 1h 58m 05.5416s, 93.486 mph/150.451 km/h; **2** Dario Franchitti, GB, 1h 58m 06.1973s; **3** Vitor Meira, BR, 1h 58m 16.1951s; **4** Scott Dixon, NZ, 1h 58m 16.7283s; **5** Hélio Castroneves, BR, 1h 58m 18.0465s; **6** Dan Wheldon, GB, 1h 58m 18.9910s; **7** Jeff Simmons, USA, 1h 58m 19.4170s; **8** Danica Patrick, USA, 1h 58m 21.2833s; **9** Sam Hornish Jr, USA, 1h 58m 21.8785s; **10** Bryan Herta, USA, 1h 58m 24.0987s; **11** Tony Kanaan, BR, 1h 58m 46.2052s; **12** Ed Carpenter, USA, 79 laps; **13** Kosuke Matsuura, J, 79; **14** Scott Sharp, USA, 79; **15** Buddy Rice, USA, 75; **16** Ryan Brisce, AUS, 67 (DNF-handling); **17** Tomas Scheckter, ZA, 44; **18** Jeff Bucknum, USA, 9 (DNF-handling).
Most laps led: Dixon, 40.
Fastest race lap: Kanaan, 1m 18.6820s, 105.234 mph/169.357 km/h.
Fastest qualifying lap: Dixon, 1m 17.0344s, 107.484 mph/172.979 km/h.
Championship points: **1** Castroneves, 441; **2** Hornish Jr, 440; **3** Wheldon, 422; **4** Dixon, 420; **5** Meira, 383; **6** Kanaan, 358.

PEAK ANTIFREEZE INDY 300, Chicagoland Speedway, Chicago, Illinois, USA, 10 September. Round 14. 200 of the 1.520-mile/2.446-km circuit, 304.000 miles/489.241 km.
1 Dan Wheldon, GB, 1h 33m 37.2662s, 194.828 mph/313.545 km/h; **2** Scott Dixon, NZ, 1h 33m 37.4559s; **3** Sam Hornish Jr, USA, 1h 33m 37.4985s; **4** Hélio Castroneves, BR, 1h 33m 39.9575s; **5** Ed Carpenter, USA, 199 laps; **6** Vitor Meira, BR, 199; **7** Tony Kanaan, BR, 199; **8** Jeff Simmons, USA, 199; **9** Scott Sharp, USA, 199; **10** Tomas Scheckter, ZA, 199; **11** Kosuke Matsuura, J, 199; **12** Danica Patrick, USA, 199; **13** Buddy Rice, USA, 199; **14** AJ Foyt IV, USA, 198; **15** Bryan Herta, USA, 198; **16** Sarah Fisher, USA, 198; **17** Jeff Bucknum, USA, 198; **18** Marco Andretti, GB, 198; **19** Marty Roth, USA, 160 (in garage).
Most laps led: Wheldon, 166.
Fastest race lap: Hornish Jr, 25.2500s, 216.713 mph/348.766 km/h.
Fastest qualifying lap: Hornish Jr, 25.4134s, 215.319 mph/346.523 km/h.

Final championship points
Drivers
1 Sam Hornish Jr, USA, 475; **2** Dan Wheldon, GB, 475; **3** Hélio Castroneves, BR, 473; **4** Scott Dixon, NZ, 460; **5** Vitor Meira, BR, 411; **6** Tony Kanaan, BR, 384; **7** Marco Andretti, USA, 325; **8** Dario Franchitti, GB, 311; **9** Danica Patrick, USA, 302; **10** Tomas Scheckter, ZA, 298; **11** Bryan Herta, USA, 289; **12** Scott Sharp, USA, 287; **13** Kosuke Matsuura, J, 273; **14** Ed Carpenter, USA, 252; **15** Buddy Rice, USA, 234; **16** Jeff Simmons, USA, 217; **17** Felipe Giaffone, BR, 142; **18** Buddy Lazier, USA, 122; **19** Eddie Cheever, USA, 114; **20** Jeff Bucknum, USA, 97; **21** Ryan Briscoe, AUS, 83; **22** PJ Chesson, USA, 54; **23** Marty Roth, USA, 36; **24** Michael Andretti, USA, 35; **25** Sarah Fisher, USA, 32; **26** Massimiliano 'Max' Papis, I, 16; **27** AJ Foyt IV, USA, 16; **28** Roger Yasukawa, USA, 14; **29** Jaques Lazier, USA, 13; **30** Airton Daré, BR, 12.
Bombardier Rookie of the Year: Marco Andretti.
Chassis Manufacturers: **1** Dallara, 137; **2** Panoz, 45.

Bridgestone presents The Champ Car World Series Powered by Ford

All cars are Lola B2/00-Ford Cosworth XFE.

TOYOTA GRAND PRIX OF LONG BEACH, Long Beach street circuit, California, USA, 9 April. Round 1. 74 laps of the 1.968-mile/3.167-km circuit, 145.632 miles/234.372 km.
1 Sébastien Bourdais, F, 1h 40m 07.670s, 87.268 mph/140.444 km/h; **2** Justin Wilson, GB, 1h 40m 21.766s; **3** Alex Tagliani, CDN, 1h 40m 28.155s; **4** Màrio Dominguez, MEX, 1h 40m 30.282s; **5** Cristiano da Matta, BR, 1h 40m 44.470s; **6** Andrew Ranger, CDN, 1h 41m 02.594s; **7** Jan Heylen, B, 1h 41m 09.318s; **8** Katherine Legge, GB, 1h 41m 09.878s; **9** Will Power, AUS, 73 laps; **10** Antonio Pizzonia, BR, 73; **11** Dan Clarke, GB, 72; **12** Charles Zwolsman, NL, 67 (DNF-accident damage); **13** Nelson Philippe, F, 46 (DNF-transmission); **14** Jimmy Vasser, USA, 24 (DNF-driveshaft); **15** Bruno Junqueira, BR, 1 (DNF-accident damage); **16** AJ Allmendinger, USA, 0 (DNF-accident); **17** Paul Tracy, CDN, 0 (DNF-accident); **18** Oriol Servia, E, 0 (DNF-accident).
Most laps led: Bourdais, 70.
Fastest race lap: Bourdais, 1m 07.931s, 104.294 mph/167.845 km/h.
Fastest qualifying lap: Bourdais, 1m 06.886s, 105.924 mph/170.467 km/h.
Championship points: **1** Bourdais, 35; **2** Wilson, 27; **3** Tagliani, 25; **4** Dominguez, 23; **5** Da Matta, 21; **6** Ranger, 20.

GRAND PRIX OF HOUSTON, Reliant Park, Houston, Texas, USA, 13 May. Round 2. 96 laps of the 1.690-mile/2.720-km circuit, 162.240 miles/261.000 km.

1 Sébastien Bourdais, F, 1h 59m 57.021s, 81.154 mph/130.604 km/h; **2** Paul Tracy, CDN, 1h 59m 58.259s; **3** Màrio Dominguez, MEX, 1h 59m 59.308s; **4** Nelson Philippe, F, 2h 00m 00.688s; **5** Justin Wilson, GB, 2h 00m 01.061s; **6** Andrew Ranger, CDN, 2h 00m 02.372s; **7** Will Power, AUS, 2h 00m 03.007s; **8** AJ Allmendinger, USA, 2h 00m 04.710s; **9** Cristiano da Matta, BR, 95 laps; **10** Bruno Junqueira, BR, 93; **11** Alex Tagliani, CDN, 90 (DNF-accident); **12** Oriol Servia, E, 87 (DNF-accident); **13** Jan Heylen, B, 82; **14** Katherine Legge, GB, 81; **15** Charles Zwolsman, NL, 69 (DNF-accident); **16** Dan Clarke, GB, 33 (DNF-mechanical); **17** Nicky Pastorelli, NL, 29 (DNF-mechanical).
Most laps led: Dominguez, 63.
Fastest race lap: Bourdais, 1m 00.176s, 101.103 mph/ 162.710 km/h.
Fastest qualifying lap: Dominguez, 58.026s, 104.850 mph/ 168.739 km/h.
Championship points: 1 Bourdais, 68; **2** Dominguez, 50; **3** Wilson, 48; **4** Ranger, 40; **5** Tagliani, 35; **5** Da Matta, 34.

TECATE GRAND PRIX OF MONTERREY PRESENTED BY ROSHFRANS, Parque Fundidora, Monterrey, Nuevo Leon, Mexico, 21 May. Round 3. 76 laps of the 2.104-mile/ 3.386-km circuit, 159.904 miles/257.341 km.
1 Sébastien Bourdais, F, 1h 39m 50.252s, 96.099 mph/154.656 km/h; **2** Justin Wilson, GB, 1h 39m 53.318s; **3** AJ Allmendinger, USA, 1h 40m 04.384s; **4** Paul Tracy, CDN, 1h 40m 37.474s; **5** Alex Tagliani, CDN, 1h 40m 48.030s; **6** Màrio Dominguez, MEX, 1h 40m 49.034s; **7** Andrew Ranger, CDN, 1h 40m 49.554s; **8** Oriol Servia, E, 1h 41m 04.208s; **9** Cristiano da Matta, BR, 1h 41m 05.210s; **10** Bruno Junqueira, BR, 75 laps; **11** Will Power, AUS, 75; **12** Charles Zwolsman, NL, 75; **13** Dan Clarke, GB, 75; **14** Katherine Legge, GB, 75; **15** Nicky Pastorelli, NL, 74; **16** Jan Heylen, B, 71; **17** Nelson Philippe, F, 0 (DNF-accident).
Most laps led: Bourdais, 47.
Fastest race lap: Bourdais, 1m 14.529s, 101.630 mph/ 163.558 km/h.
Fastest qualifying lap: Bourdais, 1m 13.253s, 103.401 mph/ 166.407 km/h.
Championship points: 1 Bourdais, 102; **2** Wilson, 77; **3** Dominguez, 69; **4** Ranger, 58; **6** Tagliani, 56; **6** Tracy, 54.

TIME WARNER CABLE ROAD RUNNER 225, The Milwaukee mile, Wisconsin State Fair Park, West Allis, Wisconsin, USA, 4 June. Round 4. 197 laps of the 1.032-mile/1.661-km circuit, 203.304 miles/327.186 km.
1 Sébastien Bourdais, F, 1h 45m 03.946s, 116.101 mph/ 186.846 km/h; **2** Justin Wilson, GB, 1h 45m 07.559s; **3** Nelson Philippe, F, 1h 45m 09.587s; **4** AJ Allmendinger, USA, 1h 45m 22.450s; **5** Oriol Servia, E, 196 laps; **6** Katherine Legge, GB, 195; **7** Andrew Ranger, CDN, 194; **8** Dan Clarke, GB, 191; **9** Charles Zwolsman, NL, 191; **10** Nicky Pastorelli, NL, 183; **11** Will Power, AUS, 155 (DNF-mechanical); **12** Jan Heylen, B, 67 (DNF-electrics); **13** Cristiano da Matta, BR, 31 (DNF-mechanical); **14** Màrio Dominguez, MEX, 4 (DNF-accident); **15** Bruno Junqueira, BR, 1 (DNF-accident); **16** Paul Tracy, CDN, 1 (DNF-accident).
Did not start: Alex Tagliani, CDN (abandoned after practice).
Most laps led: Bourdais, 117.
Fastest race lap: Bourdais, 22.285s, 166.713 mph/ 268.299 km/h.
Fastest qualifying lap: Bourdais, 21.182s, 175.394 mph/ 282.270 km/h.
Championship points: 1 Bourdais, 136; **2** Wilson, 105; **3** Ranger, 75; **4=** Dominguez, 69; **4=** Allmendinger, 69; **6** Philippe, 61.

GRAND PRIX OF PORTLAND PRESENTED BY G.I. JOE'S, Portland International Raceway, Oregon, USA, 18 June. Round 5. 105 laps of the 1.964-mile/3.161-km circuit, 206.220 miles/331.879 km.
1 AJ Allmendinger, USA, 1h 48m 32.853s, 113.989 mph/ 183.447 km/h; **2** Justin Wilson, GB, 1h 48m 38.273s; **3** Sébastien Bourdais, F, 1h 48m 38.859s; **4** Bruno Junqueira, BR, 1h 49m 09.221s; **5** Cristiano da Matta, BR, 1h 49m 12.405s; **6** Dan Clarke, GB, 1h 49m 23.140s; **7** Paul Tracy, CDN, 1h 49m 25.149s; **8** Nelson Philippe, F, 1h 49m 25.530s; **9** Andrew Ranger, CDN, 104 laps; **10** Oriol Servia, E, 104; **11** Alex Tagliani, CDN, 104; **12** Charles Zwolsman, NL, 103; **13** Katherine Legge, GB, 103; **14** Màrio Dominguez, MEX, 103; **15** Jan Heylen, B, 103; **16** Tonis Kasemets, EE, 102; **17** Nicky Pastorelli, NL, 101; **18** Will Power, AUS, 92.
Most laps led: Allmendinger, 100.
Fastest race lap: Power, 59.259s, 119.314 mph/192.017 km/h.
Fastest qualifying lap: Junqueira, 57.631s, 122.684 mph/ 197.441 km/h.
Championship points: 1 Bourdais, 162; **2** Wilson, 132; **3** Allmendinger, 102; **4** Ranger, 89; **5=** Tracy, 76; **5=** Dominguez, 76; **5=** Philippe, 76; **5=** Da Matta, 76.

GRAND PRIX OF CLEVELAND PRESENTED BY US BANK, Burke Lakefront Airport, Cleveland, Ohio, USA, 25 June. Round 6. 95 laps of the 2.106-mile/3.389-km circuit, 200.070 miles/ 321.981 km.
1 AJ Allmendinger, USA, 2h 00m 22.619s, 99.722 mph/160.487 km/h; **2** Bruno Junqueira, BR, 2h 00m 25.898s; **3** Oriol Servia, E, 2h 00m 26.124s; **4** Alex Tagliani, CDN, 2h 00m 29.327s; **5** Jan Heylen, B, 2h 00m 33.650s; **6** Màrio Dominguez, MEX, 94 laps; **7** Dan Clarke, GB, 94; **8** Katherine Legge, GB, 94; **9** Will Power, AUS, 94; **10** Nelson Philippe, F, 93; **11** Andrew Ranger, CDN, 92; **12** Tonis Kasemets, EE, 91; **13** Justin Wilson, GB, 77 (DNF-accident); **14** Cristiano da Matta, BR, 75; **15** Charles Zwolsman, NL, 68 (DNF-mechanical); **16** Paul Tracy, CDN, 41 (DNF-accident); **17** Nicky Pastorelli, NL, 22 (DNF-accident); **18** Sébastain Bourdais, F, 0 (DNF-accident).
Most laps led: Allmendinger, 36.
Fastest race lap: Philippe, 57.508s, 131.836 mph/212.169 km/h.
Fastest qualifying lap: Allmendinger, 56.283s, 134.705 mph/ 216.787 km/h.
Championship points: 1 Bourdais, 166; **2** Wilson, 140; **3** Allmendinger, 135; **4** Ranger, 99; **5** Dominguez, 95; **6** Tagliani, 90.

MOLSON GRAND PRIX OF TORONTO, Exhibition Place Circuit, Toronto, Ontario, Canada, 9 July. Round 7. 86 laps of the 1.755-mile/2.824-km circuit, 150.930 miles/242.898 km.
1 AJ Allmendinger, USA, 1h 38m 01.286s, 92.386 mph/ 148.681 km/h; **2** Paul Tracy, CDN, 1h 38m 03.137s; **3** Sébastien Bourdais, F, 1h 38m 03.720s; **4** Justin Wilson, GB, 1h 38m 05.456s; **5** Cristiano da Matta, BR, 1h 38m 08.047s; **6** Alex Tagliani, CDN, 1h 38m 09.669s; **7** Will Power, AUS, 1h 38m 10.949s; **8** Bruno Junqueira, BR, 1h 38m 13.463s; **9** Charles Zwolsman, NL, 85 laps; **10** Andrew Ranger, CDN, 85; **11** Màrio Dominguez, MEX, 83; **12** Oriol Servia, E, 76 (DNF-accident); **13** Nelson Philippe, F, 76 (DNF-accident); **14** Katherine Legge, GB, 65 (DNF-accident); **15** Tonis Kasemets, EE, 49 (DNF-mechanical); **16** Jan Heylen, B, 44 (DNF-mechanical); **17** Dan Clarke, GB, 14 (DNF-accident).
Most laps led: Allmendinger, 38.
Fastest race lap: Tagliani, 1m 00.461s, 104.497 mph/ 168.172 km/h.
Fastest qualifying lap: Wilson, 58.182s, 108.590 mph/ 174.759 km/h.
Championship points: 1 Bourdais, 191; **2** Allmendinger, 168; **3** Wilson, 165; **4=** Tagliani, 110; **4=** Ranger, 110; **6** Tracy, 108.

WEST EDMONTON MALL GRAND PRIX PRESENTED BY THE BRICK, JAGflo Speedway, Edmonton, Alberta, Canada, 23 July. Round 8. 85 laps of the 1.973-mile/3.175-km circuit, 167.705 miles/269.895 km.
1 Justin Wilson, GB, 1h 40m 30.635s, 100.112 mph/161.114 km/h; **2** Sébastien Bourdais, F, 1h 40m 35.954s; **3** AJ Allmendinger, USA, 1h 40m 40.581s; **4** Oriol Servia, E, 1h 40m 43.285s; **5** Paul Tracy, CDN, 1h 40m 47.244s; **6** Will Power, AUS, 1h 40m 58.438s; **7** Andrew Ranger, CDN, 84 laps; **8** Màrio Dominguez, MEX, 84; **9** Dan Clarke, GB, 84; **10** Charles Zwolsman, NL, 82; **11** Tonis Kasemets, EE, 82; **12** Alex Tagliani, CDN, 78 (DNF-accident); **13** Katherine Legge, GB, 73; **14** Nelson Philippe, F, 69 (DNF-accident); **15** Bruno Junqueira, BR, 54 (DNF-mechanical); **16** Jan Heylen, B, 10 (DNF-accident); **17** Nicky Pastorelli, NL, 4 (DNF-accident); **18** Cristiano da Matta, BR, 0 (DNF-accident).
Most laps led: Bourdais, 55.
Fastest race lap: Wilson, 59.200s, 119.980 mph/193.089 km/h.
Fastest qualifying lap: Bourdais, 58.560s, 121.291 mph/ 195.199 km/h.
Championship points: 1 Bourdais, 221; **2** Wilson, 198; **3** Allmendinger, 193; **4** Tracy, 130; **5** Ranger, 127; **6** Dominguez, 120.

SAN JOSÉ GRAND PRIX PRESENTED BY TAYLOR WOODROW, San José street circuit, California, USA, 30 July. Round 9. 97 laps of the 1.443-mile/2.322-km circuit, 139.971 miles/ 225.261 km.
1 Sébastien Bourdais, F, 1h 38m 00.168s, 85.694 mph/137.911 km/h; **2** Cristiano da Matta, BR, 1h 38m 06.854s; **3** Justin Wilson, GB, 1h 38m 08.268s; **4** Nelson Philippe, F, 1h 38m 11.227s; **5** Màrio Dominguez, MEX, 1h 38m 12.315s; **6** Will Power, AUS, 1h 38m 13.125s; **7** AJ Allmendinger, USA, 1h 38m 13.456s; **8** Oriol Servia, E, 1h 38m 16.088s; **9** Charles Zwolsman, NL, 1h 38m 16.626s; **10** Nicky Pastorelli, NL, 1h 38m 21.748s; **11** Jan Heylen, B, 1h 38m 25.528s; **12** Katherine Legge, GB, 90; **13** Andrew Ranger, CDN, 80 (DNF-accident); **14** Alex Tagliani, CDN, 52 (DNF-accident); **15** Paul Tracy, CDN, 51 (DNF-accident); **16** Dan Clarke, GB, 49 (DNF-mechanical); **17** Bruno Junqueira, BR, 2 (DNF-accident).
Most laps led: Bourdais, 69.
Fastest race lap: Bourdais, 49.678s, 104.569 mph/ 168.288 km/h.
Fastest qualifying lap: Bourdais, 48.989s, 106.040 mph/ 170.655 km/h.
Championship points: 1 Bourdais, 255; **2** Wilson, 224; **3** Allmendinger, 210; **4** Dominguez, 141; **5** Ranger, 135; **6=** Da Matta, 134; **6=** Servia, 134.

GRAND PRIX OF DENVER, Denver street circuit, Colorado, USA, 13 August. Round 10. 97 laps of the 1.657-mile/ 2.667-km circuit, 160.729 miles/258.668 km.
1 AJ Allmendinger, USA, 1h 44m 59.557s, 91.852 mph/147.821 km/h; **2** Bruno Junqueira, BR, 1h 45m 20.145s; **3** Dan Clarke, GB, 1h 45m 49.818s; **4** Will Power, AUS, 1h 45m 55.472s; **5** Nelson Philippe, F, 1h 46m 13.744s; **6** Paul Tracy, CDN, 96 laps (DNF-accident); **7** Sébastien Bourdais, F, 96 (DNF-accident); **8** Justin Wilson, GB, 96; **9** Katherine Legge, GB, 96; **10** Charles Zwolsman, NL, 95; **11** Jan Heylen, B, 95; **12** Nicky Pastorelli, NL, 27 (DNF-mechanical); **13** Màrio Dominguez, MEX, 21 (DNF-mechanical); **14** Andrew Ranger, CDN, 18 (DNF-mechanical); **15** Oriol Servia, E, 14 (DNF-mechanical); **16** Alex Tagliani, CDN, 0 (DNF-accident).
Most laps led: Allmendinger, 45.
Fastest race lap: Bourdais, 1m 00.314s, 98.902 mph/ 159.168 km/h.
Fastest qualifying lap: Bourdais, 59.096s, 100.941 mph/ 162.449 km/h.
Championship points: 1 Bourdais, 275; **2** Allmendinger, 243; **3** Wilson, 240; **4=** Philippe, 149; **4=** Dominguez, 149 **6=** Tracy, 146; **6=** Power, 146.

CHAMP CAR GRAND PRIX OF MONTREAL, Circuit Gilles-Villeneuve, Ile-Notre-Dame, Montréal, Québec, Canada, 27 August. Round 11. 67 laps of the 2.709-mile/4.360-km circuit, 181.503 miles/292.101 km.
1 Sébastien Bourdais, F, 2h 01m 09.290s, 89.886 mph/144.658 km/h; **2** Paul Tracy, CDN, 2h 01m 10.688s; **3** Nelson Philippe, F, 2h 01m 12.040s; **4** Dan Clarke, GB, 2h 01m 12.410s; **5** Will Power, AUS, 2h 01m 15.649s; **6** Nicky Pastorelli, NL, 2h 01m 16.722s; **7** Alex Tagliani, CDN, 2h 01m 17.611s; **8** Charles Zwolsman, NL, 2h 01m 17.700s; **9** Jan Heylen, B, 2h 01m 19.819s; **10** Màrio Dominguez, MEX, 2h 01m 19.908s; **11** Antonio Pizzonia, BR, 2h 01m 20.556s; **12** Bruno Junqueira, BR, 66 laps; **13** Katherine Legge, GB, 61; **14** Justin Wilson, GB, 48 (DNF-accident); **15** Andrew Ranger, CDN, 36 (DNF-accident); **16** Oriol Servia, E, 30 (DNF-accident); **17** AJ Allmendinger, USA, 14 (DNF-mechanical).
Most laps led: Bourdais, 38.
Fastest race lap: Bourdais, 1m 22.325s, 118.462 mph/ 190.646 km/h.
Fastest qualifying lap: Bourdais, 1m 20.005s, 121.897 mph/ 196.175 km/h.
Championship points: 1 Bourdais, 310; **2** Allmendinger, 248; **3** Wilson, 248; **4** Philippe, 175; **5** Tracy, 173; **6** Power, 167.

CHAMP CAR GRAND PRIX OF ROAD AMERICA, Road America Circuit, Elkhart Lake, Wisconsin, USA, 24 September. Round 12. 51 laps of the 4.048-mile/6.515-km circuit, 206.448 miles/332.246 km.
1 AJ Allmendinger, USA, 1h 54m 43.700s, 107.967 mph/ 173.756 km/h; **2** Bruno Junqueira, BR, 1h 54m 44.375s; **3** Sébastien Bourdais, F, 1h 54m 44.688s; **4** Oriol Servia, E, 1h 54m 46.337s; **5** Justin Wilson, GB, 1h 54m 47.463s; **6** Dan Clarke, GB, 1h 54m 48.446s; **7** Charles Zwolsman, NL, 1h 54m 49.237s; **8** Andrew Ranger, CDN, 1h 54m 51.059s; **9** Jan Heylen, B, 1h 54m 52.368s; **10** Paul Tracy, CDN, 1h 54m 52.718s; **11** Alex Tagliani, CDN, 1h 54m 56.872s; **12** Màrio Dominguez, MEX, 1h 55m 03.851s; **13** Will Power, AUS, 50 laps; **14** Nelson Philippe, F, 50; **15** Juan Càceres, ROU, 50; **16** Katherine Legge, GB, 45 (DNF-accident); **17** Tonis Kasemets, EE, 14 (DNF-mechanical).
Most laps led: Bourdais, 28.
Fastest race lap: Bourdais, 1m 44.133s, 139.944 mph/ 225.218 km/h.
Fastest qualifying lap: Clarke, 1m 55.123s, 126.585 mph/ 203.718 km/h.
Championship points: 1 Bourdais, 338; **2** Allmendinger, 280; **3** Wilson, 269; **4** Tracy, 184; **5** Philippe, 182; **6** Junqueira, 177.

LEXMARK INDY 300, Surfer's Paradise street circuit, Queensland, Australia, 22 October. Round 13. 59 laps of the 2.795-mile/4.498-km circuit, 164.905 miles/265.389 km.
1 Nelson Philippe, F, 1h 50m 50.985s, 89.259 mph/143.648 km/h; **2** Màrio Dominguez, MEX, 1h 50m 51.713s; **3** Alex Tagliani, CDN, 1h 50m 57.039s; **4** Paul Tracy, CDN, 1h 50m 58.223s; **5** Andrew Ranger, CDN, 1h 51m 00.362s; **6** Bruno Junqueira, BR, 1h 51m 01.232s; **7** Charles Zwolsman, NL, 1h 51m 07.834s; **8** Sébastien Bourdais, F, 1h 51m 09.963s; **9** Andreas Wirth, D, 1h 51m 13.180s; **10** Antonio Pizzonia, I, 1h 51m 35.071s; **11** Ryan Briscoe, AUS, 58 laps; **12** Will Power, AUS, 58; **13** Oriol Servia, E, 43 (DNF-mechanical); **14** Jan Heylen, B, 42 (DNF-accident); **15** Katherine Legge, GB, 42 (DNF-accident); **16** AJ Allmendinger, USA, 18 (DNF-accident); **17** Dan Clarke, GB, 12 (DNFaccident).
Did not start: Justin Wilson, GB (injured in practice).
Most laps led: Philippe and Power, 13.
Fastest race lap: Tracy, 1m 33.776s, 107.298 mph/ 172.680 km/h.
Fastest qualifying lap: Power, 1m 31.403s, 110.084 mph/ 177.163 km/h.
Championship points: 1 Bourdais, 353; **2** Allmendinger, 285; **3** Wilson, 269; **4** Philippe, 214; **5** Tracy, 209; **6** Dominguez, 198.

GRAN PREMIO TEMEX PRESENTED BY BANAMEX, Autfidromo Hermanos Rodriguez, Mexico City, DF, Mexico, 12 November. Round 14. 66 laps of the 2.774-mile/4.464-km circuit, 183.084 miles/294.645 km.
1 Sébastien Bourdais, F, 1h 51m 31.146s, 98.504 mph/158.526 km/h; **2** Justin Wilson, GB, 1h 51m 34.674s; **3** Will Power, AUS, 1h 52m 17.682s; **4** Bruno Junqueira, BR, 1h 52m 35.169s; **5** Alex Tagliani, CDN, 1h 52m 49.179s; **6** Oriol Servia, E, 1h 52m 59.891s; **7** Nelson Philippe, F, 1h 53m 01.143s; **8** Andrew Ranger, CDN, 65 laps; **9** David Martinez, MEX, 65; **10** Buddy Rice, USA, 65; **11** Charles Zwolsman, NL, 65; **12** Antonio Pizzonia, BR, 65; **13** Jan Heylen, B, 65; **14** Ryan Briscoe, AUS, 64; **15** Andreas Wirth, D, 64; **16** Katherine Legge, GB, 63; **17** Màrio Dominguez, MEX, 59 (in pit); **18** Dan Clarke, GB, 7 (DNF-mechanical).
Most laps led: Wilson, 40.
Fastest race lap: Bourdais, 1m 27.644s, 113.943 mph/ 183.373 km/h.
Fastest qualifying lap: Wilson, 1m 24.801s, 117.763 mph/ 189.521 km/h.

Final championship points:
Drivers:
1 Sébastien Bourdais, F, 387; **2** Justin Wilson, GB, 298; **3** AJ Allmendinger, USA, 285; **4** Nelson Philippe, F, 231; **5** Bruno Junqueira, BR, 219; **6** Will Power, AUS, 213; **7** Paul Tracy, CDN, 208; **8** Alex Tagliani, CDN, 205; **9** Màrio Dominguez, MEX, 201; **10** Andrew Ranger, CDN, 200; **11** Oriol Servia, E, 196; **12** Dan Clarke, GB, 175; **13** Charles Zwolsman, NL, 161; **14** Jan Heylen, B, 140; **15** Cristiano da Matta, BR, 134; **16** Katherine Legge, GB, 133; **17** Nicky Pastorelli, NL, 73; **18** Antonio Pizzonia, I, 43; **19** Tonis Kasemets, EE, 34; **20** Andreas Wirth, D, 19; **21** Ryan Briscoe, AUS, 11; **22** David Martinez, MEX, 19; **23** Buddy Rice, USA, 11; **24** Jimmy Vasser, USA, 7; **25** Juan Càceres, ROU, 6.
Nation's Cup
1 France, 397; **2** England, 331; **3** United States, 292; **4** Canada, 292; **5** Brazil, 266; **6** Mexico, 209; **7** Australia, 209; **8** Spain, 192; **9** Netherlands, 163; **10** Belgium, 137; **11** Estonia, 34; **12** Germany, 19; **13** Uruguay, 6.
Rookie of the Year: Will Power.

NASCAR Nextel Cup Series 2005

The following races were run after AUTOCOURSE 2005–2006 went to press.

DICKIE'S 500, Texas Motor Speedway, Fort Worth, Texas, USA, 6 November. Round 34. 334 laps of the 1, 500-mile/ 2.414-km circuit, 501.000 miles/806.281 km.
1 Carl Edwards, USA (Ford Taurus), 3h 19m 0s, 151.055 mph/ 243.100 km/h; **2** Mark Martin, USA (Ford Taurus), 3h 19m 00.584s; **3** Matt Kenseth, USA (Ford Taurus), 334 laps; **4** Casey Mears, USA (Dodge Charger), 334; **5** Jimmie Johnson, USA (Chevrolet Monte Carlo), 334; **6** Tony Stewart, USA (Chevrolet Monte Carlo), 334; **7** Denny Hamlin, USA (Chevrolet Monte Carlo), 334; **8** Dale Earnhardt Jr, USA (Chevrolet Monte Carlo), 334; **9** Elliott Sadler, USA (Ford Taurus), 334; **10** Kurt Busch, USA (Ford Taurus), 334.
Pole position: Ryan Newman, USA (Dodge Charger).
Drivers' championship points: 1 Stewart, 6255; **2** Johnson, 6217; **3** Edwards, 6178; **4** Biffle, 6133; **5** Martin, 6132; **6** Kenseth, 6120.

CHECKER AUTO PARTS 500, Phoenix International Raceway, Arizona, USA, 13 November. Round 35. 312 laps of the 1.000-mile/1.609-km circuit, 312.000 miles/502.115 km.
1 Kyle Busch, USA (Chevrolet Monte Carlo), 3h 02m 23.0s, 102.641 mph/165.185 km/h; **2** Greg Biffle, USA (Ford Taurus), 3h 02m 23.609s; **3** Jeff Gordon, USA (Chevrolet Monte Carlo), 312 laps; **4** Tony Stewart, USA (Chevrolet Monte Carlo), 312; **5** Bobby Labonte, USA (Chevrolet Monte Carlo), 312; **6** Carl Edwards, USA (Ford Taurus), 312; **7** Jimmie Johnson, USA (Chevrolet Monte Carlo), 312; **8** Robby Gordon, USA (Chevrolet Monte Carlo), 312; **9** Dale Jarrett, USA (Ford Taurus), 312; **10** Travis Kvapil, USA (Dodge Charger), 312.
Pole position: Denny Hamlin, USA (Chevrolet Monte Carlo).
Drivers' championship points: 1 Stewart, 6415; **2** Johnson, 6363; **3** Edwards, 6328; **4** Biffle, 6313; **5** Martin, 6253; **6** Newman, 6208.

FORD 400, Homestead-Miami Speedway, Florida, USA, 20 November. Round 36. 267 laps of the 1.500-mile/ 2.414-km circuit, 400.500 miles/644.542 km.
1 Greg Biffle, USA (Ford Taurus), 3h 02m 50.0s, 131.431 mph/ 211.518 km/h; **2** Mark Martin, USA (Ford Taurus), 3h 02m 50.017s; **3** Matt Kenseth, USA (Ford Taurus), 267 laps; **4** Carl Edwards, USA (Ford Taurus), 267; **5** Casey Mears, USA (Dodge Charger), 267; **6** Dave Blaney, USA (Chevrolet Monte Carlo), 267; **7** Ryan Newman, USA (Dodge Charger), 267; **8** Kevin Harvick, USA (Chevrolet Monte Carlo), 267; **9** Jeff Gordon, USA (Chevrolet Monte Carlo), 267; **10** Jeremy Mayfield, USA (Dodge Charger), 267.
Pole position: Edwards.

Final championship points
Drivers
1 Tony Stewart, USA, 6533; **2** Greg Biffle, USA, 6498; **3** Carl Edwards, USA, 6498; **4** Mark Martin, USA, 6428; **5** Jimmie Johnson, USA, 6406; **6** Ryan Newman, USA, 6359; **7** Matt Kenseth, USA, 6352; **8** Rusty Wallace, USA, 6140; **9** Jeremy Mayfield, USA, 6073; **10** Kurt Busch, USA, 5974.

Not involved in chase for the Nextel Cup
11 Jeff Gordon, USA, 4174; **12** Jamie McMurray, USA, 4130; **13** Elliott Sadler, USA, 4084; **14** Kevin Harvick, USA, 4072; **15** Dale Jarrett, USA, 3960; **16** Joe Nemechek, USA, 3953; **17** Brian Vickers, USA, 3847; **18** Jeff Burton, USA, 3803; **19** Dale Earnhardt Jr, USA, 3780; **20** Kyle Busch, USA, 3753; **21** Ricky Rudd, USA, 3667; **22** Casey Mears, USA, 3637; **23** Kasey Kahne, USA, 3611; **24** Bobby Labonte, USA, 3488; **25** Michael Waltrip, USA, 3452; **26** Dave Blaney, USA, 3289; **27** Kyle Petty, USA, 3288; **28** Mike Bliss, SA, 3262; **29** Jeff Green, USA, 3241; **30** Sterling Marlin, USA, 3183.
Raybestos Rookie of the Year: Kyle Busch.
Manufacturers
1 Chevrolet, 242; **2** Ford, 222; **3** Dodge, 163.
Bud Pole Award winner: Ryan Newman, 8 poles.

2006

47th DAYTONA 500, Daytona International Speedway, Daytona Beach, Florida, USA, 19 February. Round 1. 203 laps of the 2.500-mile/4.023-km circuit, 507.500 miles/816.742 km.
1 Jimmie Johnson, USA (Chevrolet Monte Carlo), 3h 33m 26.0s, 142.667 mph/229.601 km/h (under caution); **2** Casey Mears, USA (Dodge Charger), 203 laps; **3** Ryan Newman, USA (Dodge Charger), 203; **4** Elliott Sadler, USA (Ford Fusion), 203; **5** Tony Stewart, USA (Chevrolet Monte Carlo), 203; **6** Clint Bowyer, USA (Chevrolet Monte Carlo), 203; **7** Brian Vickers, USA (Chevrolet Monte Carlo), 203; **8** Dale Earnhardt Jr, USA (Chevrolet Monte Carlo), 203; **9** Ken Schrader, USA (Ford Fusion), 203; **10** Dale Jarrett, USA (Ford Fusion), 203.
Pole position: Jeff Burton, USA (Chevrolet Monte Carlo).
Drivers' championship points: 1 Johnson, 185; **2** Mears, 170; **3** Newman, 170; **4** Sadler, 165; **5** Stewart, 160; **6** Earnhardt Jr, 152.

AUTO CLUB 500, California Speedway, Fontana, California, USA, 26 February. Round 2. 251 laps of the 2.000-mile/ 3.219-km circuit, 502.000 miles/807.891 km.
1 Matt Kenseth, USA (Ford Fusion), 3h 23m 43.0s, 147.852 mph/ 237.945 km/h; **2** Jimmie Johnson, USA (Chevrolet Monte Carlo), 3h 23m 43.338s; **3** Carl Edwards, USA (Ford Fusion), 251 laps; **4** Kasey Kahne, USA (Dodge Charger), 251; **5** Jeff Burton, USA (Chevrolet Monte Carlo), 251; **6** Jamie McMurray, USA (Ford Fusion), 251; **7** Casey Mears, USA (Dodge Charger), 251; **8** JJ Yeley, USA (Chevrolet Monte Carlo), 251; **9** Mark Martin, USA (Ford Fusion), 251; **10** Kyle Busch, USA (Chevrolet Monte Carlo), 251.
Pole position: Kurt Busch, USA (Dodge Charger).
Drivers' championship points: 1 Johnson, 355; **2** Mears, 316; **3** Kenseth, 308; **4** Kahne, 295; **5** Earnhardt Jr, 287; **6** Martin, 275.

UAW-DAIMLERCHRYSLER 400, Las Vegas Motor Speedway, Nevada, USA, 12 March. Round 3. 270 laps of the 1.500-mile/ 2.414-km circuit, 405.000 miles/651.784 km.
1 Jimmie Johnson, USA (Chevrolet Monte Carlo), 3h 02m 13.0s, 133.358 mph/214.618 km/h; **2** Matt Kenseth, USA (Ford Fusion), 3h 02m 13.045s; **3** Kyle Busch, USA (Chevrolet Monte Carlo), 270 laps; **4** Kasey Kahne, USA (Dodge Charger), 270; **5** Jeff Gordon, USA (Chevrolet Monte Carlo), 270; **6** Mark Martin, USA (Ford Fusion), 270; **7** Jeff Burton, USA (Chevrolet Monte Carlo), 270; **8** Greg Biffle, USA (Ford Fusion), 270; **9** Casey Mears, USA (Dodge Charger), 270; **10** Denny Hamlin, USA (Chevrolet Monte Carlo), 270.
Pole position: Biffle.
Drivers' championship points: 1 Johnson, 540; **2** Kenseth, 488; **3** Kahne, 455; **4** Mears, 454; **5** Martin, 430; **6** Busch (Kyle), 403.

GOLDEN CORRAL 500, Atlanta Motor Speedway, Hampton, Georgia, USA, 20 March. Round 4. 325 laps of the 1.540-mile/ 2.478-km circuit, 500.000 miles/805.477 km.
Race scheduled for 19 March but postponed due to bad weather.
1 Kasey Kahne, USA (Dodge Charger), 3h 28m 24.0s, 144.098 mph/231.903 km/h; **2** Mark Martin, USA (Ford Fusion), 3h 28m 25.928s; **3** Dale Earnhardt Jr, USA (Chevrolet Monte Carlo), 325 laps; **4** Jeff Gordon, USA (Chevrolet Monte Carlo), 325; **5** Tony Stewart, USA (Chevrolet Monte Carlo), 325; **6** Jimmie Johnson, USA (Chevrolet Monte Carlo), 325; **7** Paul Menard, USA (Chevrolet Monte Carlo), 325; **8** Kyle Petty, USA (Dodge Charger), 325; **9** Dale Jarrett, USA (Ford Fusion), 325; **10** Reed Sorensen, USA (Dodge Charger), 325.
Pole position: Kahne.
Drivers' championship points: 1 Johnson, 690; **2** Kahne, 640; **3** Kenseth, 612; **4** Martin, 600; **5** Mears, 554; **6** Gordon (Jeff), 539.

FOOD CITY 500, Bristol Motor Speedway, Tennessee, USA, 26 March. Round 5. 500 laps of the 0.533-mile/0.858-km circuit, 266.500 miles/428.890 km.
1 Kurt Busch, USA (Dodge Charger), 3h 21m 19.0s, 79.427 mph/ 127.826 km/h; **2** Kevin Harvick, USA (Chevrolet Monte Carlo), 3h 21m 19.179s; **3** Matt Kenseth, USA (Ford Fusion), 500 laps; **4** Carl Edwards, USA (Ford Fusion), 500; **5** Bobby Labonte, USA (Dodge Charger), 500; **6** Mark Martin, USA (Ford Fusion), 500; **7** Greg Biffle, USA (Ford Fusion), 500; **8** Kyle Busch, USA (Chevrolet Monte Carlo), 500; **9** Ryan Newman, USA (Dodge Charger), 500; **10** Kasey Kahne, USA (Dodge Charger), 500.
Pole position: Stewart, USA (Chevrolet Monte Carlo).
Drivers' championship points: 1 Kenseth, 782; **2** Kahne, 774; **3** Johnson, 763; **4** Martin, 750; **5** Busch (Kyle), 677; **6** Earnhardt Jr, 664.

DIRECTV 500, Martinsville Speedway, Virginia, USA, 2 April. Round 6. 500 laps of the 0.526-mile/0.847-km circuit, 263.000 miles/423.257 km.
1 Tony Stewart, USA (Chevrolet Monte Carlo), 3h 36m 56.0s, 72.741 mph/117.066 km/h; **2** Jeff Gordon, USA (Chevrolet Monte Carlo), 3h 36m 57.083s; **3** Jimmie Johnson, USA (Chevrolet Monte Carlo), 500 laps; **4** Dale Earnhardt Jr, USA (Chevrolet Monte Carlo), 500; **5** Kyle Busch, USA (Chevrolet Monte Carlo), 500; **6** Elliott Sadler, USA (Ford Fusion), 500; **7** Kevin Harvick, USA (Chevrolet Monte Carlo), 500; **8** Brian Vickers, USA (Chevrolet Monte Carlo), 500; **9** Jamie McMurray, USA (Ford Fusion), 500; **10** Scott Riggs, USA (Dodge Charger), 500.
Pole position: Johnson.
Drivers' championship points: 1 Johnson, 933; **2** Martin, 874; **3** Kenseth, 873; **4** Kahne, 832; **5** Busch, 832; **6** Earnhardt Jr, 824.

SAMSUNG/RADIO SHACK 500, Texas Motor Speedway, Fort Worth, Texas, USA, 9 April. Round 7. 334 laps of the 1.500-mile/2.414-km circuit, 501.000 miles/806.281 km.
1 Kasey Kahne, USA (Dodge Charger), 3h 37m 55.0s, 137.943 mph/221.997 km/h; **2** Matt Kenseth, USA (Ford Fusion), 3h 38m 00.229s; **3** Tony Stewart, USA (Chevrolet Monte Carlo), 334 laps; **4** Denny Hamlin, USA (Chevrolet Monte Carlo), 334; **5** Kevin Harvick, USA (Chevrolet Monte Carlo), 334; **6** Jeff Burton, USA

(Chevrolet Monte Carlo), 334; **7** Scott Riggs, USA (Dodge Charger), 334; **8** Martin Truex Jr, USA (Chevrolet Monte Carlo), 334; **9** Mark Martin, USA (Ford Fusion), 334; **10** Bobby Labonte, USA (Dodge Charger), 334.
Pole position: Kahne.
Drivers' championship points: 1 Johnson, 1063; **2** Kenseth, 1048; **3** Kahne, 1017; **4** Martin, 1017; **5** Stewart, 966; **6** Earnhardt Jr, 951.

SUBWAY FRESH 500, Phoenix International Raceway, Arizona, USA, 22 April. Round 8. 312 laps of the 1.000-mile/1.609-km circuit, 312.000 miles/502.115 km.
1 Kevin Harvick, USA (Chevrolet Monte Carlo), 2h 54m 51.0s, 107.063 mph/172.302 km/h; **2** Tony Stewart, USA (Chevrolet Monte Carlo), 2h 54m 53.774s; **3** Matt Kenseth, USA (Ford Fusion), 312 laps; **4** Carl Edwards, USA (Ford Fusion), 312; **5** Clint Bowyer, USA (Chevrolet Monte Carlo), 312; **6** Kasey Kahne, USA (Dodge Charger), 312; **7** Jimmie Johnson, USA (Chevrolet Monte Carlo), 312; **8** Bobby Labonte, USA (Dodge Charger), 312; **9** Jeff Burton, USA (Chevrolet Monte Carlo), 312; **10** Jeff Gordon, USA (Chevrolet Monte Carlo), 312.
Pole position: Kyle Busch, USA (Chevrolet Monte Carlo).
Drivers' championship points: 1 Kenseth, 1218; **2** Johnson, 1209; **3** Kahne, 1167; **4** Martin, 1152; **5** Stewart, 1141; **6** Gordon (Jeff), 1045.

AARON'S 499, Talladega Superspeedway, Alabama, USA, 1 May. Round 9. 188 laps of the 2.660-mile/4.281-km circuit, 500.080 miles/804.801 km.
Race scheduled for 30 April, but postponed due to rain.
1 Jimmie Johnson, USA (Chevrolet Monte Carlo), 3h 30m 00.0s, 142.880 mph/229.943 km/h; **2** Tony Stewart, USA (Chevrolet Monte Carlo), 3h 30m 00.120s; **3** Brian Vickers, USA (Chevrolet Monte Carlo), 188 laps; **4** Jeff Burton, USA (Chevrolet Monte Carlo), 188; **5** Jamie McMurray, USA (Ford Fusion), 188; **6** Matt Kenseth, USA (Ford Fusion), 188; **7** Kurt Busch, USA (Dodge Charger), 188; **8** Carl Edwards, USA (Ford Fusion), 188; **9** Scott Riggs, USA (Dodge Charger), 188; **10** Robby Gordon, USA (Chevrolet Monte Carlo), 188.
Pole position: Elliott Sadler, USA (Ford Fusion).
Drivers' championship points: 1 Johnson, 1394; **2** Kenseth, 1373; **3** Stewart, 1316; **4** Kahne, 1213; **5** Martin, 1210; **6** Gordon (Jeff), 1173.

CROWN ROYAL 400, Richmond International Raceway, Virginia, USA, 6 May. Round 10. 400 laps of the 0.750-mile/1.207-km circuit, 300.000 miles/482.803 km.
1 Dale Earnhardt Jr, USA (Chevrolet Monte Carlo), 3h 05m 27.0s, 97.061 mph/156.205 km/h; **2** Denny Hamlin, USA (Chevrolet Monte Carlo), 3h 05m 27.572s; **3** Kevin Harvick, USA (Chevrolet Monte Carlo), 400 laps; **4** Greg Biffle, USA (Ford Fusion), 400; **5** Kyle Busch, USA (Chevrolet Monte Carlo), 400; **6** Tony Stewart, USA (Chevrolet Monte Carlo), 400; **7** Carl Edwards, USA (Ford Fusion), 400; **8** Ryan Newman, USA (Dodge Charger), 400; **9** Sterling Marlin, USA (Chevrolet Monte Carlo), 400; **10** Clint Bowyer, USA (Chevrolet Monte Carlo), 400.
Pole position: Biffle.
Drivers' championship points: 1 Johnson, 1521; **2** Stewart, 1466; **3** Kenseth, 1422; **4** Martin, 1345; **5** Harvick, 1313; **6** Earnhardt Jr, 1305.

DODGE CHARGER 500, Darlington Raceway, South Carolina, USA, 13 May. Round 11. 367 laps of the 1.366-mile/2.198-km circuit, 501.322 miles/806.800 km.
1 Greg Biffle, USA (Ford Fusion), 3h 42m 36.0s, 135.127 mph/217.466 km/h; **2** Jeff Gordon, USA (Chevrolet Monte Carlo), 3h 42m 36.209s; **3** Matt Kenseth, USA (Ford Fusion), 367 laps; **4** Jimmie Johnson, USA (Chevrolet Monte Carlo), 367; **5** Dale Earnhardt Jr, USA (Chevrolet Monte Carlo), 367; **6** Ryan Newman, USA (Dodge Charger), 367; **7** Kyle Busch, USA (Chevrolet Monte Carlo), 367; **8** Mark Martin, USA (Ford Fusion), 367; **9** Jeff Burton, USA (Chevrolet Monte Carlo), 367; **10** Denny Hamlin, USA (Chevrolet Monte Carlo), 367.
Pole position: Kasey Kahne, USA (Dodge Charger).
Drivers' championship points: 1 Johnson, 1686; **2** Stewart, 1593; **3** Kenseth, 1592; **4** Martin, 1487; **5** Earnhardt Jr, 1460; **6** Gordon, 1391.

COCA-COLA 600, Lowe's Motor Speedway, Concord, Charlotte, North Carolina, USA, 28 May. Round 12. 400 laps of the 1.500-mile/2.414-km circuit, 600.000 miles/965.606 km.
1 Kasey Kahne, USA (Dodge Charger), 4h 39m 25.0s, 128.840 mph/207.348 km/h; **2** Jimmie Johnson, USA (Chevrolet Monte Carlo), 4h 39m 27.114s; **3** Carl Edwards, USA (Ford Fusion), 400 laps; **4** Mark Martin, USA (Ford Fusion), 400; **5** Matt Kenseth, USA (Ford Fusion), 400; **6** Jeff Burton, USA (Chevrolet Monte Carlo), 400; **7** Greg Biffle, USA (Ford Fusion), 400; **8** Jamie McMurray, USA (Ford Fusion), 400; **9** Denny Hamlin, USA (Chevrolet Monte Carlo), 400; **10** Reed Sorensen, USA (Dodge Charger), 400.
Pole position: Scott Riggs, USA (Dodge Charger).
Drivers' championship points: 1 Johnson, 1861; **2** Kenseth, 1752; **3** Martin, 1652; **4** Stewart, 1630; **5** Earnhardt Jr, 1590; **6** Kahne, 1569.

NEIGHBORHOOD EXCELLENCE 400 PRESENTED BY BANK OF AMERICA, Dover International Speedway, Delaware, USA, 4 June. Round 13. 400 laps of the 1.000-mile/1.609-km circuit, 400.000 miles/643.738 km.
1 Matt Kenseth, USA (Ford Fusion), 3h 38m 27.0s, 109.865 mph/176.811 km/h; **2** Jamie McMurray, USA (Ford Fusion), 3h 38m 27.787s; **3** Kevin Harvick, USA (Chevrolet Monte Carlo), 400 laps; **4** Jeff Burton, USA (Chevrolet Monte Carlo), 400; **5** Kyle Busch, USA (Chevrolet Monte Carlo), 400; **6** Jimmie Johnson, USA (Chevrolet Monte Carlo), 400; **7** Kasey Kahne, USA (Dodge Charger), 400; **8** Greg Biffle, USA (Ford Fusion), 400; **9** Mark Martin, USA (Ford Fusion), 400; **10** Dale Earnhardt Jr, USA (Chevrolet Monte Carlo), 400.
Pole position: Ryan Newman, USA (Dodge Charger).
Drivers' championship points: 1 Johnson, 2011; **2** Kenseth, 1937; **3** Martin, 1795; **4** Earnhardt Jr, 1729; **5** Stewart, 1718; **6** Kahne, 1715.

POCONO 500, Pocono Raceway, Long Pond, Pennsylvania, USA, 11 June. Round 14. 200 laps of the 2.500-mile/4.023-km circuit, 500.000 miles/804.672 km.
1 Denny Hamlin, USA (Chevrolet Monte Carlo), 3h 47m 52.0s, 131.656 mph/211.880 km/h; **2** Kurt Busch, USA (Dodge Charger), 3h 47m 53.328s; **3** Tony Stewart, USA (Chevrolet Monte Carlo), 200 laps; **4** Brian Vickers, USA (Chevrolet Monte Carlo), 200; **5** Matt Kenseth, USA (Ford Fusion), 200; **6** Greg Biffle, USA (Ford Fusion), 200; **7** Kasey Kahne, USA (Dodge Charger), 200; **8** Scott Riggs, USA (Dodge Charger), 200; **9** Jeff Burton, USA (Chevrolet Monte Carlo), 200; **10** Jimmie Johnson, USA (Chevrolet Monte Carlo), 200.
Pole position: Hamlin.
Drivers' championship points: 1 Johnson, 2145; **2** Kenseth, 2097; **3** Martin, 1907; **4** Stewart, 1888; **5** Kahne, 1866; **6** Earnhardt Jr, 1850.

3M PERFORMANCE 400 PRESENTED BY POST-IT PICTURE PAPER, Michigan International Speedway, Brooklyn, Michigan, USA, 18 June. Round 15. 129 laps of the 2.000-mile/3.219-km circuit, 258.000 miles/415.211 km.
Race scheduled for 200 laps, but shortened due to rain.
1 Kasey Kahne, USA (Dodge Charger), 2h 10m 19.0s, 118.788 mph/191.170 km/h (under caution); **2** Carl Edwards, USA (Ford Fusion), 129 laps; **3** Dale Earnhardt Jr, USA (Chevrolet Monte Carlo), 129; **4** Greg Biffle, USA (Ford Fusion), 129; **5** Reed Sorensen, USA (Dodge Charger), 129; **6** Jimmie Johnson, USA (Chevrolet Monte Carlo), 129; **7** Casey Mears, USA (Dodge Charger), 129; **8** Jeff Gordon, USA (Chevrolet Monte Carlo), 129; **9** Kurt Busch, USA (Dodge Charger), 129; **10** Kevin Harvick, USA (Chevrolet Monte Carlo), 129.
Pole position: Kahne.
Drivers' championship points: 1 Johnson, 2295; **2** Kenseth, 2221; **3** Kahne, 2051; **4** Earnhardt Jr, 2020; **5** Martin, 1989; **6** Stewart, 1928.

DODGE/SAVE MART 350, Infineon Raceway, Sears Point, Sonoma, California, USA, 25 June. Round 16. 110 laps of the 1.990-mile/3.203-km circuit, 218.900 miles/352.285 km.
1 Jeff Gordon, USA (Chevrolet Monte Carlo), 2h 57m 36.0s, 73.953 mph/119.015 km/h; **2** Ryan Newman, USA (Dodge Charger), 2h 57m 37.250s; **3** Terry Labonte, USA (Chevrolet Monte Carlo), 110 laps; **4** Greg Biffle, USA (Ford Fusion), 110; **5** Kurt Busch, USA (Dodge Charger), 110; **6** Carl Edwards, USA (Ford Fusion), 110; **7** Jeff Burton, USA (Chevrolet Monte Carlo), 110; **8** Elliott Sadler, USA (Ford Fusion), 110; **9** Boris Said, USA (Ford Fusion), 110; **10** Jimmie Johnson, USA (Chevrolet Monte Carlo), 110.
Pole position: Busch (Kurt).
Drivers' championship points: 1 Johnson, 2434; **2** Kenseth, 2333; **3** Kahne, 2121; **4** Martin, 2113; **5** Earnhardt Jr, 2105; **6** Burton, 2034.

PEPSI 400, Daytona International Speedway, Daytona Beach, Florida, USA, 1 July. Round 17. 160 laps of the 2.500-mile/4.023-km circuit, 400.000 miles/643.738 km.
1 Tony Stewart, USA (Chevrolet Monte Carlo), 2h 36m 43.0, 153.143 mph/246.459 km/h (under caution); **2** Kyle Busch, USA (Chevrolet Monte Carlo), 160 laps; **3** Kurt Busch, USA (Dodge Charger), 160; **4** Boris Said, USA (Ford Fusion), 160; **5** Matt Kenseth, USA (Ford Fusion), 160; **6** Elliott Sadler, USA (Ford Fusion), 160; **7** Casey Mears, USA (Dodge Charger), 160; **8** Jamie McMurray, USA (Ford Fusion), 160; **9** Kevin Harvick, USA (Chevrolet Monte Carlo), 160; **10** Clint Bowyer, USA (Chevrolet Monte Carlo), 160.
Pole position: Said.
Drivers' championship points: 1 Johnson, 2501; **2** Kenseth, 2488; **3** Earnhardt Jr, 2234; **4** Kahne, 2209; **5** Stewart, 2202; **6** Martin, 2177.

USG SHEETROCK 400, Chicagoland Speedway, Chicago, Illinois, USA, 9 July. Round 18. 270 of the 1.500-mile/2.414-km circuit, 405.000 miles/651.784 km.
1 Jeff Gordon, USA (Chevrolet Monte Carlo), 3h 03m 59.0s, 132.077 mph/212.558 km/h; **2** Jeff Burton, USA (Chevrolet Monte Carlo), 3h 03m 59.461s; **3** Kyle Busch, USA (Chevrolet Monte Carlo), 270 laps; **4** Kevin Harvick, USA (Chevrolet Monte Carlo), 270; **5** Dale Earnhardt Jr, USA (Chevrolet Monte Carlo), 270; **6** Jimmie Johnson, USA (Chevrolet Monte Carlo), 270; **7** Reed Sorensen, USA (Dodge Charger), 270; **8** Kurt Busch, USA (Dodge Charger), 270; **9** Clint Bowyer, USA (Chevrolet Monte Carlo), 270; **10** JJ Yeley, USA (Chevrolet Monte Carlo), 270.
Pole position: Burton.
Drivers' championship points: 1 Johnson, 2651; **2** Kenseth, 2600; **3** Earnhardt Jr, 2394; **4** Burton, 2327; **5** Kahne, 2303; **6** Martin, 2291.

LENOX INDUSTRIAL TOOLS 300, New Hampshire International Speedway, Loudon, New Hampshire, USA, 16 July. Round 19. 308 laps of the 1.058-mile/1.703-km circuit, 325.864 miles/524.427 km.
1 Kyle Busch, USA (Chevrolet Monte Carlo), 3h 12m 51.0s, 101.384 mph/163.161 km/h; **2** Carl Edwards, USA (Ford Fusion), 3h 12m 51.406s; **3** Greg Biffle, USA (Ford Fusion), 308 laps; **4** Mark Martin, USA (Ford Fusion), 308; **5** Kevin Harvick, USA (Chevrolet Monte Carlo), 308; **6** Denny Hamlin, USA (Chevrolet Monte Carlo), 308; **7** Jeff Burton, USA (Chevrolet Monte Carlo), 308; **8** Kasey Kahne, USA (Dodge Charger), 308; **9** Jimmie Johnson, USA (Chevrolet Monte Carlo), 308; **10** Scott Riggs, USA (Dodge Charger), 308.
Pole position: Ryan Newman, USA (Dodge Charger).
Drivers' championship points: 1 Johnson, 2789; **2** Kenseth, 2721; **3** Burton, 2478; **4** Busch (Kyle), 2455; **5** Martin, 2451; **6** Kahne, 2445.

PENNSYLVANIA 500, Pocono Raceway, Long Pond, Pennsylvania, USA, 23 July. Round 20. 200 laps of the 2.500-mile/4.023-km circuit, 500.000 miles/804.672 km.
1 Denny Hamlin, USA (Chevrolet Monte Carlo), 3h 46m 12.0s, 132.626 mph/213.441 km/h; **2** Kurt Busch, USA (Dodge Charger), 3h 46m 13.510s; **3** Jeff Gordon, USA (Chevrolet Monte Carlo), 200 laps; **4** Brian Vickers, USA (Chevrolet Monte Carlo), 200; **5** Kevin Harvick, USA (Chevrolet Monte Carlo), 200; **6** Jimmie Johnson, USA (Chevrolet Monte Carlo), 200; **7** Tony Stewart, USA (Chevrolet Monte Carlo), 200; **8** Bobby Labonte, USA (Dodge Charger), 200; **9** Jeff Burton, USA (Chevrolet Monte Carlo), 200; **10** Martin Truex Jr, USA (Chevrolet Monte Carlo), 200.
Pole position: Hamlin.
Drivers' championship points: 1 Johnson, 2939; **2** Kenseth, 2842; **3** Burton, 2621; **4** Busch (Kyle), 2582; **5** Harvick, 2563; **6** Martin, 2557.

ALLSTATE 400 AT THE BRICKYARD, Indianapolis Motor Speedway, Speedway, Indiana, USA, 6 August. Round 21. 160 laps of the 2.500-mile/4.023-km circuit, 400.000 miles/643.738 km.
1 Jimmie Johnson, USA (Chevrolet Monte Carlo), 2h 54m 57.0s, 137.182 mph/220.773 km/h (under caution); **2** Matt Kenseth, USA (Ford Fusion), 160 laps; **3** Kevin Harvick, USA (Chevrolet Monte Carlo), 160; **4** Clint Bowyer, USA (Chevrolet Monte Carlo), 160; **5** Mark Martin, USA (Ford Fusion), 160; **6** Dale Earnhardt Jr, USA (Chevrolet Monte Carlo), 160; **7** Kyle Busch, USA (Chevrolet Monte Carlo), 160; **8** Tony Stewart, USA (Chevrolet Monte Carlo), 160; **9** Carl Edwards, USA (Ford Fusion), 160; **10** Denny Hamlin, USA (Chevrolet Monte Carlo), 160.
Pole position: Jeff Burton, USA (Chevrolet Monte Carlo).
Drivers' championship points: 1 Johnson, 3124; **2** Kenseth, 3017; **3** Burton, 2749; **4** Harvick, 2733; **5** Busch (Kyle), 2733; **6** Martin, 2712.

AMD AT THE GLEN, Watkins Glen International, New York, USA, 13 August. Round 22. 90 laps of the 2.450-mile/3.943-km circuit, 220.500 miles/354.860 km.
1 Kevin Harvick, USA (Chevrolet Monte Carlo), 2h 52m 27.0s, 76.718 mph/123.465 km/h; **2** Tony Stewart, USA (Chevrolet Monte Carlo), 2h 52m 27.892s; **3** Jamie McMurray, USA (Ford Fusion), 90 laps; **4** Robby Gordon, USA (Chevrolet Monte Carlo), 90; **5** Carl Edwards, USA (Ford Fusion), 90; **6** Scott Pruett, USA (Dodge Charger), 90; **7** Elliott Sadler, USA (Ford Fusion), 90; **8** Ryan Newman, USA (Dodge Charger), 90; **9** Kyle Busch, USA (Chevrolet Monte Carlo), 90; **10** Denny Hamlin, USA (Chevrolet Monte Carlo), 90.
Pole position: Kurt Busch, USA (Dodge Charger).
Drivers' championship points: 1 Johnson, 3241; **2** Kenseth, 3117; **3** Harvick, 2918; **4** Burton, 2879; **5** Busch (Kyle), 2871; **6** Martin, 2815.

GFS MARKETPLACE 400, Michigan International Speedway, Brooklyn, Michigan, USA, 20 August. Round 23. 200 laps of the 2.000-mile/3.219-km circuit, 400.000 miles/643.738 km.
1 Matt Kenseth, USA (Ford Fusion), 2h 57m 39.0s, 135.097 mph/217.418 km/h; **2** Jeff Gordon, USA (Chevrolet Monte Carlo), 2h 57m 39.622s; **3** Tony Stewart, USA (Chevrolet Monte Carlo), 200 laps; **4** Kasey Kahne, USA (Dodge Charger), 200; **5** Mark Martin, USA (Ford Fusion), 200; **6** Dale Earnhardt Jr, USA (Chevrolet Monte Carlo), 200; **7** Greg Biffle, USA (Ford Fusion), 200; **8** Reed Sorensen, USA (Dodge Charger), 200; **9** Denny Hamlin, USA (Chevrolet Monte Carlo), 200; **10** Elliott Sadler, USA (Dodge Charger), 200.
Pole position: Jeff Burton, USA (Chevrolet Monte Carlo).
Drivers' championship points: 1 Johnson, 3365; **2** Kenseth, 3307; **3** Harvick, 3048; **4** Martin, 2970; **5** Stewart, 2959; **6** Gordon (Jeff), 2931.

SHARPIE 500, Bristol Motor Speedway, Tennessee, USA, 26 August. Round 24. 500 laps of the 0.533-mile/0.858-km circuit, 266.500 miles/428.890 km.
1 Matt Kenseth, USA (Ford Fusion), 2h 57m 37.0s, 90.025 mph/144.882 km/h; **2** Kyle Busch, USA (Chevrolet Monte Carlo), 2h 57m 37.591s; **3** Dale Earnhardt Jr, USA (Chevrolet Monte Carlo), 500 laps; **4** Scott Riggs, USA (Dodge Charger), 500; **5** Jeff Gordon, USA (Chevrolet Monte Carlo), 500; **6** Denny Hamlin, USA (Chevrolet Monte Carlo), 500; **7** Carl Edwards, USA (Ford Fusion), 500; **8** Ryan Newman, USA (Dodge Charger), 500; **9** Jeff Burton, USA (Chevrolet Monte Carlo), 500; **10** Jimmie Johnson, USA (Chevrolet Monte Carlo), 500.
Pole position: Kurt Busch, USA (Dodge Charger).
Drivers' championship points: 1 Johnson, 3499; **2** Kenseth, 3492; **3** Harvick, 3178; **4** Busch (Kyle), 3097; **5** Gordon (Jeff), 3091; **6** Hamlin, 3070.

SONY HD 500, California Speedway, Fontana, California, USA, 3 September. Round 25. 250 laps of the 2.000-mile/3.219-km circuit, 500.000 miles/804.672 km.
1 Kasey Kahne, USA (Dodge Charger), 3h 27m 40.0s, 144.462 mph/232.490 km/h; **2** Dale Earnhardt Jr, USA (Chevrolet Monte Carlo), 3h 27m 43.427s; **3** Clint Bowyer, USA (Chevrolet Monte Carlo), 250 laps; **4** Carl Edwards, USA (Ford Fusion), 250; **5** Jeff Gordon, USA (Chevrolet Monte Carlo), 250; **6** Denny Hamlin, USA (Chevrolet Monte Carlo), 250; **7** Matt Kenseth, USA (Ford Fusion), 250; **8** Kyle Busch, USA (Chevrolet Monte Carlo), 250; **9** Tony Stewart, USA (Chevrolet Monte Carlo), 250; **10** Dale Jarrett, USA (Ford Fusion), 250.
Pole position: Kurt Busch, USA (Dodge Charger).
Drivers' championship points: 1 Kenseth, 3638; **2** Johnson, 3629; **3** Harvick, 3296; **4** Gordon (Jeff), 3251; **5** Busch (Kyle), 3244; **6** Earnhardt Jr, 3226.

CHEVY ROCK & ROLL 400, Richmond International Raceway, Virginia, USA, 9 September. Round 26. 400 laps of the 0.750-mile/1.207-km circuit, 300.000 miles/482.803 km.
1 Kevin Harvick, USA (Chevrolet Monte Carlo), 2h 57m 37.0s, 101.342 mph/163.094 km/h; **2** Kyle Busch, USA (Chevrolet Monte Carlo), 2h 57m 37.153s; **3** Kasey Kahne, USA (Dodge Charger), 400 laps; **4** Dave Blaney, USA (Dodge Charger), 400; **5** Mark Martin, USA (Ford Fusion), 400; **6** Greg Biffle, USA (Ford Fusion), 400; **7** Ken Schrader, USA (Ford Fusion), 400; **8** Matt Kenseth, USA (Ford Fusion), 400; **9** Jeff Burton, USA (Chevrolet Monte Carlo), 400; **10** Scott Riggs, USA (Dodge Charger), 400.
Pole position: Denny Hamlin, USA (Chevrolet Monte Carlo).
Drivers' championship points: 1 Kenseth, 5050; **2** Johnson, 5045; **3** Harvick, 5040; **4** Busch (Kyle), 5035; **5** Hamlin, 5030; **6** Earnhardt Jr, 5025.

SYLVANIA 300, New Hampshire International Speedway, Loudon, New Hampshire, USA, 17 September. Round 27. 300 laps of the 1.058-mile/1.703-km circuit, 317.400 miles/510.806 km.
1 Kevin Harvick, USA (Chevrolet Monte Carlo), 3h 06m 21.0s, 102.195 mph/164.467 km/h; **2** Tony Stewart, USA (Chevrolet Monte Carlo), 3h 06m 21.777s; **3** Jeff Gordon, USA (Chevrolet Monte Carlo), 300 laps; **4** Denny Hamlin, USA (Chevrolet Monte Carlo), 300; **5** Brian Vickers, USA (Chevrolet Monte Carlo), 300; **6** Elliott Sadler, USA (Dodge Charger), 300; **7** Jeff Burton, USA (Chevrolet Monte Carlo), 300; **8** JJ Yeley, USA (Chevrolet Monte Carlo), 300; **9** Dave Blaney, USA (Dodge Charger), 300; **10** Matt Kenseth, USA (Ford Fusion), 300.
Pole position: Kevin Harvick, USA (Chevrolet Monte Carlo).
Drivers' championship points: 1 Harvick, 5230; **2** Hamlin, 5195; **3** Kenseth, 5189; **4** Gordon (Jeff), 5180; **5** Burton, 5166; **6** Martin, 5155.

DOVER 400, Dover International Speedway, Dover, Delaware, USA, 24 September. Round 28. 400 laps of the 1.000-mile/1.609-km circuit, 400.000 miles/643.738 km.
1 Jeff Burton, USA (Chevrolet Monte Carlo), 3h 34m 21.0s, 111.966 mph/180.192 km/h; **2** Carl Edwards, USA (Ford Fusion), 3h 34m 28.955s; **3** Jeff Gordon, USA (Chevrolet Monte Carlo), 400 laps; **4** Kurt Busch, USA (Dodge Charger), 400; **5** Greg Biffle, USA (Ford Fusion), 400; **6** Martin Truex Jr, USA (Chevrolet Monte Carlo), 400; **7** Bobby Labonte, USA (Dodge Charger), 400; **8** Clint Bowyer, USA (Chevrolet Monte Carlo), 400; **9** Denny Hamlin, USA (Chevrolet Monte Carlo), 400; **10** Matt Kenseth, USA (Ford Fusion), 399.
Pole position: Gordon (Jeff).
Drivers' championship points: 1 Burton, 5351; **2** Gordon (Jeff), 5345; **3** Kenseth, 5333; **4** Hamlin, 5333; **5** Harvick, 5297; **6** Martin, 5276.

BANQUET 400 PRESENTED BY CONAGRA FOODS, Kansas Speedway, Kansas City, Kansas, USA, 1 October. Round 29. 267 laps of the 1.500-mile/2.414-km circuit, 400.500 miles/644.542 km.
1 Tony Stewart, USA (Chevrolet Monte Carlo), 3h 17m 22.0s, 121.753 mph/195.943 km/h; **2** Casey Mears, USA (Dodge Charger), 3h 17m 32.422s; **3** Mark Martin, USA (Ford Fusion), 267 laps; **4** Dale Jarrett, USA (Ford Fusion), 267; **5** Jeff Burton, USA (Chevrolet Monte Carlo), 267; **6** Carl Edwards, USA (Ford Fusion), 267; **7** Kyle Busch, USA (Chevrolet Monte Carlo), 267; **8** Brian Vickers, USA (Chevrolet Monte Carlo), 267; **9** Clint Bowyer, USA (Chevrolet Monte Carlo), 267; **10** Dale Earnhardt Jr, USA (Chevrolet Monte Carlo), 267.
Pole position: Kahne.
Drivers' championship points: 1 Burton, 5511; **2** Hamlin, 5442; **3** Martin, 5441; **4** Kenseth, 5427; **5** Harvick, 5415; **6** Gordon (Jeff), 5391.

UAW-FORD 500, Talladega Superspeedway, Alabama, USA, 8 October. Round 30. 188 laps of the 2.660-mile/4.281-km circuit, 500.080 miles/804.801 km.
1 Brian Vickers, USA (Chevrolet Monte Carlo), 3h 10m 23.0s, 157.602 mph/253.636 km/h (under caution); **2** Kasey Kahne, USA (Dodge Charger), 188 laps; **3** Kurt Busch, USA (Dodge Charger), 188; **4** Matt Kenseth, USA (Ford Fusion), 188; **5** Martin Truex Jr, USA (Chevrolet Monte Carlo), 188; **6** Kevin Harvick, USA (Chevrolet Monte Carlo), 188; **7** Jeff Green, USA (Chevrolet Monte Carlo), 188; **8** Mark Martin, USA (Ford Fusion), 188; **9** Carl Edwards, USA (Ford Fusion), 188; **10** Bobby Labonte, USA (Dodge Charger), 188.
Pole position: David Gilliland, USA (Ford Fusion).
Drivers' championship points: 1 Burton, 5598; **2** Kenseth, 5592; **3** Martin, 5588; **4** Harvick, 5565; **5** Hamlin, 5547; **6** Earnhardt Jr, 5492.

BANK OF AMERICA 500, Lowe's Motor Speedway, Concord, Charlotte, North Carolina, USA, 14 October. Round 31. 334 laps of the 1.500-mile/2.414-km circuit, 501.000 miles/806.281 km.
1 Kasey Kahne, USA (Dodge Charger), 3h 47m 29.0s, 132.142 mph/212.661 km/h; **2** Jimmie Johnson, USA (Chevrolet Monte Carlo), 3h 47m 30.624s; **3** Jeff Burton, USA (Chevrolet Monte Carlo), 334 laps; **4** Dale Earnhardt Jr, USA (Chevrolet Monte Carlo), 334; **5** Bobby Labonte, USA (Dodge Charger), 334; **6** Kyle Busch, USA (Chevrolet Monte Carlo), 334; **7** Tony Raines, USA (Chevrolet Monte Carlo), 334; **8** Carl Edwards, USA (Ford Fusion), 334; **9** Joe Nemechek, USA (Chevrolet Monte Carlo), 334; **10** Brian Vickers, USA (Chevrolet Monte Carlo), 334.
Pole position: Scott Riggs, USA (Dodge Charger).
Drivers' championship points: 1 Burton, 5763; **2** Kenseth, 5718; **3** Harvick, 5674s; **4** Martin, 5661; **5** Earnhardt Jr, 5657; **6** Hamlin, 5626.

SUBWAY 500, Martinsville Speedway, Virginia, USA, 22 October. Round 32. 500 laps of the 0.526-mile/0.847-km circuit, 263.000 miles/423.257 km.
1 Jimmie Johnson, USA (Chevrolet Monte Carlo), 3h 44m 00.0s, 70.446 mph/113.373 km/h; **2** Denny Hamlin, USA (Chevrolet Monte Carlo), 3h 44m 00.544s; **3** Bobby Labonte, USA (Dodge Charger), 500 laps; **4** Tony Stewart, USA (Chevrolet Monte Carlo), 500; **5** Jeff Gordon, USA (Chevrolet Monte Carlo), 500; **6** Casey Mears, USA (Dodge Charger), 500; **7** Kasey Kahne, USA (Dodge Charger), 500; **8** Jeff Green, USA (Chevrolet Monte Carlo), 500; **9** Kevin Harvick, USA (Chevrolet Monte Carlo), 500; **10** Kyle Petty, USA (Dodge Charger), 500.
Pole position: Kurt Busch, USA (Dodge Charger).
Drivers' championship points: 1 Kenseth, 5848; **2** Harvick, 5812; **3** Johnson, 5807; **4** Hamlin, 5801; **5** Burton, 5800; **6** Earnhardt Jr, 5754.

BASS PRO SHOPS 500, Atlanta Motor Speedway, Hampton, Georgia, USA, 29 October. Round 33. 325 laps of the 1.540-mile/2.478-km circuit, 500.500 miles/805.477 km.
1 Tony Stewart, USA (Chevrolet Monte Carlo), 3h 29m 23.0s, 143.121 mph/230.814 km/h; **2** Jimmie Johnson, USA (Chevrolet Monte Carlo), 3h 29m 24.129s; **3** Dale Earnhardt Jr, USA (Chevrolet Monte Carlo), 325 laps; **4** Matt Kenseth, USA (Ford Fusion), 325; **5** Greg Biffle, USA (Ford Fusion), 325; **6** Jeff Gordon, USA (Chevrolet Monte Carlo), 325; **7** Carl Edwards, USA (Ford Fusion), 325; **8** Denny Hamlin, USA (Chevrolet Monte Carlo), 325; **9** Joe Nemechek, USA (Chevrolet Monte Carlo), 325; **10** Robby Gordon, USA (Chevrolet Monte Carlo), 325.
Pole position: Kenseth.

Provisional championship points
Drivers
1 Matt Kenseth, USA, 6008; **2** Jimmie Johnson, USA, 5982; **3** Denny Hamlin, USA, 5943; **4** Dale Earnhardt Jr, USA, 5924; **5** Jeff Burton, USA, 5924; **6** Kevin Harvick, USA, 5887; **7** Jeff Gordon, USA, 5862; **8** Mark Martin, USA, 5807; **9** Kasey Kahne, USA, 5798; **10** Kyle Busch, USA, 5759.
Not involved in chase for the Nextel Cup
11 Tony Stewart, USA, 4298; **12** Carl Edwards, USA, 4013; **13** Greg Biffle, USA, 3771; **14** Casey Mears, USA, 3616; **15** Brian Vickers, USA, 3589; **16** Kurt Busch, USA, 3577; **17** Ryan Newman, USA, 3475; **18** Clint Bowyer, USA, 3475; **19** Bobby Labonte, USA, 3330; **20** Scott Riggs, USA, 3301; **21** Martin Truex Jr, USA, 3250; **22** Dale Jarrett, USA, 3246; **23** Elliott Sadler, USA, 3245; **24** Jamie McMurray, USA, 3214; **25** Reed Sorensen, USA, 3131; **26** Dave Blaney, USA, 3013; **27** Robby Gordon, USA, 3007; **28** Jeff Green, USA, 2980; **29** JJ Yeley, USA, 2931; **30** Joe Nemechek, USA, 2916.
Raybestos Rookie of the Year: Denny Hamlin.
Manufacturers
1 Chevrolet, 255; **2** Dodge, 189; **3** Ford, 183.
Bud Pole Award winner: Kurt Busch, 6 poles.

Results of the Texas, Phoenix and Homestead races will be given in AUTOCOURSE 2007–2008.

Other NASCAR Races

BUDWEISER SHOOTOUT, Daytona International Speedway, Daytona Beach, Florida, USA, 12 February, 70 laps of the 2.500-mile/4.023-km circuit, 175.000 miles/281.635 km.
1 Denny Hamilton, USA (Chevrolet Monte Carlo), 1h 10m 18.0s, 149.360 mph/240.371 km/h; **2** Dale Earnhardt Jr, USA (Chevrolet Monte Carlo), 70 laps; **3** Tony Stewart, USA (Chevrolet Monte Carlo), 70; **4** Scott Riggs, USA (Dodge Charger), 70; **5** Jimmie Johnson, USA (Chevrolet Monte Carlo), 70; **6** Matt Kenseth, USA (Ford Fusion), 70; **7** Mark Martin, USA (Ford Fusion), 70; **8** Jamie McMurray, USA (Ford Fusion), 70; **9** Joe Nemechek, USA (Chevrolet Monte Carlo), 70; **10** Dale Jarrett, USA (Ford Fusion), 70.
Pole position: Ken Schrader, USA (Ford Fusion).

NEXTEL OPEN, Lowe's Motor Speedway, Concord, Charlotte, North Carolina, USA, 20 May. 30 laps of the 1.500-mile/2.414-km circuit, 45.000 miles/72.420 km.
1 Scott Riggs, USA (Dodge Charger), 30 laps; **2** Jeff Green, USA (Chevrolet Monte Carlo), 30; **3** Brian Vickers, USA (Chevrolet Monte Carlo), 30; **4** Denny Hamlin, USA (Chevrolet Monte Carlo), 30;

5 JJ Yeley, USA (Chevrolet Monte Carlo), 30; **6** David Stremme, USA (Dodge Charger), 30; **7** Jeff Burton, USA (Chevrolet Monte Carlo), 30; **8** Sterling Marlin, USA (Chevrolet Monte Carlo), 30; **9** Robby Gordon, USA (Chevrolet Monte Carlo), 30; **10** Ken Schrader, USA (Ford Fusion), 30.
Pole position: Riggs.

NASCAR NEXTEL ALL-STAR CHALLENGE, Lowe's Motor Speedway, Concord, Charlotte, North Carolina, USA, 20 May. 90 laps of the 1.500-mile/2.414-km circuit, 135.000 miles/217.261 km.
1 Jimmie Johnson, USA (Chevrolet Monte Carlo), 90 laps; **2** Kevin Harvick, USA (Chevrolet Monte Carlo), 90; **3** Jeff Gordon, USA (Chevrolet Monte Carlo), 90; **4** Carl Edwards, USA (Ford Fusion), 90; **5** Ryan Newman, USA (Dodge Charger), 90; **6** Bobby Labonte, USA (Dodge Charger), 90; **7** Dale Jarrett, USA (Ford Fusion), 90; **8** Kyle Petty, USA (Dodge Charger), 90; **9** Dale Earnhardt Jr, USA (Chevrolet Monte Carlo), 90; **10** Scott Riggs, USA (Dodge Charger), 90.
Pole position: Kasey Kahne, USA (Dodge Charger).

Indy Racing League (IRL) Indy Pro Series

All cars are Dallara-Infiniti.

MIAMI 100, Homestead-Miami Speedway, Florida, USA, 26 March. Round 1. 67 laps of the 1.485-mile/2.390-km circuit, 99.495 miles/160.122 km.
1 Jeff Simmons, USA, 36m 41.3232s, 162.712 mph/261.860 km/h; **2** Nick Bussell, USA, 36m 41.3431s; **3** Jay Howard, GB, 36m 41.8860s; **4** Arie Luyendyk Jr, NL, 36m 42.5110s; **5** Bobby Wilson, USA, 36m 46.4660s; **6** Jon Herb, USA, 36m 46.4964s; **7** Geoff Dodge, USA, 36m 46.6773s; **8** Brett van Blankers, CDN, 36m 47.3426s; **9** Marty Roth, USA, 36m 47.4303s; **10** Wade Cunningham, NZ, 66 laps.
Fastest race lap: Herb, 28.4669s, 187.797 mph/302.230 km/h.
Fastest qualifying lap: Howard, 28.6512s, 186.589 mph/300.286 km/h.

INDY PRO SERIES GRAND PRIX OF ST PETERSBURG, Streets of St Petersburg, Florida, USA, 1/2 April. 2 x 40 laps of the 1.800-mile/2.897-km circuit.
Round 2 (72.000 miles/115.873 km).
1 Raphael Matos, BR, 52m 00.4498s, 83.065 mph/133.680 km/h; **2** Jeff Simmons, USA, 52m 00.9573s; **3** Jay Howard, GB, 52m 03.0319s; **4** Nick Bussell, USA, 52m 05.6278s; **5** Jonathan Klein, USA, 52m 06.2538s; **6** Chris Festa, USA, 52m 07.1086s; **7** Matthew Hamilton, USA, 52m 09.5675s; **8** Bobby Wilson, USA, 52m 17.1472s; **9** Brett van Blankers, CDN, 39 laps; **10** Alex Lloyd, USA, 38.
Fastest race lap: Matos, 1m 08.4165s, 94.714 mph/152.427 km/h.
Fastest qualifying lap: Matos, 1m 07.1409s, 96.513 mph/155.323 km/h.

Round 3 (72.000 miles/115.873 km).
1 Raphael Matos, BR, 50m 38.1317s, 85.316 mph/137.302 km/h; **2** Jay Howard, GB, 50m 43.8523s; **3** Alex Lloyd, GB, 50m 44.6265s; **4** Jeff Simmons, USA, 50m 44.8522s; **5** Jonathan Klein, USA 50m 48.0750s; **6** Bobby Wilson, USA, 50m 58.2720s; **7** Matthew Hamilton, NZ, 50m 59.5655s; **8** Chris Festa, USA, 51m 04.3503s; **9** Jon Herb, USA, 51m 27.9412s; **10** Nick Bussell, USA, 39 laps.
Fastest race lap: Matos, 1m 07.9642s, 95.344 mph/153.442 km/h.
Pole position: Festa.

FREEDOM 100, Indianapolis Motor Speedway, Speedway, Indiana, USA, 26 May. Round 4. 40 laps of the 2.500-mile/4.023-km circuit, 100.000 miles/160.934 km.
1 Wade Cunningham, NZ, 32m 29.3233s, 184.679 mph/297.213 km/h; **2** Jay Howard, GB, 32m 30.0122s; **3** Jaime Câmara, BR, 32m 45.1243s; **4** Chris Festa, USA, 32m 53.7006s; **5** Alex Lloyd, GB, 32m 53.9640s; **6** Jonathan Klein, USA, 33m 08.6909s; **7** Bobby Wilson, USA, 33m 08.6983s; **8** Geoff Dodge, USA, 33m 11.8442s; **9** Tom Wood, CDN, 33m 11.9456s; **10** Nick Bussell, USA, 33m 13.1517s.
Fastest race lap: Howard, 48.1931s, 186.749 mph/300.543 km/h.
Pole position/fastest qualifying lap: Cunningham, 1m 36.5546s, 186.423 mph/300.018 km/h (over two laps).

CORNING 100, Watkins Glen International, New York, USA, 4 June. Round 5. 27 laps of the 3.370-mile/5.423-km circuit, 97.730 miles/157.281 km
1 Bobby Wilson, USA, 1h 10m 23.6380s, 77.555 mph/124.813 km/h; **2** Wade Cunningham, NZ, 1h 10m 26.9175s; **3** Phil Giebler, USA, 1h 1m 27.2002s; **4** Jaime Câmara, BR, 1h 10m 28.8001s; **5** Jonathan Klein, USA, 1h 10m 30.4235s; **6** Jay Howard, GB, 1h 10m 41.3457s; **7** Brett van Blankers, CDN, 1h 10m 48.8392s; **8** Jon Herb, USA, 1h 10m 50.9746s; **9** CR Crews, USA, 1h 10m 52.7803s; **10** Matthew Hamilton, NZ, 1h 11m 12.9927s.
Fastest race lap: Wilson, 1m 54.2848s, 106.156 mph/170.841 km/h.
Fastest qualifying lap: Wilson, 1m 53.2403s, 107.135 mph/172.417 km/h.

LIBERTY CHALLENGE, Indianapolis Motor Speedway (Road Course), Speedway, Indiana, USA, 1 July. Round 6. 23 laps of the 2.605-mile/4.192-km circuit, 59.915 miles/96.424 km.
1 Alex Lloyd, GB, 35m 53.516s, 100.159 mph/161.190 km/h; **2** Graham Rahal, USA, 35m 54.184s; **3** Jonathan Klein, USA, 23 laps; **4** Raphael Matos, BR, 23; **5** Nick Bussell, USA, 23; **6** CR Crews, USA, 23; **7** Phil Giebler, USA, 23; **8** Jon Herb, USA, 23; **9** Bobby Wilson, USA, 23; **10** Logan Gomez, USA, 23.
Fastest race lap: Lloyd, 1m 27.085s, 107.685 mph/173.303 km/h.
Fastest qualifying lap: Rahal, 1m 25.581s, 109.580 mph/176.353 km/h.

SUNBELT RENTALS 100, Nashville Superspeedway, Lebanon, Tennessee, USA, 15 July. Round 7. 77 laps of the 1.300-mile/2.092-km circuit, 100.100 miles/161.095 km.
1 Jay Howard, GB, 39m 57.0934s, 150.332 mph/241.936 km/h; **2** Jaime Câmara, BR, 39m 59.4639s; **3** Jonathan Klein, USA, 40m 01.0812s; **4** Tom Wood, CDN, 40m 01.3007s; **5** Wade Cunningham, NZ, 40m 03.3382s; **6** Nick Bussell, USA, 40m 10.5560s; **7** Bobby Wilson, USA, 40m 10.9477s; **8** Sean Guthrie, USA, 40m 17.2164s; **9** Chris Festa, USA, 40m 17.4518s; **10** Brett van Blankers, CDN, 40m 20.0158s.
Fastest race lap: Cunningham, 26.3177s, 177.827 mph/286.185 km/h.
Fastest qualifying lap: Cunningham, 25.9338s, 180.459 mph/290.421 km/h.

MILWAUKEE 100, The Milwaukee Mile, Wisconsin State Fair Park, West Allis, Wisconsin, USA, 22 July. Round 8. 100 laps of the 1.015-mile/1.633-km circuit, 101.500 miles/163.348 km.
1 Jaime Câmara, BR, 46m 28.0393s, 131.060 mph/210.920 km/h; **2** Wade Cunningham, NZ, 46m 28.7007s; **3** Jonathan Klein, USA, 46m 29.0219s; **4** Bobby Wilson, USA, 46m 30.2020s; **5** Nick Bussell, USA, 46m 31.2337s; **6** Thiago Medeiros, BR, 99 laps; **7** Jay Howard, GB, 98; **8** Brett van Blankers, CDN, 97; **9** Tom Wood, CDN, 93; **10** Michael Crawford, USA, 18.
Fastest race lap: Cunningham, 26.0099s, 140.485 mph/226.089 km/h.
Fastest qualifying lap: Cunningham, 24.7254s, 147.783 mph/237.834 km/h.

BLUE GRASS 100, Kentucky Speedway, Fort Mitchell, Kentucky, USA, 13 August. Round 9. 67 laps of the 1.480-mile/2.382-km circuit, 99.160 miles/159.583 km.
1 Jay Howard, GB, 37m 57.3271s, 156.752 mph/252.268 km/h; **2** Jonathan Klein, USA, 37m 57.3461s; **3** Wade Cunningham, NZ, 37m 57.5267s; **4** Travis Gregg, USA, 37m 57.5407s; **5** Sean Guthrie, USA, 37m 57.6409s; **6** Nick Bussell, USA, 37m 58.0610s; **7** Bobby Wilson, USA, 37m 58.1783s; **8** Chris Festa, USA, 37m 59.1833s; **9** Ben Petter, USA, 37m 59.4640s; **10** Mike Potekhen, USA, 66 laps.
Fastest race lap: Wilson, 27.9927s, 190.335 mph/306.315 km/h.
Fastest qualifying lap: Klein, 28.1321s, 189.392 mph/304.797 km/h.

CARNEROS 100/VALLEY OF THE MOON 100, Infineon Raceway, Sears Point, Sonoma, California, USA, 26/27 August. 2 x 30 laps of the 2.300-mile/3.701-km circuit. Round 10 (69.000 miles/111.045 km).
1 Wade Cunningham, NZ, 48m 32.8171s, 85.278 mph/137.242 km/h; **2** Alex Lloyd, GB, 48m 33.4189s; **3** Nick Bussell, USA, 48m 34.0496s; **4** Jonathan Klein, USA, 48m 38.6698s; **5** Bobby Wilson, USA, 48m 41.5982s; **6** Mike Potekhen, USA, 48m 44.6400s; **7** Jaime Câmara, BR, 48m 45.5338s; **8** Ryan Justice, USA, 48m 46.3997s; **9** Micky Gilbert, USA, 48m 47.0920s; **10** Jay Howard, GB, 29 laps.
Fastest race lap: Lloyd, 1m 24.6860s, 97.773 mph/157.350 km/h.
Fastest qualifying lap: Cunningham, 1m 22.9324s, 99.840 mph/160.677 km/h.

Round 11 (69.000 miles/111.045 km).
1 Alex Lloyd, GB, 49m 03.7303s, 84.383 mph/135.801 km/h; **2** Bobby Wilson, USA, 49m 09.9703s; **3** Jonathan Klein, USA, 49m 10.8066s; **4** Wade Cunningham, NZ, 49m 26.5484s; **5** Jay Howard, GB, 49m 29.0259s; **6** Mike Potekhen, USA, 49m 30.1887s; **7** Scott Mansell, GB, 49m 34.5083s; **8** Ryan Justice, USA, 49m 35.5266s; **9** Daniel Gaunt, NZ, 49m 40.6806s; **10** Micky Gilbert, USA, 50m 23.5140s.
Fastest race lap: Cunningham, 1m 24.1080s, 98.445 mph/158.432 km/h.
Fastest qualifying lap: Cunningham.

CHICAGOLAND 100, Chicagoland Speedway, Chicago, Illinois, USA, 9 September. Round 12. 67 of the 1.520-mile/2.446-km circuit, 101.840 miles/163.896 km.
1 Wade Cunningham, NZ, 49m 09.3796s, 124.305 mph/200.050 km/h; **2** Jonathan Klein, USA, 49m 09.9893s; **3** Jay Howard, GB, 49m 10.0240s; **4** Alex Lloyd, GB, 49m 10.4288s; **5** Chris Festa, USA, 49m 10.4841s; **6** Arie Luyendyk Jr, NL, 49m 10.6598s; **7** Mike Potekhen, USA, 49m 10.7477s; **8** Nick Bussell, USA, 49m 11.5111s; **9** Tom Wood, CDN, 49m 12.3873s; **10** Ben Petter, USA, 49m 13.4148s.
Fastest race lap: Wood, 28.7135s, 190.572 mph/306.697 km/h.
Fastest qualifying lap: Howard, 28.9870s, 188.774 mph/303.803 km/h.

Final championship points
1 Jay Howard, GB, 390; **2** Jonathan Klein, USA, 386; **3** Wade Cunningham, NZ, 379; **4** Bobby Wilson, USA, 343; **5** Nick Bussell, USA, 319; **6** Jaime Câmara, BR, 298; **7** Alex Lloyd, GB, 294; **8** Chris Festa, USA, 205; **9** Brett van Blankers, CDN, 179; **10** Raphael Matos, BR, 154; **11** Jon Herb, USA, 126; **12** Jeff Simmons, USA, 122; **13** Mike Potekhen, USA, 121; **14** Tom Wood, CDN, 116; **15** Arie Luyendyk Jr, NL, 105; **16** Matthew Hamilton, NZ, 105; **17** Geoff Dodge, USA, 104; **18** Sean Guthrie, USA, 99; **19** CR Crews, USA, 86; **20** Scott Mansell, GB, 77.
Rookie of the Year: Jay Howard.

Yokohama presents The Champ Car Atlantic Championship powered by Mazda

All cars are Swift 016.a-Mazda Cosworth.

CHAMP CAR ATLANTIC CHAMPIONSHIP, Long Beach street circuit, California, USA, 9 April. Round 1. 32 laps of the 1.968-mile/3.167-km circuit, 62.976 miles/101.350 km.
1 Andreas Wirth, D, 49m 48.261s, 75.868 mph/122.098 km/h; **2** Raphael Matos, BR, 49m 49.101s; **3** James Hinchcliffe, CDN, 49m 51.320s; **4** Simon Pagenaud, F, 49m 52.129s; **5** Graham Rahal, USA, 49m 58.140s; **6** Danilo Dirani, BR, 49m 59.662s; **7** Robbie Pecorari, USA, 50m 02.930s; **8** Alex Barron, USA, 50m 05.173s; **9** Leonardo Maia, BR/USA, 50m 06.208s; **10** Alan Sciuto, USA, 50m 06.970s.
Most laps led: Wirth, 32.
Fastest race lap: Matos, 1m 16.058s, 93.150 mph/149.910 km/h.
Fastest qualifying lap: Wirth, 1m 16.082s, 93.121 mph/149.863 km/h.

CHAMP CAR ATLANTIC CHAMPIONSHIP, Reliant Park, Houston, Texas, USA, 13 May. Round 2. 36 laps of the 1.690-mile/2.720-km circuit, 60.840 miles/97.912 km.
1 Andreas Wirth, D, 51m 00.134s, 71.573 mph/115.186 km/h; **2** Simon Pagenaud, F, 51m 05.676s; **3** Jonathan Bomarito, USA, 51m 07.468s; **4** James Hinchcliffe, CDN, 51m 08.450s; **5** Danilo Dirani, BR, 51m 09.585s; **6** Alan Sciuto, USA, 51m 09.976s; **7** Steve Ott, USA, 51m 12.238s; **8** David Martinez, MEX, 51m 14.127s; **9** Leonardo Maia, BR/USA, 51m 14.337s; **10** James Davison, AUS, 51m 14.742s.
Most laps led: Raphael Matos, BR, 19.
Fastest race lap: Bomarito, 1m 05.562s, 92.798 mph/149.343 km/h.
Fastest qualifying lap: Matos, 1m 05.263s, 93.223 mph/150.028 km/h.

CHAMP CAR ATLANTIC CHAMPIONSHIP, Parque Fundidora, Monterrey, Nuevo Leon, Mexico, 21 May. Round 3. 32 laps of the 2.104-mile/3.386-km circuit, 67.328 miles/108.354 km.
1 Graham Rahal, USA, 44m 52.255s, 90.029 mph/144.887 km/h; **2** Simon Pagenaud, F, 44m 55.826s; **3** David Martinez, MEX, 45m 05.205s; **4** Jonathan Bomarito, USA, 45m 06.279s; **5** Stephen Simpson, ZA, 45m 08.884s; **6** Andreas Wirth, D, 45m 14.288s; **7** Alan Sciuto, USA, 45m 15.950s; **8** Alex Barron, USA, 45m 16.501s; **9** Joe D'Agostino, USA, 45m 30.487s; **10** Leonardo Maia, BR/USA, 45m 31.535s.
Most laps led: Rahal, 32.
Fastest race lap: Rahal, 1m 23.206s, 91.032 mph/146.502 km/h.
Fastest qualifying lap: Rahal, 1m 23.217s, 91.020 mph/146.482 km/h.

TRINITY CARPET 100k, Portland International Raceway, Oregon, USA, 18 June. Round 4. 40 laps of the 1.964-mile/3.161-km circuit, 78.560 miles/126.430 km.
1 James Hinchcliffe, CDN, 47m 22.170s, 99.507 mph/160.141 km/h; **2** Ryan Lewis, GB, 47m 26.290s; **3** Andreas Wirth, D, 47m 29.296s; **4** Alan Sciuto, USA, 47m 30.209s; **5** Danilo Dirani, BR, 47m 40.671s; **6** Raphael Matos, BR, 47m 46.333s; **7** David Martinez, MEX, 47m 46.679s; **8** Daniel Gaunt, NZ, 47m 47.130s; **9** Leonardo Maia, BR/USA, 47m 47.393s; **10** Tim Bridgman, GB, 47m 49.709s.
Most laps led: Lewis, 31.
Fastest race lap: Joe D'Agostino, USA, 1m 05.680s, 107.650 mph/173.245 km/h.
Fastest qualifying lap: Graham Rahal, USA, 1m 04.628s, 109.401 mph/176.065 km/h.

CHAMP CAR ATLANTIC CHAMPIONSHIP, Burke Lakefront Airport, Cleveland, Ohio, USA, 24/25 June. 2 x 32 laps of the 2.106-mile/3.389-km circuit.
Round 5 (67.392 miles/108.457 km).
1 Graham Rahal, USA, 37m 22.829s, 108.172 mph/174.086 km/h; **2** Simon Pagenaud, F, 37m 24.706s; **3** Andreas Wirth, D, 37m 25.301s; **4** Jonathan Bomarito, USA, 37m 31.967s; **5** Raphael Matos, BR, 37m 32.366s; **6** Carlos Mastretta, MEX, 37m 37.192s; **7** Leonardo Maia, BR/USA, 37m 38.357s; **8** Danilo Dirani, BR, 37m 39.071s; **9** Joe D'Agostino, USA, 37m 41.707s; **10** David Martinez, MEX, 37m 42.092s.
Most laps led: Pagenaud, 23.
Fastest race lap: Rahal, 1m 04.744s, 117.100 mph/188.456 km/h.
Fastest qualifying lap: Wirth, 1m 06.470s, 114.060 mph/183.563 km/h.

Round 6 (67.392 miles/108.457 km).
1 Graham Rahal, USA, 37m 17.341s, 108.437 mph/174.513 km/h; **2** Richard Philippe, F, 37m 32.559s; **3** Steve Ott, USA, 37m 33.354s; **4** Robbie Pecorari, USA, 37m 38.025s; **5** Simon Pagenaud, F, 37m 42.110s; **6** Leonardo Maia, BR/USA, 37m 42.784s; **7** Joe D'Agostino, USA, 37m 44.535s; **8** Jonathan Bomarito, USA, 37m 45.632s; **9** Alan Sciuto, USA, 38m 05.305s; **10** David Martinez, MEX, 38m 05.821s.
Most laps led: Rahal, 32.
Fastest race lap: Wirth, 1m 04.255s, 117.992 mph/189.890 km/h.
Fastest qualifying lap: Pagenaud, 1m 04.678s, 117.221 mph/188.648 km/h.

CHAMP CAR ATLANTIC CHAMPIONSHIP, Exhibition Place Circuit, Toronto, Ontario, Canada, 9 July. Round 7. 38 laps of the 1.755-mile/2.824-km circuit, 66.690 miles/107.327 km.
1 Robbie Pecorari, USA, 45m 08.363s, 88.645 mph/142.661 km/h; **2** Jonathan Bomarito, USA, 45m 10.929s; **3** Ryan Lewis, GB, 45m 17.696s; **4** Simon Pagenaud, F, 45m 18.273s; **5** Alex Barron, USA, 45m 34.266s; **6** James Hinchcliffe, CDN, 45m 37.692s; **7** Joe D'Agostino, USA, 45m 38.263s; **8** David Martinez, MEX, 45m 48.055s; **9** Raphael Matos, BR, 45m 48.353s; **10** Leonardo Maia, BR/USA, 45m 48.819s.
Most laps led: Percorari, 38.
Fastest race lap: Graham Rahal, USA, 1m 05.487s, 96.477 mph/155.265 km/h.
Fastest qualifying lap: Rahal, 1m 04.969s, 97.246 mph/156.503 km/h.

CHAMP CAR ATLANTIC CHAMPIONSHIP, Finning International Speedway, Edmonton, Alberta, Canada, 23 July. Round 8. 36 laps of the 1.973-mile/3.175-km circuit, 71.028 miles/114.308 km.
1 Simon Pagenaud, F, 41m 54.492s, 101.691 mph/163.656 km/h; **2** Graham Rahal, USA, 42m 05.000s; **3** Andreas Wirth, D, 42m 14.494s; **4** Richard Philippe, F, 42m 22.842s; **5** Danilo Dirani, BR, 42m 23.617s; **6** Jonathan Bomarito, USA, 42m 25.958s; **7** Joe D'Agostino, USA, 42m 28.987s; **8** Tim Bridgman, GB, 42m 39.440s; **9** Colin Fleming, USA, 42m 39.883s; **10** Robbie Pecorari, USA, 42m 46.131s.
Most laps led: Raphael Matos, BR, 28.
Fastest race lap: Pagenaud, 1m 05.647s, 108.197 mph/174.126 km/h.
Fastest qualifying lap: Matos, 1m 05.333s, 108.717 mph/174.963 km/h.

CHAMP CAR ATLANTIC CHAMPIONSHIP, San José street circuit, California, USA, 30 July. Round 9. 45 laps of the 1.443-mile/2.322-km circuit, 64.935 miles/104.503 km.
1 Raphael Matos, BR, 50m 03.045s, 77.843 mph/125.276 km/h; **2** Ryan Lewis, GB, 50m 04.893s; **3** Danilo Dirani, BR, 50m 08.400s; **4** Tim Bridgman, GB, 50m 10.833s; **5** Leonardo Maia, BR/USA, 50m 11.284s; **6** David Martinez, MEX, 50m 11.834s; **7** James Davison, AUS, 50m 12.326s; **8** Justin Sofio, USA, 50m 16.443s; **9** Simon Pagenaud, F, 50m 12.742s; **10** Carlos Mastretta, MEX, 50m 17.653s.
Most laps led: Matos, 45.
Fastest race lap: Graham Rahal, USA, 55.666s, 93.320 mph/150.185 km/h.
Fastest qualifying lap: Matos, 55.495s, 93.608 mph/150.648 km/h.

CHAMP CAR ATLANTIC CHAMPIONSHIP, Denver street circuit, Colorado, USA, 13 August. Round 10. 35 laps of the 1.657-mile/2.667-km circuit, 57.995 miles/93.334 km.
1 Graham Rahal, USA, 50m 36.984s, 68.746 mph/110.637 km/h; **2** Raphael Matos, BR, 50m 38.272s; **3** Simon Pagenaud, F, 50m 40.450s; **4** Alan Sciuto, USA, 50m 42.553s; **5** Andreas Wirth, D, 50m 43.614s; **6** Robbie Pecorari, USA, 50m 49.762s; **7** James Hinchcliffe, CDN, 50m 50.444s; **8** Danilo Dirani, BR, 50m 50.957s; **9** Colin Fleming, USA, 50m 51.718s; **10** David Martinez, MEX, 50m 52.239s.
Most laps led: Rahal, 35.
Fastest race lap: Rahal, 1m 06.945s, 89.106 mph/143.402 km/h.
Fastest qualifying lap: Rahal, 1m 06.798s, 89.302 mph/143.718 km/h.

CHAMP CAR ATLANTIC CHAMPIONSHIP, Circuit Gilles-Villeneuve, Ile-Notre-Dame, Montréal, Québec, Canada, 28 August. Round 11. 26 laps of the 2.709-mile/4.360-km circuit, 70.434 miles/113.253 km.
Race scheduled for 27 August, but postponed due to rain.
1 Graham Rahal, USA, 49m 40.829s, 85.064 mph/136.898 km/h; **2** Simon Pagenaud, F, 49m 40.902s; **3** James Hinchcliffe, CDN, 49m 55.493s; **4** David Martinez, MEX, 49m 56.436s; **5** Leonardo Maia, BR/USA, 50m 01.708s; **6** Alan Sciuto, USA, 50m 02.012s; **7** Raphael Matos, BR, 50m 08.208s; **8** Michael Patrizi, AUS, 50m 12.471s; **9** Richard Philippe, F, 50m 16.389s; **10** Colin Fleming, USA, 50m 18.580s.
Most laps led: Rahal, 21.
Fastest race lap: Antoine Bessette, CDN, 1m 45.706s, 92.260 mph/148.478 km/h.
Fastest qualifying lap: Hinchcliffe, 1m 32.171s, 105.808 mph/170.281 km/h.

BOSPOKER.COM CHAMP CAR ATLANTIC GRAND PRIX OF ROAD AMERICA, Road America Circuit, Elkhart Lake, Wisconsin, USA, 24 September. Round 12. 18 laps of the 4.048-mile/6.515-km circuit, 72.864 miles/117.263 km.
1 Jonathan Bomarito, USA, 47m 23.451s, 92.251 mph/148.463 km/h; **2** Raphael Matos, BR, 47m 24.157s; **3** Andreas Wirth, D, 47m 24.863s; **4** Robbie Pecorari, USA, 47m 29.476s; **5** Ryan Lewis, GB, 47m 30.160s; **6** Danilo Dirani, BR, 47m 31.046s; **7** Joe D'Agostino, USA, 47m 31.222s; **8** Alan Sciuto, USA, 47m 33.054s; **9** David Martinez, MEX, 47m 36.100s; **10** Mike Forest, CDN, 47m 40.314s.
Most laps led: Matos, 9.
Fastest race lap: Matos, 1m 59.174s, 122.282 mph/196.793 km/h.
Fastest qualifying lap: Matos, 2m 01.130s, 120.307 mph/193.616 km/h.

Final championship points
1 Simon Pagenaud, F, 258; **2** Graham Rahal, USA, 242; **3** Andreas Wirth, D, 227; **4** Raphael Matos, BR, 205; **5** David Martinez, MEX, 179; **6** Jonathan Bomarito, USA, 178*; **7** Danilo Dirani, BR, 178; **8** Alan Sciuto, USA, 167; **9** Leonardo Maia, BR/USA, 161; **10** James Hinchcliffe, CDN, 160; **11** Robbie Pecorari, USA, 147; **12** Joe D'Agostino, USA, 123; **13** Ryan Lewis, GB, 110; **14** Alex Barron, USA, 96; **15** Richard Philippe, F, 86; **16** Tim Bridgman, GB, 72; **17** James Davison, AUS, 69; **18** Justin Sofio, USA, 54; **19** Steve Ott, USA, 48; **20** Colin Fleming, USA, 45.
* Net 10 points deduction for incident with Maia at Road America.

Rookie of the year: Simon Pagenaud.

A1GP World Cup of Motorsport

All cars are Lola-Zytek.

2005-2006

The following races were run after AUTOCOURSE 2005–2006 went to press.

A1 GP, Eastern Creek International Raceway, Sydney, New South Wales, Australia, 6 November. Round 4. 19 and 35 laps of the 2.442-mile/3.930-km circuit.
Sprint race (46.398 miles/74.670 km).
1 France-Nicolas Lapierre, 30m 32.582s, 91.146 mph/146.684 km/h; **2** Portugal-Alvaro Parente, 30m 41.281s; **3** Brazil-Nelson Angelo Piquet, 30m 41.677s; **4** Ireland-Michael Devaney, 30m 45.067s; **5** Great Britain-Robbie Kerr, 30m 50.055s; **6** Switzerland-Neel Jani, 30m 52.566s; **7** Netherlands-Jos Verstappen, 30m 57.138s; **8** Malaysia-Alex Yoong, 30m 59.418s; **9** Canada-Sean McIntosh, 31m 00.468s; **10** Italy-Enrico Toccacelo, 31m 02.402s; **11** Australia-Will Davison, 31m 03.008s; **12** Pakistan-Adam Khan, 31m 10.694s; **13** Russia-Roman Rusinov, 31m 11.600s; **14** New Zealand-Jonny Reid, 31m 12.646s; **15** USA-Bryan Herta, 31m 22.492s; **16** China-Tengyi Jiang, 31m 23.701s; **17** India-Armaan Ebrahim, 31m 25.335s; **18** Japan-Hayanari Shimoda, 18 laps (DNF-accident); **19** Austria-Mathias Lauda, 18; **20** Lebanon-Basil Shaaban, 11 (DNF-accident); **21** South Africa-Stephen Simpson, 8 (DNF-accident); **22** Mexico-Salvador Durán, 3 (DNF-accident); **23** Germany-Adrian Sutil, 3 (DNF-accident); **24** Czech Republic-Tomás Enge, 0 (DNF-accident).
Fastest race lap: France, 1m 19.751s, 110.233 mph/177.402 km/h.
Fastest qualifying lap: France, 2m 37.036s, 111.964 mph/180.187 km/h (over 2 laps).

Feature race (85.470 miles/137.550 km).
1 France-Nicolas Lapierre, 1h 00m 54.068s, 84.205 mph/135.514 km/h; **2** Great Britain-Robbie Kerr, 1h 00m 56.547s; **3** Switzerland-Neel Jani, 1h 00m 57.086s; **4** Netherlands-Jos Verstappen, 1h 00m 57.593s; **5** Malaysia-Alex Yoong, 1h 00m 58.955s; **6** Australia-Will Davison, 1h 00m 59.499s; **7** Portugal-Alvaro Parente, 1h 01m 00.070s; **8** New Zealand-Jonny Reid, 1h 01m 02.989s; **9** Brazil-Nelson Angelo Piquet, 1h 01m 03.108s; **10** USA-Bryan Herta, 1h 01m 03.896s; **11** Pakistan-Adam Khan, 1h 01m 05.010s; **12** Lebanon-Basil Shaaban, 1h 01m 07.071s; **13** India-Armaan Ebrahim, 1h 01m 08.343s; **14** Ireland-Michael Devaney, 1h 01m 26.140s; **15** Canada-Sean McIntosh, 26 laps (DNF-suspension); **16** Japan-Hayanari Shimoda, 25 (DNF-accident); **17** China-Tengyi Jiang, 22 (DNF-accident); **18** Austria-Mathias Lauda, 17 (DNF-accident); **19** Czech Republic-Tomás Enge, 17 (DNF-accident); **20** Russia-Roman Rusinov, 7 (DNF-accident); **21** Mexico-Salvador Durán, 7 (DNF-accident); **22** Germany-Adrian Sutil, 7 (DNF-suspension); **23** Italy-Enrico Toccacelo, 6 (DNF); **24** South Africa-Stephen Simpson, 1 (DNF-accident).
Fastest race lap: France, 1m 21.015s, 108.513 mph/174.634 km/h.
Pole position: France.

A1 GP, Sepang International Circuit, Selangor Darul Ehsan, Kuala Lumpur, Malaysia, 20 November. Round 5. 15 and 30 laps of the 3.447-mile/5.548-km circuit.
Sprint race (51.711 miles/83.220 km).
1 France-Alexandre Prémat, 29m 21.541s, 105.679 mph/170.073 km/h; **2** Switzerland-Neel Jani, 29m 22.772s; **3** Great Britain-Robbie Kerr, 29m 26.606s; **4** Brazil-Nelson Angelo Piquet, 29m 28.334s; **5** Netherlands-Jos Verstappen, 29m 29.514s; **6** New Zealand-Matt Halliday, 29m 34.703s; **7** Ireland-Ralph Firman, 29m 35.423s; **8** Malaysia-Fairuz Fauzy, 29m 37.323s; **9** Portugal-Alvaro Parente, 29m 41.932s; **10** USA-Bryan Herta, 29m 42.386s; **11** India-Armaan Ebrahim, 29m 42.935s; **12** Germany-Timo Scheider, 29m 44.648s; **13** Pakistan-Adam Khan, 29m 46.755s; **14** Japan-Hayanari Shimoda, 29m 47.788s; **15** Canada-Sean McIntosh, 29m 48.949s; **16** Czech Republic-

Tomás Enge, 29m 51.551s; **17** Italy-Enrico Toccacelo, 29m 52.712s; **18** Austria-Mathias Lauda, 29m 53.179s; **19** Mexico-Luis Diaz, 29m 55.912s; **20** China-Tengyi Jiang, 29m 58.622s; **21** South Africa-Stephen Simpson, 9 laps (DNF-electrics); **22** Lebanon-Khalil Beschir, 9 (DNF-suspension damage); **23** Indonesia-Ananda Mikola, 5 (DNF-accident damage); **24** Australia-Will Davison, 4 (DNF-tyre).
Fastest race lap: France, 1m 55.373s, 107.569 mph/173.115 km/h.
Fastest qualifying lap: Switzerland, 3m 48.962s, 108.406 mph/174.463 km/h (over 2 laps).

Feature race (103.421 miles/166.440 km).
1 France-Alexandre Prémat, 1h 00m 06.495s, 103.235 mph/166.140 km/h; **2** Switzerland-Neel Jani, 1h 00m 11.051s; **3** Czech Republic-Tomás Enge, 1h 00m 22.184s; **4** Italy-Enrico Toccacelo, 1h 00m 30.233s; **5** Malaysia-Alex Yoong, 1h 00m 38.136s; **6** New Zealand-Matt Halliday, 1h 00m 39.192s; **7** USA-Bryan Herta, 1h 00m 39.832s; **8** Germany-Timo Scheider, 1h 00m 41.876s; **9** Ireland-Ralph Firman, 1h 00m 42.240s; **10** Brazil-Nelson Angelo Piquet, 1h 00m 45.883s; **11** Australia-Will Davison, 1h 00m 56.978s; **12** South Africa-Stephen Simpson, 1h 00m 58.334s; **13** Japan-Hayanari Shimoda, 1h 01m 04.243s; **14** Indonesia-Ananda Mikola, 1h 01m 11.734s; **15** Mexico-Luis Diaz, 1h 01m 28.935s; **16** Netherlands-Jos Verstappen, 1h 01m 53.803s; **17** Lebanon-Khalil Beschir, 29 laps; **18** Portugal-Alvaro Parente, 29; **19** Canada-Sean McIntosh, 21 (DNF-accident damage); **20** Great Britain-Robbie Kerr, 20 (DNF-wheel); **21** Austria-Mathias Lauda, 17 (DNF-gearbox); **22** Pakistan-Adam Khan, 4 (DNF-accident damage); **23** China-Tengyi Jiang, 1 (DNF-accident).
Disqualified: India-Armaan Ebrahim, 11 laps (received outside assistance).
Fastest race lap: Netherlands, 1m 56.001s, 106.986 mph/172.177 km/h.
Pole position: France.

A1 GP, Dubai Autodrome, United Arab Emirates, 11 December, Round 6. 15 and 30 laps of the 3.349-mile/5.390-km circuit.
Sprint race (50.238 miles/80.850 km).
1 Switzerland-Neel Jani, 26m 56.613s, 111.874 mph/180.043 km/h; **2** Italy-Enrico Toccacelo, 27m 04.860s; **3** Czech Republic-Tomás Enge, 27m 05.637s; **4** Ireland-Ralph Firman, 27m 06.574s; **5** Canada-Sean McIntosh, 27m 07.805s; **6** Indonesia-Ananda Mikola, 27m 10.009s; **7** France-Nicolas Lapierre, 27m 10.539s; **8** Portugal-Alvaro Parente, 27m 11.497s; **9** Great Britain-Robbie Kerr, 27m 12.050s; **10** Malaysia-Alex Yoong, 27m 13.234s; **11** Netherlands-Jos Verstappen, 27m 14.223s; **12** South Africa-Stephen Simpson, 27m 14.919s; **13** USA-Phil Giebler, 27m 18.655s; **14** Japan-Hayanari Shimoda, 27m 19.980s; **15** New Zealand-Matt Halliday, 27m 25.478s; **16** Pakistan-Adam Khan, 27m 26.010s; **17** Austria-Mathias Lauda, 27m 27.301s; **18** Mexico-Salvador Durán, 27m 28.282s; **19** China-Tengyi Jiang, 27m 31.732s; **20** India-Armaan Ebrahim, 27m 41.498s; **21** Australia-Will Davison, 14 laps (DNF-gearbox); **22** Germany-Adrian Sutil, 2 (DNF-accident damage); **23** Brazil-Nelson Angelo Piquet, 1 (DNF-electrics).
Did not start: Lebanon-Basil Shaaban (accident on out lap).
Fastest race lap: Switzerland, 1m 47.238s, 112.433 mph/180.943 km/h.
Fastest qualifying lap: Switzerland, 3m 31.918s, 113.790 mph/183.127 km/h (over 2 laps).

Feature race (100.476 mph/161.700 km).
1 France-Nicolas Lapierre, 56m 17.068s, 107.108 mph/172.374 km/h; **2** Great Britain-Robbie Kerr, 56m 20.782s; **3** South Africa-Stephen Simpson, 56m 23.758s; **4** Portugal-Alvaro Parente, 56m 25.067s; **5** China-Tengyi Jiang, 56m 47.856s; **6** Canada-Sean McIntosh, 56m 48.411s; **7** Austria-Mathias Lauda, 56m 51.510s; **8** Mexico-Salvador Durán, 56m 52.570s; **9** Netherlands-Jos Verstappen, 56m 53.213s; **10** Australia-Will Davison, 56m 53.414s; **11** Italy-Enrico Toccacelo, 56m 54.000s; **12** Germany-Adrian Sutil, 56m 54.916s; **13** New Zealand-Matt Halliday, 57m 06.192s; **14** India-Armaan Ebrahim, 57m 06.516s; **15** Japan-Hayanari Shimoda, 29 laps; **16** Lebanon-Basil Shaaban, 29; **17** Switzerland-Neel Jani, 27; **18** Czech Republic-Tomás Enge, 27; **19** Pakistan-Adam Khan, 26 (DNF-accident damage); **20** USA-Phil Giebler, 26 (DNF-electrical fire); **21** Ireland-Ralph Firman, 7 (DNF-gearbox electrics); **22** Indonesia-Ananda Mikola, 5 (DNF-accident); **23** Brazil-Nelson Angelo Piquet, 4 (DNF-electrics); **24** Malaysia-Alex Yoong, 2 (DNF-spin).
Fastest race lap: Ireland, 1m 46.497s, 113.215 mph/182.202 km/h.
Pole position: Switzerland.

A1 GP, Durban street circuit, KwaZulu-Natal, South Africa, 29 January. Round 7. 20 and 40 laps of the 2.040-mile/3.283-km circuit.
Sprint race (40.799 miles/65.660 km).
1 France-Alexandre Prémat, 31m 06.730s, 78.682 mph/126.625 km/h; **2** Great Britain-Robbie Kerr, 31m 06.973s; **3** Switzerland-Neel Jani, 31m 12.580s; **4** Ireland-Ralph Firman, 31m 12.890s; **5** Czech Republic-Tomás Enge, 31m 15.236s; **6** New Zealand-Matt Halliday, 31m 16.353s; **7** Germany-Timo Scheider, 31m 16.842s; **8** Portugal-Alvaro Parente, 31m 20.796s; **9** Australia-Will Davison, 31m 28.829s; **10** Mexico-David Martinez, 31m 39.510s; **11** Pakistan-Enrico Toccacelo, 31m 43.305s; **12** Canada-Sean McIntosh, 31m 45.990s; **13** USA-Phil Giebler, 31m 48.861s; **14** India-Armaan Ebrahim, 32m 32.445s; **15** Austria-Mathias Lauda, 32m 33.866s; **16** Netherlands-Jos Verstappen, 19 laps (DNF-accident); **17** Lebanon-Basil Shaaban, 18 (DNF-spin); **18** China-Tengyi Jiang, 17 (DNF-accident); **19** Brazil-Nelson Angelo Piquet, 16 (DNF-spin); **20** South Africa-Stephen Simpson, 13 (DNF-electrics); **21** Indonesia-Ananda Mikola, 0 (DNF-accident); **22** Italy-Max Busnelli, 0 (DNF-accident); **23** Malaysia-Alex Yoong, 0 (DNF-accident).
Fastest race lap: Ireland, 1m 19.614s, 92.243 mph/148.451 km/h.
Fastest qualifying lap: France, 2m 36.841s, 93.648 mph/150.710 km/h (over 2 laps).
Toccacelo was allowed to race the Pakistani entry, although he was ineligible for points.

Feature race (81.598 miles/131.320 km).
1 Netherlands-Jos Verstappen, 1h 00m 46.099s, 80.567 mph/129.659 km/h; **2** Switzerland-Neel Jani, 1h 00m 47.873s; **3** Portugal-Alvaro Parente, 1h 00m 48.064s; **4** New Zealand-Matt Halliday, 1h 00m 50.451s; **5** South Africa-Stephen Simpson, 1h 00m 55.532s; **6** Italy-Max Busnelli, 1h 00m 56.834s; **7** Austria-Mathias Lauda, 1h 01m 16.222s; **8** France-Alexandre Prémat, 1h 01m 23.316s; **9** Brazil-Nelson Angelo Piquet, 1h 01m 49.730s; **10** Canada-Sean McIntosh, 36 laps; **11** Germany-Timo Scheider, 35 (DNF-suspension); **12** China-Tengyi Jiang, 35 (DNF-spin); **13** Pakistan-Enrico Toccacelo, 31 (DNF-spin); **14** Mexico-David Martinez, 30 (DNF-spin); **15** Lebanon-Basil Shaaban, 27; **16** Malaysia-Alex Yoong, 25 (DNF-spin); **17** Ireland-Ralph Firman, 14 (DNF-spin); **18** India-Armaan Ebrahim, 10 (DNF-accident); **19** Indonesia-Ananda Mikola, 10 (DNF-accident); **20** Great Britain-Robbie Kerr, 9 (DNF-accident damage); **21** Australia-Will Davison, 2 (DNF-accident); **22** USA-Phil Giebler, 2 (DNF-accident).
Disqualified: Czech Republic-Tomás Enge (at 7 laps, after stalling and being started by his team at the pit exit).
Fastest race lap: Brazil, 1m 18.178s, 93.938 mph/151.178 km/h.
Pole position: France.

A1 GP, Sentul Circuit, Bogor, West Java, Indonesia, 12 February. Round 8. 18 and 36 laps of the 2.464-mile/3.965-km circuit.
Sprint race (44.347 miles/71.370 km).
1 France-Nicolas Lapierre, 24m 03.360s, 110.610 mph/178.009 km/h; **2** Great Britain-Robbie Kerr, 24m 10.341s; **3** Mexico-Salvador Durán, 24m 11.387s; **4** Malaysia-Alex Yoong, 24m 14.682s; **5** Switzerland-Neel Jani, 24m 16.220s; **6** Ireland-Ralph Firman, 24m 17.094s; **7** Netherlands-Jos Verstappen, 24m 17.864s; **8** New Zealand-Matt Halliday, 24m 19.669s; **9** Japan-Hayanari Shimoda, 24m 22.074s; **10** Czech Republic-Tomás Enge, 24m 26.482s; **11** Indonesia-Ananda Mikola, 24m 26.666s; **12** Germany-Timo Scheider, 24m 27.761s; **13** Austria-Mathias Lauda, 24m 32.882s; **14** Italy-Max Busnelli, 24m 35.547s; **15** USA-Phil Giebler, 24m 39.755s; **16** Australia-Marcus Marshall, 24m 41.317s; **17** Lebanon-Basil Shaaban, 24m 48.545s; **18** India-Armaan Ebrahim, 25m 03.649s; **19** Portugal-Alvaro Parente, 27m 23.194s; **20** Brazil-Christian Fittipaldi, 17 laps; **21** South Africa-Stephen Simpson, 15; **22** China-Tengyi Jiang, 5 (DNF-gearbox); **23** Canada-Sean McIntosh, 1 (DNF-accident).
Fastest race lap: France, 1m 19.394s, 111.714 mph/179.786 km/h.
Fastest qualifying lap: Great Britain, 2m 34.257s, 114.996 mph/185.067 km/h (over 2 laps).

Feature race (88.695 miles/142.740 km).
1 Canada-Sean McIntosh, 55m 55.779s, 95.149 mph/153.128 km/h; **2** Malaysia-Alex Yoong, 55m 57.710s; **3** Australia-Marcus Marshall, 56m 08.396s; **4** Brazil-Christian Fittipaldi, 56m 09.779s; **5** Switzerland-Neel Jani, 56m 12.288s; **6** Netherlands-Jos Verstappen, 56m 17.625s; **7** New Zealand-Matt Halliday, 56m 17.998s; **8** France-Nicolas Lapierre, 56m 18.477s; **9** USA-Phil Giebler, 56m 22.092s; **10** Great Britain-Robbie Kerr, 56m 38.748s; **11** South Africa-Stephen Simpson, 57m 10.293s; **12** Germany-Timo Scheider, 57m 28.763s; **13** Czech Republic-Tomás Enge, 35 laps; **14** Indonesia-Ananda Mikola, 35; **15** India-Armaan Ebrahim, 35; **16** Italy-Max Busnelli, 31 (DNF-spin); **17** Portugal-Alvaro Parente, 31 (DNF-driveshaft); **18** Austria-Mathias Lauda, 24 (DNF-accident damage); **19** Ireland-Ralph Firman, 21 (DNF-gearbox); **20** Mexico-Salvador Durán, 18 (DNF-accident); **21** China-Tengyi Jiang, 11 (DNF-bodywork); **22** Lebanon-Basil Shaaban, 7 (DNF-accident); **23** Japan-Hayanari Shimoda, 0 (DNF-accident).
Fastest race lap: Ireland, 1m 19.029s, 112.230 mph/180.617 km/h.
Pole position: France.

A1 GP, Parque Fundidora, Monterrey, Mexico, 26 February. Round 9. 18 and 36 laps of the 2.104-mile/3.386-km circuit.
Sprint race (37.871 miles/60.948 km).
1 France-Alexandre Prémat, 29m 20.743s, 77.431 mph/124.613 km/h; **2** Switzerland-Neel Jani, 29m 21.026s; **3** Italy-Enrico Toccacelo, 29m 21.617s; **4** Netherlands-Jos Verstappen, 29m 22.884s; **5** Czech Republic-Tomás Enge, 29m 34.296s; **6** USA-Bryan Herta, 29m 40.822s; **7** Malaysia-Alex Yoong, 29m 43.613s; **8** Germany-Timo Scheider, 29m 44.100s; **9** Canada-Patrick Carpentier, 29m 46.979s; **10** Austria-Patrick Friesacher, 29m 47.654s; **11** Great Britain-Robbie Kerr, 29m 49.444s; **12** Indonesia-Ananda Mikola, 29m 59.203s; **13** Lebanon-Graham Rahal, 30m 02.149s; **14** Brazil-Christian Fittipaldi, 30m 11.492s; **15** China-Tengyi Jiang, 30m 12.464s; **16** Australia-Christian Jones, 30m 33.185s; **17** South Africa-Stephen Simpson, 9 (DNF-electrics); **18** New Zealand-Matt Halliday, 4 (DNF-accident); **19** Portugal-Alvaro Parente, 4 (DNF-accident); **20** Japan-Hayanari Shimoda, 3 (DNF-accident); **21** Ireland-Ralph Firman, 0 (DNF-accident); **22** Mexico-Salvador Durán, 0 (DNF-accident).
Fastest race lap: Netherlands, 1m 21.583s, 92.841 mph/149.413 km/h.
Fastest qualifying lap: France, 2m 45.848s, 91.340 mph/146.997 km/h (over 2 laps).

Feature race (75.743 miles/121.896 km).
1 France-Alexandre Prémat, 52m 26.709s, 86.654 mph/139.455 km/h; **2** Netherlands-Jos Verstappen, 52m 27.489s; **3** Switzerland-Neel Jani, 52m 30.234s; **4** Germany-Timo Scheider, 52m 31.297s; **5** Italy-Enrico Toccacelo, 52m 31.703s; **6** Great Britain-Robbie Kerr, 52m 38.211s; **7** Czech Republic-Tomás Enge, 52m 41.549s; **8** New Zealand-Matt Halliday, 52m 45.537s; **9** Austria-Patrick Friesacher, 52m 45.849s; **10** Portugal-Alvaro Parente, 52m 46.286s; **11** Malaysia-Alex Yoong, 52m 49.709s; **12** Brazil-Christian Fittipaldi, 52m 50.270s; **13** USA-Bryan Herta, 52m 50.585s; **14** Lebanon-Graham Rahal, 52m 52.226s; **15** Canada-Patrick Carpentier, 35 laps; **16** Indonesia-Ananda Mikola, 35; **17** China-Tengyi Jiang, 35; **18** South Africa-Stephen Simpson, 35; **19** Australia-Christian Jones, 20 (DNF-accident); **20** Ireland-Ralph Firman, 16; **21** Mexico-Salvador Durán, 6.
Did not start: Japan-Hayanari Shimoda.
Fastest race lap: France, 1m 21.100s, 93.394 mph/150.303 km/h.
Pole position: France.

A1 GP, Mazda Raceway Laguna Seca, Monterey, California, USA, 12 March. Round 10. 16 and 40 laps of the 2.238-mile/3.602-km circuit.
Sprint race (35.811 miles/57.632 km).
1 Mexico-Salvador Durán, 31m 07.422s, 69.036 mph/111.102 km/h; **2** France-Nicolas Lapierre, 31m 09.193s; **3** Portugal-Alvaro Parente, 31m 15.462s; **4** Great Britain-Robbie Kerr, 31m 20.213s; **5** Ireland-Ralph Firman, 31m 31.812s; **6** Canada-Patrick Carpentier, 31m 33.449s; **7** Germany-Timo Scheider, 31m 33.838s; **8** New Zealand-Matt Halliday, 31m 37.896s; **9** USA-Bryan Herta, 31m 38.456s; **10** Australia-Ryan Briscoe, 31m 42.069s; **11** South Africa-Stephen Simpson, 31m 43.393s; **12** Austria-Mathias Lauda, 31m 59.182s; **13** Brazil-Christian Fittipaldi, 32m 01.622s; **14** Netherlands-Jos Verstappen, 32m 02.688s; **15** Pakistan-Adam Khan, 32m 05.098s; **16** Switzerland-Giorgio Mondini, 32m 07.900s; **17** China-Tengyi Jiang, 32m 20.430s; **18** Czech Republic-Tomás Enge, 15 laps; **19** Italy-Massimiliano 'Max' Papis, 15; **20** Indonesia-Ananda Mikola, 12 (DNF-accident); **21** Lebanon-Graham Rahal, 9 (DNF-accident); **22** Malaysia-Alex Yoong, 7 (DNF-spin).
Fastest race lap: Mexico, 1m 37.343s, 82.774 mph/133.211 km/h.
Fastest qualifying lap: Mexico, 2m 30.744s, 106.902 mph/172.042 km/h (over 2 laps).

Feature race (89.527 miles/144.080 km).
1 Mexico-Salvador Durán, 1h 00m 52.974s, 88.229 mph/141.990 km/h; **2** Germany-Timo Scheider, 1h 00m 55.016s; **3** Great Britain-Robbie Kerr, 1h 00m 56.091s; **4** Portugal-Alvaro Parente, 1h 01m 03.394s; **5** Canada-Patrick Carpentier, 1h 1m 07.157s; **6** Ireland-Ralph Firman, 1h 1m 13.779s; **7** Italy-Massimiliano 'Max' Papis, 1h 01m 16.173s; **8** Australia-Ryan Briscoe, 1h 01m 17.210s; **9** Austria-Mathias Lauda, 1h 01m 22.203s; **10** Malaysia-Alex Yoong, 1h 01m 23.046s; **11** Pakistan-Adam Khan, 1h 01m 24.365s; **12** New Zealand-Matt Halliday, 1h 01m 24.951s; **13** Switzerland-Giorgio Mondini, 38 laps; **14** France-Nicolas Lapierre, 37 (DNF-battery); **15** USA-Bryan Herta, 37 (DNF-handling); **16** Czech Republic-Tomás Enge, 34 (DNF-spin); **17** China-Tengyi Jiang, 33 (DNF-spin); **18** Brazil-Christian Fittipaldi, 29; **19** Indonesia-Ananda Mikola, 28 (DNF-throttle); **20** Lebanon-Graham Rahal, 27 (DNF-spin); **21** Netherlands-Jos Verstappen, 17 (DNF-penalised and gave up); **22** South Africa-Stephen Simpson, 3 (DNF-accident).
Fastest race lap: France, 1m 17.951s, 103.366 mph/166.350 km/h.
Pole position: Mexico

A1 GP, Shanghai International Circuit, China, 2 April. Round 11. 15 and 30 laps of the 3.387-mile/5.451-km circuit.
Sprint race (50.806 miles/81.765 km).
1 Malaysia-Alex Yoong, 28m 17.807s, 107.729 mph/173.373 km/h; **2** Great Britain-Darren Manning, 28m 27.648s; **3** Mexico-Salvador Durán, 28m 28.224s; **4** Ireland-Michael Devaney, 28m 31.712s; **5** Indonesia-Ananda Mikola, 28m 36.978s; **6** Czech Republic-Tomás Enge, 28m 38.622s; **7** France-Alexandre Prémat, 28m 43.148s; **8** New Zealand-Matt Halliday, 28m 43.546s; **9** Australia-Ryan Briscoe, 28m 44.477s; **10** Brazil-Christian Fittipaldi, 28m 51.550s; **11** South Africa-Stephen Simpson, 28m 51.661s; **12** Pakistan-Adam Khan, 28m 52.011s; **13** Portugal-Alvaro Parente, 28m 54.155s; **14** USA-Phil Giebler, 28m 55.382s; **15** Germany-Sebastien Stahl, 28m 59.296s; **16** Italy-Enrico Toccacelo, 29m 02.699s; **17** China-Qinghua Ma, 29m 18.770s; **18** Lebanon-Graham Rahal, 14 laps; **19** Netherlands-Jos Verstappen, 12 (DNF-gearbox); **20** Austria-Mathias Lauda, 5 (DNF-mechanical); **21** Canada-Patrick Carpentier, 1 (DNF-accident); **22** Switzerland-Giorgio Mondini, 1 (DNF-accident).
Fastest race lap: Malaysia, 1m 52.508s, 108.379 mph/174.419 km/h.
Fastest qualifying lap: Malaysia, 3m 43.700s, 109.016 mph/175.445 km/h (over 2 laps).

Feature race (101.613 miles/163.530 km).
1 Czech Republic-Tomás Enge, 59m 23.250s, 102.661 mph/165.216 km/h; **2** Malaysia-Alex Yoong, 59m 29.971s; **3** Australia-Ryan Briscoe, 59m 33.103s; **4** New Zealand-Matt Halliday, 59m 49.716s; **5** Pakistan-Adam Khan, 59m 51.433s; **6** France-Nicolas Lapierre, 59m 54.682s; **7** Canada-Patrick Carpentier, 59m 56.707s; **8** Mexico-Salvador Durán, 59m 57.665s; **9** Italy-Enrico Toccacelo, 1h 00m 11.625s; **10** USA-Phil Giebler, 1h 00m 14.581s; **11** Lebanon-Graham Rahal, 1h 00m 24.903s; **12** Portugal-Alvaro Parente, 1h 00m 30.175s; **13** Austria-Mathias Lauda, 1h 00m 30.670s; **14** South Africa-Stephen Simpson, 1h 00m 31.090s; **15** Great Britain-Darren Manning, 1h 00m 33.172s; **16** China-Tengyi Jiang, 1h 00m 40.604s; **17** Netherlands-Jos Verstappen, 1h 01m 07.725s; **18** Germany-Sebastien Stahl, 1h 01m 13.244s; **19** Brazil-Christian Fittipaldi, 28 laps; **20** Switzerland-Giorgio Mondini, 7 (DNF-accident damage); **21** Indonesia-Ananda Mikola, 1 (DNF-accident); **22** Ireland-Michael Devaney, 1 (DNF-accident).
Fastest race lap: Mexico, 1m 52.546s, 108.343 mph/174.360 km/h.
Pole position: Malaysia.

Final championship points
1 France, 172; **2** Switzerland, 121; **3** Great Britain, 97; **4** New Zealand, 77; **5** Malaysia, 74; **6** Brazil, 71; **7** Netherlands, 69; **8** Ireland, 68; **9** Portugal, 66; **10** Canada, 59; **11** Mexico, 59; **12** Czech Republic, 56; **13** Australia, 51; **14** Italy, 46; **15** Germany, 38; **16** USA, 23; **17** South Africa, 20; **18** Indonesia, 19 Austria, 14; **20** Pakistan, 10; **21** Japan, 8; **22** China, 6.

2006–2007

A1 GP, Circuit Park Zandvoort, Netherlands, 1 October. Round 1. 12 and 41 laps of the 2.875-mile/4.627-km circuit.
Sprint race (34.501 miles/55.524 km).
1 South Africa-Adrian Zaugg, 18m 03.570s, 114.624 mph/184.470 km/h; **2** Mexico-Salvador Durán, 18m 05.842s; **3** France-Nicolas Lapierre, 18m 06.504s; **4** Germany-Nico Hülkenberg, 18m 09.760s; **5** Great Britain-Darren Manning, 18m 15.577s; **6** New Zealand-Matt Halliday, 18m 18.510s; **7** USA-Phil Giebler, 18m 26.008s; **8** Canada-James Hinchcliffe, 18m 27.341s; **9** Netherlands-Jeroen Bleekemolen, 18m 27.851s; **10** Switzerland-Sébastien Buemi, 18m 28.348s; **11** China-Cheng Congfu, 18m 28.895s; **12** Malaysia-Alex Yoong, 18m 29.455s; **13** Australia-Ryan Briscoe, 18m 30.236s; **14** Brazil-Tuka Rocha, 18m 31.887s; **15** Ireland-Michael Devaney, 18m 41.921s; **16** Lebanon-Basil Shaaban, 18m 47.735s; **17** Czech Republic-Tomas Kostka, 18m 48.333s; **18** Greece-Takis Kaitatzis, 19m 13.239s; **19** Indonesia-Ananda Mikola, 19m 18.509s; **20** Pakistan-Nur Ali, 19m 24.405s; **21** Singapore-Christian Murchison, 4 laps (DNF-accident); **22** India-Armaan Ebrahim, 0 (DNF-accident); **23** Italy-Alessandro Per Guidi, 0 (DNF-accident).
Fastest race lap: South Africa, 1m 29.125s, 116.132 mph/186.897 km/h.
Fastest qualifying lap: South Africa, 2m 55.531s, 117.932 mph/189.792 km/h (over 2 laps).

Feature race (117.878 miles/189.707 km).
1 Germany-Nico Hülkenberg, 1h 10m 31.238s, 100.293 mph/161.405 km/h; **2** USA-Phil Giebler, 1h 10m 39.108s; **3** Australia-Ryan Briscoe, 1h 11m 04.857s; **4** Netherlands-Jeroen Bleekemolen, 1h 11m 07.111s; **5** Mexico-Salvador Durán, 1h 11m 11.559s; **6** Italy-Alessandro Per Guidi, 1h 11m 13.854s; **7** Great Britain-Darren Manning, 1h 11m 25.571s; **8** Switzerland-Sébastien Buemi, 1h 11m 30.620s; **9** China-Cheng Congfu, 1h 12m 00.897s; **10** Indonesia-Ananda Mikola, 1h 12m 08.727s; **11** New Zealand-Matt Halliday, 1h 12m 20.377s; **12** Brazil-Tuka Rocha, 40 laps; **13** Canada-James Hinchcliffe, 40; **14** Ireland-Michael Devaney, 40; **15** Greece-Takis Kaitatzis, 40; **16** Singapore-Christian Murchison, 40; **17** Malaysia-Alex Yoong, 37; **18** India-Armaan Ebrahim, 34 (DNF-accident); **19** France-Nicolas Lapierre, 31 (DNF-gearbox); **20** Czech Republic-Tomas Kostka, 25; **21** Lebanon-Basil Shaaban, 18 (DNF-accident); **22** Pakistan-Nur Ali, 17 (DNF-accident); **23** South Africa-Adrian Zaugg, 0 (DNF-accident).
Fastest race lap: Malaysia, 1m 29.989s, 115.017 mph/185.102 km/h.
Pole position: South Africa.

A1 GP, Automotodrom Brno Masaryk Circuit, Brno, Czech Republic, 8 October. Round 2. 10 and 38 laps of the 3.357-mile/5.403-km circuit.
Sprint race (33.573 miles/54.030 km).
1 Malaysia-Alex Yoong, 18m 02.946s, 111.605 mph/179.610 km/h; **2** Canada-James Hinchcliffe, 18m 04.580s; **3** France-Nicolas Lapierre, 18m 05.677s; **4** China-Cheng Congfu, 18m 07.608s; **5** Czech Republic-Tomás Enge, 18m 09.038s; **6** USA-Phil Giebler, 18m 09.629s; **7** Mexico-Salvador Durán, 18m 13.702s; **8** Switzerland-Sébastien Buemi, 18m 15.376s; **9** Great Britain-Robbie Kerr, 18m 16.350s; **10** Brazil-Tuka Rocha, 18m 17.965s; **11** Netherlands-Jeroen Bleekemolen, 18m 18.444s; **12** Lebanon-Graham Rahal, 18m 22.439s; **13** Ireland-Michael Devaney, 18m 24.590s; **14** Italy-Alessandro Per Guidi, 18m 27.685s; **15** Australia-Karl Reindler, 18m 35.868s; **16** Indonesia-Ananda Mikola, 18m 37.457s; **17** India-Armaan Ebrahim, 18m 37.794s; **18** Singapore-Denis Lian, 18m 48.030s; **19** Greece-Nikos Zahos, 18m 48.642s; **20** Pakistan-Nur Ali, 19m 05.312s; **21** South Africa-Stephen Simpson, 4 laps (DNF-master switch/electrics); **22** New Zealand-Jonny Reid, 1 (DNF-accident damage); **23** Germany-Nico Hülkenberg, 0 (DNF-accident).
Fastest race lap: Malaysia, 1m 47.296s, 112.643 mph/181.281 km/h.
Fastest qualifying lap: New Zealand, 3m 30.053s, 115.078 mph/185.198 km/h (over 2 laps).

Feature race (127.576 miles/205.314 km).
1 Malaysia-Alex Yoong, 1h 10m 47.815s, 108.120 mph/174.002 km/h; **2** Czech Republic-Tomás Enge, 1h 10m 55.151s; **3** Mexico-Salvador Durán, 1h 10m 56.780s; **4** Germany-Nico Hülkenberg, 1h 10m 57.657s; **5** Canada-James Hinchcliffe, 1h 11m 00.799s; **6** Great Britain-Robbie Kerr, 1h 11m 01.857s; **7** New Zealand-Jonny Reid, 1h 11m 02.434s; **8** China-Cheng Congfu, 1h 11m 19.190s; **9** Netherlands-Jeroen Bleekemolen, 1h 11m 20.077s; **10** Switzerland-Sébastien Buemi, 1h 11m 21.068s; **11** South Africa-Stephen Simpson, 1h 11m 21.736s; **12** Lebanon-Graham Rahal, 1h 11m 23.016s; **13** Ireland-Michael Devaney, 1h 11m 39.809s; **14** Brazil-Tuka Rocha, 1h 11m 40.271s; **15** Indonesia-Ananda Mikola, 1h 11m 41.485s; **16** Australia-Karl Reindler, 1h 11m 53.502s; **17** USA-Phil Giebler, 1h 12m 16.504s; **18** India-Armaan Ebrahim, 37 laps; **19** Singapore-Denis Lian, 37; **20** Italy-Alessandro Per Guidi, 37; **21** Greece-Takis Kaitatzis, 19 (DNF-spin); **22** Pakistan-Nur Ali, 10 (DNF-driveshaft); **23** France-Nicolas Lapierre, 1 (DNF-engine).
Fastest race lap: USA, 1m 47.820s, 112.096 mph/180.400 km/h.
Pole position: Malaysia.

Provisional championship points
1 Germany, 20; **2** Mexico, 19; **3** Malaysia, 17; **4** Canada, 11; **5** Czech Republic, 11; **6** Great Britain, 11; **7** USA, 10; **8** Netherlands, 9; **9** Australia, 8; **10** China, 8; **11** France, 8; **12** South Africa, 7; **13** Italy, 5; **14** New Zealand, 5; **15** Switzerland, 4; **16** Indonesia, 1.

Results of the remaining races will be given in AUTOCOURSE 2007–2008.

Grand Prix Masters 2005

The following race was run after AUTOCOURSE 2005–2006 went to press.

All cars are Reynard-Nicholson McLaren Cosworth.

ALTECH GRAND PRIX MASTERS OF SOUTH AFRICA, Kyalami, Midrand, South Africa, 13 November. 30 laps of the 2.649-mile/4.263-km circuit, 79.467 miles/127.890 km.
1 Nigel Mansell, GB, 50m 55.154s, 93.639 mph/150.697 km/h; **2** Emerson Fittipaldi, BR, 50m 55.562s; **3** Riccardo Patrese, I, 51m 15.816s; **4** Andrea de Cesaris, I, 51m 16.854s; **5** Derek Warwick, GB, 51m 17.007s; **6** Hans Stuck, D, 51m 18.355s; **7** Christian Danner, D, 51m 19.272s; **8** Eddie Cheever, USA, 51m 27.359s; **9** Jan Lammers, NL, 51m 27.932s; **10** Eliseo Salazar, RCH, 51m 38.573s; **11** Patrick Tambay, F, 52m 06.738s; **12** René Arnoux, F, 52m 07.890s; **13** Jacques Laffite, F, 13 laps (DNF-accident); **14** Stefan Johansson, S, 2 (DNF-spin).
Did not start: Alan Jones, AUS (neck injury in practice – withdrawn before qualifying).
Fastest race lap: Mansell, 1m 36.390s, 98.932 mph/159.216 km/h.
Fastest qualifying lap: Mansell, 1m 33.428s, 102.069 mph/164.263 km/h.

2006

All cars are Delta Motorsport-Nicholson McLaren Cosworth.

THE QTEL GRAND PRIX MASTERS OF QATAR, Losail International Circuit, Qatar, 29 April. 24 laps of the 3.343-mile/5.380-km circuit, 80.231 miles/129.120 km.
1 Nigel Mansell, GB, 52m 06.000s, 92.397 mph/148.699 km/h; **2** Christian Danner, D, 52m 06.562s; **3** Eric van de Poele, B, 52m 07.174s; **4** Eddie Cheever, USA, 52m 09.016s; **5** Derek Warwick, GB, 52m 09.420s; **6** Pierluigi Martini, I, 52m 11.710s; **7** Jan Lammers, NL, 52m 13.044s; **8** Stefan Johansson, S, 52m 14.339s; **9** René Arnoux, F, 52m 15.068s; **10** Riccardo Patrese, I, 52m 15.423s; **11** Patrick Tambay, F, 52m 21.506s; **12** Emerson Fittipaldi, BR, 52m 35.788s; **13** Andrea de Cesaris, I, 16 laps (DNF-spin); **14** Eliseo Salazar, RCH, 13 (DNF-electrics); **15** Hans Stuck, A, 5 (DNF-steering).
Fastest race lap: Martini, 1m 49.116s, 110.293 mph/177.499 km/h.
Fastest qualifying lap: Mansell, 1m 46.926s, 112.552 mph/181.135 km/h.

GRAND PRIX MASTERS OF GREAT BRITAIN, Silverstone Grand Prix Circuit, Towcester, Northamptonshire, Great Britain, 13 August. 28 laps of the 3.194-mile/5.140-km circuit, 89.428 miles/ 143.920 km.
1 Eddie Cheever, USA, 1h 01m 08.625s, 87.755 mph/141.228 km/h; **2** Eric van de Poele, B, 1h 01m 25.302s; **3** Christian Danner, D, 1h 01m 45.180s; **4** Hans Stuck, A, 1h 02m 02.139s; **5** Alex Caffi, I, 1h 02m 11.648s; **6** Riccardo Patrese, I, 1h 02m 15.492s; **7** Pierluigi Martini, I, 1h 02m 54.980s; **8** Emerson Fittipaldi, BR, 27 laps; **9** René Arnoux, F, 27; **10** Andrea de Cesaris, I, 26; **11** Patrick Tambay, F, 25; **12** Stefan Johansson, S, 24 (DNF-puncture); **13** Jan Lammers, NL, 15 (DNF-accident damage); **14** Eliseo Salazar, RCH, 8 (DNF-spin); **15** Derek Warwick, GB, 2 (DNF-accident damage); **16** Nigel Mansell, GB, 2 (DNF-differential).
Fastest race lap: Danner, 2m 00.537s, 95.389 mph/153.513 km/h.
Fastest qualifying lap: Danner, 1m 36.916s, 118.637 mph/190.928 km/h.

Result of the Kyalami race will be given in AUTOCOURSE 2007–2008.